MOOROSI

A South African king's battle for survival

By Graham Fysh

Published by

LifeTime Creations

Seattle, Washington

Cover designed by Gavin Fysh

Second edition

ISBN 978-0-9628987-3-0

To my wife

MARCIA

without whose loving patience, understanding, support and advice I
could never have written this book.

ACKNOWLEDGEMENTS

My thanks go to Bruce Ramsey for his excellent editing and counsel, to Letlatsa Moqalo, who guided me around Moorosi's mountain, to Ed Harowicz for drawing the maps, and to those countless dedicated people in universities, libraries, archives and bookstores around the world who helped me gather the material for this work. I am particularly grateful to the staff at Lesotho National Archives in Maseru, the Morija Museum and Archives in Lesotho, the National Library of South Africa, and the Western Cape Archives and Records Service.

ABOUT THE AUTHOR

Graham Fysh was born and raised in South Africa where he worked for 20 years as a journalist for major South African newspapers and weekly newsmagazines. He covered a wide spectrum of topics, including the world's first successful heart transplant and politics at the time of apartheid.

He traveled extensively covering the then turbulent political events in Southern Africa, observing conflict in the sub-continent first hand.

In 1980 he moved to Seattle where he earned a master's degree in communication from the University of Washington. He worked at Seattle-area newspapers for a total of 15 years writing on business and investment before devoting his time to researching and writing this book. He and his wife live in Seattle. They have three children and seven grandchildren.

AUTHOR'S NOTES

- The currency used at the time of the events in this book was the British pound (£), which was divided into 20 shillings, with each shilling worth 12 pence. In today's money, one 1870's pound would be worth roughly R1 000 (South African); US$100; or £60 sterling.
- For the most part, I have retained the names of places used by the colonial government at the time in which the events in this book take place. For example, I use the then-official colonial name of Basutoland even though many inhabitants referred to it as The Lesotho, the name it was given (without "The") when it gained independence in 1966. The Orange River, the name I use, was known by the Baphuthi and Basotho as the Senqu River.

But I have made changes to some of the names used in documents at the time — for example, I refer to the people as Baphuthi and Basotho, in line with today's spelling. Also, Moorosi was often spelled Morosi or Moirosi and Moorosi's son Lehana was referred to by the colonial authorities as Doda.

— Graham Fysh

Preface

This story of the little-known 1879 war between the British Cape Colony and the Baphuthi people, led by King Moorosi, in what was then known as Basutoland (today's Lesotho) is the result of seven years of research and writing.

Determined to uncover all I could about the war and the events that led up to it, I traveled several times to historical sites in Lesotho — a country that I had already visited many times, starting at age 20 when two friends and I rode on horseback into the rugged mountainous interior.

I searched archives in Cape Town, the Lesotho capital Maseru and Morija (the first mission station in the country), and I scoured rare books and government documents, consulting them in libraries and buying scores from used book stores around the world.

When I began, I hoped I would be able to find a skeleton of information on which to build a novel. When I was done I found I had enough information to flesh it out into a compelling story that adheres closely to the historical record.

I came to know unforgettable characters, uncovered a gripping adventure story, and gained new insight into the colonial era in Africa, the results of which continue to influence events on the continent today.

The people are more captivating and the story line is more absorbing, more filled with surprises and more meaningful than anything I could have invented.

The cover illustration appeared in The Graphic, a London publication, on February 7, 1880.

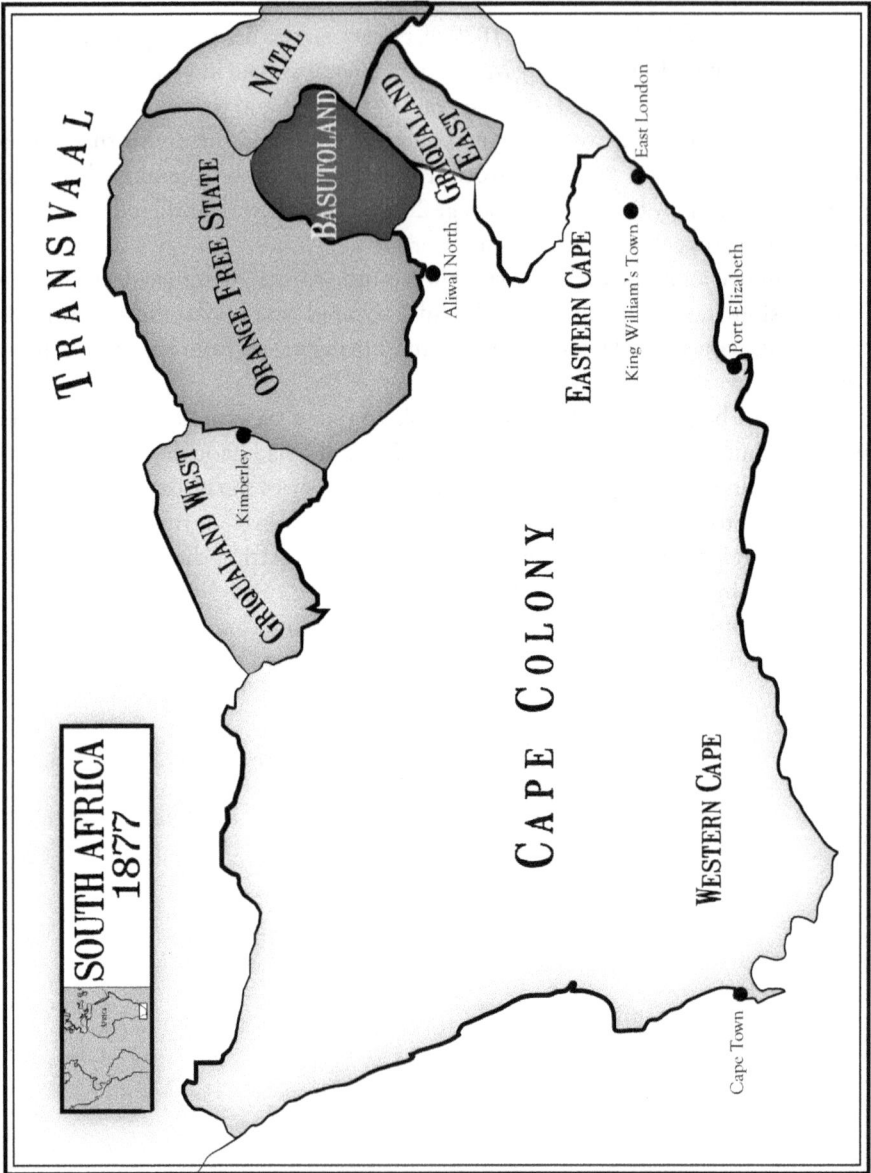

SOUTH AFRICA
1877

TRANSVAAL

NATAL

BASUTOLAND

ORANGE FREE STATE

GRIQUALAND EAST

GRIQUALAND WEST
Kimberley

Aliwal North

EASTERN CAPE
King William's Town

East London

Port Elizabeth

CAPE COLONY

WESTERN CAPE

Cape Town

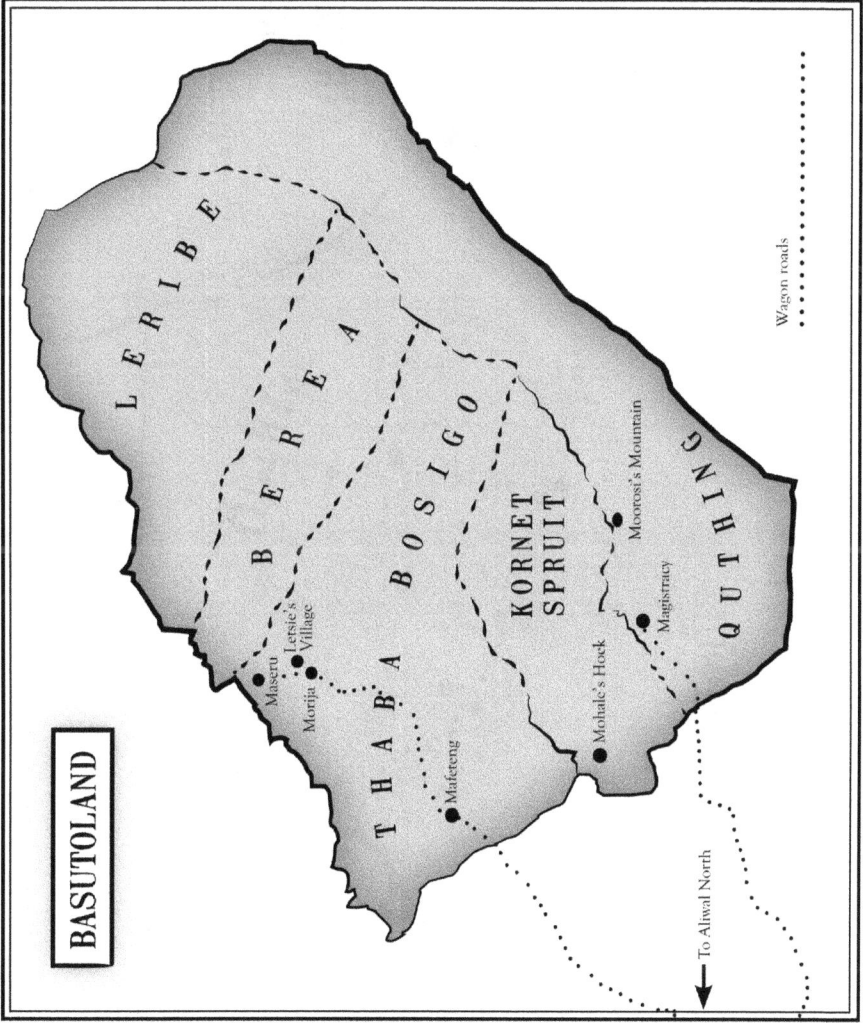

BASUTOLAND

LERIBE

BEREA

THABA BOSIGO

KORNET SPRUIT

QUTHING

Maseru
Lersie's Village
Morija
Mafeteng
Mohale's Hock
Moorosi's Mountain
Magistracy

Wagon roads

To Aliwal North

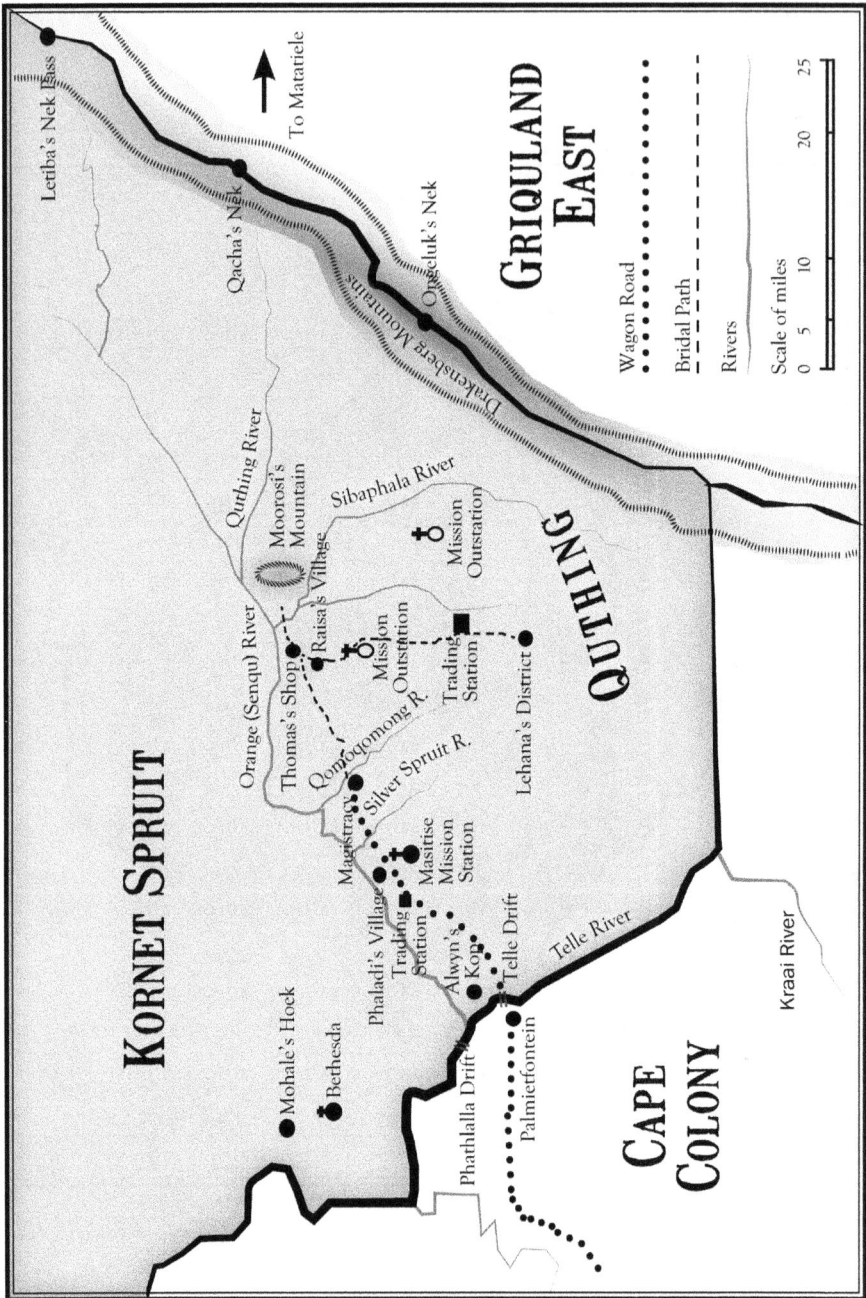

KORNET SPRUIT

GRIQULAND EAST

QUTHING

CAPE COLONY

Leriba's Nek Pass

Qacha's Nek

Ongeluk's Nek

To Matatiele

Drakensberg Mountains

Quthing River

Moorosi's Mountain

Sibaphala River

Mission Outstation

Orange (Senqu) River

Raisa's Village

Thomas's Shop

Mission Outstation

Qomoqomong R.

Trading Station

Lehana's District

Silver Spruit R.

Magistracy

Masitise Mission Station

Phaladi's Village

Trading Station

Alwyn's Kop

Telle Drift

Telle River

Kraai River

Mohale's Hoek

Bethesda

Phathlalla Drift

Palmietfontein

Wagon Road
Bridal Path
Rivers

Scale of miles
0   5   10   20   25

I

Quthing, Basutoland — Tuesday, May 22, 1877

Harvest time is here. But Raisa is not reaping this crop. He is ruining it. He lifts his ax and crashes it down alongside a healthy green corn stalk, sending a plume of dust snaking into the air. He raises it once more and, gaining leverage from the 3-foot handle attached at right angles to the iron arrowhead, plunges the ax into the other side of the stalk. In a slow, steady rhythm, he hacks at earth on either side of the corn stalk again and again until the roots are loosened and he can pull up the plant and throw it to the side.

This time of year hundreds of similar fields in Quthing, the land of the Baphuthi people, are ready for harvesting. Some will be harvested now; many will be allowed to grow for another three or four weeks. But Raisa is not waiting. He moves to another plant, less than a foot from the first, and destroys it, too, keeping time like the slow beat of a bass drum.

As the sun arcs across the northern sky, he systematically uproots each plant. His self-imposed task is demanding. The plants are tall and strong. He continues down one row and up the next, stalk after stalk. Behind him broken plants lie at all angles, some piled on top of one another, others alone, all pointing in haphazard directions.

Alerted by neighbors, a woman runs to the field, pleading with him to stop. "This is my field," MaLebenya screams. "These are my crops. What are you doing, Raisa?"

"You know what I am doing and why I am doing it," Raisa replies.

"I do not want you to do this," MaLebenya continues. "I tended to these plants. I weeded them. And I watered them. I am planning to harvest them soon. Stop what you are doing. These crops are mine."

Raisa ignores her. He is bent on destroying the field. No one will stop him.

MaLebenya runs at him, screaming and pushing against his chest with one hand while trying to grab the ax with the other. Raisa shoves her aside, causing her to fall between the corn stalks.

She realizes that, without help, she cannot stop Raisa from what he is doing. Raisa resumes his task.

MaLebenya pulls herself up and moves away. At 34, she is in her prime of life and, some among the Baphuthi would say, too young to be a widow. It was only a few weeks ago that they mourned the death of her husband from a fever; an unusual event in a largely healthy community. Now she is suffering a second loss. Her eyes fill with tears and her body shakes with anger as she grapples with the futility of protest. "Stop what you are doing," she screams again at Raisa, as he hacks away at the plants.

Her screams attract others.

MaLebenya turns to the gathering crowd, many of them family members who, like her, live in Raisa's Village. "Will none of you help me?" she pleads. "This man is destroying my plants. Help me stop him."

The crowd watches anxiously, some sympathizing with MaLebenya's plight. But no one dares interfere. For one thing, Raisa is MaLebenya's late husband's brother, making this a family quarrel. For another, Raisa is a Baphuthi sub-chief or headman. He holds sway over the people who live in his village, a collection of round mud huts with thatched cone-shaped roofs, which forms part of the territory ruled by King Moorosi, the leader of the Baphuthi people. Raisa's powers are subject only to the Baphuthi chiefs above him and to Moorosi himself.

MaLebenya's husband had plowed the field and sowed the corn seed. After that, as custom demanded, she had tended to it as it grew, and, now that he has died, had been planning to harvest and store the corn to see her through the approaching winter. Ground into meal and turned into porridge for herself and her children, it was to have been her subsistence.

Now her brother-in-law is taking away her means of survival.

Working in the rectangular stone-built trading store that he built a few years ago alongside a European-style house, Joseph B. Thomas — one of only a handful of whites in Quthing — is not far from the commotion in Raisa's village. But in the five years he has run his store in Quthing he has made it a policy not to become involved in local disputes. His motive is to make money operating a trading store, not to advance any political or religious agenda.

Besides, he needs to keep on the right side of the chiefs. Because the European system of private property is unknown here, he needs their permission to operate on the land, which belongs to all the Baphuthi, but is allocated by chiefs to people to build their huts, plant their crops, graze their cattle and, in his case, establish a trading store.

Thomas found, too, that buying and selling goods was not practiced in Quthing before he arrived, although some Baphuthi had become acquainted with it when traveling outside their homeland, particularly to work on the diamond mines in Kimberley, some 120 miles to the west.

It has been a profitable business. This outlet, known as Thomas's Shop, is the largest of three stores that Thomas operates in Quthing. As the Baphuthi line up to sell him their hides, wool and grain, which he will resell to the Cape Colony at considerable profit, he makes small talk as he weighs what they have brought. He swaps jokes in the rich language of the Baphuthi people. They, in turn, choose from a variety of goods, such as blankets and clothes imported from the white-run Cape Colony to the south and even from England.

Today the Baphuthi tell him of the dispute involving Raisa and MaLebenya. Thomas listens, but gives no indication of more than a passing interest. Apparently a headman is destroying a widow's crop. But, as long as it doesn't affect him and his daily trading, Thomas is staying out of it.

As the afternoon sun reaches its zenith across the African sky and starts its journey back toward the mountaintops, MaLebenya grows weary of protest. She slumps among tall grass near the field, her body shaking with anger and disillusionment, sobbing quietly.

With darkness spreading across the scrub-covered mountains, Raisa's task is complete. MaLebenya's crop is destroyed and cannot be replaced.

MaLebenya is furious at what Raisa has done. But she knows a way to get back at him.

Quthing — Friday, May 25, 1877

The Baphuthi people have been lining up outside the semi-completed stone-built magistracy since dawn. Most have traveled for some hours on horseback, although a few have walked for hours and even days.

They have come to this compound alongside the Qomoqomong River, a name whose clicks imitate the sound of horses walking along the rock-strewn bed, to seek travel passes or to pay their hut taxes to Hamilton Hope, who three weeks ago became the first — and only — colonial magistrate in Quthing.

Hope, representative of whites who first settled in the south more than 200 years ago and steadily expanded north before reaching this region a decade ago, is donning his formal clothing in the thatched-roofed round Baphuthi hut in which he is living until his house is completed.

It is unnecessary to pay much attention to his black bow tie and white shirt as they are mostly covered by his long, prematurely gray beard, but he does so anyway. His collar, after all, can be seen as he turns his head from side to side. Peering into a small mirror, he buttons his black waistcoat and coat and tugs on his black trousers.

Tall and strongly built, Hope carries himself with an air of confidence that borders on intimidation. He appears older than his 38 years. His piercing blue eyes, topped by thick black eyebrows, reinforce his authoritative bearing.

Almost four months ago Hope received a letter appointing him "resident magistrate for the district of Quthing in the territory of British Basutoland."

But Hope is doing more than simply extending colonial rule to another district of Basutoland. He is, in effect, extending it to another country. Arguably Quthing should not have been included as a district of Basutoland at all. When the British drew the boundary lines for the territory, in a pattern familiar with their actions around the world, they paid little heed to the local tribal groups and grouped the Baphuthi people in one country with the Basotho.

Yet the 5,000-strong Baphuthi people speak their own language and have remained independent, although they have always lived as friendly neighbors along-

side the Basotho. Even as the rest of Basutoland has come increasingly under colonial control, this independence has continued, largely because the wide Orange
River dividing Quthing from the rest of Basutoland often is impassable, making it
almost impossible to govern the territory effectively from Mohale's Hoek, the seat
of government for neighboring Kornet Spruit under which it fell.

The extent of colonial government in Quthing, therefore, has been to collect
hut tax from the people through Moorosi.

Until now. Until Hope's arrival.

The idea for the Quthing post originated with Charles D. Griffith, Governor's
Agent, who is the Cape Colony's Basutoland administrator.

"We need a fifth resident magistrate to those already serving in four districts
across Basutoland — Leribe, Berea, Thaba Bosigo and Kornet Spruit," he told the
authorities in the Cape.

"Moorosi is about the wildest and most uncivilized of any of the chiefs in
Basutoland. We need to bring him to his senses."

Hope strides across the 100 yards to his half-built house where he takes his
seat behind a desk on the porch. It is nine o'clock and he has opened for business.
Although he has been here for three weeks, so far only a trickle of Baphuthi have
come to pay their taxes,10 shillings for each hut, or to seek passes to work outside
the country. But today he is surprised at how many are here to see him. Clearly the
messengers he sent to tell the people that hut taxes must be paid to him by June 1
have been effective.

Five hundred feet above Hope, on the slopes of a rock-crested hill, an 80-year-
old man mounted on a horse holds the reins with one hand and a long-barrelled
gun with the other. A blanket helps to ward off the cool morning wind.

King Moorosi is remarkably lithe, even though he has fought several battles
and has experienced a lifetime of physical challenges while leading his people. Although he walks with an awkward gait as a result of an ankle injury 10 years ago in
a battle, he has aged well, helped by the brisk mountain air, constant exercise and,
for the most part, a plentiful supply of nutritious food. He sits erect on his horse,
making full use of his 5-foot-7-inch height.

His skin is fairer than that of most Africans, resembling, those whites who
meet him say, that of the Arab people. Around his neck is a leather necklace. From
it hang beads, bones, small goat horns, baboon's fingers, claws of wild birds, porcu-
pine quills and other totems that he has collected over the years. Each has a meaning and a purpose, for Moorosi is revered not only as king, but also as a rainmaker
and diviner among his people. His long earrings — which his people jokingly call
"rings of governing" — are a trademark, their jingling announcing his approach.

Moorosi's intellect matches his physical ability. As is the case with most
Baphuthi people, he shows no sign of losing his mental skills with age. He is self-
confident, speaks eloquently and thinks quickly. Intensely independent, he is proud

of his people, the land they occupy, his ancestors and their way of life. He is a strong leader, a good shot and a shrewd fighter.

So strong is his leadership that others — Khoisan people, whom many call Bushmen, and members of the Thembu people from the south — have been absorbed into the Baphuthi nation. Moorosi himself has two Khoisan women among his dozen wives, a gesture of respect to the mountain people who first lived here back in the mists of time and a common practice in ancient kingdoms.

Indeed, it was the Khoisan who brought him his first two horses, some 50 years ago, which they stole in a raid on a white farm to the south. Later his people acquired hundreds of horses from which today's smaller Basotho ponies, adept at negotiating the narrow mountain paths of the area, were bred.

As Moorosi watches Hope at work in the valley below, he wonders how his ancestors would have viewed this white government official come to live in their midst. He thinks of his ancestors, his father Mokuoane, the son of Mokhoebi, the son of Thibela, the son of Khanyane, the son of Tsele, the son of Kobo, the son of Titi, the son of Langa.

For 40 years, since the death of his father, these ancestors all have watched over him as he has led his people. Now he looks to them for wisdom as Hope's arrival marks the beginning of a new era for the Baphuthi, one through which he must lead them to ensure their survival as a people. He will welcome Hope — even though he had originally told the white authorities that he did not want a government official on his land — because Baphuthi custom demands they welcome strangers. He will respect Hope. He will learn from him. But he will watch Hope's actions carefully, particularly should they impinge on his realm.

Hope looks up at the man first in line.

The man holds out a cloth bag tied tightly at the top and filled with corn.

"Why are you giving that to me?" Hope asks, through a translator.

"I am paying my hut tax, boss. They said we should pay our taxes to you."

"The hut tax is 10 shillings."

"I do not have money."

"I must have money. I must have 10 shillings."

"This corn is worth 10 shillings."

"How do I know that? I don't know what that corn is worth. It could be worth five shillings or five hundred shillings for all I know."

"I have no money. I have only corn. Where can I get money? The chiefs, when they collect our hut tax for the white government, they take corn."

"I am the chief now. I collect your hut tax now. And I do not take corn. You must find 10 shillings and bring it to me."

The man, who took a day to ride from his home in the mountains, turns away.

The next man in line walks up to Hope.

"I've paid my hut tax, now I'm looking for a pass, boss," he says.

"Where do you wish to go?"

"To Kimberley."

"All you people want to go to Kimberley," Hope replies. "Why do you want to go there?"

"For work, boss. I need to work on the diamond mines there to get money."

"What will you do with the money? Buy brandy and guns?"

"No, boss. I will spend some there on food, but I will also save the money and bring it back to my family."

"You are lying to me. I can see it in your eyes. I cannot allow you to go."

The man stares at Hope in disbelief.

"My brother..."

"What about your brother?"

"The magistrate in Kornet Spruit, the one across the river who was our magistrate before you came onto our land, two months ago he gave my brother a pass to go to Kimberley."

"Well, you are not your brother. And I am not the magistrate in Kornet Spruit. He is still there. I am now the magistrate here, in Quthing, in charge of you Baphuthi people. I am not letting you leave. Next."

The man pauses, taking in what he has heard. Downcast, he walks away slowly.

"Who's next?"

As the sole government official in the district Hope enjoys the power the new office provides him. After serving for four years as a clerk to his brother-in-law Emile Rolland in Mafeteng, to the west in the Thaba Bosigo district, he now has been promoted to magistrate in an area where no magistrate has served before. Now he can wield power in his own right.

Here Hope, earning a comfortable £450 a year rather than the £170 he earned in Mafeteng, will ensure that colonial law, colonial standards and colonial order will be imposed on the Baphuthi people. Collecting hut taxes and issuing passes is just the start. He will make his mark on the territory, which stretches 40 miles at its widest point from east to west and 120 miles from south to north. He will do so with a strict application of colonial law and a tough approach that will brook no opposition, bringing the "untamed" Moorosi to his senses in no uncertain way.

He will do so alone. His wife of 13 years, Emma Cecile, whom he calls Mimmie, and his mother-in-law, Elizabeth Rolland, 74, who lived with the couple after the death of Elizabeth's French-born missionary husband four years ago, live in Burghersdorp, 60 miles to the south, in the Cape Colony. For now, they will not join him.

As Moorosi watches the movement in the valley below, he is joined by Letuka, the son of his first wife and presumed heir to the kingship when Moorosi dies. Letuka, also armed and covered with a blanket, lines up his horse alongside his father and looks down on the scene below.

"The first white man who came to live among us was the missionary Ellenberger," Letuka recalls. "He is a good man. He teaches our people and our children well. He is away now, and his work is being done by the men he trained. But he told us he would return. We know he will come back soon.

"Then came Thomas, the trader and the white men who help him. We are content for them to be here. They give us money for our food and sell us goods we can use. But now here is a man from the white government. I'm not sure about him."

Moorosi nods. "I share your fear, my son. Over many years, I have fought those who have wanted to take away our country from us. I protected our land. I kept our people together. I kept our right to rule ourselves. I retained our freedom.

"Seven years ago I placed my people and my land under the protection of the British, who had protected the Basotho people from the white farmers, the Boers, who fought us to take our country away from us for farms for themselves. I was reluctant, but I followed in the footsteps of the great Basotho leader Moshoeshoe, who asked the British to protect his people from the Boers, which they did. I looked up to Moshoeshoe as a father and so I asked the British to protect me, too.

"The British protected us. The Boers did not attack us any more.

"But then the British handed over the Basotho land and our land to the Cape Colony. At first, I thought the Cape Colony people would be like the British people. But I worry that the people from the Cape do not want only to protect us, they want to govern us. And now the colonial government is putting a white man on our land, among our people. Why does he need to be here?"

Letuka is silent. Ellenberger the preacher and Thomas the trader have been joined by Hope the administrator. A new religion, a new economy and now a new government, all from outside.

"I did not want him to come here," Moorosi continues, talking almost to himself. "When I met two months ago for a whole day with Griffith, the Kornet Spruit magistrate Austen, and Hope, I told them I did not want Hope to come here. I told them I did not want a magistrate. I told them I had not asked for one. I told them the magistrate in Kornet Spruit was enough.

"I asked them, What is wrong with the way I govern my people? My people love me and respect me. They are happy. Their crops are good. Their cattle are fat. Why do you want to send this man here? What do you want from us?

"Griffith told me this man Hope would help me to run the country and would be good for us. He said I would still govern my people. He said Hope will consult me on important matters before he takes any action. We will make sure he does."

"Next!" Hope calls to the line of waiting Baphuthi. "Who is next?"

A man walks forward.

"What do you want?"

"I want to pay my hut tax."

"Do you have 10 shillings?"

"Yes, magistrate. I have the 10 shillings."

Hope takes the money and sets about recording the man's name in his inch-thick record book. "What is your name?"

"My name?"

"Yes, your name. Don't you have a name?"

Hope is interrupted by a 20-strong group approaching from the direction of the Qomoqomong River. At its head is MaLebenya, talking loudly and waving her hands in the air. Those walking alongside her or accompanying her on horseback join in an animated discussion.

It has been three days since Raisa destroyed her cornfield, but MaLebenya's anger has not dissipated. Now, accompanied by family members, she has walked 15 miles to come here, to bring her complaint against Raisa to the white official.

Hope notes that the woman at the head of the group is talking with Abraham Sighata, the Basotho man he recently appointed chief constable and who is standing guard outside his hut about 100 yards away.

He continues recording the man's name, trying to ignore the commotion and leaving it to Sighata to handle, at least for now.

"I want to see the magistrate," MaLebenya tells Sighata. "I want to complain about what Raisa has done to me. I am angry. I want the magistrate to punish him."

Her family members join in, some arguing for and others against MaLebenya.

"You will have to wait at the end of the queue," Seghata says.

"What is going on down there?" Hope shouts.

"She says she has a complaint against one of King Moorosi's headmen."

Aha. A complaint against a headman. That's what he wants to hear.

"Tell her I will hear her complaint," Hope says, motioning to the others in the line to make way for MaLebenya.

His penetrating ice-blue eyes stare at her. "What is your complaint?"

Moorosi tugs on the reins of his horse, directing it toward a path that leads down the mountainside. His earrings swing from side to side and his necklace bounces up and down in time with the horse's lope.

As he moves lower down the hillside, he looks again at the scene below him. He sees MaLebenya moving to the head of the line. "Find out why she is there," he tells Letuka. "I want to know what she is telling him."

Cape Town — the same day

Some 600 miles south of Basutoland, Sir Henry Bartle Edward Frere is making his first public appearance in Cape Town as the new British-appointed governor-general of the Colony of the Cape of Good Hope.

As he takes his place this afternoon on the steps of the Houses of Parliament alongside the other dignitaries, he looks out on the crowd gathered in the streets to celebrate the opening of the new session of the Cape colonial Parliament.

The ceremony follows a day of festivities yesterday to mark Queen Victoria's birthday, a public holiday. A ball to celebrate the event was held last night and attended by members of Parliament, some of whom have taken several days to travel as far as 700 miles from other parts of South Africa for the parliamentary session.

The Cape of Good Hope Colony, first settled by the Dutch in 1652 and established as a British colony in 1814, is now home to 828,000 people — 235,000 of them white, 120,000 mixed-race, 98,000 aborigines officially called Hottentots, 10,000 Malay, and 365,000 black, mostly Xhosa-speaking, living in the north-eastern part of the colony. The Cape Colony was granted self-rule almost six years ago, but the ultimate power still lies in Britain, a power that Frere, as governor-general and therefore the queen's representative here in Cape Town, intends to wield. After all, Britain is the most powerful nation in the world, supported by the most powerful army. It rules the seas and has colonized large parts of the globe. As Frere is fond of saying, "The sun never sets on the British Empire."

When Lord Carnarvon — Britain's colonial secretary in the cabinet of Conservative Prime Minister Benjamin Disraeli — offered him the position early this year, Frere at first was inclined to turn him down, telling the British cabinet minister that he did not relish the position.

At 61, he was happy to bask in the glow of his achievements over the years in British India, for which he was knighted. As *Sir* Bartle Frere, he is admired and respected among his peers.

But the Fourth Earl of Carnarvon explained he wanted Frere to do more than be governor-general. He wanted him to implement a solution for all of South Africa that he had been seeking for two years — a confederation of disparate and often antagonistic white-run colonies and self-proclaimed states under one umbrella. Instead of the Transvaal, Orange Free State, Natal, Griqualand West, Griqualand East and the Cape Colony each governing themselves, they would be one unit, with each having a degree of self-rule, in one parliament under British supervision.

Confederation on similar lines was working in Canada, Carnarvon told Frere, and he was convinced it could work in South Africa, too. After that job was done, he had told Frere, he would appoint him the first governor-general of the newly established confederation, to be called the South African Dominion.

The offer was too tempting for Frere to resist.

Now, on South African soil for fewer than two months, Frere is taking on the challenge. He knows that he will have to spend more time assessing the situation on the ground. He will have to acquaint himself with the complex South African mix of colors and languages: The whites scattered around the country, the mixed-race people in the western Cape Colony and the black people of various tribes, nations and languages to the north, some of whom live on colonial land, but many of whom still largely govern themselves.

To Frere it is an unwritten rule that the confederation will be run only by people of European descent. The native people who do not want to live under the

Europeans will have to be convinced to do so or, if necessary, be forced to do so. Black areas not yet annexed to the white-run colonies will need to be annexed. The better educated and "more civilized" black people will be represented in the colonial parliament by whites — administrators, missionaries — who could speak for their interests.

He is aware, too, that some in high places in the Cape Colony are opposed to confederation, preferring their white-run colonies to remain separate, and are ready to test his political and leadership abilities to the full. He is willing to take on the challenge. He won in India. He will win here, too.

After greeting the crowd, Frere makes his way into the House of Assembly. Standing on a raised platform at the front of the assembled members, he places his prepared speech on the dais before him.

"In meeting you for the first time since my appointment as Her Majesty's Representative in South Africa, I am fully impressed with a deep sense of the responsibility attached to the high office which Her Majesty the Queen has been graciously pleased to confer upon me," he intones, "and with the most earnest desire to cooperate with you in all matters tending to promote the prosperity of this colony and the welfare of its people."

He paints a picture of a peaceful colony, saying, "I am glad to be able to assure you of the satisfactory state of affairs on the frontier, and among the native tribes which have come under our rule."

Those members of Parliament who represent the eastern districts on the frontier — to the southeast of Basutoland — are surprised to hear that the state of affairs in their area is "satisfactory." Just the opposite. Given the deteriorating relations between the white settlers and the indigenous black inhabitants to the north, many believe war to be imminent. They are even more surprised when Frere adds, "Our relations with the adjacent independent native tribes are of a friendly character, and I think we may confidently believe that the feeling of alarm and uneasiness which for some months existed, more especially on our eastern border, has now entirely passed away."

A murmur runs through the House. "Entirely passed away?" Frere, many members fear, is confusing an absence of open war with permanent peace.

To them, the eastern border remains filled with unease and they find his rose-colored depiction naive. Frere soon reveals, however, that his purpose is union or confederation into one South Africa, for which legislation is being introduced in the British Imperial Parliament in London, and the region needs to be peaceful to achieve that goal.

Frere adds that measures to annex several black-occupied territories to the Cape Colony will be introduced in the Cape parliament — a move toward confederation.

As for Basutoland, Frere knows only that it exists and little more. Because it is almost entirely occupied by indigenous people, no members of the colonial Parliament directly represent the territory, which they are content to leave to the colonial administrators to govern, a job that, according to occasional newspaper reports from the territory, they appear to be doing well.

Paris — The same day

David Frederic Ellenberger and his wife Emma have been in Europe for more than two years, recuperating from 15 years of spreading the Gospel among the Basotho and most recently the Baphuthi people — work that left them exhausted.

They have sought to relax and regain their strength for their return early next year, when they would have been away from Africa for three years. They are as eager to get back to their work as they know the Baphuthi people are for them to return.

Few who were acquainted with the couple were surprised to find that they needed time off. Ellenberger filled every day of his time among the Baphuthi trying to cope with the insidious demands of two passions.

One was to spread the Gospel. He ran schools and churches, visiting people in the far-flung areas of the mission field, counseling those who wished to become Christians, encouraging those who had converted to the faith, and preparing for Sunday services. If a moment passed when he had nothing to do, he would create a new task to ensure his time did not pass unused.

His other driving force was to record the history and customs of the people. He would sit down to his recording duties after dinner until 1 a.m. and waken at 6 a.m. to get in study time before mission work demanded all his attention.

Those long hours, lack of sleep and incessant work are why, people always assume, he looks so frail. His face, framed between a black beard and a sharply receding hairline, is drawn; his eyes look tired. But Ellenberger always has appeared frail and weak. For a while, his father-in-law refused him permission to marry Emma because he believed the man would become a physical burden to his daughter.

Nevertheless, it seemed Ellenberger was determined to counter any suggestions of perceived frailty. Driven by his overriding desire and determination to spread the Christian message, he never allowed tiredness or physical pain to be an excuse.

Even here in Paris, Fred Ellenberger finds it difficult to relax completely. He has supervised the printing of thousands of copies of the New Testament in Sesotho, the language of the Basotho people — which most of the Baphuthi people can speak, in addition to their own language of Sephuthi — and the printing of other Christian works, also in Sesotho. But nevertheless the rest has done him good.

He has visited Yverdon in the Swiss canton of Vaud where he was born on April 14, 1835. He has walked down some of the Parisian streets where he moved as a teenager and he has visited the church where he first felt the call to devote his life to mission work. He also has visited the church where, at the end of his studies, on October 11, 1860, when he was 25, he married Emma Hartung, then 23, whom he met while visiting his brother, who was married to Emma's sister.

Ellenberger also has spent many hours at the offices of the Paris Evangelical

Missionary Society which he joined at age 21. There, after studying medicine for a year, he studied theology for four years, learning how to preach to people who had never heard the Christian message before and did not speak French or English. He and Emma left for Basutoland soon after his ordination.

Now he and Emma have just returned from a speaking tour of Switzerland and France. They have told people of the great need for the teaching of the Gospel in Basutoland, of the Baphuthi whom they have come to love, of the great expanse of treeless mountains and valleys unlike anything in Europe, and of the great king Moorosi who has become Ellenberger's close friend.

At 42, Ellenberger is satisfied he has been on the right path. He is determined he will pursue his life's mission and return to Quthing within a year.

Today Ellenberger is visiting with Georges Steinheil, a 19-year-old Swiss studying theology at the Maison des Missions in Paris who plans one day to work in Basutoland as a missionary.

"I have heard that you are Swiss, also studied at the Maison des Mission in Paris and are a member of the Paris Evangelical Missionary Society," Steinheil says.

Ellenberger nods in agreement, adding, "Not only that. Your name is Georges and my wife and I named our youngest son Georges. He was born here in Paris just a year ago, on June 6th."

Steinheil laughs. "A good name. But, seriously, I am told that if anyone understands the Baphuthi and Basotho people and how to reach them with the Gospel, that person is you. I want you to tell me all about it. Do not spare any details. We have time and I want to learn."

Ellenberger is delighted at the company of someone who intends to follow the same path he took nearly two decades ago. He will be pleased to share the knowledge of 16 years in Basutoland and in particular the last 11 years in Quthing.

Soft-spoken and erudite, Ellenberger is the best source Steinheil could have found. In his missionary work in Basutoland, Ellenberger has made a point of asking all he meets to tell him their history and details of their ancestors, going back as far as they can. Only then will he tell them about the God who is more powerful than all their ancestors.

When he began his mission work, Ellenberger explains, the bulk of the missionaries in Basutoland were based at Morija, in the eastern part of the country. There the first mission station had been set up by Paris Evangelical Missionary Society pioneers Eugene Casalis, Thomas Arbousset and Constant Gosselin in 1833.

"But I wanted the Missionary Conference to send me to an area to which no missionaries had been. They said I would need to have patience. I would need first to work with another missionary, getting to know the area and the people. I reluctantly agreed. It made sense.

Ellenberger tells how he worked at a mission station called Hebron for two years, learning to speak Sesotho.

Then the Missionary Conference placed him under Gosselin in a place they called Bethesda — house of mercy —after the pool in Jerusalem at which Jesus healed the sick. It was about three miles from Mohale's Hoek in the Kornet Spruit district of southern Basutoland.

"Many of the people I worked among were Baphuthi, led by King Moorosi," Ellenberger explains. "They are a distinct nation, but they are closely linked to the Basotho people. Although they have a different ancestry, the Baphuthi share most of the beliefs and customs of the Basotho.

"Almost 40 years ago Moorosi placed his people under the protection of Moshoeshoe, the Basotho leader who had united the Basotho people against attacks from others, including the Zulus.

"Later the greatest threat to the Basotho people was from the Boers, the Dutch word for farmers, who occupy an area to the west and southwest they call the Orange Free State. They arrived in the 1830's after trekking north from the western Cape because they wanted to be free from British rule. Also they favored slavery and the British had abolished slavery in the Cape. They settled on farms in the area that formed part of the land the Basotho called their own.

"The Boers accused the Basotho of raiding their farms and stealing their cattle, which some undoubtedly did. But the Boers had pushed their way deep into Basotho territory, settling on their land and forcing their people to work as slaves on their farms and in their homes.

"Eventually, the tensions broke out into open war. Twice.

"The Boer commandos took our cattle. When they burned the village near us, I sheltered people at the mission station. The Boers saw me as a traitor; a white man who respected and helped the Basotho people.

"Because he was afraid that he would be overwhelmed and defeated by the Boers, Moorosi consolidated his people in their territory to the west of the Orange River and northwest of the Telle River, an area called Quthing.

"Moshoeshoe, determined to maintain his people's land and independence, presented a strong force to the Boers. But he could see that both sides were formidable. He preferred to seek peace. The British, who opposed the Boers, but had been adopting a hands-off attitude, stepped in and Moshoeshoe agreed to place the Basotho under British rule to protect them against the Boers.

"For the most part, it worked. The wars ended. The Basotho lost some territory when new boundaries were drawn up by the British and they were consolidated on their remaining land. In addition to losing land, the other price the Basotho paid for gaining British protection was that they were under British sovereignty and would be subject to British law.

"A few months later a messenger arrived from Moorosi saying, 'Cross the Orange River and help us. What will become of us if you abandon us?' "

"Aha," says Steinheil. "Your own mission station in a new territory. The move you had always wanted to make."

"Yes. When I arrived there the chief and his people gave me a very warm welcome. Moorosi presented me with an ox, which was immediately slaughtered to feed the many refugees from Bethesda.

"The Baphuthi king told me I could choose anywhere I liked for the mission station. After a week I came across an area called Masitise. The place was ideal. Not only was there sufficient land and water to establish a village for the Christians, but, being hidden above the valley on the slopes of a hill, it was particularly good from a defensive point of view. We worried about the Boers. We were afraid they might pursue us there. But they never did.

"Three weeks later Moorosi met me there and we agreed on the boundaries of the station. We also resolved questions relating to springs, land for fields, grazing ground and so on."

Ellenberger says he took his wife and children to settle with him at Masitise in January 1867. On their arrival, they found the Baphuthi people had built three huts for them.

"It was a wonderful gift to us, but unfortunately they were too small to accommodate my family. I did not have much money so I built a two-roomed house, but I realized that it, too, would soon be too small for the needs of my family, as Emma was pregnant.

"I asked God to show me how He wanted us to live there; I was sure it was His will that we were there. But I couldn't see how I could build a house big enough for us. Then one day I made the most amazing find."

Emma enters the room. A donor is waiting in the parlor.

"I quite understand," Steinheil says. "Why don't we meet again next week?"

London — The same day

Since his return from a brief stint in West Africa a few months ago, Alexander Granville has found few prospects for employment. He has no immediate need to work; he can continue to live with his parents in their comfortable home, attended by three female servants — a domestic nurse, a parlor maid and a cook. But he is not one for an idle life. At 29 he finds Broom in the county of Durham dull and without adventure.

When he hears from friends about the Cape Frontier Armed and Mounted Police Force in the Cape Colony, his interests are aroused. He visits the Cape of Good Hope Government Emigration Agency office in London.

"It's an excellent job and an exciting one," the agent tells him. "You will receive good wages, rapid promotion and be working in a foreign country with a good climate." The agent picks up completed forms and waves them at Granville. "You will also be among a fine group of people. I know. I have been signing them up quickly. In fact, you had better sign up now or else you might be too late."

The agreement is for three years and includes free passage to Cape Town. Granville will earn more than he is likely to earn in London, will work in the clean air, open countryside and warm weather and will find adventure.

He signs the agreement.

Granville's father, Augustus Granville, vicar of St. Edmund the King in Bearpark, in the Durham Diocese, supports his decision. But his mother, Ellen, does not relish the thought of her son leaving for Africa. Although she will have her three other sons and two daughters — all of them younger — at home, she fears for Alex. After all, one does not enlist in a police force on a frontier where fighting is taking place without being exposed to serious dangers.

Her son is quick to reassure her. "I will be helping to keep order, not going into an armed battle. So do not worry, mother, it will not be as dangerous as it sounds."

Granville is told to report in two days to the Union Steamship *Teuton* in Southampton from where he will leave for Port Elizabeth in the Cape Colony and, from there, by train to King William's Town. He has little time to prepare for what he is convinced will be the greatest adventure of his life.

Quthing — Tuesday, May 29 1877

Hope, who has picked up only a smattering of the local languages, listens intently as Sighata translates MaLebenya's complaint against headman Raisa.

The translation is not the best. Even Hope can tell that. To help in this regard, he is looking forward to the imminent arrival of an assistant — Charles J. Maitin, who is on his way from Maseru where he has been an assistant resident magistrate.

But right now Hope needs to make sure he understands.

He dips his pen in the ink pot and writes at the top of a new page, "In the Court of the Resident Magistrate, District Quthing, on Tuesday 29th May, 1877 appeared before me, Hamilton Hope, Resident Magistrate for the above district, MaLebenya, who being duly sworn states..." It is the first entry in the court book.

As he hears how Raisa turned MaLebenya's corn field into a patch of dirt, Hope's eyes light up and his body tenses with anticipatory excitement. Here is an opportunity to make his mark. Not only will he be assisting a defenseless widow who clearly has been wronged by a vindictive headman, but he also will be introducing his authority — and that of the colonial power — to the Baphuthi people in a practical and demonstrative way.

It serves Hope's agenda, too, that the complaint is against a sub-chief, or headman, under a son of Moorosi. It is but a start to his challenge to Moorosi himself.

Clearly, Hope reasons, the case is open and shut. The field belongs to the woman. Witnesses saw Raisa perpetrate the act. Raisa is not only guilty of trespass and destruction, he is also guilty of treating a woman like a piece of property.

Hope recalls the words of John Austen, the senior magistrate in the Kornet Spruit district to the west, that "the inferiority of the female sex is found to exist among all heathen or uncivilized nations." Austen — who argued that only education could place the woman in her proper position as wife and mother and center of domestic comfort and happiness — had written this four years ago in a paper submitted to a commission of laws and customs of the Basotho. Hope had made a thorough study of the commission's report.

Hope has little respect for Austen, now in his early fifties. He looks down on him because Austen is of mixed race — in Cape Colony terms, a colored man — and has little education from books. Yet this man was expected to impose justice on other people. No wonder people said Austen's kind of justice was crude, even though, they added, it was effective.

Yet Hope has to concede that Austen's knowledge of local customs, habits, thoughts and motives is extensive. How, then, when even Austen could write these comments, could anyone with civilized morals believe that Raisa's actions were anything but wrong?

"I am going to issue a summons against Raisa," Hope tells MaLebenya. "It will instruct him to appear before me to answer the charges you have leveled against him. I want you to return here on Monday. I will then give you the summons to take to him." Hope is expecting Maitin to be here on Monday when he can translate the summons for him.

Hope is confident he will pronounce Raisa guilty — what possible defense could he have? — and sentence him. Of course the principles of British justice demand he give him a hearing. But above all, he will be firm and authoritative.

Hope learned firmness and discipline from his father, William Hope, a graduate of England's Sandhurst military college and major in the British Seventh Fusiliers. In June 1846, when Hamilton was 7, Major Hope emigrated with his family to Cape Town. His skills at administration were soon recognized and, after a stint as a government clerk, he was appointed Auditor-General of the Cape, a post he held until his death in 1858, almost 20 years ago, at the age of 51.

Hope, then 19, remembers the emphasis his father put on serving one's country and doing what was right under the law. His father was a strict disciplinarian. He is convinced his father would have been proud were he to see him now.

Hope will show his superiors in the colonial office that he is taking control in spite of his relatively short experience. The people, too, will realize his will is strong and his justice swift. He will not hesitate to punish them — severely if necessary. No longer, he believes, will they be able to continue their barbaric, uncivilized and unproductive way of living or to practice their heathen customs.

Paris — The same day

Steinheil reminds Ellenberger that when they were interrupted he mentioned an amazing find he had made in the early days at the Masitise mission station.

"Yes, it was amazing," Ellenberger replies. "I climbed up the hill on the west of the flat slope I had chosen for the mission station and, in an area I had not explored before, I saw a cave under an enormous rock. The people told me that, years before, Bushmen had lived there. Later porcupines had burrowed into it. As I examined it, I realized that this cave could be turned into a home. The front was about 80 feet long and I reasoned I could safely dig back into it for at least 15 feet. I could dig down so that the ceiling would be about 6 feet high.

"At the back of the cave, on the left, in a corner, a small spring provided fresh water. I could incorporate that in our kitchen-pantry area."

Ellenberger tells Steinheil how he used bricks to fill in the 60-foot-wide front of the cave, including a front door in the center and two windows on each side. He also closed in both sides on the left and right with walls and, in each fitted a window. On the inside, he covered the bricks with mud, which he whitewashed.

"You built it yourself?"

"Yes, I did. I divided the house into four rooms, each 15 feet square. The first room on the left, that closest to the kitchen, was the dining room. Alongside was the living room, to which the front door gave access. The main bedroom, which included a big steel bed with a mattress made of dried corn leaves and a baby's cradle for the child who was soon to be born, lay alongside the living room and, at the end was the children's room.

"I had my own mission station. My own house. My own people, the Baphuthi, among whom I would work."

"You must have been pleased."

"I felt fulfilled, doing what I was called to do, all those years before, here in Paris. God was giving me the greatest opportunity of my life to serve him.

"Today the cave house and my original two-roomed house are home to eight children, who range in age from one to 15, and who will all soon be there with me and Emma again."

Ellenberger adds that Moshoeshoe died eight years ago, and that Moorosi and the Baphuthi pay loose allegiance to Letsie, Moshoeshoe's senior son, who took over the reins as paramount chief of the Basotho from his father.

"Are the British still in control over the Baphuthi people?" asks Steinheil.

"Not directly," Ellenberger replies. "When, almost 10 years ago, the Boers abandoned their attempts to conquer Basutoland the British continued to provide protection for the country, but lost interest in it and six years ago they handed over administration of Basutoland to the Cape Colony, which has been more vigorous in asserting control over the territory, which it sees as a prosperous agricultural area it can exploit and whose people can form a ready supply of labor.

"When I left, the Cape administration had exerted little direct control over Moorosi and the Baphuthi people, although I believe that is now changing."

"How did you preach to the people?"

"I went out among them. I did not wait for them to come to me. I spread the word among them and, after people became Christians, I established two outstations, run by Baphuthi converts.

"I also built schools where we taught them the Bible and how they should live, as well as school subjects. Emma helped me in teaching at the school and preparing services. She also led sewing groups for the women."

"How many of the people have become Christians?"

"When I left, a few hundred were living active Christian lives. Indeed, two great Baphuthi Christians are now helping to run the mission station while we are away. The Missionary Conference estimates the number of Christian adults in all of Basutoland has grown above 5,000."

"And the total population of Basutoland is...?"

"Around 150,000."

Ellenberger describes how he added a building in which to work, where he stored all his books on mission work among the Basotho. In that room, too, he operated a printing press for several years. The press had been shipped to Basutoland by missionary Samuel Rolland, who, in 1841, had printed several of the earliest books in Sesotho on it.

"Incidentally," Ellenberger says, "Rolland's son works as a magistrate in the north of Basutoland and his daughter is married to Hamilton Hope, who I understand is the new magistrate in the Baphuthi area."

Steinheil nods. "Has Moorosi been receptive to the Gospel?"

"He shows some interest, and he and I talk often about the Gospel, but his heart remains in his ancient customs. It is difficult for him and others to discard those ways. I think he will become a Christian one of these days. He is an intelligent man, speaks well and is self-confident. He dislikes war, but is not as ardently anti-war as are some other leading Basotho.

"These people love proverbs and folklore and storytelling," Ellenberger continues. "Especially humorous stories. The listeners roar with laughter even though they might have heard the story many times.

"It is probable that this love of story telling is partly responsible for the purity of their languages. Debased, ungrammatical speech as among the Europeans is unknown among the Basotho and the Baphuthi. "

"Interesting," Steinheil says. "Sloppy language causes sloppy thoughts. I hope we do not influence the Baphuthi that way. Talking of adopting our ways, have the people's customs changed since you arrived there?"

"Yes, they have. Those who have become Christians are increasingly adopting European customs and clothing, but the majority continue to follow the old customs and traditions while paying respect to the British and now the colonial authorities — a presence, as I have explained, that the Basotho and Baphuthi accepted because to them it appeared to be essential for their survival."

Ellenberger explains that the men build the huts. Almost all Basotho work in the fields. They plant corn, millet and sorghum, beans, sugar cane, watermelon, pumpkin, gourds, calabashes, tobacco and hemp. Now and then they eat meat, which is cooked on a stick, stuck in the ground near a fire. A major part of their diet is thick milk, kept in a skin bag. Most of their food is eaten cold.

"Owing to their simple diet and healthy way of life, the Basotho live to a great age," Ellenberger says. "It is said that years ago people who lived to be 100 to 120 years were not uncommon; and that their health and intelligence remained unimpaired to the end of their days."

Most of their time is spent in the open air, the missionary continues. The Baphuthi are well-built people who can last for days without food and recover well from most injuries. They also can go without sleep for days.

"Even as I hope to teach these people, I think I will learn something from them," Steinheil comments, with a smile.

"I think we all can. Yet I don't want to give the impression that they are never ill," Ellenberger adds. "The people do become sick and they have doctors who treat them. Some of these doctors are impostors. Some have knowledge only of certain diseases," Ellenberger notes. "Others have studied and have a considerable knowledge of diseases and the medicinal properties of plants."

This knowledge often has to be bought and those who have it guard it, he continues. Several head of cattle is not too high a price to pay for a secret remedy. Sometimes charlatans combine witchcraft and medicine. They throw divining bones, condemn a fellow tribesman as carrying an evil spirit and order him to be cast out and sometimes thrown over a cliff and killed.

Steinheil shakes his head. He has heard stories of witchcraft and feels called to replace these practices with Christian beliefs.

"Yet, apart from such occasional incidents, you find little crime among the Basotho and the Baphuthi," Ellenberger adds. "Violence is rare. It is all the more remarkable because, even now, there is little police supervision. The people seem to have a natural love of order and respect for authority. They show an almost superstitious respect for their king. He runs the judicial and political systems and he is the guardian of the land and all its natural resources."

"Sounds like the divine right of kings," says Steinheil.

"It is. Here's another thing," Ellenberger continues. "Family is more important to them than to us. The Basotho and the Baphuthi look to the family for support, friendship and sustenance. When you have no food, no house or no cattle, your family will ensure you do not sleep in the cold and you do not starve. If someone in your family dies, the rest of the family will take you in and care for you. It is considered bad to break the family bonds.

"Their custom, or law, holds the head of the family responsible for the conduct of its members, the village for that of its households and the tribe for the behavior of its village communes. The tribe is a big family that extends outward. Individual rights, such as we have here in France are unknown to the Basotho.

"Morality is so dependent on the social order that, as Casalis has noted, any breakdown in this order is likely to be followed by degeneracy and anarchy.

"The family and tribal bonds extend even beyond the grave. You have to know who you are descended from. You have to have regard for your ancestors."

He explains that he has traced Basotho and Baphuthi family history back a long way. He has drawn up an extensive genealogy of the people.

Steinheil adds, "I have heard it said that the Basotho people arrived here from the north only a few generations ago."

"My studies have shown that is untrue," Ellenberger replies. "These people have lived in and around this part of Africa for much longer than a few generations. Their memories, passed on from generation to generation, are amazing. I have been able to trace some families back 30 generations."

"Let's see," Steinheil responds. "If you take a generation as 30 years, that means you have traced their genealogy back 900 — almost a thousand — years?"

"Indeed."

"But how can that be? They have no written records. Do you mean to tell me they have remembered their genealogy?"

"They have. Just as the Bible records who begat whom, so do these people. The only difference is that the genealogies in the Bible are today written and those of the Basotho and Baphuthi remain oral. And just as it was important to the Jewish people to know who was in the royal line of descent, so it is important to the Basotho, too. The reasoning is the same. If you can trace your ancestry to a line of kings, you are considered to be royalty, too.

"Because the lines of descent are unwritten, unraveling their history and separating truth from the tangle of tradition is not an easy task. I could spend the rest of my life doing so and never end. But I have been able to verify ancestors by comparing the oral history of one clan with that of another. When I find the same ancestor occurring in a number of them, I have to accept that person as real."

"Yes, that makes sense," comments Steinheil, intrigued by what he is hearing. "What else do you know about their history?"

"The Baphuthi moved to the region now known as Basutoland from the north after a dispute with a clan in Tugela, which is now home to the Zulu people," Ellenberger says. "They arrived around 1720 when they settled among the Bafokeng in the area that is now northwestern Basutoland. The Bafokeng introduced them to iron hoes. Later the Baphuthi migrated south, to where they live today.

"There, they came across the Bushmen, who lived in caves, in holes in the ground, or under skins spread on poles. They were hunters. They lived off wild animals, many of which have now disappeared from the land.

"The Baphuthi were, and still are, farmers. They built huts, planted their fields and raised cattle. Boys were taught by their fathers to herd stock, to cultivate the ground and to use weapons. Girls were taught by the matrons obedience, courtesy, housekeeping and cooking and also to assist in the work of the fields. The difference between the two peoples was very great. Some of the Bushmen moved away. Others were absorbed into the Baphuthi people.

"There is much more," Ellenberger says. "I need to stop now, but next time we meet I'll have things about the Baphuthi people to tell you that will astound you."

II

Quthing — Thursday, May 31, 1877

Hope is working on the summons to be issued against Raisa — he must make sure it is legally correct — when Lemena walks in and asks to speak with him. Hope is delighted. Another member of the Baphuthi nation is recognizing his authority.

Lemena, a son of one of Moorosi's lesser wives, has no need of an interpreter. He learned to speak English while working on the diamond fields at Kimberley. At 45, he is a fast learner and enthusiastic about all that he tackles.

He talks quickly, gesturing with his hands.

"I want to tell you of something that took place before you got here," he tells Hope, wagging his finger. "I think it is important that you know about this, sir, because now you represent the white government here and you are a wise man."

Hope glares back at Lemena.

"I would prefer it if you did not wag your finger in my face," he says. "I am the magistrate here and you need to show me respect."

Lemena ignores Hope's reprimand. "You say you are bringing your law to us. I want to talk to you about the law and what I did. You will be pleased with me."

The tall, slim Baphuthi relishes this opportunity to make a good first impression on this man who represents justice, even if it is the white man's justice. Lemena regularly calls people to account for acts that he regards as wrong. If he had his way, he would be sitting in Hope's seat dispensing justice.

He turns back in front of Hope, bending his body forward until his face is in line with Hope's face. Hope instinctively leans back. "Before you arrived here, I caught a man who was trying to cheat Mr. Buckland, the shopkeeper." Lemena waves a finger in a southerly direction to illustrate where the incident took place.

Hope feels his personal space is being invaded. Being face to face also suggests Lemena is his equal. No black people are his equal or ever will be.

"Sit down!" he says. Lemena sits across from Hope and leans across the desk.

"Are you referring to Mr. Henry Buckland, the trader who works for Mr. Thomas?" Hope asks, trying to maintain his magisterial presence. "Does he run the shop near the Masitise mission station?"

"Yes, sir, he does," replies Lemena, banging his hand on the desk to express his approval. "That is the man. You are right, magistrate. You are right. His name is Mr. Buckland."

"Very well. How was the man trying to cheat Mr. Buckland?"

"This man, he told Mr. Buckland that he had been sent by Mr. Stephenson, who runs another shop in the south, in the Cape Colony," Lemena continues, pointing south. "He said Mr. Stephenson had sent him to borrow 15 shillings. The man said he would take the 15 shillings to Mr. Stephenson."

"Slow down," says Hope. "This man was a native?"

"Yes, sir. He was a Maphuthi. He said Mr. Stephenson had sent him."

"He said he was bringing a message from Mr. Stephenson?"

"Yes. That is right."

"And the message was that Mr. Stephenson wanted to borrow 15 shillings from Mr. Buckland?"

"Yes, you are right."

Lemena bangs his hand on the desk once more. Hope shudders. "You are right, magistrate. You are right."

"Good," Hope says. "I understand so far."

Lemena chuckles with excitement.

"But I knew that Mr. Stephenson had not sent the man there and that he was trying to cheat Mr. Buckland."

"How did you know that?"

"My good magistrate, I know all that is going on around here. I knew from his voice, from the way he spoke, that the white man did not send him. I just knew Mr. Stephenson had not sent him.

"If Mr. Stephenson had wanted to borrow 15 shillings from Mr. Buckland he would not have sent that man. He would have sent someone like me. He could have trusted me."

"Very well. Continue."

"This man — he is a bad man, a very bad man — said he would take the money to Mr. Stephenson. But I knew that he would keep the money.

"I was standing a little way off when I heard this man talking like this. Then I went up to Mr. Buckland and I told him that the man was trying to cheat him. Mr. Buckland was very happy that I had warned him. He said he would not give the man the 15 shillings.

"The man who wanted to take the money to Mr. Stephenson was angry. He said he was not a cheat. He said he had spoken to Mr. Stephenson. He said Mr. Stephenson had asked him to deliver the message because he had to stay and run the store and could not deliver the message himself. He asked me how I could say he was a cheat when he was not a cheat."

Lemena wags his finger again.

"I asked you *not* to shake your finger at me, Lemena," Hope insists. "As your magistrate, I demand that you treat me with respect."

Lemena continues undeterred. "But then I spoke to him some more. I spoke to him and asked him questions until the man admitted he had not spoken to Mr. Stephenson. I told him he was a bad man for trying to cheat the shopkeeper. I said Mr. Buckland buys our wool, our eggs, our chickens and our mealies and he sells us good things we can use. We should not cheat him.

"Mr. Buckland and I decided we would let the man go if the man gave us his gun as a punishment. The man was afraid because he thought we might punish him more, so he handed over his gun. Mr. Buckland said I could keep it as a reward.

"When Mr. Stephenson arrived at the shop a few days later I was there again. He thanked me. But he said that the gun should be sold and the money divided between him and me. I did not want to do that because I felt that I was the one who had done the good work and not Mr. Stephenson. I told Mr. Stephenson I had left the gun at home and I would think about what he said about selling the gun.

"Now I am coming to you to tell you what good work I have done in seeing that the law was upheld and to ask you to let me sell the gun and to keep the money for myself as a reward for what I did. I want you to tell me that I do not have to share the money with Mr. Stephenson."

Hope listens intently. He clears his throat and responds in his magisterial voice.

"Neither you nor Mr. Stephenson have suffered any damages," he says. "Yes, Lemena, you did good work in reporting the thief, but you do not deserve any reward for that."

Lemena sits back, his eyes reflecting incredulity. No reward?

Hope continues. "You were merely doing your duty. Mr. Stephenson did not lose or gain any money. In fact, no one suffered any damages in this case. No one deserves any compensation."

Lemena is taken aback. He stands up and shakes his finger at Hope. "Are you saying we should give the gun back to the man who owned it — the man who tried to cheat Mr. Buckland?" Lemena asks.

"Don't you shake your finger at me, Lemena," Hope responds.

Lemena looks at his hand as though it has done something wrong and lowers it to his side. "Must we give the gun back to the bad man who told lies?"

"No," Hope continues. "It is good that the man had to give up the gun as a punishment for what he did wrong. But neither you nor Mr. Stephenson deserve to have the gun.

"I order you to bring the gun to me."

Lemena leaves disillusioned. He does not like what this wise-looking man with the gray beard and black clothes has ordered him to do. He did a good deed for which he should be rewarded and is reluctant to give up the gun. What will the magistrate do with it? Will he give it to the white trader Stephenson? Is that why he wants it? Do these white people want to help one another rather than the Baphuthi people? He was looking for praise, not punishment.

Lemena will visit Moorosi, tell him what has happened.

Moorosi, and not the magistrate, is still his king and is a wiser man than this new magistrate.

Quthing — Monday, June 4, 1877

The summons is ready. It has been drawn up by Hope and translated by Charles Maitin, Hope's new clerk and translator, who arrived in Quthing yesterday.

The son of French missionaries who settled among the Basotho 34 years ago,

Maitin, 31, was born and bred in Basutoland. Being brought up among the people, Maitin has a thorough knowledge of the Sesotho language, which most of the Baphuthi can speak.

The summons Maitin has translated orders Raisa to present himself in court on Thursday, June 14 to answer charges that he destroyed a corn field belonging to MaLebenya. He must show cause, it says, why, if he is found guilty, he should not be punished.

When MaLebenya arrives in the afternoon Hope instructs her to see that Raisa receives the summons.

"You are to give it to him and tell him that he must do what it says," Hope explains. "It tells him to come here on June 14th and present himself to this court. We will then try him for what he has done. If we find him guilty, we will punish him."

MaLebenya smiles as Maitin translates. She likes the "punish him" part. She also likes this new man who speaks their language and who seems so wise.

"I will take it to him," she says.

When Lemena hands him the gun, Moorosi is pleased.

For some time, the Baphuthi leader has considered Lemena something of a rebel against Baphuthi tradition. This son is different than his other sons. Perhaps he is more like his mother, but he has been more inclined to imitate the white man. He learned to speak English and he likes to use it. Now he laughs and he gestures like white men. He spends time at the trading stores, not buying anything, but talking to the traders and learning from them about the white man's ways.

Moorosi has been afraid that Lemena will become like a white man and no longer be a true Baphuthi. But Lemena is not speaking like a white man now.

"My father, you are a wiser man than the magistrate," Lemena says. "He wants me to give him this gun, which I received for catching a man who tried to cheat a white trader. But I would rather give you the gun because I know you will keep it safe and not give it to the white men like the magistrate will do."

Moorosi is impressed. Lemena might act like a white man, but in his heart his son is Baphuthi.

Quthing — Thursday, June 7, 1877

MaLebenya's uncle, Mapeshoane, arrives at the magisterial compound to speak to Hope. "It is about Raisa," Mapeshoane says nervously.

"What about him?" Hope asks.

"I want to report what he has just done."

"I know what Raisa has done. I am going to try him for destroying a corn field. I have already issued a summons against him."

"That is not why I am here," Mapeshoane responds. "I have a different complaint against Raisa."

Aha, Hope thinks. Could be more evidence against this cruel, vindictive sub-chief.

"What is your complaint?" asks Hope.

"Raisa has seized MaLebenya's small children," he says. "These are children I would like to help raise now that MaLebenya's husband is dead. But Raisa is insisting that they are his children now. MaLebenya said I should come to you and you can make Raisa give us the children."

Hope has reason to be even more confident of his challenge to the Baphuthi chieftaincy. "This is clearly wrong," he mutters as he records the details in his official book. "Who does this man Raisa think he is?"

Hope carefully records a statement from Mapeshoane, translated by Maitin. He writes out another summons against Raisa, demanding that he release the children to their mother and her uncle. He sets the date of appearance as June 14, the same as that on the first summons. After Maitin translates the summons, Hope hands it to Mapeshoane.

"Take this summons to Raisa," he says. "Tell him he is to appear here on June 14th to answer this charge as well as that relating to the destruction of the corn field."

Quthing — Friday, June 8, 1877

The widow MaLebenya makes her way to Raisa's compound to present Hope's summons to him.

Raisa and his first wife occupy a round, windowless hut with a thatch roof, through which air can escape, enabling a fire to be built in the center. His hut is near the entrance to the bush-surrounded kraal, which encompasses the huts in which his other wives and children live and in some of which food is stored.

MaLebenya ascends the steep path to the ledge on which the huts stand. Behind it rises a flat-topped hill 400 feet high, crowned with a 50-foot circular wall-like rocky outcrop. A chill remains in the air this early in the wintry morning, even though the sun already is starting to warm the bush-covered hill.

The mat that hangs over the doorway to Raisa's hut is rolled down, indicating he does not want to be disturbed. Although Raisa has angered her, MaLebenya stops short at entering the hut as that would be breaking a strict moral code among her people.

Raisa has seen his late brother's wife approaching. He emerges from his hut and walks forward to meet her.

"Have you come to say I was right?" he asks. "Have you learned your lesson?"

MaLebenya does not reply. She thrusts the summons toward him.

"What's this?" Raisa asks, grabbing the piece of paper.

"It says you must go to the magistrate and tell him why you destroyed my crop," replies MaLebenya. "He says it's wrong and that you should not have done it."

The words are inflammatory. Who is this new magistrate to accuse him of doing wrong? What does he know about right and wrong? Raisa perceives also that the document represents more than a demand for an explanation for his action. It is a challenge to his authority.

"This man Hope is interfering in matters on which he has no authority. I will ignore this meaningless paper," he says, thrusting the summons back in MaLebenya's hands.

"It says you must be there on Thursday next week," responds MaLebenya. "At the magistrate's office along the Qomoqomong river where the wagon road ends."

Raisa curls his upper lip in a sneer. "That might be what it says," he shouts back. "But does that mean it is what I will do?"

Cape Town — Monday, June 11, 1877

Sir Bartle Frere is realizing that establishing a South African confederation is not going to be as straightforward as he had thought.

He has been told that tensions are rising between white settlers and the indigenous black inhabitants on the Cape Colony's eastern frontier. To Frere the reports from the easterners sound much like those he heard before the Indian Mutiny of 1857 and he now sees them as significant, even though he ignored them in his speech at the opening of Parliament and many in the western Cape Colony dismiss them as little more than blustering.

If true — and if they worsen — the tensions could prove to be a setback for the confederation cause.

Among his tasks, therefore, will be to ascertain the true state of affairs on the eastern border of the Cape Colony and to determine how the area will need to be managed to ensure that confederation will be successful.

Paris — The same day

"You were going to tell me something about the Basotho people that would surprise me," says Georges Steinheil. "I think you used the phrase, 'astound you' if I recall."

Ellenberger smiles and leans back in his chair. "You will recall I said that, through a combination of tradition, language and customs, we can trace the Basotho people — including the Baphuthi — farther back than I have described so far," he says. "We have found out, for example, that the Bafokeng, who introduced the Baphuthi to iron hoes and whom I mentioned earlier, migrated from Egypt or Ethiopia to the south of Africa. It must have taken centuries.

"But we can go back even farther, back even before the time of Christ. I believe — and I am not alone in this belief — that today's Basotho people are descendants of Semitic people who lived in the Middle East thousands of years ago. We have found a strong link between the customs of the Basotho and those of the ancient Hebrews."

Steinheil's eyes light up. "Now that you mention it, I have heard that Europeans who first arrived in the country said the Basotho varied in color from light brown to dark black, even in the same families."

"Indeed," Ellenberger responds. "The reason, we believe, is that they reflect the original people from whom they sprang. Their lighter skin color and Arabian-like features represent their Middle Eastern origin; their blackness reflects their intermarriage as they made their way down through Africa.

"My fellow missionaries have described some of the Basotho people as almost Arab or Persian in their appearance. As one put it, 'they are tall, beautifully built, with aquiline noses, upright foreheads and lips almost as thin as those of Europeans.'

"Of course, I noticed those characteristics myself when I first arrived there. The missionary Eugene Casalis records his initial observations in his book when he notes, and I think I am quoting him correctly, 'Their skin was soft, bronze rather than black, their limbs robust and well modeled.' He also says that in the case of the Basotho aristocracy their eyes are more prominent, their noses less flattened and their lips thinner, more like those of Europeans than Africans.

"These people also carry the culture of the people from whom they originally sprang. In short, these people are not barbaric. They are not savages, as the white colonial authorities often say. Nor can they be described as truly heathen, another epithet often thrown their way by the Europeans. We believe these people among whom I have been preaching the Gospel are descendents of a Middle Eastern people whose beliefs and customs are recorded in the Old Testament."

Steinheil sits up straight.

"Recorded in the Old Testament?"

Ellenberger nods. He explains that the theory of links between the Basotho people and the ancient Hebrews is strongly held by the missionary Casalis, who recorded his thoughts in the book from which he earlier quoted and which Casalis wrote 16 years ago, in 1862.

Steinheil notes that Casalis is now director of the Maison des Missions in Paris.

Among Casalis's evidence, Ellenberger continues, is the similarity of words in Setswana — closely related to Sesotho — and other languages spoken in Africa, such as those in the Congo, the Comoro Islands and Delagoa, as well as Swahili. Casalis also identified a number of words in languages of the Batswana and Basotho people that appeared to be of Hebrew origin.

Ellenberger takes out Casalis's book, *The Basotho*, flips through the pages to one containing a chart that Casalis drew up.

"Look here, the Hebrew word for children, *bene*, is *bana* in Setswana. It is the same in Sesotho. To repent — a term associated with religious beliefs and likely to be retained if the beliefs are similar — is *bakah* in Hebrew and *baka* in Setswana and Sesotho. The Hebrew for to swear, or attest, is *anah*; in Sesotho it is *ana*."

He flips through a few pages and reads to Steinheil from Casalis' book: "We might further notice, as bearing resemblance to the Hebrew, the forms of the verbs, the suffixing pronouns, the frequent use of the noun as adjective, and of the verb as adverb, the manner in which the comparative and superlative are formed, and several interesting idioms."

Ellenberger reads on, "We find nothing of a savage nature when we seek the reflection of their thoughts and feeling in the vocabulary and grammar of their respective idioms, which, if they do not display a degree of civilization similar to our own, may, without hesitation, be said to reproduce that of the patriarchal era."

Ellenberger adds an observation of his own. The women who adorn themselves with the traditional Basotho dress wear round their loins a girdle of twisted grass called the *thethana*, which word, he explains, may be derived from the Hebrew *thanah*, meaning a fig tree, of the leaves of which Adam and Eve are said to have made themselves aprons. "So," he laughingly adds, "you see, their language goes right back to the origin of mankind.

"Here's another example. The Baphuthi, like the Basotho, begin their month on the new moon. So did the ancient Babylonians, Hebrews and Romans. They also begin the civil day at sunset, and count days from evening to evening, which the Jewish people still do."

Ellenberger adds that the common law of the Basotho and the Baphuthi also appears to have been passed on from thousands of years ago. The system of land tenure, in which the land belongs to the nation under the chief, excludes any concept of private land ownership. That system and the major principles of the Basotho common law are largely identical with those of the patriarchal dispensation of the Old Testament.

"Being there is like living among the patriarchs of old," says Ellenberger.

Although their customs appear to have remained the same over the ages, Ellenberger adds, belief in one powerful God like that of the Hebrews appears to have waned. Instead they worship their ancestors and attribute to them a divine power for good and evil. But the concept of God appears occasionally. Some missionaries, such as Samuel Rolland, say by using the word *Molimo* the Basotho designate the Great Lord Creator of their several tribes.

"There is an ancient prayer that means 'New gods, pray for us to the God of old,' in which the Basotho invoke the Deity through the mediation of the spirits. You could argue that this points to the necessity of mediation between God and man. We, too, believe in Jesus as a mediator."

Steinheil leans forward, fascinated. "Why, then, do the people name themselves after animals? I understand that the Baphuthi, for example, are named after the *phuthi* or duiker, which I gather is a variety of antelope."

"Yes," replies Ellenberger. "Duikers used to abound in that area, but they have almost all gone now, as a result of hunting.

"I believe that these emblems are, to the Baphuthi and other Basotho clans, symbols of the Divine Being, just as the Ark of the Covenant was the symbol of

God for the Israelites of old. They wanted more than just to rely on the mediation of their ancestors, who were invisible. They wanted something tangible to symbolize the God of old to which they could pray and from whom they could seek aid.

"But to return to the law," Ellenberger continues. "It is, of course, not written down, but is passed down from generation to generation. It is accepted among the people. They do not question it; they do not seek to alter it. They all know instinctively what the law is. And that law, as I mentioned, is strikingly similar to that of the Hebrews.

"As I said, the Baphuthi law holds the head of the family responsible for the conduct of its members, the village for that of its households and the clan for the behavior of each of its village communes. Individual rights are virtually unknown. Families and villages are more important than the individuals that comprise them."

Ellenberger opens his Bible and turns to Deuteronomy 25:5.

"Here's an example of Baphuthi custom being the same as that of the ancient Hebrew people," he tells Steinheil. "Let me read it to you. 'When brothers reside together, and one of them dies and has no son, the wife of the deceased shall not be married outside the family to a stranger. Her husband's brother shall go in to her, taking her in marriage, and performing the duty of a husband's brother to her.'

"The ancient Hebrews took this system seriously.

"As we read in verses 7 to 10: However, if a man does not want to marry his brother's wife, she shall go to the elders at the town gate and say, 'My husband's brother refuses to carry on his brother's name in Israel. He will not fulfill the duty of a brother-in-law to me.' Then his brother's wife shall go up to him in the presence of the elders and pull his sandal off his foot and spit in his face. And she shall answer and say, 'So shall it be done to the man who does not build up his brother's house.' And the name of his house shall be called in Israel, 'The house of him who had his sandal pulled off.'

"The Bible also has other references to the system, known as the levirate," Ellenberger adds, "going back as far as Genesis. In that book, chapter 38, we read that Er, Judah's firstborn, was put to death by the Lord. Then, in verse 8, we read: 'then Judah said to Onan, 'Lie with your brother's wife and fulfill your duty to her as a brother-in-law to produce offspring for your brother.'

"This same approach, followed by the Hebrews so long ago, is reflected in the evidence given to the Commission on Laws and Customs of the Basotho, which sat in Cape Town four years ago. I have a copy of it." Ellenberger searches among his papers for the commission report.

"Ah, here it is. Let me read you the evidence given to the commission by George Tladi Moshesh, son of the late Chief Moshoeshoe. When he gave evidence, George Moshesh was working for the government as sub inspector of Basutoland police.

"He wrote, 'If the husband dies, his wife, or wives, belong to his eldest surviving brother who is to raise up seed to his deceased brother by taking them to wife himself or giving them to other men as wives.

" 'If the deceased has left any children, the son of the first wife will be his heir, and can claim all the children born to his deceased father's wives, and all cattle given for any of these children belong to him.

" 'The maternal uncle of every married woman is called the *malome* and he has a right to a portion of the cattle given for his niece. He is expected to take care of his niece and her children, and to supply her with anything which she may require, such as a kaross — tanned skins tied together to form a covering.'

"You may be struck by the similarity between how the Bible describes the Hebrew law and how George Moshesh describes the Basotho law 2,500 years later. If anything the law is stricter among the Baphuthi and the Basotho than it was among the Hebrews. Here, the widow is compelled to remain in the family. The purpose is to preserve the family line, which was important for the Hebrews, and is today for the Baphuthi. The Bible is filled with references to family lines. You will recall that Jesus' ancestry was traced back to David. Such ancestry gave him legitimacy in the eyes of the Jewish people. And so it is today among the Baphuthi and Basotho. If you can trace your history back to the family line of a famous chief or king, then your people hold you in high esteem.

"As I have told you, I have been able to trace the history of these people back a thousand years," Ellenberger adds. "To them, the lines of descent are just as important as they were to the Hebrew people. Moorosi, the Baphuthi king, can trace his ancestry back over eight generations.

"It is also a way of preserving the family's property. Women are granted access to land through their husbands. But when a woman's husband dies her land can be taken away from her for any reason. She holds the land by virtue of being a man's wife, not in her own right. Although action might not be taken against a woman who refuses to marry her brother-in-law, her land can be taken away.

"The widow also must often leave her male children behind with her deceased husband's family. The emphasis is on the family, its heritage and its land rather than on the individual.

"I can say a lot more about their customs — and I have not even touched on the three major issues on which major clashes occur with the colonial government and the missionaries. They involve the *lebollo*, or circumcision and sometimes cruel and merciless initiation rites that young men undergo under seclusion to mark their transition to manhood, the *sethepu*, or polygamy, and the *bohadi*, or the practice of giving cattle to a father for the privilege of marrying his daughter.

"As Casalis notes, we see evidence of these three practices, too, among the ancient peoples of the Middle East. For example, the age of the administration of the initiation rite is about the same as that of Ishmael, when he and his father Abraham received the sign of the covenant. Many Hebrew kings had multiple wives. King Solomon had 700. Also, Basotho marriages are conducted in the same way as among the Etruscans, the ancient Romans and the Arabs. The parents of the man pay a value, often called a dowry, to the parents of the woman he is to marry.

"Casalis points out that it is a curious coincidence that, at the rate of remuneration awarded to young shepherds in the southern part of Africa, a Basotho man, in order to acquire sufficient means to procure a wife, would be obliged to serve for the same number of years as Jacob did to the father of Rachel and Leah.

"I might add that I heard a Basotho say when he heard this Bible story, 'Jacob gave cattle for his wife. Did this stop God from loving and blessing him?'

"Also, the custom that forbade the marriage of Rachel before that of Leah still exists in full force among the people in Basutoland."

Sometimes, Ellenberger adds, events in the Bible become more understandable if one knows the culture of Basutoland. "For example, Casalis has pointed out that among the Basotho if an accident should happen to the younger children, or if they conduct themselves badly, the father lays the blame on the eldest son. That is why the Basotho have no problem in understanding why Reuben was so worried about his brother Joseph. It was Reuben who probably came up with the idea of putting blood on the coat of many colors and showing it to his father. He wanted to free himself from blame for the disappearance of Joseph. If his father had blamed him for what had happened, he might have disinherited him.

"We find Judah, to whom the birthright was to be transferred, saying to Jacob, 'Send Benjamin with me, and we will arise and go. I will be surety for him; of my hand shalt thou require him. If I bring him not to thee, then let me bear the blame forever.' Our ideas and customs make us less likely to grasp the deeper meaning of this pledge, but the Baphuthi and Basotho have no difficulty understanding it.

"The practice of sacrifice is familiar to the Baphuthi and Basotho, too. Some offer victims as a method of averting domestic or public calamities. It is therefore an easy transition for them to understand that Jesus died for their sins."

Ellenberger rises from his chair. "I believe I have tired you. I have been talking for far too long."

Steinheil also stands up. "Not at all," he replies.

"Are there any issues that I have not discussed?"

"I wonder what you think of the new magistrate. You mentioned him, but did not elaborate. Do you think he will do some good for the Baphuthi and help them to follow the Christian way?"

Ellenberger pauses, tugs at his beard, looks away from Steinheil, and stares toward the wall. "Let me think about that. I will try to answer the question when we talk again later, perhaps in a day or two."

Steinheil is intrigued. He judges from Ellenberger's reaction that this question is not easy for him to answer.

Maseru — Tuesday, June 12, 1877

Letsie, approaching 70, the paramount chief of the Basotho people to whom the autonomous Baphuthi clan pay nominal allegiance, seldom leaves his village and his *khotla*, or meeting place, where his messengers bring him news from his people, missionaries, and from government officials. Overweight and unwieldy, he walks slowly and prefers to rest rather than walk even short distances, because of his weight and the gout that afflicts his feet. Yet, even though he seldom mixes with his people, he wields great personal influence over them. Many are his relatives as he has 50 wives and has sired many children.

Having learned the virtues of peace from his father Moshoeshoe, Letsie is unwilling to stir up hostility with either the black nations or the white colonists. He has always got on well with the Zulu, Mpondomise and Bapedi people. Although less friendly with the Xhosa-speaking Gcaleka, Ngqika and Mfengu people to the south, he has no desire to antagonize them.

He also enjoys friendly and confidential relations with the administrators of the Cape Colony. He needs the British and the Cape colonists to protect his people from the Boers of the Orange Free State, with which his country shares a border. Letsie is not one to stir up trouble with anyone. Compromise works just fine for him.

Yet, as he meets today with his chiefs, he expresses his concern about the government's recent actions. He and his chiefs are becoming increasingly worried that confederation as advocated by Frere could mean that Basutoland's degree of independence would be taken away. Instead of being a territory administered by the colony on behalf of Britain, they would be absorbed into the white-run Cape Colony. They fear that the protection they enjoy under the British government's supervision over the colonial administration would be gone; in its place would be direct rule by the colonial government.

They are not alone in fearing confederation. Other black leaders have told the Basotho that they, too, fear confederation is a plot by the whites to extend their power across all of Southern Africa, absorbing any and all black territories.

Recently there was a rumor that, under confederation, Basutoland would be annexed to the Free State rather than the Cape Colony and that they would be governed by the Boers, their most recent enemies in war. The Basotho relaxed when this rumor was denied, but they remain fearful of encroaching white power.

They feel equally threatened by the proposal by the Prime Minister of the Cape Colony, John Molteno, that, instead of confederation, the Cape should annex adjoining territories. Both confederation and annexation would put the white government more firmly in control. And proponents of neither policy have consulted the Basotho, or expressed any concern about the effects on the Basotho.

Still, these are only proposals and so the Basotho chiefs agree to continue to cooperate with the government. But they will watch the situation closely.

Quthing — The same day

Mapeshoane makes his way to Raisa, bearing his summons. Raisa is quick to recognize the similarity of the piece of paper to that brought him earlier by MaLebenya. "What? You are bringing another piece of paper from the magistrate?"

Mapeshoane backs off slightly. He thrusts the summons toward Raisa, who refuses to take it. Mapeshoane places it on the ground between them.

"He says you must return the children," he tells Raisa. "He says I am the person who must help MaLebenya take care of the children of my niece."

"Hope knows nothing. I do not accept him. I do not accept his authority. I will not do anything he tells me to do because he is not my chief."

Raisa kicks the summons, propelling it toward Mapeshoane.

"Take that back as my answer."

Quthing — Wednesday, June 13, 1877

Having been ordered twice by the new government official to appear tomorrow, Raisa realizes that the time has come to speak with his king. Raisa is reluctant to obey the order, but is nervous about the implications of defying the magistrate, who represents the powerful white government to the south.

Raisa is convinced he acted correctly in destroying MaLebenya's corn field. After all, she had refused to become his wife, as she should have done when her husband died. She also had refused to let him become the father to her children.

Clearly she had been influenced by the white people's thinking. Why else would she disobey? Why else would she go against everything that was right and just? He was prepared to do the right thing, but she rebelled and did the wrong thing.

So he had taken away the corn field, which no longer belonged to her. It was her husband's corn field and, although she had tended it, she no longer had any right to it. The field would have become his if she had become his wife. But she did not want to give it to him, so now the field belonged to the people and must be returned to the people — without its crop.

Leaving his village, he rides on horseback along the Orange River for several miles until he reaches Moorosi's stronghold, a flat-topped mountain that the Baphuthi chief over the last decade has turned into a fortress.

The 1,500-foot mountain appears similar to many around it. On three sides it consists of sheer rock cliff faces. But on the fourth, facing south, the less-sheer rock face drops from the summit to a 150-foot-long plateau before dropping off farther to level ground.

What sets the mountain apart is the size and nature of its flat top. The summit stretches for 600 yards from north to south and is about 300 yards wide. Here Moorosi has established a self-sustaining village. In addition to two round stone-and-thatch huts, one of which is his headquarters, Moorosi has built two stone houses where he has accumulated a stockpile of rifles and ammunition, many given to him by his people and others purchased with cattle and corn from those who have worked in the diamond fields and brought back weapons. Never-failing springs provide fresh water and caves and openings in rocky outcrops on the edges of the mountaintop furnish shelter for hundreds.

Moorosi has emulated Moshoeshoe, the man he so much admired, who set up his headquarters on a flat-topped mountain called Thaba Bosigo, near Maseru, from where he defended himself when attacked. Moorosi has made his mountain even more impregnable than Thaba Bosigo. Here he feels safe.

At the base of Moorosi's Mountain, Raisa dismounts and sets out to climb to the top of the mountain where he will meet his king. With large strides, he ascends the twisting path along the side of the plateau, around the side of the mountain, up a series of rocky ledges, each about two feet high, and along a path that leads to the top.

As he climbs, he notes that Moorosi is building up his defenses. His people have built a series of six-foot-high stone-and-earth walls, that, along with natural rock formations, serve not only to block the path of an unwanted intruder, but to create protection for armed men to fire on intruders. Even as Raisa makes his way along and around the walls, men are piling on more stones, now and then leaving small holes through which they can fire.

Told by lookouts who is approaching, Moorosi walks a short way down the path to greet Raisa. Together they make their way around stone fences at the top of the mountain to Moorosi's hut, outside which the chief quietly takes a seat.

The view from here is commanding. To the southwest, the mountain drops sharply before giving way to the Orange River, which carves its way around the mountain. From the other side of the river, the land climbs mountains and dips into valleys across many miles as far as the eye can see. To the east, the land flattens out for a distance and crosses a river before rising to the bush-covered slopes of the next mountain, beyond which lie more mountains. To the south, across a valley, stands a rocky outcrop about half the height of Moorosi's Mountain, keeping watch as a sort of sentinel.

The scene imbues the viewer with a sense of supremacy.

Before they discuss the issues surrounding the corn field and custody of MaLebenya's children, Moorosi and Raisa talk of the magistrate and what his presence here means for the Baphuthi people.

"You have already asked these people to come here," Raisa reminds Moorosi. "You asked for their protection and you let us become British citizens. You accept money from the government to collect the hut tax for them."

"You are right," Moorosi replies. "I have already accepted a degree of colonial rule and I am not opposed to some of the things the government has brought. If they spend the hut tax to improve the conditions of our people, as they have said they will, I will not object.

"Also, I do not object to sending our children to the missionary schools. It is good that our people learn to read and to write. But we do not want Christianity forced on us. We will decide for ourselves. The missionaries teach us to live in ways that are different from our ways. We do not want to change our ways and it is only those teachings that fit in with our traditions that we will accept."

"How much attention should I pay to the magistrate's authority?" Raisa asks.

"We also do not want the government telling us how we should live," Moorosi replies. "When Moshoeshoe allowed our people to be protected by the British government, he did not surrender our laws and customs.

"Now these white government people from the Cape have taken over from the British and they want to tell us how to live. We are not happy if they force us to live under their laws and show allegiance to their leaders.

"We have agreed to let some of them be here. But we did not give the land to them. It it is our land. I cannot give it away. You cannot give it away. My sons Letuka and Lehana cannot give it away. Not even Lemena, with his European ways, can give it away.

"It belongs to our people, to all of us. Without our land, we are nothing. It provides us with our food. It is where we graze our cattle. It is where we walk and run and sleep and where our children grow up.

"The magistrate in Mohale's Hoek asked us to collect hut tax. We agreed to give it to them to use for us. But they asked us first to help them collect it. They respected me as the leader of the Baphuthi people. They knew they would need to ask me first before they could do anything on our land.

"Now they have jumped over the river and established themselves in our territory. Now they are here, on our land. We welcome strangers, but they must respect our land. It is our land. It is not their land."

Raisa stands up. He thrusts his hands forward to emphasize his words.

"The magistrate says I am wrong to have taken away MaLebenya's field."

"MaLebenya was wrong to have gone to the magistrate," Moorosi replies. "I did not tell her she could go to the magistrate. If she was unhappy with your actions, she should have come to me. I am thinking what action we should take about MaLebenya going to the magistrate and about the magistrate listening to MaLebenya without referring the matter to me. We are discussing it at our *khotla*."

"MaLebenya must marry me," Raisa adds. "She must obey me. Her sons will be my sons. She and her family belong to me now and I will see to her needs. But the field is no longer hers. It belongs to the people. She can keep her husband's cattle, which now also become my cattle. But she cannot keep my brother's plot of land."

Moorosi remains seated. He looks up, into Raisa's eyes.

"What you say about the plot is right. But it also is true that in each case we should look in fairness at the people involved and at the obligations of support.

"It also is our custom for you to discuss with MaLebenya's uncles what must happen to her children. Did you hold a *khotla*?"

"No, my king, I did not hold a hearing. I did not think that Mapeshoane was a true uncle."

"Perhaps he is a true uncle. Perhaps he is not a true uncle. How can I know unless he comes to speak to me?"

"But he has not come to you," Raisa responds. "He has gone to the magistrate."

"Yes, and so has MaLebenya. You did what is right. But MaLebenya is a rebellious person who refuses to accept your decision. She listens to the missionaries and the government with their new ideas, ideas that are not our ideas. Their ideas will break up our families. They will leave widows alone, unable to care for themselves. MaLebenya and Mapeshoane should have come to me. I would have held counsel and decided whether you acted in the right way."

"What then should I say to the magistrate? He has instructed me to appear before him. Should I stay away? Or should I go before him?"

Moorosi stands up, indicating the discussion is at an end.

"This matter is one that I must judge, not the magistrate. MaLebenya must come to me. You must come to me. And I will be the judge."

Raisa makes his way down the mountain, twisting and turning around the stone walls to his horse waiting patiently below. He is unsure what to do.

Yes, Moorosi is his leader, the man he calls his father. He will obey Moorosi because he is king of all the Baphuthi. He does not trust Hope or accept his authority over the land because it is not Hope's land. Hope has no say over MaLebenya because she is not his brother's widow.

But he has heard that the white government is powerful. It has policemen and soldiers. Raisa fears what Hope will do to him if he fails to appear before him.

Quthing — Thursday, June 14, 1877

The scene is set for the hearing against Raisa on the charge of destroying a corn field. The widow, MaLebenya, and her uncle Mapeshoane are sitting on a bench in Hope's living room that doubles as his courtroom until one is built. Maitin, presenting the government's case, is ready to translate. Hope, fitted out in his magisterial clothes, is ready to proceed.

Only one person is missing.

Raisa.

"Did you give him the summons?" Hope asks MaLebenya and Mapeshoane.

They did.

Perhaps, Maitin suggests, Raisa cannot read and simply set it aside out of ignorance. "Before you take further action, your honor, may I respectfully submit that you should make sure he understands what the summons says."

Hope reluctantly agrees.

He sets Raisa's court appearance at Monday, June 18. He calls a policeman, Isaak Masin, to the front of the court and instructs him to tell Raisa of the change.

"You must make it clear to him that he needs to be in court on Monday," he says. "Explain it to him as you would to a child." He tells MaLebenya and Mapeshoane to be back on Monday.

Outside, Maitin talks with MaLebenya.

"You need to help the policeman explain to Raisa that he needs to be here on Monday. He obviously does not understand."

"I did make it clear to him," MaLebenya says. "He did understand. But he said he would not be here. He told Mapeshoane the same thing."

Maitin turns to Mapeshoane.

"What happened when you delivered the summons?"

"He rejected it," replies Mapeshoane. "He threw it on the ground."

Maitin asks the two witnesses to wait and calls to Hope inside the house.

"I think you need to reconvene the court hearing," he says, "and listen to what these two have to say about the delivery of the summons."

Their stories make Hope furious. Raisa does not misunderstand. He is not unaware of the time demands of the summons to face trial. He is being antagonistic. Hope will not tolerate such an attitude. He represents the law and must be obeyed.

"You were messengers of this court," he tells Mapeshoane and MaLebenya. "His actions are unacceptable."

Hope issues a criminal summons against Raisa for contempt of court. To erase any claim of misunderstanding, he instructs Chief Constable Sighata to take the summons to Raisa and to read it aloud to the sub-chief. Hope scraps the earlier order and extends the date for the court appearance. The new summons demands that Raisa appear on Thursday, June 21 to answer the charge. He tells the two witnesses to be present, too.

Raisa is not surprised when Sighata approaches on his horse in the late afternoon. He had expected the magistrate to send someone to get him. As the constable dismounts, Raisa strides toward him, holding a short spear above his head. As the official approaches, Raisa thrusts his hand forward, stabbing toward him in a gesture of hostility.

The constable steps back. He understands the reason for tension. He works for the colonial government, which he knows Raisa and Moorosi distrust. Yet he does not expect Raisa to be so angry.

"Why are you acting like that toward me, Raisa?" he asks. "I have come only to bring you a piece of paper, not to attack you."

Raisa pulls back slightly, but keeps his spear at the ready. "I know why you are here," he says. "I have received enough pieces of paper from this new magistrate. I do not need another one."

Sighata remains calm. "This is a new piece of paper. It's not the same as the earlier ones. I will read it to you," he tells Raisa.

"You do not need to read it to me."

The chief constable persists. He looks around and calls to Raisa's family members and friends "Come and listen," he says. "I want you all to hear this so you can bear witness that Raisa heard it." The others move closer, more intrigued than volunteering to be witnesses.

The chief constable slowly reads the summons aloud. Twice.

"You must respect and obey this summons," he tells Raisa. "You must not treat it with contempt. You must do as the magistrate says. You must be in court to answer the summons on Thursday, June 21st. You must also tell him then why you were not there before." He hands the contempt-of-court summons to Raisa, who throws it on the ground.

Paris — Friday, June 15, 1877

Ellenberger leans back in his chair, tugs at his beard and coughs nervously.

"Your question — what I think of the new magisterial presence — is a complex one to answer," he says. For the first time since he has met Steinheil, Ellenberger seems unsure of himself.

"I know that some of the missionaries have aligned themselves with the British and Cape Colonial administrations. Some, like Emile Rolland, have switched from being missionaries to becoming administrators. Other missionaries have advised the Basotho to obey the laws imposed by the British, and now the colonial administration.

"These missionaries believe that the administration's laws are closer to the way the Basotho should live than are the Basotho customs. They believe it is a Christian administration and is promoting a Christian way of life. They see themselves and the administration as working together. I understand that approach. But I also believe it is not as easy as that. And a few missionaries support my view.

"Being a magistrate means you are representing a legal system being imposed on the people. You sit in judgment and you have the power to sentence people to long terms of imprisonment. You have no jury. You are the sole judge of right and wrong and what punishments need to be imposed. If you impose the law firmly you are only doing your job well.

"I believe that administrators and missionaries are following different paths.

"Ours is the path of persuasion.

"I did not go to Masitise to force anyone to become a Christian. That would be fruitless. People do not become Christians out of fear. They become Christians because they decide that is the way of life they should follow. In the eyes of God, of what value is belief arrived at through fear?

"The administration, on the other hand, is following the path of power.

"Hope is imposing his will — the will of the government — on the people. It does not matter whether they are persuaded that he is right. He is going to impose his will on them anyway.

"There is another path," he continues.

"That is the path of profit.

"It is found among the people who have set up trading stations on the Baphuthi land, such as a man named Thomas who has set up three trading stations in Quthing. It goes without saying that they are not there to spread Christianity. Neither are they there to impose laws. They are there to make money.

"Because that is their goal, they tend not to interfere with others whose goals are different. Yet, the paths cross. If exposure to the white man's way through the magistrates or the missionaries means the people buy more European goods, the traders are happy."

Steinheil adds: "I would imagine there are times, too, when the traders try to influence the administration so they will have good conditions under which to trade."

Ellenberger nods.

"That is true. That is another way the paths cross. At times, they run parallel. At other times they cross."

"And now the path of persuasion, which you represent, is about to cross with the path of power," Steinheil continues. "Is there not the chance that they will join together? Surely you should welcome the presence of the administration. If they impose their standards and their justice on the people, you will benefit because it is in essence a Christian justice."

"Perhaps," Ellenberger responds. "But I have been working among the Baphuthi for six years without the direct presence of the administration. I have worked in peace. There has been no conflict. The people, if I may say so myself, respect and even love me. Those who disagree with me and do not want to become Christians often tell me so and simply stay away. They do not try to drive me out. Now, with the arrival of Hope I am told trouble is stirring.

"We missionaries have not always seen eye to eye with the authorities. We understand the people and see much through their eyes. We do not always like what we see in the administration and the way they act. But I expect I will know a lot more of how the paths are interacting when I return."

Quthing — Monday, June 18, 1877

Hope relaxes in the office that he has set up in his living room as the late afternoon sun shines through the small window, lighting up the dust with its rays. He puffs at his pipe.

"I am really pleased you are here to help me as a clerk and interpreter. I think I will give you the title of Justice of the Peace."

Maitin smiles. The position is a senior one for a man aged 30.

"Griffith also has given me permission to appoint you agent of the post office. Of course, the number of letters passing through here is small, but the work will pick up in time. For this, you will be paid 6 pounds a year, with an allowance of 3 pounds a year, making a total of 9 pounds."

Maitin smiles again.

"I understand that you have been thrust into office quickly," Hope continues. "But now that you have been here a couple of weeks, I thought it appropriate that we review the duties of this office and discuss the way in which I plan to run it."

"I will be happy to do that, Mr. Hope," Maitin replies.

"I think we know why we are here," Hope continues. "We are preparing the native minds to understand and receive good government. Along with that goes respect for the law, for truth and for justice. Soon they will realize the benefits of good government and that will free them from the torpor of barbarism.

"Above all, it is important that we maintain peace and good order.

"And the native people understand that. Only their chiefs want to retain their hold on power to perpetuate their barbaric ways. In that regard, I think the Baphuthi people, under Moorosi, are far behind the other branches of the Basotho tribe in civilization or industry. I'm told that when their food supplies dwindle following a drop in the rainfall, they suffer because they do not have any reserve grain. They live from year to year, supplementing their grain with roots and berries to eke out a meal.

"The traders have been of little help. They do nothing to encourage industry among the natives and appear to be undercharging for the produce that they buy from them and overcharging for the things they sell them. Also, the people are abject slaves to superstition. They have witch doctors who throw bones and say all kinds of mumbo jumbo.

"Nevertheless, things are getting off to a good start. I have just received permission from Griffith to appoint more policemen. In addition to Sighata and the other three working for us, Griffith has approved the appointment of a corporal and the transfer of two privates from Mohale's Hoek and two privates from Mafeteng, as well as additional policemen, making a total of nine."

"The transferees are all Basotho and are not from the local Baphuthi people," Maitin points out. "They will not be able to speak the local language."

"Of course," Hope replies, brushing any concerns aside. "They will be loyal to us and not to the local people. And most of the Baphuthi can speak Sesotho anyway. We have a fairly strong police force, we have initiated a survey, we are mapping the territory, we will soon institute a census to ensure that all pay the hut tax — and now we have had our first court hearing.

"I have also requested £60 from Griffith to build a lock-up, where we can hold up to 10 prisoners," Hope adds.

"Griffith suggested I establish our magisterial compound at Alwyn's Kop, a mile or so this side of the Telle River," Hope continues. "But I preferred this spot at the end of the wagon road near another river. They call it the Komo...something river, don't they?"

"The Qomoqomong river," says Maitin.

"Right. I'll leave you to do the clicks. This place is closer to where the people live. The wagon road provides us with a good passage to the border. It means we can bring all we need by ox wagon.

"The stream here provides a steady supply of water. The ground is fertile. We can grow vegetables, graze our horses and have cattle here. When she joins me, my wife Mimmie can even have a flower garden here if she wants one."

Hope pauses and Maitin seizes the opportunity to talk.

"I think Griffith thought the site he suggested could be better protected. Here we are surrounded by hills on three sides and could be subject to surprise attacks."

"Yes, he would say that. But there have been no attacks on our magistrates here in Basutoland since the Cape Colony took over the running of the country six years ago. There has been trouble to the south, but the Basotho are a step above those people. They have accepted us and, apart from the inevitable troublemakers, they are respectful, obedient and loyal.

"I worked as a clerk in Mafeteng for five years for Mimmie's brother, Emile Rolland. We collected the hut tax, we held trials, we sentenced people, we conducted surveys. All without any problems. You just have to be strict with these people and show them who is in charge. Then they respect you and cooperate with you."

"I think Griffith believes Moorosi is more rebellious than the other chiefs," Maitin ventures.

"He underestimates my power to tame Moorosi," Hope counters. When I visited Moorosi with Griffith and Austen a couple of months ago, the sly old man argued for hours; we spent almost a day there. Eventually he had to concede. There is no way he can be left on his own to run this territory the way he has done for so long. We need government control here. Just look at this case with that woman that I heard today. These barbarians are cruel and vindictive. It is time they were brought into the 19th century and understood what justice and morality really are."

Hope can afford to discount Griffith's authority. Or, for that matter, anyone's authority. Communications across Basutoland are slow. Mail posted from Quthing and carried on horseback will take two or three days, depending on the state of the rivers and weather conditions, to reach Griffith in Maseru, some 100 miles away by road. From there, the post takes five days to reach the seat of government in Cape Town. Telegraph lines have reached Aliwal North in the Cape Colony, to the south, but have yet to reach Basutoland. Because he is unable to consult anyone above him on decisions that have to be taken urgently, in most cases Hope will tell the authorities only what he has done, not what he intends to do.

Maseru — The same day

As resident magistrate overseeing all of Basutoland, Charles Duncan Griffith, 47, comes from a long line of men who served in the British police and armed forces. His great-grandfather John Griffith was high sheriff of Penpompren in Wales. His grandfather was a captain in the Royal Marines. And his father, Charles Griffith, was a first lieutenant of the Royal Marines before he settled in South Africa in a Welsh party that arrived in Port Elizabeth in 1820. There, his father served as barracks master at Grahamstown.

Charles Griffith was born 10 years after his father arrived in South Africa and was introduced to military life at an early age. At 14 he was assisting his father in the barracks and getting to know the soldiers who moved in and out.

At 18, Griffith joined the just-established Frontier Armed and Mounted Police where he was stationed at Queenstown. He soon demonstrated his leadership ability, becoming a captain during a frontier war in which he narrowly escaped

death by starvation and fever, even as he was avoiding spear and gun attacks from
the Ngqika people. At 20, he was displaying coolness and professionalism.

After serving as a lieutenant in the frontier wars of 1851 and 1852, Griffith
made his first visit to Basutoland in 1855 on a mission for the then governor of the
Cape, Sir George Grey, to the Basotho leader Moshoeshoe. Grey praised Griffith
for the energy and efficiency he showed on that visit.

At the age of 28, Griffith left the military and Grey appointed him to a series of
magisterial posts in the eastern Cape. In his civilian posts, Griffith turned his loyal
military approach into a commitment to open-minded justice, following the letter
of the law and displaying fairness, persuasion and tact. He was praised repeatedly
for strict impartiality in his dealings with the settlers' black neighbors, refusing to
support those white settlers who treated all black people with suspicion.

Six years ago the then newly appointed governor of the Cape, Sir Henry
Barkly, appointed Griffith as Resident Agent in Basutoland in place of James Henry Bowker who set up the first magistrate's office under British rule.

Since taking the office, Griffith has been at pains to ensure that relations with
the Basotho chiefs have been cordial. For the most part he has allowed the chiefs
to conduct their own affairs, interfering in them only when he deems it necessary.

He has imposed colonial rule gradually, trying to become a friend rather than
a ruler. So much so, that he has on occasion been called "father" by the people.

Initial reports from Hope concern him that the man might be too strict. But,
ever the bureaucrat, he is more concerned right now about the way Hope has presented his request for reimbursement for £28 and 10 shillings to pay for his wife
and mother-in-law's move from Burghersdorp to Aliwal North.

"Sir," he writes to Hope. "With reference to your letter of the 9th instant sub-
mitting an account for £28-10-0, I have the honor to return the account to you
and to state that I cannot comply with your request with regard to recommending
the account for approval, for the very obvious reasons that it is not made out in
compliance with Government notices No. 370 of 1856, No. 853 of 1858, No. 460
of 1858, and No. 323 of 1859, Pages 58 & 59 of Book of Circulars & Government
Notices — I wish to draw your attention particularly to Government Notice No.
323 of 1859.

"I have, etc., etc.

"Col. Charles D. Griffith, Govrs Agent."

That should show Hope that he will not tolerate anything but precise adher-
ence to the rules.

Quthing — Wednesday, June 20, 1877

As evening approaches, Hope is ready to retire for the night when two men
who identify themselves as sons of Raisa arrive at the door.

"Our father will not be coming to see you tomorrow," one of them — who has
worked in the diamond mines and can make himself understood in English — tells

Hope. "But he might come the next day."

Hope glares at the two men standing outside the door. His eyes reflect his irritation at being treated with such contempt.

"Did he tell you to say that?"

"Yes."

"Tell him that is not satisfactory," he says. "Explain to him that when I issue a summons I expect it to be obeyed. He must appear before me tomorrow, Thursday morning, to answer the charges. There is no alternative. I insist he obey this order."

The men do not reply. They do not fully comprehend what he is telling them, but they can understand that he does not accept Raisa's explanation.

They stand quietly before Hope, showing no emotion and no surprise. They have delivered their message. That is all Raisa told them to do.

"Tell him this," Hope continues, irritated by the men's apparent unconcern. "Tell him that he has lost all right to debate with me whether he will or will not appear before me tomorrow. If he does not obey the summons it will be my duty to order my chief constable to arrest him and to bring him in as a prisoner."

The young men continue to show no reaction. They hesitate, unsure whether the discussion is over or whether they should wait to hear more.

"You have heard what I have to say," Hope adds, raising his voice and speaking slowly and deliberately in the hope that doing so will ensure the message gets through to the men and that they show some reaction. "Tell your father I want to see him in the courtroom tomorrow or I will have him arrested."

The men are quiet.

Hope waves his hand, motioning to them to leave. The men gather the conversation is over. They turn away and leave.

Quthing — Thursday, June 21, 1877

It is 9 o'clock in the morning on which Raisa is due to appear in court. Although the headman sent his sons to say he would not be here, judicial procedure requires that Hope hold the hearing anyway. It also is possible that Raisa might have changed his mind after his instruction to his sons that he must appear today.

MaLebenya and Mapeshoane are ready to give evidence should Raisa arrive. They wait outside in the weak winter sunshine. MaLebenya sits on a grassy patch opposite the building while Mapeshoane stands.

A small gathering of Baphuthi have gathered to observe the trial, the first of its sort on Baphuthi soil. Among those gathered is Lemena, who is determined to continue his observation of white justice.

As Hope waits in his office to give Raisa a chance to change his mind and attend the hearing, the mail arrives from Maseru. Among the few letters is the one from Griffith. As he unseals the folded blue paper, another letter falls out. It is Hope's request for the transportation allowance for his wife and mother-in-law that he sent two weeks ago to Griffith. Griffith has returned it. Why?

Hope stares in disbelief at Griffith's explanation as to why it has been returned. Is it not clear to Griffith that he was asking for £28-10-0 as a transportation allowance for his wife and mother-in-law who could not stay with him because of the dangers of his post? What difference does it make whether he wrote it using exactly the right forms? What does Griffith think he is doing here in Quthing? Spending all day looking up the proper procedure?

Hope re-reads the letter, then seizes it at each side, ready to tear it into little pieces. But reason takes over; he has no chance of receiving the allowance if he destroys Griffith's letter outlining what he should do. He sighs with resignation and takes up his pen, taking pain to make sure that his request is correctly submitted.

"This had better be acceptable," he mumbles to himself. "I cannot afford to waste all day ensuring it is in the right format. How does Griffith know which are the right notices to be followed anyway? Does he sit there reading them all day?"

When Raisa fails to arrive by 11 a.m., Hope, still smarting from Griffith's letter, summons Sighata and two constables.

"His sons visited me last night and told me he would not come today," he tells them angrily. "Well, you know, I don't care what his sons said. Raisa must appear in court today. Go and arrest him. And bring him here."

"Where will we look for him?" Sighata ventures.

"How should I know?" Hope replies gruffly. "That is why I am sending you to find him. He will be in his village, I suppose. I am telling you to bring him here. Now you go and bring him here, you understand?"

The men do not dare to reply. They set off. Hope retires to his office.

An hour later Hope hears talking outside the courtroom.

"We met him on the way," Sighata says, pointing to Raisa, who is slowly dismounting from his horse. "He says he was on his way here."

Hope — convinced Raisa did not intend to come to court and made up the story that he was on the way here — asks Maitin to convene the court. Lemena and the others gather once more to watch.

Hope composes himself with the dignity that should be accorded a magistrate and says he will start with the contempt-of-court charge. Raisa, he explains, did not obey the summons to appear last Thursday — a week ago. That action showed disrespect for the court.

"It is clear that you did not intend to appear in court today either," Hope says sternly. "Your sons came to tell me last night you would not be here. I had to send policemen to arrest you.

"Have you anything to say in your defense?"

Raisa listens to the translation from Maitin, but remains silent.

"I said, Have you anything to say in your defense?"

Maitin repeats the question.

"I have nothing to say."

"Do you admit that you failed to obey the summons, that you failed to appear in court when you were summonsed to do so?"

Raisa listens intently to Hope's questions as Maitin translates them. They have nothing to do with MaLebenya and the corn field. They appear strange questions.

"The magistrate knows I did not appear," he says to Maitin.

"Don't you be cheeky to me," Hope responds when he hears the translation. "Did you appear or did you not appear?"

Raisa drops his head and stares at the ground. "I did not appear, boss."

"You are to call me: your honor."

"Yes, your honor."

"Very well." Hope fixes his eyes rigidly on Raisa. "I am fining you 5 pounds for contempt of court. You are to remain in a hut here until the fine is paid."

Raisa, not quite sure what he is supposed to do next, remains where he is. It is as well that he does so. The next step, Hope explains, is to hear the charges of destroying a corn field and taking custody of two minor children.

After being sworn in, MaLebenya and Mapeshoane give their evidence. MaLebenya tells how Raisa destroyed her corn field and Mapeshoane describes how Raisa came to his hut and took MaLebenya's young children.

"Well," says Hope after the evidence is complete, "is what they have said correct? Is that what happened?"

Raisa, afraid of being called cheeky and of saying "no" to this angry man, looks down. "It is," he says.

"Have you nothing to say in your defense?"

Raisa continues to look down at the floor. He remains silent.

"Well, then I find you guilty of unlawful destruction of property and the abduction of two minor children," responds Hope. "You have admitted what you did and what you did was wrong."

The next question catches Raisa off guard.

"And are you sorry it happened?" Hope asks.

At first, Raisa is unsure how to respond. He is not inclined to challenge this man who appears to have so much power. Also, Raisa fears one should not disagree with a white man in authority. He has heard that white people become angry when you say "no" to them. His people's traditional friendliness to others also demands that he say "yes."

"Are you sorry it happened?" Hope repeats; the irritation in his voice is clear.

Better agree to this question, too.

"Yes," Raisa replies.

"I am pleased to hear you apologize. This woman whose corn field you destroyed is the wife of your dead brother. She is a relative and still you did this to her. I will not tolerate such action from you again. Do you understand?"

"Yes," Raisa responds.

"You have done something that is wrong under the law. You have harmed someone — and someone even related to you — without any reasonable cause. You need to be punished for what you have done."

"Yes."

He orders that Raisa should compensate MaLebenya with three bags of corn and that he should pay the five pounds fine for contempt of court directly to him. A murmur runs through the crowd; they are surprised at the severity of the sentences. Five pounds is a lot of money and three bags of corn is a lot of food, both representing a substantial portion of any man's wealth.

After a collection of money from villagers, Raisa hands five pounds to Hope.

"Good. You are free to go and there is no need to keep you in custody," Hope says. "You must bring me the three bags of corn within the next week. I will pass them on to MaLebenya. That way I will know you have paid her.

"I trust you are contrite for what you have done and that you are satisfied with the judgment of the court?"

"Yes," says a submissive Raisa, with no outward show of emotion and not quite sure what the question was.

"And," Hope adds, "you will in future obey the law and all orders of the court?"

"Yes."

Hope's eyes light up. Already, his influence is being felt. At first Raisa was clearly rebellious. Now he is sorry for what he has done, is willing to apologize and obey the law in the future. Hope has achieved an important victory for the rule of law. Griffith cannot fail to commend him for his judicial achievements — even if he fails to complete the right form for his transportation request.

Raisa turns and leaves the courtroom. Accompanied by members of his family and friends, he sets off on his way back to his village. He reviews the trial in his mind. The evidence was brief; Hope did not have the patience that a Baphuthi chief has when he presides over trials. He did not listen to many witnesses and to Raisa it seemed that Hope had made up his mind before hearing any evidence. He must tell the king what has happened.

Lemena watches Raisa leave. He turns to Sighata.

"Is this not strange? We punish a woman for not doing the right thing in our law. The white government in its law punishes us for punishing the woman.

"Now," he adds with a twinkle in his eye, "will we punish the government for punishing us for punishing the woman?"

III

Quthing — Friday, June 22, 1877

Hope has just sent off his amended request to be reimbursed for £28 and 10 shillings when, shortly after lunchtime, he sees a group of Baphuthi heading toward his compound. He wonders why they are here. When he sentenced Raisa yesterday, the headman paid his fine and was contrite and submissive, so it could not relate to that, could it?

At first, there are only a few. But the Baphuthi keep coming and soon Hope estimates they are 500 strong. Many of the men are armed, either with spears or with guns.

He is concerned because they are carrying weapons, but their demeanor appears peaceful and their mood, although somber, does not appear threatening.

Yet some of the men at the back of the crowd, unseen by Hope, are far from somber. They are in a party mood. One wears a goat's beard around his face, mocking Hope's long gray whiskers. When the others see it, they point and laugh so loudly that they double over. Another pulls his blanket up to his neck and smooths it in an imitation of the magistrate's "uniform." He stands rigid and looks stern. Pointing at one of his fellow Baphuthi, he says, "You must be whipped." This, too, evokes laughter.

The armed men give way to allow Moorosi, riding on his white horse, to move through the crowd toward Hope. Moorosi is accompanied by his sons Letuka and Lehana and his leading advisers. Raisa rides nearby.

Moorosi stops as he reaches Hope, standing outside his house.

"I and my people have come here to greet you as my magistrate," he says. "I told them, Come all of you, my children, that I may introduce him to you. I wish you to hear for yourselves everything that he says to me."

Hope is suspicious of Moorosi's motives, given the chief's reputation for a rebellious attitude and the events of the last few weeks that culminated in yesterday's trial. But he accepts the king's words at face value and calls on his policemen to bring two chairs, one for him and one for Moorosi. He invites Moorosi to sit. Moorosi walks slowly and eases himself into the chair. The old chief is starting to show his age, Hope notes, although he clearly remains fit. Many in the crowd draw closer and sit on the grass in a group around the men. Others talk among themselves and watch from a distance.

Moorosi and Hope ask after each other's health, discuss the weather and the state of the crops and share an occasional laugh. If Moorosi has come to confront the magistrate he shows no such intention, which makes Hope wonder why he is here. Is it mere coincidence that it follows yesterday's trial?

After a while, Moorosi says he will ride to the mission station at Masitise where he will sleep for the night. He suggests they should meet again tomorrow.

Hope agrees. No sense rushing the meeting.

He will find out more about Moorosi's intentions tomorrow.

Quthing — Saturday, June 23, 1877

The next morning, Hope awakens to the steady hum of speaking among a large gathering. Outside his house is a crowd larger than the one yesterday. It could number as many as 600. He notices that today every man is armed. They carry guns or spears; some carry many spears in bags slung across their shoulders.

Questions swirl in his mind. If Moorosi's motive is only to continue yesterday's rather superficial meeting why are the men armed? Is today's meeting going to turn into an armed confrontation over his sentencing of Raisa?

If Moorosi is indeed seeking confrontation and these men attack him and Maitin, they would have no chance of escape. His small police force would be no match for this crowd.

Reflecting on the somewhat celebratory mood of the people, he thinks, "Perhaps they are holding a ball and the opening celebration today will be to slit my throat."

But Hope is hardly faint of heart. And, in a broader sense, he is not alone. He is confident that behind him stands not only the colonial government, but ultimately the British government and Queen Victoria herself.

He walks outside.

"What do they say?" he asks Maitin, who has been talking to the crowd.

"They say they are waiting for Moorosi to arrive," his assistant replies. "He told them to be here again today. And to bring more people with them. They say that is all that they know."

Before long, Moorosi arrives, riding on his white horse. A group of men who, Hope assumes, are his family and leading advisers, accompany him.

Moorosi rides up the slight incline that leads to Hope's house. He dismounts, greets Hope and Maitin, and asks them to gather with him for a pitso, a traditional gathering at which important matters are discussed.

Talking is better than fighting, Hope thinks.

A constable provides chairs for him, Maitin and Moorosi. Maitin sits to the side, ready to translate.

Thoughts of a plot against him still coursing through his mind, Hope decides he should take the initiative. He tells Moorosi he has one stipulation before they start talking.

"What is that, magistrate?"

Hope rises and turns to face the onlookers, preferring to address them directly than to cede his authority to Moorosi. Asking Maitin to translate, he says, "I am glad that you have come to see me. I send you my greetings. But you must first put away your weapons — your guns and your spears. If you do not do that, I will not talk with you at all."

Moorosi's face tightens. Hope already is doing what he did with Raisa: bypassing him as the leader of the Baphuthi people. Hope is taking it on himself to give instructions to his people in front of him. And it is a demand that the Baphuthi men weaken themselves.

Stunned, he remains silent.

Hope adds, "Go on then, put away your weapons. With weapons, there will be no talk. Without weapons, there will be talk."

The people are hesitant. They look to Moorosi for guidance. Carrying their weapons is a tradition — and they see no good reason to set them aside now.

Moorosi, carrying a rifle, also is reluctant to give up his weapon. He turns to his sons. They gather and talk.

Hope waits expectantly. He senses that he has disrupted their plan and counts it a gain.

Moorosi discusses with his sons whether he should upbraid Hope for addressing their people directly. They conclude it is better to remain friendly because they have important matters to discuss.

Weapons are a tougher issue. But, after a lengthy debate and with reluctance, Moorosi and his advisers decide to concede this issue for the duration of the pitso. Moorosi steps forward, turns to his people and gives the order to disarm. Led by Moorosi, the men place their arms in a pile.

 Hope is relieved. The tension lessens. He has thwarted the plan. He has taken control.

Moorosi launches into the first item to be discussed at the pitso. Hope has exceeded his bounds by sentencing Raisa. Griffith had reassured him he would remain king and would continue to implement the Baphuthi laws and customs. Now Hope is overriding that agreement by interfering.

Moorosi therefore wants to clarify what laws Hope plans to implement and how much they impinge on Baphuthi law. This will be his first move in a lengthy pitso on the subject of authority.

"I have brought all my people to hear the laws read so that they may know them," Moorosi says.

Hope, encouraged by Moorosi's apparent intent that his people obey the law, asks Maitin to read the regulations set out in "Courts of Law." He explains that amendments have been made recently and will be read to the people when they are available. For now, they will hear the existing version.

Moorosi listens intently as Maitin reads the laws:

Each of Basutoland's four districts will have a magistrate. The magistrates will hold trials. Serious offenses are to be tried by three magistrates presided over by the senior magistrate. Death sentences must be confirmed by the governor. The scale of punishments and fines is laid down; females are not to be sentenced to a whipping. The magistrates are given criminal as well as civil jurisdiction.

Marriage by force is unlawful. Church marriages have the same validity as traditional Basotho marriages. A man who marries in Christian or civil union cannot take another wife. The marriage is to be registered and a fee of 2 shillings and sixpence paid. The amount of the dowry is also to be registered. In the event of a parent dying, the survivor has custody of the children until the boys are 18 and the girls 16. Widows can remarry, but the children of the first marriage are to remain in the custody of a person selected, if possible, from among the relatives. Questions of inheritance or guardianship shall be decided by Basotho custom.

Moorosi and Raisa exchange glances, but say nothing.

The right to allot land is vested in the governor. The chief in each district will have to provide the governor's agent with a list of the people to whom land has been given. A tax of 10 shillings a year is payable on June 1 for each hut except that a polygamist has to pay 10 shillings for each wife's hut as well as his own and an unmarried man who has a hut of his own is taxed 10 shillings.

The governor's agent is empowered to issue trading and hawking licenses valid for up to a year and may refuse to grant or renew a license at his discretion. The sale of spirituous liquor is prohibited. Firearms and ammunition may be sold only with the sanction of a magistrate.

Maitin stops reading. "Those are the courts of law," he says.

It was just as he thought, Moorosi says to himself. Even should he accept them — which he is reluctant to do — the colonial laws do not directly cover many issues, such as Raisa's destruction of the corn field. Hope was intruding in affairs outside his law that he did not understand.

Moorosi turns to the crowd. "You have heard the law," he says. "Those who have not yet paid their hut taxes for this year should pay up as soon as they can. You also heard again today, as you heard when Mr. Hope was installed as a magistrate, that they want you to obey the laws of the colonial authorities. But I am your king and you are responsible to me for following our laws and customs."

Moorosi turns back to Hope, sits down, and continues talking.

"I have a matter to raise with you," Moorosi tells him. "I hear my children crying because they say you have fined them as much as five pounds because they had not attended your court. In addition, in our country we do not fine people for damage done to corn fields. What you have done is wrong and is against the laws of our people.

"I am very unhappy with you because you did not ask my consent for all that you did. You cannot do anything without first consulting me."

Moorosi directs his attention once again to the crowd. "Who told you, my people, that you should bring your complaints to this man? It is only today that I am introducing him. You have not met him before. Why do you go to a man whom you have never met? Today, I am showing you the man who has been given me by the government, to help me. He has brought his own laws with him. You have heard them.

"But we still have our laws. I am your king. He is not your king.

"How is it that some of you go around me, that you go to the magistrate, the man you have never met until today, instead of to me?"

Moorosi turns to Hope.

"You did not ask my permission for what you did to Raisa," he says. "The agreement that I made with Mr. Griffith was that you would work here under me and be responsible to me. You did wrong to order Raisa to appear before your court. You should have come to me first.

"So the summons you issued to him is wrong. These matters are not covered in the 'courts of law.' These are matters on which I should rule."

Hope remains silent. What had started out as a conversation has become a confrontation. He knows that he needs to be firm, to assert his authority, but, while he is considering his best course of action, he will let Moorosi speak fully first and then respond.

Moorosi stands, turning again to the people gathered around him.

"Are you my people or are you the government people?" he asks. "If you are government people, you are fools."

Still addressing the crowd, he turns and points to Hope. "Do you obey him?" He swings back, points to himself and faces the crowd.

"Or do you obey me?"

The crowd responds immediately. "We obey you," they shout in near-unison.

This support for Moorosi puts the magistrate over the edge. Hope stands, glaring at Moorosi. "How dare you?" he sputters, enraged at Moorosi's attitude toward a representative of the white government.

"How dare you?" he says again to Moorosi. "How dare you challenge my authority?" His face reddens with fury. "How dare you indulge in this display of insubordination?"

Hope turns to the crowd.

"Your chief agreed to be under the government," he says. "I do not need his permission to do anything here. I am not subordinate to him. He is subordinate to me. Every man and woman may appeal to me and bring complaints to me before he complies with the judgments of the chief and headmen. You must not expect me to send cases to the chief. The chief must send cases to me."

Moorosi is quiet. He watches his people, trying to gauge their reactions to Hope's outburst. They, too, are quiet. They appear taken aback by Hope's angry disrespect of their king.

Hope pauses, even more angry that he is eliciting no response from Moorosi or from the people.

"This meeting is over."

Motioning to Maitin and his constables to follow him, he walks into his house, taking his chair with him.

The people in the crowd talk animatedly. Hope has turned his back on their king and on them, which is not only rude but also threatening. They are unimpressed with the white man who claims to bring justice and a superior way of life. This is not justice, this is an attack on their tradition, their culture and their king.

Sitting in his office, Hope's fury turns to concern. He fears that his direct challenge to Moorosi might invite a violent response from the people gathered around his house.

He tries to attend to his work, but his mind is outside. He hears the people talking and wonders what they are saying. He knows their pile of weapons is right there.

Maitin suggests Hope should sit down with Moorosi to talk further.

"You will recall that when Griffith introduced you to Moorosi, at first Moorosi would not accept you. He said he did not want you to be his magistrate."

"Yes, but then Griffith told him he had to accept me."

"Precisely. He opposed Griffith's suggestion, but backed down after a day of talking. Perhaps he will do so again. The Basotho people prefer to talk matters over in lengthy discussions. Time is not pressing to them. Moorosi brought up the issue of who is in charge in order to stimulate a debate with you, perhaps in the hope that you might resort to some acceptance of his authority, not to cause you to turn your back on him and walk away."

Hope says he understands. But he has reservations.

"If I go out there now and say I want to talk with him, it will be a sign of weakness. It will look as though I am recognizing him, giving him authority he does not have. He needs to accept that I am in charge here now and he is not.

"Did you hear him say that I should have consulted with him before I sentenced Raisa? And that what I did was wrong? What preposterous impertinence. He needs to accept my authority. I know the difference between right and wrong and I know that I am right and he is wrong. These are British subjects and they need to accept British law. He needs to consult with me and ask me what he should do, not the other way around.

"But then what can you expect from a cattle-thieving, war-mongering witchcraft-believing barbarian?"

Hope rises from his chair, running his hand through his thinning hair.

The only solution right now, he decides, is for the crowd to dissipate. He cannot allow Moorosi to stir them up against him.

He calls one of his chief constables, Isaak Masin.

"Tell Moorosi he should return the chair on which he is sitting," he says. That should persuade him that the pitso is over.

To Moorosi the request is another sign of rudeness and disrespect for him as king. "Go to the magistrate and say I am still using it," he tells Masin.

"I cannot tell him that. He has told me to fetch the chair and I am here to take it back to him."

Moorosi calls a man from his circle of advisers. He is in no mood to talk directly with Hope any longer.

"Go in there and tell the magistrate that I am still using it."

Inside, Hope is aware from the reactions of the crowd that his demand for the chair has caused resentment. He covers his mistake with a lie. He tells Moorosi's messenger that he was not the person who requested that the chair be returned and Moorosi can continue to use it.

Moorosi is not placated. If it was not Hope, who was it? From whom else would the policeman have taken an order? Maitin? But why then did the policeman say Hope wanted the chair? The lie, he concludes, is another illustration of Hope's arrogant and disrespectful attitude toward him.

Almost three hours have passed. The crowd continues to mill around outside the magisterial offices. Hope and Maitin attempt to work, but regularly glance through the window. It is past midday; surely the people will return home soon.

A messenger from Moorosi walks to the door. Maitin speaks with him and then turns to Hope. "Moorosi wants to talk with you."

Hope considers the proposal. Perhaps the situation can be saved.

"He is having second thoughts," Hope tells Maitin. "Perhaps you are right. He has thought it over and learned his lesson. I will talk with him because he has approached me and I am not lowering myself by going to him."

But this time, the conversation will take place on Hope's turf, in his house, away from the crowd and their weapons.

"Tell him he can come inside here and talk with me."

Moorosi enters the house, his son Lehana carrying the chair. Lehana places it in the room and Moorosi sits on it. With Maitin acting as interpreter, Moorosi tells Hope he is disappointed that he left the meeting. The object of a pitso, he explains, is to discuss matters. A pitso can work only if people are allowed to talk without interruption, to make their wishes known in a straightforward way, and to answer one another until they have nothing more to say. They must talk and talk and talk.

Hope shakes his head in disagreement.

"Let me sum up what happened," he says. "You came here today with other subjects of Her Majesty the Queen to greet me as the chief government officer in this district. Although I had not summoned a pitso, I was pleased to see you and consented to your request to conduct such a meeting. But immediately after we read the regulations about the courts of law — at your request, I might add — you began to behave in an unseemly manner.

"When your people, in answer to a question from you, declared their intention of obeying you rather than me, I could not, consistent with my duty as a government officer, remain in the pitso any longer.

"Do you think I could sit still and listen to you insulting the government and, by implication, the queen? Also, I cannot accept your statement that before they make representations to me in my court they must ask your permission."

Moorosi repeats his assertion that he, and not Hope, is the ultimate authority in the area.

"When I met with Mr. Austen and Mr. Griffith and you were there, did they not say that in all cases you, the magistrate, would be subordinate to me?" he asks.

"Did they not say that the people living on this side of the river as well as those of my people on the other side of the river were still my people? Did they not say my people would continue to be allowed to bring their affairs to me? I could go on settling them because they are still equally my children.

"You misunderstood what they said," Hope replies. "Or else the interpreter translated the words incorrectly."

Hope reaches across his desk and picks up the government document from which Maitin had earlier read.

"Here is the law. I can have it read to you again if you wish."

"I have heard what your law says," Moorosi replies. "I am talking about what I was told at that meeting with Mr. Austen and Mr. Griffith. I am talking about who is the king of my people and who has the authority over them.

"When Mr. Austen was our magistrate, sometimes he used to send people back to me and tell them first to report their cases to me."

"If he did that, he was acting inconsistently with the orders of the government," Hope replies. "My most earnest wish is to govern this district well and I will deal justly with everyone. But I will govern in the way that I decide I should.

"You agreed to be placed under British protection. I represent the queen and the authority of the Cape Colony. You need to respect me and to accept my judgment.

"Although you admit you are under the government, you seem to expect government to come down to your level and adopt your customs and let you dictate to the magistrate. That is not the way it is. If you behave well, I will consult you, but every man must come to me and obtain my approval before he complies with the judgments of chiefs and headmen.

"The government is first and the chief second."

"To our people, their king is first," responds Moorosi. "I cannot accept your judgment on our matters. You need to agree that, in all cases, whether civil or criminal, you will first report to me. Once you have my permission you can start proceedings. But you cannot judge any cases until you have consulted me.

"If you do not do that, you will be killing me. You will be destroying my authority over my people."

That is what Hope has every intention of doing.

"You went too far in judging Raisa," Moorosi continues. "Your authority as magistrate here is not valid. You cannot act until I have authorized you to do so. You must restore Raisa's fine."

Hope is tired of the discussion, which has been continuing for far too long. The same points are being repeated and his workday — he tries to stop working early on a Saturday afternoon — is drawing to an end.

"I can see that you are refusing to listen to any of my arguments or to heed them," he says. "I am being patient with you, but I cannot continue arguing back and forth if you will not accept what I say. Tomorrow is Sunday and I will not be at work. Let us meet again on Monday."

Moorosi agrees. He does not want to end the debate; it is only getting started. But he realizes it is getting late.

"Very well. We will meet again on Monday."

He leaves the office.

Hope, who had been concentrating on the conversation with Moorosi, suddenly becomes aware that the people are singing outside. To him, it sounds like a war dance.

He looks through the window and sees that the people have picked up their weapons from the pile in which they had placed them after he had instructed them to put them down. Holding their spears and guns aloft in their right hands, they raise their knees high as they dance. They chant in unison, repeating the same phrases over and over.

Hope wonders what they are singing. Although the weather is cool, their bodies already are sweating as they pick up the pace.

Hope's apprehension turns once again to fear as he realizes the strength of the force that is potentially arraigned against him.

But he cannot believe that Moorosi will use their conversation to rouse up his followers against him. After all, the debate will continue on Monday.

His thoughts are interrupted by the sound of a shot. Within seconds, it is followed by another shot. Then another. The dancing turns into pandemonium as the people scatter.

Hope and Maitin shudder, unsure how to react.

Minutes later, chief constable Abraham Sighata enters the room.

"A man has been shot dead," he says.

Aliwal North — The same day

Mimmie Hope sits alongside her mother on the porch. Although their house lies along a main road in the first colonial town settled in the Eastern Cape, it is quiet. It also provides her a degree of security. Should she need help, her neighbors will come running.

She recalls the time five years ago when she was living with her brother, Emile Rolland, who was an assistant magistrate in Mafeteng.

There she met Hamilton Hope, the man who was to be her husband. Hammy, as she calls him, was a clerk. She was impressed with his manliness, his strong moral convictions and his desire to protect and love her.

She and her widowed mother lived for a while with her husband in Mafeteng, but, when he was transferred to the wilds of Quthing, Hammy suggested that they move to her old home town of Burghersdorp.

A month ago he sent them money to move to a house in Aliwal North. He would build a house in Quthing, he had said, in which they would live once he had settled into his new post. So far, he has not mentioned moving in any of his letters.

Mimmie's brother Emile now works for Griffith in Maseru. It is somewhat ironic, she thinks, that her husband and her brother should be linked in this way, both working for the same government 100 miles apart.

Mimmie grew up on her father's mission station in what is now the Orange Free State. She remembers the Boers attacking them because they befriended the Basotho and because the Boers believed that the mission station was on land that should be theirs.

She remembers the sense of foreboding she felt before the attack and for reasons she cannot explain she feels it again. She has at times suffered under her husband's violent temper and is wary of his strong-armed approach.

She turns to her mother. "I wonder what Hammy is doing now," she says. "I am concerned about him, mother. I am afraid that he will lay down the law too strongly and that the chief Moorosi, who is said to be wild and rebellious, will fight back."

"I am sure he can look after himself," Elizabeth Rolland replies. "Your father and I found the Basotho people not warlike at all until they were attacked by the Boers."

"That's what I worry about. I am afraid they will feel they are being attacked. I hope Hammy knows what to do.

"Please pray for him, mother."

Quthing — The same day

The dense mass of almost 600 Baphuthi surge forward to see the shot man lying on the ground. Their dancing forgotten, they shout, push and argue as they scramble for a look at the body. Guns and spears wave in the air. Now and then further shots are fired into the air, contributing to the chaos and creating frenzy.

Hope walks slowly and tentatively out of his house. His first task is to make certain that the shooting was not aimed at him or his staff. When he sees the concentration around the man on the ground, and sees his constables in place, he relaxes somewhat. Had the incident been devised to attack him, or his policemen, surely they would have done so by now.

Hope knows murder is highly unusual among the Basotho and Baphuthi people. They sometimes have gone to war, and sometimes they kill a person accused of witchcraft. But Hope has heard no reports of Baphuthi people murdering one another. Suicide, too, is virtually unknown. Hope reminds himself, too, not to jump to conclusions. He has no idea why the shot was fired, who fired it and who was hit. He does not even know if the person is really dead.

Unwilling to become directly involved — he is the magistrate, not the police — he instructs unarmed policemen, headed by Sighata, to investigate. He watches as they make their way through the crowd. Soon they disappear into the human mass, which continues to be uncontrolled and unruly.

When the policemen do not return, he fears the crowd might have mobbed them. He decides that he had better take charge after all. He had claimed control over law and order in Quthing in his confrontation with Moorosi. Now he had better demonstrate it. He will go and see for himself.

Casting aside the danger, Hope plunges into the seething mass of people. A frightened Maitin follows close behind him. The crowd parts for the two white men.

At the center of the turmoil is Moorosi. He is arguing furiously with Sighata, who has arrested the apparent shooter.

"Do not lay your hands on him," Moorosi says. "Let him go. I am here. I am in charge and I will see that he is put on trial. I assume all you want is your reward."

"I am not looking for a reward; I am only doing my work," Sighata responds, looking fearfully at the men around him holding spears above his head.

Moorosi pulls the accused man away from the constable and turns to Hope. "Here, sir, is the man who killed the one lying on the ground," he says.

"Why did he do it?" asks Hope.

"You question him yourself," Moorosi says, pushing the man toward Hope. He will watch carefully to see how Hope handles the situation. This will be a test of the white man, who is supposed to be working for him, and his justice.

Hope and Maitin briefly examine the man lying on the ground. He is indeed dead, killed by a shot to the right side which appears to have penetrated his heart.

"You come with me to the courtroom," he says to the man identified as the one who fired the shot.

Unsure what to do about the body, Hope decides to let the Baphuthi see to that. He turns toward his house, Maitin with him. A knot of men follow them through the crowd.

Before he enters the courtroom, Hope delivers another lecture. With Maitin translating, he turns to face the crowd, which falls silent.

"You see what has happened," Hope says. "This is why I told you not to bring guns and spears to a meeting. Now this has happened. I want all of you to put down your weapons again. Then I will proceed with the hearing."

The men ponder the request. Moorosi, still questioning witnesses, is apparently unaware of what Hope has said. They opt to obey the magistrate and place their weapons in a pile once again.

In his house, Hope has the prisoner brought before him. Onlookers crowd outside the window. Moorosi now has returned and stands among them, near the front.

The man, Kabi, says the gun misfired three times. He tried to fire it a fourth time, but had forgotten that the ramrod, used to load the musket, was inside it. When he tried to cock the gun, it was too strong for him and went off. The man was killed when the ramrod was fired from the gun.

"I do not know why you needed to try to fire your gun," Hope says. "But I find it impossible on this evidence to decide whether this killing took place by accident or not."

Hope instructs the chief of Kabi's village to act as security and to bring the prisoner before him in the future when Hope issues a summons.

Hope is pleased that Moorosi appears to have deferred to him to judge the case. It seems that Moorosi is unaccustomed to dealing with incidents like this, presumably because they are so rare and so serious. Now believing he needs to press home his advantage, he invites Moorosi, accompanied by his son Letuka and his senior advisers, to continue the conversation that was interrupted by the shooting incident. The men sit together in the house.

Referring to the shooting, Hope comments, "Consider this, Moorosi. Suppose you or I had been killed by that ramrod, what would the people say?"

Hope is merely raising the question as a talking point, to bolster his suggestion that no arms should be brought to a meeting. But Moorosi takes it as a suggestion that he and Hope could be involved in an armed confrontation. "Ah, chief," he says. "Your statements are predictive. What you say is likely to happen."

The men are silent for a moment as both consider the implications of such a thought.

Hope suggests they return to the discussions of the morning. Moorosi asks Hope why he left so abruptly. "You turned your back on us, which is a sign of disrespect among our people," he says.

"Do not accuse me of disrespect," Hope replies. "You were the one who was disrespectful. I was responding to your actions. You chose to act in an unseemly manner. The people made a public display of their support for you as opposed to the government. In response to a direct question from you, they said they would obey you rather than me. I could not, consistent with my duty as a government officer, remain any longer.

"You need to understand, Chief Moorosi, that I am in charge here now. I am the authority. I am the person your people need to obey, not you."

Moorosi repeats his contention that he remains the leader. Any action Hope takes without his approval will be resisted, he says. "I will tell my people not to obey your policemen unless I have given the police permission to act against them — even if the policeman wants to arrest someone. For example, I did not give permission for Raisa to be tried, but I did give permission for you to question the man accused of the shooting."

Hope sits up straight in his chair. He must make clear to the chief where he stands. "You do not have the authority to give me permission to do anything," he says firmly. "I am the one who gives or withholds permission. You must accept that, Moorosi."

Moorosi is as firm in his rejection of Hope's argument.

The men continue to talk. Neither will concede any ground, and each is determined to persuade the other. When the sun sets they agree to talk again on Monday.

Hope leaves the meeting fearful that Moorosi might have to be forcefully brought in line. To do that, Hope feels he needs a stronger police force to back him up. He writes a report to Griffith outlining what happened, including Moorosi's insistence on final authority, and asks for Griffith's instructions.

"I will maintain the stand I have taken, but as I expect open resistance to be offered to the constables should they be ordered to arrest any person, as Moorosi was at no pains to hide the fact that such would be the case, I beg you to take into consideration the incalculable advantage of crushing any such resistance at once, and to strengthen my hands by augmenting my police force."

Cape Town — Monday, June 25, 1877

The 1877 session of the Cape Parliament, which began in Cape Town on May 25, is in full swing, reflecting the optimism members feel about the economic progress being made in the colony. In the western Cape railways and harbors are being constructed and European immigrants are arriving in considerable numbers. In the eastern Cape, the construction of a bridge over the Kei River will soon take place. Irrigation by farmers is being promoted as a means of increasing the productive power of the country.

But members representing the eastern Cape argue that defense is a stronger priority. A frontier defense commission headed by John Gordon Sprigg, a farmer in the district of East London, reports to Parliament that farmers in the eastern Cape are living "on the brink of a volcano." The whites have expanded into black territory and colonists fear that the black people will rise up against them, the commission asserts, proposing an additional £150,000 a year be spent on defense and recommending the increase of the Frontier Armed and Mounted Police from 900 to 1,200 men. The commission also recommends that volunteers be encouraged to enlist in the defense forces.

The westerners say these reports are exaggerated and refuse to provide the requested additional expense.

Quthing —The same day

Light rain is falling this Monday afternoon as Moorosi, followed by about 100 Baphuthi, arrives at Hope's house to continue Saturday's discussions. Unwilling fully to concede to Hope's instruction that they do not carry weapons, the men are armed with their traditional spears, but none carries a gun.

Hope, for now, is satisfied with the compromise. He feels less threatened by spears, which — although they can effectively be hurled as far as 150 yards at an enemy — are most effective only in close-up fighting.

Hope and Moorosi sit outside. Hope, making sure Moorosi is seated on a chair, says he would like to speak first. Moorosi agrees. After all, a pitso is intended as a general meeting at which everyone can speak for as long as they like.

"First, I want to make clear that the language that you used at our last meeting was disloyal to the government," Hope says, speaking loudly so all can hear. "I am warning you, and that includes all the chiefs and all the common people, that, if it is repeated, I will not allow such disrespect to pass unnoticed. You will then be liable to be treated as rebels. We do not like rebels and we treat rebels in the way that they deserve."

Hope is laying down a direct challenge to Moorosi. The Baphuthi onlookers wonder how Hope will enforce his will as he does not appear to have much armed support, although they have heard that armed forces are ready to the south and assume they can be called to fight here.

Hope once again goes over the laws, telling the crowd that it is their duty to obey him because they are British subjects.

Moorosi holds up his hand, as is customary at a pitso, to take his turn. He is quick to counter the magistrate's argument, declaring that even though he might be a British subject, he is the supreme chief in his land; Hope is his subordinate.

During the Sunday break, Hope considered ways to allow the chief limited — albeit meaningless — powers to try to appease him. He plays that card now. He agrees that Moorosi has the right to arbitrate in civil cases if both sides request it, but he also adds that Moorosi cannot enforce cases and has no right to fine any person in criminal cases or to seize their property in civil cases.

He then tries to add a sweetener.

"You receive a stipend from the government for administering the hut tax," he adds. "I will generously increase that from 20 pounds a year to 50 pounds. You should be satisfied with that." Moorosi suggests it should be closer to 100 pounds.

Hope does not respond, but the mention of the hut tax moves the debate from the general to the specific. Raising the issue of Lemena and the gun, Moorosi says he and Lemena have reached an agreement. He, not Hope, has been the arbitrator.

"I ordered Lemena to bring the gun to me," Hope says. "Instead he seems to have given it to you. Now you must give that gun to me."

"I do not wish to give the gun to you," an adamant Moorosi says. "I stand in the place of the thief. It is better that the gun be given to me than returned to the thief as you suggested."

Hope sighs. "I did not suggest that the gun be returned to the thief. I, too, stand in the place of the thief. I ordered that the gun be handed over to me, as the government representative."

"Lemena did not want to give you the gun. He brought the gun to me," Moorosi continues. "He said, 'Now the gun is in the hands of my father.' This case already has been settled by me. Now you want to overrule me."

Hope plays the money card again, hoping this one will be more successful.

"Very well, bring the gun to me and I will pay you for it on behalf of the government."

That puts a whole new aspect on the case.

"You will pay me for the gun?" Moorosi asks. He ponders the offer. Selling the gun to the magistrate will not be yielding power to him; it will simply be a sale.

"I will sell you the gun."

A gasp runs through the crowd.

Hope beams. That was easy — amazing how money can change minds.

Moorosi realizes too late that he has, in effect, yielded power to the magistrate by agreeing to sell him the gun. Feeling he has been tricked, Moorosi vows silently that he will not hand over the gun and will not accept the money. But he is afraid he can no longer recant what he said.

The light rain has now become heavy and a cold wind adds to the worsening conditions. So the men continue their conversation indoors where the space allows only Maitin, acting as translator, and Moorosi's son Letuka, acting as an adviser to Moorosi, to be present. Without the crowd present, the discussion becomes more intimate.

"I would like to tell you of another issue with which I am dealing," Moorosi says. "I am angry that the people in a village near here — Lebetsa's village — are selling *joala*. For nearly a year now I have been telling the people to stop doing so."

Joala is a potent alcoholic drink brewed locally from sorghum. Unlike *leting*, which is only slightly alcoholic, *joala* is said to keep on fermenting in the stomach. Hope has seen the effects of overimbibing on the drink, which causes severe headaches, bloodshot eyes, indigestion and renders the drinker ill for several days.

Some Baphuthi mix *joala* with brandy brought from the Cape Colony, making the effects even worse. Hope believes Moorosi, who like all good chiefs takes pains to stay sober, does not want his people to drink *joala*. But Moorosi is not concerned about the effect of the *joala* on his people; if they want to drink it, they can do so. He is upset because the liquor is being sold in the European way, rather than given as a gift, in the Baphuthi way.

Moorosi believes that asking strangers to pay for food and drink is contrary to a basic custom in which he and his people believe. This custom is reflected in the Biblical injunction to the ancient Hebrews to show love to strangers as recorded in the book of Leviticus — "the stranger that dwelleth with you shall be unto you as one born among you, and thou shalt love him as thyself." Moorosi is against foreign greed-inspired concepts undercutting traditional Baphuthi hospitality.

Hope has no understanding or appreciation for this cultural custom and cannot identify with it. His immediate reaction therefore is to conclude that Moorosi is concerned about the harm, not of being uncaring to a stranger, but of strangers' imbibing a strong drink.

"I will not allow such a thing in my district," says Moorosi.

"Nor will I allow it," Hope replies.

Moorosi continues, "I know it will spread to other things, too, and will not stop at *joala*. Soon it will spread to bread and they will not only be selling *joala*, but will be asking sixpence from visitors to give them bread.

"The result will be that, if people visit from a distance, they will go thirsty and hungry because they will not have the money to buy the *joala* and the bread. This is not our way. We show hospitality to visitors. We share what we have with them."

Hope nods, failing to grasp the real intent of Moorosi's complaint, but satisfied that they are agreeing on a ban on the sale of a potent alcoholic drink.

"You are quite right," he says. "It should not be allowed. Give me the details and the names of those involved and I will inquire into the matter and take the appropriate action." The suggestion reopens the rift between the men once more.

Moorosi steps back, lines of anger crossing his face.

"No," he says. "I have held a hearing. I have ordered the people to pay a fine. They will not do this again. I am merely telling you about this so you will know that I am seeing that my people do the right thing."

"To whom will they pay the fine?" asks Hope.

"To me, of course."

"Here is a perfect example, Moorosi. Let me make it clear: You have no jurisdiction in this matter. It is my responsibility. I will fine them and they will pay a fine to me."

"I will never submit to you in this regard," Moorosi retorts. "I will judge the cases. I will not surrender my independence to you."

"It is too late to talk of independence. You are not independent. You and your people are subjects of the British crown. I am a representative of that government."

"I have never given my country to the government to control. I have agreed only that the government will protect me and my people."

Moorosi outlines another example to indicate that he is in charge of his land. When he allots a man a piece of ground to plant crops, the man pays him a goat for the privilege. "The goats are given to me," he explains. "I am the ruler. I decide how people can use our land."

Hope sighs. Clearly Moorosi still does not understand.

"No, Moorosi, those kind of payments no longer belong to you. You heard what the 'courts of law' say. This land is subject to the British crown and to the Cape Colony, which I represent. I decide who can occupy the land and whether they should pay for the right to use it. The British law is applicable here.

"You are acting like Langalibalele who opposed the Government and was killed as a result."

A flash of anger crosses Moorosi's face. Mention of Langalibalele arouses a variety of emotions. It talks to him of deceit.

Langalibalele was a rainmaker who earned a strong reputation and great respect across southern Africa. He was the ruler of a 7,000-strong tribe, the Hlubis, who lived in the Drakensberg mountains that form the Natal-Basutoland border.

In 1873 the Natal colonial government regarded Langalibalele as a rebel and sent an armed force after him. To avoid capture, Langalibalele fled into Basutoland.

Figuring that Langalibalele would seek sanctuary with a chief named Molapo, Charles Griffith offered Molapo a share of the Hlubi herds if he would help the government arrest Langalibalele.

Molapo cooperated. He invited Langalibalele to seek refuge, but he also told Griffith where they would meet, so that when Langalibalele arrived Griffith was there with troopers to arrest him. Langalibalele was imprisoned on Robben Island; Molapo accepted a reward of 2,000 head of cattle, an action regarded by the Baphuthi as a serious act of treachery against not just the Basotho people, but all the black people of South Africa.

Mention of Langalibalele, therefore, does not sit well with Moorosi. He sees it as a threat that the same thing could happen to him.

"No, magistrate, do not compare me with those that are dead to their people and are no longer their leaders. I am only discussing these matters with you as the leader of my people. You may threaten to kill me, but I will not hand over any of my authority to you."

Hope sighs. He has become frustrated at this seemingly endless back-and-forth discussion about who has legal authority over the Baphuthi people. He swallows hard, looks down and resists the forces welling up within him to stand up and shout at this wild rebellious barbarian and demand that he hand over his authority to him, that he obey and respect him — or else.

"I must warn you that your language is rebellious," he says as calmly as his emotions permit. His tapping foot reveals his frustration.

Moorosi, detecting Hope's anger, remains unbowed. He repeats his contention that he will not yield to Hope. These matters might seem small, but they are symbolic of the wide cultural differences that divide them.

Letuka leans forward and quietly urges his father to be more cooperative. He fears what the magistrate might do.

Encouraged that he at least is making headway with Moorosi's son, Hope stands. It is time, he decides, to lay down the law.

"Very well, Moorosi," he says, looking down at the seated chief and straight into his eyes. "I have been patient with you. I have taken a great deal from you. Now you are openly defying the government.

"I want to warn you, before it is too late, that if you openly resist me as magistrate, you will regret it. And the responsibility for doing so will be yours."

He waves his hand toward the door, indicating Moorosi should leave.

Moorosi rises. Hope has indicated he will not listen to any response, so, as he walks out, Moorosi turns to Letuka. "In spite of what the magistrate says, I will not give up the gun that Lemena gave me," he says. "I will fine those who sell *joala*. And I will keep the goats in payment for the use of the land."

Outside, all but the most devoted of Moorosi's followers — no longer part of the discussion — have left, driven away by the constantly falling rain.

Moorosi replays the confrontation in his mind. He recalls Hope's reference to Langalibalele. He recalls the times when his kingdom extended to the south, when the white authorities misled him and tried to usurp his authority. Now the white authorities are trying to mislead him again.

But he remembers Moshoeshoe's words: "Try to achieve peace rather than war; show kind deeds to your enemies and you will shame them into cooperation."

Perhaps, he reasons, it is time to try to meet Hope halfway, to offer him cooperation rather than confrontation. Better to yield a little to achieve peace than to wage war — that was the great leader's philosophy.

Moorosi notes that Hope's policemen will need to have more land on which to plant their crops. He agreed to let Hope establish the compound, but the policemen will need land beyond that.

And he is the one who is in charge of the land. It is his to assign.

Here is a way he can exercise his authority while showing Hope some respect. He will assign an additional area to Hope as a gesture of goodwill.

He sends his chief messenger and son-in-law, Mafetudi, who has waited patiently in the rain, to tell Hope to meet him the next morning so that he may show him the ground that he will allot for the constables to plant their crops.

Mafetudi returns with the message that Hope refuses to meet him because Moorosi is refusing to recognize his authority. Specifically, Moorosi is retaining Lemena's gun even though he said he would sell it to Hope, he opposes Hope's authority over the *joala* sellers, and he is keeping the goats that he received for the land. These matters must be resolved before Hope will meet with him again.

"I will not yield on those matters," Moorosi says. "But, in spite of his hardheaded attitude, I will assign his policemen a good piece of land. That is our custom. That is what Moshoeshoe taught us to do. I will show him two things at once — that I am in control of the land and that I am showing goodwill to him.

"But now it is raining too hard. Let us return tomorrow to complete this task."

Hope is irritated at his lack of progress. He writes again to Griffith: "I trust that you will see the urgent necessity of at once stamping out any attempt at open resistance, which resistance seems only too likely to be offered. I cannot allow matters to remain in status quo, nor yet let them drift until further and more serious complications arise. Hence I have the honor most earnestly to request that you will lose no time in giving me definite instructions as to how you wish me to act in the event of me being openly and forcibly resisted.

"You may depend upon my not precipitating matters, but at the same time I shall go steadily on, as I told Moorosi. I will do my duty, and let those who resist me by force take the consequences."

Quthing — Tuesday, June 26, 1877

The messenger who knocks on Hope's door in mid-morning says he has been sent by Moorosi to invite him to see a garden plot that he has set aside for Hope's policemen.

Hope is convinced the offer can mean only one thing. Moorosi is demonstrating that he has control over the land and he, and he alone, will determine who may occupy it. Yet this is Cape Colony government land; it became such when Moorosi ceded control of it to the British — and now by extension to the Cape Colony — eight years ago. Now the government is surveying the land to determine how it will be used and divided up. In time, the concept of communal property will be phased out. Parcels will be sold to the highest bidders.

But before he discusses the issue of land, Hope wants to resolve yesterday's confrontation and to get Moorosi to back down on the authority issue. Then the issue of who owns the land will follow.

"I will not go to see the garden plot until he has given me a satisfactory apology for all the things he said yesterday," he tells the messenger.

Later another messenger arrives. He repeats the invitation. Hope responds in the same way, as he does when a third messenger brings the same offer.

Moorosi is not about to accept "no" for an answer. The chief, accompanied by his senior sons and advisers, arrives at Hope's house around 2 p.m. He would like to show Hope the garden plot, he says.

Hope invites the group inside. Here, surrounded by the trappings of authority, he feels less vulnerable.

He insists that the chief and his retinue remain six feet from him at the one side of the room. He faces them with his two constables and the police corporal and asks Maitin to interpret. This is to be no casual discussion.

"Tell me again why you are here," he says.

Moorosi repeats the invitation sent earlier by his messengers. "I would like to show you the parcel of land I have set aside for your policemen so that they can plant their crops there."

Hope has no time to wait for Griffith's advice and assistance. He must deal with Moorosi now. Impatient and determined, he stares into Moorosi's eyes.

"Your offer is an attempt to show that you have some sort of control over me, isn't it? You want to prove that you have control over the land. You expect that, by accepting your offer, I will concede your authority over the land and submit to you.

"Well, let me tell you, Chief Moorosi, you cannot tell me what the policemen who work for the government can and cannot do. You cannot tell them where to plant their crops. You cannot tell me what I can and cannot do. I am in charge here. I have the authority.

"Yet you have the temerity to challenge me. You are seeking a confrontation with me — and let me tell you if you want one, you will get one.

"So, I must ask you again, chief. Will you submit to my authority? If you will, I will shake your hand as a faithful British subject. If not, I will regard you as a rebel. And I will treat you accordingly. I am sure you know what happens to rebels."

The atmosphere in the room is tense. The men are more or less evenly divided in numbers, with five on Hope's side and six on that of Moorosi. They stare across the room at each other, fearful of the consequences of the direct threat Hope is making to Moorosi. Although Moorosi remains outwardly calm, he is taken aback at Hope's sudden confrontational attitude when he is trying to show goodwill. He remains silent.

Hope continues to stare at Moorosi.

"Well?" he asks. "What do you have to say?"

Moorosi looks across at Letuka, at Lehana and at Lefata. Their faces are stern and resolute, but Letuka in particular shows signs of fear. He says this is not a good time to fight and urges Moorosi to back down. They are on Hope's turf. Lefata agrees with Letuka, but Lehana favors continued confrontation.

The Baphuthi king turns back to face Hope. He knows he is on dangerous ground, but the issue of who is in control over the Baphuthi people, their land and their lore, is vital. The tribe's moral code, its very way of life, is vested in him.

He cannot concede. He must assume Hope is returning to the debate that began at yesterday's pitso. Moorosi will try to explain his motives once more.

"I am unhappy with what you said yesterday," he tells Hope. "You threatened me and you said you would go against me. You said you would act against the people who were selling *joala* and that you would fine them."

"Yes, I did say that yesterday," Hope replies.

"What do you say today?"

"I say the same today. And I will say the same tomorrow. You must understand, Chief Moorosi, that I have the power to force you to do as I say. I am not alone here. Mr. Maitin, here, and my policemen, over there, are only part of the power that I bring with me. I bring the whole authority and force of the government with me. If you do not listen and accept my authority, I will force it on you. The fines and the whippings I have administered on cattle thieves are only a small representation of what I can do when people will not listen.

"You agreed to be subject to the British government. I represent the Cape Colony, which represents the British government. You are therefore subject to me. That is the way it is."

Moorosi is silent. Hope seems bent on confrontation, not on discussion. This is not the way a debate is supposed to work.

He starts to take a step forward, to challenge Hope physically and directly. Then he thinks better of it and moves back.

"Well, what do you say, Moorosi?" Hope asks.

The Baphuthi leader is silent.

"Do you agree with me?" Hope asks Moorosi.

After a long pause, Moorosi bows his head and turns his eyes away from the magistrate.

Hope repeats his assertion. "You agreed to be a British subject," he says. "As a British subject, you must obey the British government. I am the representative here of the British government. You must therefore obey me. By failing to obey me you and your advisers are the aggressors. You are challenging my authority. By doing so you are forcing me to use the power I have to punish you.

"And, make no mistake about it, I will punish not only you but your councillors, too."

Turning to face Moorosi's sons, he says, "You are the ones who are forcing my hand. I am not the aggressor. You are the aggressors. You are fighting against me. I am not fighting against you. The law says you must obey me. By failing to obey the law, you are fighting against me. You are advising your father to fight against me. Why do you do that? If you cooperate there will be no reason for me to use any sort of force."

The men say nothing, but their eyes and gestures express their feelings. Letuka and Lefata say Moorosi should back off; Lehana says he should stand his ground.

Hope turns once again to look into Moorosi's eyes.

"I have to ask you, therefore: Are you willing to cooperate or do you want to force my hand with all the consequences that will bring? Am I right? Do you agree with me?"

Hope's demeanor is authoritative, demanding, threatening, intimidating.

He raises his voice. "Do you agree with me, Moorosi?"

For the first time with Hope, Moorosi feels real fear. He has heard that, in a previous posting, Hope has gone so far as to order even chiefs to be whipped. Hope has made it clear that serious offenders will be sent to Cape Town where, cast into an alien culture, they will be put to work on building a new breakwater. Better to die than to be sent there.

Moorosi sees not only Hope the man, but Hope the government with an army behind him. He recalls Nehemiah Moshesh, a chief in Griqualand East, who was charged with conspiring to wage war against the government, and was cruelly forced to yield.

He feels cornered, like a snake under a rock.

His sons feel the same pressure.

Fear. Not only for themselves, but for their people.

Concerned that the confrontation could lead to violence, Lefata advises his father, "I think you should yield in this matter." Letuka agrees. "My father, put an end to this. Give Mr. Hope the answers he wants and let us go. We will fight against him another time." Lehana, morose and sullen, says nothing.

Moorosi weighs up the advice. It is customary in Baphuthi society for a father to show respect for the advice he is given by his sons and advisers. Two of his sons are advising him to concede. He reflects on the deepening confrontation and ponders the repercussions of prompting some sort of violent reaction from Hope.

"I agree," he says, quietly. He quickly adds, "Although I am dissatisfied." The message is clear. Hope is forcing him to yield in words, but not in spirit.

"Aha." Hope is brimming with the pride of accomplishment. "And so you give in to me on these issues?"

"I give in about the *joala*," Moorosi says reluctantly.

"And?"

"And the goats."

"And?"

"And the gun." His words do not seem real to him. He must make it clear, however, his agreement comes not from persuasion but from coercion. "But I give in grudgingly," he adds.

Moorosi is disillusioned. He thought he had an agreement with the colonial government. Griffith had told him he would remain in charge of his people and their affairs. He thought Hope would be subservient to him. Now Hope is bent on destroying him.

Seeking to explain that his action in yielding has come as a result of pressure and not conviction, he returns to the issue of the *joala*.

"Mr. Hope, you have treated me unjustly in taking away a matter from me on which I have already given judgment. I have already ruled on the matter about the beer. Now you are taking that away from me. Your action shows that you think I am nobody in this land."

Hope, delighted by Moorosi's concession, is quick to respond, "No, you are still somebody." He will still need Moorosi to carry out his orders, to collect the hut tax and generally to keep order.

"You are an important person, Moorosi. I need you to help me," Hope says magnanimously.

He moves forward and takes Moorosi's hand. He shakes it vigorously.

"Remember what I said?" he asks. "I said if you agreed to do your duty as a loyal subject of the queen we would shake hands and give three cheers to the queen. So let's go outside and do just that."

As Moorosi and his contingent leave the room and as the people still gathered outside watch, Hope excitedly shouts, "Hip, hip, hooray. Hip, hip, hooray. Hip, hip hooray. May God save the queen." Moorosi and his sons simply watch in silence.

Hope suddenly bursts into singing. "God save our gracious Queen, Long live our noble Queen, God save the Queen: Send her victorious, Happy and glorious, Long to reign over us: God save the Queen."

The onlookers are bemused. These white people are strange. Their dance of celebration and their war chants are neither inspiring nor rhythmical.

"Now let us go and look at the garden," Hope says, a satisfied look on his face and his mood changed from belligerence to friendliness. "Let me see whether I agree that it is a suitable place for my policemen to grow their crops."

Moorosi walks alongside Hope, leaving with superficial peace between the men. But in Moorosi's heart there is no peace.

Hope is proud of himself. Today he broke the back of Moorosi's rebellious attitude. He was strong and resolute. That approach is the only way to deal with these people and in particular the sly, villainous Moorosi.

Before the day is over, he describes his victory in a report to Griffith. His supervisor must know how diligently he has worked and what he achieved today not just for the Cape Colony but for the British government.

"I do not wish to exaggerate the seriousness of this affair," he writes to Griffith. "But, at the same time, judging from the bearing of all his tribe, from Moorosi's own words, and from information which I have received from his messenger Mafetudi, I believe that we have reason to be specially thankful that no false step on the part of Government brought matters to a crisis, until I had succeeded in putting Moorosi into a false position, when I was able to show his councillors that they were the aggressors, and would be punished accordingly if I was unable to uphold the dignity of the Government without using force.

"Trusting that my management of this matter may meet with your approval."

Hope, proud of his achievement, is anxious that his action in this matter reach Griffith as soon as possible, but he is concerned that Griffith has not responded to his earlier letters and he wonders whether he is reading them; perhaps they are not written following the correct format as outlined in a hundred sets of regulations.

He turns to his clerk and translator.

"Take these reports to Maseru. I would like you personally to report to Griffith on what has happened. I have acknowledged your assistance in my letter and praised you for your coolness throughout the whole affair."

Maitin is cautious. "That puts quite a burden on you," he says. "Remember that the new pass laws come into effect on July 1 — just five days away. From then on, you will have to issue passes for crossing the border in to the Cape Colony."

"I remember. But I do not think we will have a rush for passes. Mostly they will want passes to buy brandy at those canteens across the border where our rules banning the sale of brandy do not apply. I will refuse them more often than I grant them.

"They will have to provide me with good reasons before I grant them passes. Do not be concerned. It will not consume too much of my time. It does not take long to say no. It is more important that you travel to Maseru. Griffith must know of the victory I achieved today."

"I will leave in the morning," Maitin replies.

Maseru, Basutoland — Wednesday, July 4, 1877

When Maitin arrives in Maseru and tells him Hope is concerned that he has received no reply to his earlier letters, Griffith is apologetic. "I was in Bloemfontein when the first letter arrived," he says. "I read it only this morning."

Griffith reads the latest letter that Maitin has brought with him. It confirms his fears that Hope is trying to take charge too quickly and drastically.

Maitin reports that he feared for his life when Hope confronted Moorosi and the 600 armed men.

"I know it is wrong to criticize the actions of my superior," he says. "But I feel constrained to tell you that Mr. Hope appeared not to understand that a pitso is a time of frank discussion when it is considered normal for a common man to criticize a chief, sometimes fairly strongly.

"I felt Mr. Hope should have welcomed the opportunity to have heard Moorosi's views so that he would have known how the chief was thinking and could have acted more appropriately. Instead, Mr. Hope brought about a confrontation with Moorosi by storming out of the pitso in anger."

"I appreciate it that you told me of your concerns, Mr. Maitin," Griffith replies. "I know it is not easy for you to do. But I agree with you and I came to the same conclusion when reading Mr. Hope's report. I have attended many pitsos and I know the way they work.

"I am worried, too, that Mr. Hope appears to be relying on being backed by armed forces. But war is brewing on the eastern frontier and the troops are needed there. It will not be possible at this stage to send troops north to Quthing.

"Right now, physical force is not an alternative. Mr. Hope must temper his firmness with diplomacy and understanding to reduce the tension with Moorosi."

Griffith chose Hope for the magistrate's position as he saw Hope as a firm, somewhat stubborn man who, in the way a good military leader would act, would stand his ground. But now he is afraid that those attributes have proven dangerous; the situation needs tact and diplomacy, neither of which is Hope's strong suit.

Griffith writes to Hope in an attempt to persuade him to be less autocratic. An arch diplomat, Griffith first blames "the extraordinary behavior of the old Chief, who appears to have been worked up to a state of excitement by bad advisers or by some other cause," and praises Hope's "patience and firmness."

But he adds: "It will, however, be very necessary for you to be most careful and judicious in carrying out the judgments and orders of your court, to see that they are not carried out by your policemen, etc., with too high a hand. Every possible care must be taken to prevent any of Moorosi's supporters being forced into open resistance or bringing on a crisis, as I am not in a position to say that you will receive any physical support if such an unfortunate result should happen.

"In any case in which resistance is shown to the execution of any orders or judgments of your court, it will be necessary for you before proceeding to extremities to make a full report on the subject to me so that I may be able to get instructions from the government before matters are brought to a climax."

Turning down Hope's request for more policemen, he writes, "The idea of crushing any resistance at once by physical force would require a very large body of men, which it is out of the question to suppose the Government would approve of; and I am decidedly of opinion when matters have reached such a state that 12 men will not be sufficient to support your authority, then it is quite clear that 50 or even 100 men would be inadequate for such a purpose."

He directs Hope to "substitute diplomacy and moral persuasion for physical force or high-handed proceedings."

Griffith's years of experience have taught him that political advancement often is a two-sided effort. He not only must tone down Hope's intransigence, but also must seek cooperation from Moorosi whom he suspects conceded to Hope only under great coercion and will remain resistant to his rule.

He will approach the king in two ways. He will send a messenger to "tell Chief Moorosi that the course he is pursuing will inevitably bring trouble upon himself and upon his people." Secondly, on Monday he will send two of his most trusted messengers — Inspector George Moshesh and Sub-Inspector Sofonia Moshesh — to Letsie's headquarters near Maseru.

"You are to ask Chief Letsie to send an official messenger to the Chief Moorosi," he will say. "The messenger, whom you will accompany to the chief, should explain to Chief Moorosi what Chief Letsie's position is toward his magistrate. He should also inform Chief Moorosi that, although government has no intention of depriving him of his position as chief, it expects from him that he will place no obstacle in the way of his people availing themselves of their rights as British subjects to bring their complaints before their magistrate.

"In other words, Chief Moorosi must allow the Baphuthi people to lodge complaints with Mr. Hope and be satisfied to allow Mr. Hope to judge them and take any action he sees fit."

He hopes that the messengers both from Letsie and from him will have the effect of changing Moorosi's attitude toward Hope. Should Hope show flexibility — and given that Moorosi yields ground on some issues — the chances of Moorosi cooperating with Hope in the future are promising, Griffith believes.

Griffith also signs approval for the spending of £60 on a lock-up at the magisterial compound, for which he has received approval from Cape Town.

"Before you go, I need to write one more letter for you to take with you," Griffith tells Maitin. He hands it to him.

"With reference to your letter of the 25th ultimo relative to a transport account for £28-10-0 returned to you under cover of my letter of the 18th ultimo, I beg to inform you that Colonial Office circular of the 8th of August, 1853, page 57 of Book of Circulars, to which you refer me, rather tends to prove the unreasonableness of your charges than alters my opinion with regard to them.

"Again, let me draw your attention to Government Notice No. 323 of 1859, page 59 of Book of Circulars, in which you will find it distinctly stated 'that the allowance is granted, not upon the principle of defraying the officers' actual expenses, but simply by way of aiding him,' etc. etc."

He signs the letter, then adds a postscript:

"P.S. I may further point out to you that it is absurd in the face of it to expect the government to pay the expenses of the conveyance of your family to Aliwal North, just as well might you have sent them to Cape Town and then expect the Government to pay for their transport. — C.D.G."

He seals the letter and hands it to Maitin.

Even in the case of money, Griffith mutters to himself, Hope acts without thinking. He spends the money to move his family, realizes how expensive it is, and then expects the government to refund it to him.

He is not impressed.

At home on his mountain fortress, Moorosi is having second thoughts about yielding to Hope the week before. He was intimidated and should never have backed down on the three issues.

Moorosi sends a messenger to the magistrate regarding the court order fining Raisa three bags of corn. "Tell Hope I am referring the matter to the chief Letsie and, until I hear from him, I have told Raisa he must not pay the fine," he says.

Maseru — Saturday, July 7, 1877

Griffith, told by Hope of Moorosi's order to Raisa not to comply with his judgment, fears that the magistrate might act precipitously.

So he writes again to Hope, requesting "that you will not act hastily in this matter and that before using any harsh recourse I hope you will try and explain matters to the Chief Raisa and get him to comply with your judgment without the necessity of your having to enforce it."

He adds he will send a messenger to Moorosi advising him to submit to his magistrate's authority and pointing out the danger of the course he is pursuing.

Thaba Bosigo, Basutoland — Thursday, July 12, 1877

Letsie, the king of all the Basotho, faces a dilemma. On the one hand he wants his people to retain the protection of the British and, by extension, now the Cape Colony. But protection is one thing and control is another. From the time it took over the administration of Basutoland five years ago, the Cape Colony has been steadily undermining the power of the chiefs. The disinterest of the British is giving way to a more aggressive policy by the Cape Colony.

True, Letsie admires Griffith. The "white chief" is a kind, understanding man whom he and many of his people call "father," a term of respect that is not easily given. But, at the same time, Letsie is concerned that Griffith is under pressure to tighten the Cape's rule. He wonders how long Griffith will be able to resist the government's steady implementation of its laws in place of the Basotho customs.

He wishes the situation would stay the same so there would be no confrontation, which he dislikes. He believes it is unwise to confront the white government in the way Moorosi is doing. At least not yet. Diplomacy might yet work. That is what his father Moshoeshoe would have tried.

So Letsie decides to do as Griffith requests. He sends a messenger to Moorosi suggesting he attempt to seek cooperation rather than confrontation with Hope.

Quthing — The same day

Hope explains to the workmen the kind of building he wants for the lock-up. He has bought the materials and the building should be completed quickly. The courtroom and offices will follow; the jail must be built first.

He uses a shovel to outline the dimensions of the building, 18 feet long and 8 feet wide. The walls should be 8 feet high and have an iron roof.

This jail will help him considerably. Should Raisa fail to pay the three bags of corn representing his compensation to MaLebenya, for example, this would be the place to put him.

But he needs more to bolster his position. He sends a request to Griffith for six carbines — a shorter version of the popular Snider-Enfield rifles — "and accoutrements" for the use of the police stationed at Quthing. A more strongly armed police force will help him maintain law and order.

Quthing — Monday, July 16, 1877

Moorosi has listened to the arguments from the messengers sent by Letsie and Griffith that he cooperate with Hope and be obedient to the person placed here by the British queen for his "protection and edification."

Already, he has reluctantly yielded to Hope on a few issues, and now he will verbally accede to the request from Letsie and Griffith that he avoid confronting Hope directly. But he will demonstrate to Hope that he remains in charge. He will do so by conducting his own trial of Raisa, in his own way, on his own terms.

Having listened to the stories of MaLebenya and Raisa as well as of those who saw the destruction of the corn field, the Baphuthi king understands why Raisa acted as he did. But, Moorosi concludes, although Raisa acted in line with Baphuthi custom, he overstepped the mark. The force was too strong. He should have relied more on persuading her to marry him rather than punishing her for her refusal.

Today he meets with Raisa and MaLebenya in a *khotla* in front of his hut. He instructs Raisa to pay a fine for overstepping the boundary between persuasion and punishment. But, Moorosi tells Raisa, he is not to pay the fine to him and certainly not to the magistrate, but to MaLebenya. In that way, he will compensate her.

Raisa reluctantly accepts Moorosi's ruling. He offers MaLebenya two goats and one pound, eight shillings.

"That is not enough for the damage he did to my corn field," the widow responds. "He caused me a lot of suffering. He took away everything I had."

Raisa increases the offer to a two-year-old ox and £1. MaLebenya accepts.

With the £5 he paid earlier to Hope for the contempt of court charge, Moorosi reckons Raisa has paid the equivalent of £10 altogether. It is a goodly sum.

MaLebenya leaves the meeting and makes her way to the magistrate's house. She will tell him that she has received sufficient compensation for Raisa's actions against her and that Hope no longer has to seek out Raisa and force him to pay. The action against the sub-chief has been concluded.

As Raisa and MaLebenya leave, Moorosi calls the deputation that has been awaiting his reply for Letsie. "Tell him Raisa has already paid the fine," he says. "There is nothing more for the magistrate to do. Tell Letsie and tell Griffith that the matter is over. I have sorted it out."

Moorosi is satisfied that justice has been done. And this time it has been done without the magistrate and his laws and customs. He, not Hope, has exercised his authority over his people. That is as it should be.

His actions today will show Hope who really is in control. And never again will he allow Hope to gain the upper hand.

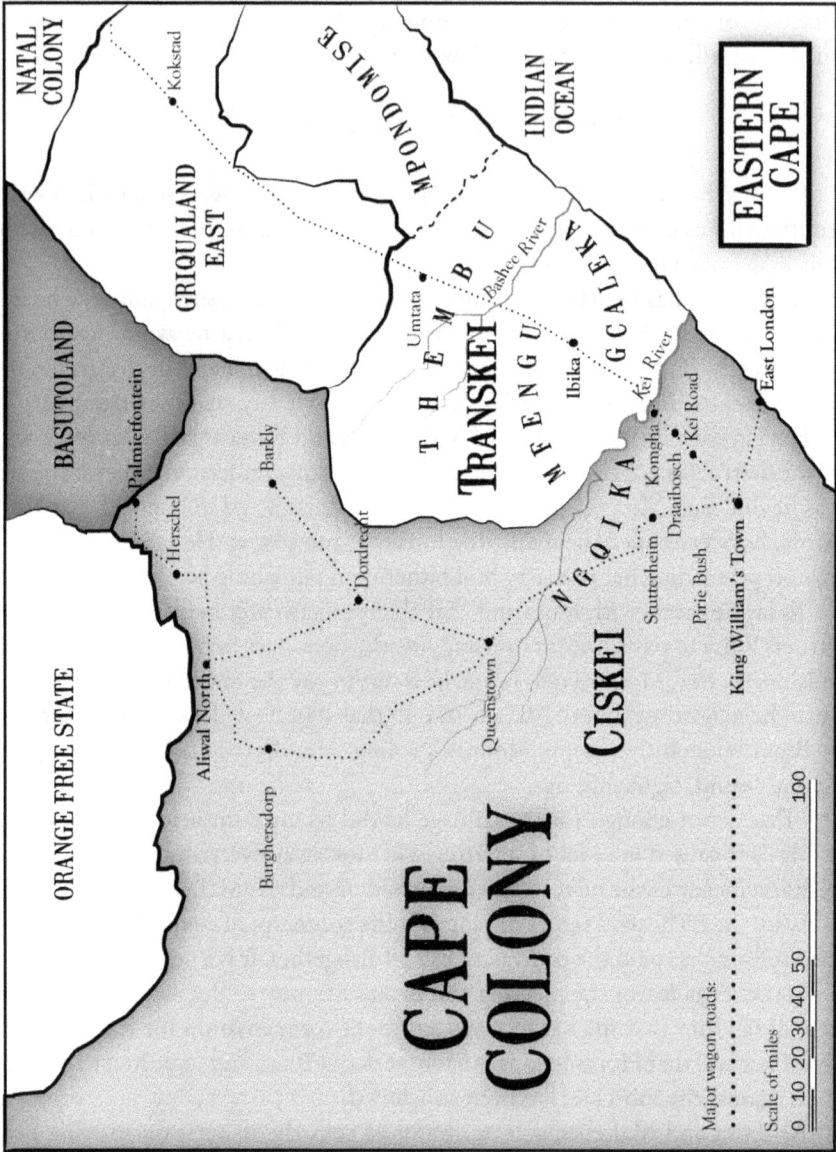

EASTERN CAPE

NATAL COLONY

Kokstad

GRIQUALAND EAST

MPONDOMISE

INDIAN OCEAN

BASUTOLAND

Palmietfontein

T H E M B U

Bashee River

Umtata

GCALEKA

Barkly

TRANSKEI

Ibika

Kei River

East London

Herschel

Dordrecht

M F E N G U

Kei Road

Komgha

Draaibosch

Stutterheim

Pirie Bush

King William's Town

Aliwal North

Queenstown

N G O I K A

CISKEI

ORANGE FREE STATE

Burghersdorp

CAPE COLONY

Major wagon roads:

Scale of miles

0 10 20 30 40 50   100

IV

King William's Town, Eastern Cape — Wednesday, August 1, 1877

Granville awakens and rubs his eyes. The sun's first rays are flickering through the windows of the seven-room barracks that he shares with 60 other members of the Frontier Armed and Mounted Police.

The barracks is a short distance outside King William's Town, 200 miles south of Quthing, home to 9,000 whites who live largely in expansive Victorian homes in the city center, with 90,000 black people living in "locations" or shanty towns, around the town. It is the last major town before the Kei River, which marks the boundary between the Ciskei — the land on the white settlers' side of the Kei River — and the Transkei — the land over the Kei River. Although both areas are home to clans of the Xhosa nation, the Ciskei, home to the Ngqika, is colonial territory and the Transkei, home to the Gcaleka, Mfengu and Thembu, lies outside the colony, although missionaries and traders have set up there.

Granville glances at the bed next to him. His fellow newcomer to the force is stirring. "Ready for drill?" he asks 30-year-old Robert George Scott, who, born and raised in Cambridgeshire, was also recruited in England a little less than a month ago. Scott pushes himself up in his bed.

"I suppose I am." Scott has the sour-looking face and surly eyes of a man who does not do well in the morning.

The two, who first met on the *Teuton*, which had brought a number of recruits from England, got to know one another at the coastal port of Port Elizabeth, south-east of King William's Town, when lined up to receive their formal issue — a red blanket, biscuits and tinned salmon — and became friends. Although from different parts of England, they were both educated at grammar schools and raised in affluent homes and share a similar reaction to barracks life.

"Each day we do the same thing. You know, drill, breakfast, stable fatigue and then sit around and do nothing," Granville says.

"Don't forget roll call," Scott reminds Granville, reflecting his early-morning anger at the world. "The one at five o'clock in particular. I am never quite ready to face the world then. Then the one at nine o'clock."

"Now those are exciting events," Granville sarcastically retorts. "Did you think it was going to be like this when you joined up?"

"Not quite," Scott replies. "Although my father, who is a fleet surgeon in the Royal Navy, did say that life in military service can be dull at times. The problem is that we are still a police force, not a military unit."

"Well, I must say that I joined up precisely because it was a police force and not a military force. I thought —"

A voice comes from the bed alongside Granville. "Do you two have to talk so

83

loudly? Some of us like to get in a little extra sleep, you know." The voice is that of Swedish-born Peter Brown, who came to South Africa with his parents and has also recently signed up. He has adopted the last name of Brown, changing it from the original Brun. He sports sideburns long enough to meet his extended mustache, forming a W across his face.

When told of the discussion, Brown says the boredom and lack of order appear about to change.

"I have noticed frontier farmers visiting the barracks and speaking in urgent tones with the officers. These visits are followed by calls on some of the men to track down cattle thieves among the Gcaleka and Ngqika. These incidents are accompanied by rumors of an imminent uprising among the black people.

"And I hear that today we're all going to have to sleep dressed so we can be ready for action."

Eastern Cape — Friday, August 3, 1877

Behind the rumors reaching Granville and his fellow recruits are rising tensions between two Xhosa-speaking clans, the Gcaleka and the Mfengu. The source of the strain emanates largely from the Gcaleka who feel squeezed between the Mfengu, the Thembu to the east, the white settlers and the sea.

The Gcaleka have long regarded the Mfengu as inferior and now detest them for being subservient to the oppressive colonial government, following European customs and serving in white-run military forces.

Relations between the Gcaleka and the white settlers are also strained. Led by King Sarhili, paramount chief of the Xhosa, the Gcaleka fought against the white settlers from 1850 to 1852. The Gcaleka were defeated and forced into a peace treaty in which they lost land, on which the white settlers settled the Mfengu. The Gcaleka have never lost their desire to retrieve the land, particularly as the Mfengu takeover forced them to move Sarhili's Great Place, or headquarters — which in 1857 was on land that is now in the heart of the Mfengu territory — farther west to where it is today.

Adding to the tension, the Cape Parliament has annexed the Mfengu territory. The Gcaleka fear it will not be long before the whites take all their land and force them to work for them as servants and farm laborers, robbing them of their freedom, their culture and their heritage.

Young Gcaleka warriors, some armed with weapons bought from money earned on the diamond mines and the expanding railroad, are confident they can defeat not only the Mfengu, but also the white settlers.

The Gcaleka are emboldened by other events in South Africa. In the Transvaal, the Bapedi chief, Sekukuni, has held his own against the Boers, showing that the white firepower can be beaten. In Natal, the Zulu king Cetshwayo is raising his voice against white encroachment and has sent messages of support to Sarhili.

Nevertheless, war is not inevitable. Tensions might rise, but, like tinder-dry brush, they cannot turn into a conflagration without a spark.

Today, enmity is set aside for a marriage feast at a Mfengu village on the border of Gcaleka territory. Although they might be at loggerheads as nations, many of the Gcaleka and Mfengu people are hospitable to one another at a local level. So yesterday the Mfengu organizers of the feast crossed the Gcuwa River, three miles northwest of Butterworth, to borrow pots from the Gcaleka to brew beer. The pots were gladly given.

Today, the young Gcaleka chief Mxoli, and a few of his followers have crossed the river to join in the Mfengu festivities. The organizers of the feast do not object. Today is a day for celebration, not recrimination.

But, after feasting for a while, Mxoli is dissatisfied. The refreshments they are served seem sparse. The Mfengu should serve them — the proud Gcaleka — with a plentiful supply of beer, particularly as they lent them the pots.

"You Mfengu are hiding the beer," Mxoli shouts. "You Mfengu never want to share your beer with other people. You are keeping a reserve of beer to drink when we are gone."

The family organizing the feast is angry. Who do these Gcaleka think they are? A shouting match ensues.

"We have no beer left."

"You did not give us enough; we lent you our pots."

"You are not organizing this feast. We gave you beer."

"You hardly gave us any beer at all."

"You do not decide how much beer we should give you."

"We deserve to be treated better than this."

A Mfengu man grabs a stick. Mxoli staggers backward from a blow to the head. Soon widespread fighting breaks out in which Mxoli and his companion Fihla are severely beaten and a Gcaleka is killed. Outnumbered, the Gcaleka are driven back across the river.

The matter is not over. A man has been killed, but, more significantly, a proud Gcaleka chief has been struck by a lesser Mfengu. Such action cannot be tolerated. The rest of the Gcaleka will hear of this insult.

A spark has dropped in the tinder-dry brush of Gcaleka-Mfengu relationships.

Cape Town — Friday, August 10, 1877

Set off by the marriage feast quarrel last week, skirmishes have occurred over the past week between the Mfengu and the Gcaleka. The skirmishes pose a dilemma for Native Affairs Secretary Charles Brownlee and the Molteno government running the Cape Colony. They fear that if they fail to intervene and leave the two nations to fight it out, the Gcaleka will easily defeat the pro-government Mfengu, whom they outnumber in men and arms, take over their land, which has just been annexed to the Cape Colony, and thereby present a challenge to the colonists.

Should they intervene, however, the face-off between two black peoples would almost certainly turn into a black-white war as the colonial troops would be seen as taking the Mfengu side.

For his part, Sir Bartle Frere worries that a war on the eastern frontier could not only be damaging to the colony's economy, but also could hold back his drive to create a confederation uniting all the territories in South Africa in two years.

Because the members of Parliament in Cape Town differ on how serious the situation is, Frere decides to travel to the area and assess it for himself and to see whether he can prevent the outbreak of wider hostilities. He will travel by sea to East London in a little over a week — on August 18 — and from there to King William's Town, where he should arrive in early September.

Because his appointment as governor-general included the post of "High Commissioner in regard to the relations between the South African colonies and the native tribes," Frere accepts that, after he has found out for himself first hand what is happening on the borders of the colony, he will be the one to take the reins, negotiate some sort of peace and, if necessary, use the British military forces to implement it.

Carnarvon had said that a strong hand would be required to implement confederation. Frere is prepared to apply one.

Maseru — Saturday August 11, 1877

As reports continue to reach them of possible war on the eastern frontier, the Basotho chiefs and their missionary advisers are perturbed that the effects of the war will impact them. Right now, they worry that the colonial government is using tax money gathered in Basutoland to fund its war preparations.

When they first began collecting hut tax in Basutoland eight years ago, the authorities promised that it would be used only for the good of the Basotho people. It would be spent to upgrade roads, fund the administration and make other improvements.

Recently, however, the colonial ministry announced it would take £10,000 from a reserve fund belonging to the Basutoland government to pay for the mounted police on the frontier. After some members of the Cape parliament objected that this move was unfair to the Basotho, the government opted to go a step further. Instead of taking only a one-time sum to bolster the troops, Parliament last week approved a measure combining the revenues of Basutoland with those of the Cape Colony, rendering it impossible to track where the revenue generated in Basutoland is spent.

In an editorial today in *The Little Light of Basutoland*, a newspaper produced by the missionary community at Morija, the authors note that the hut tax always has been "cheerfully collected and readily paid" because the people believed it would be used to benefit Basutoland.

"It must be borne in mind that the Basotho are as yet unrepresented in the Cape Parliament, and that although their revenues are now thrown into the colonial treasury they have no voice in the employment of the funds. Simple justice seems to require some modification in the present order of things."

Eastern frontier — Friday, August 24, 1877

Told that the skirmishes between the Mfengu and Gcaleka are becoming more serious, Brownlee feels compelled to send a Frontier Armed and Mounted Police troop to the mission station at Butterworth to keep the feuding groups apart — and to protect the pro-government Mfengu. To ensure that the order sends the right message, he asks Colonel John Eustace, resident magistrate with Sarhili, to explain to the Gcaleka king that the move is directed at restraining the Mfengu rather than supporting them against the Gcaleka.

"Tell him it is aimed at keeping the peace while we inquire into the circumstances that led to the fighting in the first place," he says. "It is not directed at attacking Sarhili."

Eustace sends his clerk, West R. D. Fynn, to relay the message.

But the Mfengu, encouraged by the news that the police are soon to arrive, counteract the message by telling the Gcaleka that the white police will help them drive them into the sea. They follow this boast with crossing the border and stealing a few Gcaleka goats and ambushing those who pursue them to retrieve the goats.

When several Gcaleka men are killed in the incident, Sarhili starts preparations for an attack on the Mfengu and their white allies. "I cannot tolerate it that so many sons of their fathers have been killed by these Mfengu dogs," the chief says.

He summons all the Gcaleka men to his Great Place, or Holela, to have a black war-mark applied to their heads by the war doctor Ngxito and to ready themselves for an all-out attack on the Mfengu.

Quthing — The same day

Hope rules the fatal shooting among the crowd outside his magistracy a month ago was an accident for which no one should be tried. He also decides to close the case against Raisa. MaLebenya has told him she is satisfied with the amount ultimately paid by Raisa and he will accept that because she was the complainant. He is convinced that had it not been for his action Moorosi would not have intervened and Raisa would not have paid any damages. So he feels vindicated.

But that gain is diluted by Hope's increasing frustration at the administration's reaction to his confrontation with Moorosi. Although he is proud that he forced Moorosi to back down on several issues, that he forced Raisa to pay compensation, and that he successfully prosecuted two stock thieves, he perceives that Griffith is still unhappy with his work. Griffith, it seems to him, implicitly blames him for Moorosi's rebellious attitude.

He is still smarting from Griffith's instruction of a few weeks back that "in any case in which resistance is shown to the execution of any orders or judgments of your court, it will be necessary for you before proceeding to extremities to make a full report on the subject to me so that I may be able to get instructions from the government before matters are brought to a climax."

He has pondered that phrase for a long time. What does "before proceeding to extremities" mean? Does it imply his earlier actions were extreme? Does it mean he should ask Griffith what to do in all court cases and then do only what Griffith says?

He succeeds in getting Moorosi to back down, and this is how he is rewarded?

He cheers up a little, however, when he receives a letter from Griffith approving his request for a draft of £128 "for building a court room and offices at your seat of magistracy."

Again, however, the approval is accompanied by more of Griffith's criticism.

"Be so good as to return the enclosed receipts for the above account," Griffith writes, "duly signed and witnessed" — and then the sting — "with as little delay as possible."

Not content with that barb, Griffith adds, "I must also impress upon you the necessity of rendering accounts in duplicate duly signed and witnessed as soon as the building is completed, and at the same time return any balance which may be unexpended."

That's the problem with Griffith. Always treating him like an incompetent child.

King William's Town — Friday August 31, 1877

The Town Hall is crowded to capacity. Even the upstairs gallery is full. Towns people and farmers have gathered here because they are afraid that clashes between the Gcaleka and the Mfengu threaten them.

Just on Wednesday, the Mfengu were attacked by a force of Gcaleka numbering 10,000. After a short clash, the Gcaleka voluntarily withdrew, and the police had no need to intervene. But the latest attack has led some to conclude that the skirmishes already have turned to war and that the frontier police will have to intervene, to protect the "good natives" against the "bad natives."

After hearing a number of speeches on the nature of events on the border, some more charged with emotion than others, the meeting agrees to adopt a resolution that will be passed on to the government. The resolution, prepared at a preliminary meeting last night, and approved at tonight's meeting, makes it clear that the people want the authorities in Cape Town to know that they want change, they want action, and they want it now.

"This meeting is of the opinion that the critical situation of affairs on the Transkeian border has been, and is still, of a most disastrous character, entailing already loss which cannot be estimated," the resolution reads. The Government should take "immediate and vigorous action for the suppression of the recent outbreak," which "can be attributed to the lack of a vigorous native policy," and should not deal leniently with the offenders, it says.

The resolution is to be sent to the governor, Sir Bartle Frere, and the prime minister, John Molteno.

King William's Town — Monday, September 3, 1877

On his arrival in King William's Town, Frere has his first indication of the state of affairs in the town. An inrush of people from the surrounding farms has filled all the hotel and home rental rooms. As a result, there is nowhere for Frere to stay except in the barracks of the British 24th regiment.

As he settles in to his rather rugged quarters, he hears reports that the fighting between the Mfengu and the Gcaleka is not only gathering force, but also increasingly moving on to land occupied by the white settlers. The police are battling to keep control and are in danger of being overrun. Frere is concerned, too, that farming and other industries are being brought to a halt. The impact on the local economy could be far-reaching and could have ripple effects all the way to Cape Town.

Frere concludes the easterners were right when they said they had something to fear. The situation is worse than he recalls from the Indian mutiny. He feels he has no choice but to stay in King William's Town. The Gcaleka and their land must be brought under control and to do so strong police action is essential.

A first step, he decides, is to negotiate an end to the fighting by talking directly with the Gcaleka leader Sarhili to try to broker a peace accord between the Gcaleka and the Mfengu. He sends a message to Sarhili saying he is ready to listen to his grievances and he will be at the mission station in Butterworth to hear them.

Cape Town — Tuesday, September 7, 1877

Secretary of Native Affairs Charles Pacalt Brownlee knows the eastern Cape well. Born there 56 years ago on his father's mission station in the Ciskei, he played a major role over the years in peace treaties between the whites and the Xhosas. By the mid-1860s he became the most important administrator of affairs on the frontier. Former Governor Sir Henry Barkly had called him "better acquainted with the language and customs of the natives on the eastern frontier than anyone else in the colony."

Yet, although he might know the Xhosa people well, he has never doubted that he knows well what is best for them. He sees the government's policy as a "civilizing mission" of the blacks by the whites. "Our frontier magistrates are expected in every way to foster and encourage everything tending to the elevation of the colored races," he has said.

Brownlee's approach also is to impose such a "civilizing mission" cautiously. He knows from experience that pushing rapid change invokes retaliation. Act slowly, but surely and steadily and your chances of success are greater.

His goal of victory without violence, however, demands diplomatic skill, sound judgment and calm reasoning, not all of which he possesses.

Even though Brownlee has not come to know the Baphuthi people as well as other black people, he assumes they are little different than the Xhosa-speaking people, such as the Ngqika and Gcaleka, and the Zulu people. He applies the same approach to them as he would to any other black group.

Today he sets aside the Gcaleka-Mfengu conflict for a while and directs his attention to providing an assessment of events in Quthing, which, as a part of Basutoland, he oversees. He has received regular reports on the situation there and the time has come to react to them.

Protocol demands he address his letter to Griffith. At the same time, he knows Hope will read a copy of the letter and so, in effect, he will be addressing him, too.

Judging from Griffith's letters to Hope, Brownlee knows that the veteran magistrate is concerned that Hope might have a tendency to act injudiciously and high-handedly. But the best approach, Brownlee decides, is a positive one. He will praise Hope for what he did, couching Hope's action in terms of persuasion rather than confrontation, thereby emphasizing the need to avoid violence. He will say Hope is in the right and Moorosi is in the wrong, but, bearing in mind Griffith's concerns, he will subtly warn him not to move too fast.

He underestimates, however, the strong feeling of independence from the rest of the Basotho people that Moorosi and the Baphuthi harbor. "Moorosi, as one of the old and leading chiefs of Basutoland, cannot be ignorant of the wishes and instructions of Mosheshoeshoe, as well as of the conditions under which the Basotho came under British authority," he writes. "Moreover, he has before his eyes the example of Letsie, Molapo and Masupha, his superior chiefs, who are in every way subordinate to the magistrates placed over them.

"It is therefore altogether incomprehensible to Government why Moorosi adopted the extremely objectionable course taken by him. Such a course is only calculated to encourage insubordination in the Basotho, and lead to resistance of authority.

"If Moorosi had any reasonable grievance or complaint to be redressed, he should have gone in a proper and becoming manner to Mr. Hope; and if thereupon he failed to receive due attention, he should then in the next place have gone direct to yourself (Griffith).

"It is well for Moorosi and his people that things turned out as they did, and that he eventually succumbed to Mr. Hope's authority, otherwise stringent measures would have been necessary, and must undoubtedly have been employed to bring him to a proper sense of his position and duty towards the Government."

He tells Griffith that, as Moorosi and his people have resolved to "behave properly and submissively in future," the government desires "to let bygones be bygones," and to accept Moorosi's more recent acts as proof that he intends to conform to the law and "support the magistrate in the good government of his people."

But he adds an indirect warning to Hope not to take matters in his own hands without consulting Griffith first: "Government fully approves of the instructions given by you to Mr. Hope in connection with this matter, more especially in the case of the chief Raisa," he writes to Griffith. It would have been prudent, Brownlee says, to use every method to impose the magistrate's decision "without resort to force."

No sooner has the letter been sent than Brownlee's attention is forced back to events in the eastern Cape once more.

Prime Minister Molteno summons Brownlee to his office. He is concerned that Frere's presence in the eastern Cape will usurp his authority there. Although Frere, as the governor-general appointed by Britain, should not be directly involved in the day-to-day affairs of the self-governing Cape Colony, Molteno suspects that Frere's background as, in effect, a dictator in India and his desire to implement confederation will lead him to take more action than he should.

"I would like you to travel to the border," he tells Brownlee. "You will then be in a position to monitor what Frere is doing and, if necessary, intervene. In addition, should war break out there I will need you to be my eyes and ears."

King William's Town — Tuesday, September 11, 1877

"I am afraid my mission to talk sense into Sarhili failed," Frere tells Lieut.-General Sir Arthur Thurlow Cunynghame, overall commander of the frontier forces.

"I sent the chief a message saying I was to arrive in Butterworth where I would be pleased to meet with him," he continues. "But over two days Sarhili sent various messages putting off a meeting. He provided all kinds of excuses. He even sent his sons to cancel an appointment.

"I soon got the message. He had no intention of speaking with me."

Cunynghame is not surprised. "It seems that these people have no intention of settling anything," he says. "They are eager to fight. And not just against the Mfengu. Already, the fighting is spreading into settler territory."

"Attacks on the settlers are not the only reason we have to proceed against Sarhili," Frere responds. "Mfengu territory is colonial territory; any attack on the Mfengu is an attack on us.

"We need to start moving more aggressively against him soon. And our best method of doing so is to use the Frontier Armed and Mounted Police. What do you know about their commandant, Colonel Bowker?"

"Well, Colonel James Henry Bowker, to give him his full name, has served in a number of offices and conducted several wars over the last 35 years," Cunynghame replies, consulting his papers. "He also has been in administrative positions, having served as governor's agent in Basutoland from 1858 to 1870 before returning to police and military duty.

"He is a capable man and likeable enough. But at 55, I fear he is getting too old for military service and his health is failing. He suffers from rheumatism, complains about shortness of breath and says he feels tired. I think it is time for him to step down."

"How will he feel about vacating the position?" Frere asks.

"He has made it clear to me that he would welcome it."

"Very well. And I think he should do so before the conflict spreads any further. But who do we find to replace him?"

The men discuss the senior officers in the Mounted Police and men in other military ranks.

Soon they have decided on a replacement for Bowker.

"In this case I will need to consult with the Prime Minister before I move any further," Frere says. Within the hour he sends a telegram and before the day is out he receives a favorable reply.

Maseru — Thursday, September 13, 1877

The message turns Griffith's world on its end.

Dated Tuesday, September 11, it was telegraphed by the Under-Colonial Secretary in Cape Town, acting on orders from Frere, to the closest telegraph office, in Aliwal North, and sent by express mail to Maseru.

It reads: "Bowker is ill. Would it inconvenience you much to proceed to King William's Town to relieve him without delay, and, if so, what arrangements do you suggest for the discharge of your duties in Basutoland? Reply by telegram."

Griffith thought his days in active military service were over, but now he finds himself called into action to take a major role in what looks like becoming the ninth frontier war between the colonists and the black indigenous people. He needs to drop everything and go.

He sits quietly for a while, considering the implications. What will happen to his wife and 11 children, the youngest of whom, Owen, turned a year old on Wednesday? Who will run the Maseru office? What will be the reaction of the Basotho people? What will be the impact on operations at Quthing? How will Hope handle Moorosi while he is away?

Soon another telegram arrives, also from the Under-Colonial Secretary.

"As Mr. Bowker is ill and unable to discharge his important duties, the Government wishes you to proceed to King William's Town at once to take command of the Police," it reads. "This is most urgent. You will be granted leave as soon as possible to return for your family. Please reply per telegraph and report when you can be in King William's Town. You would not be asked to incur this inconvenience if the matter were not most pressing, the Governor being on the spot."

A third telegram says the governor wants him to be in King William's Town four or five days after he receives the order. Griffith does not question the order any further. How can he after three telegrams? He informs his assistant — Hope's brother-in-law, the missionary-turned-government-official Emile Rolland — that he will be filling in for him.

"When are you leaving?" Rolland asks.

"Molteno wants me to get down to King William's Town in four or five days."

"That means you will be leaving immediately as it takes five days to get there."

"I need a day to get ready. I will leave early on Saturday morning."

"This is really short notice. How long will you be gone?" Rolland asks.

"I am not sure. I assume it will depend on how long the hostilities last," Griffith says. "I am afraid I am going to be dumping everything in your lap, my dear Mr. Rolland. The most serious situation right now, of course, is what has been happening in Quthing. I am aware he is your brother-in-law, but I think you need to keep a close watch on Mr. Hamilton Hope. He is inclined to act high-handedly and I am concerned that the situation between him and Chief Moorosi could flare up."

"I wish you were here to continue to handle it."

"I wish I could be, too. But duty calls. The main aspect to watch is that Mr. Hope should avoid using force to get Moorosi to cooperate with him. He should talk with him, reason with him and point out the futility of countering him before he tries to force him. I am afraid that Mr. Hope has a short fuse and so I have advised him to consult with me before he takes any further significant action against the Baphuthi chief or sub-chiefs. Now, of course, while I am away, the duty to restrain Mr. Hope where necessary will fall on you."

Griffith intends to leave his wife and children in Maseru at least for a few weeks. "I am not sure at this stage what arrangements will be made for them to join me in King William's Town, where I assume I will be based," he says. "Please see that they are well cared for while I am away, Mr. Rolland."

Griffith replies to the telegram, agreeing to accept the position and suggesting to the authorities that Rolland take his place while he is away.

He walks to his house and tells his wife the news.

Maseru — Saturday, September 15, 1877

As Griffith sets off for the eastern Cape, Rolland's first act as the temporary governor's agent is to postpone the annual meeting of colonial magistrates that Griffith had planned. He does not feel adequate addressing those matters with such short notice.

Rolland tells the authorities in Cape Town that he will hold the annual meeting once they have chosen Griffith's replacement. For now, he will ask individual magistrates to hold their own meetings with the Basotho chiefs and explain the amended rules and regulations that Griffith had intended to cover at his meeting.

Eastern Cape — Thursday, September 20, 1877

The camp on the Kabousie River looks like a suitable place for Griffith to spend the night. Although it is early afternoon, he has been traveling for six days, has encountered heavy rains, and is tired. Here he can rest before proceeding tomorrow to King William's Town where he is to report to Sir Bartle Frere.

Cunynghame, commander of the frontier forces, also happens to be staying on the river bank for the night. When Griffith tells him his name, Cunynghame says, "Aha. You are the resident magistrate of Basutoland." Griffith nods as the general continues, "And you have been sent by the governor to take command of the frontier police." Griffith nods again. "And your appointment is the result of the continued indisposition of the commandant of that force."

The men are interrupted by the arrival of the contractor who conveys the post between King William's Town and Queenstown. "General," he shouts as he drives up. "The war cry has gone forth in Sarhili's country; the natives have risen."

Cunynghame responds immediately.

"Inspan the mules," he directs soldiers at the camp. "I must travel immediately to King William's Town. You might want to join me, Griffith. I believe if we leave now we can be in King William's Town tonight."

Letsie's Village — Friday, September 21, 1877

Last week's news that Griffith has been called to serve on the colony's eastern frontier has so shocked Letsie that he has become seriously ill, causing violent pain and fever to course through his body for several days. He had come to trust Griffith's calm, friendly and understanding approach, seeing him as a brother who was as interested in his welfare and those of his people as much as any white official ever could be.

Now he feels as though a rock has given way under his feet and he does not know where to turn. Without Griffith, he is left to deal with a government he distrusts, with people who do not understand him or care for his welfare. How will he and his people manage without their confidante and advocate?

Unaware that Griffith is already in the Eastern Cape, he believes he must protest this move with as big a demonstration of political power as he can summon to ensure that Griffith remains at his post. He calls 31 of his sons, counsellors and senior chiefs to his village to draw up a petition to the government in Cape Town.

Letsie's brothers, Tsekelo — who has a good knowledge of English gathered on an extended visit to England — and Masupha, gather paper and pen. The paramount chief says the protest should be addressed to Sir Bartle Frere.

After much discussion, the group draw up their message:

"The Petition of the undersigned humbly sheweth: That your petitioners have heard with great grief that it is the intention of your Excellency's Government to remove from his position at the head of affairs in Basutoland our present Governor's Agent, Charles D. Griffith, Esq. That your Petitioners have been struck with dismay at this news, and not only they, but everyone else in Basutoland, from the old man with hoary head to the woman and the child.

"That your Petitioners, together with all the inhabitants of Basutoland, have enjoyed extraordinary benefits through the able and just manner in which the Governor's Agent has governed the country — saving it from invasion and war, overruling disputes, reconciling hostile factions, and establishing in the hearts of all confidence and security. Your Petitioners have, with all the people in Basutoland, felt that with such a man at the head of affairs they could rest in confidence.

"He has endeared himself to everyone, and we look upon him as the greatest and best gift her Most Gracious Majesty has bestowed upon this land, and we contemplate with grief and consternation the prospect of that gift being taken away. Your Petitioners are unrepresented in Parliament, and have no other means of making their prayers and wishes known, but by such humble Petition as the present."

Letsie adds an additional paragraph asking at least to postpone Griffith's departure and for Frere to visit Basutoland to enable Letsie and the other chiefs to have "an opportunity of personally and by word of mouth expressing their wishes and prayers to your Excellency."

Letsie hands the petition to his chief messenger Ntho, and tells him to take it to Rolland and ask him to send it to the government in Cape Town.

Ibika, Transkei — Saturday, September 22, 1877

Granville and his fellow soldiers in the Frontier Armed and Mounted Police have arrived in Ibika as part of a force of 13 officers and 295 non-commissioned officers and men. They have made camp, thrown up earthworks and taken steps to prepare for war. In four or five days, they are told, their new commandant, Charles Griffith, will arrive to replace James Henry Bowker.

"I wonder what the new commandant will be like," Granville comments to Scott after returning from a grueling day-long patrol. "I gather that Griffith has been the British resident magistrate in Basutoland. Some of the men suppose he is much better suited for that position than commanding us."

Eastern Cape — Wednesday, September 26, 1877

Frere insists on daily meetings with the Cape Colony's Commissioner of Crown Lands and Public Works, John Xavier Merriman, and Secretary of Native Affairs Brownlee, both of whom have arrived in King William's Town. On today's agenda is the petition from Letsie and 31 chiefs and councillors asking that Griffith's departure from Basutoland be canceled or postponed.

"Clearly, we cannot concede to anything like that," Frere says. "Griffith is already here. There is absolutely no way we can send him back to Basutoland."

He tosses the petition across the table to Brownlee.

"Will you please respond on my behalf? I am too busy now to do so. Tell them we are pleased with their respect for Griffith, and it is a good thing that they have learned to obey him. These natives respect someone who shows who is in charge."

Brownlee remains silent as Frere continues talking. "Make it clear to them we are the ones who make the decisions about where Griffith will work, not them. They have no right to tell us what to do. They want me to visit there. There is no way I can do that any time soon. Tell them I will visit them as soon as circumstances permit. That leaves it wide open. Show me what you write before you send it."

Brownlee nods.

"Now let's get on to more important matters," Frere continues. "I thought it important to start this first meeting with a summary of events as they now stand.

"The good economy that the Cape Colony has been enjoying has changed things here," he says, trying to make clear he understands Southern Africa even though he has been here for a little more than six months. "Many black people are working on white farms, others on the diamond mines in Kimberley and others in the ports of East London and Port Elizabeth."

Seeing no indication of disagreement, he continues. "The arrangement up to now, whereby the black people ran their own affairs in the Transkei, is no longer viable. They will have to be annexed to the Cape Colony, will need to become civilized and subservient to the government."

"One tribe has accepted this situation and I think we can call them our friends. They are the Mfengu. For generations, they had been subservient to the Gcaleka. Now the Mfengu have sought our help against their stronger enemy.

"Over the past two months, since August 3 in fact, the Gcaleka have been attacking the Mfengu, crossing into their territory and stealing their cattle, sheep and goats. We have had to send in our forces and restore some semblance of peace. But the Gcaleka persist in their attacks.

"I have tried to talk with the Gcaleka leader, Sarhili, but he was unwilling to meet with me. I have sent him a message telling him that I hold him responsible for all transgressions he has made into the Mfengu territory.

"Yesterday, just such a transgression took place. It resulted in a bloody fight under adverse circumstances in rough terrain. Inspector G.B. Chalmers and a group of 180 men were returning to their camp at Idutywa when they saw 5,000 Gcaleka attack a Mfengu kraal in the area called Gwadana.

"With the help of a group of Mfengu, our men from the Frontier Armed and Mounted Police engaged the attackers, as they had been instructed to do.

"They fared less than well. They managed to keep the Gcaleka at bay for two hours, but panicked when their seven-pounder gun collapsed on its carriage.

"The Mfengu fled and Chalmers, fearing his whole force was at risk, ordered his men to retire. Six of our troopers were killed. The incident, being called the Battle of Gwadana, has shaken everyone here in King William's Town.

"Gentlemen, we cannot allow such a setback to occur again. The troops in Ibika now under Colonel Griffith are ready to enter Gcalekaland where, helped by 2,000 Mfengu, they will subdue Sarhili and his Gcaleka."

Ibika, Transkei— Thursday, September 27, 1877

Granville is a member of a party of some 25 men sent from Ibika to travel the six miles to Gwadana and recover the bodies of the men killed in the battle there. As they reach the top of a hill about four miles from Gwadana, Granville and Brown turn and look down the valley where they see a force of 3,000 Gcaleka, armed and dressed for war, moving toward them.

After a brief discussion, the men abandon their mission to recover the bodies and head back to Ibika where they report what they have seen to Griffith. He instructs them to prepare for an attack, which he fears will come soon.

The only brick structure at Ibika serves as a house, store, shop and stable belonging to John Barnett, a trader who has lived there with his family for several years.

The police have commandeered Barnett's building, which they have surrounded by a wall built of earth and a ditch.

Tents housing the troops surround the building.

The men are ready for battle.

Transkei — Friday, September 28, 1877

Both sides — the Mounted Police at Ibika and the Gcaleka at Sarhili's Great Place — are dug in, watching each other by means of scouts sent out regularly to reconnoiter movements. Each is waiting for the other to attack. The colonial soldiers were told last night to sleep in their army uniforms, ready to spring into action at any minute.

When, by midday, no signs of any attacks appear imminent, Granville and Brown are among a group instructed to return to Gwadana to gather the six bodies.

As they reach the slopes of the mountain at which the battle took place, Granville half-walks and half-runs down the bush-covered hill to the valley below. He is unprepared for what he sees.

One body is covered with huge gashes from a spear. He and Brown count 17 deep wounds.

"Look at that," says Granville. "Can you imagine the force that must have taken as the savages repeatedly thrust their weapons into poor old Evans?"

"These blacks are barbarians," Brown mutters under his breath.

From stories told by the survivors and noting the scene before them, the men piece together what must have happened.

When the order to fall back was given, a man named Van Hohenan assisted Evans into his saddle. As he did so, he was shot in the hip. Both men rolled to the ground, unable to escape, and were viciously attacked.

Evans's coat was so full of holes that the Gcaleka considered it not worth taking as a booty of war. Van Hohenan was wearing good boots. Finding them difficult to remove, the attackers cut off his feet at the ankle joint.

Granville notices an aspect common to all the bodies. "Do you see how they have all had their clothes stripped off them and their stomachs ripped open?"

"I have heard that this is what they always do to the men they kill in battle," Brown says. "I have heard they eat these internal organs, believing it will give them strength. I had heard it, but this is the first time I have seen it. Hearing about it is not like seeing it."

"These people are cruel," Brown shouts. "They are damned uncivilized barbarians." He kicks a rock with his boot in an attempt to give vent to his anger. "I cannot wait to avenge these deaths. I will tear their bodies apart in the way they tore these men's bodies apart."

Granville recalls his mother's fear that he will face danger in Africa. He remembers reassuring her that all would be well. But she was right. Today he has met the raw reality of the conflict into which he has been thrust.

The scene the men face catapults them into a new reality, one they had not anticipated when they signed up for the Mounted Police. This is more than the adventure of traveling on horse back through the frontier of Africa, in a world that most Englishmen will never see. It is more than sleeping overnight in a small tent among the bushes away from any signs of civilization. It is more than the aches and pains of nights spent in the bush. It is more than the sweat of digging ditches and piling up earthworks. It is more than the discipline of drilling exercises and learning to use a rifle. It is even more than the adrenaline of firing on the enemy.

It is facing the prospect of death — a cruel, vicious death.

The horror they see around them will shape their emotions forever.

Granville stares at the disfigured bodies, an immobilizing numbness creeping through him as the scene seeps into his mind.

Brown's anger grows. He knew these men. He served with them. He ate with them at the mess table.

Slowly, reluctantly, the men load the bodies on to horses to convey them to Ibika for burial.

Ibika — Saturday, September 29, 1877

After two days of waiting, Granville looks out over the scrubland at eight o'clock on a cloudy morning and sees 7,000 to 8,000 Gcaleka troops massing a mile and a half away.

The 308 colonial soldiers hurriedly eat breakfast. They have opened boxes of ammunition and placed them behind the walls. Shells and case-shot are in position near the guns. Barrels of water are set in convenient positions around the enclosure, which is protected by sandbags.

"All we can do now is wait," Granville says to Scott. The sight of the distended bodies at Gwadana have not left him and he finds it difficult to contain the fear that he might suffer a similar fate.

Scott, puffing on his pipe, grunts in agreement.

"I am going to take off my coat so I can be freer to fire," says Granville.

Scott does the same. "I hear that Sarhili is there with them," he says. "One of the prisoners we captured said Sarhili told his men he wants to 'sweep those white tents off the hill,' the sight of which disturbs him. He wants to overrun us and join up with the Ngqika and form one big front to prevent us invading his territory."

The soldiers fear the battle is not going to be easy. They are vastly outnumbered by the thousands of Gcaleka, and they know it.

It is close to 10 a.m. when the Gcaleka begin moving forward.

"Where are they now?" Granville asks. "Can you see them?"

"They have dipped into a hollow, " says Scott. "They are using the ridge as a cover. I expect they will appear quite suddenly. We had better be ready."

Now numbering close to 10,000, the Gcaleka emerge from the hollow, running toward the camp at Ibika, shouting and holding spears and guns above their heads. As they approach the camp, 2,000 Mfengu, fighting under white leadership, advance toward the Gcaleka.

As the two forces clash, six Mfengu are struck by spears and killed. The Mfengu retreat to an area alongside the fortified camp and the Gcaleka withdraw into the hollow. The quiet returns.

In the early afternoon, the Gcaleka, armed mainly with spears, but some rifles, regroup and begin their advance once more. As they appear in six or seven dense columns over a ridge 500 yards away, Griffith, watching from his command post, orders the men to fire the Armstrong seven-pounder cannon. But the shells go over the heads of the approaching warriors. The rocket tubes are more effective, two charges bursting in the midst of a column.

Led by a couple of senior colonial officers, the Mfengu launch another onslaught on the approaching Gcaleka. But soon they retreat once more; the huge body of warriors is too much for them.

As the Gcaleka continue to advance, the soldiers behind the earthworks fire shell after shell into the approaching warriors. But the Gcaleka keep coming, in waves, hurling their spears and firing their guns and reaching within 50 yards of the earthworks before they are beaten back by the troopers' withering fire. As they retreat, they are hidden for a while behind a hill.

When the Gcaleka reappear to resume their attack, Granville, Scott and their fellow troopers pour shell, case rockets and bullets into them with devastating impact. The troopers are using .557 Snider-Enfield rifles, which are single-shot but breech-loading and can fire 10 rounds a minute, with a range of 600 yards. The Gcaleka have a number of long guns, but many are muzzle-loading and in comparison they cannot sustain any sort of firepower attack. The Gcaleka rely on sheer numbers to advance on the colonial forces. They forge ahead, confident that some eventually will reach close enough to fling their spears at the soldiers and bring them down.

At times, the Gcaleka retreat, but soon regroup and advance once more. With each advance, more and more bodies lie scattered on the ground.

The fighting continues for much of the day until, around 5 p.m., the Gcaleka gather for a final attempt. They charge, shouting war songs. Again, the battery of fire from the camp mows them down and they stumble over bodies of their own men before falling themselves.

With darkness closing in, the remaining Gcaleka turn and flee, leaving bodies, guns, blankets and spears behind them as they take off into the bush. Sub-Inspector Alan MacLean calls on his Mfengu troops to advance. Seeing their enemies wither in the face of the colonial assault, the Mfengu chase the Gcaleka deep into their territory before returning to Ibika.

With the fighting over, Granville makes a quick check of his friends. The brick house is peppered with shot and he assumes many troopers must have been hurt and possibly even killed. But his check shows the mounted police have lost no one. An artilleryman has been wounded in the neck, but it is no more than a scratch.

"They fired too high," comments Scott, "although I see that some of our horses were hit. I must say that I admire their courage. They just kept coming and coming. I think they thought if they sent enough men they would overrun us."

"That's apparently the way it usually works for them," says Granville. "Had they known how few of us were actually in this camp they might have been even bolder. What got them this time was our big guns, assisted, of course, by our Sniders. I don't think they had ever experienced them before. They just could not understand why they were not getting through to us. If they had been able to attack us at close range, I am afraid we would have been destroyed. We have some good men among us, but our forces are not disciplined or hardened to fighting at close range. And Griffith is really the only capable officer we have."

"True," responds Scott. "But if we had, say, 200 men on horses armed with sabres, I think we would have ended this war today."

During the evening the Gcaleka creep up to the battlefield to remove the bodies of their dead. Gcaleka prisoners report as many as a thousand lost their lives.

Griffith is eager to take advantage of his victory and push on into the Gcaleka territory. But he is going to have to wait a few days until their supplies of ammunition and food are replenished.

Paris — Sunday, September 30, 1877

Fred Ellenberger is concerned about the reports from South Africa. He has heard from missionary colleagues of the trouble between Moorosi and the new magistrate Hamilton Hope. He has read in the newspapers of trouble on the eastern frontier of the Cape Colony, and he fears that should war break out it might have ripple effects on the people in Basutoland.

"We need to return to Masitise," he says to Emma. "I want to be there to help my people, to advise them and to protect them."

"I, too, feel we should return," Emma replies. "I want to continue my teaching and I want to help you with your work. But I am worried that you are not physically ready to return. You look wan. You are thin."

"Do not be concerned at how I look, my dear Emma," Fred replies. "My strength has returned; I am sure of that. But before we leave, I feel we must do one more trip around the cities of Europe, particularly in France and Switzerland. We must tell the people of the great need among the Basotho and Baphuthi people, of the work we are doing at Masitise.

"But we should not return before we have gathered enough funds to see us through the months and years ahead which could be turbulent if the stories I hear are correct."

Emma agrees. "When do you feel we should return to Masitise?" she asks.

"Early next year," Fred replies. "Let us pray that conditions do not deteriorate further by then."

King William's Town — Friday, October 5, 1877

At the start of today's daily meeting with Brownlee and Merriman, Frere tells them that Cunynghame has appointed Griffith a colonel and commander of the troops on the eastern side of the Kei River, where they are preparing for an all-out attack on the Gcaleka and their land.

"Talking of Griffith, here is the letter I have drawn up as your response to Letsie's petition asking that Griffith return to Basutoland," Brownlee says. It is addressed to "Chief Letsie and other children of Moshesh."

"Greeting. His Excellency the Governor directs me to say that he has with the highest satisfaction read your Petition addressed to him in regard to the removal of your late chief, the Governor's Agent. It is most gratifying to the Governor to find that after a period of six years residence among you, Mr. Griffith regrets his leaving you, and that you regret his leaving."

Frere interrupts. "Six years? He has been there that long?"

"Yes, sir."

"Continue."

"When Mr. Griffith first came among you, you did not know him, but you have learnt to know, respect and love him."

"Love him? Love him? We are talking about an administrator here."

"I understand that, sir. But Mr. Griffith has endeared himself to these people. That much is clear from their petition." "Very well. Keep that in, if you must. But add the words 'and obey him' after 'respect and love him.' We need some balance."

"So it would read, …'you have learnt to know, respect and love him, and to obey him.' Is that right?"

"Let's say, 'and above all to obey him.' That puts it above the concept of love."

"It will then read, 'You have learnt to know, respect and love him, and above all to obey him.' Is that how you would like it to read?"

"Yes."

Brownlee notes the amendment. He continues reading the response that he has drawn up.

"In removing Mr. Griffith from your midst the Government honors him, and at the same time honors you. He has accomplished great things among you."

Frere says he thinks "great things" is a little vague. "Talk about the actual things he has done."

Brownlee suggests adding, "he has established the rule of law" and "he has initiated measures for your improvement."

Frere nods vigorously.

"Then add something like, 'You have not looked to Mr. Griffith as much as you have looked to his measures.' I want to make it clear that they respect Griffith because he is a firm administrator who has implemented British rule, not because he is a nice person."

Brownlee is tempted to ask, "How do you know that? You had never even heard of Griffith until a few weeks ago." But he holds back and writes down Frere's suggestion, shortening it to "You have not looked so much to Mr. Griffith as to his measures."

"You can also add, 'and now the Government requires that he do elsewhere what he has done for you' after that. In other words, Griffith has been a forceful administrator in implementing the law in Basutoland and now we want him to be a forceful administrator in leading the police against Sarhili."

"What else have you written?" Frere asks.

Brownlee reads, "But of this you may rest assured that, in appointing a successor to Mr. Griffith, the Government will appoint a man who will follow in the course Mr. Griffith has so ably marked out, and one you so highly approve of."

"That's good," Frere comments. "Pray continue."

"The Governor, like yourselves, regrets that the necessity should have arisen for the removal of Mr. Griffith from Basutoland." Because Frere is interested in the wants of "all Her Most Gracious Majesty's people," the letter concludes, "it is his intention to visit Basutoland as soon as circumstances admit, and then he will have an opportunity of hearing fully what you wish to say, and to give you his views and advice."

Frere leans across and looks at Brownlee's notes.

"Is that it?"

"Yes."

"Good. You have presented my views well in the second part of the letter. I would make only one change. Instead of 'the wants of all her Most Gracious Majesty's people,' I would like you to write 'the wants of all her Most Gracious Majesty's children.' We need to make it clear that the relationship here between the government and the Basotho people is closer to that of father and child than adult to adult."

Brownlee takes up his pen and makes the change.

"I will see that this letter is sent tomorrow," he says.

Quthing — The same day

News of the fighting on the eastern frontier reaches Moorosi by word of mouth. Although the Gcaleka are Xhosa and so speak a different language and have different customs, the Baphuthi king feels an affinity with them. He assisted them with food during a great famine 20 years ago and 12 years ago the Gcaleka assisted the Baphuthi in fighting the Boers.

Moorosi knows that the Gcaleka want to run their own affairs, as he does. They resent the intrusion of the white government and laws, as he does. They are prepared to resist the colonial government, as he is.

He is disturbed to learn that Griffith is the man leading the attack against the Gcaleka. His mind goes back to the meeting at his mountain fortress five months ago when Griffith and Austen introduced Hope to him. Suddenly it all springs into context. Moorosi had the impression then that Griffith was promising him a large degree of autonomy, but now it is clear Griffith misled him. Hope — who worked for Griffith — is doing all he can to take away his autonomy.

"If Griffith will fight against the Gcaleka because they want to retain their autonomy, surely he also will fight against me if I seek to retain mine," he reasons. And if Hope was appointed by Griffith and worked for him until recently, it follows that Hope is following Griffith's lead.

What, then, should he do to resist this intrusion?

Moorosi asks his advisers — doctors and rainmakers — what his next moves should be with regard to Hope. He, too, is a diviner and he has his ideas. Now he is interested in knowing theirs.

The men, who throw their divining bones like dice, are used to identifying evil spirits, diagnosing illnesses and searching for lost stock. Often the bones will say whether a wife has cheated on her husband. The bones will say whether a person is bewitched and what sacrifice is necessary to exorcise the evil spirit. Should a chief contemplate a raid, the bones will say what ointments will make his followers invulnerable. They will indicate the direction in which to hunt or search for lost stock.

Now Moorosi wants to hear what the bones say about a white man; about Hope. It's an unusual request, but not beyond their powers.

The doctors throw their bones. Crouched beside them, they examine the way the bones have fallen and read them in the way that British people read tea leaves.

"The bones show this man Hope is trouble," they say. "He has come like a lion into our territory, ready to spring when the time is right. He will make small moves as he creeps up on our people. But one day he will pounce, just as the whites are pouncing on the Gcaleka.

"The crops are not good this year. Since Hope arrived, the rain has become less. Before he came, the crops were good.

"Our ancestors, who speak to us through these bones, are troubled by what they see."

Never afraid to profit from his practice, one of the doctors adds, "But he can be stopped. We can ward off his evil powers. You will need to protect yourself from him with medicine, which I can make if you will pay me a goat for each piece."

"Do so. I will pay you," says Moorosi.

The bones confirm what Moorosi suspected. They serve to prompt him into action. He must move while Griffith's attention is diverted elsewhere. But he believes, too, in caution. As Moshoeshoe did, he should try to assert his authority through a combination of diplomacy and threats. He should be friendly at times, but assertive at others. If he can put those principles into action, he might be able to prevent an outright attack on his people.

Reluctant to move unilaterally, he will wait for an incident to occur. It needs to be the right incident and he needs to be ready to move when it happens. By the end of the day he has devised his plan of action.

King William's Town — The same day

Shortly before 7 p.m., Sir Bartle Frere arrives at the Town Hall where about 500 settlers have assembled, filling the hall to capacity. Frere stands behind the table set out at the far end of the hall for him. He is aware that part of his strategy in managing the war effort here is to get support for his methods and tactics. He will try to achieve that goal tonight.

"I have been asked to outline for you my views of the situation here at the base of operations on the eastern frontier," he says. "I will try to do so tonight.

"As I am sure you are aware, we have moved all regiments and disposable artillery across the Kei River to the border of the Gcaleka territory northeast of here. We have made forays into the areas occupied by the Gcaleka, who are headed by Chief Sarhili, and killed a large number of Gcaleka fighters.

"We are taking this action because we cannot allow Sarhili to live in a state of semi-independence that is not easily classified according to any rules of international law. Indeed, there are 10 or 12 other tribes in this area that are living in various stages of anomalous dependence. Some are fully annexed to Her Majesty's dominions by Acts of Parliament and Orders in Council, even as others are in various transition stages toward that state.

"Our initial forays into Gcalekaland have been successful. The conflict could continue for a while yet.

"But let me say that I believe, no matter how great the sacrifices our troops might be required to make, the British and colonial forces will ultimately be the victors in this struggle. That struggle is between law and anarchy, between civilization and barbarism.

"I think that no true-hearted Englishman, no lover of civilization, no one who prefers law to anarchy and peace and lawful industry to war and idle license will fail to do homage to the courage and patriotism of our troops and those who support them."

The residents applaud politely. Frere, gaining confidence, clasps his hands, with his forefingers extended to touch the table in front of him.

"I would like to inform you that today I issued a proclamation stripping Sarhili of all power and authority as a chief. "

More applause.

"In addition, we have annexed all his land. It is now part of the Cape Colony. Pending approval from the imperial authorities, which I am sure will be forthcoming, Gcalekaland is to be ruled directly by officers appointed by the government of the colony.

"No longer will Sarhili be able to lead his people in their barbaric ways, as he has done for so long. He will have to abrogate his power. We will impose civilized standards of government on the land and its people. It will be subject to all the laws of the Cape Colony.

"We will give to every native person the right to acquire private property in the land by individual title, as opposed to tribal communism. In their system the chiefs control who lives where, but individual natives cannot own the land themselves; apparently they all own it. Such a situation will cease to exist in Gcalekaland from now on.

"Eventually, as the native people become property owners and become civilized, we will grant to them the same rights as other residents of other provinces in the colony. We will deal with them much as the English Government dealt with Wales and the Highlands of Scotland when the present order took the place of the old tribal system of chiefs and their followers in the mountain regions of Britain.

"Some propose segregation. They say we should create a separate state of Gcalekaland under the direct control of the Secretary of State in England, which shall exclusively belong to the natives and shall be entirely independent of colonial interference.

"But I believe that such plans are impractical. They would be a curse to the unfortunate natives compelled to inhabit them and to the population under European law that may be living in those areas.

"In addition, the English government would apparently be responsible for cattle thefts across the border and all the other disorders and irregularities usually committed by the natives. Such a system of creating a native reserve would also require money to start it, even if it could ultimately be made self-supporting.

"But why do we want to segregate the races anyway? Are many of them not living amicably and prosperously side by side with you in many parts of the colony, working on your farms and providing labor in the towns?"

A murmur runs through the crowd. Frere senses that not all agree with him, but he continues.

"My policy is that of fusion of the races," he explains. "By this, I mean social and political fusion." Again, a murmur runs through the crowd.

"I want you to understand that by fusion I mean leaving the two races distinct, but living side by side in the same districts, with equal rights and equal chances of social and political progress, as Celts and Saxons live in Wales and Scotland or Czechs and Germans in Bohemia."

A middle-aged man rises from the audience.

"Sir Bartle, I would respectfully point out that this is not Britain or Europe," he says, pointing his finger at Frere. "The native people have not reached a level of civilization that even approaches ours."

"I understand that," Frere responds. "But look at the Western provinces of the colony. Political fusion already exists there, and it is not confined to those districts."

The man remains standing.

"Perhaps. But they are not threatened by natives. Here we are being threatened. We are not concerned about political fusion, we are asking for protection. You might have proclaimed that Sarhili is stripped of all his power, but he and his army can still attack us."

Frere explains that his policy would ensure peace and protection by civilizing the natives and annexing their territory to the Cape Colony. With the implementation of the law will come peace.

A woman seated toward the back of the hall rises. She speaks quietly, but forcefully.

"I have spoken with some of the Gcaleka people who live on the outskirts of town," she says. "They are in touch with their people in Gcalekaland. They say that their people do not want to attack the whites. Their only quarrel is with the Mfengu."

"Their actions do not match their words," Frere replies. "We have numerous reports of cattle thieving and attacks on settlers' farms."

The woman insists that such attacks are not as frequent as is claimed.

"Indeed, you are wrong," Frere responds. "It is a serious problem."

"Do you have any figures to back up your assertion?" the woman asks.

"We have had many reports of cattle theft."

"But have you recorded them? Have you a list of them?"

Frere has to admit he has seen no such list.

A man seated near the front jumps up and turns to direct his remarks to the woman. "Our farm was threatened," he says. "We had to move into town to protect ourselves. Who knows what has happened to our possessions on the farm and to our cattle while we have been living in town?"

"Thank you," says Frere, relieved at the support.

The woman is persistent. "You say your farm was threatened. Was it attacked?"

"I do not know, but I have heard that my neighbor's farm was ruined," the man responds.

"I believe this is more rumor than substance," the woman adds. "I think if you let the people run their own affairs and do not take over their land, they will be less of a threat," she says. "If they can run their own affairs, why would they want to attack us?"

"They want to attack us because they do not want us here keeping law and order and running an efficient administration," Frere intervenes. "They are barbarians who know no civilized laws. They are determined to drive the settler population out of this area and into the sea."

"I do not believe that is true," the woman counters. "They have their own laws and keep to them. They want only to run their own affairs. If the police and their officers would leave them alone, they would soon be at peace with us."

"I disagree with you," Frere responds. "This whole affair started when the Mfengu and Gcaleka attacked one another and then turned on us. They do not understand what peace means. All they want to do is fight, both against one another and against us. Our duty is to bring civilization to these people. And I want to assure you we will do that."

The woman sits down, shaking her head.

An older man in the audience rises.

"The natives told me the Gcaleka are selling cows to buy guns," he says. "I can prove it. I can also state from 40 years' experience as a soldier in four wars that when the natives sell their cows for weapons they are up to something."

A woman seated toward the front jumps to her feet.

"My native servant told me that Sarhili is a leader with amazing powers. He says Sarhili was put inside a large hut, which was set on fire and he came out without a hair of his head touched."

The meeting is starting to get out of hand. Frere decides the time has come to end the discussion. "If there are no further questions, I declare the meeting closed."

A groan goes up from part of the crowd, followed by muttering.

As the crowd leaves, John Gordon Sprigg works his way forward and introduces himself to Frere. "I am a farmer in the area and the member of the Cape parliament for East London," he says. "I was impressed with what you said. You make a lot of sense and your policy accords with what I believe. I am alarmed that our police and armed forces seem concerned only with cattle thieving and individual attacks. They are not concerned about the big political picture. Your moves to annex the land and take control are the only way to bring order and peace to the frontier."

Frere takes an instant liking to Sprigg. Serious and earnest, he appears to be an intelligent and capable man. Frere believes it is possible that Sprigg can be of help not just in the region, but also in the cause of confederation.

"We should meet again," he says.

Ibika, Transkei — Monday, October 8, 1877

Griffith has had trouble switching back into the role of military commander. In this position, he needs to plan and lead attacks against the enemy, to direct his men to kill. These decisions are disturbing to him. Over the years as magistrate he has come to see war as a last resort, preferring to cultivate compromise; to choose diplomacy above death.

But his task now is not to decide between diplomacy and war. His task is to carry out the instructions of the government.

"You are to break up the Gcaleka army," Cunynghame told him. "Destroy the kraals so the fighting men cannot rally again, and capture the people's cattle so they can be forced into submission. Allow those who wish to surrender to do so."

Griffith has had an initial success. Up to a thousand Gcaleka were killed at

Ibika. Yet the war has only begun. Sarhili still controls most of his territory.

Although a lack of sufficient ammunition and food continue to prevent him from making an all-out advance into Gcaleka territory at this stage, Griffith determines the next step is to swing from defense to offense and attack Sarhili's Great Place. He will inflict as heavy a blow as possible on the enemy, taking his capital. That objective can be realized with the supplies he has at present.

As evening approaches, Griffith orders the men to gather to take their marching orders. They are to start tomorrow at first light and march in two formations to the Great Place, about an hour's ride away, and seize it.

"You will meet resistance on the way, I am sure of that, and that will slow you down so it might take you several hours to reach your goal. The enemy is well armed and can fight effectively at close range, as you know. But you are better armed and more skilled in warfare.

"I am relying on you to represent the Cape Colony, Britain and the Queen in this assault on the enemy. God save the queen!"

The men raise their guns and cheer, repeating in unison, "God save the queen!"

The Ninth Frontier War is about to be launched — officially.

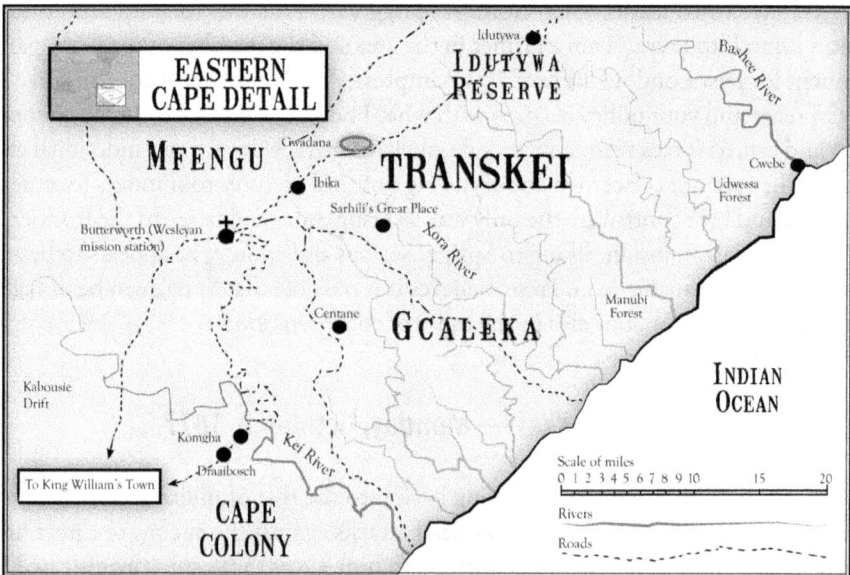

Gcaleka territory, Eastern Cape — Tuesday, October 9, 1877

It is 2 a.m. as the men tumble out of their tents and prepare to march on King Sarhili's Great Place. The skies are clear and bright moonlight will help them find their way to the Great Place and surprise the sleeping Gcaleka.

Griffith leads two troops of mounted police. One is headed by Inspector David Hook and the other by Captain Robinson. Thousands of Mfengu, under colo-

nial command, are instructed to march from three points. Volunteers from local
farms form another group. The first stage in the battle has begun.

Granville is in Robinson's group, which is proceeding along a road leading to a
trading station close to the Great Place.

After about six miles, they leave the road and move to a hill where they look
down on Sarhili's Great Place. Below them is a slope that descends to an area with
a spattering of thorn trees, beyond which is the Xora River.

The Great Place, consisting of several huts, is on the near side of the river. Behind the kraal and the river is a perpendicular hill, rising almost half a mile and
blocking an escape route to the north. But, Granville notes, the Gcaleka can escape
down the river, which flows eastward toward the Manubi Forest and the coast.

Granville waits as the other troops gather for the attack. They report no resistance on their way here, so clearly the decision to move at night was sound. The
Great Place is quiet. Everyone appears to be asleep.

Eventually the Mfengu arrive. All the men are assembled.

Robinson sends out word that they are to wait until sunrise so they can see
clearly. The signal is to be a bugle call. They wait quietly, speaking only in whispers.

Little more than an hour later, daylight begins to spread across the veld, casting
long shadows and lighting up the scene ahead of them.

The bugle sounds.

Granville and his fellow soldiers leave their horses at the top of the hill, run
down the slope, and start firing from 200 yards.

They continue to fire as they run. Hundreds of other soldiers move with them.
The cannon rumble down the slope and fire over their heads into the kraal.

The surprise is complete.

Confused and unprepared, the Gcaleka run from their huts, taking the only
escape route open to them, along the river to the east. The troops follow, pouring
fire on the fleeing men, women and children.

Granville runs over the uneven veld, trying to avoid being snagged by thorn
trees. He fires now and then on the men fleeing ahead of him.

Some of the Gcaleka fall, hit by the rifle fire. Others continue fleeing. No one
remains behind.

As the Gcaleka reach a flat spot to the east of the Great Place, they turn and
fire back at the troops pursuing them and hurl spears in their direction. But they
cannot hold the position. As they head for the safety of trees ahead of them, the
troops invade the now-deserted Great Place, seizing cattle, sheep and corn and setting fire to the huts.

An hour later, the bugle sounds again, announcing the order to retreat.

For the government troops, the first phase of the Ninth Frontier War has been
successful. Sarhili, his family and his followers have been ousted and their Great
Place looted and burned. But Granville wonders aloud why the cannon were not

used more effectively and why troops were left on the hill in reserve. Those men could have been used to great effect in the attack, he tells Scott.

He wonders, too, why the retreat was sounded when the Gcaleka reached the edge of the trees. "Surely, it would have made sense to have pursued them," Granville argues. "Now they can go back to the kraal and rebuild it."

With dusk approaching, Griffith addresses the men at Ibika.

"The operation was a great success and I want to thank you all for the part you played in it," he says. "According to our initial count, 80 Gcaleka were killed. Our losses amounted to two Mfengu killed, three wounded and two policemen slightly wounded. Two men of Bowker's Rovers were wounded, one severely.

"Our casualties have been small in comparison with the loss sustained by the enemy," Griffith continues. The effect on the enemy morale is great. Their defeat showed them they cannot stand against us, even in their own country, or their own stronghold. We captured a vast quantity of loot.

"Unfortunately we did not have the ammunition and the rations to continue to pursue them. We will give you instructions on the next mission soon."

Granville and Scott return to their quarters, shaking their heads.

"I am sure if we had pursued them to the end of their country Sarhili would have had to surrender, particularly after his Great Place was destroyed," Scott says.

"You are right. He has not been subdued," says Granville. "He will simply return. We should have continued to pursue him while he was still on the run."

Quthing — Thursday, October 11, 1877

Hope is settling into his new offices. After receiving permission and money from Griffith a few weeks ago before the resident magistrate left for the eastern frontier, he has constructed a courtroom 27 feet by 14 feet and two side rooms, each 10 feet square. The rooms are sparsely furnished and the walls are rugged. But the structures represent the colonial presence. They also allow Hope and Maitin to conduct their business and store their records away from their houses, which, together with the lock-up and the new offices, form the magisterial compound.

Hope, sitting in his office alongside the courtroom, uses a lull in the daily work routine to discuss recent matters with Maitin.

"I have noticed the number of requests for passes has decreased lately," he says. "The natives don't seem as eager to work on the diamond mines as they were when I first got here."

"Why do you think that is?" asks Maitin.

"I'm not sure. I suppose they don't need the money. It seems to me that more are returning from the mines, too. The local population appears to be growing."

"The natives who go to the mines tend to save up for something and when they have enough money, they buy it and return home," says Maitin.

"And then they stop working."

"Yes, it appears that way. They do not have any desire to save more money once they have what they want. Talking of earning money, I have sent a letter to Rolland urging him to increase your allowance for acting as interpreter. I have explained that your role is really important to me."

"Thank you, sir. I am grateful."

"Of course. It is due to your good interpreting work that I am able to keep in touch with what the people are saying. In that regard you said you wanted to tell me about reports you have heard."

"Yes, sir," Maitin says. "One concerns the chief Tjali who, as you know, speaks Xhosa, but is aligned with Moorosi. I am told that he is sympathetic to Sarhili and the Gcaleka and that his thinking is that, if the white authorities can send Griffith to fight against the Gcaleka, why would they not send him to fight against them?"

"If they want a fight, they will get one," says Hope. "I need to ask Rolland to provide special provision for us should any emergency arise."

"I will keep you apprised of any further reports I might hear in that regard."

"Please do, Mr. Maitin."

"I have also heard other reports that tell of a group of shepherds who, apparently without any flocks of their own to tend, stole goats from a nearby kraal at night, slaughtered them and ate them.

"Another case of stock theft," Hope replies. "It's the most serious crime around here. Since I have arrived, these are about the only crimes I have had before me, except, of course, for the case of Raisa and the corn field. So far, I have had no murders and no assaults. I suppose that is because we are here. If we were not here, you can be sure there would be many cases of violence. I checked the figures last night. So far, in the five months since I set up my office as magistrate here, we have had seven cases of stock theft, or little more than one a month."

"To these people, cattle, sheep and goats are their wealth," explains Maitin. "They are as important possessions to them as jewelry or fine china is to us. Now, with the lack of rainfall, animals are even more important as a source of food."

"I am not sure how they tell which are their goats and which are other people's goats with this ridiculous system of common grazing," counters Hope. "If this were the Cape Colony, you would know your goats because they would be on your farm and another man's goats because they would be on his."

"I think even without fences you would know which were your goats," replies Maitin, with a smile. "But often — as is apparently what happened in this case — the stock is stolen out of the kraals where they are kept for the night. So they know exactly whose animals they are stealing."

"Perhaps. But all goats look alike to me." Hope stands up. He is tired of the conversation.

"In any event, we should send Sighata to arrest the people who have stolen the goats so that they can be tried. They must learn that even when food is scarce, stealing is against the law. After a good whipping, they will have second thoughts about doing it again.

"And it will give us a further opportunity to put our courtroom to use and to establish ourselves as the authority around here."

Maitin excuses himself and walks outside where MaLebenya has been waiting patiently for some time to hear how the discussion with Hope has gone. "Did you tell him about the men who stole the goats?" she asks. "Yes, I did," Maitin replies. "He is going to have them arrested."

MaLebenya smiles. "Does it please you that I give you this information?"

"Yes, it is very helpful," Maitin replies. If hearing more information helps him to get to know MaLebenya better that would be good, too.

Gcaleka territory — Saturday, October 13, 1877

Sarhili gathers his advisers around him to discuss their next moves. The mood is one of sorrow and anger.

The Gcaleka are particularly upset that one of their major leaders died at Ibika. Nita was a doctor and a rainmaker who had promised to lead them to victory as she had done before. They had believed she was invulnerable to attack. But at the battle of Ibika she had been killed — shot in the head by a bullet fired from the colonial troops as she led the warriors into battle.

It was a moment of truth; a somber time to grasp at reality. A gun can kill from a distance with just one shot. And it could kill someone who was strong and able as equally as one who was weak. True, the Gcaleka have used guns for some years, but they have not understood how to use them in battle. And they do not have enough arms to counter the guns of the whites.

But the deaths of Nita and a number of sub-chiefs in the battle have left the Gcaleka thirsty for revenge and determined to fight on. They have heard of Frere's proclamation that Sarhili has been stripped of his authority as a chief. But to the Gcaleka the ruling makes no sense. No outside power can deprive Sarhili of a right to which he was born. Sarhili remains chief, the land remains theirs and its occupation by colonial forces must be resisted.

They will fight to the death if necessary to defend their homeland.

As the discussion continues, Sarhili's son and chief adviser, Sigcawu, advises caution, suggesting that his people do not let their emotions control them. His name means "spider" and he reflects the tactics of the patient arachnid that snares its prey rather than venturing out to catch it.

"We must be wise," Sigcawu says. "We must realize that these white men have many guns and we have only a few guns. They also have cannon that can fire long distances and the cannon balls land right among us, sometimes when we cannot even see where the firing is coming from. We have to fight mostly with spears. We fight well with our spears when we come close to the white men, but we have to get past their guns and that is not easy."

He outlines a strategy that he says they must adopt to beat the whites waging war against them. The men listen intently. The spider has spoken. They respect his wisdom and will do as he says.

Quthing — Monday, October 15, 1877

The message from the chief constable is not what Hope wanted to hear.

"I went with two of my policemen to arrest the young shepherd boys who stole the goats," Sighata tells Hope, seated in his office at the start of a new working week.

"When we got there, Moorosi was there. He refused to allow us to arrest the boys."

"What did he say?"

"He said he is the chief and he had already tried the boys for stealing the goats."

Hope is furious. Once again, Moorosi is interfering in the judicial process. "He has already tried them?"

"Yes, sir."

"Did he say what he had done with them?"

"Yes, sir. He said he had fined their parents six times the value of the stolen goats. They had already paid him the fine. He said the matter was over and there was no need to arrest the boys.

Hope calls to Maitin in the adjoining office.

"Did you hear that?" he says as Maitin enters the room. "Moorosi has taken the law into his own hands. He has fined some shepherd boys for stealing the goats. Sighata has just told me that Moorosi stopped him from arresting them. Moorosi said he had taken care of it.

"Can you believe this man's guile? I thought he had learned his lesson last time I confronted him and forced him to back down. I thought he had accepted that I am the authority here."

"It does appear he is intent on rebelling against your rule here," Maitin ventures.

"Appear?" Hope blusters. "He *is* rebelling against my rule. "We cannot allow this to continue, Mr. Maitin. We have to stop him from doing this and explain to him in no uncertain terms that he is not the law here. I am."

Hope calls Sighata.

"I want you to go to the place where the goats were stolen. I want you to arrest the people responsible.

"I do not care whether Chief Moorosi says he has already tried and sentenced them. We need to disregard that action as illegal and irrelevant. They are to be tried in a proper court of law."

Sighata asks what he should do if Moorosi refuses to let him arrest the people, as he did before.

"You are to confront the chief and tell him that the magistrate has sent you and he must be subservient to my orders. Remind him of what happened before and how he was forced to back down. Does he want that to happen again?"

Nervous about confronting Moorosi, Sighata reluctantly agrees to return to the village.

Transkei — Thursday, October 18, 1877

As the military operation to take control of Gcaleka territory gets under way once again, Griffith forms his forces into three columns. Each consists of about 600 white colonial forces assisted by 200 Mfengu and pro-government Thembu.

Griffith addresses them.

"We have received reports that Sarhili wanted to talk peace with us after the last attack," Griffith says. "But he had his chance to talk peace when he refused to see the governor. Now he has felt the taste of our forces. He has lost 1,500 men in recent battles. His headquarters, the Great Place, has been destroyed. His tribe has been broken up. There is no longer room for a peace treaty. There is room only for surrender. Gcalekaland is now colonial territory. All its people are under our rule. Our next step is to ensure that Sarhili, who has lost his powers as a chief, is completely subdued so that he does not even think of attacking us again.

"We believe we now have enough ammunition and food rations to conduct this attack. So let's go ahead and do it properly."

Griffith instructs the leaders of two columns to march in swaths 12 miles apart to the sea through the heart of Gcaleka territory.

"You are to burn down the kraals of those who fail to surrender and to shoot any who actively resist," he says. "You are to treat well those who surrender, but make clear they are now under colonial control. No longer is Sarhili their chief; the government is in control. Our plan is to scour the entire Gcaleka territory and to squash all plans they might have to rise against the colonial forces ever again."

Ibika — Monday, October 22, 1877

For four days, the combined forces of the Frontier Armed and Mounted Police, Mfengu and volunteers have been scouring the land of the Gcaleka people. The Gcaleka have offered little resistance. The soldiers report that the Gcaleka, who have broken up into small groups are moving eastward.

As he prepares to continue, Griffith receives a visit from Cunynghame, who asks Griffith for his assessment of the campaign.

"We are driving the whole Gcaleka people before us," he tells Cunynghame.

"Where are they going?"

"I believe they are leaving Gcalekaland and dispersing among other tribes. I also suspect that Sigcawu — Sarhili's son and a cunning strategist — might be planning a surprise attack. My scouts have questioned people in the surrounding areas, but no one professes to know where Sarhili and his forces are hiding.

"But we are ready for such an attack. Gcalekaland will soon be vacated."

To Cunynghame the victory seems too easy.

He tells Griffith that Sarhili and Sigcawu must be found. Capturing them will ensure that the colonists control not only the land itself, but also its people.

Quthing — Wednesday October 24, 1877

Early summer rain is falling lightly outside as Hope speaks to Maitin.

"I have received an instruction from Mr. Rolland to travel to Maseru to attend the annual Basotho pitso on Thursday next week," Hope tells him. "He also has asked me to speak.

"After that, I will be involved in discussions with Mr. Rolland and my fellow magistrates before I travel to Aliwal North to spend a couple of weeks with my wife and mother-in-law. My plans are to return in about five weeks, toward the end of November, depending on how much rain falls and the condition of the roads.

"By the way, I also have applied to Mr. Rolland for 100 pounds to repair the road between here and Palmietfontein.

"While I am gone you, my dear Mr. Maitin, will be in charge here."

Maitin looks perturbed. Five weeks is a long time. "What about the boys who stole the goats? Do you want me to pursue that matter while you are away?"

"I think that can wait until my return. Sighata failed in his second attempt to arrest them, but we did prosecute two cases of stock theft in the past three weeks.

"Our policemen are to continue to spread the message around the villages that all cases of criminal wrongdoing must be brought here and not to Moorosi or any of his subordinates. All cases, no matter how small, must be brought before me. Should any incidents be reported to you while I am away, I would like you to record them and to set a date for the trials from November 26th."

Maitin remains concerned. Over recent weeks, he has spent an increasing amount of time with MaLebenya who continues to live in a hut close to the magisterial compound. Not only has she become a friend, but also a source of information from family members in Raisa's village.

"MaLebenya has told me of rumors that Moorosi is planning to reassert his authority among the Baphuthi," he tells Hope.

"She has told me that Moorosi remains firm in his demand that you accept his position as king and ruler. He demonstrated his power in the case of the stolen goats, but is concerned that you have not heard the message and are continuing to interfere in Baphuthi matters.

"Others also have told me of the rumors."

Some, he says, even go so far as to say that, should Hope fail to acknowledge Moorosi's authority, Moorosi plans to expel Hope from the district by force.

"One informant told me that Moorosi has seen what has happened to Sarhili and the Gcaleka people and he fears that the same thing is going to happen here," Maitin says. "If Griffith can attack the people there, take over their land and give it to the whites, he thinks you are planning to do the same thing here and he wants to prevent that happening."

"Stuff and nonsense," Hope says. "He would not dare to challenge me with any sort of force. I think what you are hearing is rumor and nothing more."

Hope casts aside any thought of an uprising against him and government rule. His mind is on his meeting at Maseru and his trip to his wife and mother-in-law.

But Maitin is worried. "What am I to do should Moorosi take some sort of action while you are away? Is there any way I can consult with you?"

"Yes, by messenger, but there will be a week's delay," says Hope. "Fear not, Mr. Maitin; I am sure you can handle anything that should occur."

V

King William's Town — Thursday, October 25, 1877

The decision seems logical to Secretary for Native Affairs Brownlee: Give Bowker — former commandant of the Frontier Armed and Mounted Police — Griffith's post as senior magistrate in Basutoland. After all, Bowker set up the office in Maseru eight years ago. His service then was widely praised.

It's a simple switch of roles. Now that Bowker has been replaced by Griffith, surely it makes absolute sense to send Bowker back to Maseru and to replace Griffith there. Bowker's rheumatism has rendered him unfit to lead a police force, but it does not prevent him from serving in his former office position in Maseru.

Frere approves. Brownlee notifies Bowker of his appointment and suggests he take up his new office as soon as possible. He also notifies Rolland he should return once more to the role of assistant to the senior magistrate as soon as Bowker arrives.

Maseru — Thursday, November 1, 1877

Today is the day for the Maseru pitso, or annual meeting, at which the Basotho chiefs gather with the magistrates to discuss events in the country and to tell them what is on their hearts. It is an opportunity, too, for the magistrates to bring the chiefs up to date on any changes in the administration or any new regulations that are to be put into effect. It serves as an effective two-way communication channel.

Rolland had hoped Bowker would have arrived in time to lead the meeting, making it a fine introduction to his second tenure as senior resident magistrate. But Bowker is suffering from a severe bout of rheumatism and has been detained at his home in Pietermaritzburg, in Natal colony. Rolland considered postponing the meeting until Bowker arrived, but it was too late to inform all concerned. So he is going ahead with the meeting as planned.

Once all the chiefs and headmen have taken their places outside the magistracy, many on horseback, Rolland greets them. With him, sitting outside the magisterial offices, are magistrates from the five districts, including Hope from Quthing, and several missionaries who have traveled from Morija, 25 miles south of Maseru.

Rolland attributes the Basotho turnout, which is smaller than he had hoped it would be, to Griffith's absence. He notes, too, that Paramount Chief Letsie and Chief Molapo, are not there, although both have sent their sons and headmen.

Rolland reminds the gathered Basotho that this meeting is their chance to speak their minds. "It is therefore a matter of regret that all who have the good of their nation at heart should not avail themselves of it," he adds. "Here all those who are chiefs or those who are of lower rank may speak freely to the government, but let each man who speaks remember that he must speak with reflection, true words that he thinks will be for the good of the people. That is the object of the meeting."

He starts by outlining recent events.

"With regard to what the government has done here during the past year, I may tell you that a new district has been made over the Orange River. There was no one at hand there to collect revenue, issue passes and settle complaints, and the people were put to great inconvenience when the river was full. The Government, therefore, found it necessary to give Moorosi's people over there a magistrate and Mr. Hope has been appointed."

Rolland outlines the new laws, an updated version produced in March by a government commission that first met in December 1872. Many chiefs and people were called to give evidence to the commission and spoke freely about the changes that should be made, Rolland says. Now, after four years of deliberation, the laws have been published.

"This is the way the government works," Rolland tells the gathered Basotho. "It consults the views and feelings of the people, and then enacts laws that seem the best. The amended laws are not very different from the old, as you will see. I have had a number of copies printed in Sesotho for your information, and I will now ask George Moshesh to read them to you."

After Moshesh reads the laws, several chiefs comment that, although the commission might have listened to what the Basotho people said, they did not necessarily follow their suggestions. And the people who sat on the commission were all whites who thought like white people.

Disregarding their comments, Rolland says he would like to draw the listeners' attention to the section about passes for traveling outside Basutoland. "Any one leaving the country without a pass will be fined," he says. "Also, the annual hut tax is due on Monday, November 5. I will give you time to pay it, but you must pay it as soon as you can."

Rolland leans down and picks up a packet. "I am now placed in a difficult position," he says. "I have a certain packet which I am ordered to deliver publicly and the man to whom it belongs is not here. The packet is this beautifully embossed letter from Sir Henry Barkly (governor of the Cape Colony before Sir Bartle Frere was appointed) to Letsie and the other sons of Moshoeshoe. Where is Letsie?"

A few among the crowd respond, "He is not here." Someone says, "He is sick."

"If he is sick," Rolland continues, "where is his eldest son, Lerothodi?"

No one responds. He is not here either.

This is not the first time Letsie has failed to attend a pitso and it annoys Rolland. He adds, "The queen grants you this annual opportunity of speaking to her, and Letsie is always sick, so is Molapo. I cannot help thinking that this is an excuse, and, as representing the government, I tell you, frankly, I am dissatisfied."

He warms up to the topic.

"This absence of the principal chiefs is a bad thing. It is not bad for the government, but bad for the chiefs, and for you all. It shows that they do not care any longer what becomes of the people, nor anything about their welfare. That was how Dibe, Moshoeshoe's uncle, lost his chieftainship, and allowed it to slip into the hands of the younger branch. Should such a thing happen again, don't blame the government."

The crowd murmurs.

Rolland hands the engraved letter to Masupha, as the highest ranking chief there, asking him to deliver it to his eldest brother, Letsie.

He then introduces Hamilton Hope, the new magistrate of Quthing district.

"The difficulties of a magistrate are great," Hope tells the attendees, "but if every man helps his magistrate to see that the law is kept, those difficulties will be easily overcome. If you obey the laws you will prosper and eventually become a great nation. A country cannot progress without law and order. Let every man assist his magistrate. I greet you all, and I am glad to see so many present."

Rolland asks whether the chiefs have any comments.

"I know you are dissatisfied that Chief Letsie and other chiefs are not present," George Moshesh says. "The reason is that they are old and they are infirm. Besides, they know that the government will manage everything all right. I think, too, that what they want to say will be said by their delegates."

Rolland nods.

After further discussion, Tsekelo, a brother of Letsie, spurs the horse on which he is sitting and moves it forward. Clearly he has something important to say.

The crowd watches intently. They are aware that Tsekelo, dressed today in European clothes and wearing a tall hat, recently returned from a visit to England where, over several months, he learned much about how the English people live, talk and think.

Tsekelo has told his fellow Basotho that he gained respect for the English for their learning and their achievements. He soon discovered, however, that the Basotho were considered uneducated heathens who needed to be taught to become civilized. The British considered their way of life superior to any in the world. He also found out that it did not help to insult the British or to express opposition to their system; they were convinced they were right, that their culture was the only culture that had any merit, and they would not consider any contrary thoughts.

So, when discussing politics with the British, the method Tsekelo had found most effective was firstly to praise them — they loved that — and to concede that they had nothing but good intentions for the Basotho people. Secondly, he would assert his rights as a British citizen; he could express his thoughts more openly that way. Above all, he learned to cultivate and enhance the natural Basotho ability to express disagreements in a quiet, inoffensive manner.

So today he will try to use what he has learned.

"I greet you Bakwena," Tsekelo says. "We are thankful to the government for this pitso. It is truly a 'calling together,' an 'invitation' to us. We are glad to have it, and we know it is a great boon.

"We are all British citizens and so we are Englishmen although our color is black. And we have here the Englishmen's privilege of speaking freely and of grumbling, and here again the government can speak to us as a people. We can tell the government everything as we used to tell our kind father Moshoeshoe. Such is the indulgence granted to us, a man can here mention the veriest trifles."

Tsekelo swings around and points to a man sitting on the ground to his right.

"You there," he says.

The man jumps up.

"If you like you may tell the government your hen-roost was robbed last night."
The man protests that it was not robbed.

Tsekelo laughs. The crowd laughs with him, recognizing Tsekelo's reference is hypothetical. In effect, Tsekelo is saying: You tell me I am a British citizen and I am free to say what I want to say, and I am about to exercise that freedom, so do not dare stop me.

"What we like in the Queen's government is the freedom we enjoy and the justice of its administration," Tsekelo continues. "This was why we refused to come under the Free State. This was why we refused to be annexed to Natal where a despotic law then prevailed. We, therefore, elected to join the Cape Colony and its father England. We wanted peace and rest."

The crowd cheers.

Rolland and the other magistrates smile with delight. Hope leans forward. If only Moorosi were this cooperative, his life would be a lot easier.

For Tsekelo, his approach is like hunting an antelope. Move slowly, approach it from the side. Act relaxed and be sure the wind is blowing from the antelope toward you so he does not smell your presence. Even creep slowly away from it for a while so its defenses are down. Plan your strategy correctly and eventually you will be in a position to hurl your spear at the unsuspecting antelope from close range.

"I came prepared to protest strongly, very strongly in the name of our Basotho against our not having been consulted beforehand in the framing and publishing of these new regulations, but Mr. Rolland has cut the ground from under my feet, and I am silenced."

He is, of course, not silenced.

"Mr. Rolland has shown what I had overlooked, that we *were* consulted. We were given an opportunity of expressing our views, and today we have another such opportunity. It is as if the matter were submitted to our Houses of Parliament. Were it not so, I would have walked away today.

"You say we are in a backward state, and are unfit to legislate for ourselves, but still we like at least to be consulted. That is our due as men.

"But what I would always protest against would be if the government were suddenly to proclaim laws without warning. What we want is to be politically educated, consulted, and made partakers in whatever new legislation may be initiated. And if any one is found objectionable, we can consider the issue and then we are free to submit the matter to government."

Did you get the message, government? Did you see through the sarcasm? We want to have a say over the laws. We want to be joint legislators; we do not want you telling us what we should do as you have just done.

The pitso continues. At its end, Rolland sums up the meeting, answering Tsekelo's plea to be made participants in the legislative process.

"Some of you have remarked that the chiefs were not consulted in making these new laws. I have already told you that they were, and again last year you were told at this pitso that the new laws would soon be established, but none of the chiefs took the trouble to inquire.

"Was this from indifference, or was it because you fully trusted the government? I think the latter. You all know full well that the government never has, and never will, treat you ill."

As Tsekelo rides away, he wonders whether Rolland and the other magistrates got the message that the chiefs who stay away and prefer to say nothing are unhappy with the government deciding what is right for them. Their silence shows disagreement, not agreement.

But were he to see into the mind of Hamilton Hope he would know his message was too subtle and had completely missed its mark.

Transkei — Tuesday, November 6, 1877

Sir Arthur Thurlow Cunynghame, commander of the British and colonial forces on the eastern frontier, reviews the campaign against the Gcaleka with Griffith and his senior officers.

Over the course of 18 days, the men made a clean sweep of the Gcaleka territory, driving the people ahead of them, burning down vacated kraals and seizing the people's corn. The result: The Gcaleka, who appear to have fled, no longer have huts in which to live and would have little to eat should they return. An operation originally intended to defeat the Gcaleka turned into a scorched earth campaign.

Although he has reservations about the long-term effects of this action, in an official despatch to Sir Bartle Frere, Cunynghame commends Griffith for carrying out his orders "with correctness and judgment."

"Commandant Griffith has been unremitting in his endeavors to carry out to the best advantage his military operations, in which he has been very successful," he writes. "The whole of the country known as Gcalekaland has been entirely freed of the enemy, much cattle has been taken, and the enemy routed from their strongest position. Circumstances lead to the indication that the termination of this war is not far distant."

At camp headquarters in Ibika the troops are less happy.

"The Gcaleka have not been defeated," Granville says. "From what I hear, they are already starting to return to the areas from which we drove them."

"Yes," responds Brown. "They will return. We should have followed them and destroyed them."

Scott, his boots shaking the wooden floor, enters the room.

"Have you heard the news?" he asks.

"What news?"

"At Griffith's request, more troops are being sent and we are to march on Gcalekaland again. I hope we do it properly this time."

Quthing — Thursday, November 15, 1877

Moorosi believes his plan to push quietly against Hope is working. His refusal to allow the men to be arrested by Hope's policemen was effective. As a result, the magistrate yielded to him on the issue of the stolen goats, recognizing his authority to punish the offenders.

He must push this advantage further and discuss matters with Hope in another pitso. Perhaps this time, given his victory over the stolen goats, he will advance his cause more effectively and persuade the magistrate to back off.

Transkei — Friday, November 16, 1877

Griffith's men are exhausted. After seemingly endless days of marching in the rain and mud, they have covered almost every square mile of the deserted territory, burning huts, seizing cattle and gathering stores of food, but have come into contact with only a few Gcaleka. The horses, too, are tired. The provisions are almost gone and the rugged terrain and wet weather make it difficult for the supply wagons to reach the men with food and ammunition because virtually no roads exist in most of the area.

Some of the men are sick with fever and dysentery. All need a rest. The Mfengu and Thembu fighting with them are anxious to return home.

Griffith orders most of the troops to return to Ibika, but sends a team to guard the Bashee River near the sea to prevent the return of the Gcaleka — who presumably have fled north — to their land. He thanks the settler volunteers for their services and allows them to go home.

The news spreads throughout the colony. The war is over, the Gcaleka cease to exist as a community. Their land has been taken. Their chief and leaders have fled.

Merriman, the de-facto war minister, is beaming. He had feared, he confesses, that the fighting would have been much worse. "We can now move toward setting apart about 500 farms of 300 acres each for occupation by Europeans," he tells Frere. "Clearly, they will select the most fertile areas. The less fertile areas will be given to the Mfengu. What is then left will be open to occupation by those Gcaleka who, we believe, will return, surrender, give up their arms and agree to live under British rule."

In the barracks in King William's Town, Griffith sits alone, on the edge of his bed. He sees again in his mind's eye the shooting, the shouting and the shelling as his men chase the panicked Gcaleka.

He sees the vivid orange and red of the huts on fire. He sees the troops pillage food from the deserted kraals and capture the disoriented cattle. He sees the fury in their eyes, reflecting those streaks of cruelty and hatred every soldier needs to perform his task efficiently.

Griffith had been determined to lead the operation with his head and not his heart. He would serve his country as he had been trained — as a good soldier, following orders. But, unable to ignore the murmurs of his heart entirely, he had tempered his instructions with compassion. He had opted to do so with the least loss of life possible. He had instructed his men to force the enemy to flee. Rather let them depart their land than depart this earth.

At least, Griffith consoles himself, the loss of life was not as great as it could have been. He and his men might have driven people from their land and destroyed their means of survival, but they had not killed people unnecessarily and had avoided needless cruelty and suffering.

The thoughts tumble through his head, vying with one another for primacy.

But enough of this. He had implemented justice fairly and with compassion. He will struggle to be content that he served both his country and his conscience.

Maseru — The same day

It is nearly six years since the colonial government in Cape Town officially took over the running of Basutoland from the British, but it appears to the acting governor's agent Emile Rolland — who has worked for the government for those six years and is now 41 — that the colonial authorities are still stuck in the past.

He writes to Brownlee, the Secretary for Native Affairs, in Cape Town.

"I beg most respectfully to draw your attention to an error in the colonial office letter No. 949 A of the 3rd Instant in which this territory is called 'British Basutoland.' As this is an error of frequent occurrence in official documents, I have thought it might be worth while to bring it to your notice. By Section IV of Act No. 12 of 1872 the official designation of the territory is deemed to be 'Basutoland.'"

As Rolland folds the letter, he suddenly realizes that perhaps Griffith's penchant for petty bureaucratic accuracy has rubbed off on him.

No matter, he will send it anyway. Perhaps the government in Cape Town will be using the correct designation by the time Bowker arrives — if he ever does.

Quthing — Monday, November 19, 1877

Maitin feared something like this might occur in Hope's absence. For more than an hour, groups of armed Baphuthi have been gathering at the Quthing magistracy tethering their horses and talking loudly to one another. Their numbers have been steadily increasing for some hours; now hundreds are here.

Maitin's mind jumps back to the occasion five months ago when a large gathering of armed Baphuthi, led by Moorosi, confronted Hope. He recalls how threatened he felt when the men asserted that Moorosi was their leader and they would obey him and not Hope.

He feared for his life when a man was shot among the crowd and Hope insisted on plunging his way into their midst and urging that he follow. At any time, he thought on that occasion, a verbal or physical spark could cause the people to turn on them.

How should he respond now?

Maitin approaches a man who is leading one of the groups.

"Why are you here?"

"King Moorosi told us to come because a pitso is being held here today," the man responds. "He told us to bring our weapons."

"I know of no pitso," Maitin replies. "Did he say what the pitso would be about?"

"No."

Maitin is debating whether he should tell the crowd to leave as no pitso is to be held, when a man makes his way to the front. Maitin recognizes him as Moorosi's messenger, Mafetudi.

"King Moorosi is coming to pay a friendly visit to Mr. Hope," Mafetudi says. "He wants to talk about things that friends discuss with one another. Last time they met they did not have a chance to talk as friends. Now he wants to do so."

"Mr. Hope is not at home. He has gone for some days. I suggest you tell Chief Moorosi that he should postpone his visit. I will pass the message on to Mr. Hope when he returns."

As the messenger leaves to convey the message to Moorosi, Maitin retreats into the relative safety of the office where he discusses the situation with the policemen. They are as puzzled as he is.

"Look at them," says sergeant Isaak Masin. "They are walking around and talking as though it is a party. I don't think they know why they are here, either. Their king told them to come here and so they are here. That is all."

"At least they look relaxed," replies Maitin. "They do not seem bent on any sort of confrontation."

Later, the messenger returns. "King Moorosi says to thank you for the information. When Mr. Hope comes back, we will ask him to set a day for a pitso."

The messenger shouts to the crowd to leave. Maitin heaves a sigh of relief.

Quthing — Thursday, November 22, 1877

Hope disembarks from the new scotch cart that he bought with government money in Aliwal North while visiting his wife and mother-in-law. He has been on the road for three days.

He wastes little time conferring with Maitin, who describes the arrival of armed men four days ago. Hearing what happened, Hope becomes convinced that Moorosi does not want a pitso. He wants a confrontation.

"I have been giving this matter some thought while I have been away," he tells Maitin. "I listened to what the Basotho said at the Maseru pitso and discussed their attitudes with the other magistrates. I'm convinced Moorosi is more rebellious than any of them. He is rash and fearless. He is clearly defying the government.

"I have done what I believe is right to counter the chief. I do not know what else I can be expected to do. During our private discussions in Maseru, Rolland kept quoting Griffith's letter to me in which he warned me not to precipitate any crisis. He said, too, that he would be unable to back me up with force should matters get out of hand. Rolland also quoted Brownlee's letter to me that by being 'calm, firm and reasoning' I will be more effective than if I use force.

"Calm, firm and reasoning.

"I'll try to be calm. I think I have shown I can be firm and, well, I have reasoned with him over and over again. I don't know whether I'll succeed. But I'll try.

"I will set out my message to Moorosi in writing so that the authorities can see what I have said to him. Then they will be unable to second-guess me."

Hope sits at his desk and, in careful neat handwriting, sets down his words on paper. The letter will be passed on to Maitin to translate.

"Yesterday I returned to my office and was informed by Mr. Maitin of your message sent to me by Mafetudi," he writes. "I was much pleased with the words you sent me by him. I will also be very glad to see you; for, as you say, when we last met we had so many affairs which we were forced to talk over in order that we might understand each other, that we had no time for friendly discussion.

"Mr. Maitin advised you to postpone your visit because I was absent, and I was very glad to hear this, as I should have missed seeing you, my friend, had you come when you first intended."

He reads over what he has written. He smiles as he reads the words "my friend." Those are "calm and reasonable" words.

He lays down one stipulation; one with which he is sure the authorities in Maseru and King William's Town will agree. "I trust that you will not bring trouble on yourself and your children by omitting to tell all your friends to leave their arms at home when they come to this or any other friendly meeting."

He has no intention of facing the same armed threat he faced before.

After Maitin has translated the letter, Hope hands it to the chief constable, Abraham Sighata. He tells him to read it to Moorosi and to wait to see whether he has a reply. Hope also suggests that Sighata remind Moorosi of the events in the eastern Cape and to bear in mind what has happened to his friend Sarhili.

Quthing — Friday, November 23, 1877

As Moorosi listens to the letter from Hope, read to him by Chief Constable Sighata, he is pleased that Hope is ready to see him again and to discuss the issues causing trouble between them. He is also anxious to hear from Hope about the pitso in Maseru. He likes that Hope calls him friend.

But he balks at one stipulation: That he and his people leave their weapons at home.

"I will not leave my guns at home when I go to a pitso to speak with a chief," he tells Sighata. "Tell the magistrate I cannot leave my weapons. It is our custom to take our weapons with us wherever we go. Even when I move among my people I take my spears."

Moorosi gestures toward Sighata.

"You know that is the case," he tells him. "If you don't know, anyone here can tell you. It is our custom. Let me remind you that when a Baphuthi is initiated into the privileges of manhood, the elders place a weapon into his hands. The weapon is a sign of manhood. With his weapon he is to defend his chief, his country and himself.

"We say, 'Hold on to your arms.'

"Tell the magistrate that when a bull goes out to pasture, he does not take off his horns and leave them in the kraal. They are part of him. He uses them to defend himself. He gores his assailant if he is attacked.

"The horns are part of the bull and our weapons are part of us, too.

"Even when I visited Moshoeshoe I would take my weapons with me. Even when I go from one hut to sleep in another I go carrying my quiver of spears to the place where I sleep.

"Abraham Sighata, explain my view to the magistrate for me. Tell him I would be weak if I were unarmed. I would be walking around naked.

"Even when I go to pay my hut tax, I go with these arms to the magistrate's office. The weapons do not prevent me from paying tax. I pay it anyway. No one tries to stop me from paying the tax because I have a weapon with me.

"If the magistrate replies that I must leave my weapons behind, he is telling me he refuses to see me. What matters is where your heart is. These weapons cannot hurt anyone unless your heart is crooked. I will visit the magistrate with a happy heart, not a crooked heart. That is what is important."

Sighata points out that sometimes weapons are fired even though no harm is intended.

"I understand that accidents can happen," Moorosi replies. "The last time we met a man was shot by accident. I understand that. Accidents can happen anywhere at any time. There was no danger to the magistrate.

"Tell the chief that I will attend this pitso with a glad heart. The arms mean nothing. They are only the appendages of manhood. True manhood is in the heart.

"I am pleased that the magistrate has informed me of his return and I am pleased that he has agreed that we should meet. But Mr. Hope must not listen only to what the lips say when he and I speak to each other. What matters is what is in the heart. Please convey my very best greetings to Mr. Hope and also to Mr. Maitin."

As he mounts his horse, Sighata promises to convey Moorosi's sentiments, but he already knows what the answer will be.

Quthing — Saturday, November 24, 1877

Hope remains convinced that Moorosi has an ulterior motive in bringing the weapons with him to the pitso.

"All that contention about arms being a part of him and his people is utter nonsense," he tells Maitin. "He wants to back up with force his assertions about being the ultimate authority here. He knows he can stand up to me more effectively with a crowd of armed followers behind him than without them."

Hope's first reaction is to tell Moorosi he must leave his weapons at home or else the pitso is off. But he realizes, too, that, as Rolland emphasized in Maseru, he needs to keep communication open. After some thought, he decides to start with the positive and move to the negative. He will first set a date for the meeting: Monday December 3, a little more than a week away. He will follow with the negative: Whatever Moorosi might say, no one — neither him, his staff nor Moorosi and his people — should be armed.

In the meantime he will send copies of his correspondence with Moorosi to Rolland in Maseru. Let Rolland advise him. In that way, at least Rolland will not be able to criticize him afterward.

He sits down to write to Rolland immediately so he can catch the Monday post. The letter, starting from Quthing early on Monday, should reach Maseru by Wednesday morning. Hope should receive Rolland's reply by Saturday morning, two days before the planned meeting with Moorosi.

Hope also decides to cover himself more fully by sending a message to Brownlee, the Secretary for Native Affairs, who is still in King William's Town. The message will go by horse cart to Palmietfontein, where the recently extended telegraph line now ends, and from there by telegraph to King William's Town. "Brownlee will receive my message in a day or two. What is the use of modern means of communication if you cannot use them, right?"

Maitin has learned not to respond to rhetorical questions from Hope. He fears that, after only a night's sleep back in Quthing, Hope already is departing from the calm, reasoned approach pressed upon him by Rolland and Griffith.

The letters are insurance; Hope still expects to do as he thinks best — and the message from Moorosi has stirred him up.

"It is all very well for them to sit in their offices in Maseru and King William's Town, or wherever they happen to be, and warn me not to act with a high hand," he says. "But what would they do if they were here? How would they act if they were faced with an aggressive and defiant chief, backed by hundreds of warlike armed savages, who is determined to subvert my authority? And to chase me out of the country if necessary? Or to kill me if that will achieve his aim?

"And the man who told me not to be so high-handed, whom we now should correctly call *Colonel* Griffith, has himself been leading troops against Sarhili. Why is he acting correctly when he makes war, yet I am *not* acting correctly when I ask for a few score troops to back me up against a rebellious chief?

"I will do my work here to the best of my ability. I will bring justice and civilization to these savages and I will do it effectively — whatever it takes. When they see what I have achieved, they will thank me for my work.

"One thing is for sure. I will not tolerate arguing once more with Moorosi with a force of armed warriors arraigned against me without some sort of armed force backing me up. Either it is unarmed against unarmed, or armed against armed. In equal numbers. Otherwise, I do not meet with him at all."

He pens a telegram to Brownlee to be sent via Palmietfontein.

"Moorosi is to be here on 3rd December to repeat his old argument. Has warned the whole tribe to assemble armed. District a good deal unsettled at this, and at exaggerated reports of what he is going to do. I sent a message to warn him not to bring guns or spears; he sent civil reply, but says he insists upon the guns. I think he does not believe the news I have given him about Sarhili's collapse. This being a direct defiance, please send me instructions at once, meanwhile I will act as before. Have reported to Rolland, who will send letters by post."

Now, Hope decides, he will await the replies from Rolland and from Brownlee. Their responses will determine the approach he will need to take on December 3.

King William's Town — Tuesday, November 27, 1877

With the war against the Gcaleka for all purposes over, Frere is preparing to return to Cape Town, and to continue on Lord Carnarvon's design for confederation. But at today's briefing in the British barracks, Merriman, the cabinet member who has become the colony's de-facto war leader, informs Frere of disturbances among the Ngqika, original occupants of the land on which the whites settled who live throughout the territory.

"We believe that the Ngqika are being stirred up by the Gcaleka, who as you know are living outside their territory," Merriman tells Frere. "I believe we have no choice in the matter but to break up this rebellion by entering the areas in which the Ngqika are most populous and depriving their chief, Sandile, of his power. We have a good excuse to act against them; through their attacks on our farms, they have broken the law."

Frere is taken aback. If the confederation is to work, the country needs stability. He had thought the war was over when the Gcaleka were driven from their land. Now he fears more trouble lies ahead.

Quthing — Tuesday, November 27, 1877

Hope has been concerned for some time that he knows little of what the average Baphuthi is thinking. Maitin provides reports — particularly through

MaLebenya, with whom Maitin has become too friendly in Hope's opinion — but he is not sure whether her reports reflect general opinion among the Baphuthi.

Today he hopes he is making an advance in that respect. He has before him a man named Mokhoa. He is there because he told one of Hope's policemen, Constable Monaheng, of a conversation that he overheard between Letsie and Austen after the recent pitso in Maseru. Monaheng told Hope and Hope told Monaheng to bring Mokhoa to him to tell his story.

Mokhoa is nervous. He has heard of the severe sentences Hope has imposed, often including many lashings, and of Hope's bursts of anger. He is concerned that, when Hope hears his story, he will have him whipped or even thrown in jail.

"I did not hear anything," he says.

"I heard you say it," Constable Monaheng counters. "I do not lie."

Makhoa realizes he is in a corner. He looks across at Hope, who reassures him that he will not be punished if he tells the truth about what happened.

There is no way out, Makhoa concludes. He must speak.

Makhoa says he heard Letsie complain about passes being refused to people to work in the Cape Colony, preventing them from leaving Basutoland to earn money to pay the hut tax.

"He also said a woman brought a claim against Raisa and Mr. Hope fined Raisa excessively. Mr. Austen then said that he knew that Moorosi had objected to the establishment of a magistrate on his land, but he at last consented because he wanted to obey government. Mr. Austen also said that he had told Moorosi if he had any complaints against his magistrate he could bring them to him in Mohale's Hoek. Yet, he said, Moorosi never had brought any complaints to him."

Letsie had said there were wars to the south, but his people are faithful and pay their hut tax, Makhoa adds. But Letsie said that if matters continued and passes were refused, then there would be war here, too.

"Letsie took the cap off his head and threw it on the ground and said, I swear that if we are treated in this way there will be a war."

Maitin looks up from his writing.

"How far were you away from Letsie when he said this?" he asks.

Makhoa looks outside through the open door.

"About as far as the jail over there," he says. "Mr. Austen was close to me."

"So you could hear clearly what they were saying?"

"Yes."

"What would you say if Letsie or Mr. Austen were to deny your story?"

"I would still insist on it. It is the truth."

Once Makhoa has left, Hope paces up and down for a couple of minutes. He stops, swings around and fixes his eyes on Maitin.

"I cannot let this pass," he says, his voice suddenly growing strident and anger boiling within him. He is disturbed that Letsie was reporting his actions to Austen and that it led to a heated discussion. He also resents the inference that Austen took Letsie's side against him and acted as though he were Hope's superior. Bring the complaints against Hope to me, he had said, and I will sort them out.

But most disturbing is that Letsie threatened war if passes were refused.

"The attitude indicated by this statement cannot be tolerated," Hope says. "Letsie is said to be cooperative with colonial rule. Griffith spoke highly of him, at least in terms of peaceful cooperation. If Letsie can threaten war, imagine what a rebellious chief like Moorosi must be thinking."

Maitin suggests the report might be inaccurate. The story is told by only one man. "Perhaps we should wait until we hear from Mr. Austen or from Letsie."

"But that will take time," Hope responds. "What is Austen going to say? Can he deny it? It sounds plausible." He sits down, strokes his beard and looks at the papers and books on his desk, thinking.

He looks up at Maitin.

"I think these statements explain in some way why Moorosi is so determined to oppose me and why he insists on being armed when he meets with me. He has heard these stories and he probably thinks he can depend on Letsie's support. He will no doubt arrive for the meeting next Monday with about a thousand armed men to make as formidable a demonstration as possible.

"He will use that threat of force to insist that he is in charge here and that he will resist my administration — or else.

"Yes, we will ask Mr. Rolland to obtain an explanation from Letsie for his behavior. And, yes, I have asked Mr. Rolland for orders on what to do about the pitso. I am hoping he will send me a reply as soon as he receives the letter on Wednesday; I should receive the reply on Saturday. But can I afford to wait that long?"

Hope rises from his desk once more.

"In the meantime, I need to show Moorosi that, even though he thinks he can get support from Letsie, he will not be able to use that as a lever against me. What I need is to have a visible armed force in place here so that Moorosi will know that I can back up what I say."

Maitin knows that when Hope is determined to do something, nothing will stand in his way. But he feels obliged to respond.

"You will no doubt recall that Mr. Griffith..."

"*Colonel* Griffith," interjects Hope.

"Colonel Griffith said he cannot send any police force to back you. They are committed elsewhere."

"I do recall that. But Colonel Griffith is now in Ibika, the war with Sarhili is over, and his forces are idle. Before, he might not have had any troops available. Now he does. I fail to understand how he can tell me he cannot send forces to back me up when he can launch a war against Sarhili."

He shakes his head in annoyance, his beard swaying from side to side. He stops and shakes his finger at Maitin. "In any event, I do not plan to ask Colonel Griffith for troops. Nor do I plan to ask for any police to be stationed here."

"What, then, if I may ask, is your plan, Mr. Hope?"

"I will request West Fynn, who is in charge of the troops at Kraai River 50 miles to the south, to send as strong a patrol as he can spare — say forty or fifty men — to the border of Moorosi's territory, at Palmietfontein, less a day's ride from here.

"I will tell him that I need the troops to be there no later than Sunday, December 2nd. That will put them in place a day before the pitso with Moorosi. The news that they are there will reach Moorosi and he will be reminded that the government is watching his actions and is prepared to restrain him with force if necessary.

"I will ask Fynn's men to remain at Palmietfontein and not enter Quthing without instructions from me. You see, if the men come here to meet Moorosi's force a collision will inevitably take place. But when Moorosi hears that the men are in position at Palmietfontein, ready to attack, he undoubtedly will abandon the idea of the so-called pitso, which I suspect is a way to confront me with an armed force once more. He will postpone it to a later date. At that time we also may have an even stronger force to back us up."

Maitin is concerned Hope is relying on armed force to back up his position, a tack that Colonel Griffith had earlier admonished him not to take. But Maitin knows better than to disagree with Hope.

Hope writes a letter to Fynn, and orders Maitin that it be sent "by special express post if necessary." Only six days remain before the pitso and he needs to have the troops in place by then.

Maseru — Wednesday, November 28, 1877

It is more than a month since Acting Resident Magistrate Emile Rolland was told Bowker would take over the office and Bowker still has not arrived.

Realizing he cannot put pressing matters indefinitely on hold while waiting for Bowker, Rolland decides he needs to step in and try to calm the troubles engulfing the Quthing magistracy.

After reading the letters and statements from Hope that arrived in this morning's post and studying carefully Hope's report of the events immediately following his return from the pitso in Maseru, Rolland accepts that Moorosi will not easily back down on his demand that his people be armed at the pitso. Nor will Hope back down on his demand that the men come unarmed.

It appears to be a recipe for conflict that, sparked by an incident, could easily get out of hand.

Rolland would like to travel to Quthing himself to try to calm the situation. But such a journey will take a few days in preparation and travel time and he cannot risk being out of the office for that long should Bowker arrive. He needs to do something now. The pitso is less than a week away.

Firstly, he will order that the pitso planned for December 3 be postponed, providing breathing room. Secondly, he will send a message to Letsie, asking for his help. Then he will write a letter to Moorosi, which he will enclose with the letter to Hope, instructing Hope to see that Moorosi receives it.

Rolland ponders what he should say to Moorosi. But he cannot ponder for long. A new daily police express service will ensure that his letter arrives in Quthing by noon the following day, but he must complete his letter today so that he can get it in the Thursday morning express post, which will reach Quthing on Friday, three days before the pitso planned for Monday. Doing so will provide Hope enough time to send the letter to Moorosi before Monday.

Rolland's approach to Moorosi will be colonial and British. Even though his father was French, Rolland was born in South Africa to a mother of British descent and grew up with English as his home language. Even though Rolland spent only four years in Britain, he is thoroughly British as any born and bred British national.

In line with that approach, he regards Moorosi as a disobedient child, as one who needs to show respect to the authorities and to obey them because it is the right and only thing to do. To Rolland the British, and now the colonial authorities, have brought light into darkness for people who were mere savages. The British system is civilized and just. Its basis in Christian principles underpins it with moral authority. There can be no question the British system of government is superior to anything anywhere else in the world.

British rule is in the best interests of the Basotho people themselves. Left to their own devices, Rolland believes, they will wallow in heathenism.

Unlike Hope, who grew up in a home with a military and administrative background, Rolland was reared in a missionary home. His approach, therefore, is rooted in persuasion and conviction and an appeal to a higher standard. To Rolland, the Baphuthi people will accept the colonial system because they will be persuaded that it is just and in their best interests, although he believes, too, that government officials should bring about such persuasion by speaking quietly, but firmly, making clear that they are in charge and not tolerating any attitude other than complete obedience and profound respect. Like children, the natives will be persuaded by the higher reasoning, will obey and will be subservient.

In his letter to Moorosi, therefore, Rolland believes he needs to show firmly that the government holds the power and that Moorosi needs not just to obey, but to obey happily; not merely to be content with British rule but to show how admirable it truly is.

He writes a letter to Moorosi in English, which he will then translate for onward delivery to the chief. Hope will be sent both versions, the English original for him to read and the other for him to send to Moorosi.

"Your words have greatly amazed me," Rolland writes to Moorosi. "I am sure that the Queen's government will also be greatly astonished to learn in what way Moorosi speaks to his magistrate."

Moorosi's duty, he continues, is to go to Hope unarmed, no matter what his custom might be. By not obeying Hope's instruction to leave his arms at home, he has shown no respect for the magistrate, let alone the queen's government.

"You say there is no harm in carrying arms if a man's heart is right, and that arms are only dangerous when the heart is crooked. Yes, but when you come with armed bands how will the magistrate see into your heart to ascertain if you come with white hearts or with hearts of another color? Supposing that the governor came to you with many armed warriors, what would you think of it? Would you not conclude that he had come to fight you?

"In the old time you used to go armed to chief's meetings, because, very often, warlike expeditions were ordered and planned at these meetings. Now, under the Queen's government, all that is over; there are no longer any warlike expeditions to which the people may be summoned by the chief.

"But all that is beside the question. The great thing is that it is not you, Moorosi, who must dictate your customs to the Queen's government; it is the Queen's government which must teach you its custom, and that is that people do not attend a pitso armed.

"We are not like God who can see into men's hearts whilst they are afar off; we are only men, and when we see armed men coming to us, we suppose they want war. Although your words may deny it, your actions call out in a loud voice.

"No, Moorosi, your duty is to obey and humble yourself. If you go about with bands of armed men after you have received an order to the contrary, it will be impossible for the government to recognize you as a subject. A bull that carries its horns with it in order to gore its assailant (to use your own words) is very like an enemy."

He tells Moorosi the pitso is off. It is not Moorosi's place to take the initiative and dictate to the government that a meeting shall take place.

"I entreat you to recognize that you have done wrong and to remain peacefully at home," he writes. "If you have any cause for dissatisfaction bring your complaint to your magistrate or to me. The government does not wish to prevent any man from speaking his mind or bringing forward his complaint. What will not be permitted is the use of threats."

The correct way to discuss a matter is to sit down in council and discuss it, Rolland adds. "That is the way men behave. To flaunt your weapons is not manliness, it is only the bragging of a bully."

Rolland says he plans shortly to visit Moorosi, concluding: "My words to you are the advice of a true friend."

Rolland folds the letter and instructs it to be sent to Moorosi via Hope.

In his letter to Hope, Rolland feels caught between Hope's lack of diplomacy and the rightness of his cause.

"I am of the opinion that the greatest caution and prudence should be exercised in this matter," he tells Hope, "and that there is everything to gain from delay, whilst on the other hand no advantage can possibly accrue from a pitso held at the suggestion of this unruly chief and which will give him the opportunity of being insolent to his magistrate and of contrasting his large physical resources, in the shape of a body of armed men, with the (to the native eye) defenseless and weak position of the magistrate.

"The chief Moorosi is evidently trying to make use of these armed demonstrations in order to convince his people of his power and supremacy, being unaffected by the presence of the magistrate, and to a tribe of ignorant barbarians no argument could be more conclusive, especially if the demonstration be accompanied by a defiant bearing."

He adds that he will send a messenger to Letsie, asking him to remonstrate with Moorosi, and that he intends to visit Moorosi himself, if needed.

Rolland adds, "It is quite impossible for me to give you any specific instructions. If, for example, Moorosi should, in spite of my letter, come down with his armed followers, you would have a good reason for declining to attend the pitso, by alleging the order contained in the letter.

"In any case, your wisest policy will be to keep quiet, avoid trials of strength, gain time, and allow the moral influence of the government to gain ground insensibly as it has in the more advanced districts.

"Should Moorosi visit you, unless there are special reasons to make it advisable, I should counsel that you receive him in your office, or at your residence, and that you should avoid giving him any opportunity of making a display before his people of his power and eloquence, a display which must necessarily be at your expense as long as he remain in his present sentiments.

"You will continue to exercise that friendliness and forbearance which you have already shown under trying circumstances, and to bear in mind that your highest and most lasting triumphs will be those which are the most gradually and noiselessly obtained, and that profound tranquility is the most successful result of good government.

"In all other matters you must use your own judgment and discretion, in which I have every confidence."

He hopes this coordinated action will calm matters in Quthing.

Quthing — Thursday, November 29, 1877

Unaware as yet of Rolland's efforts to delay the event, Hope is preparing for Monday's pitso. In addition to his request to West Fynn for a police presence on the border, he will ask Rolland to boost the police presence at his magisterial compound. Use of the Police Postal Express will ensure that the request reaches Rolland tomorrow, giving him time to send reinforcements by Monday. In that way, he will at least have a stronger back-up should Moorosi turn violent.

Fearing that Rolland will turn down his request to move additional police to Quthing, he couches his request as a response to stock theft. The request is not a total fabrication. Stock theft is a problem and he could do with additional police to counteract it.

In one letter, therefore, Hope informs Rolland of his request for additional troops from Fynn.

He then writes a separate letter to Rolland requesting more police in light of the increasing number of stock thefts. He points out that the thieves are using footpaths to take the cattle out of the territory and he requires several additional policemen to man the paths and watch for stock thefts.

He places the letters in separate envelopes so that Rolland will not believe that the two requests are related.

Maseru — Friday, November 30, 1877

As he reads the copy of Hope's letter to West Fynn that reaches him today, Rolland crashes his fist on the desk. Who does Hope think he is? And what does he think he is doing? It is bad enough that Moorosi calls up an armed band to confront Hope at the magistracy. Hope now counters by summoning troops to the border. And the 40 or 50 men on the border would be no match for the thousand or so warriors that Moorosi would be able to summon and so they would not serve as a threat, nor would they force Moorosi into docile submission. They would serve only as a provocation.

The arrival of an armed force at Palmietfontein would suggest an attack on Moorosi is imminent. The people would not see it as a precaution or as a mere symbol of authority. They would see it as the start of a build-up of forces against them and their chief. They know of the war against Sarhili to the south; now they would see the buildup as the first moves in a war against Moorosi.

Surely, Rolland mutters to himself, Hope should have listened when Griffith warned him before that no forces could be sent. Could Hope not read? Did he not understand Griffith? Could it possibly have been any clearer than it was?

Above anything else, Hope had been told to leave the responsibility of taking drastic action with the resident magistracy in Maseru. Yet here he is taking it upon himself to send his request directly to Fynn.

Even though Hope is his brother-in-law, Rolland feels constrained to tell him he has dangerously overstepped the mark. He fears that his actions will upset Mimmie, who eventually will hear of them. But another part of him suspects that Mimmie will understand the reason for his words. In any case, he must say what needs to be said.

"Your action in calling for troops to go to Palmietfontein," he writes, "meets with my most serious disapproval. As a counter-demonstration to anything Moorosi may do, it is most inadequate and is only calculated to irritate and provoke that chief without overawing him," he continues. "Moreover, the arrival of an armed force under such circumstances might produce a scene on both sides of the Telle River, amongst a population so given to spreading false and exaggerated rumors.

"If Moorosi supposes you have been instrumental in it, your moral influence with him will be greatly undermined."

Rolland reminds Hope of the instructions given him by Griffith that he is to take no action without reporting to the Maseru office and to leave the responsibility for action with the Maseru magistrate.

"If you assume the responsibility of communicating directly with the government and the F.A.M. Police, except under the gravest circumstances, I cannot be answerable for what may happen in the future.

"Under these circumstances, I should feel obliged if you would inform Mr. Fynn that it will no longer be necessary for him to send the patrol as requested by you.

"I trust that the disturbance caused by Moorosi's armed demonstration, which is the only cause I can see for the present uneasiness, will, by this time, have passed away. We are not at present in a position to meet force with force, nor is it desirable; and our only wise policy is to keep quiet as much as possible to avoid giving the chiefs opportunities of displaying their physical superiority."

Rolland notes another letter from Hope requesting additional policemen to be sent to the magistracy to combat stock theft. He casts it aside for later.

Rolland then turns to Hope's report of the conversation said to have taken place between Letsie and Austen. But he cannot accept its veracity. It simply does not ring true. For one thing, he does not believe Letsie would talk that way to Austen, nor would he throw his cap to the floor in anger and threaten war. Furthermore, Austen would not allow Letsie to speak in such a disrespectful way without some sort of response.

Rolland believes the report is a gross exaggeration at best. But, just in case, he will check with Austen.

In the afternoon, Rolland visits Letsie and outlines the reports of his statement to Austen that he has received from Hope. Letsie is quick to respond that he did not threaten war when he spoke with Austen.

The reports of his discussion with Austen, he says, are untrue.

"But these reports — rumors if you will — that you threatened war almost certainly have been conveyed to Chief Moorosi," Rolland says. "It does therefore seem that Chief Moorosi might be under the impression that you are threatening, or at least predicting, war and that might embolden him to do the same," Rolland says. "I would like to ask you to send your most confidential messenger to Chief Moorosi, tell him these reports are untrue and tell him to keep quiet and to submit to the orders of the government. Warn him, too, against making any armed demonstration."

Letsie ponders Rolland's request. He empathizes with Moorosi, but he is not inclined to foment confrontation. He believes in keeping on the good side of the authorities right now rather than confronting them directly. He does not believe that the best tactic is to threaten physical force, as Moorosi appears intent on doing. At least not now. His father taught him to resort to war only when all else has failed and to treat enemies with respect. That way they would be less inclined to attack you, invade your territory and steal your cattle.

His father Moshoeshoe had entrusted his people to the British authorities for protection. Letsie has not forgotten how, when the Basotho territory was being snatched by the Boers, the British stepped in and set a boundary beyond which the Boers were not to go. Although the Basotho lost a large slice of land on the western boundary, some of the land seized by the Boers was returned. Were protection to be removed, Letsie's people might face renewed attacks from the Boers or Zulus — and invasion could prove to be a worse fate than living under colonial laws.

Better to live under a degree of oppression than to have no land and no independence at all. Should the original British protective shield turn into a colonial spear and they find that the colonial intrusion is as bad as an invasion from the Boers or the Zulus, only then will the balance have swung.

Letsie sees, too, what has happened to Sarhili. Letsie's people are good fighters and are well armed and would fare better than those of Sarhili, but they are not yet ready to take on the colonial forces, even with the guns they have bought with money earned from working on the diamond mines in Kimberley.

So it is that Letsie smiles, nods and agrees with Rolland to send a messenger to Moorosi. Doing so will keep Letsie on the good side of his protectors and will remind Moorosi not to provoke the colonial powers. At least not now.

Quthing — Saturday, December 1, 1877

The letter from Rolland, which arrived in the post at noon, leaves Hope steaming. He has sent a message to Moorosi canceling the pitso as Rolland requested. But Rolland's instructions do not anger him as much as the way the letter is written.

He goes over it once again, re-reading the reprimand on his decision to request Fynn to move troops to Palmietfontein. The reprimand is so blunt that he begins to fear that his position as magistrate might be in jeopardy.

But Hope decides to fight back. He must reassert the necessity of his action. He must explain that, with the pitso due on Monday, he needed to act soon and could not wait for instructions by post on what to do. Had he followed strict protocol, he would have sent his request to Rolland, who would then send it to Brownlee, who would then reply to Rolland, who would then reply to him. But by then, the pitso would have come and gone.

Hope drafts a letter to Rolland explaining that his brother-in-law is not present in Quthing, does not understand the threat he is facing from Moorosi, and fails to understand that he needs an armed force, not to provoke Moorosi, but simply to back him up. "It would serve as a display, not a threat," he writes.

Having second thoughts, he deletes the word "display" and writes "protection."

He adds a paragraph arguing that he still needs an armed force to back him up. Moorosi could arrive at any time with hundreds of armed men and demand to speak with him. Hope is convinced the chief is bent on seeking a confrontation, attacking him and ousting him from Quthing.

He reads the letter over once more, deleting sections and substituting others. He takes up a fresh sheet of paper and writes out the letter again.

He reminds himself that he could jeopardize his position should he become too assertive. He reads Rolland's comments once again. Rolland's language is as strong as diplomatic talk will allow. He notes that Rolland has instructed him to tell Fynn to move the forces away from the border.

Fear reasserts itself and pushes fury into second place. He decides he had better do as he is told. Fuming, he crumbles the letter and throws it on the floor.

He begins with the required acknowledgment: "I have the honor to acknowledge the receipt of your letter of the 28th ultimo, enclosing letter for Moorosi." He says he has sent the letter with his chief constable to the Baphuthi chief.

With that out of the way, fear and fury vie in his mind as he once again tackles a response to the letter of reprimand. Like a true soldier, he must stand his ground. But, like a good whist player, he must recognize when the cards go against him.

The only way out is to find a compromise of some sort. If only there were a way, he thinks, he could go back in time and erase his request to Fynn. Yet there is a way he can partially do that. "I have also just received yours of 30th ultimo," he continues, "and have the honor to state that I had already seen my mistake, and sent to countermand Mr. Fynn, telling him not to come."

The letter is uncharacteristically short for someone who even writes long telegrams. So be it. It is a lie and lies are better short.

He signs the letter and readies it for the next post.

Now he needs to ask Fynn not to move his troops after all. And to mark the instruction with yesterday's date.

Dating the letter the day before Hope sent it does not help it arrive earlier. Fynn already has moved almost 50 men to the border.

News of their arrival soon reaches Moorosi on the word-of-mouth pipeline that stretches across the kingdom. Why, the chief asks himself, are they there? Is it a coincidence that the pitso was postponed and the troops gathered on the border at the same time? Do the colonists want to fight rather than talk?

Moorosi wanted to conduct a long conversation with Hope, to get to know him better and to ask him not to usurp his authority. He wants to comply with Letsie's request that he act with tact. But that attempt at dialogue has been answered with an armed threat.

Now, even as the colonial authorities are telling him that he should not arm his men, they are arming theirs. Is it because they want to attack him without facing any resistance?

It all makes sense. They think they can score as easy a success over him as Griffith did over Sarhili.

They deceive themselves.

He calls his messenger, Mafetudi.

"Go to the people who live between the magistrate's office and the Telle River. Inform them they are no longer to come to the pitso. Tell them they should move closer to the border and watch with guns and horses at the ready.

"They will see that there are armed police across the border.

"Should the police cross the Telle, they are to defend themselves and attack them.

"But they are not to cross the river if the colonial men stay on the other side. They are to attack only if the troops cross the river into our territory."

Transkei — Sunday, December 2, 1877

It is a routine patrol, geared more toward practice than anything else. About 150 police and volunteers, including Granville and Brown, are scouting along the Xora river. They camped last night near Sigcawu's burned kraal — a symbol of the flight of the Gcaleka six weeks ago — after leaving Ibika early yesterday.

Now it is late afternoon and they are heading toward Holland's Shop, a trader's post near a village called Mzintzani. With them are two wagons laden with food and baggage and two horse-drawn field guns.

A low rumble of voices and singing some distance away alerts them. As they look across the countryside to ascertain the source, hundreds of armed warriors appear on a nearby hill, heading their way.

"They're back!" yells Granville, who is near the head of the group. "The Gcaleka are back! And they are heading our way."

Inspector William Bourne, leader of the group, has seen them, too. "Head for Holland's Shop," he shouts. "It recently burned down, but we are going to have to use whatever earthworks are there to defend ourselves."

Minutes after arriving at the former trading station, the men place the guns in position and load them. They fasten the horses and oxen to the wagons. They take up their positions behind the rough defenses near the shop.

With the Gcaleka ready to attack, Bourne turns to one of the men.

"Tell Colonel Griffith what has happened and that we will need reinforcements," he says. The man rides off.

The men watch as a large number of Gcaleka emerge from a deep valley about a half-mile away. Soon the warriors massed against them number 500.

Captain Zachary Bayly, who has arrived to take charge of the soldiers, orders 20 policemen to advance down the hill to turn back the Gcaleka. But when Bayly realizes they stand no chance against the large number massed against them, he orders them to return to the top of the hill. Most do so, but three of the policemen run after their horses, which have broken loose.

Two succeed in reining in their horses and reaching the hill, but one, named Wellesley, is shot in the hip and then speared to death. The battle has claimed its first victim.

The Gcaleka fall back to reinforce their numbers and prepare for a concerted attack.

It is 6:30 p.m. when the Gcaleka, now a thousand strong, storm the small colonial force and surround their position. The sun is setting, but a full moon helps to bathe the battlefield in light.

"They're all around us," Granville notes. "We have nowhere to go. We have to fight them off or we're goners."

For 90 minutes, the fighting is continuous. Panicked by the cannon fire, the horses and oxen break loose and run into the Gcaleka hands.

The men succeed in holding back the Gcaleka, whose firing is wild and inaccurate. Nevertheless, stray bullets kill Henry Philip Baron, a Cape Town volunteer, and injure a number of others.

As the sky darkens, the Gcaleka withdraw.

"None too soon," says Bourne. "Our ammunition is exhausted."

"But we did succeed in killing many of them," says Brown.

"Yes, we succeeded in beating them off," Bayly says. "But I fear that this attack is just the start of a concerted attempt by the Gcaleka to regain their territory."

VI

King William's Town — Tuesday, December 4, 1877

Scouts report to William Raymond, deputizing for Fynn— who is occupied at Palmietfontein — that large parties of Gcaleka are gathering in both the north and south of the territory from which they were forcibly driven a little more than a month ago.

Raymond, in turn, reports to Griffith who realizes what he should have expected all along — that those Gcaleka who had eluded his forces had been lying low, both within their territory and across the Bashee River, and they have now returned to reclaim it.

Griffith, in turn, reports to Frere what has happened and asks for reinforcements to build up the military forces once more.

The war against the Gcaleka — the Ninth Frontier War — has not ended.

Before the day is over, moves are under way to collect an active force on the border, including the drafting of soldiers from as far away as Cape Town.

Quthing — Wednesday, December 5, 1877

Fynn is puzzled by the change of orders from Hope, whose latest letter has reached him in Palmietfontein, but, as an obedient soldier, he does as he is told.

As Fynn's troops dismantle their tents and leave Palmietfontein, Moorosi's armed and mounted men across the Telle River watch with fascination.

For Moorosi, the withdrawal is a victory. Clearly, once he placed his men near the border, the colonial soldiers were out-matched. Had he not moved his men into position, the colonial forces might have marched right up to the magistrate's office and perhaps beyond, with the aim of backing Hope's assertion that he is in control in Moorosi's territory and possibly even challenging him head-on.

The sudden withdrawal gives Moorosi confidence that taking on Hope with force will have the desired effect of causing him to back away from asserting his authority.

Once all the colonial troops have left, Moorosi tells his men on the border they can return to their homes. He will call on them once more should it become necessary. For now, the recent events have shown that their mere presence has the effect of frightening off the colonial troops.

Maseru — The same day

Acting Resident Magistrate Emile Rolland regards it as a good sign that he has received no express letters from Hamilton Hope in the last two days. The cancellation of the pitso, his letter to Moorosi, the withdrawal of the troops from the border, and his admonition to Hope to avoid the appearance of seeking armed confrontation all seem to have had an effect. As far as he can tell from a distance, calm has settled over the area.

Rolland reports to Secretary for Native Affairs Brownlee that Hope committed "an error of judgment" in acquiescing to Moorosi's holding a pitso at the magistracy and thus giving that unruly chief an opportunity for a trial of strength and that he had "erred again" by summoning the police to the border, "a step which might have occasioned a general scare."

"As far as I can ascertain everything has quietened down," he adds, "but I think that it may be necessary that I should not delay much in going down and holding a kind of inquiry. I should be glad if you will instruct me as to whether you would approve of my doing so."

In sorting the letters that have accumulated on his desk, Rolland comes across one from Hope sent last week, while the concern about the pitso was at its height, requesting that he send additional police to Quthing. He had pushed it aside at the time and forgotten about it.

He sighs. Another letter. He has lost count of how many Hope has sent in the last week. This one, however, he identifies as another attempt by Hope to bolster the armed forces surrounding him; the stock theft story is simply an excuse to talk him into providing more policemen.

He decides to call Hope's bluff.

"You will be good enough to inform me from whom the stock is stolen and by whom it is supposed to be stolen, whether by persons in your district or by outsiders, and whether the stock is taken by the footpaths you mention out of your district or into it. On these and other points the information contained in your letter under reply is too insufficient for steps to be taken in the matter."

That, Rolland reasons, should dispense with that request.

King William's Town — Saturday, December 8, 1877

Aware that the return of the Gcaleka almost certainly means a resumption of the war, Governor-General Frere is re-reading an editorial in *The Guide*, a newspaper published in King William's Town, which was scathing in its criticism of Griffith.

"The enemy was simply allowed to escape from us," the writer contends. In the opinion of those who fought in the war, the white settlers, volunteers and burghers under Griffith's command had been brought within easy reach of the Gcaleka, but had been kept back from a direct attack, allowing the Gcaleka to run away and hide in the bushes along the Bashee River, the writer added.

"Either, the volunteer soldiers concluded, Colonel Griffith's hands were tied by senior officers or he was an ineffective commander."

The country does not relish operations to be carried out in any spirit of revenge, the writer continues, "but it certainly does require that steps should be taken to put down lawlessness and plunder within our borders and to secure a permanent peace beyond them." Achieving that "cannot be satisfied with any half measures."

Frere, concerned about the British revulsion at the "half-measures" already taken, is thankful that Griffith did not slaughter thousands more of the Gcaleka people. After all, Britain is his constituency, Carnarvon is his superior, under whom he is working, and Carnarvon is responsible to the British voters who would balk at any moves to slaughter the Gcaleka in a wanton display of cruelty.

Yet even the Cape Town newspapers, of whom Frere had thought better, have criticized Griffith for being, in effect, too humanitarian.

But now, Frere must turn his attention not only to the renewed fighting in Gcaleka territory, but also to the rising tensions in the colonial-run Ciskei between the Ngqika people under Sandile and the white settlers — a situation that threatens to turn into civil war.

Reports reach him daily of Ngqika preparing for hostilities. They are selling sheep and cattle at unusually low prices to buy blankets, tinder boxes and butcher's knives, all to equip them for a life in the bush. They are not driven to take these measures through hunger or scarcity, but because they are determined to fight, Frere is told.

Meanwhile, white traders worry that their stores will be looted and farmers fear their stock will be stolen.

Quthing — Monday, December 24, 1877

Two challenges face the Baphuthi people as the summer heat bears down on the mountainous territory. One concerns the conflict between their chief and the magistrate. The other is an increasingly worsening drought. The rains have been few and far between. Small and less hardy corn, sorghum and millet plants, planted just a few months ago, are withering under the relentless sun. The vegetables, too, are not as vigorous as they should be by this time of year. Unless plentiful rains fall soon, many plants will die. Meanwhile, the supplies from the last harvest, which were not as plentiful as in previous years, are dwindling. Many Baphuthi are supplementing their stored grain with roots and berries.

Livestock are still plentiful and the expansive grazing areas still include some areas of green grass. But the Baphuthi do not want to slaughter too many cattle to supplement their food supply. Cattle are their wealth and their sources of milk and future herds.

The situation is worsened by the arrival of those Baphuthi who have worked for years on the diamond fields in Kimberley. In returning to their families and friends, they place additional strain on the grain supplies.

Many blame Hope for the ailing crops. He has been ardent in attempting to challenge their king, collect hut tax and throw offenders in jail. But he has done little to help them with food. To many it appears — in spite of what he says — that

Hope is bent more on hurting than on helping them.

But they appreciate the help given by Thomas and other traders who have been assisting the Baphuthi by selling them grain from other parts of the country, even though their prices are high.

For their part, the Baphuthi Christians are waiting for the Ellenbergers to return. Fred Ellenberger is a wise man, a kind man and has done many things to help the Baphuthi people. Emma Ellenberger teaches them many things that help them. They believe things will improve when the Ellenbergers return.

They will gather tomorrow, Christmas Day, at the church built by Ellenberger to celebrate the birth of Jesus and to ask Him to help them, too.

Transkei — Tuesday, December 25, 1877

For some time, Sarhili, caught between the drive to retake his land and his fear of the colonial firepower, has asked to be given a temporary amnesty to discuss peace terms with Colonel Eustace, resident magistrate in the Gcaleka territory and effectively the colonial government's representative in the area. Today, after many messages sent back and forth on the conditions, the men arrive for the meeting. Both are unarmed and are alone except for an interpreter.

Eustace assures Sarhili that his life will be spared and he will be provided with land on which he can live if he surrenders. Sarhili responds that he wants to remain as the head of his people and live among them on their land. If this request is granted, he says, he will stop fighting.

"I desire peace," he says. "I am prepared to live under the government, but I also would like to live in my country and lead my people."

Eustace indicates that nothing but Sarhili's unconditional surrender would satisfy the government, who would dictate where Sarhili could live and would stipulate that he could no longer rule his people.

Such terms, Sarhili says, are unacceptable to him.

The talks fail. Sarhili goes back into hiding.

King William's Town — Wednesday, December 26, 1877

Rebuffed in his attempt at a settlement, and determined to obtain his country back, Sarhili has devised a way to boost his forces. He has formed an alliance with the Ngqika leader Sandile, who, encouraged by Sarhili's resistance, wants to regain control over land in the Ciskei that was taken away from him by the settlers many years ago.

The men have agreed that they can be more powerful as a combined force.

Two events today mark the start of the joint operations.

A force of Gcaleka, returning from their hiding places within their territory and from across the Bashee River, attack a Frontier Armed and Mounted Police patrol led by Griffith through territory he had thought was still deserted.

Griffith orders his men into a defensive position and they beat back the Gcaleka, but not before some of Griffith's men are killed and several wounded.

The message is not lost on Griffith, who sends a messenger to King William's Town requesting more troops. Unless the area is continuously patrolled, he says, the Gcaleka territory will be repopulated and the clearing of the territory in recent months will be rendered ineffective.

For his part, Ngqika leader Sandile marks the start of the joint operation by cutting off communications between King William's Town and the Transkei. He seizes and burns the Draaibosch Hotel on the main road between them.

The renewed fighting and reports of the joint operation have put many white settlers in a state of panic. As exaggerated accounts tell of stock losses and the prospect of a combined attack against them spreads, they hold public meetings to protest the lack of government action. They form vigilante committees as the frontier towns prepare to defend themselves.

At a large meeting at a town known as Kei Road, farmers threaten to take the law into their own hands and shoot every black man that ventures on their land.

Hundreds of men are streaming into the Eastern Cape from Cape Town responding to calls for reinforcements.

The growing turmoil leads Frere to urge the Cape colonial government to set up a permanent force to protect the frontier districts.

Maseru — Monday December 31, 1877

Rolland is reflecting on the events of 1877 as he prepares to write his annual report for the Minister of Native Affairs in Cape Town. As he reads through the reports from the six magistrates in Basutoland, he concludes that progress has been made during the year.

The main event he decides, was the transfer of Griffith from the post he filled so long and ably. Rolland ponders why the move upset the Basotho people so much. He concludes the reason is that the Basotho people are accustomed to personal rather than amorphous government rule. They look to a chief, and Griffith was their respected white chief alongside their Basotho chief, Letsie.

The Basotho never have identified with a political system, a set of laws or a dogma, he reasons. They have identified themselves with a person who embodies those elements: the king, or paramount chief, and the sub-chiefs who lead them. A chief would not be expected to establish new laws, or introduce a new system. He would be expected to act in terms of the unchanging mores and customs that have existed for generations.

So it was that when the British and later the Cape Colony began to implement their governmental system the Basotho people put their trust in the man introducing it. Here was a new chief, whom they expected to work alongside their old chiefs, to respect them and their traditions, to help them and protect them from their enemies.

Griffith excelled at that, Rolland believes. He understood the Basotho character, imposed justice impartially and handled emergencies with tact. He displayed a kind disposition toward the people. He succeeded in never setting himself up as an opponent of the Basotho chiefs, rather working alongside them. In doing so, he won the hearts and the confidence of the Basotho chiefs and people alike.

When he went to fight against the Xhosa-speaking Gcaleka, the Basotho did not identify with the people he was fighting against. They believed they were superior to the Xhosa and that Griffith recognized this. Griffith was their father, not the father of the Gcaleka.

Rolland suspects that such feelings are not shared by Moorosi and the Baphuthi. Not only have they had fewer direct dealings with Griffith, but they see Griffith's representative, Hope, as an enemy of their chief, a man setting out to impose his traditions and customs on them rather than working with them.

The Baphuthi are more likely to identify with the Gcaleka and the Ngqika. Their ties of history and geography with the Xhosa-speaking people are stronger and they see Griffith's attack on the people to the south as something that could well be directed at them.

Rolland accepts that he has been an inadequate replacement for Griffith. He has tried, but failed to win the people's confidence in the way Griffith did. He can sense this lack every time they ask him when Griffith will return. He hopes Bowker will be a good replacement as, by all accounts, he, too, won the hearts and minds of the Basotho when he first served in the post.

This "paternal" attribute seems to run counter to Frere's belief that it is possible to turn the attention of the Basotho away from "men" to "measures," Rolland reasons. The very being of the Basotho is to react to men, not measures. To the Basotho, measures are attributes of specific men, they cannot be separated.

In Quthing Hope has tried to corral Moorosi, a task that Austen, the magistrate at Kornet Spruit, had found impractical. Here, too, Rolland muses, the people have looked to the man more than the measures. Even though the laws and system of administration are the same, Hope has not been a Griffith-like person to the Baphuthi.

Same measures, different man.

Rolland is grateful that Quthing is quiet for now. He hopes Moorosi has accepted Hope, and that Hope has found his feet. But he fears that the man — not necessarily the measures — has been found wanting and that will continue to be a source of friction.

Cape Town — The same day

The proclamation, issued on the last day of the year, is titled "Spread of rebellion to Ngqika." It is published in an extraordinary edition of the Government Gazette in the name of "His Excellency the Right Honorable Sir HENRY BARTLE EDWARD FRERE, Baronet, Member of Her Majesty's Most Honorable Privy

Council, Knight Grand Cross of the Most Honorable Order of the Bath, Knight Grand Commander of the Most Exalted Order of the Star of India, Governor and Commander-in-Chief of Her Majesty's Colony of the Cape of Good Hope in South Africa, and of the Territories and Dependencies thereof, and Her Majesty's High Commissioner, &c., &c., &c."

It reads:

"Whereas certain Ngqikas and other evil-disposed persons, who have recently been engaged in armed rebellion and acts of aggression against Her Majesty the Queen and her liege subjects within the Colony and the Dependencies thereof, have entered the districts of Stutterheim and Komgha within this Colony, with arms in their hands, and have incited other evil-disposed persons there being to acts of aggression and outrage against the peace and safety of this Colony:

And whereas certain persons residing and being within the said districts of Stutterheim and Komgha have given and are giving refuge and succor, countenance and support to the said Ngqikas and other evil-disposed persons:

And whereas it is expedient the measures should be taken for the most speedy repression of the said outrages, and punishment of the aggressor before mentioned, and those who have rendered them refuge, succor, countenance and support as aforesaid:

"Now, therefore, I hereby proclaim and direct that, after the promulgation of these presents, martial law shall be enforced throughout the said districts of Stutterheim and Komgha and I, moreover, direct that all persons, other than those in the military, naval, police, burgher, militia, volunteers, or other armed forces of Her Majesty the Queen, or Her Colonial Government, who shall be found within the said district with arms in their hands, and all those who shall give succor, refuge, countenance, or support to such persons, shall be treated as rebels and summarily punished as such.

"GOD SAVE THE QUEEN"

That, reasons Frere, should provide them with sufficient power to disarm the Ngqika, dissuade them from joining the Gcaleka in a joint attack, and thwart their uprising.

Quthing — Friday, January 18, 1878

In checking out his 1877 tax receipts and the recent preliminary census, Hope has noticed that five widows in Lehana's district did not pay their hut taxes.

He discusses the situation with Maitin, back from his week's leave of absence. The government needs to gather taxes from everyone, he says. The money is used to run the administration in Basutoland and taxes cannot be allowed to go unpaid. It is the law and it must be obeyed.

"In Baphuthi custom, when a widow is beyond child-bearing age and has not remarried her son is responsible for seeing to her welfare," Maitin explains. "Therefore, I would assume that the widows' sons would be seen as being responsible for paying the taxes."

"Very well," Hope responds, "let us tell them that the widows' sons should pay the taxes."

He dispatches his senior police officer, Sighata, to tell the men that if they do not pay the taxes for their mothers, they will be summonsed and face punishment.

King William's Town — Saturday, January 19, 1878

The event being held in the Town Hall in King William's Town is as elaborate as such events get in this little piece of Victorian England. Attendees are dressed in their finest clothes. Military leaders are decked out in their full gear. Indeed, anyone who is anybody in "King" is here.

The occasion is the investiture of Charles Duncan Griffith with the insignia as a Companion of the Order of St. Michael and St. George. The presentation, arranged before the recent flare-up in the war, is to recognize Griffith for his meritorious services in driving the Gcaleka out of their country, destroying their huts and fields, and forcing their leader Sarhili into hiding somewhere along the Bashee River and thereby rendering Gcaleka land available for annexation and occupation by white farmers.

Performing the ceremony is the governor, Sir Bartle Frere, who tells Griffith: "Her Majesty has been graciously pleased to confer this insignia on you.

"The insignia are the badges of fraternity with men who in every continent and climate have done good service to the Empire beyond the narrow seas which encircle the British Isles. The brotherhood to which you now belong has its members wherever the flag of the British Empire is flying. Amidst the snows of Canada, the palm groves of the Western Indies, of Equatorial America and Africa, through the vast continent of Australia and New Zealand, on every coast of the Indian and Pacific Oceans, on the shores of China and Japan, and in many a classic Isle and promontory of the Mediterranean, you will meet companions — men who, like yourself, have served their country as brave and faithful citizens, who have spent their lives in fighting the battle of civilization, of light and progress, against every form of danger and difficulty."

Frere says the award not only recognizes Griffith, but those who served with him and "hurled back the hosts of warriors."

He concludes: "The good service of that day has been so promptly acknowledged by Her Majesty's Government that the battle clouds are hardly yet rolled away. Let us hope for better days, when you and the good men who work with you shall have restored peace to this land."

Quthing — Tuesday, January 29, 1878

The five men stand silently in Hope's courtroom, listening to the charges against them. All the accused men — Maikela, who is a headman, and four other

Baphuthi — fall under the jurisdiction of Moorosi's son Lehana.

Through a translator, Hope tells them their widowed mothers have failed to pay their hut tax. "You are responsible for collecting or paying the tax," he says, "and so I am charging you with failure to do so."

The men show no outward reaction.

"Do you admit that your mothers are quite active and have gardens that they cultivate?"

"Yes," the men say.

"They have separate fields, which they are well able to attend to?"

"Yes."

"Good. When I find a woman is really too old or infirm to support herself, I give her a certificate of exemption. But in this case, these women have their own separate gardens, which they are able to cultivate. Is that not so?"

"Yes."

"They then have no excuse for not paying the hut tax. Why then have you not gathered the hut tax from them or paid the tax for them?"

As the headman, Maikela answers on their behalf.

"These taxes are a burden on us. The widows must not pay the taxes. We are responsible for them. But we do not have the money to pay their taxes and also our own taxes.

"Mr. Austen, the magistrate in Mohale's Hoek, when he sent his men to collect the hut tax from this area, he said these widows do not have to pay the tax."

"Mr. Austen exempted them?"

The men agree.

Hope is taken aback. They are unlikely to have made up such an explanation. For a brief moment, he considers telling them if that is the case then they are free to go. But he cannot back down now. And who is to say Austen is right? Although he has more experience, Austen does not have the education that he does. And the law is clear. Everyone who is capable of working in their fields must pay hut tax, even if someone pays it on their behalf.

Hope quickly recovers. He cannot back down. He must keep to his original decision.

"So what you are saying is that because Mr. Austen exempted you, I must exempt you too?"

"Yes."

"Do I look like Mr. Austen?" he asks the men.

"No, you do not look the same," Maikela says. "But you and the other magistrates all live in the same kind of village. Two horses do not look alike, but they eat the same grass in the same village and they carry the same people on their backs."

Hope accepts that Maikela's contention, couched in the symbolism favored by the Baphuthi, is reasonable. In their eyes, Austen is equal to Hope. But Hope is unwilling to concede the point completely. He would show himself as weak and lacking in judgment should he suddenly change his mind and throw out the case.

Instead, he will toss the issue back at the accused men.

"Very well," he says. "I will need proof that you are not lying to me. I will give you 14 days to go to Mr. Austen and get from him a certificate of exemption."

The men, after listening to the translation, ask what a "certificate of exemption" is. After an explanation from Maitin, they say that they understand.

"If I receive no proof of exemption, you will need to pay me a total of five pounds for the widows' hut taxes."

Hope declares the hearing over.

The men leave the courtroom and gather outside.

"I do not understand why Hope says we must show him we are not lying," Maikela tells the others. "We are telling the truth, why does he not believe us? He says we must go to Mohale's Hoek. But the river is full and difficult to cross. Why does this magistrate not know what the other magistrate did?"

"Why cannot he ask the Mohale's Hoek magistrate what he did?" asks one of the men. "He wants us to talk to that man, Austen. Why must we do it? Why does he not do it?"

Their opposition to Hope's ruling goes further. Their mothers are part of their family. They, as sons, are responsible for their mothers, who were already old when their fathers died. The gardens that their mothers cultivate are the family fields, granted by Lehana. The family already is paying hut tax, so why should their mothers pay it again?

Hope, they argue, is trying to assign to their mothers responsibilities that they do not have. Their widowed mothers occupy the same position as children in Baphuthi custom — and just as their children do not pay hut tax, so, too, must their widowed mothers not pay it. To say that they owe the hut tax in their own right is implying that their sons have not looked after them. It is an insult and demeaning to them, their sons.

Hope also says that they must take the hut tax from their mothers to pay it to him. How can they do that to their mothers, who depend on them in their old age? Taking from their mothers would be wrong and would show them to be unworthy sons.

"In the same way that Hope punished Raisa for doing the right thing, so now Hope is punishing us for doing what is right," Maikela says. "Raisa upheld his family responsibility; we, too, want to uphold our family responsibility. Yet the magistrate wants us to abandon our obligations as sons and become irresponsible like the white people. I found when I worked in Kimberley that many of the white people do not take care of their families. He wants us to act like we are not really men. He wants us to act like the white men. Hah!" He shakes his head in disgust.

The men know what will happen if they fail to obey Hope's instruction. He will act as he has in the past, sending a policeman with a summons. If they resist, the policeman will arrest them and Hope will punish them.

But Hope is not their chief. He does not understand them and shows no concerns for their way of life. Lehana is their headman. Moorosi is their king. They know, as all Baphuthi do, what is right and what is wrong and they keep to those ways. Hope wants to impose false laws on them, laws that want to take away the love and support they have for their mothers.

Moorosi understands. Lehana understands. Even Austen understands. But Hope does not want to understand and is always looking for ways to punish them.

They climb on their horses, return to their village and report back to Lehana, a son of Moorosi and their headman, to seek his counsel on what they should do.

Quthing — Friday, February 1, 1878

Lehana has traveled two days to ask Hope to explain the hut-tax charges.

Hope sighs, muttering to himself about the inability of these people to understand anything.

He goes over the case, explaining that the widowed mothers must pay the hut tax and, if Austen has given exemption, the men must show him proof of such exemption.

Lehana listens intently.

"What if the men do not agree that their widowed mothers have to pay the hut tax?" he asks. "The mothers are members of their family. They are not separate families. The mothers do not have rights of their own. Their rights are the rights of their sons.

"And the sons do not have the money to pay the hut tax for themselves as well as for their widowed mothers."

Hope, feeling under pressure, but determined to stand by his decision, replies that his ruling was that they do need to pay the tax.

"I do not care whether you agree or disagree with my decision," he tells Lehana. "That is irrelevant. The law is clear, even if it makes the sons feel bad and regardless of whether they have the money. If the mothers cannot pay it and the sons do not have it, they will have to find it."

When Lehana remonstrates further, Hope holds up his hand, indicating he should stop. "I cannot argue with you any further, Lehana. If they do not bring proof of exemption from Mr. Austen, I will fine them. But if they still disagree with my verdict, they are free to appeal my ruling."

"To whom do they appeal?" Lehana asks.

"They can appeal to the resident magistrate in Maseru."

Lehana shakes his head and looks down. The men cannot cross the river to get to Austen in Mohale's Hoek right now, let alone Maseru.

It is apparent Hope does not understand and does not want to understand.

Concluding that further discussion is futile, Lehana leaves for his village.

As Hope sits alone in his office, feelings of frustration well up within him. He might have erred on the hut-tax issue, but he cannot reverse his decision; that would not only embarrass him in front of the Baphuthi people, but also lessen his effectiveness as an administrator and judge. But at the same time he fears he will be condemned for his action. Already, he can see the letters from Rolland telling him he is wrong. In diplomatic language, of course. He will be blamed for disagreeing with Austen — of all people. It will be another black mark against him.

It feels to Hope as though he is being thwarted in everything he does. He should not be so "high-handed." He should not have arranged a pitso with Moorosi. He should not have called on Fynn to move his men to the border. He should not ask for more armed policemen. And now he is sure he will be told he should not have charged the men.

What does the government want from him? Do they want him to control Moorosi, or do they want him simply to cooperate with the Baphuthi leader and allow him to take control?

"How can I complete the task that they have assigned me if I am criticized for every move I make? How can I serve my country when they stand in my way?"

Perhaps, he reasons, he can get rid of his frustration by working for a different authority. He writes to Rolland, placing himself at the disposal of the government for military service. At least there his services will be appreciated.

King William's Town — Wednesday, February 6, 1878

Over the past three weeks, as tensions on the border of the Eastern Cape rise, the Prime Minister of the Cape Colony, John Molteno, has met 10 times with Frere since arriving here a week ago to investigate the situation for himself. Some meetings have lasted as long as four hours and they have become increasingly bitter and contentious.

Molteno insists his colonial militia be independent of the governor. The militia, composed of burghers, stationed in the local towns, and volunteers from the surrounding farms believe in the complete subjection of the native people to the white government. Frere has maintained, however, that the colonial forces are unruly and unnecessarily cruel. Their vendetta against the native people has become one of hatred, whereas British rules of engagement call for fairer treatment for the native people who must be persuaded to become loyal subjects of the Empire.

Frere is determined that his approach be implemented. As governor and head of the native reserves, he insists he is commander of the combined forces and is prepared to wield that power. Molteno disagrees; Frere is only the governor-general and is an adviser to the government, not an administrator.

The men are at loggerheads and their disagreement has turned into a personal vendetta.

Today Molteno tells Frere that only one solution seems possible — his resignation. He is convinced that Frere will not take him up on it. After all, he has been elected by the people and enjoys a substantial majority support in the colonial legislative assembly.

But, to his surprise, Frere replies that the resignations of Molteno and Merriman and any other cabinet ministers who support them will be accepted.

Molteno, having had his bluff called, withdraws his resignation.

"I am left in that case with no alternative," Frere responds, "but to dismiss you."

Frere's act is unprecedented in the history of British constitutional government. The governor knows he will face criticism, but the alternative, in his view, is tacit agreement with gross acts of injustice that can lead only to a conflagration that will burn with it any plans for South African confederation.

Frere needs to look beyond the cabinet and the majority party to find a new prime minister. So Frere will turn to the local farmer who impressed him when he talked with him after he delivered his speech a few months ago in the Town Hall. He will ask Gordon Sprigg, member of parliament for East London and a leading member of the opposition group in the legislative body, to become prime minister.

As soon as word of Molteno's dismissal reaches him, Brownlee tenders his resignation as secretary for native affairs.

The government of the Cape Colony has been forced to take a radical turn at a time when an epidemic of rebellion against its rule is sweeping through the Xhosa people, leading, it is now clear, to a joint uprising between Gcaleka and Ngqika against the white settlers.

Transkei — Thursday February 7, 1878

As daylight tries to break through a heavy cover of dark clouds moving in from the west, Alexander Granville stands among the pitched tents that surround the colonial troops' piled-up stores and ammunition.

He senses that Round Two in the Ninth Frontier War is about to begin. Round One marked the clearing of the Gcaleka from their ancestral land. Round Two will consist of thwarting their attempt to return. This camp at Kentani, occupied by 415 colonial troops and 200 pro-government Mfengu, is in the heart of what was once the land of the Gcaleka people. So when they return this is where they will come to evict the new occupiers of their land.

Granville stands on the crown of a low hill, three sides of which slope gently down to a stream below, in a position fortified by a deep semicircular 400-yard-long trench in the form of a square with a gun at each corner. Nearby is a square laager of wagons. His eyes look down the slope to level ground, interspersed with trees and shrubs, that extends about a mile before rising to another hill. He suspects that the bush will afford a modicum of cover for an attacking force, the members of which could avoid fire by running from one tree or shrub to the next.

As he watches, the cloud cover drifts closer and descends lower until the entire area around the camp is darkened. The clouds reduce the temperature, but it remains warm. Granville has been here long enough to know the weather is not atypical; it is the heart of summer and the rainy season.

Granville, along with the other fighting men, is oblivious to the dramatic change in the government yesterday. The news from King William's Town will reach the camp at the earliest only later today. In any event, the men have more pressing matters on their minds. They have been warned that thousands of Gcaleka, determined to reclaim their land, are massed over the horizon where the Ngqika have joined them in their thousands in a planned joint uprising against colonial rule. In response, the colonial soldiers have deepened the trench.

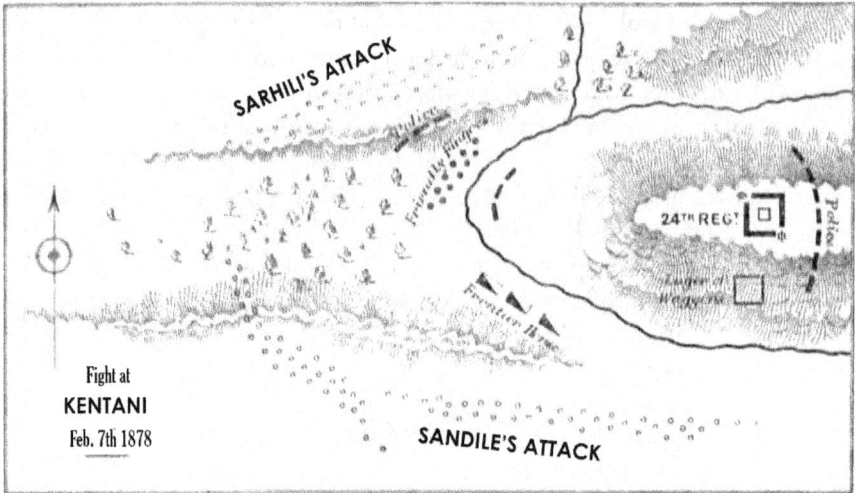

Adapted from a map in "My Command in South Africa" by General Sir Arthur Thurlow Cunynghame

The Gcaleka king, Sarhili, has gathered his best fighting men in the bush at Tala, about a mile from the colonial camp at Kentani. With him is Sigcawu, the man they call "spider," who told his father when the war began almost four months ago to flee with his people and to wait across the Bashee River until the colonial soldiers left.

Now here they are again, ready to drive off the invaders and reclaim their land.

Also advising Sarhili is Xito, a tribal priest whose duties are to perform sacrifices, to sniff out those who seek to inflict injury on those who would use witchcraft on the chief and his house, and to prepare warriors for battle.

"We will attack this morning," Sarhili tells his people. "The weather is good for an attack. It will hide us as we approach them. We will attack the camp and take the white soldiers and their Mfengu supporters by surprise. Our scouts tell us that we outnumber them by many, many people."

Sarhili outlines his plan to the Ngqika leader, Sandile, who also has gathered his warriors. "Now is the time for you to join us," Sarhili says. "As we attack the invaders and drive them away, we will seize their ammunition and their food, which will support us if we need to make further attacks to take back our land."

But Sandile is hesitant. His advisers think attacking the camp is a bad idea. It is taking on too much too soon, they say. Better to build up their forces first.

"I think we should first make a raid on the Mfengu," he replies. "We will weaken the Mfengu and lessen their ability to fight with the whites against us. We also will obtain much spoil to add to our strength when the whites attack us."

"I do not support that idea," Sarhili responds. "We must not wait for the whites to attack us, which they will do if we attack the Mfengu. We must attack them first." He is adamant that the time is now.

He turns and asks his men, "Are you ready to fight?"

The men shout their support for Sarhili in unison. Hung around their necks are charms from Xito to protect them in battle. On the forehead of each man is a black spot, the mark of war. They are ready to do battle — for their chief, to take back their land, and to preserve their way of life.

"The spirits of our mighty ancestors are watching," says Xito. "They are telling us we will win."

"*Amandla,*" the Gcaleka shout as they raise their spears and dance in a semicircle. "*Amandla.* We have the power. We have the strength to do this."

The Ngqika leader, Sandile, remains skeptical.

"We will let you take the lead," he says. "We will follow you at a distance and watch what happens."

Sarhili, convinced his men can achieve victory without the Ngqika, agrees. "So be it," he says. "We will be there first to gather the spoils." He divides his men into three columns of about a thousand each, with Sigcawu, Xito and a sub-chief named Kiva leading the columns.

"Let's go," he shouts.

Granville peers through the low clouds to the hills opposite them. Perched on them are enemy scouts, whom Granville points out to his colleagues Robert Scott and Peter Brown as they emerge from behind the tents and stand alongside him.

"Looks as though they are up to something," he says.

"They are," Scott responds. "Our Mfengu scouts have reported that the enemy intends to attack us today. They came here breathless at 4:30 this morning and told us that the forces poised to attack us are beyond number."

"I hope there are not *that* many," Granville responds.

"I do not care how many there are," says Brown. "Once they get into range of our guns, they won't know what has hit them, just as happened before."

The discussion is interrupted by the camp commander, Captain Russell Upcher, appointed to the post by Griffith, who remains in King Williams Town. "There is no time to waste," he shouts. "Strike the tents and when you are done enter the trenches so you cannot be seen."

Upcher orders the men to place the 9-pounder cannon at the southwestern side of the hill and the 24-pounder rocket tube in the middle, facing the route most likely to be taken by the attackers.

Granville and Scott join the others in the trench.

Suddenly, a heavy downpour drenches the men. They stay at their posts, enduring the rain as best they can. Pools of mud gather at the base of the trenches and their boots become soggy.

At 6 o'clock, the rain eases, leaving behind large pockets of mist on the ground ahead. Upcher decides not to wait for the enemy, but to attempt to draw them out. He orders 10 policemen and 100 soldiers on horseback into the field to serve as a scouting party and to entice the Ngqika and Gcaleka from their hiding places.

As the men on horseback advance to the level ground, the mist clears enough for them to see a wide mass of Gcaleka less than 1,800 yards away. The number shocks Upcher. He sends an urgent message to Captain Robinson who is camped with another force not far away, asking for support.

"I see them," shouts Sigcawu as the colonial riders appear through the mist below the Kentani hill. "They are coming to find us. Let us attack them first."

Yelling and holding up their spears, the men charge from the north, toward the Kentani camp. Soon the ground is covered with a mass of Gcaleka warriors, hurtling forward. On the southern side of the hill, at a respectable distance, are the Ngqika, numbering two or three thousand, moving cautiously ahead.

"They think the men on horseback are our entire force," Scott comments as the men, hidden in the trench and unable to look out, hear the sound of the approaching warriors. "They are in for a surprise."

When the Gcaleka, advancing from the northwest, reach 500 yards from the camp, the colonial horseback riders turn and ride back up the hill.

"They are afraid and they are running away," shouts Sigcawu. "Get them."

The Gcaleka, yelling even louder, start to hurl their spears and discharge their guns at the retreating men, but the mist and the fast pace of the men on horseback prevent them from reaching their targets.

"After them!" Sigcawu says. "We have them on the run. Take the camp and gather the spoils!"

The Ngqika, massed to the south, believe the colonial troops are all but beaten. They run to join the Gcaleka. Now 5,000 warriors are advancing on Kentani.

The 300 men in the trenches stand up and fire.

The Gcaleka suddenly realize that the defenders at Kentani have many more men than the hundred who had confronted them. Fearful, they slow their pace. As they do, the mist thickens, reducing visibility to almost zero. The firing stops.

Moving slowly, and using the mist as a shelter, the Xhosa warriors creep forward. They cannot see the hill, but they know they are getting closer.

Thirty minutes pass. The white and Mfengu troops on the hill catch only glimpses of their enemy below through gaps in the mist. The Gcaleka warriors occasionally can see their enemy above them, but not clearly enough to attack. They edge steadily forward.

Gradually, the fog starts to dissipate. Suddenly, as if someone had whipped a cloth off a table, the cover is gone and the scene on the level ground below the colonial camp is bathed in early morning light. It takes the colonial soldiers only a few seconds to see that the Gcaleka and Ngqika, now only about 150 yards away, have made good use of the fog.

"Look at that," says Scott. "There are thousands and thousands of them and they are right below us." Granville nods nervously, but says nothing.

Now that they can see the warriors approaching, the men on the hill open up with volley after volley from their Martini-Henrys. Others put the cannon and the rocket tube into action. The Mfengu, however, are armed only with muzzle loaders, which cause little damage.

Scores of Gcaleka and Ngqika fall as the large-caliber bullets tear into their ranks. Others hurl their spears toward the trenches, but the distance is too great for them to reach the target. Some try to shoot back.

Even as their men fall around them, the warriors advance on Kentani. Soon spears are starting to reach the soldiers in the trenches, who duck even as they fire on the approaching fighters.

For three hours, the battle rages on. At times, the Gcaleka and Ngqika fall back under the gunfire, but then their spears no longer can reach the trenches. After a while, the warriors brave the colonial fire and advance once more, only to fall back again under the relentless fire.

At 10:30 a.m. Robinson and the reinforcements arrive; they enter the trenches and start firing alongside their colonial colleagues.

The additional men and the accompanying firepower turn the tide. As hundreds of Ngqika and Gcaleka are killed, the others turn and run.

"Out of the trenches and after them," Upcher orders. "Charge!" Granville, Scott and Brown join the pursuit as the 9-pounder cannon fires into the fleeing men ahead of them.

The colonial fighters race over the bodies of fallen Ngqika and Gcaleka, shooting ahead of them as they run. Others charge on horseback, firing from their sides as they go.

Within minutes the battle is over. The Ngqika and Gcaleka have fled, leaving behind 400 dead.

The colonial soldiers return to the camp wearing the smiles of victory. They have lost only three Mfengu. Four Mfengu and one colonial policeman have been wounded. "It will be some time before they attempt that again," Brown says, smiling broadly. Scott and Granville nod vigorously.

Sixty-two-year-old Sarhili is a broken man. This battle was decisive. It was more intense than anything his people faced when they fled Griffith's advancing troops a few months ago. Today his men gave their all and failed. His chieftainship itself has been found wanting.

"We must return across the Bashee River into the land of the Bomvana," he tells his men. "It will be a long time before we are able to fight these colonists again. Their firepower is too strong. We must hide where they cannot find us."

Xito insists that they can return and fight. Their men are strong and brave. The "spider," Sigcawu, says he has more plans to achieve victory. "I will not become a dog of the white man," insists Keva. "I will never rest until I have driven them out of our land."

"All your tough talk is of no use," replies Sarhili. "I do not want more of my people to be killed for nothing. For now we will leave our land and, across the river among the Bomvana, who will shelter us and provide us with hiding places, we will discuss how we can return later to take it back."

Sandile — after reminding Sarhili that he did not believe the attack was wise in the first place — says his Ngqika people, too, will find refuge where the colonists will not find them.

"We will return to our territory across the Kei River," he says. "There we will hide in the rugged country along the lower river. There we will discuss how we can defeat the settlers. But, for now, we must accept that the future does not look good for us. These people who say they are superior to us have today shown us that, when it comes to the use of guns in war, perhaps they are."

News of the victory reaches Griffith at the military barracks in King William's Town. He has mixed feelings. As a commander of the joint forces, he takes pride in the accomplishment. But he is disappointed that the victory had to come at the cost of so many Gcaleka and Ngqika lives.

Nevertheless, he reasons, the lesson is that armies like the Gcaleka and Ngqika can be defeated by standing up to them with superior firepower and mowing them down. He sighs. If that is how it has to be, then so be it.

Quthing — Monday, February 11, 1878

When messengers from the south bring him news of the defeat of Sarhili and Sandile, Moorosi ponders its meaning.

He reaches several conclusions.

One is that any thought of ousting the white government from their territory by armed force should be set aside until they can buy more guns. Although the two Xhosa chiefs had thousands of people under their command, and they did have firearms, they were largely using spears to attack guns.

His second conclusion is that the colonial forces had an advantage by fighting from a hill, looking down on their attackers. Moorosi had found for himself in earlier battles that those on higher ground have an advantage. From now on, he will ensure he always defends himself from higher ground.

A third conclusion is that he must fight with his mind. A lion usually does not run straight at an antelope, warning it and giving it a chance to escape. The lion stalks his prey, slowly and carefully. He watches until the time to spring is right. Sarhili acted too soon, without thinking through his strategy. Moorosi, too, must be careful not to act too soon.

The messengers told Moorosi how, at Kentani, a small group of white police went out first and tricked Sarhili and Sandile into believing the white forces were small. They told him how Sarhili thought the government force was only about 100 strong which is why the Ngqika chief Sandile set aside his initial judgment that the attack would fail and ordered his men to join it. They told Moorosi, too, how the rest of the colonial soldiers, hidden on the hill, jumped up into sight when the forces commanded by Sarhili and Sandile came into range.

It was a clever trick. He vows to use such tricks. He must avoid confronting the government soldiers directly. He must have his warriors draw them into a trap, make the government people think his forces are small so that they will not summon big forces to attack them. Then the Baphuthi will come out from hiding and overpower them. The white government people will be frightened away and will be hesitant to attack the Baphuthi people again.

It will also help if the government thinks Moorosi is not involved and that only a small group of Baphuthi people oppose them.

He will do to the white authorities what the white authorities did to Sarhili and Sandile.

He calls Lehana to his mountain fortress to tell him what to do.

Quthing — Thursday, February 14, 1878

Sixteen days have passed since Hope instructed Maikela and the four other accused men to obtain proof from Austen of their hut-tax exemption. Hope has heard nothing. He told them to return in 14 days; he has given them two additional days. No one can accuse him of being unfair, of being "high-handed."

Clearly, the men are purposefully ignoring him. He is afraid, too, that Rolland will not back him up. He feels threatened on both sides.

Adding to Hope's frustrations is his receipt of a copy of a letter Rolland sent to the Secretary of Native Affairs in King William's Town. The letter is in response to Hope's request to be transferred to a military post.

"Although I do not doubt that Mr. Hope might do good service," the acting senior magistrate writes, "I cannot see my way clear to recommending his proposal unless the Government should see fit, in accepting it, to replace Mr. Hope at Quthing by some other officer experienced in the native service."

In other words: "No."

He has no choice but to pursue as best he can the issue about the men accused of not paying the hut tax for their widowed mothers.

Quthing — Saturday, February 16, 1878

Isaak Masin, the sergeant, knocks on the door of Hope's office.

"What is it?"

"I have something to report, Mr. Hope. For the past week Lehana has gathered all his men, armed with guns and spears. They are assembled in the mountains behind his village. They have orders that if you send your constables to arrest Lehana, Maikela or anyone else, they are to shoot the constables.

"I am told, too, that Lehana has told his father, Moorosi, about the situation."

"Very well. Thank you for informing me. You have done well."

The report has elevated the hut-tax dispute to a new level and makes Hope temporarily forget his frustration with Rolland. He will not allow these men to defy him. He will not tolerate their disobedience. He will show them he cannot be intimated by a display of force. This action is a challenge to him personally. Hope writes out a summons. He calls chief constable Abraham Sighata.

"I want you to go to Maikela and serve this writ on him," he says. "Take four men with you. There are four others who must be served the writ, so I am sending five of you, one of you for each of them. Tell them they must pay the hut taxes for their mothers, or face the consequences.

"You must all be unarmed. I am afraid that if you are armed, they will want to be armed, too, and I do not want Moorosi or any of his people to accuse me of breaking the rules that I set up for him. I demanded that he approach me unarmed and so when you approach his people you, also, must be unarmed."

He warns Sighata the men might resist, might be backed by an armed force and that Lehana is likely to help them. But should he encounter resistance, he should not create a disturbance. It is sufficient to serve the summons and return.

When Sighata and the four constables arrive on horseback at his village, Maikela is nowhere to be seen. But the rocky outcrop behind the village is lined with 70 to 80 men, all armed. The men see them arrive, but show no reaction.

"Let's go to Lehana's village," Sighata tells his constables. "I am sure we will find Maikela there."

They do.

"We have come from the magistrate to demand that you pay the five pounds you owe in hut tax for your mothers," Sighata tells Maikela.

"You must ask Lehana about that," Maikela replies. "He is my headman."

Lehana steps forward. "I will not allow them to pay the money," he says. "As their headman, I have decided that they do not need to pay the tax."

"If they think they don't have to pay, why have they not brought a paper from Mr. Austen to show they don't have to pay?" asks Sighata.

"Why should they go to another government person?" replies Lehana.

"I have not been sent here to argue with you," replies Sighata. "I am here to serve this summons on you and to obtain payment for the hut tax."

"I have already told you I will not allow them to pay the tax. We have no payment to give you," says Lehana.

Sighata turns to the constables accompanying him. "Let's go back to Maikela's village and see whether we can obtain the tax there," he says.

As they ride to Maikela's village, a group of men, all armed with spears, follows them, all also on horseback.

At Maikela's village, the government representatives see the armed men are still on the rocky outcrop. Sighata notes that the cattle are still in the kraal and have not been released to graze in the fields for the day.

"Come," he says to the men with him. "We will take two cows. That will take the place of the hut tax they owe."

To the men who followed them on horseback, the policemen's action is tantamount to theft. As Sighata and the assistant ready their ropes to seize the cows, they hear yelling from the mountainside above them. The armed men who were gathered behind the rocks above, run down the slope, waving their sticks and spears above their heads. "Stop," they shout. "Leave those cattle alone!"

King William's Town — The same day

The messenger brings Frere a telegram that sends shock waves through his body. Lord Carnarvon, the architect of the policy of confederation and the man who sent Frere to South Africa to carry it out, has resigned following a dispute with his cabinet colleagues over the sending of a British fleet to the Bosphorous.

For a while he feels lost and strangely alone.

But soon he realizes that the Conservative-led British Parliament had approved the confederation plans. It is almost certain, then, that Carnarvon's replacement as colonial secretary, Sir Michael Hicks-Beach, will continue the policy.

Frere, knowing Hicks-Beach, believes he is likely to take a hands-off approach. He will leave Frere with a free hand to solve the "native problem" in South Africa and pave the way for confederation. And that could enable Frere to achieve his goal more effectively than would have been possible under the supervision of Carnarvon. Carnarvon's departure might therefore not be as bad as he first feared.

Quthing — The same day

Sighata throws a noose over the cow's head and pulls it tight. He is determined not to be intimidated, believing that the men would not dare to attack him and his police cohorts. But, as the armed men running toward him show no signs of slowing down and continue to yell insults, Sighata has second thoughts.

He releases the cattle as the armed men reach the kraal. The men stop. Maikela tells them to lower their weapons, which they do. Sighata, imitating Hope, addresses Maikela and the men gathered around him.

"You have refused to pay the tax," he says. "Now you have refused to allow me to receive other payment representing the tax you owe. You are now liable not only to pay the hut tax, but also to be punished by the payment of a fine. You have brought no evidence that Mr. Austen exempted your mothers from the tax. So, even though you did not appear in court, Mr. Hope has imposed a five-shilling fine on each of you. That makes five pounds for the hut tax and an additional amount of two pounds and one shilling for the fine, making a total of seven pounds and one shilling that you each need to pay.

"You are making it bad for yourselves. If you had let me take the cattle, that would have been payment for the hut tax and the fine and the matter would be over. Now you are liable to be punished even more. I will report this to Mr. Hope."

The armed men watch quietly as Sighata and the four constables ride away.

On hearing of the events, Hope decides that Lehana must be included in the people charged over the hut-tax issue. He is convinced he is inciting Maikela and the others not to pay the taxes.

Hope is convinced, too, that Moorosi also is behind the stand-off on the issue. So he decides, too, to take the matter to Moorosi himself. He will play on Moorosi's desire to be involved in administering the territory.

"I have another duty for you," he tells Sighata. "I want you to go to Moorosi and tell him I need his help. Ask him to let me know where Lehana is so I can summons him and obtain the hut tax and the fines that these people owe."

As Sighata sets off, Hope writes to Rolland in Maseru. This time he wants to ensure his actions meet with Rolland's consent. After summarizing the events, he writes, "I think you will agree with me that I should summons Lehana on a charge of instigating the people in his ward to resist the authority of the magistrate. I do not, however, expect that Lehana will attend upon a summons of this kind; and I also doubt if Moorosi will be able, truthfully, to deny having advised Lehana to this course. I shall have a reply from Moorosi tomorrow, which I will send to you. Moorosi has been very quiet for some time, and I imagine this is merely a pretext to cause some excitement without which he apparently thinks he cannot exist."

Quthing — Monday, February 18, 1878

Sighata tells Hope that he has spoken with Moorosi, who denies all knowledge of Lehana's conduct, expresses his greatest regret for what happened and asks Hope to be merciful to his erring children.

The message sounds false to Hope. He is convinced Moorosi knew of the events surrounding the widow's hut tax. For him to deny all knowledge of it does not ring true. Hope perceives Moorosi is avoiding direct confrontation, leaving Lehana and Maikela to lead the defiance against him.

Hope's suspicions are confirmed when a policeman who lives in Lehana's village reports to him on a conversation he had with Molasso, a son of Moorosi's chief messenger, Mafetudi. "Molasso said he had been given a message by Moorosi to send to Lehana, saying Lehana had done right and should maintain his stand."

Another policeman, who lives in Lehana's ward, also has a report. "I am told that Maikela and the four other men tried twice to come here and pay you, but Lehana threatened to kill them if they did," the policeman says. "To make sure he does not pay the tax, Lehana has kept Maikela a prisoner in his hut. All the people from the surrounding villages have fled to the mountains with their cattle."

The hut-tax confrontation has developed from a small trial into a contest once again between Hope and Moorosi.

Hope issues a criminal summons against Lehana and Maikela, as well as the 30 who threatened Sighata and the constables to appear before him on Thursday.

When he reports the latest events to Rolland, Hope is sure that the acting chief magistrate will turn to Letsie for help to resolve the issue. But he is convinced, too, that Letsie and Moorosi are working together behind his, and Rolland's, back.

"I would respectfully suggest that an appeal to Letsie in this matter will most probably only result in another deputation being sent to Moorosi as in December last and end in a more cleverly planned scheme being hatched between those two chiefs to be developed upon in the next favorable opportunity."

Quthing — Wednesday, February 20, 1878

Hope's policemen have been able to round up 16 of the 30 Baphuthi who threatened Sighata and his constables. The accused men now stand before Hope in his courtroom, charged with interfering with the administration of justice.

The men plead guilty and Hope fines them two head of cattle each.

In some ways it is a hollow victory. Although the men surrendered when confronted, Hope is aware they did little more than follow Lehana's orders in threatening the policemen. His real quarrel is with Lehana who is continuing to subvert his authority. But his policemen report that Lehana and his cohorts have left their village and are in the mountains, presumably hiding in one of the many caves along the Qomoqomong or any of the other rivers in the area.

Sending his constables to try to track them down will be an exercise in frustration. How then to get Lehana?

The only way is through Moorosi, Hope concludes. The chief almost certainly knows where his son is and is probably spurring him on. He needs to bring Lehana to book to reassert his authority and get rid of this hut-tax issue. He sends word through his policemen that he would like to see Moorosi's messenger, Mafetudi, in his office.

"Tell your chief that he has often said that he is anxious to show his loyalty to the government," Hope tells Mafetudi, who arrives in the late afternoon. "I am now offering him an opportunity to prove his loyalty and also a way to remove any suspicion that he is involved in the matter concerning the payment of hut tax for the five women. He can do so by seeing that his son Lehana appears before me in my court."

He adds a sweetener: "Tell the chief I send him my best wishes and my hope that all these affairs will end quietly and quickly and all will be peace again."

Mafetudi sets off to take the message to Moorosi at his mountain stronghold.

Quthing — Thursday, February 21, 1878

Fred Ellenberger walks past the first house he built when he arrived at Masitise 11 years ago. It looks as good as when he built it.

He climbs the twisting stone stairs through the trees. As he reaches the top step, the cave house comes into sight. He sighs with relief and satisfaction when he sees it. It, too, is still there, just as he left it. The row of 60 aloes lining the open space in front of the house on the edge of the steep drop to the cattle enclosure below are still there. He is home. He has returned to work among the people he loves.

Satisfied after a brief walk-through that the house is in good order and the books and papers he left behind are all there, he walks back to the wagon in which he brought Emma, their family and belongings back to the mission station.

Soon the news gets around. The Ellenbergers have returned. People emerge, seemingly from nowhere, flocking around Fred and Emma.

They alternately laugh with joy, sing and try to tell the couple all that has happened since they left. They carry the missionaries' supplies up to the cave house. They reassure them the mission work was well conducted by local evangelists, but, they are quick to add, they are pleased to see their spiritual leaders back. And they try to tell them everything all at once.

The Ellenbergers listen patiently, tired after their journey over the rugged African roads, but anxious to hear the news.

Fred Ellenberger's senior pastors tell him of the new government presence that has moved into the area. The magisterial compound and police camp, his people tell him, lies a little more than two miles away where a magistrate named Hamilton Hope is imposing direct government rule on the Baphuthi people. They tell him, too, of the trouble that has arisen between Moorosi and the magistrate. The missionary listens intently. Normally, he is not involved in politics. But these events are affecting his people's lives. He cannot ignore them.

Before he moved to Masitise, Ellenberger occasionally took up causes on behalf of the Basotho people against the government, but mostly had agreed with the British laws — involving marriage, for example — that accorded with a Christian perspective. When he moved to Masitise, he found little reason to become involved in the government relations with the people as the colonial administration, still based in Mohale's Hoek, had little influence in the area beyond collecting hut tax. Austen did little to impose colonial law on the people directly.

Now a magistrate, police post, court and jail two miles away present a whole new dispensation. One of his most trusted evangelists, Philemon Seboka, tells him the tensions between Hope and Moorosi have become thwart with danger.

"At one stage, we thought there might be a violent conflict when King Moorosi and hundreds of armed men gathered at the magisterial compound," he tells Ellenberger. "We heard them singing war songs and we were afraid."

Tensions lessened a few months ago, but now are growing again, Seboka says. "This time the magistrate is angry because some of the widows are not paying their hut tax." He tells Ellenberger how the sons defended their mothers, Lehana defended the sons, and they are now hiding in caves. "The magistrate wants to find them and punish them, but he has been unable to do so."

Ellenberger, not one to waste time, decides he must do what he can to reduce tensions as soon as possible. He will visit Hope tomorrow.

Quthing — Friday, February 22, 1878

After spending the morning in further discussions with his Baphuthi staff, Ellenberger rides on horseback to Hope's offices. After the men swap stories of their backgrounds and the reasons they are there, Ellenberger gets to the point. Though French is his primary language, he speaks in English. "I have heard of disputes between you and Moorosi, whom I know quite well, and I wondered whether I could help perhaps to reconcile some differences that you and he might have," Ellenberger says. "In the past, he visited me from time to time and kept me in touch with what was going on. I have not yet been to see him as I arrived only yesterday morning. I thought I would speak with you first."

Hope senses another threat. He has had enough criticism from Griffith and Rolland for his actions. Now this man comes here to tell him what to do. What does a holier-than-thou missionary know about government? He jumps to the conclusion that because Ellenberger is friendly with Moorosi he will take Moorosi's side against him. After all, the missionaries are known for siding with the native people against the government.

"Will you be instigating the chief to challenge my authority?"

Ellenberger is taken aback.

"Not at all," he says, trying to remain calm. "Sometimes confrontations come from misunderstanding. Because I think I understand Moorosi and his people, their traditions and their beliefs, I might be able to help you to understand him better and work with him more effectively."

"I understand him perfectly well," Hope responds. "He is cunning, crafty and rebellious. Now he has turned to lying as well. He refuses to accept that I am in charge here now and he shows a reluctance to accord me the respect that I and my office deserve. The only way to deal with him is to show him in no uncertain terms where the authority lies around here.

"Reasoning does not work with these people. They do not understand what reasoning is. They respond only to power and, where necessary, the use of force to back that power. I am not afraid to confront him and to show him the error of his ways. No longer can he carry on as though he is the only authority around here. Nor do I accept his ridiculous assertion that I fall under him."

Ellenberger listens quietly, takes a deep breath, and responds.

"I believe it is important to understand that King Moorosi has ruled his people here for many decades," Ellenberger says. "He carries on a long line of rule that extends into history. Until you arrived here, he was, for all practical purposes, subject to no other authority except when it came to collecting hut taxes — and that itself was only a recent introduction. Now that you have arrived and are asserting your authority it will disturb him. He sees his power challenged and potentially usurped."

"I'm surprised at your attitude, reverend," Hope responds. "You are spreading Christianity among these people; we are bringing them a Christian government."

"True," Ellenberger responds. "We do preach Christianity. But we don't believe in forcing people to become Christians. We try to persuade them that their sins will be forgiven and they will live happier and more fulfilled lives if they are Christians."

Hope is quick to respond. "But these people practice polygamy, witchcraft and barbarism. We must impose the laws that enable them to live as Christian people and as civilized people. The British laws are Christian laws. The laws of these people are heathen laws."

"Their customs are not necessarily heathen," Ellenberger responds. "Some of their values are similar to ours and those of the Israelites.

"They might not all know of the ten commandments, but they respect and honor many of them.

"Of course, doing so does not make them Christians, but they are not wild savages either. These people are orderly and law-abiding within their code of conduct. I am sure you have found that crimes of violence are rare."

Hope is quiet. True, he has had to deal with few such offenses. But he is suspicious of the track that Ellenberger is following.

"A natural love of order and respect for authority are part of the Baphuthi character," Ellenberger continues. "That is why you probably have found they are reluctant to criticize you or to argue against you.

"It doesn't mean they agree with you. It is that they respect you and are being polite to you."

"I find little respect from Moorosi," Hope responds. "He argues with me continuously. He does not always say yes."

"I cannot speak for him and I am not here to defend him and all that he does," responds Ellenberger. "But he and the Baphuthi people accept that they need British protection from their enemies and so are willing to accept your presence here as a representative of the British."

"You are right," Hope says.

"Moorosi agreed to come under British protection when his district fell under the magistrate in Kornet Spruit. Indeed, he found it an admirable set-up. If Letsie attempted at any time to tyrannize him, he could appeal to the government. As long as he paid as much hut tax as he and his people could conveniently spare, he went on his way, deciding civil and criminal cases as he chose, always taking care that the fees of court amounted to a comfortable sum for himself.

"He referred a case to the magistrate at Kornet Spruit only when he found he could not extort money or cattle from the wrongdoers."

"That might be true," Ellenberger says. "I am not suggesting that Moorosi is without fault. But I would suspect that he and his people believe the Cape Colony's motive is to annex this territory so they can secure the bounty of this fertile land for the monetary benefit of the Cape Colony."

Hope rises from his chair and steps back, physically and symbolically distancing himself from Ellenberger.

"And that is what you are going to be telling them?

"That is the way in which you will incite them to action against us? That is the way in which you will make them restless?

"Whose side are you on?

"You, a Frenchman and a European, criticize the English people and you take the side of the black people against us."

Ellenberger remains calm, even as Maitin, roused by Hope's rising voice, emerges from the adjoining office.

"Please understand, Mr. Hope. I am telling you what these people believe, not what I tell them to believe.

"There is a difference.

"I have yet to speak to them to any extent about you and what you are doing here. I am suggesting how I believe they feel based on what I have learned about them since first moving here 11 years ago.

"We need to understand other people's points of view.

"But we need to go further.

"We need to understand why they hold that point of view. That is key."

Hope is defiant.

"I suggest you turn from supporting these people and their heathen beliefs and uncivilized way of life to helping to show them that they are wasting the government's time and resources by trying to rebel against our authority.

"We are here to stay. And we will impose civilized government on these savages whatever it takes to do so."

Maitin looks at Ellenberger and back at Hope.

His face carries a look of confusion. Why is Hope so angry? What did Ellenberger, who clearly is a quiet, moderate man, say to cause him to act this way?

Ellenberger, realizing it is of little value to continue, promises to return to talk again. He mounts his horse and rides home.

The missionary is deeply worried now. Hope's attitude is a strong contrast to that of Griffith and Rolland.

Ellenberger's next move will be to talk with Moorosi. He will inquire into the tax issue and see whether he can convince the men to meet somewhere in the middle. Although he fears that persuading Hope to take a less belligerent attitude will be a tough hill to climb, he will try nevertheless. He owes it to his people.

VII

Quthing — Saturday, February 23, 1878

This is Hope's first summer in Quthing and today, with the temperature climbing, he is finding that by mid-afternoon his small stone walled office has become a baking oven. His official English heavy clothing adds its own complement of heat, causing perspiration to run down his body. His face is red and his breathing labored.

Outside, the Baphuthi are sitting in the shade of the occasional trees, dressed in only the barest of clothes. For him to do the same would be to act like a savage. He is above them and must sit in his office, wear his official clothes and sweat. Only tomorrow, Sunday, might he be able to find some respite from the heat in his house, which, with its thicker walls, is a little cooler than this office.

The heat also affects his thinking. He feels anger boiling within him, ready to be taken out on the nearest victim. He is aware his temper is usually short and he does his best to control it. But today it has no length; it is poised to spring.

He has been thinking all day of ways to capture Lehana. He is angry at Lehana. He is angry at Moorosi for sheltering him. He is angry because he has been unable to control them, the reason he was sent here in the first place. He is angry because his supervisors are accusing him of failing. He is angry because he feels he is failing.

Looking back, perhaps he has failed. Moorosi intervened and finalized the Raisa case. Moorosi settled the issue of the stolen goats. Moorosi never gave him the gun that Lemena handed over. Austen's ruling on the widows' tax seemed more acceptable than his. The planned pitso with Moorosi was canceled. He had been ruled wrong to have called up the troops to the border.

He pours himself a glass of brandy and water, hoping it will provide a measure of relief. He has worked all day and, although it is only mid-afternoon, the time for his end-of-the-day drink is soon approaching; all he is doing is taking it a little earlier — and with a little less water.

Yesterday he had a lecture from the missionary, just returned from France with his other-worldly, anti-European attitude. Does Ellenberger really think these black savages have any decency in them? Any redeeming features at all? Even Ellenberger, as a minister of the Gospel, is against him, failing to realize the good work he is doing for Christianity.

As he takes a gulp of the brandy and water, Hope glances down at the recent correspondence from Rolland, neatly copied over into a one-and-a-half-inch lined book. He takes more gulps and tops up the glass with more brandy as he reads them through again. The letters remind him of how angry he felt when he received them.

The alcohol fuels his fury, driving him away from blaming himself to blaming others for all that has happened. Griffith, Rolland, Austen. They are all to blame.

He has not failed. They have failed him.

His brother-in-law never helps him, never praises him, only hinders him. How can he be expected to apply the law when Rolland tries to block his every move?

Look at these recent letters.

On December 7, in reply to his request for more policemen to combat stock theft: "You will therefore be good enough to inform me from whom the stock is stolen and by whom it is supposed to be stolen, whether by persons in your district or by outsiders."

Hope looks up at the stone wall opposite him and addresses it as an interested bystander. Supposed to be stolen. *Supposed* to be stolen. He is accusing me of lying."

He looks down at the letter again. "The information is too insufficient for steps to be taken in the matter."

Hope addresses the wall once more. "The stock *is* being stolen. I don't know who is stealing it. If I did know, I would apprehend them. I need policemen to find out these things. That's why I asked for them."

Hope flips over a couple of pages.

January 20: "With reference to your letter of the 29th ultimo requesting to be supplied with a pack saddle. I have the honor to inform you that officers traveling on duty are expected to make their own arrangements and are for this purpose allowed to charge for traveling expenses. I can therefore not recommend your application." Always no, no, no. If Austen had asked, he would have received a pack saddle. But not me. Austen is the perfect magistrate. He is always right; his requests are always honored. Nothing ever goes wrong in his district. Nobody rebels against *him*. He even knows how best to handle taxes on widows. But let him come here and see what he can achieve against this malicious Baphuthi king.

February 16: After he told Rolland of reports from a secret informant on the intention by Tjali, the chief who lives on land presided over by Moorosi, to support Moorosi against the government, Rolland shot back, "I think it extremely improbable that he should have disclosed an intention to rebel to a Mosotho, an alien, and to him a natural enemy. This part of your informant's letter should be received with extreme caution and investigated if possible and the man punished severely if it proves to be false." Rolland does not trust my informants. He trusts informants sent by Austen, but he wants me to punish my informant because he, the great and wonderfully wise Rolland, knows my informant is lying. He knows. He can see right into men's minds from a hundred miles away.

Hope recalls how his requests for more ammunition, for more policemen and for help from the Cape Colony were all turned down. When he went around Rolland and ordered back-up forces to be sent to Palmietfontein, he was countermanded. You need no help. Battle on your own. Fight Moorosi with one hand tied behind your back.

Rolland might be Mimmie's brother, but Hope has had enough of his superior attitude. He had hoped Rolland would be better than Griffith. And, for a while, he was. But he has now proven to be the same. And it does not stop with Griffith or

Rolland; his attitude has poisoned the higher ranks of government, too. Even the Secretary of Native Affairs had advised him not to be so "high-handed."

Do these people have any idea how wily this rebellious old chief is? Do they really think they would have handled him any better? But, then, he assumes the Native Affairs Secretary was influenced by the attitudes of Griffith, and now Rolland. "I see it in every letter. I am always wrong. They are always right.

"When does Rolland ever say, 'Thank you?' When does he ever say, 'Well done?' They say that to Austen all the time, but never to me. And he's a colored man!"

He gulps the rest of the brandy in the glass, takes up his quill, dips it in the ink and writes. He will tell Rolland exactly what he thinks of him and his government superiors.

When he has completed the letter, he places it for delivery by the next post.

As the afternoon drags on and his rage intensifies with the rising heat, Hope adds more brandy to his glass, drinks a mouthful, and picks up another piece of blank paper. The first letter was not forceful enough, hinting rather than telling. He will send another, stronger letter to Rolland.

Quthing — Monday, February 25, 1878

When he receives Hope's message relayed through Mafetudi, Moorosi is impressed because, by asking him to find Lehana, Hope is recognizing his authority. Hope is acknowledging that he is powerless in this case to act without him.

"Tell the magistrate that I thank him and praise him," he tells Mafetudi.

Moorosi has no intention of helping the magistrate to achieve his aim of finding his son Lehana and punishing him. Nevertheless, at this stage, he will give Hope the impression that he is helping him.

He will use his messenger, Mafetudi, as an unwitting part of the plot to deceive Hope.

"You are to go to the village and tell Lehana that I want him to accompany me to the magistrate's office," he tells Mafetudi. "After you give the message to Lehana, take my message of thanks to Hope. I am flattered that he is recognizing my authority and seeking my help."

The sun is setting as Mafetudi returns to Moorosi, saying he could not find Lehana in his village. He decided it best to return to Moorosi for further instructions before proceeding to Hope's office. Moorosi nods. That is as he expected. He knows Lehana has left his village and is hiding in a cave. But it will enable Mafetudi to tell the magistrate truthfully that Moorosi instructed him to find Lehana and he could not find him.

Now Moorosi will go further in meeting the magistrate's request for cooperation. He will do the same as he did with Raisa and MaLebenya, when the magistrate eventually conceded his right to judge the matter, and with the issue over the stolen goats, when Hope abandoned the matter after Moorosi acted on the case.

Moorosi turns and goes into his hut. After a short while he emerges with a rag, folded and tied at the corners, which he hands to Mafetudi.

"Give this to the magistrate. Tell him it is from Lehana and it is from me."

Quthing — Wednesday, February 27, 1878

Mafetudi arrives on horseback, conveys Moorosi's message of thanks to Hope and tells him that Moorosi had sent him to tell Lehana to accompany him to the magistrate.

"I am pleased to hear that the chief is ready to cooperate with me in imposing the law," replies Hope, who has recovered somewhat from his bout of weekend anger, although it remains simmering below the surface. "Did you do as he said? Did you give Lehana the message? When will Lehana and the chief be here?"

Mafetudi takes each question at a time.

"I arrived at Lehana's village yesterday, gathered the people together and asked them where Lehana was," Mafetudi reports. "I told them I had been sent by King Moorosi to take him to the magistrate. They all said they had no idea where he was."

As Mafetudi is speaking, Hope notices he is holding a piece of rag.

"What do you have there?"

"This is King Moorosi's appeal to you on behalf of Lehana," he says.

Hope opens the rag. It contains nine pounds and five shillings — two pounds more than the total owed him for payment of the hut tax and the fines.

He looks up at Mafetudi.

"What does this mean?" he asks.

"This is King Moorosi's offering to you," he says. "He has weighed up the situation and decided that Lehana should have collected hut taxes from the widows. The taxes have now been paid and, because you represent the government that imposes the taxes, the taxes must be paid to you.

"King Moorosi also has imposed a fine on Lehana. In a spirit of friendliness, he wants you to accept the fine as well as the taxes that should have been paid. Here they are."

"This is not the right way to do this," Hope tells Mafetudi. "Lehana must come here, he must stand in front of me, I must try him and he must admit his wrong. Lehana must pay the penalty himself. I cannot have Chief Moorosi deciding the issue and then paying the taxes and the fines. Also, I suspect Lehana never paid this money. The chief is paying the tax and the fine himself to shield Lehana and to prevent him from appearing in my court.

"He is playing with me."

He thrusts the rag back into Mafetudi's hands. "Take the money. Tell him that I do not want it. He has played with me long enough."

Mafetudi is taken aback. He holds out the rag and its contents once more toward Hope. "He wants you to have it," he tells him. "He wants to pay the penalty for Lehana and the five men."

Hope folds his arms so that Mafetudi cannot put the rag in his hands once more. "I have told you, Mafetudi, I will not accept it."

Hope's caustic tone causes Mafetudi to move backward. He does not want to anger the magistrate and be faced with charges of insubordination himself.

"Yes, magistrate," he says and walks out the door.

"I know what Moorosi is doing," Hope tells Maitin. "He is acting as the authority here. He is trying to defeat me. Again. He is trying to show me that he is able to collect the tax because the Baphuthi people look to him as their chief. He is saying they will obey him, but not me.

"If I accept this money I will, in effect, be telling Moorosi that he is in charge and that I should approach him when I want the law obeyed. You will recall that he first offered me 3 pounds and five shillings and I rejected that. Now, he comes and offers me more. He seems to think that if he offers me enough money the whole matter will go away and he will be victorious once more.

"But it is not about the money. I see this old man's game. He told Maikela and the others who were charged not to pay the tax because that would be acceding to my authority. Now he comes along and collects the tax and a fine. He even increases the fine. He is trying to prove that he is the authority that they obey, not me."

Hope's face reddens as his anger rises.

"No. No. No.

"I want to see Lehana punished and humiliated for inciting his followers to disobey me. I want to see him brought to trial. I want him to be responsible to me, not to his father. I want the people to see that I am the authority here, not Moorosi. And I will not impose only a fine on him. He would not suffer at all from such a punishment, particularly if his father is gathering contributions from people in the village to pay to him. No. I would rather throw him into jail for what he has done."

"But could you keep him here?" Maitin ventures. "In our small lock-up?"

"You are right, Mr. Maitin," Hope responds. "We would have to send him to work on the breakwater in Cape Town."

Hope knows the Baphuthi consider this punishment a fate worse than death. Most Baphuthi find it hard to survive for long away from their mountain homeland in a strange culture doing work unlike anything they have done before. That is why Hope regards being sent to Cape Town as an appropriate punishment for the worst offenders.

"I must take a hard line on this issue," Hope says. "These people must understand who is running affairs around here and what the implications are of disobeying me."

Hope calls Sighata.

"Go to Lehana's people," he tells him. "Tell them I will not receive their hut tax and their fines if they are paid through Moorosi. I want them to pay the fines and the taxes to me because I am the authority, not their chief Moorosi."

"And tell them I will refuse to grant them passes to leave this area until this matter is settled."

Maseru — Wednesday, February 27, 1878

The rancorous letters from Hope take Rolland by surprise. He understands Hope's frustrations. He knows the work is difficult. And he knows Hope can lose his temper.

But for Hope to take out his frustrations on him is unacceptable. He leaves the letters on his desk for several hours, returns to them and re-reads them. They are damning in their accusations of him and others in the government. They are acts of insubordination. Hope should lose his position for writing letters like these.

The Hamilton Hope he knows is an intense hard working, intelligent person, serious and determined. Clearly his emotions have blurred his senses, causing him to exaggerate perceived wrongs. Rolland is unsure why Hope wrote what he did and suspects that Hope was acting irrationally when he wrote the letters.

For the sake of his sister, he will give his brother-in-law another chance.

"I have the honor to acknowledge the receipt of two letters from you dated 23 instant," he writes.

"As I cannot but think that you will regret what you have probably unadvisedly written both with regard to direct expressions as well as to covert and implied sentiments, I shall defer any reply until you have had an opportunity of withdrawing or amending these letters."

He sets the offending letters aside, readying them to be discarded. Better that no one else ever sees them.

King William's Town — Monday, March 4, 1878

William Ayliff has been in his post as Native Affairs Secretary for only a few days, but is bringing himself up to speed on issues concerning the native affairs administration he now heads.

As he reads through the reports on the situation in Basutoland, the events in Quthing stand out.

To him it seems clear that Hope has created problems that might not have existed had he handled affairs better.

Why, he wonders, did Hope not believe the men who said that Austen had exempted their widowed mothers from paying hut tax? Would they have invented that story? Surely they would have assumed that Hope would check with Austen, which is what he should have done, but did not do?

And why did Hope not accept the payment made by Moorosi for the hut tax and the fine?

He shares his views with Rolland in a letter.

"Judging from the report of Mr. Hope, I infer that the whole affair originated in the fact of certain widows now being asked for hut tax who had been exempted by Mr. Austen," he says. "If such is the case, and Mr. Austen with his large experience in the management of the Basotho saw fit to do so, it is a subject of regret that Mr. Hope should not have followed out Mr. Austen's view, whatever his own may have been; and it seems from the tone of the report that Mr. Hope has allowed temper more than prudence to guide him in the matter.

"Mr. Hope's refusal to accept even a portion of the hut tax when tendered was perhaps not the wisest thing he could have done, the fact of any portion being tendered being an acknowledgment of liability for the whole, and might well have been taken as a part of the debt.

"It seems hardly fair to those of Lehana's people who have been willing and anxious to have the matter settled by offering to pay the debt with the fine, that receipts for hut tax or passes should be refused them.

"The government gladly accepts your idea that force may not be needed," Ayliff writes, concluding the letter to Rolland by saying that Hope should know that calling in troops "could only be resorted to as a resource when every other effort had failed."

Basutoland, — Tuesday, March 12, 1878

Heavy rains have swollen rivers and rendered the road across the mountains from Pietermaritzburg in Natal Colony harder to negotiate than usual. But James Bowker, 56, is finally on his way to his appointment as new resident magistrate at Maseru.

He realizes he should have been in his office in January, two-and-a-half months ago, or even earlier. But his rheumatism had played up again and he had waited for the severe summer rains to ease off. That strategy did not work out, however. The rains have come late this year, slowing his progress even further.

The driver assures Bowker that once they have crossed this river they will not have long to travel. Although the roads will be muddy, they should be in Maseru tomorrow.

As his cart and the wagon carrying his goods wait at a river crossing that is deeper than usual, Bowker talks with another traveler also waiting for the river to abate before crossing. Bowker is a big man. Taller than 6 feet and heavyset, he towers over many of his contemporaries, giving him an advantage in negotiations.

As the two men sit down and talk, Bowker tells his new-found fellow traveler that he will once again be the most senior colonial official in Basutoland, the position he occupied some years ago. "The move will be something of a homecoming for me," he says. "It is a switch of roles, too, as Griffith, who took over the post from me, has replaced me as commandant of the Frontier Armed and Mounted Police. Now I will take his position as governor's agent in Basutoland."

As the hours pass, Bowker tells the traveler his story. Unmarried, he is the youngest of 11 children born to Miles Bowker, a settler who arrived at Port Elizabeth in 1820, and his wife Ann. He was introduced to the reality of frontier violence at the age of 13 when skirmishes broke out with a neighboring group of black people. The Bowkers, who lived on an extensive farm at Tharfield, near the Eastern Cape coast, were warned to take refuge at a church in nearby Bathhurst. He and his brothers tied the family silver and other valuables in an old tablecloth and buried them on the farm.

The attacks were beaten off and attempts to set fire to the thatch on the church roof failed. "But, even though we returned to our farm and tried to find where we had buried the treasure, we never could do so," he says.

"It has never been found?"

"Never."

He again came up against the reality of frontier life when he was 24 and the family, who had moved to Thornkloof farm, near King William's Town, successfully defended themselves against an attack by 300 natives, Bowker continues. He later became active in military service, fighting in three wars on the eastern Cape frontier. An accomplished negotiator, he helped settle several boundary disputes.

"Pushing humility aside, I must tell you that I was once recognized for outstanding bravery," Bowker adds. "During a skirmish, I outstripped my men by several yards and fought off four natives in a hand-to-hand fight until my men came to my aid."

Bowker tempered physical adventure with a streak of compassion.

"I recall the time when I was serving in the Mounted Police during a skirmish with the Ngqika in 1864," he says. "A Basotho man, who had been living among the Ngqika, fired toward me, but missed me and killed my horse. As the Basotho man ran off, I fired at him, hitting him in the arm, and causing him to fall.

"As I approached him, the man cowered, expecting me to kill him. But I bound up his arm and let him go.

"Many years later when I was traveling in a wagon in Basutoland, buying cattle, I stopped at a kraal at sundown. The Basotho people crowded around me. One stared at me closely and then disappeared.

"Within an hour, the man was back, bringing a sheep, milk and vegetables and carrying a bundle of firewood on his head. 'I offer these gifts to the man who broke and mended my arm,' he told me."

It is a story that Bowker loves to tell. It and other incidents have endowed him with a reputation for combining his military prowess with humanity, which gives him the ability to broker disputes between antagonistic groups of farmers and natives.

"I suffer from rheumatism which means I often have to retire from my duties and rest," Bowker adds. "After a few months, however, I gain new energy and I am ready to spring into action once again. That is what has happened now. After ill health caused me to step down as head of the F.A.M. Police last year, I am now ready to take on my old post in Basutoland."

"When did you occupy the post previously?" the traveler asks.

"Ten years ago, when I was 46," Bowker replies. He explains that he was appointed high commissioner of Basutoland, which was recovering from its wars with the Orange Free State. He served for three years before handing over the reins to Griffith, and returning to military service.

"Did you find you had to be firm with the Basotho people?" the traveler asks. "How did you force them to obey the colonial laws?"

"I found little resistance among the Basotho to colonial rule," Bowker replies. "At first, they were ready to accept almost anything for protection against the Boers. But as time progressed, dissatisfaction arose now and then.

"I must say that sometimes I felt I had more resistance from the missionaries," he says. "I often criticized them for opposing annexation of native territories. I believe that the natives are better governed by whites, but the missionaries always seem to take the side of the blacks against the whites, although I came to learn later they were often expressing the views of the Basotho, who dislike confrontation."

Bowker cannot resist saying that he spends a lot of his time observing and catching butterflies and has gathered one of the best collections in South Africa. He has identified 40 new species and a new genus. He has written numerous papers on the haunts and habits of butterflies and their distribution in South Africa.

"It is common to see me with a butterfly net," he says. "At times, I will amuse passersby by walking with the net wound around my head and using the rod as a walking stick." He imitates the strut for his newfound friend.

But Bowker adds, he will have little time for butterflies in his new post. "I have been told that pressing issues await my attention."

King William's Town — Friday, March 15, 1878

Frere believes it is only a matter of time before the Ngqika under Sandile are defeated. It is true that a low-level guerrilla war continues in the colonial-ruled rural areas, particularly in an area known as the Pirie bush, where the mountainous land is covered for the most part by dense bush, making it ideal for guerrilla tactics.

But Frere is convinced that the situation in the eastern Cape has calmed down enough for him to return to Cape Town, where he can work on a plan to secure the coming peace in the eastern Cape. He wants to establish a special police or defense force that will ensure that those black people who want to become part of the established order will be able to do so, and that the rebels will be kept under control.

Nevertheless, although the uprisings in the Eastern Cape have been all but defeated, trouble is stirring elsewhere. Indeed, as Frere reviews official reports from across South Africa, he concludes that the Gcaleka and Ngqika uprisings were not isolated. Nor were they accidental. They are, he is convinced, part of a general uprising against British and colonial rule across the sub-continent.

Unrest, he notes, is threatening in five regions.

In Griqualand East around the diamond mines at Kimberley, rebellion is brewing; in Griqualand West the Batlapin chief is giving trouble; in southern Basutoland, Moorosi, already disaffected, is urging his people to defy the government and is threatening to cause more trouble; in the Transvaal the Bapedi chief Sekukuni is defying the British administration; and in Natal the cross-border activities of the Zulu chief Cetshwayo, said to be the most powerful chief in South Africa, have led Sir Theophilus Shepstone to apply for more troops in preparation for a war that might break out at any moment.

Peace, he believes, will not be established until the whites have shown that they are the masters. Frere remains convinced that black people are easy to govern, but they must be actively governed and not be allowed to rule themselves. He remains confident, too, that his policy of political fusion — to subdue the surrounding tribes, to annex their land, to govern them with British law and to enable them to live like any other subjects under Her Majesty's rule — is the only way to govern the native people.

Even should the native people one day be able to participate in the government, the standards of right and wrong must be European, he believes. At issue is not skin color, he insists. At issue is the cultural norms that the people follow. A black person who speaks English, lives as the English do and honors and respects the queen is to all extent and purposes British.

But, if the black people reject the British as their masters and refuse to be trained in the British way of life, they will be forced to do so — for their own good.

Frere is determined that, no matter how strong the South African black people think they are, he will teach them who are the masters in South Africa. He is confident he has the support of Sprigg, who has made it clear his intention is to "recognize no chief whatever in the colony ... and to break up all tribes."

One duty remains. Frere replaces Cunynghame as the commander of the British forces in the eastern Cape with the Hon. F. A. Thesiger.

He sets off for Cape Town from where he will monitor and, where necessary, control the emerging events on the sub-continent.

Quthing — Monday, March 18, 1878

The cave in which Lehana is holed up with his followers is protected by stone walls, behind which armed men stand guard. Because the cave is situated above a wide valley, the guards can see every approach to it. They know when a person is nearing long before the person is aware of the cave or them.

Late this morning the guards call out that someone is approaching. As the person nears, they inform Lehana that it is a man from their village.

"He is a friend. Let him approach; I will talk with him," Lehana replies.

"I have not told anyone where you are hiding," Philemon informs Lehana. "But I went to the service at the missionary Ellenberger's church yesterday. He spoke with me afterwards and asked me whether I could get a message to you. He wants to talk with you and asks that you meet him on the path to the mission station. He will not tell the government people that you are meeting with him."

Lehana, who learned to trust Ellenberger when he was at Masitise before his visit to Europe, agrees. He follows Philemon down the hillside and along a path to the mission station.

He meets up with Ellenberger along the way and the two sit down on nearby rocks to talk. Ellenberger lays out his argument that resistance will provoke violence and bloodshed.

"I suggest you go to the magistracy and talk to Hope," Ellenberger says. "That is worth more to you than facing the possibility of armed forces attacking you and your followers."

Lehana is resolute.

"Hope never listens to the Baphuthi," he says. "He does not even let you explain how you feel or what your view is. When you answer him, he threatens to throw you in jail or be whipped for not showing respect to him. I would rather be killed by the government forces than that I should be whipped like a dog or sent to Cape Town to work on the breakwater. If I go there I will never return home."

"Would you be willing to go to Mr. Hope's office if you could be given the assurance that you would not be whipped or sent to Cape Town?" Ellenberger asks.

"If I could talk to him, if he would listen to me and if he would promise not to whip me or send me to Cape Town, I would be willing to see him. But he will not do that."

"We will see whether that is possible," says Ellenberger.

He thanks Lehana and leaves, pleased that he has hold of a potential compromise. Now he needs to find someone on the government side to assure him Lehana will not be harshly sentenced. But who? Ellenberger's previous visit to Hope was not encouraging. He needs to go over his head. He has heard that Bowker, whom he knows from the magistrate's previous service in Maseru, has taken up the office again and is planning a trip to Quthing. Bowker has a reputation as a good negotiator and a man of compassion. Ellenberger will send him a letter of welcome in the hope he might be able to talk to him about Lehana and the hut-tax issue.

Maseru — The same day

It is less than a week since he arrived in Maseru, but Bowker already is focusing on the growing confrontation between Hope and Lehana. After reading the reports from Hope and the responses from Rolland, he discusses the situation with Rolland. From the discussion, several aspects become clear to him.

One is that he needs to help to settle the matter peacefully. For one thing, he has only 70 untrained Basotho policemen he can send to Quthing. For another, the ammunition stored at Maseru is ineffective; a quick examination shows that half of the few thousand cartridges would not fire if used. In addition, he has no money in his budget to pay for colonial armed forces and, in any event, the forces are all needed in the Transkei.

A potential non-violent solution would be to withdraw the charges against Lehana, particularly as they do not seem to be well based, but doing so, Bowker decides, would depict the colonial rule as ineffective. The law must be seen to be enforced.

Bowker is convinced that to achieve resolution he needs to go around Hope. The magistrate has precipitated the trouble he is now being called upon to resolve and Hope appears unlikely to be able to broker some sort of settlement of the standoff. The government records reflect a man who is abrupt and stubborn and whose temper has a short fuse.

Bowker decides to call on his old friend paramount chief Letsie.

Letsie's Village — Tuesday, March 19, 1878

In visiting Letsie at his headquarters near the Morija mission station, 35 miles south of Maseru, Bowker is not treating him as a subordinate by summoning him to his office, but is meeting him on neutral ground. The symbolism, he is convinced, will not be lost on the paramount chief.

He asks "my true friend" to send his most trusted messenger to persuade Moorosi to help in bringing Lehana to book and to bring the matter to a peaceful resolution.

"After this discussion with you, I will go on to Mr. Hope's district," he tells Letsie. "I will be glad if upon my arrival there, I find that you have accomplished and peacefully arranged the matter in accordance with the orders you have received so that when I see Moorosi I may find all old and crooked things done away with and be enabled to commence afresh without any grievance."

Letsie nods vigorously. He says he is pleased to see Bowker back in his old position and will do all he can to help resolve the conflict.

"My messenger will leave tomorrow morning to speak with King Moorosi," he says.

Bowker decides to delay his visit to Quthing until he has heard back from Letsie.

Maseru — Monday, March 25, 1878

Just as Bowker made a special trip to Letsie, so today the paramount chief, in an unusual foray outside his village, has made the journey north to see Bowker, responding to Bowker's gesture with one of his own. Walking slowly, the chief, who recently turned 70, moves to a chair in Bowker's office and slumps into it.

"I sent my messenger to talk with Moorosi, as you requested when we met on Tuesday last week," he says. "He returned to say that Moorosi says his son Lehana will not go to see Hope. Moorosi says he does not accept that Hope is the ruler of the Baphuthi people and he does not accept the magistrate's authority to punish Lehana."

The response is not entirely unexpected. But Bowker has learned that diplomacy takes time, skill and perseverance. These moves are only round one in the battle of wills and the balancing of alternatives. The carrot has not worked. His next move will be to try the stick; experience has taught him the threat of force can be an effective diplomatic tool.

Bowker has no forces on which he can draw, but Letsie does. Faced with a threat from Letsie's men, Bowker believes, Moorosi will yield.

But how to persuade Letsie to commit his forces on behalf of the government?

"We cannot allow Lehana to continue to confront the government," he tells the paramount chief. "Not only does it mean he is not respecting our authority, it sets a bad example for others. We cannot tolerate such disobedience or disrespect."

Letsie finds the words hard. He sees the relationship between the white authorities and the Basotho chiefs as shared power, in which the white people's laws apply in some cases and the black people's laws apply in others. But he simply nods and lets Bowker continue talking.

"If Lehana continues to refuse to do as he is told, and Moorosi continues to back him in that refusal, I want to draw you a picture of what can happen to the Baphuthi and the others who live in Moorosi's territory."

Letsie listens intently.

"Let us say that Lehana persists in refusing to go to Hope's court to stand trial and to pay the fine and face the prospect of jail. Let us say that Hope calls for military help from the government to force Lehana to attend the court hearing.

"Let's say, too, that Moorosi backs Lehana in his fight against the government, meaning that all of the Baphuthi people are drawn into the fight. Then let's say that the government forces win. The next step would be for the colonial government to take over the Baphuthi territory and to divide it up and give it to white farmers. That land would be lost to the Baphuthi nation and also to the Basotho people. It would be occupied by white people.

"You have seen this happen in the south where the land that Sarhili's people once occupied has been annexed and is now being given over to white farmers."

"What then do you want me to do?" Letsie asks.

"I want you to help me with your men so that we can capture Lehana and his followers, punish them for what they have done and put this matter to rest. By using your forces you will make it unnecessary for white forces to enter the territory."

Letsie realizes that he is trapped between two tough alternatives.

On the one hand, he can cooperate with Bowker. The result will be a higher standing with the colonial government. It also will mean a removal of any threat that Moorosi would be attacked by the colonial forces and his territory taken over by the settlers.

By turning on Moorosi, therefore, he would be ensuring his people's safety, but at the price of acknowledging that the colonial power is the superior power.

On the other hand, if he refuses Bowker's request he will be seen as a rebel who, in effect, sided with Moorosi. When the whites take over Moorosi's territory, they will turn on him next.

Letsie looks down. As he thinks through the alternatives, he wonders if he has any choice at all.

After a while, Letsie looks up once more.

"Tell me what I should do."

Bowker smiles with relief.

"I think you have made the right decision," Bowker says. "I would like you to assemble some of your best warriors. Only then will Moorosi take you seriously. Only then will he understand that the consequences of disobedience are greater than simply words.

"Remember, chief, that a lot is riding on this. We need to settle this matter and to settle it quickly. If we can use your warriors, it will be far preferable than the alternative, which is to bring in the colonial forces and fight a war that Moorosi cannot win, just as Sarhili could not win."

Letsie pauses one more time. Reluctantly, he looks into Bowker's eyes and asks, "How many men do you need?"

"I think if you asked your son Lerothodi to assemble between 600 and 700 men on the border of Moorosi's territory that would be a good start," Bowker says.

Although Letsie has not appointed an heir, it is clear that his eldest son, 41-year-old Lerothodi, the leader of Basotho who live in Kornet Spruit, adjoining Baphuthi territory, will be paramount chief when Letsie dies. Lerothodi, whose name means "drop of dew" and who has 10 wives, is — in contrast with his overweight and sedentary father — a man of energy and activity even though he, too, is on the plump side. He is highly intelligent, has a quick temper and is proud and ambitious. He remains obedient to his father, knowing he must do so if he is to inherit the kingdom. Like his father, therefore, he remains outwardly loyal to the colonial administration, although he sometimes questions its motives. He lives near Mafeteng where 5,000 people recognize him as their chief. Although many of his subjects have become Christians, Lerothodi dislikes Christianity, but he does not oppose it openly.

Letsie replies, "I will instruct Lerothodi to send his men to help you."

"I think you're doing a wise thing," Bowker replies. "Have Lerothodi's forces gather in Mohale's Hoek. I'll meet them there and tell them what to do next."

Mohale's Hoek — Sunday, March 31, 1878

Bowker sees a ray of hope for reconciliation in the Lehana affair when he receives a letter from Ellenberger, who sees the possibility of compromise should Hope promise he would only fine Lehana and not whip him or send him to prison.

Bowker writes back to Ellenberger, reassuring him that such punishment will not be inflicted. Bowker says he will either conduct the trial himself or instruct Hope only to fine Lehana and no more. He asks Ellenberger to pass on the assurance to Lehana.

Yet, on deeper reflection, Bowker wonders whether his assurance to Lehana is worth anything at this stage. The situation has gone beyond the issue of the hut tax, a fear of being flogged, and has turned into a clash of wills. Feelings have hardened; neither side will easily make concessions. Indeed, the dispute between Lehana and Hope is fast becoming a matter of lesser importance. The dispute now is between the colonial government and Moorosi.

Rumors are spreading. Reports from the Orange Free State say people there believe the Baphuthi people are rising against the government and war is imminent. But the tense atmosphere is not confined to the Orange Free State. Reports filtering through to Bowker from Quthing and the northern Cape colony indicate that war fever has spread along the Orange and Telle rivers and that Thembu chiefs in the Cape Colony to the south of Basutoland are preparing to link up with Moorosi and to join him in any confrontation that might arise with the white government.

Whenever possible, Bowker has sent messages reassuring the public there is no danger; he realizes if the rumors persist it could lead many of the white people in southern Basutoland — magistrates, their assistants, missionaries, doctors and traders — to flee. Rumor might feed on itself and, combined with the hardening of feelings on both sides, erupt into a conflict that might not have materialized were it not for the rumors.

Informers have told him, too, that Lehana's plan in hiding in the cave is to induce Hope to send a party to capture him. The plan, according to the reports, is that the government forces should fire the first shot, giving Lehana an excuse to shoot back. During the ensuing conflict, a group would creep up from behind and ambush the government forces. That action would force the government to run for their lives, enabling the Baphuthi to drive the government people from the area.

Bowker continues to hope diplomacy will succeed. Although he will use Lerothodi's forces if he is forced to do so, a bloodless resolution remains his major aim.

As part of the diplomatic maneuvering, he will organize Lerothodi's forces and march them to confront Moorosi. This action might be a step closer to war, but it might also be the only way to assure peace.

As he devises his tactics, Bowker selects Palmietfontein, just south of the Telle Drift, as an ideal location for his camp. A seven-pounder placed there and aimed into Basutoland, for example, would be as effective as a regiment. Not only that. Bowker believes Palmietfontein is key to the entire Cape Colony's north-eastern border area. He often has said that the town and police camp, with roads leading in every direction, is one of the most advantageous military positions in South Africa. A wagon road runs west to Kokstad and on into Natal colony, another east into the Orange Free State and a third into Basutoland.

But he faces another obstacle. Palmietfontein is outside Basutoland and so is out of his jurisdiction. He cannot simply set up camp there. So Bowker writes to Secretary of Native Affairs Ayliff in King William's Town, requesting authority to operate in the district of Herschel, in which Palmietfontein falls.

Bowker also is unsure how motivated Lerothodi's people will be to fight against the Baphuthi. The two groups are similar in culture and Lerothodi is married to one of Moorosi's daughters. How determined would they be in a fight to the death?

So, in the midst of these preparations, Bowker decides to give negotiation another chance. He sends a message to Moorosi, offering to meet with him in a pitso.

Quthing — Tuesday, April 2, 1878

In recent days Ellenberger has met twice with Moorosi at his mission station in an attempt to persuade him to hand over Lehana for trial. Doing so, Ellenberger assures him, will avoid a violent confrontation, in which Moorosi would come off second best.

"I realize that you want to retain your independence as a chief and that you are not willing that the colonial government rule your people," Ellenberger tells Moorosi. "But I think you must realize that, if you do not try to negotiate a solution with the colonial government, you stand to lose everything.

"Is this dispute over the hut tax worth risking a war — a war that you might lose? Particularly if there is a middle way out, a way that does not involve violence on either side?"

"But I refuse to give in to him and let my son be flogged or be sent to Cape Town or to jail in Aliwal North," Moorosi replies.

"That will not happen," Ellenberger says. "Colonel Bowker has told me that will not happen."

He looks into Moorosi's eyes. "Sometimes," he continues, "we have to meet in the middle. If two people are stubborn and refuse to concede anything, they can destroy each other with their stubbornness. They fight so hard and they hurt one another so much they both lose. But if each concedes a little, well then each wins a little, too. If you are willing to yield a little by handing over Lehana, Colonel Bowker will be willing to yield on the punishment, too. I am sure of that.

"Remember, too, that Colonel Bowker is a bigger man than the magistrate. I believe you can trust his word."

"I will do all I can to yield a little ground to Bowker, but I do not trust the white people. If I yield too much to them, they will take over my country and my people. But I will do as you say. I will try to meet him somewhere in the middle and perhaps in that way we can avoid violence. But I will only yield so much."

Ellenberger, realizing that is all he can hope for, returns to Masitise, praying for peace and hoping he has helped avert an outbreak that could lead to war.

Mohale's Hoek — Thursday, April 4, 1878

Ellenberger's efforts at negotiations prove successful. Moorosi has agreed to hand over his son Lehana to the government for trial — on condition that Hope is not the magistrate and that no floggings will be administered. Bowker has assured him he will conduct the proceedings himself, that they will not be held in Hope's courtroom and that flogging will not be a form of punishment. The trial will be held in place of the pitso he had proposed. Everything is falling into place.

Bowker is making plans for any eventuality. Ayliff has given him permission to move his forces — largely Basotho provided by Lerothodi — to Palmietfontein and to operate from there. Bowker has also requested from Aliwal North a wagon load of cartridges. It will be of little use confronting Moorosi without ammunition. He must be ready for any eventuality.

An obstacle remains, however. Moorosi tells Bowker he will not attend the trial unarmed.

Bowker, working in Austen's office in Mohale's Hoek before moving to Palmietfontein, needs to resolve this remaining issue. He asks Lerothodi, who has brought his forces here, to join him and Austen for a discussion. Austen is an important attendee because he was the magistrate who had authority for Quthing before Hope's arrival, and was the one who waived the fines on the widows. Hope is in Quthing and was not invited to join Bowker in Mohale's Hoek.

"First of all, I think the trial must go ahead," Bowker says. "We cannot afford to show that we are not in charge here. Hope has charged Maikela and Lehana with instigating people not to pay their hut taxes and we must stand by it. We cannot allow our courts to be treated contemptuously or their precepts disregarded. Whether the ruling is considered fair or unfair, it must be obeyed. Failure to do so undermines our whole system of government. Now, let's see whether we can resolve this issue peacefully."

Bowker outlines the agreement he has received from Moorosi to hand over Lehana for trial.

"What do you think?" he asks. "Do you think he will honor it?"

"I am convinced he will honor it," Lerothodi replies. "But I also am convinced that he would rather declare war on the government than meet you without his people being armed. When I spoke with him, he said he is afraid that he will be caught like Langalibalele who was tricked into being arrested by Griffith after being told that he was meeting only with Basotho people who were going to show him hospitality."

Bowker knows the story well. "We will not trick him. He knows he is meeting with us and he knows what it is about."

"Yes," Lerothodi continues. "But if he and his people come unarmed he knows he will be unable to defend himself should he be tricked.

"Please, Mr. Bowker, you must agree that he come armed. I am fearful that if you do not agree he will not come and then we will face big trouble. He does not want his arms in order to shoot anyone. He does not want to wage war against you unless you attack him. All he wants to do by bringing his arms is to protect his people in case there is trouble.

"Please. It is the only way of saving the country from a war. You have never objected to armed meetings with the chiefs before. I know that for myself as I have been at meetings at which we have been armed and you have been there. Please, Colonel Bowker. You must listen to what I say."

Bowker turns to Austen, "Your opinion?"

"I agree with Chief Lerothodi on both points," says Austen. "Chief Moorosi will not back down from any agreement he might make with you. But I, too, am convinced he will not meet with you unarmed."

"So you, too, believe that I should allow him to attend the meeting armed?"

Austen hesitates for a moment and glances across at Lerothodi who is fighting back tears of concern for his people and the consequences that war could bring and whose eyes plead with him to agree. He turns back to Bowker. "If you want to pursue every avenue short of war, I think you should do so," says Austen. "After all, you yourself will be backed by an armed force, won't you?"

Bowker nods. He looks at each of the men, weighing his decision. He is nervous that if such a meeting gets out of hand, he will have an armed conflict on his hands, but he realizes that refusing Moorosi's request (and Lerothodi's passionate plea) could destroy any chances for a peaceful resolution. And, Lerothodi is right. His practice always has been to allow arms at meetings.

Lerothodi looks across at him anxiously. His face again becomes contorted in fear as he watches Bowker weigh up his decision. "Please, Mr. Bowker. Please."

Bowker raises his hand, indicating that Lerothodi should cease his pleas.

"I am a soldier as well as an administrator," Bowker says. "My people will be armed. I can see no reason, therefore, that Moorosi should not come armed."

Lerothodi is so relieved at Bowker's decision that he offers to send one of his messengers to take the news to the Baphuthi leader.

"Thank you, chief," Bowker replies. "I would like you to do that. But let's make this the final message to him. We need to move forward and hold this trial. Please tell him I must have an answer before Saturday on whether he will bring Lehana to trial. If his answer is yes, we will meet on the following Friday, April 12."

Bowker is confident that the ammunition will have arrived by then.

Lerothodi agrees. As he leaves, Bowker turns to Austen.

"This meeting of two armed forces will either prevent war or start it," he says.

Palmietfontein — Saturday April 6, 1878

Moorosi meets the Saturday deadline. He sends a message saying he is ready to meet and hand over Lehana for trial on Thursday, April 11 — a day earlier than Bowker suggested.

In preparation for any eventuality, Bowker, now in Palmietfontein, has called on Dr. Henry Taylor, surgeon to the Basutoland Police Force and stationed in Thlotse Heights, to the north of Maseru, to serve as the medical officer in charge. He has appointed King William's Town-born Captain Henry Lee Davies, 27 — proficient in the local dialects and resident magistrate from Thaba Bosigo in northern Basutoland — to oversee the 700-strong Basotho force.

As his Palmietfontein quarters, Bowker has selected an abandoned mud hut from where he can see Moorosi's territory across the Telle River. In one of the rooms he sets up a bedroom and office for himself. The other room will accommodate six white officers from the Basutoland administration who are accompanying him.

Another hut serves as a mess hall where a cook prepares meals for the colonial officers and the Basotho National Police. Lerothodi's men will have to find their own food.

During the day the senior officers fish and bathe in the river, play games involving spear throwing, and practice shooting — being careful not to use up too much ammunition. In the evening they play whist by candlelight.

A source of amusement for the officers derives from the discovery on their arrival that they have only six spoons among seven people. They decide the last one to reach the mess hall for each meal will go without a spoon. The result is much laughter at breakfast and dinner when the unfortunate victim has to consume his porridge or soup with a fork.

Another amusement for the white officials derives from their desire for female company. Young Thembu women often visit the camp to sell food and trinkets that they have made. After several visits by the attractive young women, the men have devised sweepstakes. Each contributes a shilling to the kitty for each woman present. The men then line up and ask the women to select the one whom they would most like for a husband.

As they are inspected, the men stand to attention, carefully arrange their clothing and describe their virtues and great deeds. These speeches are more for their fellow officers' amusement as few of the women can understand what they are saying.

The women, enjoying the game, carefully peruse each candidate, offering comments in their language that the men — thankfully in many cases — do not understand.

Now and then a woman will stand in front of a man for some time, carefully examining him and smiling at him. He becomes confident that he is the one. Suddenly, however, she laughs, moves off and selects another man, to the groans and laughs of the rest. Once each woman makes her selection, the favored man receives all the shillings in the kitty. The woman receives a shilling for her trouble.

Boredom is less of an issue among the Basotho under Lerothodi than is their lack of facilities. For two days they have crowded into a few huts. Many sleep outside as the first frost has not arrived and the nights remain warm.

Besides the living conditions, the Basotho have two major complaints.

One is the lack of food. For two days now many have had little to eat.

The other complaint is the apparent senselessness of the conflict. They have been instructed by their headmen to be there, but they feel the fight is not theirs. They know, too, of Moorosi's reputation as a mighty warrior and they fear many lives could be lost.

Comments one, "If Moorosi broke the white law, why does the government not send the white soldiers against him? Why should we leave our wives and our fields to fight in other people's quarrels?" Another agrees. "It is the white people who have caused this. Let them fight their own battles."

As the dissent spreads, some quietly make their way back to their homes.

Others, however, are satisfied to follow their chief, Lerothodi. If he says they should prepare themselves to fight, they will do so. Even a lack of food, their absence from their families and the unpleasant living conditions will not deter them.

This afternoon Lerothodi arrives. He moves among the men, encouraging them to stay on. By helping the whites now, he says, they will be helping their own people. By joining in with the white government, they will show them that they are honorable, trustworthy people and so the government will treat them well.

"It is better to stay on the government side in this dispute," he says. "By doing that, they will treat us well and will not fight against us as they are fighting against Moorosi."

The men listen carefully. To many, the argument makes sense.

"But we have no food," complains one man. "How can we fight without food?"

"And we are not being paid," says another. "The white government pays the people who fight for them."

Lerothodi promises he will talk to Bowker about those issues. In the meantime, he says, they should stay and be ready to fight.

Quthing — Monday April 8, 1878

Maitin offers to leave Quthing for Palmietfontein to represent Hope, who — fearful of the criticism if he leaves — is determined to stay at his post. "You need to go," he tells Maitin. "You will be safer there. But my duty is to stay here and maintain the government presence. I cannot yield to this muttering among the people about war. The law must be imposed and I will see that it is."

The threat of war is not confined to muttering. For the last two days, each evening, around dusk, Baphuthi men have been gathering around Hope's house, dancing and singing war songs. Others stand on the hillsides, yelling loudly. Maitin, translating the threats to Hope, say they tell of what they will do to Hope that night. Few details of how they would tear him apart are omitted.

Hope tries to ignore them. Although he now has 30 policemen, he knows they will be of little help against a serious attack. But he will remain in the compound. With each night that passes without incident, Hope's conviction grows that the threats are empty.

This afternoon, before the usual war-dance ritual begins, Davies, commanding officer of the Basotho troops, and Taylor, the physician, arrive at Hope's house. They explain that the officers at Palmietfontein have decided to take turns to ride the 12 miles each afternoon and spend the night with him for his protection.

Davies and Taylor have opted to take the first duty.

Hope insists he is unafraid, but accepts their offer. He says they can sleep on the sofas in his living room.

At dusk, when the Baphuthi gather to shout blood-curling threats, Taylor and Davies feel more vulnerable than they had imagined. The house is surrounded by steep hills that offer would-be attackers ample opportunity to hide until they are within yards of the house. For those inside the house there is no means of escape. A policeman stands sentry nearby, but he would be of little help. Hope, Davies and Taylor decide to take turns at keeping watch during the night.

"Let's barricade the doors and windows in case they should attack," suggests Taylor. "That way they cannot rush in without warning. I'm sure we can find enough wood. If not, we can use chairs and even this table to slow down any intruder."

Hope disagrees. "That's not a good idea," he says. "Here's what we need to do." He walks to the front door and flings it open. He lights candles, placing a couple in each room. "Our only chance of safety is by showing them we are not afraid of them," he says. "I refuse to be intimidated by these people. I have shown them who is in charge here and I have not been attacked as a result. Every time I confront them, they back off. We need to continue to do that."

The men agree Hope knows more about the Baphuthi people than they do.

About 1 a.m. the man on sentry duty bangs on the open door and calls out that an attack is imminent. "People are crawling around in the field down there," he says, pointing 50 yards away toward corn fields by the river. With only a sliver of a new moon, the men cannot see that far, but accept the sentry's warning.

Taylor has a plan.

"First, let us put out the lights," he says. He did not think much of lighting up the house in the first place. "Then we creep down to the field and, as we approach it, we fire repeatedly as soon as we see the men among the corn stalks," he adds. "That way, we will make them think we have been reinforced during the night. They will turn and run. Should this fail, they are likely to attack the house. In that case, we would be out of the house and we could creep away and hide until daybreak."

This time Hope, feeling more fearful now, agrees.

The men douse the lights, take up their rifles and sneak toward the corn field where they see the shapes in the darkness. Taylor raises his gun, cocks it and takes aim toward a shadowy figure.

"Don't shoot," shouts Davies, who is slightly ahead of Taylor.

He turns back toward Taylor and Hope and laughs.

"These are not would-be attackers. They are oxen who have escaped their compound and are eating the corn."

Taylor and Hope, hugely relieved, share the laughter. They walk back to the house and eventually fall asleep.

Palmietfontein — Tuesday, April 9, 1878

Davies and Taylor return to camp today and tell Bowker of the incident during the night. The chief magistrate is not amused.

He instructs no further expeditions be made to "keep Hope company." Instead, the magistrate should abandon his Quthing residence, as Maitin has done, and join them in Palmietfontein.

"I do not want to start a war before we have even met with Chief Moorosi," he says. "I am doing my best to avoid an armed clash and you people seem to be bent on provoking one."

The men promise they will return to fishing, bathing and playing cards to pass the time before the meeting — now rescheduled at Moorosi's request for Saturday.

Palmietfontein — Saturday, April 13, 1878

Reports reach Bowker early in the morning that Moorosi is on his way to the Telle River crossing with a body of armed men. The day Bowker feared might never arrive has arrived. And now that it has arrived he fears what its arrival could bring.

At least, the ammunition is here and during the morning the officers place their 50-strong police force in position to guard it.

Moorosi's men assemble opposite the Telle Drift. They traveled most of yesterday, slept in the vicinity overnight and now look across the rapidly flowing river, which is shallow here as it passes over a series of sandbars, toward the military outpost on the opposite river bank. Some dismount and talk animatedly; others sit quietly on their horses.

For Moorosi, this place at the junction of the Orange and Telle rivers, where his kingdom meets the northernmost boundary of the Cape Colony, is heavy with memories, both good and bad.

Here, 30 years ago, he built a fortress on the nearby flat-topped mountain the Baphuthi call Tulumoneng and the whites call Table Hill. He abandoned the fortress when war broke out between the Basotho and the Boers, believing he and his people would be safer farther into his territory.

It was near here that nine years ago Moorosi met Sir Philip Wodehouse, telling the then governor-general of the Cape he acknowledged Moshoeshoe as his chief.

Here, too, eight years ago he met with Bowker — the same man he will meet with today — to accept British protection and payment of hut tax.

This junction of rivers is a natural place for the meeting of opposing forces, whether they be hostile black nations, the Boers or the colonial government. Here they have confronted one another before — and will do so again today.

Slowly, as the sun rises and warms the earth, government officials, the Basotho policemen and the troops under Lerothodi take their places on the Cape Colony side of the river and stare across at Moorosi's men. Apprehension mixes with excitement at the confrontation ahead.

Bowker knows that crossing into Moorosi's territory with even a small armed force would be an act of war.

Hoping his protocol will be correct, Bowker crosses the ford with only a couple of men and invites Moorosi to join them on the colonial side. Moorosi accepts, signals to his followers, whom Bowker estimates at 700, to follow him across the ford. The riders, well-built men armed with rifles and spears, are ready to do battle should their chief call upon them. Many are eager to demonstrate their dislike of colonial government rule.

By 10 a.m. more than 1,600 men — the vast majority black — have gathered in two groups outside the camp's mess hut. To the south are the colonial government's men, to the north, the Baphuthi men. Their presence has changed the essence of the event. Had Bowker been the sole representative for the colonial government and had Moorosi arrived only with Lehana and Maikela the issue would be confined and there would be less chance of a wider confrontation. This has become a symbol of a deepening rift between the Baphuthi and the colonial government and the feelings on both sides that have been growing more bitter over the last year.

As they reach the designated place, Moorosi, his sons, grandsons and headmen take up their positions, with Moorosi standing in front. Near him stands a sullen-looking Lehana, angry at being forced by his father to be there, and a wide-eyed Maikela. Behind Moorosi, his sons, grandsons and headmen, totaling about 80, stand in two ranks, one behind the other. All are holding rifles. Behind them sit or crouch a dense mass of Baphuthi warriors, alongside their horses. All are armed, some with spears, others with rifles and some with both.

Seated facing them with their backs against the mess hall are five colonial authorities. In the center is Bowker, dressed in his red-coat-and-black-trouser military uniform, and next to him Austen, the magistrate at Mohale's Hoek, dressed in his magisterial garb. Taylor, the physician, sits on the other side of Bowker and alongside him is Hope, who arrived in Palmietfontein yesterday and whom Bowker has instructed to remain quiet. "You are to speak only should I ask you to speak," Bowker has told him. Maitin, sitting next to Austen, completes the official retinue.

About 70 members of the colonial-appointed Basotho National Police are gathered on either side of the officials. They clutch their rifles. Off to either side are Lerothodi's men, armed with spears and rifles, now numbering 500. Another 200 policemen brought by Austen from Mohale's Hoek are close by.

Slowly Moorosi's men and those of Lerothodi edge forward until they make two big semi-circles with Bowker, the magistrates and officers, and Moorosi, Lehana and Maikela and his retinue in the middle. The right wing of Lerothodi's force almost touches the left wing of Moorosi's force.

Bowker sizes up the situation. In his police and army days, he was present at many confrontational meetings and discussions, and faced incidents that called for careful strategy, some to discuss peace terms after a war. Now he draws on that background. Although it is unlike any other he has experienced, it contains similar elements, including a volatile mix of emotions.

As he sees it, any attempt by Moorosi's men to fire would be met with a quick response from the well-armed policemen gathered on either side of him, among them a few sharpshooters, as well as the senior officials themselves, all of whom are armed. Moorosi would hesitate to give the order to fire first unless he and his family could escape within seconds after firing, an almost impossible feat. Should Moorosi flee to his rear, he would be blocked from a hasty retreat by his own men.

Clearly, Bowker reasons, Moorosi, is aware of this. His warriors are there for insurance and to demonstrate his power, not to stage an attack. Moorosi has come to discuss, perhaps even to argue, but not to fight. Nevertheless, he is prepared for a confrontation if one occurs. The same can be said for Bowker and Lerothodi.

Yet the potential for violence lies even beyond the power of the leaders. Any stray shot, fired perhaps as a result of a misunderstanding, would ignite latent mistrust like a match cast into a field of dry grass.

Bowker pushes those thoughts aside, confident that a resolution to the conflict is well worth the risk he is taking by allowing arms at the meeting.

He is aware, too, that some in the colonial government will condemn him for dealing directly with the chiefs — Letsie, Lerothodi and now Moorosi — virtually as equals and not as subordinates. He will face that criticism later. Here, Bowker's experience convinces him that dealing with chiefs as equals is the only way to resolve this clash of wills. At the same time, he knows he must not back off the government's assertion that Lehana has done wrong by, in effect, inviting his people to rebel against colonial rule.

So much, Bowker realizes, depends on how he handles the situation.

Lerothodi's men are restless. As they look across at the Baphuthi opposite them, they, too, are nervous that shooting might result and that they might be asked to kill men whom they regard almost as brothers. But they remain at the ready because obeying their chief is more important to them than any other consideration.

Moorosi — dressed for the occasion in a silk hat and a black cloak draped over his shoulders — looks around and behind him, satisfied that his people all are there. He looks across at Bowker. The people lapse into silence and only the buzzing of insects hangs in the warm air. The king steps forward and, after shaking hands with Bowker, sits on an ammunition box, placed there for that purpose.

"Your instruction to me was to bring Lehana and Maikela here," Moorosi says quietly, looking at Bowker. The men who are gathered behind him peer forward, hoping to hear better.

"I have brought them here."

Moorosi swings his right arm outward toward the men.

"Here they are."

With that, the men lined up immediately behind Moorosi lower their bodies until each is kneeling on one leg. Their rifles rest on their thighs. The silence is broken only by the clicking sound of the men cocking their rifles, ready to be raised to their shoulders and fired within seconds. The men are acting on instructions given them earlier.

Bowker stares at 80 rifles pointed in his direction. Tension ripples through his body. He is one wrong word away from a riot. Never has he felt more responsibility than now.

"There is Lehana," Moorosi repeats. "With him is Maikela. Take them."

Bowker fears that, in spite of Moorosi's invitation, if he stands and moves across to Lehana and physically seizes him, such a move could be interpreted as a move to take him into custody and therefore a call to arms. The men with the cocked rifles are sending a message: Don't touch him or we'll shoot. Taking them now would be too dangerous.

Yet Moorosi is saying: I'm telling you to take them. He is throwing down a challenge to Bowker. That challenge encapsulates the confrontation between the Baphuthi and the government, between natives and settlers, between those who wish to follow their traditional customs and those who want to impose new ones on them — essentially between black and white.

In essence, Moorosi is saying, "You have come into my country saying you will protect me from my enemies and that you will bring us new and better ways to live. You have said we can continue to run our own affairs. But you have not allowed us to do that. You have imposed your justice that runs counter to my people's justice and you have imposed your justice harshly. You have set up your magistrate, not to assist me in my power, but to override my power with your power.

"You have treated us not as men, but like children, like disposable animals who are worth nothing but to be your servants. Now you insist I must hand my son to you for you to punish, even though in our eyes he has done nothing wrong. He has acted like a man by standing up for those whom you want to punish, by protecting them and talking for them.

"You say the punishment is for showing contempt to you by not appearing in your court. But your punishments are more harsh than is warranted by such an offense, if it is an offense. If you flog my son, an heir to my kingdom, and especially if you send him to work on the breakwater in Cape Town it will be more than he can bear. You will slowly kill him; he will be of no value to himself, to me as I become older, or to our people.

"So now you have told me I must bring him to you or you will attack me to force me to do so. You have even persuaded Lerothodi to send his men to fight against me. But you also have told me that I must trust you and you will treat him fairly. The missionary has told me that if I want you to give ground on your demands and have a peaceful outcome, I must give ground, too. Well, here I am. I am giving him to you. But you will have to bear the anger of my people if you treat him unfairly."

"Here they are," Moorosi repeats aloud. "Take them."

Bowker is aware of Moorosi's unspoken feelings, although he might not appreciate their intensity. Yet can he refuse to punish Lehana? He cannot back down and tell Lehana he is free to go; such a move would be an admission of defeat, would set a precedent, and would make the government appear weak. After all, the law says Lehana, by preventing Maikela and others from appearing in court, should be arrested and punished.

The law must be upheld.

Bowker must, therefore, take action against Lehana. Yet he must also show respect to Moorosi. He must not be seen to be undermining Moorosi's power over his people. Already, Moorosi has made a major concession in handing over Lehana.

He must find a middle way, one that enables both sides to save face. The compromise bartered by Ellenberger is such a middle way and should avoid violence. But he must be careful how he approaches it. The peaceful outcome might be available; achieving it might be more difficult. Bowker decides to lessen the chance of losing the compromise by using an intermediary.

He turns to Lerothodi.

"Bring the prisoners to me," he says.

Lerothodi walks up to Lehana and Maikela and leads them forward so that they stand between Moorosi and Bowker. Lehana and Maikela hand over their weapons to Lerothodi who lays them down alongside Bowker.

The time has come for action. Bowker knows he cannot vacillate. He must act and he must act now.

VIII

King William's Town — The same day

Compromise is off the agenda in the eastern Cape where the new commander of the combined forces, Lieutenant General Thesiger is conducting armed operations against the Ngqika, who have been seen raiding white areas from bases in the Ciskei mountains, particularly around the Pirie mission station. Thesiger is out to destroy all resistance, but he is having a tough time doing so.

Internally, he is being less than successful in uniting the colonial and British forces into an effective whole. Many of the colonial fighters tend to disobey orders, particularly from British officers. Such disaffection spreads even to the higher ranks. For example, on March 18, the colonial leader Captain Edward Yewd Brabant, a former member of the legislative assembly and now a field commandant of the Cape Colonial Forces, was said to have left his post to capture a herd of Ngqika cattle, ruining a combined action between the British and colonial forces that had been arranged for that day. Brabant said he had been ambushed. The fact remained, however, that the operation had been wrecked.

Another internal problem is that the Mfengu, drafted to fight in the battle against the Ngqika, prefer to sing, hunt game, and fire volleys in the air rather than flush out Ngqika guerrilla fighters. For them, the war was over when their enemies, the Gcaleka, were driven from their territory.

Today, therefore, Thesiger is calling off his first offensive and reassessing his strategy. Supported by the new Sprigg ministry and its aggressive approach for subjugating the black people in the eastern Cape, Thesiger is calling in reinforcements so that he can force the Ngqika to surrender.

"I am dividing the Pirie bush into 11 districts," he tell his commandants, including Griffith, the commander of the colonial forces. "Each district will have a commandant and must flush out the rebels," he says.

"If you encounter strong resistance, you're to call on other districts for support.

"We are to seal off escape routes and starve them out; the Mfengu have been instructed to capture the rebels' food supply and cattle. We are to brook no opposition. We are to force the Ngqika to surrender. There will be no middle ground. There will be no negotiation and no compromise. Is that understood?"

The men voice their agreement.

"Good. We must squash this rebellion. And we must squash it quickly."

Palmietfontein — The same day

As Lerothodi hands over Lehana and Maikela for trial and they take their place alongside their chief, Bowker rises and steps forward until he is about two yards from Moorosi.

From the outset, Bowker had insisted he needed no armed help from the Cape Colony. He turned down an offer of assistance from burghers in Aliwal North, saying this was a matter for the Basutoland government to handle. His magistrates and his police would settle it alone.

Now he wonders momentarily whether he should have asked for help from the Cape Colony. It would have been reassuring. But he shrugs those feelings aside. He can, and will, handle the situation. He can, and will, achieve a peaceful solution. There can be no other outcome.

"Chief Moorosi, I am glad to see that you have listened to the word of the government," he says. "I am pleased you have brought Lehana and Maikela here today."

Without allowing time for Moorosi to respond, Bowker turns to Hope.

"I ask that the charges be read."

Hope stands up and reads out the charges — the one part of the trial in which Bowker has agreed that the magistrate can participate. The charge against Lehana is that he instigated the people in his ward to resist the magistrate. The charge against Maikela is that he instigated people in his village not to pay hut tax. George Moshesh, who accompanied Bowker from Maseru, translates the charges.

"How do you plead?" asks Bowker.

As they hear the translation, both men reply almost simultaneously.

"Guilty."

Bowker sighs with relief. One obstacle out of the way. He responds almost immediately. "They have pleaded guilty to these charges. And I therefore find that they are guilty. The next step is to punish them for what they have done."

The men holding the rifles grasp them more firmly.

Bowker addresses Moorosi, as though he were the only person at the trial. "First of all, let me assure you that I shall not put them in prison," he tells him. "I will not send them to Cape Town, nor will I have them flogged."

Moorosi smiles in relief. The tension noticeably lessens. He had hoped that would be the case. Ellenberger had said it would be likely. But to hear it confirmed by Bowker is reassuring.

Bowker needs to make one thing clear.

"I do that out of consideration for you, his father," he tells Moorosi.

He hopes that his respect for Moorosi, not just as a chief but also as a father, will be seen in a favorable light. He does not have to wait long. The men with the rifles at the ready noticeably relax. Bowker knows now that Ellenberger was right when he said that Lehana feared flogging more than anything else.

"But..." Bowker adds. The tension rises once more.

"Lehana and Maikela have committed an offense for instigating people not to pay their taxes and for failing to appear in court when called upon to do so."

As the men with the rifles stiffen once more, Bowker realizes he must press ahead and deal with the sentencing as quickly as possible.

"Are we agreed that Lehana and Maikela have committed that offense? After all, they have pleaded guilty."

Moorosi says he agrees. Lehana and Maikela watch in silence.

Bowker continues. "They must therefore be punished for what they have done."

Silence. Now for the fine itself. Will it prove to be too harsh?

"I believe that a suitable punishment for this offense will be 25 pounds for Maikela and 100 pounds for Lehana. Those amounts are equivalent to a total of 24 head of cattle. Hand the money or the cattle to me today and the matter will be over. Do that and you, Lehana and your people, can go home in peace."

It works. The penalty is strong, but is not physical. The reaction of joy mixed with relief is immediate.

The men kneeling behind Moorosi lower their rifles and stand. Cries of *"pula, pula"* ring out from Moorosi's followers. Bowker is delighted. He is aware that *"pula"* means rain and is an expression signifying joy.

"Before you go, I want to thank you all for coming here today," Bowker says, raising his voice as talking breaks out among the assembled crowd. "I want to thank everyone for the fairness that they showed today, which enabled us to resolve this issue in a way that is acceptable to both sides. I am satisfied that now we can return to the peace that prevailed here before this event arose."

Satisfied that there is little harm that he can do now, he asks Hope to say a few words. Hope echoes Bowker's words and is followed by Austen, who says he is thankful everything turned out for the best.

With the speeches over, the hundreds of potential warriors gathered in the background break up in a disorganized mass. People, it seems, are everywhere. But they are relaxed. They are pleased. A great danger has been averted.

As the Baphuthi cross over the Telle River drift, 24 head of cattle are herded in the other direction.

Intense relief rushes through Bowker's body. He will relax and accept his achievement. But he is aware, too, that, although he might have solved the present confrontation, the underlying tensions have not disappeared.

As the crowds thin out, a tall bearded man with compassionate eyes moves toward Bowker and Moorosi.

"May I speak to you both for a minute?" he asks.

Masitise — The same day

Ellenberger sits at the table in the cave house with Moorosi and Bowker, exchanging pleasantries as they eat the evening meal his wife and the servants have prepared for them.

"Thank you for inviting us here today," says Bowker, still dressed in full military regalia. "I appreciated the letters you sent me indicating that the charged men feared being flogged or sent to work on the breakwater in Cape Town and this was a major problem. You helped a lot in enabling us to understand how Lehana was thinking and how we might respond."

"I am pleased by the outcome," Ellenberger responds. "I thought you and the chief might like to sit quietly and talk for a while before you return to your head-quarters."

"I am always pleased to visit you here in the cave house," Moorosi says qui-etly. "I am especially pleased when I can meet here with the government people." Ellenberger translates for Bowker's benefit. "I recall that you opened your house nine years ago, in 1869, for a meeting at which Colonel Bowker and I met with Sir Philip Wodehouse, who was then governor-general of the Cape Colony."

"To me that was a special visit," Ellenberger adds. "Not only did I have the pleasure of you two great men visiting with me, but never had I had anyone of such a high government position as Sir Philip in my house. After all, as governor-gen-eral, he was Queen Victoria's representative in the Cape Colony. A man of power and, I must add, a man of great compassion and diplomacy. You will recall that he brought about peace to this part of the world by drawing up the boundaries of Basutoland and giving British protection to the Basotho people within those boundaries so that they would no longer be attacked by the Boers.

"Although the British then became their rulers and Wodehouse did introduce a ban on liquor sales, a hut tax and a few regulations — which were acceptable to most people — he largely allowed the Basotho people to continue running their affairs.

"It is true that some criticize him because his boundaries caused the Basotho people to lose a large portion of their original land, which he gave to the Free State. But I am afraid that trying to regain that land would have meant a great war and might have resulted in tragedy for the Basotho people. He understood that com-promise is almost always the price we pay for peace. We have to lose something to gain something greater."

"Indeed," Bowker says. "The meeting in this room was to define the boundaries to the Baphuthi people." He turns to Moorosi. "Chief, you had already agreed to fall under the government as the other chiefs had done. You might recall that Sir Philip came to explain where the boundaries were to make them clear to us all."

"That is so," says Moorosi. "Mr. Austen, the magistrate in Mohale's Hoek who was then our magistrate, was here, too. It was here on this bench that the governor sat when he talked with us." Moorosi refers to a 10-foot three-seater bench, that Ellenberger sculptured from rock, set against the inner side of the living room, on which he is sitting. He admires the smooth contours.

"I see the governor's name is on the side," Bowker says.

Ellenberger explains that, after the Wodehouse visit, he carved out an area on the side of the bench and etched in capital letters the name "PHILIP WODE-HOUSE," which he painted white to stand out against the dark red bench.

"That's how special his visit was to me," he says. "I named the seat after him. Whenever I look at it, it reminds me of a great man of peace.

"But not everyone understood his achievements. The British government reprimanded him. Some of the Basotho people were upset that they lost some of their land. It was as though he could not fully satisfy either side. But I am afraid that often happens. When we achieve peace through compromise, not everyone appreciates it. They fear they have lost something. They think they have not just to win, but to win completely, destroying other people in the process, or else they are weak. But in thinking that way they fool themselves and are the poorer for it. When you destroy other people you destroy a part of yourself, too. You lose your moral integrity.

"Peace achieved through compromise demonstrates your values of concern and respect for others. It demonstrates love, the greatest of human values, not hate, the basest of all values.

"Peace is worth making sacrifices to achieve. Those who encourage peace are the real heroes. And I believe as Christians we should be always looking for a peaceful solution to our problems. After all, Our Lord said, 'Blessed are the peacemakers, for they shall inherit the earth.' Those who encourage war and urge victory at all costs, but do not search for a peaceful solution — well, eventually they are the losers, not the winners.

"War seldom achieves anything of lasting value for anyone — for the winners as much as for the losers. The cost of war, in lives and money, is not worth it. And war destroys our finest values. It makes us lesser human beings, turning us into cruel killers rather than compassionate lovers of our fellow humans."

He pauses and looks at Bowker and then at Moorosi.

"And that is why I am so happy today that you both prevented an outbreak that could have led to war. You ensured a peaceful outcome. Through compromise. It is a wonderful thing."

The room falls silent for a moment.

"But I fear I am preaching too much," Ellenberger continues. "As I was saying, the British government criticized Wodehouse. In his defense, after serving six years as governor, he wrote to the British Secretary of State, who had reprimanded him. He defended himself against those charges. Let me find his exact words for you."

Ellenberger retrieves a book of official records from his study: "Here it is. This is what he wrote to the British Secretary of State: 'I will ask your Grace to bear in mind that I have now been in office here longer than any governor since Lord Charles Somerset; that I have paid the most constant attention to border and native affairs; that not a shot has been fired in war by a British soldier during my government; that I have never applied to her Majesty's Government or to this parliament for the smallest sum for the purposes of war and that I have never involved the former in any difficulty.' "

The missionary puts the book aside. "Yes, he was a man of peace. And I would invite both of you to sit on that seat — the Wodehouse bench — today because that seat is a seat of peace and I am anxious to do all I can to reduce tensions, to reconcile differences between the Baphuthi and the government, and to establish a platform for an enduring peace."

Bowker, taking a seat on the bench alongside Moorosi, says he appreciates what the missionary is saying.

"I served under Sir Philip and I can identify with everything you say about the man," he adds. "It is a pity he did not serve even more than the eight years he did."

Moorosi says he is willing to compromise in the future, even as he did today. Rather than insist that Lehana go unpunished, he was willing to accept a lesser punishment in the interests of peace.

"What you did was good," Ellenberger responds.

Ellenberger senses the time is right to swing the discussion toward the Maikela affair. He expresses again his satisfaction at the outcome.

Bowker seizes the opportunity to outline his views to Moorosi.

"I want to make it clear that your son, Lehana, was fined for stirring up the people to disobey the government and its tax rules," he says. "He was punished because, in a sense, he rebelled against government rule. Lehana would have been given a lesser punishment if he had simply not paid his own taxes, which I assume he did pay. Instead, he instigated others not to pay theirs. We regard that as a serious offense."

"But he was afraid to appear in court before Mr. Hope," Moorosi responds. "Mr. Hope is a cruel man. He punishes people severely and he speaks angrily to them. Also, Mr. Hope was wrong to say the widows should pay hut taxes. Even Mr. Austen said they should not pay taxes. Why should Lehana take Mr. Hope's side and tell the people to pay their taxes when Mr. Hope is wrong? Lehana was saying the right thing. He was supporting his people against Mr. Hope. Even when I sent Mr. Hope money to pay the taxes and the fine he would not accept it.

"Now we have come with the compromise that the Rev. Ellenberger advised us to make. We have again paid the fine because we want to have peace with the government. But that does not mean that Mr. Hope was right."

Bowker is reluctant to criticize Hope in front of Moorosi. Hope represents the government and it is important that the government present a solid face to the Baphuthi people. Were they to be aware of cracks in the wall of government, Bowker fears, they would seek to exploit them just as the government exploits the differences between the native clans.

Ellenberger turns to Moorosi.

"May I suggest that if you have problems with Mr. Hope you send a message to Colonel Bowker who can help to solve them for you," Ellenberger says. "I assume, colonel, that you will be happy to respond in such a case."

"I will certainly do all I can," Bowker responds. "But we appoint a magistrate in the area because we cannot deal with every situation from far away in Maseru. He is there to represent us and you need to obey what he says."

"But sometimes he is wrong," Moorosi responds.

Realizing that tensions are rising, Ellenberger intervenes. "But I think we can all agree that it is better to talk things out rather than resort to force."

"If we can talk, that would be good," replies Moorosi. "But it is not always true that we can talk."

"I will talk whenever I can," says Bowker.

Ellenberger believes he has helped to bring the men together and to sort out some of their differences, although a divide still separates them. He hopes that to-day's discussion will persuade them that should another issue arise, they will talk rather than fight.

He tells the men once again that he is encouraged that they both modified their positions to bring about a peaceful resolution to the conflict.

"You are worthy, my friends, to sit on the Wodehouse bench," he says.

"For my part, let me say that this discussion has helped me focus my thoughts," Bowker replies. "But now you must excuse me. I must return to Maseru where I have an important action to make, one that has been advanced by this discussion. And one that I think might help restore calm to this area."

Maseru — Thursday, April 18, 1878

Back in his office, Bowker re-reads a paragraph in the letter from the new Secretary for Native Affairs, William Ayliff, that struck a chord with him when he received it this morning.

"The government is anxious that in all appointments to magistracies, care be taken to choose men not only qualified by knowledge of official routine, but also men whose judgment and ability for the fulfillment of difficult and responsible duties can be relied on," Ayliff had written.

This statement is a hint that Hope might have the knowledge, but he does not have the diplomacy or the temperament required to perform his work at Quthing. After reading through Hope's reports once more, Bowker concludes that the Maikela affair resulted largely from Hope's determination to stick to the letter of the law as he interpreted it and to refuse to concede anything to Moorosi.

Had Hope accepted the men's contention that Austen had given the widows a reprieve, the incident at Palmietfontein five days ago might never have occurred. In his mind, Bowker replays the scene with the rifles cocked and pointing in his direction, the hundreds of armed men gathered behind them. He feels anew Moorosi's challenge as the chief says, "You asked for Lehana. Here he is."

Bowker understands, too, that the Maikela affair grew out of the Baphuthi's underlying hostility toward government. But he believes that the latent hostility would not have found such outward expression had Hope acted judiciously.

In recent days he has heard reports from the Basotho that Moorosi and the Thembu, assisted by a group from across the Drakensberg mountains to the east, had been preparing to go to battle with the government had the Maikela affair not been settled at Palmietfontein. The reports make it even more apparent that Hope's intransigence had brought them to the brink of war.

Bowker decides that the time has come for Hope to go. He will be replaced by Austen, who has impressed him as a man of experience and wisdom. In addition, Austen is older than Hope, an aspect, Bowker believes, that will give him a greater presence among the Baphuthi.

He writes a letter to Ayliff recommending that Hope be replaced.

Quthing — Wednesday, April 24, 1878

Hope is furious. Bowker, with approval from Ayliff, has ordered him to vacate his office in Quthing as his duties there will end at the end of next month. He will be moved to a post at Qumbu in the Transkei where he will begin serving at the beginning of June, giving him a month to make the move. Austen, of all people, will replace him.

Steaming with fury, he throws the letter on his desk, kicks the wall and paces the floor with heavy steps. Clearly Rolland has persuaded Bowker that he should go. Why did Rolland refuse to let him take up a military position? Instead, he was to stay and follow instructions. Instructions that would not work. They set him up for failure. Now they have declared him a failure.

How many times did he ask for armed help? How many times did they say, You don't need more policemen? And now they declare that, hobbled and unable to face Moorosi with a strong show of force, he has failed.

"Come here, Mr. Maitin," he calls.

"I have been told my services are no longer required here," he says, his hands shaking as he holds the letter.

"I will be sorry to see you go," replies Maitin — to whom the decision does not come as a surprise.

"It seems that my firm commitment and my strong upholding of the law are inadequate for the government."

"Do they say that?"

"No, they do not explain why I have been moved. But I gathered from Bowker's attitude to me that I was not good enough for him. He had to take over the Lehana trial and run it his way."

Maitin ventures a response. "I do not know whether..."

Hope ignores Maitin and continues talking.

"I am proud that the Baphuthi are afraid of me because it means I am doing my job. Yes, I am firm. Yes, I am strong-willed. Yes, I am courageous.

"Are not those the very qualities required of someone in my position? The very fact that this office is still standing is testimony to my resoluteness. Even though they denied me armed back-up, I held firm.

"Who was the government officer who defied Moorosi? Who held on to this newly established magistracy when 700 armed men gathered here ready to cut my throat? For that, Griffith praised me. I still have the reports here..."

Hope searches through the papers carefully copied into a large notebook. He flips the pages impatiently.

"Here's one," he says. "It is from Griffith. It says 'you should be most careful and judicious in carrying out the judgments and orders of your court.'

"I don't suppose you would describe that as praise. But I did what he said. I was careful. I was judicious. "

He flips over the pages, searching for more references to his work. "Here's another. It is from Rolland."

Hope glances through the letter. It admonishes him for calling up troops to assemble at Palmietfontein.

"Why cannot I find the papers that praise me? I know there have been many."

He looks up at Maitin, seeking confirmation in his eyes.

"I know I have them here," he adds. "I just have to find them."

"But, wait, Mr. Hope," Maitin says. "It is not necessary that you find those letters. I know they have praised you from time to time. Let's look rather at the reason they are moving you. Matters are unsettled on the eastern frontier. They have had wars there recently and it seems as though they could have more. Could it not be that they are moving you to the Transkei because your services are required there more urgently than here?"

"I had not thought of that, Mr. Maitin. But why would they move me now when my work here is not complete?"

"Perhaps the needs in the Transkei are more urgent."

Hope is sure he is being moved because Bowker and Rolland dislike him and have succeeded in convincing the new secretary of native affairs of their views. But Maitin's suggestion provides him with a reason for leaving that he can tell his wife and mother-in-law. It is clear, too, that some people in the government still believe in him; he has not been completely removed from government office.

"Your theory of why I am being moved is unlikely to be true," he tells Maitin. "They are moving me because they are dissatisfied with what I have done here. I have failed at my task. That can be the only explanation. Colonel Bowker does not care for me. I know that from the way he treated me at Palmietfontein.

"I will write to Ayliff and protest my removal. I will call for an official government inquiry. In this way, everything will come to light. It will show what I did and why I did it, and it will clear my name. I will not meekly back down and accept this slap in the face."

Maseru — Thursday, April 25, 1878

When Bowker receives a copy of Hope's protest and his request for an inquiry, he shakes his head. He writes to Ayliff to cut it short.

An inquiry, he says, "would show the natives that there was disunion amongst us which might lead to further troubles," he writes.

He tells Ayliff he is convinced that the magistrate's arbitrary and injudicious actions were a major cause of the deepening trouble between the government and Moorosi. None of the other magistrates in Basutoland is having similar trouble, he writes.

"I need hardly comment upon the tone of Mr. Hope's letter, which speaks for itself," he adds.

But, even as Bowker hopes for a peaceful future, he learns of a new problem. Twelve fugitives have entered Quthing from Kokstad, where they attempted to burn the magistrate's house and attack the government's ammunition supplies.

Bowker decides that Austen's first action should be to capture these fugitives and place them in jail. He does not want these men to foment strife in Moorosi's territory. He is anxious therefore that Austen proceed quickly to Quthing and assume his new duties.

"It was my intention to have the transfer between yourself and Mr. Hope take effect from the 1st May next," he writes to Austen, "but the present affair being of a serious nature you will at once assume the active duties of the district, leaving Mr. Hope to wind up the affairs of his office.

"From the great distance you will be from this office, I will leave the whole matter in your hands and hope you will soon be able to give a good account of the rebels. It is almost needless for me to add that the prisoners when taken had better be sent direct to Kokstad. I shall inform Letsie and instruct him to send a trusty messenger to accompany you."

Aware that relationships between Hope and Austen are strained and that he has heard that their antagonism is already showing as the duties are transferred, Bowker gives Hope a month's leave of absence from duty so that he will be able to leave Quthing immediately and the two men will not be in the office together.

Aliwal North — Saturday, April 27, 1878

Bowker and Ellenberger might be pleased with the peaceful outcome at Palmietfontein three weeks ago, but the white settlers in the Cape Colony, who view Bowker as weak and an appeaser, are not. Their criticisms are harsh and reflect a fundamental policy difference between the settler community and Bowker.

Most settlers believe in total submission of the indigenous blacks. They seek control, not compromise. Attack, not arbitration. Subjugation, not settlement. That is why they were critical of Griffith when he failed to destroy the Gcaleka rather than chase them off their land. Now similar reasoning lies behind their attack on Bowker.

Their opinions are reflected in an editorial published today in the Aliwal North newspaper, *Northern Post*.

"The first thing that struck us as being strange was that Moorosi should have been allowed to meet Mr. Bowker accompanied by an armed retinue of several hundred men," the editorial says. "This we consider was a blunder of a very serious kind and one that ought not to be allowed to pass over without comment. The circumstances were simple: A son of Moorosi defied his magistrate (Mr. Hope). For weeks, Moorosi openly supported his son and Mr. Hope's life was for several days placed in serious jeopardy, his house being menaced by threatening agents of Moorosi's people.

"When the governor's agent (Mr. Bowker) came upon the scene he dared not proceed as he would have done in times of peace, with a couple of bat-men to Mr. Hope's magistracy, but he came with an army of Basotho, and pitched his camp some distance off, sending an ultimatum to Moorosi that unless he do certain things by a certain day the usual consequences of rebellion would follow.

"Moorosi required he should be allowed to meet Mr. Bowker with an armed demonstration and he was allowed to do so. In the meantime, the whole district of Aliwal North had been turned into a commotion. Burghers were called up, horses purchased and volunteers equipped and an expense of some £10,000 gone to in order to put a sufficient force in the field to support Mr. Bowker and, if necessary, proceed against Moorosi and Tjali who are both under Mr. Hope's jurisdiction and were virtually responsible for the disturbance."

The newspaper quotes from a letter it received from "a gentleman who was on the spot."

"It was a very critical matter," the letter read, "and the least false step might have caused a general rising of the Basotho. Their sympathies were all with Moorosi, whom they believed to be in the right. It is my firm belief that, had we acted differently than what we did, and attempted to take Lehana away, he would have been rescued and we would have been left in the lurch by Letsie's people. They would have run away and not fired a shot on Moorosi's people, and the chances are that everyone of us would have been killed."

The *Northern Post* continues: "How was the difficulty met? It was not met at all. It was evaded. Mr. Bowker fined Lehana — a rebel who had been in arms for weeks — 24 head of cattle! The colony is saddled with expenditure of some £10,000 and this district is left to suffer the losses it sustained through his and Moorosi's conduct without any reparation whatever. This is the surprising result and is most unsatisfactory.

"We ask ourselves why Mr. Bowker acted as he did, and we can only say his conduct seems to us almost inexplicable. But there is a partial explanation which we find in the attitude assumed throughout the matter by the governor's agent. His desire and his hope, he said, were that the 'Basutoland government' be able by itself to deal with and put down the internal troubles arising in that territory. He did not ask for burghers or any assistance from the Cape Colony, although men were moved up in anticipation of being required. He regarded Basutoland as a separate country, with its separate government, and would not be beholden to any other government for assistance, notwithstanding that assistance was sent forward unasked."

But Basutoland is not a separate country, the newspaper says.

"Basutoland forms part of this colony and has only a separate administration for certain specified and particular purposes. There is no such thing as a 'Basutoland government' in the sense of an independent government and it is a vicious misconception to talk of it as such. We do not know how far Mr. Bowker acted under instructions from the head of the colonial government or whether he acted without instructions. Most likely without instructions or, at least, without instructions of a very definite kind. We do not believe that Sir Bartle Frere or Mr. Sprigg would have sanctioned Moorosi being allowed to come to a meeting with the government agent accompanied by an armed following. We do not believe they would have been satisfied — or that they will now be satisfied — with a paltry fine of 24 head of cattle."

The crucial issue, the newspaper adds, is "the evil of allowing or recognizing native chiefs in any way."

"They should be done away with in Basutoland as well as here — not in a spirit of maliciousness but as a matter of high policy. The British government in South Africa cannot permit such petty chieflings as Moorosi and Tjali to threaten to disturb the peace and any overt act of a pretense to exercise the functions of a chief ought to be made punishable. These men ought to be employed as paid servants of the crown, like George Moshesh, if it is thought proper. The government have decided this matter south of the Orange River and their policy, we trust, will not stop short at the banks of the Orange River. If the Basotho will not consent voluntarily they must be made to do so under pressure."

Such views find an echo in the thoughts of Sir Bartle Frere who believes the reason for Moorosi's conduct is not as much the disputes with Hope, which are minor, but the spirit of war that has spread from the Eastern Cape into Basutoland. He remains convinced Moorosi is part of a plan hatched by the black chiefs across South Africa to unite against the settlers and to drive them into the sea.

The answer, Frere continues to believe, is to impose colonial rule across all of the region and to unite the different white-ruled areas in a confederation. The government must not think of shrinking from war because of its costs or because the people are tired of fighting, Frere says in a speech. "You must not cease to fit the front with the men required to keep up the strength till all opposition is effectively put down."

His words are supported by the *Northern Post* which says in an editorial that patriotism can never stand in the way of "teaching the natives that we are the masters now and intend to remain so in the future."

King William's Town — Monday April 29, 1878

On a visit here, Prime Minister Gordon Sprigg has an urgent task to complete before he returns to Cape Town. He walks across the wide street to the barracks to talk to Commandant-General Griffith.

"Have you been reading the reports about the meeting between Bowker and Moorosi?" he asks.

"I have and I must say I find it inconceivable that Bowker allowed Moorosi to attend the meeting fully armed," Griffith replies. "I would not have allowed it."

"Indeed. It seems that the situation was such that war was on the verge of breaking out," says Sprigg. "I can't say I appreciate what Bowker is doing there.

Not only does he arrive some three months later than his date of appointment, but when he arrives there he splits up the two offices you held because, he says, doing both is too much work. He organizes the building of a new house for himself and he moves the offices to what he says are better accommodations in a nearby school-house. He then plunges himself into the affairs relating to Moorosi and comes up with a solution that is nothing short of an appeasement and an embarrassment to the government."

"I am reluctant to criticize Bowker," Griffith says. "But I would have tackled the issue differently. I would have built on Moorosi's good relationship with Letsie to achieve a settlement of the issue that did not cause the government to lose face."

"That is the reason I have come to speak with you," Sprigg says. "I would like you to return to Basutoland and take over the office you vacated last year."

Griffith is taken aback.

"Well, I am not sure that…"

"The salary will be £1,200 a year. You will take over the house that Bowker built. I am sure we can arrange to hire or purchase it from him."

"But my duties here are not finished. We hope that the war against Sandile is drawing to a close, but it continues."

"I understand that the rebellion prevents you from taking over the duties of the office at once," Sprigg responds. "But I do believe that your presence in Basutoland is highly necessary. I would like to know, therefore, whether you are prepared to proceed to Basutoland as soon as the Government desires you to do so."

"Yes," Griffith replies, hesitantly. "Yes, I would be prepared to go."

"Very well. I will put that in writing immediately."

Back in his office, he writes a letter to Griffith: "I have the honor to request that you will at once proceed to Basutoland to relieve Mr. H. Bowker, taking over from him the duties of the office now filled by him, and that you will continue to perform those duties."

Leaving Griffith dazed at the sudden turn of events, Sprigg walks to the temporary office that Ayliff is occupying in a nearby building.

"I have spoken with Commandant-General Griffith and he is willing to proceed to Basutoland as soon as we require his services there," he tells Ayliff. "I think we require him to be there as soon as possible. I leave it to you to inform Colonel Bowker that his services will no longer be required. You might want to allow him to resign rather than face dismissal."

Cape Town — Friday, May 10, 1878

Frere is becoming increasingly frustrated at his lack of progress toward confederation. He has now been in the country for a year and yet, it seems he has done little to advance the policy for which he was sent here.

True, he has annexed some native areas to the Cape Colony and so extended the boundaries of a future confederation. But the region remains in the grip of war fever. To achieve confederation he must do something to permanently end more uprisings in the eastern Cape and thwart plans by black nations in the north and east, including Basutoland, to join forces against the colonial government.

Two actions must be taken to quell black rebellion: The colony's military forces must be strengthened and the native people must be disarmed. Of these, disarmament is the most important — and Frere knows of a model to follow. On Sprigg's arrival in Cape Town, Frere shows him the Irish Disarming Acts, allowing only those with licenses to possess arms, that were passed by the British Parliament. If it worked in Ireland, it would work here, Frere tells him.

Sprigg, agreeing that disarming the native people will go a long way to remove the threat posed to the whites, says he will sponsor the measure's adoption in parliament. So it is that, when he opens the sixth session of the fifth Cape Parliament today, Frere includes a reference in his speech to the bill for the Preservation of Peace in the Colony and the reasons he believes the legislation is necessary.

"A civil war — the outbreak of which unhappily found the defensive resources of the country without organization — has for many months past been raging on the frontier," he tells the assembled members and guests.

He promises that "the rebels will be thoroughly subdued, their power completely broken" and the groundwork for a permanent peace laid. To make sure no similar war starts again, he promises "a measure providing for the better preservation of the peace by the disarming of all persons whom it is not safe or desirable to entrust with arms" will be laid before them.

"Measures will also be submitted for your consideration, having for their object the establishment of an efficient force for the defense of the colony."

His speech receives the required polite applause.

In informal discussion among members, Frere says the intention of the new measure is to disarm all native people in the colony. "Only those who have shown themselves capable of handling weapons responsibly will be licensed to do so," he says. "All others will be given the opportunity to surrender their weapons — firearms as well as spears — peacefully."

In that way, Frere explains, all chance of native rebellions will be ended. Not only would attacks on the colony cease, but inter-tribal warfare would be ended as well. Peace would result and, in its wake, a confederation under white rule could be established.

"In my opinion," he tells members, "guns make natives fancy themselves the equals of Europeans, and this causes war between the two races. Also, if they are not disarmed, they will continue fighting inter-tribal wars.

"As far as this matter is concerned, they are children."

To boost the military, Frere sends four other bills to the House of Assembly, all involving a permanent police presence on the frontier and the introduction of legislation that will ensure proper discipline among the volunteers. The bills are: For the Organization of a Yeomanry (or voluntary) Force; For the Organization of the Inhabitants of the Colony for the purpose of defense; For the better regulation of the Volunteer Service and For the Organization of the Cape Mounted Riflemen.

The measures will be paid for with increased property taxes and excise duties.

From the initial reaction, Frere is satisfied that the disarmament measure will pass. If it does, it promises to open up a whole new dispensation in the confrontation between black and white in South Africa.

Ciskei — Saturday May 11, 1878

In spite of an occasional setback, Thesiger's forces — particularly the colonial troops led by Griffith — have been successful in sweeping the Ngqika rebels from their mountainous hideouts.

The colonial forces' plan now is to seek out and destroy the Ngqika chief Sandile, reported to be surrounded by his followers in the Pirie bush, believing that if he is killed the rebellion will end.

Maseru — Monday May 13, 1878

Bowker asks Rolland to see him in his office.

"I know I have been here for only three months, but my rheumatic problem is recurring and it is time for me to move on," he tells Rolland. "I am wracked with pain and short of breath, which makes me extremely tired, and I am unable to perform my duties in the way that they should be performed."

"But, Colonel Bowker, you have been so effective in this position," Rolland responds. "The way you handled the Maikela affair was outstanding. I thought at any stage that the situation could spill over into violence. And who knows what might have happened had that occurred?"

"Thank you, Mr. Rolland. But I have no choice in the matter. My breathing is becoming constricted, the pain is increasing, and the doctor says I must rest. I am confident that this phase will pass, as others have, but it is imperative that I stop working for at least a few months."

"When will you be leaving?" he asks.

"I am leaving for Leribe today."

"You are leaving Maseru immediately?"

"Yes, I am afraid this attack has come upon me quite suddenly. And I know from previous experience that it will tend to linger for some months.

"In Leribe I will be able to rest and there I will await instructions from the secretary for native affairs, whom I have already told of my intention to leave. I understand they will instruct Colonel Griffith to return to resume his previous office. Apparently he is occupied right now on the eastern frontier, but I am told he should be able to return in about a month.

"In the meantime, I am sure you will be able to continue performing the same duties that you have performed even as I have been in office."

Rolland has developed a respect for Bowker and his compassionate and diplomatic approach.

"I would be pleased," he says, "if before you go, colonel, we could discuss the situation here and perhaps you could give me some insight into how you would have handled it had you stayed."

"Well, the main problem, of course, is Moorosi. But I am convinced that now that Mr. Hope has been moved, Moorosi is likely to quieten down. I do think, however, that a strong police force should be stationed at Palmietfontein. If it is a permanent force it is unlikely to be seen by Moorosi as a threat, but, at the same time, there is nothing like a good reminder of force to concentrate the mind, I always say."

Rolland laughs. "Indeed you are right, colonel. I will try to ensure that such a force is maintained on a permanent basis. Do you have any other concerns?"

"Yes. I believe that the disarmament act — the so-called Peace Preservation Act — being cooked up in the Cape Parliament is worrying. Word has spread here quickly and the local Basotho have spoken to me about it. Letsie was here just yesterday. We discussed it then. I believe he might be forthcoming with a petition against it."

"But will the law be applied to Basutoland?" asks Rolland.

Bowker takes a deep breath and pauses.

"As far as I understand the situation, yes, it will be," he responds, breathing heavily. "Because Basutoland is administered by the Cape Colony I assume it will be applicable here."

"I agree that it could cause trouble," Rolland responds.

Bowker's breathing becomes easier as he continues. "As you know, I enlisted the help of Lerothodi in confronting Moorosi. I think the presence of 500 of Lerothodi's men at Palmietfontein was extremely helpful in persuading Moorosi to yield. I believe that we can effectively pit one group against the other and, in that way, keep the peace here in Basutoland. And, at the same time, we can gradually increase our control here — with the emphasis, I might add, on gradual."

Rolland understands. "And disarmament will not be helpful in keeping the peace, no matter how gradually we move."

"It certainly will not, Mr. Rolland. And that is what Letsie told me. He asked how effective Lerothodi's people would have been in helping me against Moorosi if they were not armed."

"What did you tell him?"

"I told him that disarmament will not be applied here as long as he is being called upon to fight the Queen's enemies," Bowker says.

"You told him their arms will not be taken away?"

"I told him I *thought* they would not be taken away. Obviously I cannot give any promises. It is up to the government. But I think the authorities would be foolish to implement the law here."

"Have you told the government of your views?"

"Not yet," Bowker responds. "The measure has not been passed and we do not know whether it will be implemented in Basutoland. But if they do ask I will tell them I am dead against disarming friendly tribes. I believe that if you put that law into operation in Basutoland you would at once have 20,000 men against you. I have no doubt about that. The feelings here are bitter about this new measure."

Rolland is surprised at the strength of Bowker's conviction. He notes, too, that Bowker seems to be breathing normally as he becomes more vigorous in his argument against the disarmament law.

"What about Moorosi?" Rolland asks.

"I am sure that once word reaches him — if it has not done so already — he will believe that he will be the first to fall under the act. He is a very turbulent character and he was insistent, you will recall, that he would meet with me only if he and his followers were allowed to be armed.

"Also, Mr. Hope had many altercations with him over the question of arms. The chief was angry because Mr. Hope told him he could not take arms to a pitso. But with this legislation we are not talking about simply having no arms at a pitso; we are talking about the people having no arms at all at any time.

"I believe that the passage of the act in itself, even before any action is taken, will be a cause of great dissatisfaction in Moorosi's territory and also in Basutoland generally. Already, merely a discussion of it is causing trouble."

Bowker tells Rolland that when he came to Basutoland 10 years ago the Basotho people had been thoroughly beaten by the Boers and were only too glad to accept British protection.

"When I returned here a little more than three months ago, little had changed," he continues. "They were willing to do anything I wished. The one exception was Moorosi. Others, such as Tsekelo and Masupha, are now starting to become troublesome, but I am not worried about them; they have no following among the people. But Moorosi does."

"I think they showed their willingness to do what you asked when you asked for their help in the meeting with Chief Moorosi," says Rolland.

"Yes. I had the full support of Letsie. He would have accompanied me to Palmietfontein himself and not just sent Lerothodi if I had asked him to do so."

"But Chief Moorosi is resisting Letsie, is he not?"

"Not any longer, as far as I can tell. Or, at least, not entirely. He has always looked up to Letsie as his leader. When I arrived here in March as the Maikela affair was developing I believe Moorosi was on the verge of open rebellion. He was then preparing to resist the authority of Letsie. That is why I called on Letsie for help. I thought the best plan was to get Letsie on my side.

"I can tell you now that I thought I would not get through that meeting at Palmietfontein without a fight. But at the same time I was determined to avoid it if I could and I therefore gave Moorosi every chance of agreeing to my terms. If he started a fight, I would show that the blame lay with him and I would have been supported by the rest of the country."

"Some say Letsie is moving in Moorosi's direction," says Rolland.

"I don't believe that," responds Bowker. The only problem is the matter of disarmament. I think if the government tries to impose disarmament here, you would have trouble. But from no other cause."

"So your belief is that the only ill will here is the threatened disarmament?"

"Entirely. Nothing else. I think the Basotho are a wonderful people. They are willing to pay their hut taxes, although they do complain that the money goes to building roads and conducting wars in the colony and is not used in Basutoland.

"Also, they work hard in their fields, feed themselves quite effectively and give less trouble than any other nation I know of. But I think disarmament would affect the loyalty of all the people. It could even bring on a general war.

"If you ask me, the application of disarmament to Basutoland would be insanity. The only way you could apply it would be with six regiments. And then the people would retire into the mountains. There are many fortresses, as you know, similar to the one Moorosi has in the mountains in Quthing."

"So you think that to forcibly disarm them would be a greater evil than to allow them to possess their arms?"

"Decidedly. It is moral castration. If it is applied across the whole country it will unite every black face in South Africa against us. The impact would be as strong here in Basutoland as anywhere else, and with Moorosi the strongest of all. I had thought that, with Mr. Hope out of the way, we could have peace with Moorosi. But, if this law is implemented in Basutoland, we will have trouble.

"The authorities seem to think they know best. They will dismiss me — and my views — as irrelevant. So be it."

Cape Town — Wednesday May 15, 1878

Introducing the second reading in Parliament of the Peace Preservation Bill, which most commentators call the "disarmament measure," the attorney general, Thomas Upington, removes any pretence that the measure will be fair to all races. "In no ordinary instance would that license be refused to white people," he says.

"Native persons might also come to apply for licenses, but the magistrates would have the strictest instructions not to grant such licenses, except under special circumstances."

Upington explains that the law is based extensively on the Irish Arms Act, which obliged gun owners to license their firearms.

The second reading of the bill is approved. It will now go into committee where adjustments will be made before it is sent to a third reading for approval.

Quthing — Thursday May 23, 1878

Austen is satisfied that his work in the Quthing magistracy is off to a successful start. The rebels from East Griqualand have been tracked down by Sub-Inspector O'Connor and, with the help of local police, they have been sent off to Kokstad.

The victory, however, does not impress Hope, who — even though he was placed on a month's leave of absence by Bowker two weeks ago — remains in the office, continuing to wrap up his affairs.

"You received more help in that one mission than I ever received in the entire time I was here," he complains. "They never gave me that sort of help in tracking down rebels, even though I requested it."

"I am sure they would have given it to you, too," Austen replies. "These rebels were from outside the Quthing area and so we needed help from outside."

"Hmph."

The men do not exchange words often; their dislike for one another is palpable. Austen wishes with each passing day that Hope would leave. But Hope is trying to put his paperwork in at least some sort of order. He reluctantly admits how slack he was in organizing the office, but reminds himself that he was busy on other duties.

Three days ago, Hope came across vouchers for £128 spent on the construction of the offices and court room nine months ago. He realizes that he should have sent them to Griffith when the work was completed. Today he realizes that he spent £35 and 5 shillings of his own money on the construction and never claimed it back.

He sends the vouchers and the claims to Rolland. Better late than never.

Ciskei — Friday, June 7, 1878

Making his way along the mountains on a regular patrol, Granville is the first soldier to see the body. It lies behind a large rock where it has clearly been for some time as the left side of the face and right arm have been eaten away by animals. Granville walks back down the mountain slope to Griffith, who is leading the patrol, telling him of his find.

"Our troops were here a little more than a week ago, on May 29, when we confronted a group of rebels," Griffith says, as he walks toward the rock behind which Granville saw the body. "Our count was that we killed 26 in that skirmish and seriously wounded a number of others. I suppose this man crept behind the rock during the fighting and died from his wounds."

Griffith reaches the rock. He gasps as he sees the body.

"This is the body of Sandile," he says. "I am sure of it." That beard and strong handsome features could only be those of the Ngqika leader.

In the past few weeks, Sandile had been trying to make peace with the authorities. But the government had refused his offer, insisting on unconditional surrender. Now this.

King William's Town — Saturday June 8, 1878

On hearing that the body has been positively identified as that of Sandile, the commanding officer, Thesiger, telegraphs Frere in Cape Town saying he is "of the opinion this war may now be considered virtually at an end."

Frere declares an amnesty for Ngqika rebels who wish to surrender, allowing them to return to their homes.

The rebellion in the Ciskei has collapsed.

To prevent an uprising such as that of the Ngqika from occurring again Colonel Samuel P. Jarvis, stationed in King William's Town, has been appointed the first commandant-general of a newly created Defense Department, which organizes the military forces into a single organization along the lines that Frere had proposed. Jarvis oversees the new Cape Mounted Riflemen, reorganized as a military unit from the Frontier Armed and Mounted Police, which will be disbanded.

Granville, Scott and Brown, along with most other members of the Frontier Armed and Mounted Police, are assigned positions with the new Cape Mounted Riflemen and ordered to duty at Ibika.

Quthing — Tuesday June 11, 1878

Ready to leave, Hope looks out on the valley, brown from the dry winter.

He will miss the area. He will, believe it or not, miss the people, too. Although the position was a lonely one, it was challenging. If only the government had supported him more, he would have been able to achieve much more.

He is sorry Mimmie could not have spent time with him here.

He loads his wagon and harnesses the oxen. He must not look back. What he has done, he has done. What has happened has happened. Now he must look forward to a new post, new people and, inevitably perhaps, new problems. But he is determined to face them with the same fortitude and resilience with which he faced the problems that Moorosi presented.

Cape Town — Friday, August 2, 1878

After debating the Bill "for the better Preservation of Peace within the Colony" the legislature is ready today to vote on it. The bill as amended, says that the governor (Frere), with the advice of the executive (led by Sprigg), may proclaim areas "within which it shall not be lawful to possess arms or ammunition without a license." Government officials, its military and police are exempt. The governor also may authorize "certain persons" to grant licenses to "proper persons" to possess arms and ammunition and to license arms dealers.

The Bill provides for a fine of £500, more than a year's earnings for many, and imprisonment and seven years' hard labor for offenders.

Following suggestions from members of the opposition in the committee debate, no racial groups are mentioned in the legislation. But members know whites will be given licenses and blacks will not. Disarm the natives and they will be unable to fight any prolonged war. The law will, as its name implies, preserve the peace within the colony — peace meaning the inability of the black people to defend themselves against the white authorities.

After a brief debate, members — anxious to return home after a long session — approve the Bill. In a few days Frere will approve it and the disarmament measure will become law.

Maseru — Wednesday, August 14, 1878

Is it something in the Quthing air? Rolland asks himself as he goes over the requests made by Austen in the past six weeks. They sound similar to those Hope made while he was in office there.

Although everything appears peaceful, Austen has requested an increase in the detachment of police and money to improve the buildings.

Rolland writes to tell Austen that these matters "must be left in abeyance until the arrival of Mr. Griffith in Maseru."

Rolland approves a request by Maitin — who had been instructed to leave Quthing and take up a position in the north of Basutoland — to remain in Quthing as justice of the peace. Rolland wonders what the attraction is, but he approves the request, adding that a final decision should await Griffith's return.

Quthing — Monday, September 16, 1878

MaLebenya, a regular visitor at the magisterial compound at Quthing, has become a Christian after attending services at one of Ellenberger's outstations and has tried to adopt much of the colonial way of life. She respects and admires the men who run the government and none of them more than Maitin, with whom she regularly visits.

Today MaLebenya is here again, telling Maitin that reports are circulating among the Baphuthi that sheep and goats in Lehana's village have been seized and slaughtered by those living outside the village.

"Here is what I have heard," she says. "Five months ago, when King Moorosi and Mr. Bowker were meeting with the Rev. Ellenberger at Masitise, three of Lehana's followers — including Dethlama and Thaba, who are both Moorosi's sons, but from different wives — rode into the Cape Colony where they stole horses, sheep and goats. They knew that the white government authorities were with Mr. Bowker at Masitise and so they thought they would not be apprehended.

"Before they could return, the men were arrested in the colony for stock theft, were tried and were sent to jail in Aliwal North. But they escaped from the jail."

"Yes, we are aware of that," Maitin replies. "Mr. Austen sent a message to the chiefs to look out for them. But we have received no reports that they returned to Quthing."

"Well they did and are living with other men in caves near Lehana's village,"

MaLebenya continues. "Now these men have angered other Baphuthi because they have stolen sheep and goats from the people in the nearby village and are slaughtering and eating them. I know this because the men have been talking with their wives and friends who have given them cooking utensils and places to sleep. They have told us not to say where the men are hiding, but I am telling you because I think they must be arrested. They have done wrong and are still doing wrong in stealing other people's animals."

"So," says Maitin. "These people not only are sheltering the escaped prisoners, but also are thieves who have robbed sheep and goats from their own villagers. They are as guilty as the escaped prisoners themselves."

"That is right," MaLebenya says.

Maitin thanks her for the information.

"Keep me in touch if you hear any more," he says. He wants to add, "And even if you don't hear anymore," but he resists the temptation.

Maitin tells Austen of his conversation.

"We need to take action immediately," Austen says. "But I do not think we should send out our policemen to arrest them. The area in which they are hiding has a labyrinth of caves and it will not be easy for a small group of policemen to track them down and capture them."

"How do we bring them to justice then?" Maitin asks.

Austen bears in mind warnings from Bowker to be diplomatic with the Baphuthi. He knows that a major source of friction between Moorosi and Hope was the authority of the chief and that Hope would deliberately withhold Moorosi from any decision making.

"I think this case is one in which we need to involve Moorosi," he tells Maitin. "After all, Moorosi does not condone stock theft and they deliberately acted while they knew Moorosi was occupied at Masitise. So they were trying to deceive Moorosi, too.

"By enlisting the help of Moorosi in capturing these people I will not only achieve my aim of arresting the stock thieves, but I will also keep Moorosi content that he is involved in the running of the territory."

He summons a policeman.

"I want you to go to Chief Moorosi," he says. "Tell him that I request him to bring about the capture of these thieves — Dethlama and Thaba as well as the others who are helping them — for trial. Tell him I know that he does not want the property of innocent people to be injured."

Austen decides to use the strong family ties among the Baphuthi to his advantage.

"Tell Chief Moorosi, too, he is to put pressure on the thieves by seizing the stock that belongs to these men's parents and friends. The stock will be kept in security until the thieves are caught. In that way, their parents will tell their sons to cooperate with the law.

"He has a week to carry out my instructions. If I find he is acting promptly and taking steps toward resolving this situation, I will extend that week, but if not then I will take the matter into my own hands."

Austen wants to avoid this incident flaring up into a contest of authority with Moorosi, as so often happened with Hope.

Quthing — Friday, September 20, 1878

Moorosi, sitting outside his hut on the top of his mountain fortress to the north of the magistracy, scans the sky, as he does each morning, for an indication of the weather headed his way. Off to the west, fluffy gray clouds move slowly toward his redoubt. They hold a hint of rain, but one that might not be realized.

It has been more than a year, perhaps even two years now, that the rain has been insufficient for their crops. Here, on the mountain, they have stored food, but the supplies are not plentiful. The lower leaves on this year's corn plants are brown and many are not growing strongly. Already, some of the Baphuthi people are on meager rations and, if the crops do not grow, many more will follow.

"Lemena, come over here and sit with me," he says. "What can you tell me about the drought?" Moorosi asks. "I am now an old man. I have seen many harvests. I have seen many droughts. But I have never seen a drought as bad as this one.

"Lemena, when will the rains come?"

"Perhaps they will come only when the colonial government goes away from here," replies Lemena. "They brought the drought with them."

"You are right, Lemena. Look at how brown the grass is."

The brownness of the long grass, heightened by the contrast with the green shrubs alongside creeks in the valleys, is unusual for spring. By now rain should have transformed it into a sea of light green. The men gaze down at the Orange River as it flows slowly past the mountain. It seems tired and forlorn, as if also suffering from a lack of sustenance. Beyond it, the valleys, normally lush with the first hints of summer's grain and vegetable crops, appear singed. They look morose and sullen.

For the men, it is a physical portrait of colonial rule.

"They sent a magistrate here who said he would show us how to live better lives, who told us we did not know what we were doing," Moorosi continues. "He said his way was better. But, I ask you Lemena, you who know the white man's ways, is it really better?

"Is it really better when they want to put us in jail and flog us for doing things that they think are wrong but we know are right? Or for doing things they think are right but we know are wrong?

"Is it really better when they make it clear that they want to take away our land and turn it into farms for the white settlers as they have done in the south? Is it really better when they tell us we must follow their customs and not our own? Are they happier than we are? Are their families stronger than ours?

"Is it really better when the result is a tearing apart of our people, a fighting between the new ways and the old ways?

"Is it really better when the worst drought we have ever known moves across the country like a thousand ravenous antelopes?"

"No, king, it is not," says Lemena.

"Now I hear from messengers from the chiefs at Thaba Bosigo that the white men want to take away our weapons from us. They want to make it so that we cannot fight back against what we know to be wrong. We must not allow that to happen. We must fight to keep our weapons.

"They are destroying our ways. They are not helping us with our crops now the rains have stopped. Now they want to destroy our ability to defend ourselves."

"Do you think the new magistrate is better than the old one?" asks Lemena.

"I am not sure whether he will be better," the chief replies. "We will have to see. He did say that the widows need not pay the hut tax. So perhaps he will be better. Perhaps he will be more like Bowker than like Hope.

"But I am afraid of what the big power to the south wants to do; they are more powerful than Austen. I am afraid that they want to take our land from us, as they did with Sarhili and others who have resisted them.

"When they have taken away our land they will put up fences and white men's houses as they are doing on the Gcaleka land. The land will no longer belong to our people, it will belong to individual white people. One man will own the same amount of land that can provide food for 50 of our people. He will get many more crops than can feed him and he will sell them for money. We will be left with nothing. They will destroy our crops and plant their own. We will have to work for them and we will have to follow their laws. Our people will be broken.

"I am old and I will have to suffer for only a short time if that happens. But you are young and many of my people are young. What hope is there for them if the white government comes and takes away everything they have? What help is it to them if they are protected from their enemies but are not protected from the people who say they are their protectors?"

As Moorosi looks down at the ground, Lemena slowly rises and walks toward the highest point on the flat-topped mountain. He looks down again at the scene below, casting his eyes north and south. He wonders how it will be if the valleys were to be filled with white farms, with the Baphuthi people working on them, forced to do the white farmer's bidding every day of the year, while the white farmer sits back and becomes fat and lazy.

Lemena knows from his travels to Kimberley that that is what happens when the white man takes over the land. He has seen children being taken and forced to work like slaves for white farmers.

The images tumble through his mind. He does not like what they portend.

Lemena swings around and walks back to Moorosi.

"We must stop them," he says. "We must resist the colonial authorities and their rule. We are better without them."

"But how can we do that?" asks Moorosi. "They beat Sarhili, chased him out of his land. And now we hear they killed Sandile, too. Those chiefs were working together. Now they are defeated."

"We will not be defeated," Lemena replies. "We can be as powerful as the white soldiers are. Our people can shoot well, better than Sarhili and Sandile's people and even better than the white people."

Lemena is interrupted when a messenger from Austen appears on the path.

"I have a message from the magistrate," he says.

As the messenger outlines Austen's request to apprehend the men responsible for stock theft, Moorosi ponders his position.

He asks the messenger to walk away, out of earshot, and he turns to Lemena.

"What is your advice on this matter?" he asks.

"I do not think we should help the magistrate at all."

Moorosi shakes his head.

"We must be wise. If we let him have the stock thieves he talks about, he will be quiet and not go after my son Lehana and all the others living in the caves. They will be free to continue their plans to help us resist the government. We must be willing to compromise. We must give up a little to gain a lot. That is what the missionary told me. Perhaps we must give up these men to gain more."

He does not wait for Lemena to comment, but calls to the messenger.

"Tell the magistrate he must leave it to me," he says. "I will take the action that is needed."

Quthing — Saturday, September 21, 1878

Austen is pleased to hear that Moorosi will help apprehend the stock thieves, but in the last few days he has concluded the stock theft is a symptom of a deeper problem.

He outlines his conclusions to Maitin.

"I have pieced together reports from informants on the stock thefts committed while Lehana and his men were holed up in caves. From them, I have built a picture of about 30 men, led by Lehana, three of whom are the prisoners who escaped from the jail at Aliwal North, who are living in caves in the mountains on meat from stock stolen from the villagers and are said to be plotting to eject the government from Quthing.

"Their original plans were to entice government troops to cross the Telle and confront them in a battle. They were confident they could win and send the troops fleeing back across the border, at which time they would oust the magistrate and his staff from the territory. Their plans were thwarted, however, at the meeting with Bowker when Moorosi agreed to hand over Lehana for sentencing.

"But I fear their sentiment remains intact. They might not have exactly the same plans now, but I believe they are determined to resist the colonial presence here in every way they can.

"Any incident, no matter how trivial, that involves an intrusion of colonial rule provides them with an excuse to rebel.

"I am convinced the young tyrant Lehana is trying to mislead his father. The old chief Moorosi has seen the danger that could arise in an all-out battle and is anxious to avoid that. Lehana wants to fight; Moorosi is afraid of an all-out battle.

"The immediate task facing me now is to see that the two men accused of stealing sheep and goats from Lehana's village are brought to justice. After that I can take steps to act against those who stole stock across the border and thereby get at the heart of the rebellious group."

Natal Colony — Monday, September 23, 1878

With the Eastern Frontier and Basutoland outwardly calm, Frere is ready to deal with the next threat to confederation. He is today in Pietermaritzburg, the capital of Natal, where he is being received by Sir Henry Bulwer, the lieutenant-governor of the crown colony.

Frere is convinced the powerful Zulu king Cetshwayo plays a key role in the plot to combine black forces against the colonists and to drive them into the sea.

Frere sees Cetshwayo as fundamentally aggressive, unstable and unpredictable. He is convinced that Cetshwayo encouraged black rebellions in the Transkei and he could decide to attack the colonists in Natal at any time.

In addition, the confederation cannot be formed with the unpredictable Cetshwayo in power, Frere believes. Zululand, which abuts the Natal colony, must be under white control.

But not all the Natal colonists agree with Frere. Bulwer, who has been trying to smooth over the disturbed relations with the Zulu king for two years, believes Cetshwayo, handled properly, will back down and that his actions are mainly defensive.

Over the objections of Bulwer, Frere has called for reinforcements for the British troops in Natal, has moved troops from the Eastern Frontier into the colony, and has sent detachments toward the Zulu frontier.

Frere has demanded that Cetshwayo break up the *amabutho* system, a form of conscription, under which young Zulus serve as soldiers under the king. Frere also has demanded that Cetshwayo leave his kraal and accept a British residence as his homestead.

As Frere feared, the king has refused to comply with either request. Frere concludes that the Zulu military machine can be dismantled only with force and this time he will use British, not colonial troops, to do so. He believes they are better trained and more motivated than the colonial forces. The British, he is convinced, know how to wage war.

For more than five months, General Thesiger has been in Natal, planning the attack on Cetshwayo on Frere's orders. He knows it will be a graver undertaking than the wars in the Transkei and the Ciskei.

"If we are to have a fight with the Zulus," Thesiger says, "I am anxious that our arrangements should be as complete as possible to make them.

"Half measures do not work with natives. They must be thoroughly crushed to make them believe in our superiority."

Quthing — Wednesday, September 25, 1878

Austen is pleased when Dethlama and Thaba, prompted by Moorosi, answer the summons and report for trial on stock theft.

When tried by Austen, the men confess their guilt.

He sentences each to six months' imprisonment with hard labor and they are placed in the lock-up built by Hope.

But Austen's task is not yet done. The testimony at the trial confirmed his belief that the men did not act alone. He is convinced Lehana was behind the stock thefts and the two men who appeared before him for trial are, in effect, sacrificial lambs. Austen needs to apprehend and convict Lehana to remove the person most responsible for the turmoil among the Baphuthi people. With Lehana out of the way, Moorosi will be more conciliatory.

This is Austen's big chance to expand the colonial presence and maintain peace.

Having gained Moorosi's cooperation in the case against Dethlama and Thaba, he will enlist his support once more. He sends a message to the Baphuthi king, telling him that the king needs to ensure that his son Lehana and a grandson, Thladi, appear before him on a charge of stock theft.

Maseru — Friday October 11, 1878

As Griffith settles into his Maseru office once more, Rolland attends a gathering of 27 Basotho chiefs who present him with a statement that they would like him to translate and deliver.

It is addressed to Griffith and reads:

"Our hearts are filled with a wonderful gladness at hearing of your arrival in Basutoland and we ask you to receive herewith our greetings with which we welcome your coming into this territory.

"This day we are in truth satisfied that the Queen does indeed love the Basotho people, since she has once more yielded you back to us, you whom we know to be greatly regarded by the colony!

"Our hearts were wrung and died within us on the day that you departed from our land, when we heard that you had gone away for good; but today we are comforted by consolations which have filled our hearts with rejoicing; sorrow has come to an end now that you have been given back to us.

"Today the country breaks out into gladness because of its blessedness; we shall sow our corn, we shall progress in the knowledge of the laws, we shall sleep sweetly now that he whom we call 'Chief,' 'Father,' 'Mother,' is once more brooding over us. Rain!

"Oh! Our master, our joy is one that cannot be told, our hearts are overflowing, but we will not say many things, we wish to show our love by our deeds!

"We give thanks, 'Darling of the Warriors,' that you have returned among us covered with the fame of fresh deeds of valor, and it is with self-glorifying hearts that we sing the praises of our Hero. Your praises are the glory of us your children, and all give thanks for the protection with which God has shielded you from danger.

"May the Lord bless you, Sir, you and your family; and grant you many years in this land and may the Basotho nation learn through you to honor and love the law.

"God save the Queen!

"God save the 'Darling of the Warriors!'

"We salute you our honored Chief, may God pour upon you endless blessings. We are your subjects and children."

Maseru — Wednesday, October 16, 1878

Today Griffith, after spending a week organizing his office, addresses a challenge from his own government which he fears will render his second term of office in Maseru radically different from the first.

Awaiting him is a letter from the Prime Minister, Gordon Sprigg, written from King William's Town.

"The disarmament, as you are probably aware, is proceeding very successfully from the sea right up to (the area known as) Wodehouse," Sprigg writes. "Levey is now having a meeting with his people on the subject. Blyth had a meeting with the Mfengu on Wednesday, and they expressed their willingness to give up their arms whenever required and in the course of the month the thing will be done. The natives in the Idutywe Reserve will be disarmed at the same time.

"I want you now to commence with the Basotho. Assemble the leading men and acquaint them with the native policy of the present government, which I believe you thoroughly understand to be a government ruling over a barbarous people in the proper sense of the word.

"Tell them that they are not to be allowed to arm themselves and everybody else, but that our superior intelligence is to be beneficially exercised on their behalf, that they are to be held in hand and guided and trained with the view of raising them out of barbarism into civilization.

"Tell them that the proof of manhood is not the possession of a gun, but the capacity to observe and maintain order and to assist in advancing the moral and material prosperity of the community. The guns after delivery will be valued and each man will receive compensation — and an assurance that the government recognizes its duty to protect the people from oppression and will perform that duty.

"If you report to me that the people are willing to submit to the orders of the government in this respect then a day or days can be appointed for the delivery of the arms, spears, etc...

"If you find any unwillingness on the part of the Basotho you will oblige me by informing them that the government are resolute in the matter and are determined to carry it out, but I prefer doing it with the consent of the people.

"I suppose you may experience some difficulty with Moorosi, but you will know how to deal with him. If he is obstinate and you require a force to overcome him it shall be supplied. After the bulk of the natives in the several frontier districts is disarmed the Peace Preservation Act will be proclaimed making it illegal to carry a gun without a license and when that is done I shall feel somewhat more easy than I do at present."

Griffith does not like what he reads. He is an obedient soldier and administrator and will do what his government says. But he is fearful of the reaction of the Basotho and Baphuthi people. He finds a way to stall Sprigg by resorting to the letter of the law, a favorite resource.

He writes back:

"Your note of the 5th October in re disarming the Basotho has just reached me and of course your orders will be obeyed whatever they are. I wish, however, to point out to you that by Act No. 12 of 1871 — The Basutoland Annexation Act: Section II — it is provided that no act passed by the colonial parliament shall extend or be deemed to extend to this territory unless such act shall be extended thereto in express words contained therein or in some other Act of Parliament or unless the operation thereof shall be extended to such territory by the Governor by a proclamation.

"Under these circumstances the disarming act does not at present apply to this territory and cannot legally be put in force here."

Realizing that the government will surely have its way and extend the measure to Basutoland anyway, Griffith ponders the rest of Sprigg's letter. He is afraid that the measure's effect will be disastrous, in other parts of the country as well as in Basutoland. In the eastern Cape the law was applied first to the Mfengu because of their cooperation with the whites. In spite of what Sprigg says, Griffith knows the Mfengu handed over their arms in a spirit of bitter discontent. After all, they argued, they had fought for the white government against Sarhili and Sandile. Now their reward was to hand over their arms. It did not make sense.

Griffith knows, too, that a similar situation exists in Basutoland where Letsie and his son Lerothodi have cooperated with the government against less cooperative clans, including Moorosi and his Baphuthi.

Griffith also is amazed that Sprigg cavalierly promises to back Griffith with a force to overawe Moorosi. From where will the force come? Will the government be willing to pay for it?

So Griffith continues his letter by telling Sprigg that he has not the slightest doubt that Moorosi will refuse to give up his arms and will resist any attempt to take them.

As for the show of force, Griffith suggests that at least two seven-pounder mountain guns with ammunition and two armed rocket tubes should be "collected quietly at Palmietfontein and arrangements made for provisioning a sufficiently strong force at the same place when it becomes necessary to enforce the law." The purpose, Griffith suggests, would be to intimidate Moorosi before moving in to disarm his people.

Griffith trusts that, although Sprigg tends to be lacking in understanding the subtleties of human behavior, he will get the point — it is easy to fling around phrases like "overcome" the chief without considering how large a force would be required to do so.

Before continuing the letter, Griffith asks Rolland what he thinks of Sprigg's order to disarm the Basotho people and apparently start with Moorosi.

"I do not think it is a good idea," Rolland responds, recalling his conversation with Bowker. "Moorosi will oppose it in every way he can. So, I suspect, will Chief Masupha. The others might go along with it, but they will do so with reluctance."

"I agree, but given that the government intends to do this, don't you think we should prepare the people for it?" Griffith replies. "I was thinking that we should summon all the Basutoland magistrates here and tell them about it. A good time will be at the pitso that we have planned for next Thursday. We can inform the ordinary people as well as the magistrates what the government proposes.

"A time has not yet been set for the disarmament. So, in the meantime, if we get them used to the idea and say it is coming some time in the future they will less aggressively oppose it than if we suddenly announce one day that they are to hand over their arms to us. It will at least help to pave the way, although I am sure they will still oppose it."

"A good idea," replies Rolland. "We can also get their reaction to the proposal so that we have some idea what to expect."

"Yes. In addition to the pitso, I think we should have Mr. Austen let Moorosi know about it and gauge his reaction to it."

Griffith takes up his letter to Sprigg once more, tells him about the plan to announce the disarmament plans at the pitso and adds: "The only way to prevent any resistance is to show a bold front and to have a sufficient force to put down at once any attempt at resistance." The meaning behind Griffith's diplomatic words are clear: You have been warned, Mr. Prime Minister, there will be trouble if you try to impose this measure in Basutoland.

He hopes Sprigg will grasp the meaning behind his words.

London — Thursday, October 17, 1878

The Conservative-led British Home Government tends to side with Natal lieutenant governor Sir Henry Bulwer's contention that the Zulu are not the warmongers that Frere believes they are. In a reply to Frere's request for British reinforcements to attack the Zulu, Colonial Secretary Sir Michael Hicks-Beach writes:

"Her Majesty's Government are not prepared to comply with the request for a reinforcement of troops. All the information that has hitherto reached them with respect of the position of affairs in Zululand appears to them to justify a confident

hope that by the exercise of prudence, and by meeting the Zulus in a spirit of forbearance and a reasonable compromise, it will be possible to avert the very serious
evil of a war with Cetshwayo; and they cannot but think that the forces now at
your disposal in South Africa, together with the additional officers about to be
sent, should suffice to meet any other emergency that might arise, without a further
increase to the imperial troops."

The letter will anger Frere, however, who is convinced the British government
has no idea of how serious the threat posed by Cetshwayo really is.

Maseru — Thursday, October 24, 1878

Thousands have gathered for Griffith's pitso, the first since his return. Four
resident magistrates from the area around Maseru are here, as are several missionaries belonging to the French Protestant Missionary Society and the recently arrived Roman Catholic Mission. Traders and several white investors in the country
are there. Once again, Letsie, the paramount chief, is absent, but the next in rank,
Chief Masupha, is there. Also among those who are absent is Moorosi, although
there are those among the crowd who will report to him everything that is said.

The leaders of Basutoland are here today because they have been told that
Griffith has important issues to raise at the meeting.

Griffith is the first to speak. He begins with warm greetings and apologizes for
having left the previous year without having said goodbye.

He reports that "after several months' fighting the Gcaleka have been driven
out of their country and all their cattle taken, hundreds of the people killed, also
many of the chiefs killed and taken prisoner and their chief Sarhili is now hiding
himself away like a wolf. The Ngqika have shared the same fate, only in a worse
degree; their old Chief Sandile and many other chiefs have been killed."

After describing the destruction and suffering, he adds: "From all I have told
you I hope you will learn a lesson and see what the result of rebellion is. The Gcaleka
and Ngqika were living in much the same way as you are. No one bothered them
or interfered with them and yet they were not satisfied. The chiefs listened to bad
advisers, and thus brought themselves and their people to destruction. And thus
will it ever be with people who rebel against the just and mild rule of the Queen.

"During the time that I was away from this country, I heard of the unsettled
state of the Baphuthi and the proceedings of Moorosi and his son Lehana, which
news astonished me very much, as when I left the country I thought all the chiefs
and people in the country were loyal subjects of the Queen, but when I heard
that Moorosi and the Baphuthi came to meet Mr. Bowker at Phathlalla Drift all
armed with guns and spears, as if they were going to meet an enemy, my astonish-
ment knew no bounds and to this day I cannot understand what Moorosi and the
Baphuthi meant by such conduct."

Up to this point, Griffith's message is clear: Opposing the government does
not pay. Those who rebelled in the eastern Cape had their country seized and their

people killed. And bearing arms to confront the government, as Moorosi did, is not a good idea.

Having laid the groundwork, Griffith moves to the major issue: disarmament.

Griffith explains that the government will call on the people to disarm. His listeners understand that, in this context, "people" means black people and that it means them. The mood of the crowd perceptibly changes. The Basotho listen attentively as Griffith says that the Thembu, the Mfengu "and all other tribes in the colony and under British rule will have to do so."

Many, he adds, have shown their loyalty by giving up their arms at once.

"This policy has been adopted by the government because it wishes the country to be at peace," he says. "The government says the people have no use for guns as there is no game in the country to shoot, that if they are allowed to keep their guns they will only fight with each other. The government will protect everyone.

"I mention these matters to you today because you Basotho will also be called upon to give up your arms and I hope you will all do so willingly; and you will suffer no loss by doing so, as it is the intention of the government to pay you the value of your guns."

The Basotho raise issues relating to the power of the chiefs and the imposition of colonial norms on their daily living, but they have little to say on the issue of disarmament, largely because they have just heard about the Peace Preservation Act. Few are willing to discuss it now. They need time to consider it and want first to discuss it with family and friends. But those who do respond to Griffith's announcement on disarmament reluctantly accept it. After all, it comes from their white "father" whom they so greatly respect. Says government-supporter Sofonia Moshesh, "Though we may be called upon to make a painful sacrifice like Abraham, we can do it. We will find it bitter; but what the government sees fit to do must be right."

Still, the concession comes more from a desire to be polite and avoid confrontation rather than agreement. Clearly Moshesh does not like the idea. The disarmament issue is likely to be the one to ignite anti-government feelings in the months ahead, particularly among the Baphuthi, who are not represented at the pitso, but who will soon hear about it.

Masitise — Friday, November 1, 1878

Moorosi climbs the winding stone staircase to the cave house and asks Emma Ellenberger whether her husband is there. She tells him he is in the new church he is building. Moorosi finds him there.

"I have heard that Mr. Griffith held a pitso and he said there that the government is to force our people to give up their arms," he tells Ellenberger. "No longer will we be able to own rifles, let alone carry them. Even spears will be forbidden.

"The white authorities and their allies, the police, will be armed. I and my people will be left like bulls without horns. When the government wishes to impose its will on us it will be able to do so with force and we will not have the ability to fight back."

Ellenberger reassures Moorosi that, according to his information, the law has not yet been imposed in Basutoland, even though it has been passed by the Parliament in Cape Town.

"But Mr. Griffith says that it will be imposed on us."

Ellenberger speaks quietly, reassuringly. "My missionary colleagues and I are opposed to this measure," he says. "We are sending a message to the government in Cape Town that we think they should not impose this law on the people of Basutoland.

"So do not take any action now that you might regret later. Do not try to fight the authorities on this. We are doing what we can to stop them. We cannot stop the law, but we can ask them not to impose it on this country."

Moorosi sits for a while and thinks.

"What you say is good," he replies. "You can talk to the white people for us because you know what we think. They will listen to you even though they do not listen to us. I hope that now you can help us with this bad law. It will destroy us as a people, it will take away all my power as a chief and it will mean we will have to obey the white people's laws whether they are just or not."

Ellenberger holds up his hand.

"You must not seek to fight against the white authorities with your weapons," he says. "As you know, I am a man of peace. I do not want to see anyone fighting. I believe that God is unhappy when he sees anyone fighting. That is why I suggest you should not attack the government with your guns. You should be patient and let us, the missionaries, talk to the government about this. Give us time to see whether we can stop them from imposing the law on you and your people.

"In the meantime, I suggest that you do not take your weapons when you meet with the magistrate. Doing so will only make them fear you and will give them reason to want to take away your arms."

In his heart, Moorosi fears an attempt to disarm his people is inevitable. He has had many dealings with the white authorities and he knows that the government does not suggest one thing and do another; it does what it says it will do. And it does not always listen to the missionaries.

"I want to talk to you about another matter," Ellenberger says. "I have heard that the magistrate wants you to tell Lehana and Thladi that they must appear in the magistrate's court to face trial and I would like to suggest that you tell the men that they must appear in court."

"But they are afraid of what the magistrate will do to them," says Moorosi.

"This magistrate is not like the other one," Ellenberger replies. "He does not order men to be whipped in the way the other magistrate did. Only the other day I heard that he had asked permission from Mr. Griffith to withdraw a sentence of lashes that Hope had imposed on a man.

"So you need to tell them they must not be afraid, but must act as good citizens and appear before the court. God wants us to obey the authorities that He has put there for our good.

"If Lehana did not commit the offense of stock stealing, the magistrate will find him not guilty. If he finds him guilty he must face the consequences because stock stealing is not right."

"But I do not know where the men are," Moorosi says.

"King, I know that you can find out where they are," Ellenberger says. "If you do not do so and you do not send them to trial then the magistrate is going to call in other people to help him find them and we will have a battle on our hands. That is another reason you should tell them to appear in court.

"We do not want to have a war over a matter that is not big enough to warrant one."

Moorosi accepts Ellenberger's advice and decides he will tell Lehana and Thladi to appear before Austen in court. But they will not be the only ones in court. He will attend the session himself and help the magistrate make his decision.

Quthing — Tuesday, November 12, 1878

Persuaded by Moorosi to appear in court, Lehana and Thladi are here, ready to face trial.

Word of the trial has spread. The small courtroom is filled with about 30 spectators, the maximum that can be accommodated without causing some to faint for lack of air. A few — including Lemena who arrived early to ensure he could get a seat — occupy the few benches and the rest stand.

Moorosi sits in the front row, alongside Lehana and Thladi, ready to come to their defense.

Some 70 more spectators stand outside, jostling one another for a view. Those closest to the door say they will report to those outside.

Austen is pleased to note that none of the crowd is armed. They are quiet and calm.

Maitin, serving as the clerk of the court, stands.

"I call the case of the Queen versus Lehana and Thladi," he says.

"What is the charge?" asks Austen.

"The accused are charged with the crime of being accessories before and after the act of theft and with receiving stolen property," Maitin intones.

The crowd is silent as Maitin translates the charge, explaining that it means that the men might not have committed the thefts themselves, but that they caused others to commit them, which is an equally offensive act, and that they took possession of the goods that had been stolen.

"How do you plead?" asks Austen.

The men protest that they are innocent.

The first witness takes the stand and the testimony begins.

Now, Austen thinks, is my chance to put the troublemaker Lehana away for good, in a place where he will no longer be able to stir up trouble among the Baphuthi people. He believes he owes that to the cause of law and order and the future of colonial rule in the territory.

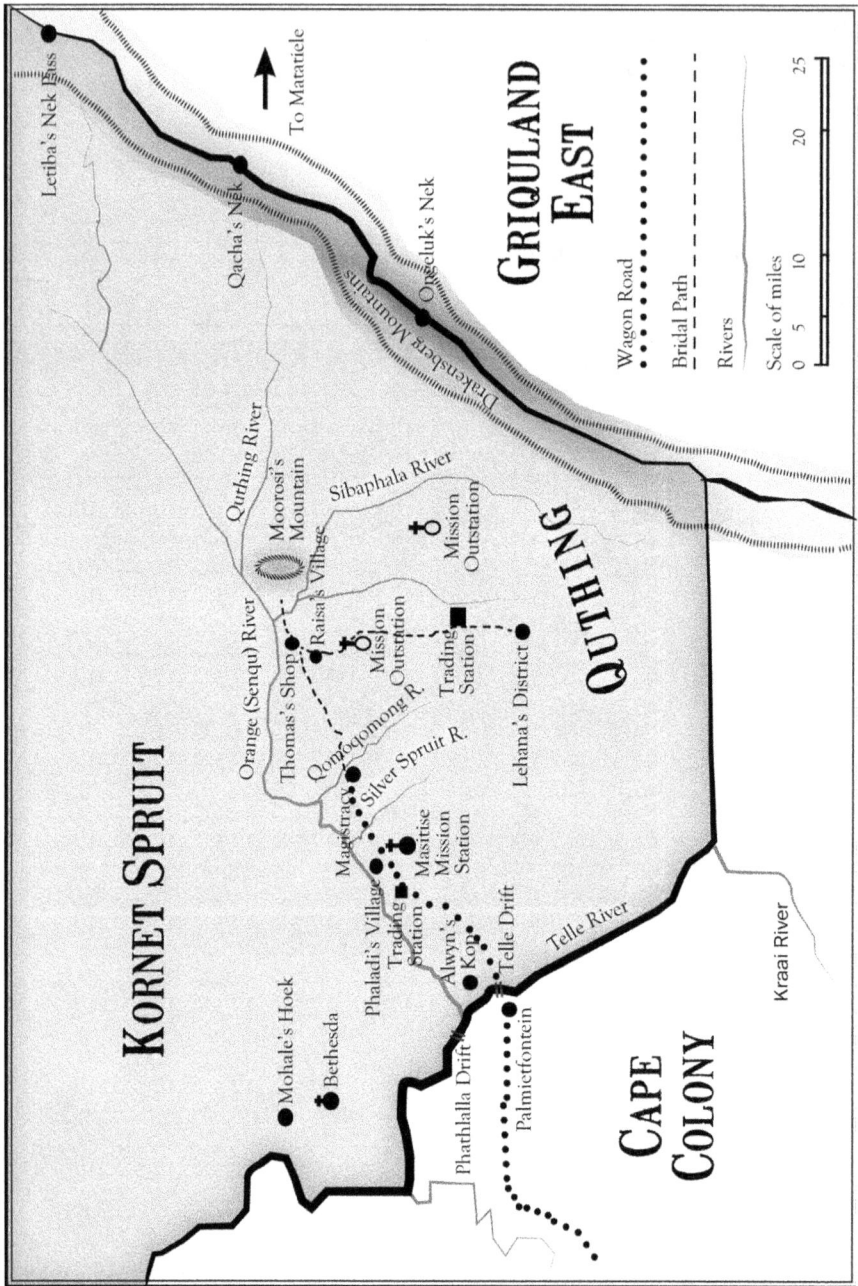

IX

Quthing — Friday, November 15, 1878

For three days, witnesses have testified that they heard that Lehana, his son Thladi and others crossed the border twice to steal cattle in the Cape Colony — firstly when Lehana was awaiting trial in the Maikela affair and secondly after he was fined by Bowker at the meeting at Palmietfontein. The cattle provided food for the thieves and their 20 followers holed up in a cave in Quthing, the witnesses said.

Some said they saw Lehana riding toward the border and later heard that he had returned with stolen cattle.

Lehana and Thladi insisted they were innocent of the charges laid against them. They said no direct evidence had been produced to show that they had either stolen the cattle or ordered the thefts. None of the witnesses had heard the men specifically instruct anyone to steal cattle, nor did they see them stealing cattle.

The question before Austen now is: Although no direct evidence has been presented that Lehana stole cattle and Thladi assisted him, is it a reasonable assumption that they must have done so or, at the least, took no steps to stop it?

As sole judge and jury, Austen finds himself influenced by two factors, neither directly related to the theft charges. He is convinced Lehana was not hiding in the cave simply to escape capture from the contempt charges leveled against him by Hope. Austen believes Lehana's plan was to taunt colonial forces into invading Baphuthi territory, giving him the justification for hitting back and thereby starting a rebellion against colonial rule.

The other factor is Austen's belief that Bowker imposed too lenient a sentence on Lehana at Palmietfontein. Because he was not imprisoned, Lehana could return to his cave and continue to foster his incipient rebellion against the colonial government. Now, Austen believes, is his chance to impose the sentence Bowker should have imposed.

Finding Lehana guilty would, therefore, serve a dual purpose. Not only would justice be done in the stock-stealing case, but imprisonment would remove Lehana and Thladi, and their influence, from the Quthing district. Without their influence, Austen is convinced, the Baphuthi people would be more cooperative and respectful of the government. No longer would Moorosi be subject to persuasion by his wild, aggressive and rebellious son.

Austen clears his throat.

"Does anyone want to say anything more?" he asks. The court room is silent.

"Very well, I will deliver my verdict."

Austen summarizes the case, outlining the charges and the evidence presented to him. The crowd of onlookers listens in silence. He reaches the end of his summation and he instructs the accused men to stand.

231

"Lehana, I find you guilty of the crimes as outlined in the charge sheet. I am convinced that you committed the stock theft, you encouraged others to assist you in stealing the cattle, sheep and goats and that you took the animals to your hideout in the caves along the Orange River.

"Thladi, I find you guilty of receiving stolen property. There is not enough evidence to find that you actually stole stock, but I am convinced that you lived off that stock when you knew it had been stolen."

A few members of the crowd gasp, but for the most part they are quiet. The verdict was not entirely unexpected. Their main concern is the punishment.

Austen continues.

"Lehana, you were the leader of this group that hid in the cave," he says. "Because you are a headman and because you are able to influence more people — and because I am convinced you took a leading role in the thefts — I am going to give you a harsher sentence than the one I will impose on Thladi.

"I want to point out that I cannot tolerate such action as you have both taken. The law condemns stock theft as a serious offense and this court will not take it lightly.

"Lehana, I sentence you to four years' imprisonment with hard labor.

"Thladi, I sentence you to two years' imprisonment with hard labor.

"The police will take you to the jail near this courtroom where you will start to serve your sentence immediately. Later you will be taken to another jail in the Cape Colony.

"The court is dismissed."

A cry of shock rises from the crowd. To fine a man is one thing, but to put him in prison, to remove him from his family and his people is another. Under Baphuthi laws, Lehana likely would have been told to return the stolen cattle and would have been fined an amount equal to the stock he had stolen. Imprisonment as a punishment is a concept brought by the white people.

But, even if imprisonment is accepted as a form of punishment, why was he not given six months imprisonment as the other convicted stock thieves were? That was the worst case that Moorosi had imagined. The reason for relief when Bowker sentenced Lehana at Palmietfontein was that the magistrate did not impose a harsh jail sentence on him. With this sentence, there is no relief. The king is devastated.

Lehana is shocked. He stands still, looking down. His heart drops. Above all, he cherishes his freedom, his ability to go where he wishes, to enjoy his family and to sit for hours and to eat and talk with those close to him. Take those freedoms away and he is nothing. Without being close to his family, he might as well cease to exist.

Thladi, too, is downcast. Like Lehana, he stands motionless.

They are bitter and angry. Why did they listen to Moorosi and agree to the trial? He said he would protect them — and now look at what has happened.

The policemen place the men in the jail, give them prisoners' shirts and blankets, and secure the door with a lock. The prisoners reluctantly put on the shirts and throw the blankets on the ground.

Already in the jail are Dethlama and Thaba, sentenced by Austen to six months in September, and two other men sentenced recently to a short jail term.

"Did the magistrate also send you to jail?" asks Dethlama.

"For four years." Lehana spits out the words angrily as he and Thladi look around them. The stone walls are about eight feet high and the building is covered with an iron roof. The mud floor is smooth from the trampling of others who have preceded them in the jail. The realization sinks in that their freedom has been taken from them. The years of the sentence — particularly in contrast with that of Dethlama and Thaba who have a little more than three months left to serve, seem like forever.

As a rat scurries away through a hole under the wall, the men wish they could follow it. They wonder how long they will be kept in this ill-smelling, dark confinement before being sent elsewhere. Austen said they would be sent to other jails. Would the others be any better — or worse?

Moorosi, still numb from the severity of the sentence, slowly rises from the bench in the court room on which he had been sitting. These sentences are wrong. Lehana is being punished not for stock theft, but for defiance. He is being put away because he is seen as a threat to them. Surely, the evidence was not sufficient to convict his son and grandson of the charges. But even if it was, Lehana and Thladi do not deserve such harsh punishment.

Not only will his love for his son and grandson not allow him to rest in peace while they are being held in the government's prison, but he will also lose the counsel and support of the one who has become his favorite son and so to whom the chieftainship of the Baphuthi people will surely pass when he dies. In the later years of Moorosi's life four years seems an eternity. He might be dead when they are released. If the men are taken out of Basutoland, he may never see his son and grandson again.

He will devise a plan to fight back. He will not confront the authorities now lest they take that as an excuse to act against him. Of what use will he be to his people if he, too, is put in jail? He will prepare quietly.

Of one thing he is sure. He will do all he can to prevent the authorities taking his son and grandson out of Quthing to the Cape Colony.

Moorosi rides to Masitise, where he sees Ellenberger talking outside. The missionary ends his conversation and turns to Moorosi.

"How are you doing today, chief Moorosi?"

"I am not doing well," Moorosi replies as he dismounts. "I am deeply saddened by the action taken by this magistrate. You advised me to tell Lehana to appear in court. You said Mr. Austen would be fair as Mr. Bowker was fair. Now he has sent Lehana to four years in jail. He will be sent away to Cape Town. This sentence, it is too harsh. It breaks my heart to see my son and grandson treated in this way."

"I can understand your feelings," Ellenberger responds, shocked at the severity of the sentence.

"I should not have listened to you," Moorosi continues. "I did what you said I should do. You speak of the Wodehouse bench, the bench of peace. This is not the way to achieve peace. This magistrate is not sitting on that bench. I am the one who has made all the sacrifice. The magistrate has done nothing."

Ellenberger nods. He had no idea the sentence would be so harsh. He had thought it would be along the lines of that imposed by Bowker. Now Austen's action will render his efforts at peacemaking much harder and will erode Moorosi's trust in him. Yet he must hold out hope.

"I admire you for playing your part in helping to ensure peace," he says. "You have acted in a good and noble way. What you have done will help to achieve peace, to ensure that the government will not wage war on you.

"Remember, as I said, we each have to give up something to achieve compromise and thereby peace. You have given up something big. You have taken a big step to ensure peace."

Moorosi looks down at the ground. Ellenberger is a man of God, a man who speaks wisdom. But he finds this wisdom difficult to accept. He looks back up at Ellenberger. His eyes tell of his feelings of betrayal and despair more eloquently than words can do.

"Do not despair yet, King Moorosi," Ellenberger continues, trying to retain an optimistic outlook. "Perhaps Mr. Austen will change his mind. Or perhaps the authorities in Maseru will reduce the sentence."

The king raises his head and looks into Ellenberger's eyes. He sees compassion in them. He knows it is not Ellenberger who has sentenced his son. He can see that Ellenberger is saddened by what has happened. But he feels betrayed.

"I will do what I can to help you, King Moorosi. Please, I beg of you, do not despair."

Ellenberger rides to the magistracy where he urges Austen to reverse his judgment and impose a less severe sentence on the men.

"I helped you by encouraging Moorosi to bring his son for trial," he says. "He trusted me and did what I asked him to do. Now he feels betrayed because of the severity of your sentence. These men fear jail, and fear being sent to jail and hard labor in East London or Cape Town more than anything. You will recall that was the issue when Mr. Bowker held the hearing at the Telle River. When he imposed only a fine and not jail on the men they were happy and shouted with joy at the relief they felt because the men would not be sent to work on the breakwater in Cape Town."

Austen recalls it well. He was there.

"Perhaps you can do the same thing this time," Ellenberger replies. "There is still time to call them back and tell them you have changed your mind and you want to impose a less strict sentence."

Austen sighs. "You do not understand, Rev. Ellenberger," he says. "These men are not just stock thieves. They are rebels. They want to overthrow our government and chase us out of the country."

"If they do want to rebel, it is because you are imposing severe sentences on them. To achieve peace, we have to compromise, Mr. Austen. Moorosi has given up his son. I am asking you also to give up something to secure peace."

Austen displays a flash of anger. "The rebelliousness came first; the severe sentences followed," he says. "The latter is a result of the former, not the other way around."

"That may or may not be so, but, for the sake of peace, I am pleading with you to lessen the sentence," Ellenberger says. "Impose a fine — a severe one if necessary. But lift the jail sentence, or reduce it to a few months in jail here. We have been living in peace here for many years. There were no problems when you were governing Quthing from across the river in Mohale's Hoek. I would hate to see that peace shattered and all the work you have done here destroyed by this act.

"I plead with you to follow the same action as Mr. Bowker. He prevented violence breaking out by imposing a sentence on Lehana that did not involve going to jail."

"No, Rev. Ellenberger. You are looking at it in the wrong way.

"Mr. Bowker has been severely criticized for what he did. He was an appeaser. That is why he is no longer the resident magistrate in Maseru. He let Lehana and Maikela go with a relatively small fine instead of punishing them severely. If he had put them in jail, we would not have been in this situation. Lehana would not have been able to continue his rebellious ways.

"We cannot afford to make the same mistake that Mr. Bowker did. If anything, perhaps my sentence was not strong enough."

Maseru — Wednesday, November 20, 1878

When Griffith receives notice of the verdicts in today's express post, he supports the harsh sentence imposed by Austen, but realizes that keeping the convicted men in the insecure jail in Quthing can be no more than a temporary measure.

"I want your opinion on this matter, Mr. Rolland," he says. "Lehana and Thladi have been sentenced to long periods in prison and have been locked up in that small jailhouse in Quthing since their conviction last week."

Rolland nods.

"I am afraid that their confinement can be a source of trouble," Griffith says. "These men are in a rebellious mood. Already they came close to dragging us into a war. Now they are in a jail that is not meant for much more than holding prisoners overnight.

"Austen is convinced that Lehana's move to his fortified cave, under the plea that he was afraid of his magistrate, was only a pretext. The rebellion, he believes, was to have started at Lehana's fortified cave.

"Clearly, these men have to be removed from the area so that they can be prevented from continuing to foment rebellion."

"I agree that the men should be moved to the Cape Colony," Rolland says. "I have seen that jailhouse and it's not what you would call a miracle of modern engineering."

"Mr. Austen has asked me, therefore," Griffith continues, "to take steps to have the men sent out of the area, either to East London or to Cape Town, where convicts are needed to build a new breakwater at the harbor."

"I cannot quarrel with that."

"But here's my dilemma. Were I to have the authority to have the men placed in jail in a colonial institution, I would not hesitate to do so today. But I am not sure whether I have such power. I cannot instruct the authorities in the rest of the country to take our prisoners. That would be impinging on their authority. I cannot give them orders.

"At least, I believe that to be the position. It is on that issue that I seek your opinion."

Rolland considers the question.

"Can you not issue a request to, say, the magistrate at Aliwal North to hold them for a few days until they are transferred to East London or Cape Town? At least that would remove them from Quthing until permission is obtained to move them."

"I can ask, but I doubt that they would have the power to accede to my request. Even then, you see, I would in one sense be giving instructions to Mr. Halse, the resident magistrate in Aliwal North, who does not fall under my jurisdiction.

"In addition, I certainly do not have the authority to order that these men be kept in a jail in East London or Cape Town."

"But surely you can ask them?"

"We are dealing here with legal procedure which has no room for requests," Griffith replies. "But you have given me an idea. I will not ask the local authorities. I will go to the top and ask Ayliff to order the men to be held in a colonial jail. As the secretary for native affairs, he can obtain the authority of the government to send these prisoners to Aliwal North and then to the convict stations at Cape Town or East London. Thank you, Mr. Rolland."

Maseru — Monday, December 23, 1878

Today, six weeks after Lehana and Thladi were confined to the small jail in Quthing, Griffith finally has the authority to move the prisoners to Aliwal North, from where they will be transferred to East London and then to Cape Town. Griffith's request has gone through Ayliff in Cape Town and the British colonial secretary, Michael Hicks-Beach, in London.

Griffith sends the relevant permission form to Austen in Quthing, asking him to send it to Aliwal North.

Aware that the Baphuthi might try to prevent the men being moved out of Quthing, he also requests an armed escort be sent to accompany the men to Aliwal North. Griffith is confident that once Lehana is out of Quthing the spirit of rebellion among the Baphuthi will wane. Now, two days before Christmas Day, everything seems to be in place to achieve their removal before the end of the year.

Aliwal North — Wednesday, January 1, 1879

"We leave for Quthing tomorrow at dawn," Sgt. James Thorne tells four policemen who are to escort Lehana and Thladi to the jail in Aliwal North.

"Although we haven't received the formal papers, we have been informed by telegram the papers are on their way. We are aware there is some urgency to the removal of the prisoners and so we will saddle our horses at first light tomorrow. If the weather holds, we should be at the Quthing magistracy by the end of the day."

Quthing — The same day

The New Year's Day festivities have been going on for some hours in Quthing. Indeed, it has been a time of rest and relaxation at the magisterial compound for a week. Last Wednesday was Christmas Day and the following day was Boxing Day. By the time Friday and the weekend rolled around, it seemed a good idea to take a few days off until today, New Year's Day.

The holiday festivities are confined largely to the colonial authorities and the 12 policemen who work for them. It is a British concept, after all, and is just another day to most of the Baphuthi people — although a few hundred attended Christmas services at Ellenberger's church and outstations.

But, as colonial government employees, the native policemen can take part in the festivities — and do so with some eagerness. Their position entitles them to Cape brandy, banned for sale in Basutoland, and it flows freely among them today.

Now, as the sky darkens, the men are suffering the after-effects. The weather is not helping. A strong wind, carrying with it light rain, is sweeping down from the ridges around the magisterial compound, making outside duty unpleasant.

A sleepy and not entirely sober Second Class Private Mohomo is standing prison guard with Jeroboam, who shares the same rank and now shares the same impaired ability. After taking an evening meal to the prisoners, the two men sit a few yards from the entrance to the jail.

Two men on horseback pass the jail. Mohomo recognizes one as Mponya, a grandson of Moorosi, who stops his horse, dismounts and walks toward the jail where he exchanges a few words with the prisoners.

"Tell that man he has no right to come here," says Jeroboam, reluctant to do so himself. Mohomo slowly rises and walks in a zigzag line toward Mponya. He passes on the instruction.

"Why are you stopping me from seeing the prisoners?" asks Mponya. "I want to greet them."

"If you want to see the prisoners, ask the magistrate," Mohomo replies, pointing to Austen's house. "You see the magistrate's house? Go to him. Don't ask me."

Mponya pursues his argument for a while, but receives the same slurred answer. Finally, he rides off with his colleague.

Jeroboam and Mohomo check the jail door is secure with a padlock and that a bar is in place across the door, the usual nightly routine.

From the slopes of a nearby hill, Mponya and his friends look down at the jail as the policemen return unsteadily to their huts 60 yards away.

"They are going to sleep well tonight," says Mponya. "They have had a lot to drink and it still is showing. I think tonight — later when it is totally dark, the wind is hiding any noise, and the guards are sleeping — is the time for us to act.

"We'll ask some of the others to help and bring six extra horses so that they can get away quickly. My grandfather will be pleased."

Quthing — Thursday January 2, 1879

His head pounding in spite of his long deep sleep, Jeroboam walks to the jail to start his day's duties. As usual, he is to take the prisoners to work in the gardens where they will be closely guarded.

But the sight that greets him indicates that today's activities will not be usual. The jail door is closed, but the bar across it to prevent it being opened from the inside is hanging down. The padlock is missing and the door is dented about quarter of an inch deep. The damage appears to have been made with the same blunt piece of iron used to smash the padlock.

The jail is empty.

Jeroboam runs to the policemen's huts. "The jail has been broken open and the prisoners have gone," he tells Isaak Masin, sergeant of police.

A dazed Masin, also suffering from the New Year's festivities, runs outside.

"They have gone? They cannot have gone."

He looks across at the jail house, its door ajar.

They have gone.

"Why didn't you stop them?"

Jeroboam is quick to defend himself. "They broke out during the night. I was asleep." Determined not to be the scapegoat, he quickly adds, "And so were you."

The men walk slowly to Austen's house, as if delay by even a few minutes will make it easier to tell him what has happened. They know he is going to be furious.

Pietermaritzburg — The same day

Ever since he left Basutoland almost eight months ago, Bowker has wanted to speak with Frere about the situation in Basutoland. He believes Frere has little more than a cursory knowledge of what the Basotho and Baphuthi people think and feel and does not realize the effect that the disarmament act will have on them.

Bowker left Maseru partly for health reasons, but largely because he felt he could no longer implement the colonial policies and had lost their support. Since being heavily criticized for being an "appeaser," he has shared his thoughts only with close friends. Now, he decides, is the time to make himself heard — and who better to tell than Sir Bartle Frere?

He carefully crafts a letter to the governor, reminding him that he is well acquainted with the thoughts and ambitions of Basutoland's people, having served as governor's agent under the British for 12 years from 1858 to 1870 and, after a break of eight years, returning last year to serve once more, this time under the Cape Colony administration. He believes the British were right to allow the Basotho largely to govern their own affairs. He has noted with disappointment the trend away from that policy since the colonial authorities took over in 1871.

"The Basotho looked upon themselves as a nation taken into British protection," he explains, "but never by any act of theirs assented to incorporation with or subjection to the Colony of the Cape of Good Hope, to which they seemed to have been handed over in the most arbitrary fashion.

"The Basotho are quite clever enough to take unfavorable note of the fact that by such transference they became, without getting any 'quid pro quo' in the shape of representation, a province of a mere dependency."

Up to that point, Bowker notes, they had managed with the aid of Her Majesty's Commissioner, to rule and restrain themselves through their grand councils. The money collected in the hut tax was used in Basutoland.

"Under the Cape Parliament, however, they were threatened with taxation without representation; in fact, their surplus revenues were actually taken away from them without their consent and paid into the colonial exchequer."

Bowker advises Frere to take note of the strength in arms, horses and men in Basutoland.

"I must warn you, Sir Bartle, that if you do not allow them to keep their arms a Basotho war against the whites must arise, when colonists would have to face a people united against them."

Quthing — The same day

Mponya rides astride Moorosi's favorite white horse, lent to him for the occasion. Behind him are Lehana, Thladi, Dethlama, Thaba and two other released prisoners as well as the men who helped Mponya break open the jail.

They have stayed away from the regular routes to avoid detection, moving instead up and down steep hills. Now it is mid-morning; they have traveled five miles and are tired from little sleep.

They make their way to a cave that, Mponya says, will be their hideout for a few days. It is hidden in a deep valley and the government people will not be able to find them here.

"I knew you wanted to free us," says Lehana, "but for a while I thought you might not make it in time. We overheard the guards talking about men arriving soon to take us to Aliwal North and then to Cape Town to work on the breakwater."

"We knew the time was getting close," replies Mponya. "We started planning around the time of the Christmas celebrations because we knew then that the magistrate and the policemen would be distracted. Then Jantji Xaka, a Thembu, told us he had heard that white policemen would come to this office from Aliwal North on New Year's night and remove you.

"We knew we had to act soon, but we needed to find out whether King Moorosi was supporting us. Three days ago we received a message that we were to go ahead with the plans to break open the jail and release the prisoners. He sent us a key to use in the padlock.

"Some of the people who wanted to release you were afraid because the police sleep nearby and they said the policemen would shoot us.

"Then we decided a better plan would be to go to the jail and ask you whether they have a guard on the jail, when he is there, what kind of a lock the jail has, and also to tell you when you next see us pass the office that we have come to liberate you. By speaking in our language, Sephuthi, we knew that the Basotho guards would not be able to understand what we were saying.

"We sent that report to King Moorosi. We heard back that he thought our ideas were good.

"So we visited you," continues Mponya, picking up the story once more. "But we were interrupted by the policemen and could not ask you all the questions."

"Yes, that is when you whispered to me that you would return later to break open the jail and I told you not to be slow about it. 'Come quietly and do it at once,' I said. Then the policeman came up and told you to leave."

"And did we not do as you asked?" inquires Mponya, his face breaking into a smile.

"You did. But you took longer than I thought."

The men laugh.

"We did. When we tried the first time, earlier that night, we heard voices in the magistrate's office. We ran away and returned later, leaving extra horses for you knee-haltered on the hill above the jail. Then it was quiet in the office; no candles were burning and the wind was blowing strongly enough to cover any noise.

"We tried to open the padlock with the key, but it did not work. So Nepa broke the padlock with a piece of iron."

Lehana is now more concerned about the future.

"Now, tell me, what is this I hear? They are going to take away our weapons?"

"Yes, Lehana, it is true," Mponya continues. "The government says they will take away our weapons — from us and from everyone in Basutoland. Not only our rifles, but also our spears.

"All the people are talking about it. The Maseru magistrate, Griffith, held a pitso and told everyone there that there is a new law to take away the arms from all the black people in South Africa — and we will be among the first.

"When they do that, the people say, war will break out. They are talking about it in Letsie's territory and in other parts of the country. Even King Moorosi said that after we have released you we must hide the children because there might be fighting. Another reason he wanted you released before they could send you away was so that you would be able to fight with us when the government tries to take away our weapons.

"Do you really think that war will break out?" asks Thladi.

"Yes," Mponya replies. "They will come to take away our weapons. We will not want to give them up. War will break out."

"Have you found out when the government will do this?" Lehana asks.

"A messenger has been sent to Chief Letsie as he is in contact with the white government. We have not heard back from him yet. But we decided it is better that we break you out of jail so we can all fight together."

"They already are waging war on us by putting me in jail for four years," says Lehana. "I thought they would fine me and I would be told to pay back perhaps double the cattle that were stolen.

"That magistrate wants me to be sent to Cape Town because he knows that I want to resist his rule.

"They are slowly herding us like cattle into a kraal. We have to be ready to fight. But we must also be careful not to be caught and be put into jail again."

"I have made plans for us to stay here in the cave for a few days," says Mponya. "Food will be brought to us every night. Later, we will move to King Moorosi's Mountain. You will be safe there. King Moorosi has told me that he and his men are ready to fight off any attempt the government might make to recapture you."

"How could this have happened?" Austen asks when Masin tells him of the breakout.

The policemen are silent.

"Nothing like this has ever happened in Basutoland," Austen continues. "No prisoners have ever escaped. Were your policemen not guarding the jail? Why were they not on special guard? A group of policemen are due to arrive here today or tomorrow to take these men to the jail in Aliwal North."

Masin and Jeroboam say they received no instructions to post a sentry at night.

"But was that not an obvious thing to do?" Austen asks. Even as he puts the question to the men, he suffers a twinge of conscience. Because the prisoners had shown no signs of wanting to escape, Austen had given no instructions to guard them at night.

But the men, too, feel guilty and are quick to change the focus of the discussion. "This is the work of King Moorosi," Masin says. "It would not have happened if he had not been behind it."

Austen believes that is an excuse. The policemen were negligent, but it is of little use remonstrating with them now. He needs their help to get back the most important prisoners he has ever held.

He needs to act before it is too late.

"I want you, Isaak, to go to Chief Moorosi. Tell him this is a very serious offense. It will make a very bad impression on the mind of the government against him and his people, especially as it comes after the time when Lehana fostered rebellion while hiding in his cave.

"Tell him I expect him to use his utmost attempts to find and capture the men and to send them back to jail."

Isaak Masin says he will leave within the hour for Moorosi's Mountain.

In addition, Austen will launch his own search. He turns to Jeroboam.

"I want you to take Mohomo with you. You must take the same message as Isaak is taking to Chief Moorosi to the people who live in Lehana's village and the area that he oversees. I want you to go to the villages along the Silver Spruit River and the Qomoqomong River. I want you to talk to the people and find out where the escaped prisoners are hiding so we can then recapture them."

Austen retreats to his office. Suddenly, Quthing looks a lot different than it did just a few days ago when he penned his annual report. The calm of which he was so proud has gone. The leading rebel he thought he had removed from the area now is back with his people, with an even stronger reason to rebel than before. Moorosi, who clearly was not happy with the sentence imposed on his son, will be even less cooperative now.

Austen fears the chances of his policemen finding Lehana and Thladi are slim. The mountains, hills and crags offer a thousand hiding places. Unless they are lucky and find someone who will talk, it will take weeks to scour the mountains and during that time the fugitives — whose spies will keep them informed — will move continually, making the search almost impossible.

"Why did this have to happen?" he shouts, banging his fist on the table. "How could the policemen have been so careless?"

Hearing the noise, Maitin enters the room.

Austen tells him what has happened.

"But they were about to be escorted to Aliwal North," Maitin says.

"I know, I know," Austen sighs. "I have just received a letter from Griffith authorizing the move."

"Did the police not guard the jail during the night?" Maitin asks.

"Don't ask me. I haven't the faintest idea," Austen bites back with a sting in his voice that runs counter to his normal composed nature.

Maitin brushes aside the sharp retort. "Did you find out why the police weren't there when the breakout occurred? If they were there surely they would have confronted the men?"

"No, a sentry was not posted," Austen shouts back. He stands up and paces the floor. "It has happened, Mr. Maitin. It serves no purpose to go back on it now. It has happened. It's no good second guessing. It has happened."

Maitin takes a step back.

"I am sorry, Mr. Austen. I am only trying to help."

"Well, you certainly are not helping."

"I am sorry, Mr. Austen."

There is silence. Maitin has never seen Austen in such a foul mood before and is unsure what to say next.

Maitin tries to put an optimistic spin on events. "Not all hope is gone," he says. "It will all work out right if Moorosi returns the prisoners."

Austen is in no mood to be optimistic. He sits down, trying to regain his composure as he comes to grips with what has happened. "He will not do that. I am convinced Moorosi was behind this act," he says. "He is no longer working with us, my dear Mr. Maitin; he is working against us. We are back where we were two months ago," he continues, sitting at his desk once more and jabbing his finger toward Maitin. "Only matters are now worse. We have not just a rebel on the loose, but a man who is out to get me for the sentence that I imposed on him. He will stir up not just his own family, but his father, the chief himself, against me.

"I am going to have to ask for more protection."

Maitin nods. "Yes, but I am not sure that protection will be forthcoming, Mr. Austen. You know how reluctant the authorities have been to provide more..."

Maitin stops himself before continuing. He realizes he is repeating what the magistrate already knows and is angering Austen again.

"Yes, I know that, Mr. Maitin," responds Austen, desperately trying to control his emotions. "I don't think we can find these men, but we will try. I will also try to negotiate with Moorosi, to do all I can to persuade him to hand back these prisoners. As you say, his favorable reaction is the main hope I have. I have already sent Isaak to Moorosi to talk with him."

Austen pounds his fist on the desk one more time.

"Why, oh why, did this have to happen?"

Maitin returns to his office. Austen sits at his desk for what seems like an hour. He is unable to concentrate on his routine duties. If only the prison break could have been avoided. If only...

Darkness is approaching when there is a knock at the door.

"Come in."

The door is opened and a head pokes around it.

"Sergeant Thorne reporting, sir. We have come from Aliwal North to pick up the prisoners and escort them to the safety of our jail."

Quthing — Saturday, January 4, 1879

Isaak Masin returns from his visit to Moorosi in the mid-morning. He finds Austen in his office.

"I delivered your message," he says.

Over the last two days, Austen's mood has turned from anger to anxiety. He fears not just for his safety in Quthing, but also for his position as a government servant. After all, even the British government in London was involved in deciding where the prisoners should be sent. Lehana and Thladi are now known far beyond the confines of Quthing, Basutoland and even South Africa. It seems to Austen that he is operating under the eyes of the world. And he does not relish the position in which the escape has placed him.

His only chance of rescuing the situation now is to ensure somehow that the prisoners are returned to the lockup. Ironically, Moorosi is now his main hope.

"What did the chief say?" he asks Masin.

"He did not seem surprised when I told him what had happened. He said the magistrate locked them up and he should know where they are. He said he is not responsible for them. But he said nevertheless he would send two messengers to try to find them. The messengers would go to the villages that lie along the Quthing River on the road over the Maluti mountains that leads to Matatiele in the east."

"That might sound good, but, Isaak, I think we cannot rely on Moorosi to find these men for us," he replies. "He is probably sending the messengers in the wrong direction."

Masin nods. "I agree with you," he says. "He did not seem eager to find them."

As the men are talking, Jeroboam and Mohomo ride up. They have returned from their mission to Lehana's village.

"Well, what did you find?" asks Austen.

"We found no clue or trace of the men who have escaped," Jeroboam reports.

He adds that his inquiries in Lehana's village add to his suspicion that Mponya was responsible for the breaking of the lock. He was told, he says, that Mponya lives on the mountain fortress with his grandfather and was one of Moorosi's advisers during the time that Lehana lived in the cave.

Jeroboam tells him, too, that they spoke with Matsapi, one of Moorosi's sons who has broken with his father and crossed to the government side, who promised that he would help find the fugitives. "He told me his father must be involved in what has happened," Jeroboam adds. "He says no ordinary man would commit such an outrage. It must have come from the king."

Austen is glad to know that at least one of Moorosi's kin is willing to help him, though many others will aid Lehana and Thladi.

He urges his policemen to keep asking questions of anyone they think could help.

He also draws up a warrant for the arrest of Lehana and the other prisoners and asks Maitin to make several copies. He believes Moorosi was trying to mislead him in saying that the men might have sought refuge over the Maluti mountains, but he sends a copy of the warrant to Liefeldt in Matatiele just in case.

In addition, Austen offers a reward of £15 for anyone providing information that will lead to the arrest of those who broke open the jail or those who escaped.

Austen decides it is time to tackle a duty he had hoped to postpone, but knows he cannot: To notify Griffith what has happened. He writes to Griffith, telling him he believes Moorosi was behind the break, having heard that the policemen were about to arrive to move the prisoners to Cape Town.

He says he hopes to be successful in finding the men, "especially if you would sanction a reward to informers."

Austen folds the letter and places it in the box for the post that leaves tonight. He is under no illusions about how Griffith will take the news.

Maseru — Monday, January 6, 1879

Griffith is furious. Waving the letter from Austen in his hand, he strides into Rolland's office.

"Mr. Austen has allowed the prisoners to go," he tells him.

"He has released them?" Rolland gasps with disbelief.

"No, they have escaped."

Griffith tosses Austen's letter on Rolland's desk.

"And one of those prisoners is Lehana?"

"Yes."

"Did he not realize how important a prisoner he was?" Rolland responds, ignoring the letter.

"Apparently not," Griffith responds. "At least not from the way he acted. It is clear from his report that proper precautions were not taken. He does not say so specifically, but I am convinced a proper guard and sentries were not placed over the lock-up at night. Had they been, the prisoners would not have escaped."

Rolland realizes the seriousness of the situation. Lehana was known to be plotting rebellion against the government. He was the ringleader. With him out of the way the tension would have been lessened. Now he is on the loose once more, likely more rebellious than before.

Griffith continues.

"The guards were there when the prisoners were having their supper, but, after locking them up, the policemen did not return again until the next morning, when they found the lock-up empty. That much is clear from statements by the policeman and constable.

"Somebody has been very careless here."

"And you think Mr. Austen is to be blamed?" Rolland asks.

"Of course. Clearly. When last I heard, he was in charge over there. He is the person who should have given the policemen orders to guard the lock-up at night.

"Perhaps he gave them orders and the policemen did not follow his orders," Rolland ventures.

"Well, then, he should have seen that those orders were obeyed. But he does not say he gave them orders or that anybody disobeyed anything. Surely if that were the case he would have protected himself by explaining it in his report.

"No, there are no excuses for him. He is to blame."

Griffith picks up the letter once more. His eyes glance down again at the contents, which he already has read several times.

"And then he goes on to suggest that Moorosi is responsible for the break-out."

"Is he not?"

"I do not know, Mr. Rolland. But before he tries to hold Moorosi responsible he must be in a position to prove that Moorosi has aided in the escape or that he harbored them after the escape. He and his policeman Isaak are trying to throw the blame on Moorosi in order to avoid their own responsibility in not having taken proper precautions to keep the prisoners in safe custody. Before we act against Moorosi, make demands on him or hold him responsible for finding the prisoners, we need to know for sure that he organized this affair. If we do not know that, we are acting unjustly."

"Do you think he should have refrained from telling the chief about the break-out?"

"No. It is fine that Mr. Austen reported the break-out to Moorosi. I think the chief needs to know that it happened — assuming he did not already know. But I do not think Mr. Austen should go beyond that. I think it would be much better for him to work out the matter with his own police constables.

"I will inform him that he needs to take his own steps to find these men and show Moorosi that the Government is independent of him. Working through Moorosi is a mistake. It is important that we do not ask chiefs to do our work for us. Doing so only makes them believe they are still in full control of their own people, that their word still counts and that they are responsible for law and order in this country. It also gives the impression that we are weak and incapable of administering justice ourselves.

"We need to show Moorosi that the government is quite independent of him."

Rolland is afraid that the developments in Quthing might have an impact on the rest of Basutoland where the people are edgy over the disarmament act. Although few Basotho have complained to him, he has heard them mutter about it and he has noted that a number of men have become quite sullen. Open defiance of government authority in Quthing will not help.

"Will you tell Mr. Austen of your concerns?"

"I certainly will. But I will wait a few days while I make inquiries among the people here. I would be pleased if you would help me do so, too. The chiefs around here are in contact with Moorosi and we might be able to glean some information from them.

"But, unless I hear something that changes my mind, I will let Austen know how I feel about what has happened and his neglect in allowing it to happen. I am going to call on him for a full report as to what steps he took to secure the safe custody of these prisoners. When I receive his report, I will be able to judge more fully who is to blame for the escape, but I already have a good idea of what happened and who is responsible for it. I also plan to inform the Secretary for Native Affairs and to express to him my concern about Mr. Austen's actions.

"First, Mr. Hope causes trouble among the Baphuthi with his high-handed, tactless and undiplomatic attitude. Now Mr. Austen, who seemed to be getting to grips with the situation, aggravates those problems with negligence.

"If we are not careful, we will be facing an extremely serious situation in Quthing. For now, we must find Lehana and the other prisoners — particularly Lehana. At all costs."

Transkei — The same day

Hamilton Hope has produced his first annual report as magistrate at Qumbu in the Transkei. It reflects a pattern that characterized his dealings with Moorosi.

Hope says that Mhlonthlo, paramount chief of the Mpondomise, of whom he has had charge since July 1, 1878, "is a brave and warlike man and far more outspoken and straightforward than most other native chiefs; and as a natural consequence he is somewhat impatient of control.

"I believe that before I came here he had not infrequently offered a good deal of opposition to government authority; and when I was installed as magistrate of the district he expressed great dissatisfaction at my appointment.

"But I am glad to be able to say that, after one or two feeble attempts at opposing me at first, he accepted the position I allotted to him as in all things subordinate to me, and he has since then rendered me cheerful, and I may say prompt obedience in all matters."

In spite of Hope's rosy outlook, however, signs of resistance are growing to his demand that the chief be subservient to him in all matters, his frequent use of the whip, and his cracking down on the payment of arrears hut tax.

"I have many obstacles to overcome," Hope confesses. "But I do not despair."

Pietermaritzburg — Saturday, January 11, 1879

Unaware of the turn of events in Quthing, Frere is in Natal colony, where he has been since August, planning Cetshwayo's downfall with his available force of men. He has organized wagons of supplies for the troops and given instructions on how the battle will be waged. The Zulu king has been warned, but refuses to accede.

So today British troops, accompanied by several hundred pro-government natives, are invading Zululand to force Cetshwayo to agree with Frere's demands.

Quthing — Friday, January 17, 1879

The messengers sent across the mountains to Matatiele report back this morning that the magistrate M.W. Liefeldt has not seen the escaped prisoners, but will do all he can to find them. He has sent detectives to inquire in the area and will report back on what they tell him. He also has sent a copy of the warrant for the prisoners' arrest to the chief magistrate's office in Kokstad.

"Thank you," says Austen. "At least Liefeldt is trying to help."

Chief constable Masin enters the office.

"I have some good news," he says.

"If it is, it will be the first I have heard in the three weeks since the breakout."

"One of the escaped prisoners has been apprehended," Masin says. "His name is Magerman."

"But he was not one of the rebels," Austen says. "He was in the jail awaiting trial on charges of theft."

"Yes, but he can give us a clearer picture of how the break-out took place and who was responsible for it. We also have apprehended one of the accomplices in the jailbreak, a man named Mapara."

Although the men are not involved in the rebellion, they are important witnesses and Austen believes they also will implicate Moorosi as the one who planned and gave instructions for the rescue of the prisoners.

Austen instructs Masin: "I want you to put them in the jail and place additional guards at the door to ensure that Moorosi does not help them break out again to prevent them giving evidence against him." He adds, "I have just heard from Mr. Griffith that he has approved my request to increase my police force to a total of 18 men, including a sergeant, a corporal, three first-class, three second-class and 10 third-class privates. He also has agreed to send me two additional pairs of leg irons."

"Another piece of good news," Masin says.

"I suppose it is," Austen says. "Finally, they listen. It takes something like this before they realize that we need additional policemen and equipment. He also has approved my request that, as a last resort, I can send the prisoners to Palmietfontein where the officer commanding there, Captain James Surmon, will place them under guard. But, he has emphasized, this action should be taken only as a last resort."

Austen, who believes that bad news and good news both come in strings of three, has his theory proven later in the morning when he receives a visit from Moorosi's eldest son, Letuka.

Letuka tells him that even though he is the eldest son and should be the next king, his father has turned away from him and designated Lehana as his heir. "I have been out of favor because I have said he should do as the government asks, but Lehana has opposed the government," he says. "And now I am a nobody."

As a result, Letuka wants Austen to know that he has nothing to do with the break-out. He tells Austen that his brother Tesala also disagrees with their father's actions.

"Thank you," Austen says. "I am pleased to hear what you say and I would appreciate any help you can give me. Indeed, I believe you have a duty to help me find these men."

"I don't know where these men are and they will not tell me, " Letuka says. "But I think my father, King Moorosi, knows where they are."

Austen is quick to respond.

"I no longer have any doubt that the prisoners were released on your father's orders. It is all his fault. He is supporting Lehana in his plans to rebel against the government. And I am sure the escaped prisoners are now on your father's mountain.

"My informants have told me that the men want to return to the fortified cave in which Lehana hid last year. But they say that Chief Moorosi objects and says it is not yet time for them to go there. They should stay on the mountain for now."

As he leaves, Letuka says he will find out what he can. He stresses again he was not involved in the break-out and should not be punished.

Austen promises he will treat Letuka as an ally.

As Letuka rides away, a woman arrives, walking on the wagon road from the direction of Masitise.

"My name is MaLebenya," she tells Austen. "Is Mr. Maitin here?"

"He is not here today," Austen replies. "He has been sent for a few weeks to Palmietfontein. Why did you want to see him?"

"We are friends," she replies.

So this is the woman of whom Hope spoke, the one who seems to spend a lot of time with Maitin, providing him with information.

"But I do want to talk to you, too," MaLebenya continues. "I am the woman whose field was destroyed by Raisa," she says. Austen says he recalls the case; he has read about it in the records.

"I am living now at Masitise, near the home of the missionary, Rev. Ellenberger," MaLebenya says. "But I often hear from the people in the villages.

"I came here today to tell you that I am going to try to find out where Lehana and the other prisoners are."

Austen smiles. Perhaps sometimes good news comes in fours.

Natal colony — Wednesday, January 22, 1879

The rout is complete.

In a furious battle at Isandhlwana, a rampaging force of 20,000 swift and mobile Zulu warriors take the slow and cumbersome British, led by Lord Chelmsford, completely by surprise. They outwit, overwhelm and kill 900 white and 500 black soldiers — members of the Natal Native Contingent — leaving only a few of the troops alive.

C.L. Norris-Newman, the first newspaper correspondent to reach the scene, writes, "The corpses of our poor soldiers, whites and natives, lay thick upon the ground in clusters, together with the dead and mutilated horses, oxen and mules, shot and stabbed in every position and manner; and the whole intermingled with the fragments of our Commissariat wagons, broken and wrecked, and rifled of their contents, such as flour, sugar, tea, biscuits, mealies, oats, etc., the debris being scattered about and wasted as in pure wantonness on the ground."

After rampaging over the British forces at Isandhlwana, the Zulus continue on to Rorke's Drift where a small group of soldiers battles for hours to hold the group of houses that constitute a British base. Led by Lieutenants Chard and Bromhead — who are lauded as heroes for their bravery — the group holds out until sunset, when the Zulus retreat.

But, in spite of Chard and Bromhead's stand, the story of the day is that the Zulus imposed a stunning and humiliating defeat on the British, who boast the most modern weaponry and the strongest army in the world.

Quthing — Monday, January 27, 1879

The news of the British defeat at Isandhlwana five days ago has spread to Basutoland. It is stark: a black indigenous army defeated the white colonial power. Cetshwayo did what Sarhili and Sandile were unable to do. The casualties, the sources say, were the heaviest to white soldiers in any battle in South Africa and the greatest defeat suffered by the British army anywhere in the world.

The news is meaningful to the Baphuthi who have had many contacts with the Zulus over the years. Up to now the white-won battles to the south have led some Baphuthi people to believe that Africans cannot win. Moorosi's response has been that his people's independence is so important that it is better to die at the hands of the whites than to succumb. The Zulu victory has reshaped this debate. It demonstrates, as Moorosi had suspected all along, that a black army can win convincingly.

As a result, Moorosi feels more emboldened to stand up to Austen and more convinced that Lehana is right that war is the only answer. Indeed, the Zulu victory gives him a feeling approaching invincibility.

"He has completely lost his head," Mafetudi, Moorosi's chief messenger, tells Lemena. "He says the Basotho will join us in our fight against the government and we will be even more victorious than the Zulu people. He is convinced that this time Letsie's son Lerothodi will be fighting on our side — against the whites."

For the colonial authorities, the loss at Isandhlwana is a cause of consternation, alarm and dismay. They have relied on a show of force to back up their authority. They have used colonial victories in the south, such as that against Sarhili, to drive home their point that they have powerful forces to bolster their rule.

Suddenly, their power is less impressive.

The only comfort they can take is that Chard and Bromhead — the two lieutenants who held thousands of Zulu warriors at bay at Rorke's Drift — show that vastly outnumbered soldiers can defend themselves if they are determined.

During the morning, Arthur Barkly, the man who took over Austen's post at Mohale's Hoek, arrives unexpectedly at Austen's residence.

"The news from Isandhlwana is disturbing," he says. "I knew most of the officers of the regiment well. Now they have been killed by Cetshwayo and his impis.

"But it goes beyond that," he adds. "I am afraid this catastrophe is the beginning of great trouble for us. Already the Basotho people have been angered by the disarmament proposal and have been showing greater and greater resistance to colonial rule. And I hear that the Zulu people are sending messages trying to stir up the Basotho to join them against the government."

Barkly's assessment comes as a surprise to Austen.

"Our people here are quiet," he replies. "The people are not showing strong support for the would-be rebels."

"I am surprised to hear you say that," responds Barkly. "Our people around Mohale's Hoek are becoming more and more sullen every day. As they do, we are becoming more and more nervous. We feel the time is becoming perilous and I am not sure what each day might bring forth."

Austen recalls similar stirring, spread by a few discontented Basotho, when he was magistrate in Mohale's Hoek. He dismisses Barclay's reaction as unfounded.

"I doubt that matters will become that serious," he says. "The people have been talking of resistance for some time, but it is more talk than substance. They respect us and they are afraid of our armed power should we wish to wield it."

"But don't you think the events at Isandhlwana change that?" Barkly asks.

"You may be right. But all is quiet here. That's all I can say."

"I wish such quiet prevailed in my magistracy," Barkly counters. "What I am hearing is that the chiefs are waiting to see how Moorosi fares in his confrontation with you and, of course, the government generally. Any victory that he can achieve will give them even more encouragement."

Austen and Barkly discuss Lehana's conviction and the jailbreak. As they do, Barkly becomes concerned that Austen is not taking matters seriously and does not realize the degree of discontent prevailing in his district — discontent that has spread to Mohale's Hoek. After a while he concludes that the discussion is going nowhere. His hope of formulating a cohesive plan of action with Austen has faded.

"I cannot linger," he says. "My wife is expecting a child in a week or so, but it could arrive early and I need to be there. I am anxious for her safety should rebellion of some sort spill over into our district."

Soon Barkly is on his horse back to Mohale's Hoek. Surely, he thinks, Austen must understand that his conviction of Lehana, his excessive sentence and the subsequent jail break — all of which are known in Mohale's Hoek and in much of Basutoland — have prompted strong feelings against him.

He concludes that Austen is fearful to admit the truth because he knows he was responsible for the prison break and that any suggestions that the area is not peaceful will reflect badly on him.

Barkly leaves more worried about events in Quthing than when he arrived.

Quthing — Wednesday, January 29, 1879

Austen remains convinced that those Baphuthi who live close to the magistracy are harboring no feelings of rebellion. But Barkly's comments have made him wonder whether he has failed to notice rising tensions in other areas of Quthing.

So today he takes two steps. He asks Griffith to send him more arms and ammunition. And he sets off on a trip into the interior with two of his policemen to see if Barkly's information about widespread discontent is grounded.

Passing through a village, Austen talks with the people who live there, trying to gauge their feelings. He finds them reluctant to talk with him. He can assess little and realizes anew that the Baphuthi are good at hiding their feelings and often will say only what they think an inquirer wants to hear, partly out of politeness and partly out of a fear of saying something that will upset the questioner.

As he leaves the village, he and the policemen ride along a narrow mountain path. Here, he comes across a man who says his name is Japhta who lives in Lehana's village. He tells Austen he has been shown boxes of ammunition in his village and has been told that they have been sent there by Moorosi.

"The men of my village sleep with their guns at their side," Japhta says. "And they take their arms with them when they go into the fields. Some of the people in my village have taken their cattle to hide in a kloof near the source of the Sibaphala River, high in the mountains."

"Have you heard where Lehana is hiding?" asks Austen.

"They do not tell me," Japhta replies. "I told them the government will find Lehana and put him back in the jail. But they say the government will not get him again. This is not the work of ordinary men; this is the work of King Moorosi."

As he returns Austen realizes those who live near the government offices are quiet and appear, on the outside, to have little sympathy with Moorosi in the Lehana affair. But the people farther away seem to be preparing for a confrontation.

Maseru — Wednesday, February 5, 1879

Griffith rejects Austen's request that Cape Mounted Riflemen be sent to assist him in capturing Lehana, suggesting instead that Austen should gather evidence against Moorosi and be ready to charge him, but he should treat the king as innocent until charged and treat him as he did before the jail escape.

Increasingly angry at Austen's failure to keep the prisoners in the jail, Griffith writes to Secretary for Native Affairs Ayliff, "I regret to be obliged to say that I consider Mr. Austen's report very unsatisfactory, and that the escape of the prisoners is due to his carelessness in not seeing that a proper guard was put upon the lock-up every night," he writes. "He tries to excuse himself by saying that the sergeant of police with three men and the chief constable with one of his men were in their huts about sixty yards away from the lock-up; they might as well have been six miles away if they could not see or hear what was going on at the lock-up.

"The real question at issue is: Did Mr. Austen take the ordinary precautions to secure the safe custody of Lehana and the other prisoners? I have no hesitation in saying that, judging from his own report, he did not do so.

"Mr. Austen knew well the importance of securing a prisoner of Lehana's reputation as it was at his special request that I recommended to you the necessity of sending Lehana and others to the Breakwater Works at Cape Town."

Griffith has just mailed the letter when a messenger brings him a copy of the *Northern Post,* the newspaper in Aliwal North. An item catches Griffith's attention. The report says Prime Minister Sprigg has ordered two troops of yeomanry militia to move from King William's Town to Palmietfontein on the Basutoland border.

He did so without consulting him and clearly not realizing the message that such a move could send to Moorosi.

He writes to Ayliff: "If I am to be kept in ignorance of all that is taking place around me in this way, then as a simple act of justice I beg that I may in no way be held responsible for the peace and quietness of this territory."

Realizing that these moves mean it is now more important than ever that Lehana and his fellow escapees be brought to book before the situation gets out of control, he assesses the moves he can make.

He summarizes the situation: If Moorosi is innocent of orchestrating the jail-break, he can persuade Lehana to hand himself in, as before. If Moorosi is guilty of assisting Lehana, however, the Baphuthi chief will protect Lehana and prevent him from being captured.

Whichever way you look at it, Moorosi is the key and he must be confronted.

The task now is to make that confrontation swift but without allowing the tensions it will arouse to erupt into violence. As Griffith mulls over the alternatives, he realizes that a man who can help is the Basotho paramount chief Letsie. Not only can Letsie be of great influence over Moorosi, if persuaded he also can provide a strong body of fighters to bring Moorosi under control. After all, at the request of Bowker, Letsie was willing to persuade his son Lerothodi to amass an army to confront Moorosi at the Telle River.

Griffith is aware that persuading the paramount chief will not necessarily be easy. Until now Letsie has been willing to cooperate with the government; in many ways he has been the finest example of the success of colonial government in southern Africa. But the disarmament law added to growing restlessness about the steady tightening of the imposition of colonial rule, threaten to turn respect into rebellion.

In addition, rumors are rampant of growing collusion between Letsie and Moorosi. Disarmament is providing them with a common cause to oppose the government. And now comes the victory of the Zulus at Isandhlwana. The whites can be beaten. Colonialism can be beaten back.

The trend needs to be reversed. Letsie needs to stay on the government's side — and Griffith believes he is the one to do that. Letsie respects him and will be strongly motivated to help him.

But how to gain his cooperation?

Griffith ponders his strategy. Without realizing it, he echoes the argument Bowker used in his attempt to enlist Letsie's help against Moorosi. He will begin by warning Letsie of the consequences of using colonial forces to pacify Moorosi. The government will throw all it has at Moorosi, he will say, and it is inevitable that

Moorosi will lose. Cetshwayo might have won, but Moorosi has fewer men and will suffer Sarhili's fate.

Once white forces take Moorosi — he will tell Letsie — they will take his land in the same way they took Sarhili's land. From there, they will look toward other parts of Basutoland to annex as well.

So Letsie's first task should be to persuade Moorosi to hand over Lehana and the other fugitives to the authorities. Any suggestions that his territory should be annexed will be removed; Griffith would personally see to that.

Should Letsie not be entirely convinced by this argument, Griffith will tell the chief that, should he use his arms on behalf of the white government, it will have every reason to exclude his people from the disarmament law. If Letsie can use his arms to defend the Queen, why would the Queen want to take his arms away? Already, in the eastern Cape, Griffith will say, some of the native people who fought for the government have been exempted from the disarmament law.

Griffith knows he is on risky ground by making such promises; if the Cape government should decide to impose the disarmament law on the Basotho, he will be powerless to stop it. But he is confident, too, that he will be able to wield some influence over the decision.

Also, he will tell Letsie, the Basotho will be able to keep many of the cattle taken from Moorosi should the old chief fail to cooperate.

Greed and the chance to avoid disarmament, Griffith hopes, will outweigh any sympathy that Letsie might have with Moorosi. Knowing Letsie hates confrontation, he will play on that attribute as much as he can.

Griffith instructs an assistant to ready his scotch cart. He will visit Letsie in Morija and present what he believes is a convincing argument. He hopes desperately that Letsie will buy it.

X

Palmietfontein — Monday, February 10, 1879

Throughout the turmoil around the Quthing magistracy in its first two years, one man has remained at his post in the compound, quietly serving Hope and then Austen. During that time Charles Maitin — born in Basutoland to French missionaries, clerk, Justice of the Peace, translator and assistant to the magistrates — has kept a low profile, doing his work quietly and efficiently and giving advice only when called upon to do so.

But now, sent for a few weeks by Austen to Palmietfontein to observe the troop buildup there, Maitin's concern is growing and he feels the need to take a more active role in the growing stand-off. He discusses the political situation with Captain James Surmon, commander of the troops, hoping he can help to prevent an escalation. He is talking to Surmon in the barracks when he is surprised to see MaLebenya enter the room. She greets him, smiling broadly at her success in tracking him down.

"Wait for me outside. I will join you in a short while," Maitin says.

As Surmon watches MaLebenya leave, Maitin adds, "She is an informant for us." Surmon nods, but appears not to be entirely persuaded.

Maitin ends his conversation with Surmon and finds MaLebenya waiting outside.

"Why are you here? How did you find me?" he asks.

"I heard from Mr. Austen that you were here and so early this morning I set out for here. Now I am here."

"But why? I will be back in Quthing before too long."

"I miss seeing you," she tells Maitin. "And I am worried for your safety should you return to Quthing. Word is spreading among the Baphuthi that Moorosi is preparing for war. I want you to stay here."

Maitin tells her not to worry. The government will be able to control the situation.

"You do not know how the people are thinking," MaLebenya replies. "Many of them are preparing to fight. I have been talking with them to see whether I could find where Lehana is hiding as I promised Mr. Austen. No one will tell me where he is; they all say they don't know.

"But I think they do know. The reason they will not tell me is they think I will tell you and you will tell Mr. Austen."

MaLebenya says the reason for the people's anger is not only dislike of the colonial government's intrusion into their affairs, but also the move to disarm them. They are ready to fight for the right to keep their weapons. That was their tradition when they had only spears and it remains their tradition now they have rifles.

"Now they see the soldiers here at Palmietfontein," she adds. "They believe the soldiers want to come and take their guns. They also believe the white soldiers want to take Moorosi because they think he is hiding Lehana.

"People are afraid. Sometimes they think the white soldiers are coming and they run away to find cover."

A Thembu man, who has heard some of the conversation, approaches Maitin.

"I, too, have heard what the people in Quthing are saying," he says. "I believe Moorosi is preparing for war. He wants to defend himself because the troops are here and he believes they are getting ready to attack him. And nearly all the people will be on Moorosi's side. I also hear the chances are good that Tjali, the Thembu chief, whose people are spread across the border, will side with Moorosi."

London — Tuesday, February 11, 1879

Details of the defeat of the British forces in Zululand are reaching London, where Colonial Secretary Sir Michael Hicks-Beach believes that it puts the confederation policy in jeopardy.

Defeat, especially at the hands of savages, is unacceptable. And the greatest defeat ever inflicted on a British force is intolerable. It must be reversed. Cetshwayo must be crushed.

Hicks-Beach decides to send reinforcements to South Africa.

Quthing — Thursday, February 13, 1879

For some days now, Quthing chief of police Isaak Masin has been watching a man named Pindu who has been sitting under a tree or talking to people around the magistracy. Masin talked briefly with Pindu a few days ago. The man said he had fled the turmoil in the north to seek a safer area in which to stay.

But Masin is suspicious and today confronts Pindu.

"You, Pindu, you are a rebel," Masin says.

Pindu is silent.

"Yes, I know you are a rebel." Masin pokes him in the stomach. "Go on, tell me you are not a rebel."

"How can you say that?" Pindu responds. "How can you say I am a rebel?"

"I am not going to tell you how I know you are a rebel," Masin responds. "I just know you are. You are disloyal to the government. You need to be locked up in jail."

"Would I be standing here, by the courtroom and near the jail if I were a rebel? Would I not be in hiding up in a cave with the other rebels?"

"Perhaps you are here to learn our secrets, to find out what we know. You will then take the secrets back to the cave."

"You have told me no secrets. No one else has told me secrets. How can I find out secrets when you do not tell me the secrets?"

"I might not tell you anything, but you are listening to other people speaking, you are watching what we are doing. I know you, Pindu. I know you are a rebel."

"Alright, then, Isaak, let's have a test.

"If I tell you where some of the rebels are hiding and you find they are hiding there, will you then believe me that I am not a rebel? Would I tell you, a policeman, if I, too, am a rebel?"

"That makes sense, Pindu. You show us where the rebels are hiding and we will no longer call you a rebel and we will not lock you up. Wait here and I will call Mr. Austen, the magistrate."

Inside his office, Austen is reading a letter from Griffith. It reminds him of Nero who was said to have fiddled while Rome burned.

"With reference to my 'circular memorandum' of the 7th of November 1878, setting forth a uniform system for conducting correspondence in this territory, I have the honor to draw your attention to the third paragraph thereof and to explain that when your communications extend beyond the first page of a sheet of foolscap such sheet must remain intact. Should your communication be short and written on the first page, or in other words, on one side of a half sheet, then, in such case only, must the corresponding half sheet be torn off."

Typical of Griffith, Austen grunts. He instructs how pages should be torn while the world explodes around him.

"I am sorry to interrupt you, sir," Masin says.

"Yes, what is it?"

Masin recounts his talk with Pindu. Austen resists the temptation to respond, "Did he say that on a half sheet of paper, or did the message go on to a second page? And where did you tear off the page?" But he resists the temptation.

"I will talk with him." The men walk out of the office; Pindu is waiting.

"So, Pindu, you will lead us to a rebel hideout?" Austen asks.

"Yes. I will take you to where Nepha and Sieponi are hiding. They helped Lehana to break out of the jail. They are rebels. I am not a rebel. I am here because I want to be safe."

As Masin did, Austen fears Pindu might be laying a trap for them. Yet he is willing to take the chance because he desperately needs to vindicate himself. And arresting these men could lead them to Lehana.

He devises a plan to protect himself should the offer be a ruse. "Here's what I suggest, Pindu," Austen says. "You will go ahead of us, lead us to the place where the rebels are hiding and talk to them. While you are talking, we will arrive and arrest them."

Pindu agrees.

"When you arrest them you will know I am not a rebel. You will give me a place to stay where I will be safe in case they find out that I have betrayed them."

"The plan is a good one, Pindu," Austen says. "We will meet here — not tomorrow because it is a busy day for me — but on Saturday."

As Austen returns to his office, Masin prods Pindu once more in the stomach.

"If this plan works, I will not call you a rebel anymore."

The two men laugh loudly.

"I am not a rebel, Isaak. I am not a rebel. You will see on Saturday."

Quthing — Saturday, February 15, 1879

Austen leads the group of policemen toward the village. Pindu is supposed to be here talking to Nepha and Sieponi. With Austen is an informant named Mapara who is willing to identify the men who broke open the jail.

Austen carries a rifle. Rather than relying on the policemen, who botched the last attempt to find the prisoners in a cave, he is taking the lead himself.

The group approaches a stream with thick bushes near where Pindu said the men were hiding. Austen signals his men to walk slowly and hunch down.

"There they are," Masin whispers. He points ahead. Two men are standing on the path, talking. One is Pindu.

As they get closer, they hear the men arguing. Mapara, the informant, identifies the other man as Nepha, one of the men who broke open the jail. They creep closer until the men are in earshot.

"You are going to tell the magistrate where we are," Nepha says to Pindu.

"No, Nepha, I will not do that. I will not tell him where you are."

"Why then are you here?" he asks. "Why have you come to talk to me about nothing? You are a traitor."

Nepha pushes Pindu backward. Pindu slips on a stone and falls into bushes at the side of the path. "I will show you what people like you deserve," Nepha shouts at Pindu. "I will show you what it means to be a traitor to your people."

He pounces on Pindu, hitting him in the shoulders and chest.

Austen walks quickly to the fighting men. He raises his rifle.

"Nepha, you are under arrest for releasing Lehana from jail," he says.

Nepha stands upright. "You did betray us," he shouts at Pindu. "You deserve to die." He spits on the ground.

"Stop that immediately," Austen says. "You will come with me."

The policemen surround Nepha, seize him and bind his hands. Pindu realizes that if he does not reveal the whereabouts of Sieponi, who is close enough to hear what is being said, that Sieponi will track him down and possibly kill him.

"Sieponi is in the bushes over there," he says, pointing.

Austen raises his rifle and fires several shots into the bushes.

"Do not shoot anymore," a voice shouts. "We will come out."

Three men emerge from the bush. Another flees upstream. Austen orders two policemen to pursue him.

"I am here to arrest you," Austen says, pointing his rifle toward them. He turns to their informant. "Mapara, is this one of the men who broke open the jail?"

"Yes," Mapara says reluctantly as Sieponi glares at him. "He is Sieponi and he helped break open the jail. The others also helped."

The policemen tie the men's hands and escort them up the hill to where the horses are waiting. Austen and the policemen ride slowly alongside the men, who are forced to walk back to the magistracy.

As they make their way along the side of a mountain, the two policemen who pursued the fifth man join them, saying that the man got away. They identified him as Ditlame, a son of Moorosi. They also saw blood spots on the ground, indicating that Ditlame had been injured. Nevertheless, he was able to move fast through the bushes and over a hill, where they lost him.

Austen is annoyed that once again his policemen have allowed a man to escape. But he is satisfied that he has caught the ringleaders of the breakout group. And he is confident they will help him track down the prisoners, including Lehana.

Quthing — Monday, February 17, 1879

Austen's first tasks today are to obtain confessions from the men arrested on Saturday and then to try them. He orders them to stand in front of his desk and two of the policemen who accompanied him to act as witnesses.

Nepha says Moorosi himself instigated the breakout. He says he worked under instructions from Moorosi's son Somathube who was riding his father's white horse and who said he was following his father's orders. He broke open the door with an iron bar after a key Somathube had given him did not work in the padlock.

"Somathube said his father would never consent to the disarmament of the people," he says.

In his confession, Sieponi says he also acted under instructions from Somathube who said Moorosi wanted Lehana to be rescued because the white people would take him away to the colony.

Austen sentences Nepha to three months imprisonment and Sieponi to six months imprisonment, each with hard labor.

A letter awaits Maitin as, accompanied by MaLebenya, he returns from Palmietfontein. Griffith has transferred him to Mafeteng from April 1.

He will have to organize his personal life to ensure he does not go alone.

Quthing — Wednesday, February 19, 1879

Moorosi's mountain is today the scene of an urgent discussion among the Baphuthi king and senior family members. Other family members and advisers sit in a large circle facing the men.

Every man is armed with a gun or spear.

"You might have heard that the white soldiers have been sent to Palmietfontein," Moorosi tells the assembly. "I ask you, my people, the people whom I love, is this not a sign that our country is to be invaded and they are to seize me? Why would they assemble there if they do not intend to use those men to attack us?

"Has the government not said we will be punished? Have they not said they will capture us if we resist their orders?"

The listeners are quiet.

"Now, this magistrate, Austen, has fired on my son Ditlame. Fortunately, his wounds were not too bad. But Austen tried to kill him and he also shot and killed two other of our people when all they were doing was standing in the bushes with the others. Why?

"This matter about Lehana and the escaped prisoners is in the hands of Chief Letsie. He is talking with us and with Griffith in Maseru. Why is Austen acting like this and shooting us when we are talking to Letsie about these matters? Is Letsie nobody that he should be passed by in this way? Why do they not wait to hear what we have decided?

"When I attended a church service at Masitise on Sunday, the missionary Ellenberger had a long talk with me. He told me I should hand over Lehana to the government people. He said that if I do not do so, they will come after me and that Letsie and other chiefs will also send their people after me. He says that Lehana is one man and one life, but if I rebel against the government I will put the lives of all my people at risk.

"He said it is better to concede one thing than it is to be hard-hearted and to invite a war.

"I thought carefully about what he said because Ellenberger is a good man and I know that he wants the best for me and my people. That is why I asked him to be my missionary. He is a man of peace who is always looking to prevent trouble.

"But I said I did not want to do that as the last time I did so Austen wanted to send Lehana to a jail in Cape Town for four years. At the time, the missionary told me that he would talk with the government and tell them to take away the jail sentence on Lehana as Mr. Bowker did. But that did not happen. Now he wants me to hand over Lehana again because he says it will bring peace. I thought about it again and I was getting ready to hand over Lehana. But it was difficult for me to take that step because he is my son and because he will take over as king when I go.

"And now it will be worse for Lehana because he has broken out of the jail. I know they will send him away and we will not see him again. I thought I would like to talk to the magistrate about the sentence, but I could not because I am afraid he would arrest me for hiding Lehana.

"I was not sure what to do because I also want peace.

"But now the decision has been made for me. I can no longer talk to the government people or hand over Lehana. When Austen fired on our people that meant war. He showed by that action that he will shoot us if we do not do as he says. Will he shoot me if I talk to him? So I will not talk to Austen. He has started a war against us.

"Austen is an unjust man. He sentenced my son Lehana to a long term in jail for something he did not even do. If Lehana had not escaped, he would now be in Cape Town working on the breakwater and he would not be able to take over my people when I die. Now Austen shoots at Ditlame. He already has punished Lehana and my grandson Thladi. Does he want to punish all my sons? All my family? All my people?

"The white government has assembled soldiers on the banks of the Telle River because they want to invade us in the way they invaded the lands of Sarhili and Sandile. They want to destroy us in the way they tried to destroy Cetshwayo. Why do they assemble their troops there if they do not want to attack us? The white men do not assemble troops without attacking people.

"We cannot let that happen.

"They also have said they will take away our weapons. If we do not give them up, they will fight against us. I have told them our weapons are part of us just as the horns are part of a bull. But they will not listen; they say they will come and take away all our weapons from us. They want to take our arms away because they know we will be unable to defend ourselves when they invade our land.

"We cannot let that happen.

"And they will come for me, too. They will try to take me prisoner, to try me in their court and to sentence me, too.

"We cannot let that happen.

"If we let these things happen, they will take away our freedom. They will take away our land and give our land to white farmers and build European houses and European towns on our land. They will force our people to work for them on the farms and in their towns. They will break up our families. They will destroy our way of life — the way of life our ancestors taught us and that has served us well for generations and generations.

"They will take away our freedom and make us their slaves. They will rob us of our happiness and make us miserable people.

"We have tried to be good to our visitors, as our custom demands. We have accepted the magistrates on our land because we know they can teach us new things, show us new ways, and protect us from our enemies. We have tried to work with them. But now they have shown they are not interested in working with us or among us or helping us. They are interested only in destroying us.

"We say to them now: This is enough.

"If you want war, so be it.

"I would rather die fighting for my people, their land and their way of life than live under white people, forced to live according to their laws and to work for them for long hours and little money.

"So it is that we will go out and fight when they come to get us."

He stands to give his words more impact.

"If the people they send against us outnumber us and try to defeat us the way they defeated Sarhili, we will make our homes here on this mountain top where we can defend ourselves and where we can live for many months and even years. We are stronger than Sarhili. We have more ways to protect ourselves. I have fought many battles and I know we can chase away the whites so they will leave us to live on our own. They will run from us like dogs with their tails between their legs.

"I know some of you do not want to fight. You say you do not want to send your sons and your brothers into battle only to die at the hands of the white man.

"But we can do nothing else. To surrender is to give up life. You will be like a lion that is put in an enclosure where it cannot run where it wishes, where it cannot live with its family, where it cannot hunt and where it depends on people to feed it. That lion will say to itself, 'I will rather die than live like this.' But once he is put in the enclosure he cannot choose to die; he is forced to live in such a way that life has lost all meaning. It is better for that lion that he dies when they try to put him in the enclosure than to live as a captive.

"So it will be with us and with our wives, with our sons and with our daughters and with our brothers, with our sisters, with our cousins and with our uncles if the white government takes away our weapons, takes away our land, forces us to live according to their laws and makes us work for their people. It is better for us to die than to live in their enclosure."

The men around him nod in agreement.

"We will fight," they say in unison. "Wherever King Moorosi leads us, we will fight. We do not want to be like a lion in an enclosure.

"Lead us on, King Moorosi. We will fight with you."

Moorosi smiles. He is pleased at the support he receives.

"Now," he says, "we must discuss how we are going to fight. We must be prepared to attack them before they build up their strength and attack us."

Quthing — Friday, February 21, 1879

Reports of Moorosi's preparations for war and his mountaintop summit are reaching Austen. The first report is from Moeletsi, who says he accompanied Letsie's messenger when he visited Moorosi.

"During the talks between Letsie's messenger and Moorosi's people the men said, 'We are not satisfied with the government; we chiefs called the government into this country to protect us, but the government does not treat us well but kills us,'" he tells Austen.

He is followed by Petrus Damanyane, a Christian who regularly attends Ellenberger's services and has provided him with occasional snippets of information that have always proven accurate. But never has the news been as dramatic as the report he delivers to Austen today.

"I am told that King Moorosi was to leave his mountain village last night or will do so today," Damanyane says. "He is bringing all his warriors with him and he intends to make war on the government. At Raisa's village, a man named Teki told me the chief had decided to attack the camp at Palmietfontein. He will attack them before they can attack him and prevent them from helping you."

Austen feels his stomach twist into a knot. As frightening as the story is, however, he reminds himself that it could be exaggerated. Although Damanyane might have conveyed exactly what he heard, his informants might have been mistaken.

He turns to the other pro-government man who has brought information.

"Molotsi, what have you heard?" he asks.

"I have heard that on Wednesday there was a great meeting at Moorosi's Mountain," he says. "At that meeting it was decided that Moorosi and all his warriors were to come and attack the magistracy at night and release the prisoners you are holding there, the men you say helped Lehana escape.

"After releasing the prisoners, they will go to the camp on the Telle River. People say Moorosi is doing this to start the war at once before the government can bring more troops from the Cape Colony."

"This is grave news," Austen tells Maitin after the men leave. "All the stories point in the same direction and so there must be some truth in them. We cannot allow ourselves to be overrun. We have no means of defending ourselves against the hundreds and possibly thousands of men that Moorosi will bring with him when he attacks us here."

"I heard similar reports of war preparations when I was at Palmietfontein," Maitin says.

"Indeed," Austen replies, "We need to act now before Moorosi does. We cannot afford to be taken by surprise." Still smarting under the criticism of his inaction on New Year's night, Austen is determined to take the initiative.

"First, I will send policemen out as scouts to let us know when Moorosi and his warriors start to head in our direction.

"Second, I will send an urgent note to the commanding officer at Palmietfontein telling him that Moorosi intends to attack here tonight and asking him to send every available man up here at once to defend this office tonight.

"If I send the request by special messenger it should reach Palmietfontein in a few hours, giving the officer time to gather his troops and be here by nightfall."

Conceding that Austen's idea is an appropriate one, Maitin nevertheless is afraid that Austen's actions might precipitate war rather than prevent it. Already Austen has been reprimanded by Griffith. Maitin is afraid the magistrate might be overreacting and taking too much authority on himself. "Should you not inform Griffith of your intentions and gain his permission?"

"How can I possibly do that?" Austen snaps back. "He is two days' ride away — and that by express post. Don't you understand, Mr. Maitin? Did you not listen as you translated and wrote down those words from the informants? The chief is planning to attack us here tonight.

"*Tonight.*"

"With all respect, Mr. Austen, sir, I understood the informants to say that Moorosi would attack at night, but not necessarily tonight."

"They might have not used the word 'tonight', but they said he intends to start the war immediately. To me, that can mean only one thing. 'Immediately' and 'at night' mean tonight."

Maitin thinks Austen is reacting with emotion rather than reason. But another matter is uppermost in his mind. Last night, before MaLebenya returned home to Masitise, he asked her to marry him so she could accompany him to his new post in Mafeteng. She agreed. He will hold off telling Austen or any government officials for now, but he will ask Ellenberger to conduct the ceremony.

Austen notes that Maitin appears to be lost in thought. He takes the silence as agreement and instructs his staff to prepare the ox wagon should they have to leave urgently and gathers a few possessions from his home.

He writes to the commanding officer in Palmietfontein: "I have just heard from a reliable source that the Chief Moorosi sent this morning to call up all the people who acknowledge him on the northeast side of the Orange River to catch their horses and come up to him; that he is tired of seeing the forces at Palmietfontein and is coming down to attack this place tonight and kill all the officers and sweep the country down to the Telle River and stop your forces there.

"Under these circumstances I have to request that you will be good enough to march every available man up here at once, in light marching order, to defend this office tonight.

"Have also to request that you will be good enough to send an express to Captain Hook, the resident magistrate of Herschel, to move up with all his available men to the Palmietfontein Camp to cooperate with us if necessary; and I think it would also be advisable that you should ask Captain Hook to send an express to Aliwal North and telegraph this intelligence to Government."

Bearing in mind Maitin's advice about consulting Griffith, Austen adds, "I am sending an express letter to the governor's agent with this information at once."

He makes two copies of the letter for his records, seals it, summons a messenger and tells him to deliver it immediately to Palmietfontein.

His next step is to write to Griffith. Enclosing the copy of his letter to the commanding officer and outlining his course of action, he adds, "I have no other course open to me, but to take the present precautionary steps," adding, "I will stay at my post to the last."

Quthing — Saturday, February 22, 1879

Austen sleeps fitfully, expecting to hear blood-curdling yells at any time. But the night is quiet. He rises before dawn and assesses the situation: The troops he requested did not arrive, but neither did any attack. He remains convinced, however, that an assault from Moorosi's warriors could come at any time.

"As you noted, the report said he would attack at night," he tells Maitin. "We have survived one night and should be grateful for that. I expect the troops from Palmietfontein to arrive today so that we will be ready tonight."

At his mountain fortress, Moorosi considers his strategy in his fight to retain his independence and how he should defend himself against the colonial troops should they be sent to arrest him and to take his arms away from him. Most important is the degree of support he will receive from the paramount chief, Letsie. But the Basotho king has been sending him mixed messages. A message from Letsie, brought by Makhube, says "The government wants to disarm the Basotho, but Letsie will refuse to give up his arms." But in other messages, Letsie advises Moorosi to surrender Lehana and the men who broke open the jail. "If you refuse to hand over the men and want to fight against the British Government (which is the government given to me by my late father Moshoeshoe) you had better fight your own battle, wherever you like, but not in my country," one message said.

Letsie cannot have it both ways, Moorosi reckons. Either we are to fight the government or we are not to fight the government. Either we cooperate or we don't.

Moorosi calls Lemena to sit alongside him in front of his hut.

"I hear two messages from Letsie so I cannot depend on him to help me," he says. "What do you think we should do, Lemena? You have lived on the diamond mines, learned how the whites live, and how they think. What do you think?"

As they talk, men move forward to listen. Soon a hundred or more — headmen, relatives, doctors and advisers — are sitting or squatting in a semicircle in front of them.

"I do not like war," Lemena says in a quiet tone. "We are not soldiers like the whites. No one will pay us for the months to be away from our fields, hidden behind rocks or watching the roads that lead to the white government's houses. War takes men like us away from home, it makes us hungry, tired and cold. Some will die. We will lose our cattle."

His listeners nod.

"The animals that fight, they are always miserable. The lion must skulk and hide in the daytime. He has no rest. In his old age he is thin; then he is weak and his end is unhappy. But the sheep rests. He is fat and people take care of him instead of fearing him. The quiet horse is well treated and loved, but the ill-tempered one is starved and beaten. So it is with people. If we have war we cannot improve ourselves. We cannot rest.

"There can be nothing better than for a nation to be at peace."

The audience nods again. Some murmur their agreement.

For a while everyone is silent. Moorosi starts to speak. "What you say is —"

"But," Lemena interrupts, his mood turning from solemnity to shouting. "But I... But I...." He jumps up, tearing off the shirt he bought at the diamond mines.

"But I do not believe that to be true now. This shirt is holding me back. Like the civilized life I was told at the diamond mines that I would like, it is confining me. The shirt has been telling me what to say.

"No." He throws the shirt to the ground. "No, it is better to be free than enslaved. The whites' way of life is like slavery. Clothes are slavery. School is slavery. The church is slavery. These are the things that make people children all their lives when they would be men and women."

Lemena kicks the shirt away from the area in front of the hut.

"Must these things take our manhood from us? Are the whites going to come here to insult our king, Moorosi, to walk over our mountains, to trample over our graves, to steal our cattle, to take away our horses and must we, because of plows and clothes and box-shaped houses and books and things our fathers never knew, and comforts they never sought, sit still when we should spring up to defend our chief, his honor and our homes?

"The white man's houses are built only of brick. He is only a man in a house. Our home is the mountain. All the land is ours. We are above the white man.

"Let those who want King Moorosi and freedom join with me. Is not freedom worth more than a blanket from the white man's store, and the name of a Baphuthi warrior better than the name of a white soldier?"

Moorosi stands up alongside Lemena.

"You are right, Lemena," he says. "Why should I hand over Lehana? I am not willing to give up my son and I am not willing that my people give up their spears and their guns, and the way they live.

"Every man can see now that I am going to be attacked. You have made it clear to me that now I do not care what Letsie thinks because I must protect myself, my son and my family. If I don't do so, I will be a dead man."

As the Baphuthi listeners stand up, raising their fists and cheering in support of the fighting words, a messenger walks up to the hut. He says Ellenberger is asking Moorosi to meet with him. The missionary is concerned, the message says, that the state of affairs appears to be heating up and would like Moorosi to come to the cave house and sit on the Wodehouse bench.

"Tell the missionary I would like to talk with him, but I am busy right now."

Maseru — The same day

When Griffith receives a copy of Austen's request for soldiers from Palmietfontein to defend his office, his anger is once more aroused.

"Look what this idiot Austen has done now," he says, walking into Rolland's office and throwing the report on his desk. Rolland quickly reads it.

"You don't think it is a good idea to send troops to protect Austen?" asks Rolland.

"Of course it is not," splutters Griffith. "Austen is panicking. He also has asked the resident magistrate at Herschel to call out the volunteers and send them to Palmietfontein. Word of that will spread quickly and is likely to cause alarm throughout the Herschel native reserve as well as the neighboring districts.

"Imagine what the people's reaction will be when they hear that our forces are readying to fight against Moorosi."

"Does Austen have the authority to give orders to those forces?" Rolland asks.

"He does not, and I can only hope that the officer commanding at Palmietfontein would have the good sense to decline his request. In any event, I do not believe the officer would act without authorization from a more senior source.

But if he does, we could have an extremely serious situation on our hands."

"Austen believes he is facing a serious threat," Rolland responds. "He is trying to protect himself and our offices."

"Austen accepts these statements from these people named..." Griffith checks the letter; "...named Damanyane and Molotsi, which he sent me, and believes that Moorosi and his forces are about to attack him. But I don't believe Moorosi would do that," Griffith replies. "These men are scared, as natives often are, and are making this up. I do not believe Moorosi would dream of attacking Mr. Austen unless he felt sure that he had the support of Letsie, which I am convinced he has not got.

"Moorosi is an obstinate old man and will very likely continue to refuse to give up his son and the others, but he will act strictly on the defensive. I have spoken about these things with George Moshesh and other trustworthy Basotho and they agree with me.

"Letsie tells me he has sent messengers to Moorosi pleading with him to hand over his son rather than face a confrontation that could end up badly for him. We should give an opportunity for that advice to have an effect. Moorosi respects Letsie and will be inclined to go along with what he advises him to do."

"Yes, I suppose that is a good idea," Rolland says. "But Mr. Austen is worried about his own safety should these reports prove true. I know you say they are false, but can you blame him if he seeks to protect himself should they prove to be true?"

Griffith paces up and down the room. Perhaps he has been hasty in dismissing Austen's concerns. But Austen cannot be allowed to call out troops. There must be another answer.

"Very well, you have a point," Griffith says. "Let us assume, even though I do not for one moment believe it, there is good reason for Austen to believe that it is unsafe for him and the other officers to remain at their post. Then the proper step would be to go to Palmietfontein, taking with them the government chest and the records of the office.

"Calling for armed support is madness. Even if half the men stationed at Palmietfontein were to be moved north to Quthing, they would be unable to defend the buildings anyway. Given its physical situation and the number of men Moorosi would be able to muster to sweep down on it from the surrounding hills, it would be impossible to defend it.

"Also, moving armed men into the magistracy is likely to precipitate matters with Moorosi. All doubts he might have had about intentions to attack him would be wiped away. It would also cause great confusion and excitement in the Quthing District as well as Basutoland generally.

"In addition, the small force at Palmietfontein would be divided in two, leaving both vulnerable to attack. No, if Austen feels he is in danger, then his course is to fall back on Palmietfontein. It is only ten miles from his office."

"What about the prisoners?" asks Rolland. "Aren't two of them in the jail?"

"Of course, I had forgotten about them," Griffith responds. "Only two days ago I sent a letter to Austen telling him to send the prisoners to Aliwal North, using the same authorization as in Lehana's case. I don't want to learn that the same problem has occurred again and these prisoners also have escaped."

His eyes light up as he considers an additional possibility.

"Austen can leave Letuka in charge of the office. That's it. Austen has reported that Letuka, Moorosi's son and the man who was supposed to have been the heir to the kingdom, opposes his father's actions and has become a faithful supporter of the government. Letuka will see that the prisoners are kept in jail until they are transported to Aliwal North and that the office is kept safe."

Griffith telegraphs the officer commanding at Palmietfontein, telling him not to accede to Austen's request for troops. He sends a letter to Austen telling him if he really feels in danger he should leave for Palmietfontein, but he should under no circumstances call up troops to his office.

Ibika, Transkei — The same day

The orders reach Granville, Brown and Scott in their camp at Ibika. They and other members of the Cape Mounted Riflemen who have been stationed at Ibika for about eight months are to proceed to Palmietfontein, taking with them three ox-wagon loads of supplies and ammunition.

They are pleased at the chance for action after spending months conducting routine police activity.

"Something must be going on up there," Brown says. "I guess the natives are giving trouble, otherwise why would they need the ammunition? Well, I am ready to fight again. Let me at them."

The men set off along the rough road toward Basutoland.

Towed by 16 oxen each, the heavy wagons make their way slowly across the flat plain. The men know the going will be rougher as they encounter hills and rivers fed by the summer rains on the road ahead, but soon they will be in Palmietfontein, ready for action.

Quthing — The same day

It is early afternoon as Joseph Thomas closes his trading store near Raisa's village for the day, and mounts his horse on his way to spend the evening and Sunday at the home of Henry Buckland, manager of his store near Masitise. From there, he plans to travel into the Cape Colony where he needs to attend to business. He has placed his store in the hands of a Baphuthi assistant while he is away.

As he makes his way down the hill leaving his trading post, Thomas senses that something is different in Raisa's village.

At first, he is unsure what it is. Then he notices that horses are being kept near the kraals. Normally at this time of day they are in the fields where they can graze. The large group of horses in the village suggests they are being held ready for immediate use or for protection — the sort of measure taken only in emergencies.

Thomas rides down the path to Buckland's store, thinking that the recent rumors he has picked up of war readiness may be more than mere hearsay.

Buckland is waiting anxiously outside the store he runs near the Masitise mission station as Thomas rides up. "A Baphuthi man who lives nearby arrived here a short time ago and told me to remove all my stock from the country without delay," Buckland says. "I know him to be a reliable source of information."

"Why did he say you should do that?" Thomas asks.

"He said war could start at any moment."

"Who is this man?"

"He begged me to keep his name secret," replies Buckland. He points to several people in the store. "You can never be sure you are not being overheard."

He leans forward and whispers, "He is one of the leading men in the church at Masitise and is a son-in-law of Moorosi."

"It is all starting to add up," Thomas says, keeping his voice low. "I have been hearing these rumors. too. And, as I left my shop near Raisa's village I noticed the horses were being kept in the kraals.

"I am going to tell Mr. Austen about this warning and find out what he knows. I must go down to the Cape Colony for a few days. But I will return as soon as I can. It looks as though we must be ready to leave at any time."

Cooperating with government officials has given Moorosi's son Letuka a new insight into colonial attitudes and changed his thoughts on his father's confrontation with the government. He understands now, from the way they speak to him, that the government officials have nothing but contempt for his people and their values. The settlers believe that they are superior beings who are entitled to dominate his people, take over their land and turn them into servants.

He realizes that siding with the government has put him on the wrong side of his people's future. He understands why his father has transferred his favor to Lehana as his successor. Lehana has been willing to fight for his people's freedom. Now Letuka is also.

He climbs the mountain to speak with his father. "I am no longer listening to the government people," he tells Moorosi. "You are right and I have been wrong. I will fight for you and for my people against the white intruders.

"I thought the government people were trustworthy and that they were working in our interests. I thought they wanted to help us. But now the whites want to take away our weapons so they can take away our land. They are gathering soldiers to kill us if we do not listen. They want me to work for them, but I am no longer working for them. Now I am working against them. My brother Lehana was right. You cannot trust the government people.

"I will show you that I will be a good king when you are gone. I will protect our people and fight against the whites."

Moorosi is impressed. Now both his senior sons support him.

Letuka's switch of allegiance moves from one extreme to the other and now he is ready for immediate action against the whites to prove his refound allegiance to his father. Convinced the answer is to attack the whites first, he sets about gathering a group of supporters to help him, meeting on the mountain with a group of Baphuthi, including Mafetudi, Moorosi's chief messenger.

"I want you to help us," he tells them. "We will surround the magistracy during the night. We will drive away the people who live nearby. Then we will shoot the magistrate's police so they cannot help him. Then we will shoot the magistrate and make sure he is dead. Then we will destroy all those books in which they have written down what we have said and done.

"That is my plan. My father will be impressed when he hears what we have done. I will show him that it is not only Lehana that can fight for him and our people."

The group is supportive, but Mafetudi is skeptical. He can see that Letuka is hoping to regain favor with his father as heir to the Baphuthi kingdom. But he wonders whether, in his eagerness to switch back and prove himself, Letuka is going too far.

"If you kill the magistrate, the government will attack you and kill you," Mafetudi says. "I do not think that is a good thing to do. I do not think we should be killing any white people. They will come to kill us if we do. Also, our customs do not tell us to kill strangers who are living among us, but to welcome them."

Letuka jumps up. He is angry. "Don't tell us what we should do, Mafetudi. You are supposed to be my father's messenger, but I know you do not agree with all my father's views and you have given false evidence to the magistrate to protect yourself. I found that out when I was helping the whites." He turns to the others. "What shall we do with this man?"

"He will tell the magistrate what we are planning so that the magistrate will escape before we can shoot him," one of the men says.

"You are right," Letuka says, turning to Mafetudi. "You, Mafetudi, you will be a traitor. You will tell the magistrate what we are doing and you will go and warn him."

"I will not do that," Mafetudi protests. "I will not warn him."

Letuka raises his rifle and places his finger on the trigger.

"If you do, we will shoot you, too," Letuka says.

Quthing — Sunday, February 23, 1879

Usually, Austen is able to relax on a Sunday, but not today. Reports of an imminent attack continue to reach him. After a visit yesterday from Thomas, the trader, he has received similar reports — and they have been continuing this morning.

Austen feels isolated and vulnerable, particularly as Captain Surmon, the commander in Palmietfontein, has refused his request for a platoon of soldiers. The only help he received was six volunteers from the Herschel district who had read reports in the Aliwal North newspaper of unrest in Quthing. They arrived yesterday, but would be of little help in a full-scale attack.

He rises early today after a sleepless and nervous night and sees Ellenberger and another white man passing the magistracy.

"Good morning, reverend," Austen calls out, walking up to speak to him. "Where are you headed?"

"My friend, Mr. Vernet, who is from Geneva, and I are on our way to Sunday church services at our outpost at Qomoqomong. One of our church leaders, Philemon, is preaching this morning at Masitise."

"You seem calm in spite of the crisis."

"What crisis?"

"Moorosi is about to attack us."

"He is?"

"Yes, I have received numerous reports that he is about to sweep down on our magistracy, attack us and destroy our buildings and then make for the border where he intends to confront the forces at Palmietfontein."

Ellenberger is surprised. "I have heard rumors that Moorosi will protect himself against any invasion, but I have not heard of any invasion and I have heard nothing along the lines of what you describe."

"I find your response surprising, reverend," Austen replies. "All my informants have told me that the forces are being gathered for an attack. They are armed. They are aggressive. And they are ready to fight."

"My people are going about their business as normal," Ellenberger replies. "I have invited King Moorosi to the opening of my new church, which is now complete. I am expecting to hear back from him this afternoon. Should I hear of anything untoward, I will let you know."

Austen thanks Ellenberger. He shakes his head in disbelief as he walks back to his office.

Before long, people whom he regards as reliable arrive to tell him that Moorosi has sent a force of armed men to Raisa's village, a few hours' ride to the north. There they will gather more men and from there, Austen is told, Moorosi intends to attack the magistracy.

Austen is aware that Raisa has wanted revenge against the government ever since Hope fined him for destroying a widow's corn field. He also recalls the time in Mohale's Hoek when he issued a hut-tax waiver to widows in Moorosi's district. Hope's refusal to accept the waiver created resentment in Raisa's village. It is not surprising, therefore, that his village should be ready to rebel.

Austen's scouts report that Moorosi has ordered that cattle be driven to his mountain top.

More preparations for war.

Maitin joins Austen. He, too, is anxious, but cannot believe rumors that they are to be killed. He has never encountered any feelings of hostility against him among the Baphuthi people. But he accepts that if the magistracy is to be attacked he might be in the way.

"Are you sure these threats are serious?" he asks.

"I am. I think anyone would be delusional not to believe them. There have been too many reports and all are so similar. We are left with no choice but to leave here," Austen tells him. "I think we need to leave for Palmietfontein and consult with Captain Surmon and Captain Grant there."

Maitin agrees.

And so it is that the magistrate who professed two days ago that he would stay at his post to the last decides to abandon the magistracy — even without receiving Griffith's letter approving his move.

"Once we reach Palmietfontein, I will apply to the commanding officer for a couple of wagons to remove all the government property and my furniture from here," Austen says. "I will return with the wagons but I will need an armed escort. All I hope is that we can take them across the border in time."

He and Maitin pack a few personal belongings and strap them on pack donkeys. They saddle their horses. "We should be able to reach the border and safety at Palmietfontein by late afternoon," Austen says.

Maitin hesitates; he must tell MaLebenya, who is living in a hut close to the Masitise mission station, what is happening. He mounts his horse and starts to ride in her direction.

"Where are you going?" Austen shouts. "I need you to ride with me."

"I am going to... "

Austen interrupts him before Maitin can continue. "You cannot go anywhere. We have no time to lose. We must leave immediately."

Torn between his desire to inform MaLebenya and duty to his superior, Maitin hesitates. Reluctantly he turns his horse around and follows the magistrate.

Austen instructs the policemen to follow them and drive their own cattle and those of the magistracy to the border. They will take some of their belongings, such as items of clothing, on donkeys.

As Austen and Maitin ride along the wagon road to the border, they spot scouts on the hillsides above them. Austen knows they will be reporting what they see to Moorosi.

Passing the mission station at Masitise, Austen suggests they ride up to the cave house to check that Emma Ellenberger is safe in the absence of her husband.

Maitin would prefer to see MaLebenya, but realizes he has little choice but to do as Austen says.

Emma Ellenberger tells Austen and Maitin that, along with her husband, she has not heard any reports that the Baphuthi are planning to attack.

"I am convinced Moorosi is determined to fight and I am expecting him to attack the magistracy tonight," Austen tells her. "My situation has become untenable. I believe I am acting prudently by leaving."

"You mean you are leaving us to the mercy of people bent on war?"

"I do not believe that Moorosi has any quarrel with you, your husband and the mission station," Austen says. "I believe his quarrel is with us. But you are welcome to join us and seek safety across the Telle."

"Thank you, but I am sure that, as you say, the king has no quarrel with us. We intend to stay here, Mr. Austen, no matter what happens. We will trust in God to see to us and protect us. My husband quoted only yesterday the verse from Psalms, 'It is better to trust in the Lord than put our confidence in princes.' That is what we will do if there is trouble."

As Austen and Maitin prepare their horses before leaving, Ellenberger and his companion Vernet, return to the cave house.

"Mr. Austen is worried about the chief," Emma tells her husband. "He says Moorosi plans to attack the magistracy."

"Yes, he told us that earlier when we passed the magistracy on our way to the service at Qomoqomong," Ellenberger replies. "I told him I was unconcerned, but now, after talking with our people at the outstation, I am afraid there might be some reason for concern. I should tell the magistrate before he leaves."

Ellenberger walks to where Austen is getting ready to mount his horse. "I have been talking with some of our people at Qomoqomong," he tells him. "I asked them pointed questions about their chief's attitude and I now understand your concern a little better. I still do not think there is any reason to leave here, but I was able to confirm reports that Moorosi is regarded as being in open rebellion against the government. Whether that will translate to actual fighting, it is impossible to say, although I consider it unlikely, at least at this stage."

Austen asks Ellenberger to write a note outlining what he has heard about Moorosi's rebellious plans. "I would like to pass it on to the authorities," he says.

Ellenberger agrees. "I will write what I have heard, but I still do not think there is reason to panic," he says. Austen thanks him and takes the note. He will enclose it with a letter to Griffith telling him why he has fled the magistracy. Austen and Maitin wish the couple well and continue their journey.

After they have ridden four or five miles farther down the road, Austen looks back and sees a party of mounted men in the distance following them. He had seen them earlier, but now they are much closer.

"We need to move faster, Mr. Maitin; they appear to be gaining on us."

They whip their horses and donkeys, shouting at them and encouraging the slow animals to pick up speed.

Austen and Maitin round a bend and the drift over the Telle River comes into view. They can gain speed now because the rest of the road is downhill.

The men who have been following them stop at a hilltop and watch them.

As they cross the drift into the Cape Colony, Austen breathes a sigh of relief. They are safe. At least, for now.

Austen tells Captain Surmon what has happened. He says he wants to return to the magistracy to retrieve the rest of his goods.

"I would like a wagon and an armed escort," he says.

"I am afraid I cannot do that, Mr. Austen."

"Why not?"

"I have no authority to cross the Telle," Surmon replies. "We are not permitted to operate outside the Cape Colony. Even though the colony has responsibility for Basutoland, this is still the border and unless I have specific orders from the Cape colonial government, I cannot enter Basutoland. That is why I had to turn down your request a few days ago to send a group of men."

Austen is too afraid to return on his own. He will wait in Palmietfontein.

The mounted men on the Quthing side note that the magistrate is talking with a man dressed in an army uniform. They head back to report to Moorosi.

Clearly the white men are preparing for an attack, they will tell him. The magistrate has left his offices and joined the troops and has been talking with the leaders of the government army.

It adds up to one message: An attack is imminent and their king must be ready to defend himself.

Maseru — Monday, February 24, 1879

Griffith, unaware that Austen and his staff fled across the border yesterday, feels pleased with his progress in enlisting the support of Letsie. He is heartened when he receives from a messenger a copy of a message Letsie has sent to Moorosi. Clearly Letsie is trying to be a peacemaker.

"Last year, I was unhappy with the white authorities," the message says. "I was dissatisfied with them because I thought Lehana had been wrongly treated. He was sentenced to a long term in prison only because he had run away. But now, it is clear that Lehana stole horses from white men in the Cape Colony."

Griffith smiles. Letsie clearly changed his mind when presented with the white authorities' view of the situation rather than that from Moorosi.

"But the white man has taken nothing belonging to anybody," Letsie continues. "Why did Lehana capture white men's horses? Had those white men ever taken anything of Moorosi's?"

Good, Griffith thinks. He reads on.

"A great many of Moshoeshoe's sons have been imprisoned, but no one has broken open the jail to let them out. As far as I am concerned, they were justly punished. I have not yet experienced any injustice from the white men. I say to Moorosi: Are your children so very precious that they should be protected more than the children of Moshoeshoe?

"If you, Moorosi, lived in your own country, I would say nothing, but the territory that you occupy is my father's country.

"There was a time when you, Moorosi, defended my father, the great chief Moshoeshoe, while he was yet alive. Anyone who tried to attack Moshoeshoe would also be attacking you. In the same way, when you say you will fire on the white men, does it not mean that you will fire on me? I am at peace with the Queen. The inheritance from my father, Moshoeshoe, is to respect the white men because they are protecting us from our enemies.

"I believe that you should support me and, in supporting me, should support the white government."

Letsie adds in a note to Griffith: "I have sent this message with Molomo to Moorosi. I have told him he must give the men who broke open the jail to me. If he is afraid to hand them over to Austen, let him bring them here and give them to me. I will take them to the court to be tried. If they are innocent, they will be returned to him. If they are guilty they will be put in prison."

Griffith is pleased with the message, but he is concerned that the time to reach Moorosi with Letsie's message of reconciliation is wasting away; the longer the message takes to reach Moorosi, the greater the chance that events will spiral out of control. Griffith is convinced it is time for him to step into the fray. He must confront Moorosi more strongly.

Griffith calls for three of his senior policemen.

"I want you to go to Moorosi as quickly as you can," he says. "You must tell him that I demand that he surrender Lehana and the other escaped prisoners," he tells them. "Also warn him of the danger he runs, to himself and his people, if he disobeys the order that I have now sent him."

Griffith is hoping Letsie's message will have a stronger impact if it is backed up with his own. Together they will present Moorosi with the prospect of a conflict he cannot win.

He also tells Inspector George Moshesh, his most senior policeman, that not only should he ensure that Moorosi receives the messages from him and Letsie, but he should move among the Baphuthi people, trying to allay their fears and to restore their confidence in the government.

"Tell them the government does not intend to punish innocent people, but only the guilty," he says. "Tell them, too, that all who support Moorosi in resisting the orders of government must remember that they will be punished and perhaps driven out of the country which they are now occupying."

War can be prevented, Griffith believes. He is confident that the combined impact on Moorosi of his instructions to surrender Lehana, Letsie's message to do the same, and the threat that he will be forcibly removed from his territory if he does not obey, will be sufficient to cause Moorosi to back down, hand over the prisoners and agree to cooperate.

As the policemen set off for Moorosi's mountain, Griffith receives a telegram from Native Affairs Secretary Ayliff in which he says the urgency of Austen's telegram has prompted him to send Col. R.G. Southey and the 260 troops of the 2nd Yeomanry to join the troops at Palmietfontein.

Griffith laughs in a mocking way when he reads the final sentence.

"Hope this affair may be settled without the use of force."

He wants to shout so loud that the secretary can hear wherever he is, "Not if you support Austen in his panic. The more troops you send to Palmietfontein, the more likely war becomes."

Quthing — The same day

The news that Austen and his staff have fled the magistracy conveys a strong message to Moorosi. Talk, he believes, does not always reflect what is in a man's heart, but action does. The lion's roar might be a pretense; it is only when the lion starts running toward its prey that you know it means to attack.

"His flight can mean only one thing," Moorosi tells Lehana. "They are preparing for war. He is joining the white soldiers at Palmietfontein and from there they will attack us. If he were not preparing for an attack on us, why would he leave the magistracy?"

Lehana agrees. "When a snake defends its position under a rock, it does not wait in the darkness at the back of the rock for you to attack it," he says. "It comes to the front and it shows you its fangs. It shows you it is ready to fight to defend itself. So we must show the white government we are ready to defend ourselves when they come to attack us. "

"You are right, my son," says Moorosi. "Tell the men in the villages they must be ready tonight to confront the whites and to defend ourselves from their attack. They must have their weapons ready and be prepared to use them in the way that the snake shows its fangs. They must show the whites we are not afraid of them.

"We must also show our fangs to those Baphuthi who support the government. Tell our people to take their cattle. The Christians who follow Ellenberger will not support us; their cattle must be taken, too, so they will know we will not tolerate any support for the enemy.

"But also tell them not to attack the missionary. Respect him, for he does good work; he does not want to attack us and we must not attack him. It is the government that wants to attack us, to take our weapons and our land from us."

The men from the surrounding villages start to gather at the base of Moorosi's Mountain. Hundreds of Baphuthi warriors dance and chant in unison, raising their spears and their rifles, echoing the words of their lead singer Lemena. Before long, their war songs are reverberating across the valleys.

"Tonight, we will resist the invaders.

"We will drive away the government men.

"We will show them we will not be subjugated.

"We will resist their attempts to disarm us.

"We will defend our land, the land our ancestors gave us.

"Tonight we will fight to keep our freedom."

Lemena stands and faces the warriors as he sings a praise-poem to Moorosi, asking for God to bless him. The warriors wave their spears and dance in time with the rhythm of the song.

"The Protector of the son of Mokuoane,

Who darkens the sun and makes it as dusk,

Saying that the orphans should walk in the shade,

That those should live whose fathers have died.

Protect now the son of Mokuoane

As the guns point their mouths at each other

Protect the one who was born a warrior."

Lemena turns to face Moorosi:

"We're yours, son of Mokuoane,

"We're dogs, bulldogs of yours

"We'll strike with you at the nations."

The warriors raise their spears in a salute to Moorosi and shout their support, echoing the words of Lemena. "We're yours, son of Mokuoane. We're dogs, bulldogs of yours. We'll strike with you at the nations.

"We're yours, son of Mokuoane. We're dogs, bulldogs of yours. We'll strike with you at the nations."

As the intoxicating singing and dancing continues into the darkness of the night, the line between defense and attack becomes blurred. A display of defensive forcefulness transforms into a demonstration of determined firepower.

Some of the men start moving forward, eager to turn their ardor into action. As they move, others join them and the throng of advancing warriors grows in number.

Still singing and dancing, they leave the mountain. Some turn toward Lehana's village. Others take the trail to Thomas's shop.

"We're yours, son of Mokuoane. We're dogs, bulldogs of yours. We'll strike with you at the nations.

"We're yours, son of Mokuoane. We're dogs, bulldogs of yours. We'll strike with you at the nations."

Maseru — Tuesday, February 25, 1879

When he sees Maitin riding toward the Maseru magisterial compound, Griffith wonders what can have happened in Quthing to warrant his traveling the long distance to him. Seeing a look of urgency on Maitin's face, he strides to the door to greet him.

"What brings you here?"

"I have a letter from Mr. Austen that I thought it important to deliver to you myself. Mr. Austen agreed to my request to bring it to you. Once you have read it,

I will be able to elaborate on its contents."

The main content is a copy of a telegram Austen sent from Palmietfontein to the Secretary for Native Affairs "for the information of government." Once again, Griffith notes, Austen has gone over his head.

The telegram, dated Sunday February 23, reads: "I have to inform you that I found it absolutely necessary to vacate my seat of magistracy this morning. Having had reliable information that the Chief Moorosi had called a considerable armed force to come down to the village of a subordinate chief named Raisa, about two hours' ride from my office, with the intention of attacking me and all loyal people and driving the cattle toward his mountain, which he had strongly fortified."

Griffith's jaw tightens as he reads how Austen abandoned his post, leaving all his furniture and government records behind.

"But I thought...I thought he was going to stay at his post to the last," he responds in anger. "Only yesterday I received a letter that he was doing all he could to suppress reports about a supposed attack by Moorosi. He said he was fully aware of the exaggeration used by his informants. And now he leaves."

"He did intend to stay," Maitin ventures. "But..."

Griffith gives him no time to continue.

"What could possibly have happened to make him change his mind like this? First he says he will stay at his post to the end. Then he asks for armed support. When that does not happen, he gives up and abandons his post."

Maitin finds it difficult to support Austen's action. "He did intend to stay on, Colonel Griffith, but matters took a turn for the worse."

"They did, did they?" Griffith exclaims. "What turn did they take?"

"We received reports that an attack was imminent, colonel. We were told that Moorosi would attack last night."

"And did he?"

"Well, colonel, I do not know yet. I left from Palmietfontein yesterday. I slept overnight on the way and rose early today to reach here as soon as possible."

Griffith grunts. "Very well. Thank you. But let's get this straight. Mr. Austen himself told me last week that these reports of an attack originated as a result of three causes.

"One was the presence of the force at Palmietfontein. That made the Baphuthi chief and his people afraid. I had always said that would happen and advised against sending additional troops there, but, as you know, I was overridden by the authorities in Cape Town.

"A second factor was Moorosi's anticipation of an attack from us to take away his guns in terms of the new disarmament law, which, as you know, has not yet been applied here and might never be. We should have been telling him that it is not yet law.

"A third cause of these reports was undoubtedly the sad Natal disaster which has emboldened the native people around the country who see us as vulnerable in a way that they never saw before."

Maitin agrees that these were all contributory causes, but adds that the reports of an imminent attack by Moorosi were persistent. It was these reports on which Austen acted.

"Some of them came from people we know and trust," he says.

"Yes, my dear Mr. Maitin, that might be so," Griffith continues. "I am not suggesting that the people who gave you the reports were not reliable. I am suggesting that the reports themselves were not reliable. Your informants were merely passing on information that they had heard from others. Who knows where the 'others' received their information?"

"That is a good point, colonel. But surely, if I may say so, sir, the persistence and similarity of reports must testify to their veracity."

"Perhaps. But I continue to hold the view that this information has not been proven to be reliable. I am surprised that he should have found it 'absolutely necessary' to vacate his seat of magistracy, upon information that could be highly questionable. Now he is leaving the loyal natives to take care of themselves — and that in itself could drive them into the ranks of the hostile ones."

"While we were on our way to Palmietfontein," Maitin says, "we saw numerous scouts on the mountains watching our every move. Mr. Austen believes they were evidence of the pending attack."

"Not necessarily. They were probably on the look-out for the attack Moorosi's people feared from Palmietfontein."

Maitin continues. "We also saw a group of armed men on horseback following us as we left. They were gaining on us as we neared the Telle River crossing."

"They, too, must have been merely observing you, Mr. Maitin. If they had been preparing to make an attack on Mr. Austen, it would have been easy for them and the scouts on the mountains to have closed in on him. Is that not correct?"

"That is correct, colonel."

"They would have been able to cut off his retreat altogether, leaving him vulnerable to attack. No, Mr. Maitin. All the evidence shows that Moorosi's people were acting more on the defensive than being aggressive. In vacating his post, Mr. Austen has left the loyal natives to take care of themselves, which is eminently calculated to drive them into the ranks of the hostile section of the natives simply to protect themselves."

"Yes, colonel."

Griffith signals the discussion is over.

"Thank you for delivering this note, Mr. Maitin. I realize you are not the one who made the decision to abandon your magistracy and I am sure you understand that my reactions are not directed at you personally, but rather at the person whose actions brought you here."

"I understand, colonel."

"Now it is up to me to try to rescue what we can from this situation and to prevent a war. I intend to send Mr. E.O. Davies, acting resident magistrate here and one of my most senior officials, to assume the duties of acting resident magistrate at Quthing. I should consult with officials in Cape Town, but I don't have the time to wait for them to respond.

"We need to waste no time in showing the Baphuthi we will continue to run the magistrate's office as we have been doing for nearly two years. I do not want to give the impression that we have abandoned our presence there. I consider this matter so important I am sending Mr. Davies this morning to start out for Quthing.

"I would like you, Mr. Maitin, also to return to Quthing and resume your duties as magistrate's clerk there. You will work alongside Mr. Davies. Ignore, for now, my instruction that you are to move to Mafeteng next month.

"I will direct Mr. Austen at once to send the constables he took with him to Palmietfontein back to Quthing. I intend to write to Mr. Austen informing him that his actions are unacceptable and that, pending further instructions from the government on the subject, he is to take two months' leave of absence."

Hearing reports that trouble in Quthing is becoming more serious, and concerned about the safety of his three trading stations, Joseph Thomas has cut short his visit to the Cape Colony and returned to Quthing.

After checking his store near the Masitise mission station, which is operating normally, Thomas climbs the hill to Ellenberger's cave house. He asks for the missionary's opinion of conditions in the area.

"At first, I thought there was no cause for alarm," Ellenberger says. "Even when Mr. Austen fled, taking his staff with him, I had heard only occasional talk of war and I did not take that too seriously. The Christians who live near here said they were not interested in fighting against the government.

"But since Mr. Austen left I have heard disturbing news. Cattle belonging to some of my converts have been stolen and I have heard increasing reports that King Moorosi is in open rebellion. Yet there is no fighting and no indication that anything approaching war is about to break out."

"Is it safe for me to visit my trading station at Raisa's village?"

"I would think so. Although I do hear reports that Moorosi is ready to defend himself from any attack, I do not believe that the colonial forces are about to attack him. Words are one thing, actions another. There are words, but no actions as far as I can tell. I sincerely hope it stays that way.

"I intend to speak with Moorosi in the next day or two to see whether I can persuade him that the government is not about to attack him and that Mr. Austen fled to Palmietfontein because he feared an attack, not because he wanted to launch one."

Feeling somewhat reassured, Thomas nevertheless is afraid that fighting could break out in spite of Ellenberger's best efforts to calm the approaching storm. Ever the optimist, Ellenberger might not be aware of Moorosi's true intentions.

Returning to the trading station near Masitise, Thomas seizes the reins of a couple of pack horses — and ties them together. He will take them to his trading station near Raisa's village and pack his most valuable goods on them. He has heard enough to concern him, and, in spite of Ellenberger's reassurances, he wants to save at least some of the goods that represent his livelihood should fighting break out.

He sets off, riding past the vacated magistracy and on to the bridle path along the steep slopes of the Orange River to his shop near Raisa's village.

When Lemena arrives at the Quthing magistracy no one is around. Austen and Maitin have gone and so have the policemen. Even the cattle and the horses are not there. He wonders where Austen and Maitin are. Why have they left? Have they taken some sort of break from work? The Europeans like to take holidays and go away. But when they do, they leave someone in charge. It never happens that no one is around.

The door of the courtroom is broken open. Lemena assumes someone was here earlier and broke it; surely Austen would not have left it like that. It is strange to see no policemen, no magistrate, no one in the jail. He wanders into the courtroom, picks up a criminal record book, looks through it, noting the names of people charged with crimes, found guilty and their sentences, and throws it down.

Surely, the explanation for their absence cannot be that they are afraid of Moorosi. The government is strong. Hope always said he was more powerful than Moorosi. Austen seemed to be more fearful than Hope, but surely he would not run away? Whatever the men in the government might be, they are not cowards. Are they?

Perhaps they left the magistracy so they can prepare a big force across the border to invade Quthing. Why would they do that? Why would the force not join them at the magistracy and advance northward?

No explanation makes sense to him.

Lemena hears voices outside, one of which he recognizes as that of Matushela.

Five other men, including Moorosi's son Ratsuayane, enter the courtroom. Lemena smiles, ready to turn the absence of the government officials into a party. "Let's hold a court hearing," he says. He sits behind the desk in the chair in which Hope and Austen have so often sat. He takes a record book, opens it and looks around. He had always wanted to be a magistrate.

"I call the case of the Queen versus Ratsuanyane," he says.

"Ratsuanyane is here. But where is the Queen?" asks Matushela. "Are you going to call her, too?"

"Yes, the Queen will come. She will be here any minute, wearing her crown and her long robes, but in the meantime we will go on with the case." Lemena says, laughing loudly.

Ratsuanyane takes up his position in the dock.

"You are accused of stealing cattle, telling lies and being a bad boy," Lemena says. "How do you plead?"

"I am not guilty," replies Ratsuanyane as more men join the group in the courtroom to watch the proceedings. Lemena dips an imaginary pen in an imaginary ink pot (the original seems to have gone) and pretends to write in the book.

"Let's have some witnesses," Lemena continues. "Who wants to say bad things about this man?"

Nk'a, one of the newly arrived men, walks up and enters the witness stand. Lemena leans forward and intones, "Do you swear to tell the truth, the whole truth and nothing but the truth?"

"I do," Nk'a says in a deep voice.

"You must put your hand on the Bible in the witness stand," Lemena shouts. "Why did you not do that when I first asked you to swear to tell the truth? Are you so stupid that you do not know what to do? You boys are all so stupid."

Nk'a quickly obeys.

"I am sorry my magistrate. I am sorry. I will do whatever you say, my magistrate."

The group in the courtroom, which has now grown to some 20 men, are enjoying the display.

"Tell the court, did you see the accused doing something wrong?"

"He always does something wrong," Nk'a says.

"When you speak to me you must say, your honor."

"I am sorry my magistrate. I am sorry. I will do whatever you say, my magistrate."

"I said: Your honor. You must say 'your honor.' I am so important you must call me that."

The assembled crowd laughs.

"He is a bad, bad boy, your honor."

More laughter.

"Please tell the court why he is a bad, bad boy," Lemena intones.

"Because he does not do what the white people tell him to do."

"He doesn't do what the white people tell him to do? Now I know why he is a bad, bad boy. That is a very, very bad thing to do."

More laughter. This is the most fun they have had in years.

Lemena calls for quiet.

He turns to Ratsuanyane. "I sentence you to be whipped twenty-four times with the cat-o'-nine-tails."

"If he is whipped once with the cat-o'-nine-tails, is that nine whippings all at once?" asks Matushela. "How many then is twenty-four whippings with nine cats?"

"No, you are a stupid boy," Lemena replies. "It is one cat. But it has nine tails. It is not nine cats. Aw, you boys. I don't know what to do with you. You are so stupid."

As more laughter erupts, Lemena stands up from the desk and glares at the assembled men in a look reminiscent of Hope. "I am going to whip you all," he says. "I am so angry with you that I am losing my temper and I will punish you all."

His face wrinkled with mock anger, he seizes the desk with the books on it and throws it over.

Now the humor has made his onlookers realize how much they hate the system they are mocking. Suddenly, Ratsuanyane, reverting from laughter to seriousness, takes his spear and plunges it into the record books several times until they are in tatters. Others follow. Shredded books lie strewn across the floor and spears fly through the air as they are directed at any symbol of the government the men can find.

After destroying the desk and benches in the court room, the men run to Austen's house where they smash furniture and carry off clothing.

Still holding his spear, Ratsuanyane walks outside, raises his arms above his head and shakes them in victory.

"Now the government is dead," he shouts. "I must go and tell the king."

Approaching his trading station near Raisa's village, Thomas sees several Baphuthi gathered around the entrance. January, the assistant he had left in charge of the store, runs to meet him.

"I am sorry, Mr. Thomas," says January, son of a Khoisan mother and a Baphuthi father. "When I came to open the store this morning, I found it had been broken into last night. They took some things."

Thomas dismounts and enters the store. He can see that goods have been taken, although it has not been heavily looted.

"I must leave here and take as many of my goods with me as I can carry, January," he says. "It is not looking good. I will pack what I can on my horse and these two horses I have brought with me. I will return later to take the rest of my goods. I must close the store."

"What will we do without the store?" January asks. "Where will I work?"

"I am sure it will not be for long, January. I will give you extra money when this area returns to normal."

He grabs some of his most expensive blankets from the shelves, places them on the back of one of the horses, and secures them with a rope. He ties several shiny new pots to the rope.

As Thomas is attaching another set of blankets to a second horse, a number of armed men appear, almost, it seems, from nowhere. All are mounted.

"What is happening here?" asks Madekoni, as he dismounts. "King Moorosi says no goods are to be allowed to leave the country. But here the white man is getting ready to take the goods away."

Madekoni's men raise their rifles toward Thomas and January.

"Leave your goods here or we will shoot you," Madekoni says. "King Moorosi tells us the goods must stay."

For the first time as a trader here, Thomas feels real fear.

There had been minor incidents. Some people, for example, had accused him of rigging the scales when weighing their crops and wool and said he was overcharging them for his goods.

But such disputes never amounted to much and he was able to settle them amicably. For the most part the Baphuthi people have been friendly, cooperative and grateful for his services. As they sold him their farm goods and bought saddles, blankets, pots and pans from him, they enjoyed talking with him; some swapped jokes with him; some even shared their personal stories with him. When January was in charge and Thomas was away, the store operated as normal and there was no attempt to disrupt trading.

Now it seems this group of warring men are furious at him for wanting to stop trading.

"He is trying to take the goods away," Madekoni tells his men, their rifles still pointing at Thomas and January.

"Shoot him."

MaLebenya is concerned that Maitin left the magistracy on Sunday without telling her where he was going or when he would be back.

She walks to the magistracy to find out whether he has since returned.

As she nears the building, she sees all is not normal. Scores of men have gathered around the building, shouting and jumping up and down in excitement.

She runs forward and looks inside.

Maitin is not here. Austen is not here. The magistracy is filled with men destroying not only the record books, but the magistracy buildings.

They pick up large stones and fling them at the door and the windows, they lift up furniture and toss it into the field outside and they plunge their spears into the books, tearing them apart.

She watches in dismay, then screams at them.

"What are you doing? Why are you doing this?"

She is still screaming when a spear is flung from inside the building in her direction.

Thomas stands still, frozen in place.

"I said: Shoot him," Madekoni repeats.

The men are reluctant to follow the order. For one thing, Thomas is standing still and not actually taking the goods, so shooting him does not seem justified. In addition, the men have a sense of respect and fear toward whites and they also bear no personal animosity to Thomas.

As the seconds pass, Thomas, realizing that should he turn and run he almost certainly will be shot, stares at his would-be assassins. Their rifles loaded and cocked, the men remain poised to pull the triggers.

"What are you waiting for?" demands Madekoni. "Do you not know how to shoot? Let me show you what you need to do."

He cocks his rifle and raises it to his right eye. As he does, a group of men from Raisa's village, who have heard the loud talking and remonstrating and have come to find out what is happening, enter the room. It does not take them long to take in the scene. On one side stands Thomas, ashen-faced and shocked. At the other stands a group of Baphuthi men, their rifles pointing at Thomas. Madekoni seems ready to shoot.

"Put down the weapons," one shouts. "Mr. Thomas is a good man. He is our friend."

Madekoni briefly lowers his rifle and turns to face the men. He is insistent. "None of the goods must go from here. The trader wants to take his goods. He must be stopped." He raises the rifle once more and aims it at Thomas.

The men continue to try to dissuade Madekoni from shooting. "If he wants to take his goods away for a while let him do so," the man says. "He will return them soon."

Madekoni shouts back, "Our orders are not to let him take the goods."

"Don't you see, he is not taking the goods. Take the rifle off your eye and you will see he is not taking the goods."

Madekoni lowers his rifle, turning to face his challenger and pointing to the horses loaded with goods. "Look at the pack horses over there. He has put his blankets and saddles on them. He wants to take the goods."

"Well, tell him not to do so. Why do you want to shoot him? Let him leave the goods. If you shoot him, bad things will happen."

As the men argue, January leans across to Thomas. "You must leave here as soon as you can," he whispers. "These men come from the area where King Moorosi lives. They are under orders from the chief. Ride only on your own horse from here. Do not take your goods or your pack horses with you. We will look after them."

Madekoni, conceding his challenger's argument has merit, moves closer toward Thomas, his rifle lowered, but still pointing toward the trader.

"Take those blankets and pots off the horses and put them back in the store," he says.

As Thomas starts to unpack one of the horses, Ratsuanyane arrives. He is on his way to tell Moorosi of the devastation at the magistracy and is attracted by the noise in the store. He goes to investigate. He is senior to Madekoni in the Baphuthi clan which immediately places him in command.

"What is going on here?" he asks.

Madekoni lowers his rifle.

"This man Thomas, he wants to take away his goods and King Moorosi told us he must not take them away. We are following the chief's orders."

Ratsuanyane appears to ignore the reply. As Thomas pauses in his unloading, Ratsuanyane looks around the store, walks to a display stand and removes a saddle. He strides across to the shelves and takes a blanket. He hands the saddle and the blanket to Littabehbe, one of the men who arrived at the store with him.

"These are for you," he says.

Ignoring Thomas, he turns to January. "You and Madekoni are to ask Raisa for someone to help you run the store," he says. "They must see that nothing is taken away. None of the goods must leave here."

Thomas is relieved at Ratsuanyane's approach. He knows that, in the absence of Moorosi, Ratsuanyane's word is effectively law to these men. Although Thomas is unhappy with him taking charge of his store, he prefers it to losing his life.

Leaving the pack horse half-laden, Thomas walks slowly to the side of the store to his horse. Now that Ratsuanyane effectively has taken possession of the store the men's attention has turned to the inventory and whether they can share in it. They are noisy, attracting more people from the village.

Thomas gingerly mounts his horse and walks it away from the store, moving some distance before stopping to glance back. No one is following him. He digs his heels into the horse and heads south.

Cape Town — The same day

As if the situation in Natal were not enough to provide cause for concern in the colony, Ayliff now has another confrontation on his hands.

"I am worried about Basutoland," he tells Prime Minister Gordon Sprigg over dinner in the dining room at the Houses of Parliament.

Sprigg says he has been so involved with the events in Natal that he has not kept up with reports from Basutoland.

"What is the latest there, Mr. Secretary?"

"I think, Mr. Prime Minister, it is best that I provide you with a little background," Ayliff says. "A confrontation with the chief, Moorosi, started when the chief's son, Lehana, caused problems over the payment of hut taxes."

"Refused to pay them, did he?"

"That is what it amounts to, Mr. Prime Minister."

"Very well."

"He later stole cattle from the Cape Colony. He was arrested for the theft and sentenced to four years in jail. He was to be sent here to work on the breakwater when Moorosi's men broke open the jail and released him and other prisoners."

"Was he recaptured?"

"No, Mr. Prime Minister, he was not. He eluded capture."

"The magistrate, Mr. Austen, negotiated with Moorosi for his recapture to no avail. I think Lehana's jail break was the cause of all this trouble. Last week, when Mr. Austen reported to me that tension was growing in the territory, I dispatched Richard Southey, who is an experienced military leader, to take charge of the troops at Palmietfontein, just across the border."

"Yes, yes, I am familiar with Southey. He has done good work on the eastern frontier. I think he is a fine choice. Has that move succeeded in persuading this chief to hand over his son?"

"I am afraid not, Mr. Prime Minister. Mr. Austen informed me by telegram last week that he began hearing reports that he and his staff would be attacked. Indeed, he was so alarmed that he fled over the border into the Cape Colony, to Palmietfontein, where he is staying in the police station at present."

"Has the magistracy been attacked?"

"Not yet, as far as I have heard. Colonel Griffith, who, as you know is our agent in Basutoland and is stationed in Maseru, says all is quiet in the rest of the country and he is hopeful that all will end peacefully. In a telegram to me on Saturday he said he does not fear that Moorosi will act on the offensive. He thinks that Mr. Austen got frightened unnecessarily."

"Griffith is a good man. He is the same Griffith who defeated Sarhili, right?"

"That is correct, Mr. Prime Minister. I have utmost confidence in him, not just as a military leader, but also as a civil commander. So much so that I intend writing to him today to ask him to go to Palmietfontein and to inquire into the situation and report back to me. I expect he will receive my letter in about two days.

"In the meantime I will prepare to leave tomorrow for Aliwal North, from where I will travel on to Basutoland. I want to be near the scene of the action."

Quthing — The same day

Philemon, the preacher, runs up the stone staircase to the cave house.

"Reverend Ellenberger," he says. "You must come quickly."

Ellenberger follows the man down the stairs to where MaLebenya is lying.

"We bound up the wound as you taught us to do and brought her here from the courtroom on a horse," Philemon says. "We thought we should bring her to you."

The missionary removes the cloths tied over the wound and sees the bloody gash across the woman's body. He gasps.

"What happened?"

"There was destruction at the magistracy," Philemon explains. "The people, they went mad. They threw stones. They hurled spears. She was hit by a spear."

Ellenberger leans down and examines MaLebenya. She is clinging to life. Tears well in his eyes.

"She is a fine Christian woman," he says. "I am sure she did what she thought was right. I will do all I can to help her, but she has lost a lot of blood."

He stands up once more.

"How will we tell Mr. Maitin?"

"I will go," Philemon says. "I will find Mr. Maitin and I will tell him. He must know what has happened. He will be very sad."

Arriving at the trading store near the mission station after two hours of hard riding, Thomas describes his experience to Ellenberger. The missionary puts the actions down to one or two troublemakers. He is sure, he tells Thomas, that the men would not have shot him and were just blustering.

Thomas thinks Ellenberger would have had a different opinion were he to have been facing down the barrel of a rifle.

"I must add, however, that I am becoming increasingly worried about the atmosphere," Ellenberger says. "I have just tended to a woman who was hit by a spear. It might have been an accident, but it did take place during a scene of mayhem at the magistracy, I am told."

"A scene of mayhem at the magistracy?"

"Yes, Austen, Maitin and the policemen have all left for the Cape Colony."

"I noticed a number of people at the magistracy when I passed it, but I assumed all was normal and that Austen and Maitin were there," Thomas replies. "That news makes it even more imperative that I pack up my goods from my store here and leave. Henry Buckland, the man who runs the store for me, is away on holiday in the Cape Colony and the store is being run by his Baphuthi assistant."

Thomas and his helpers have gone only about half a mile when armed men on horseback ride down a hill ahead of them, shouting to those who are riding with him to stop.

"You must ride on to the border," his assistants tell him. "They are more interested in the wagon and what it is carrying than in you."

Thomas gallops south, leaving his merchandise in Baphuthi hands.

Maseru — Wednesday February 26, 1879

It is the note from Ellenberger that reaches him today which, more than anything else, has given Griffith second thoughts on his reaction to Austen. Combined with two further statements from agitated Baphuthi sent him by Austen, Griffith realizes that the magistrate might indeed have had cause to flee to Palmietfontein. For the first time, he accepts that Moorosi is in open rebellion, and conflict could erupt at any time. He regrets his reaction to Austen's flight, but brushes that aside; attending to the situation at hand is more important right now.

Griffith must do all he can now, not just to stop a war, but to prepare for one. He must act quickly and decisively. He must take charge.

First, he sends a messenger to inform the Basotho around Maseru and to the south to call out their available men and mass them on the Orange River across from Moorosi's territory. He sees no need to explain why or to question whether they will help the government. He will simply tell them they must do it.

Second, he writes to Austen to tell him to advise Southey to take possession of two houses close to the Telle River drift. Either house can easily be made defensible. Austen should also ask Southey to protect the pontoon used to cross at the Phathlalla drift at high water. Should the river rise, men would still be able to cross the river using it.

He adds a postscript: "You must do the best you can to protect all loyal natives belonging to the Quthing district. I can't suggest any way of doing it. You, on the spot, must be the best judge."

Shortly after sending the note, Griffith receives a telegram from Ayliff, which has been forwarded to him from Aliwal North where it was received two days ago. Ayliff, readying himself to leave for Basutoland, says he has read startling reports from Austen on Moorosi's plans and if the chief carries out his threat to attack Palmietfontein, he will have to be dealt with severely. "Hope that Austen's fears may prove groundless, but if well founded it is well that we should be prepared for any attack."

Griffith responds immediately. "I still have hopes of settling the Lehana affair without force," he writes, "but if I am driven to extremities, can I order Letsie to attack Moorosi and do the business using Basotho alone? I think it will be a good plan to employ them in this way; they won't have time then to think of Zulu affairs.

"Of course, I will have to hold out some inducements to them, such as the chances of looting Moorosi's cattle. This matter cannot be allowed to pass over without our punishing Moorosi severely; if this is not done we shall be the laughing-stock of the whole country."

Taking a dig at his temporary replacement Bowker and his settlement with Moorosi, Griffith adds, "Last year he was let off with a mere nominal punishment, and hence his arrogance and disobedience now."

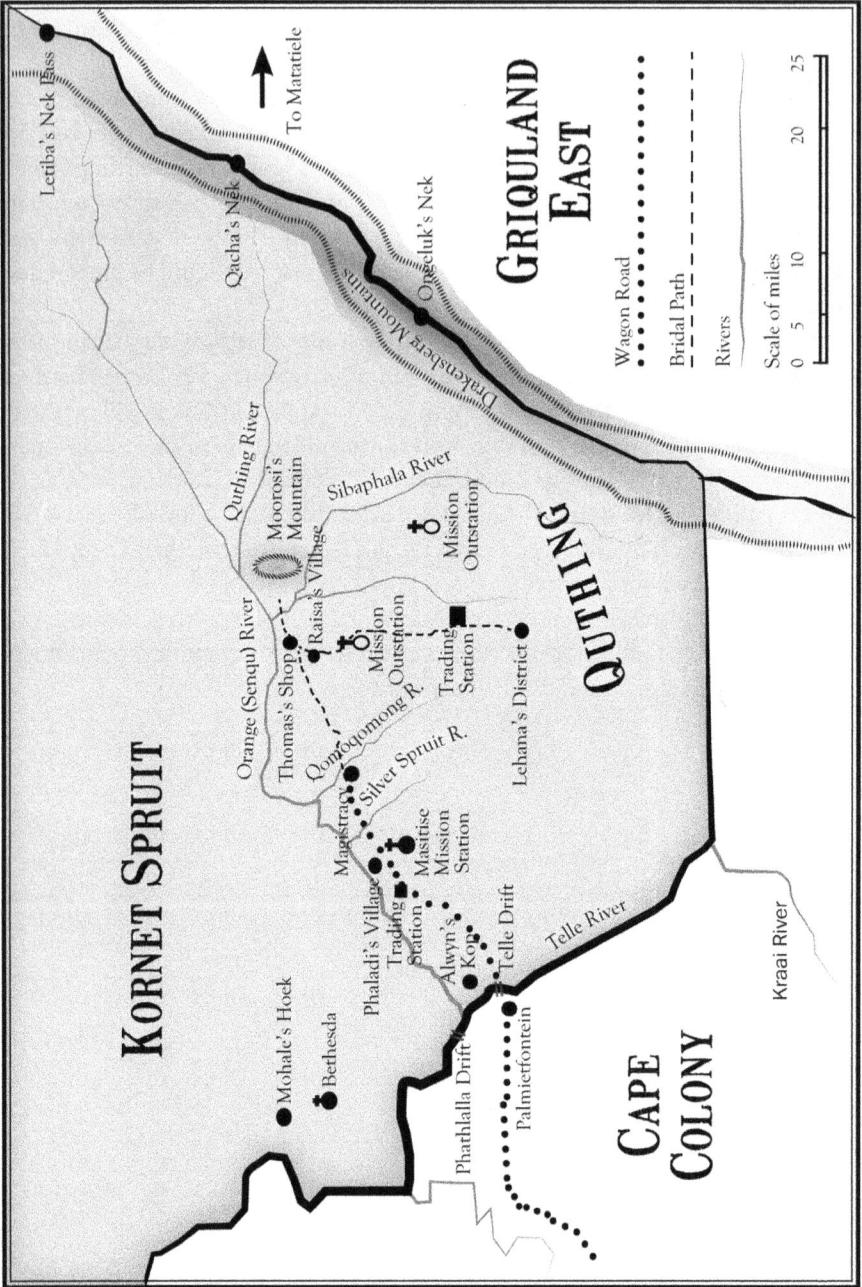

XI

Maseru — Thursday February 27, 1879

Griffith has moved from preventing an uprising to planning to put down a rebellion. The way to do it, he concludes, is to assemble a large force with mountain guns at Palmietfontein and march them into Quthing. Invasion by such a force would have a sobering effect on Moorosi, who might be driven to surrender before too much blood was shed.

Griffith must take several steps immediately.

He must withdraw Austen's two months of leave and ask him to stay on and help Southey in Palmietfontein. Austen can advise Southey on the nature of the terrain, where the roads are, and where the people live — all valuable information for an attack on Quthing.

He must change the directions he gave to Davies and Maitin, who by now should be with a party of Basotho, crossing the Orange River on their way to Quthing. He must tell them that, rather than try to take over the now-plundered magistracy, they should do all they can to give support and help to the loyal natives.

He must put together a combined force under Letsie, his son Lerothodi and other chiefs who, Griffith believes, would want to prove their loyalty to the Queen and demonstrate thereby that they should be allowed to keep their weapons.

Griffith will tell Letsie and other Basotho chiefs that, by his actions, Moorosi has thrown off the cloak under which he had been hiding and has openly rebelled against the government of the Queen.

As Griffith ponders all the actions that must be taken, all the orders that must be given and all the decisions that must be made, he feels overwhelmed. Always one for strict, careful planning and organization within a legal framework, he feels the situation is rolling out of control like a rock down the side of a hill. Part of his frustration is that he must organize a Basotho invasion force to work alongside the colonial soldiers and volunteers, but he cannot give orders to those troops who are under Colonel Southey at Palmietfontein. Instead, protocol demands he send his requests through the commandant-general at King William's Town, 300 miles to the south, which will unduly delay matters.

As he ponders the dilemma, he hits on a way out: He will ask the Cape Colony's Native Affairs Secretary Ayliff to take charge of those areas.

Griffith decides he must put his part of the plan into action as soon as he can. He will pack supplies and set off tomorrow for Mafeteng, from where he will travel to Mohale's Hoek, about five miles northwest of Palmietfontein. On the way, he will gather fighters from Letsie and the other chiefs. Because he has no authority to act outside Basutoland, he will ask them to cross the Orange River into Quthing rather than go through Palmietfontein and thereby cross into Cape Colony territory. It will not be long before he will have a large fighting force of Basotho warriors eager to prove their mettle against Moorosi.

Quthing — The same day

Moorosi, accompanied by a commando of fighting men, leaves his mountain fortress and, riding his favorite white horse, follows the course of the Orange River, a few miles down the road to Thomas's Shop.

He is distressed to find it in disarray. Goods lie strewn across the floor. The few blankets that are left lie in ragged piles. Saddles, once carefully arranged on poles, lie haphazardly on the ground. Shelves, normally filled with pots and other items for sale, are bare.

"By whose order was this shop looted?" Moorosi asks Raisa as he surveys the scene.

"I do not know," Raisa replies. "I have been keeping guard since yesterday to make sure that no more items are taken. When I am not here, others help out to make sure nothing more is taken."

"I want you to make sure that all the goods that have been taken from here are found and returned," Moorosi says. "The trader Thomas did not hurt us. He did not take things from us without paying for them. He was a guest in our land and we do not treat guests in this way. We have no argument with him. Our argument is with the government."

"I have heard that the people stopped a wagon on which Thomas had piled goods from his store near the mission station," Raisa says. "He wanted them to be taken across the border, but the people took the goods for themselves and then returned the wagon and the oxen to the missionary."

"I will have to talk with them, too, and get the goods back," Moorosi says before continuing south.

After a few hours, Moorosi, followed by hundreds of men, travels through the narrow valley of the Qomoqomong River, turns a bend in the path and comes across the scene of destruction at the magistracy.

Maitin's house, grain store and horses are untouched, reflecting his popularity with the people. But what were once Austen's office, his house and the courtroom are now little more than a pile of rubble.

Moorosi dismounts and walks into the ruins of Austen's house. The doors and windows have been smashed. Broken tables and chairs and torn mattresses give evidence of the force with which a group swept through and destroyed everything. The harmonium that he had once heard Austen play is damaged beyond repair.

In the garden alongside is a piano, its legs broken and many of its keys torn away by the force with which it was flung out of the house.

Books and drawings lie in confused heaps in the house and in the garden.

Moorosi walks to the courtroom, which he enters through a jagged hole where the door once stood. Inside, the overturned desk and benches are broken. The windows are smashed. In adjoining rooms in which records were kept, torn books and government papers lie in heaps on the floor.

He walks slowly across to the prison, where the iron bars have been wrenched off and the door — repaired after the New Year's Day breakout — broken down.

Moorosi is disturbed by what he sees.

True, he derives a degree of satisfaction that the symbol of the government's attempt to take away his people's independence lies in tatters, its dignity crushed and its authority dented. Here was where he confronted Hope and later Austen, standing up to their attempts to rule his people and their land. Here is where he experienced their so-called justice, where his son was sentenced to banishment to the Cape for a crime he did not commit. In some ways, it is good to see it all destroyed in this way.

But his satisfaction is tinged with apprehension. Although his men wrought this destruction on the magistracy without his approval, the government does not know that and will assume he orchestrated it. Yes, he had spoken to his men of sacking the magistracy, but he had told them that was a move he would make should the government forces enter his territory and try to arrest him. It was a possible plan for later, not an instruction for now.

Yet, under the intoxication of the war dances and their anger, a band of his men, including two of his sons, moved on their own, convinced that this was the action the chief wanted and was the right way to defend their freedom.

But the deed is done. It will provide the government with an excuse to attack him. Any hesitancy they might have had will now be wiped away. He and his people must prepare to fight.

While he is here, he calls on Ellenberger.

"I am sorry for what my people have done," he tells him.

"You are right to be sorry, for what they have done is wrong," Ellenberger says. "This is the government that took over from the British government, which Chief Moshoeshoe respected and agreed to obey. As one who respects Moshoeshoe, you should teach your people to respect the government and not to rebel against it."

"But we are forced to fight," Moorosi counters. "We are being threatened by the government which wants to fight against us. They put my son in jail, they have gathered soldiers just across the Telle River to fight against us. The magistrate — who shot one of my sons and killed two of our people for no reason — has left to fight with them. They want to take away our weapons so that we cannot stop them from taking away our land."

Ellenberger says that, in spite of these actions, Moorosi should hand over Lehana.

"If you hand over Lehana and you do not fight against them, they will not fight against you," he says. "I know the magistrate took strong action against your son Lehana, but you must accept that decision, hand him over and then I will intervene at a higher level than Mr. Austen and try to prevent Lehana from being sent to Cape Town. I did it before and I will do it again. Above all, you must try not to fight back because then it might be much worse for all your people.

"Even now, in spite of the damage that has been done, I believe they can still be persuaded to hold off on attacking you if you hand over Lehana and agree to help in the rebuilding of the magistracy. We, the missionaries, might also be able to persuade the government not to impose the disarmament law on Basutoland.

"Remember that God wants us to have peace. We must do all we can to achieve that and to give up some things if necessary. As I have said before, perhaps you have to give up your son's freedom to achieve peace. It is the price you must pay. In that way, we can prevent war, which will be bad for us all."

Moorosi thanks Ellenberger for his advice, but fears that the missionary does not understand the colonial government. If Moorosi follows Ellenberger's advice, the government will not only imprison his sons for an even longer time, but also try to take away his people's guns. Then they will not be able to defend themselves and his people's land and their freedom will be lost forever.

Volunteer troops and police in Palmietfontein, now at 400 and strengthened by new arrivals daily, are told they should be ready at a moment's notice for an attack on the camp and should make entrenchments for themselves. In addition to placing 40 men on guard to give advance notice of an assault from Moorosi's men, Southey issues an order that the men should keep their guns and ammunition close to their beds at night.

Moorosi sends a message to his people to meet at a cave near the mission station. With his body of fighting men gathered in the valley around him, he stands in front of the cave entrance.

"I want all the goods looted from Thomas's shops to be collected and returned to the trader," he says. "I am disappointed that you destroyed the magistracy. I understand why you acted as you did, but if you had asked me I would have told you not to attack it. But now the deed is done. We can discuss that matter when it is peaceful again. Now we no longer have peace in this land."

Pointing to the hills to the south, he adds, "The government forces are across the Telle River, waiting to attack us. Every man must be prepared to defend our land. The war is upon us.

"We need every Baphuthi to fight with us. We must persuade all our people, and that includes Christians, to fight. If they will not fight with us, we will take away their cattle. We need all our people to fight; only in that way can we achieve victory.

"Now, we must be ready for attacks from the government, for they will come. And they will come soon."

Cape Town — Saturday March 1, 1879

Secretary for Native Affairs Ayliff, ready to leave for the scene of the action in Basutoland, has been giving the rising turmoil in Moorosi's territory much thought. Earlier in the week, he heard of the plundering of the magistracy by telegram and today receives an express letter from Griffith telling of his plans to enlist Basotho against Moorosi. Ayliff has steadily pieced together a plan of action. But his plan relies more on government troops than on friendly Basotho.

Ayliff orders a strong force to be sent to support Southey at Palmietfontein and any Mfengu willing to fight with him be encouraged to do so, believing they will be better fighters than the Basotho provided by Letsie.

In correspondence with Ayliff, Prime Minister Gordon Sprigg has urged him to appoint Griffith head of the combined troops. Sprigg points out that Griffith has proven himself a competent commander, in civil as well as military affairs. And, after all, he is the government's main administrator in Basutoland. It seems that he is intent on gathering the Basotho forces together to attack Moorosi and he would encourage him to continue to do that.

Ayliff pens a telegram that he will send to Griffith by way of Aliwal North tomorrow informing him he should take over from Southey as commander of the colonial forces, which includes the 2,000 men assembled by Lerothodi, as soon as he arrives in Palmietfontein.

As such, Griffith will continue to take orders relating to civil matters from Ayliff, but will report to the recently appointed commandant-general of the defense forces— Colonel Samuel P. Jarvis, stationed in King William's Town — on military matters.

He recalls the words of Sprigg in a recent meeting that Moorosi be subdued as soon as possible.

"I cannot emphasize enough the necessity to win this war, if that is what it turns out to be," he had said. "We cannot afford another setback like that in Natal. The sooner we can subdue the native people in all parts of South Africa and take control of their territories, the quicker we can move toward Frere's plans for confederation. The sooner this chief Moorosi is brought to justice, the better."

Quthing — The same day

When Philemon hears Maitin has arrived in Phaladi's Village near Masitise, he seeks him out. "I have been going all around, from village to village, to find you," he says. "I even crossed into Palmietfontein, but no one knew where you were."

"What is it, Philemon?"

"It is about MaLebenya."

"Where is she? I was planning to meet with her today."

"She has been hurt, Mr. Maitin. Badly hurt." He pauses to let the news sink in. "Badly hurt."

He outlines how MaLebenya was struck by a spear, how he helped take her to the mission station, and how serious her wound is.

Maitin is afraid that, as a member of the government, it will be too dangerous for him to journey to Masitise under the existing conditions.

"Please return to Masitise and tell her I love her and I am praying for her and that I hope the missionary can help her survive this terrible event," he says, his eyes welling with tears. "She is precious to me. She must not die."

Mafeteng — The same day

Working in the government office in Mafeteng, where he arrived yesterday on his way to Palmietfontein, Griffith receives reports from magistrates in northern Basutoland that they are enlisting the support of the chiefs against Moorosi.

A letter from C.H. Bell in Thlotsi Heights says that Molapo, a Basotho chief, expressed "the greatest loyalty to the government."

Another report notes that Lerothodi, acting on Griffith's orders, already has attacked a group of Moorosi's people who had crossed the Orange River. The Baphuthi ran back across the river, surrendering their cattle.

Later in the day a telegram arrives from Ayliff instructing Griffith to proceed to Palmietfontein with his Basotho forces to join Southey there.

Griffith is pleased that he has been granted permission to take the Basotho into the Cape Colony and that he will be at the scene of action. He expects the war to be short and swift. Moorosi, faced by an onslaught of thousands of Basotho and colonial troops, will not know what has hit him.

Palmietfontein — Thursday, March 6, 1879

Robert Scott, on afternoon picket duty near the Telle River to prevent Baphuthi from crossing into the Cape Colony, notices them first. Several mounted and armed Baphuthi have crossed over the fast-moving river, and are riding on the Cape Colony side, toward the police horses tethered near the police station. Scott estimates their number at 20.

The Baphuthi have not seen the pickets, who are bunkered down among bushes and behind an earthworks about 100 yards east of the police station. Scott turns to Alex Granville.

"What do you make of this?"

"We have been told that they could be planning to attack. But these people don't seem intent on any kind of attack. Surely they would be charging forward and firing if they were."

"But it looks as though they might be trying to round up our horses. We cannot allow them to do that."

Granville stands up, raises his rifle, shoots in the air, and shouts.

"Leave those horses alone or we will shoot you."

The men turn their horses around, and head back across the river.

"That was easy," Granville says.

"Not so fast," Scott responds. "Look across the river. I believe they are planning to return."

On the other side of the river, the Baphuthi men shout toward the hills. More riders appear until they number about 150. This larger group crosses the river, yelling instructions and encouragement at one another. They seize two horses belonging to a trader named Jones whose house is close to the river and head back across the drift once more.

Granville jumps up again. "Return those horses!" he shouts. "They are not yours. Return those horses at once or I will shoot."

His demand is answered by a volley of fire. A shot grazes one of the pickets, who runs to the police station to receive treatment and also to alert Southey.

At the sound of the volley, hundreds more Baphuthi riders emerge from the hills, most mounted on horses, and some running alongside. They charge down the slope toward the water, yelling.

Alerted by the injured yeoman, Southey orders the alarm to be sounded and mounts his horse to see for himself close up what is happening.

The Baphuthi appear to be gathering for an attempt to capture more horses. Leading them is a man on a white horse. The pickets assume he is Moorosi, whose presence makes matters much more serious than an attempt to seize a few horses.

Granville, who is most senior among the half-dozen men behind the earthworks, takes charge. He advises the others to fire should the Baphuthi come any closer. "We shouldn't take any chances," he says. "They are armed and they are on our territory and we have every right to shoot to kill. If they get past us and attack the police station, we will be in big trouble. We are on the front line here."

As a few warriors come within 20 yards of their position, Granville issues an order to respond. He fires. Scott follows, aiming into the midst of the gathered men. A Baphuthi man falls from his horse.

The riders turn toward the pickets and fire back. The pickets return the fire.

Chaos erupts among the Baphuthi who thought the closest troops were in the police station a mile away and were not anticipating a fire fight over the horses.

The reinforcements summoned by Southey arrive. The Baphuthi and colonial forces fire furiously at one another. As puffs of smoke cloud the air and the smell of gunpowder wafts across the bush, several Baphuthi run toward the colonial soldiers, holding their spears, ready to fling them.

Scott and Granville cut down a number of them. But several succeed in evading the fire and run toward the pickets. As they do, a Baphuthi warrior hurls his spear over the earthworks directly toward Scott.

The 2,000 Basotho led by Lerothodi, and armed with spears or rifles, have crossed the Orange River into the colony using the pontoon at the Phathlalla drift.

They are somber, appearing unsure what is required of them. They have heard of the victory of the Zulus at Isandhlwana. And they have heard of rising tensions in Quthing. Now and then a rumor has rippled through their villages that war has started, but it soon proves to be false. Now they are told they are to fight against Moorosi and the Baphuthi people.

The men have been raised to believe that every man should be brave enough to be a warrior, to defend his family and his people. They have been trained to fight with their spears and many have learned how to fire the guns they have bought. They feel a sense of assurance in being ready to fight. But, although they have heard stories of war from their elders, most of these young men have known only peace in their lifetimes.

Now they are being called upon to show their prowess.

But the younger people are confused about why they are being called upon to be ready to fight. For most of their lives they have been told that the government is there to defend them from the Boers. They have heard how their fathers fought against the Boers, how they were driven from their land and faced losing all their land until the British soldiers came to their aid.

Now, however, they are not fighting the Boers. They hear that Moorosi and his people are upset with the government. The Baphuthi, they are told, want to fight against the colonial authorities because they do not like the way in which they rule them. Now Moorosi and the Baphuthi people, and not the Boers are the enemy.

They have heard, too, that the white government wants to take away their weapons from them. But now Lerothodi tells them that if they fight on the side of the government against Moorosi they will get to keep their weapons as a reward for fighting for the government. And they have been told that they will get to keep any cattle that they might capture in a fight against Moorosi.

So they have, most a little reluctantly, followed Lerothodi's instructions to gather here today to prepare for what could be a fight against a group of people with whom they really have no quarrel. Perhaps, they think, it will turn out as it did nearly a year ago when Bowker faced off with Moorosi. They will stand there, listen to the two sides argue, see them sort out their problems peacefully, and then go home. Above all, however, they will do as they are told. Lerothodi is their leader and they will follow him. If he says they must fight, they will fight.

Before they can give the situation more thought, Lerothodi instructs them to travel to Palmietfontein. It seems as though the war has already started.

Scott jumps to the side. The spear glances his leg, drawing blood, but the wound is not deep.

The Baphuthi warrior continues advancing, presumably to follow with another spear — he carries several — and a hand-to-hand attack. Granville raises his rifle and fires. A few feet away, the warrior falls, fatally wounded.

Southey summons more men. Soon members of the Cape Mounted Riflemen and the volunteer Queenstown yeomanry are tumbling out of their barracks. Half-way to the river, they kneel, load and fire on the rampaging Baphuthi whose numbers have now swollen to 450.

For more than an hour, the Baphuthi fight back with spears and rifles and the fighting becomes intense. Several Baphuthi fall from their horses. Others, on foot, collapse as the colonial soldiers' bullets find their targets. Some of the Baphuthi risk death to gather the bodies, put them on horses and take them back across the river as the firing continues around them.

The fighting is in full swing as Lerothodi arrives with his men.

Unexpectedly the man on the white horse gives instructions to retreat over the Telle River. The Baphuthi follow, abandoning most of the cattle and horses they had seized.

Southey, reluctant to cross into Basutoland, orders the troops to hold their positions.

About 20 Baphuthi have been killed in the skirmish. On the colonial side, a sergeant in the Basotho police has been shot in both legs and a trader named Kelly has suffered a superficial wound to the chest.

As a medical officer tends to Scott's wound, Southey walks across to thank Scott for his action.

"Did you see the way we made them run?" Scott says, wincing as the officer wipes away the blood and bandages his leg. "They sure were afraid of us."

Griffith urges Southey to pursue Moorosi across the border.

Southey disagrees. "We should wait for orders from Cape Town," he says. "And I think we need more fighting power. I have ordered a couple of cannon and we should wait until they arrive. We also are expecting more troops.

"Clearly, the men who crossed the border are only a small portion of the force at Moorosi's command. If they had not turned and fled, we might have been harder pressed to push back the attack. It is no good pursuing Moorosi and then finding we're unable to complete the mission."

Griffith reluctantly concedes. He wonders what would have happened should he have insisted on pursuit and taken Lerothodi's people with him. Would Southey have been able to overrule him? After all, he is the governor's agent for Basutoland and responsible for Lerothodi and his people.

He lets the issue go for now, confident that the combined forces will be more than enough to capture Moorosi, his family and his senior advisers in short order and end this uprising against colonial rule.

Quthing — Friday, March 7, 1879

Riding on his white horse, the Baphuthi king is subdued as he makes his way to his mountain fortress. His face reflects disillusionment.

When he led his troops across the Telle River, he believed he would be joined by a large number of Basotho, who had promised him support. He turns to his son

Letuka. "I had thought that even Letsie's son Lerothodi would join me with thousands of warriors," he says. "Did you not yourself tell me that?"

"It was what we heard from Lerothodi's messenger," Letuka responds. "He said you were like family. If you were attacked by the whites, Lerothodi would feel he was being attacked, too, and would come to your aid. Then I heard that he was gathering his men at Mohale's Hoek and I assumed he was there to help you."

"I thought he would help me," Moorosi continues. "I wanted to attack the settlers first, before they could gather a larger force and, with Lerothodi's support, defeat them.

"Sarhili and Sandile beat the colonial troops at first. They lost only after the colonists increased their troops. Cetshwayo showed that if you attack them first, before they are ready, it is possible to defeat the white government forces."

"That is so," Letuka replies. "The number of white soldiers just across the Telle is small, perhaps only 200."

"But now I see they are supported by Lerothodi." Moorosi sighs, looking at the ground, still shocked by the sight of his friend becoming his enemy.

"If Lerothodi will not support me, now I know that Letsie will not support me. It is not only that he will not support me; he will fight against me.

"How can that be? How could Letsie dishonor his own word? How could he turn on me and make him his enemy when two days before I was his friend? And how can I fight against my brothers?

"I want you to send a message to Lerothodi. I want you to tell him that he sent me promises of help, but now I have been completely deceived. But tell Lerothodi I will not yield. I will not let the government seek me out and try to kill me, even if it means I have to fight against him, too.

"Tell our people that they must go into the mountains and defend themselves and their cattle."

As he stands awash in disillusionment and abandonment Moorosi becomes certain of one thing. He will fight to the end against the colonial forces, even should Lerothodi fight alongside them. It is better, he believes, to die fighting than live in servitude.

He cannot turn back now. He will defend himself and his people against all who try to oust them. He is the ruler of his people, an independent ruler of his own country, not a vassal of anyone.

Palmietfontein — Monday, March 10, 1879

A note from Ayliff appointing him commander of the invasion force and placing Southey under him has emboldened Griffith. Only a week ago, he felt that the situation was spiraling out of his control. Now he feels fully in control, both as a military officer and as the chief representative of the civilian government in Basutoland.

His task is clear. He will need to impose justice on Moorosi who has made it obvious that he is a rebel against British colonial rule and so must be prevented from continuing his rebellious activities.

Griffith has learned that Moorosi's son Letuka who they recently were told was on the government side has joined his father in the rebellion. It seems that the Baphuthi people are rallying around their king and that the number of Baphuthi loyal to the colonial government might be fewer than they had hoped. The news comes as a disappointment to Griffith; he had come to like and respect Letuka even though he had never met him.

Griffith outlines his plans to his senior officers. "In order to wage this war, for that is what it is now, I will assemble a large force to invade Moorosi's territory and to arrest him, his son Lehana and other offenders," he says.

"We will need to subdue the rebellion and ensure government control is re-imposed on the territory. We can expect Moorosi to fight back vigorously. He has already shown he has no intention of yielding without a fight and he has a strong force of warriors on whom he can call, which now include Letuka.

"I will be in command of all the forces, consisting of regular troops as well as volunteers from the surrounding districts, as well as the men supplied by Lerothodi and the other Basotho chiefs. They are good fighters, men who understand the terrain and who know the thinking of the people against whom they will fight.

"We will need a few days to prepare, to ensure we have the requisite number of guns and ammunition, but we will have to move soon."

Griffith asks Maitin, for whom he developed considerable respect as the events unfolded in Quthing, to serve as his aide-de-camp and interpreter. "I need you to assist me with record keeping as well as helping me with translation when I talk with Lerothodi and the many other chiefs who will be involved in this operation," he explains.

"You proved yourself an able administrator in Quthing, where you were called upon to serve two people, one of whom in particular who could be unpredictable and with whom, I am sure, you did not always agree."

Maitin smiles. At least someone noticed.

"You also know Moorosi and his people. You speak their language and you are close to their people."

The smile disappears from Maitin's face. He looks down. Griffith does not realize just how close he has become to one Baphuthi person. Maitin wonders what he and MaLebenya would have been doing now had she been able to join him and were she not lying near death at the mission station, now that full-scale war appears imminent and Maitin is to help in the fight against the Baphuthi.

Maitin believes that, if she recovers she will wait for him so that they can be married and start a family of their own, one that would cross the cultural divide that now is precipitating war. Of course, he thinks, MaLebenya will not fight for Moorosi in word or deed. But then, he could be wrong. Perhaps her soul is still steeped in her Baphuthi roots, in spite of her run-in with Raisa. Now that he thinks of it, he has never discussed these matters with her, always assuming she was on the government's side, and, being a Christian, had adopted European ways. How would she feel about him taking this position with Griffith, in which he will assist the colonial forces to kill the Baphuthi people?

He sets those thoughts aside. He must do what he is called upon to do.

"I will perform my duties to the best of my ability," he assures Griffith, hoping that the war will prove short, and that he might someday find that MaLebenya has recovered, has returned to live in her hut at Masitise and that they will be together.

Phathlalla Drift — Saturday March 15, 1879

Griffith is anxious to move as soon as possible against Moorosi, even though Southey is still urging the colonial forces to wait until they receive instructions from Cape Town.

"Here's what I plan to do," Griffith tells Southey. "Moorosi is likely to fall back on his mountain fortress should we succeed in advancing through his front lines in the south of Quthing, which I believe we will do. So I am sending a message to Colonel Edward Brabant, who is stationed in Umtata, to bring his troops and two cannon, which I believe will be needed if we are to attack the mountain fortress."

"I have heard of Brabant," Southey replies.

"I know him well," says Griffith. "He came to the Cape Colony about 23 years ago, at the age of 16 and became a rancher in the East London district. He joined the Cape Mounted Riflemen and fought in various native wars, rising to be a captain about 10 years ago. He spent two years in politics, as a member of the legislative assembly for East London, then was appointed a field commandant of the Cape Colonial Forces four years ago. He must be about 40 now and is a colonel of the First Cape Yeomanry.

"He is a strong commander. His men know how to operate the cannon and they are good fighters; they will be of great help to us. I have instructed him to gather 150 men, to send some by way of Palmietfontein with the cannon, and to travel himself with the remainder. They are to enter Baphuthi territory to the east, where he will be able to mop up any rebel forces on his way to Moorosi's Mountain.

"Seven hundred Basotho that I have assembled and who form part of what I am calling the Basutoland Native Contingent will go to the Kornet Spruit bank of the Orange River where they will take up posts at staggered positions northward along the river as far as the mountain above Raisa's village. Their task will be to prevent rebels from crossing the river and to capture stock from any who try.

"Tomorrow, I will march with the rest of the contingent to the bank of the Telle River, from where we will advance into Moorosi's territory on Monday.

"As we advance northward, Captain Henry Davies, leading the Basutoland Police, and another group of the Basutoland Native Contingent, will march to the east, working their way around the hills toward the head of Silver Spruit River. From there, they will move back west to Phaladi's Nek, close to the village occupied by the family and friends of Phaladi, a Christian Baphuthi who lives close to the mission station at Masitise and, I am told, has renounced his allegiance to Moorosi.

"We'll meet Davies at Phaladi's village. From there, we will patrol the surrounding territory, dispersing any rebellious groups we might find or inviting them to surrender. We will send a patrol to Lehana's cave in the valley of the Qomoqomong, oust the chief's rebellious son from his hiding and bring him to face justice.

"Should Moorosi find sanctuary on his mountain we will confront the chief there directly — after capturing the rebel groups in the rest of the country. There, we will surround him and force him to surrender."

Quthing — Monday, March 17, 1879

It is an impressive show of force. At nine o-clock this morning, under skies heavy with the threat of rain, Griffith, Southey and Colonel E.T. Minto, commander of the 104-strong 3rd Yeomanry, which arrived in Palmietfontein on Saturday, cross the Telle River, accompanied by 100 Cape Mounted Riflemen, 300 Cape Mounted Yeomanry, 100 Mfengu and 2,000 members of the Basutoland Native Contingent. Maitin, serving as a special aid to Griffith, accompanies them. Their destination: Phaladi's Village, near Ellenberger's Masitise mission station.

Granville, Scott and Brown are among a contingent of the Cape Mounted Riflemen instructed to remain at Palmietfontein. They are told they will be called upon once the troops advance to Moorosi's mountain; in the meantime they should serve as a back-stop in case of trouble.

The troops under Griffith, Southey and Minto are surprised when they encounter no resistance on their 12-mile march in intermittent rain into Quthing, where they set up camp close to Phaladi's village.

Phaladi's people welcome the troops.

With the rain increasing, the men move quickly to pitch their tents. Some have to settle for sheltering under blankets.

As they work, Davies arrives with his group.

"Our march appears to have been almost as uneventful as yours," he tells Griffith in the commander's tent, raising his voice against the patter of rain on the canvas. "But we did drive off a small party of Baphuthi under Moorosi's son Ratsuanyane shortly before we arrived here. We took one of the rebels prisoner."

"Good work, Davies," Griffith replies. "Because it appears so quiet, I have instructed a large part of the Basutoland Native Contingent, who are on the other side of the Orange River under Letsie's sons Lerothodi, Bereng and Maama, to join us here, but I have just received word that they cannot cross the Orange River until the waters have abated a little."

With the tents erected, Griffith instructs the men to fortify the camp.

"We cannot afford to take any chances," he tells the men. "Moorosi might be planning a surprise attack. I need you to build earthworks to protect our camp."

The men reluctantly swash their way through the mud to start the arduous task of digging trenches and surround them with sandbags.

"Now we have a visit to make up that hill," Griffith says, pointing eastward.

Southey and the senior magistrates accompanying him join Griffith through another heavy downpour to visit the missionary, Fred Ellenberger, and his wife, Emma, in their cave house at Masitise.

The Ellenbergers invite them to dinner.

During the meal, Ellenberger tells Griffith what happened to MaLebenya.

"How is she faring?" asks Griffith.

"She is clinging to life. We are hoping that, with all the prayers being sent to heaven on her behalf, that she will pull through, but it is going to be tough."

"Was she deliberately attacked?" asks Griffith.

"No one seems to know," Ellenberger responds. "All we know is that a spear hit her, but whether it was aimed at her or whether it was flung carelessly and she happened to step into its path is unknown."

"Perhaps she was deliberately attacked," Griffith replies. "She was the first to lay a claim with Hope when he set up here as the first magistrate."

"I do not believe that to be the case," Ellenberger responds. "The Baphuthi people don't bear animosity in that way, strange as it may sound to our European minds. We are so used to thoughts of revenge that we cannot always understand how people can be so forgiving."

"In any event," Griffith says, "my men will provide aid and protection to you, your good wife and family, and to those Baphuthi living close to you who have not joined Moorosi in his revolt. Let me assure you you have nothing to fear from the rebels. We will see to that."

Ellenberger thanks him, pointing out that he has postponed the formal opening of his new church — which he had spent nine months building and can seat 400 — until next month. Moorosi is to be a special guest and he hopes the tension will have abated by then and the king will be able to attend.

"Talking of tensions abating and seeing you are sitting on the Wodehouse bench," Ellenberger says, "I would have liked to have heard you discussing a way of bringing about a peaceful resolution to this conflict."

"It is up to Moorosi to bring about peace," Griffith responds. "If he is prepared to hand over Lehana and the other escaped prisoners, and present himself for trial for his rebellious acts, we will take a big step toward resolving this issue peacefully. But as long as he resists our moves to capture Lehana and the others, and as long as he persists in attacking us, we have no choice but to go and get him."

"I am told Moorosi didn't want his people to attack the magistracy," Ellenberger replies.

"Whether he wanted them to do so is immaterial," Griffith responds. "He must take responsibility for the actions of his people. In any event, I cannot believe that he did not encourage them to do so. After all, he crossed the Telle River with his people just a few days ago and stole some of our horses. That is an overt act that belies any pretense he might have of being the defender rather than the aggressor."

Quthing — Tuesday March 18, 1879

Few people are around to notice as the man climbs under cover of darkness down the path that leads from the top of Moorosi's mountain. Now and then a shaft of moonlight falls on his face, revealing he is Mafetudi, Moorosi's messenger and confidante.

For some time now, his relationship with Moorosi has deteriorated. The rupture began when he opposed Moorosi's decision to rebel openly against the government. He kept his views to himself for a few weeks, but the disagreement broke into the open when Moorosi accused him of giving false evidence against Lehana in his trial in November.

Relationships further soured three weeks ago when Mafetudi questioned the plan to surround the magistracy during the night, kill the police and drive away all people living in the vicinity. Now, as Griffith's forces approach the mountain and it is clear that war has broken out, Mafetudi decides to break with the king he respected and served for so long. He will leave the hut he occupies on the mountain and surrender to the government.

A break in the rain makes it easier for the Basutoland Native Contingent patrols working their way across the east of the territory. They capture a few sheep in Lehana's district and chase off Baphuthi who approach them. The pro-government Basotho forces are permitted to keep the sheep, making the venture into the land of Moorosi seem more worthwhile to them.

Clear skies also enable the colonial army's rear guard to make the journey over the rough road from Palmietfontein. A string of 15 wagons, each pulled by 16 oxen, containing munitions, supplies and clothing, arrive during the day and outspan to the side of the road, close to Phaladi's village.

Shortly after their arrival, the soldiers who drove the wagons allow the oxen to roam freely. The animals graze in the corn fields carefully planted by the Christians, trampling them down as they eat them, destroying the people's ripening food supply which has grown well now that the two-year drought has been broken.

To the soldiers, the distinction between friend and foe among the native peoples is of little meaning. All the Baphuthi people are the enemy and war holds no bounds. So it is that when the Baphuthi ask the troops to remove the oxen the men respond by shooting at them and setting fire to their village.

The Christians gather their horses and head for the mission station at Bethesda near Mohale's Hoek, where they will be safe. So much for Griffith's assurances of safety.

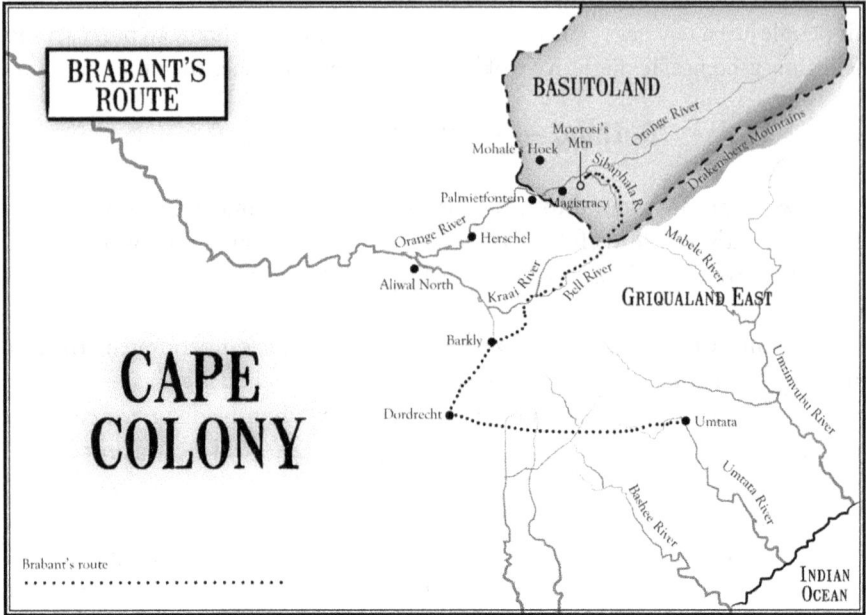

BRABANT'S ROUTE

BASUTOLAND

Moorosi's Mtn
Mohale's Hoek
Palmietfontein • Magistracy
Sibanhala R.
Orange River
Drakensberg Mountains
Orange River • Herschel
Aliwal North
Kraai River • Bell River
Mabele River
GRIQUALAND EAST
Barkly
Umzimvubu River

CAPE COLONY

Dordrecht • Umtata
Tsitsa River
Umtata River
Bashee River
INDIAN OCEAN

Brabant's route
. . . .

Barkly, Cape Colony — Thursday, March 20, 1879

For three days, Colonel Edward Yewd Brabant has been on the road with his men from Umtata, bound for Baphuthi territory.

Today, as he arrives in Barkly, a message reaches him from Griffith ordering him to send him the two cannon he carries by way of Palmietfontein.

Brabant directs a small group to take the big guns that way. The rest of his force will advance up the valley of the Kraai and Bell rivers, across the Drakensberg mountains to Moorosi's Mountain, a way that white troops have never taken.

"Because of these rains, we will have to cross several flooded rivers," the colonel tells his men.

"That might be a problem. But our presence is urgently required as war has broken out with Moorosi. We likely will encounter rebels along the way and once we reach the chief's mountain fortress with our supplies we will certainly be needed in the fighting to capture it.

"I am sure you will be up to it, no matter what conditions we may encounter.

"Once we leave here we will be out of postal or telegraphic contact with the main forces under Colonel Griffith, so we are to try to make as best time as we can and arrive at the mountain when he is expecting us."

But if the march of the last three days is any guide, Brabant fears the journey is not going to be straightforward. In traveling from Umtata to Dordrecht, they negotiated five flooded rivers. But, even though they made it in tolerably good time to Barkly, it has been raining steadily since they arrived. Fearing the journey ahead will be hazardous for their wagons, Brabant instructs his men to remain until the rains cease and the roads become passable.

Ahead of him, he has been told, is a ravine called Rebel's Kloof which is so difficult to negotiate that no timber has been brought down from the district on the other side of it for two years; it simply has been considered impossible to make the journey bearing the loads of timber. Brabant, too, has wagons and loads that need to be taken through the ravine, but he reckons he has soldiers who are able to see it done.

Quthing — The same day

The rain returns to Phaladi's Village — and Griffith's camp — during the early hours. Apart from yesterday's brief respite, heavy rain has been falling for almost a week, not only breaking the drought but also saturating the ground to overflowing.

Rivulets form in areas that previously were little more than tracks through the bushes. Together, carrying mud and debris, the newly formed streams rush to the nearest creeks, which fill to overflowing and hasten toward the Orange and Telle rivers, turning them from meandering waters into brown torrents and causing them to overflow their banks.

Every road turns into a quagmire of mud.

The mud slows the three 14-foot colonial supply wagons to a crawl as they slip and slide their way along the 14 miles to Phaladi's Village.

For three days, the drivers and leaders of the wagons have exhorted the oxen to pull harder and move faster; their voices are hoarse; their arms are weary from repeatedly whipping the oxen's backs. Their task has been frustrating at best, impossible at worst. Not only do the oxen have to work harder to pull through the mud, but the water-drenched canvases that cover the wagons add to the weight of the load.

At times, where the road crossed creeks, the mud reached up to the axles, forcing the drivers to dig the wagons out before proceeding.

Today they reach Griffith's camp.

"You are going to have to return to Palmietfontein for more supplies," Griffith tells the drivers. "You can rest tonight, but I need them as soon as possible. My men cannot conduct a war without sufficient food and ammunition."

Although the need for more supplies will delay his advance into Quthing, Griffith recalls the time during the Gcaleka war that he ran out of supplies and does not want that to happen again. If the guns he has asked Brabant to send through Palmietfontein fail to arrive in the next day or two, he will wait for them before launching an attack on Moorosi's mountain.

In the meantime, fearing a possible preemptive attack from Moorosi, Griffith instructs his men to construct an even higher earthwork around the camp.

"Place the wagons that remain here inside it and take every precaution to prevent their being taken by surprise," he tells them.

On the surrounding hills, unseen by Griffith, armed men are watching and sending reports to their king, who is now their commander in chief.

Quthing — Friday, March 21, 1879

With reports from scouts reaching Griffith that Moorosi's men are strengthening their defenses in the hills close to Raisa's village, he decides to take advantage of a lull in the rain.

He sends a messenger to instruct Lerothodi, who is camped with 1,500 men near the Orange River, to send out a patrol against the rebel Baphuthi.

The aim is not only to destroy the rebel holdouts, but also to send a warning message to the Baphuthi that the forces against them are formidable. The warning, he hopes, will persuade the men hiding in the hills to surrender.

Soon after he has sent the message, Griffith receives word that Ayliff has arrived. "He reached here faster than I thought he would," Griffith tells Maitin, who he notes has been unusually quiet and sad lately and who disappears for a couple of hours each day. Griffith considers asking Maitin what is on his mind, but assumes it is the war that has unnerved him.

Indeed, he wonders whether Maitin is even listening to what he is saying about Ayliff. "I assumed he was in Herschel yesterday, but clearly he was already in Palmietfontein," he says, raising his voice.

"Who is that?" Maitin asks.

"The secretary, Ayliff." Clearly, Maitin did not hear him the first time. "I am told he is here. Here in our camp. I am surprised he made the journey, in spite of the weather. I must confess I did not really expect him to do so. Please ask him to join me here in my tent."

Griffith shows Ayliff his plan of attack. On a piece of paper he sketches an outline of the southern boundaries of Basutoland. On the left, he draws an arrow from his camp toward Moorosi's Mountain.

"This is the attack that I will launch with the colonial troops under my command and 1,100 Basotho under Letsie's second son, Bering, on the main path to Moorosi's Mountain," he tells Ayliff. "I have instructed Lerothodi to clear out the only significant group of rebels in the way.

"My troops will surround the mountain until the guns from Brabant arrive. They should be here any day now."

He draws another line from the Cape Colony across the southern border of Basutoland along a path known as Lehana's footpath, and concludes it with an arrow pointing at Moorosi's Mountain. This, he explains to Ayliff, is the path being followed by Brabant's men, who should be well on their way.

A third arrow stretches from the northwest, from Ongeluk's Nek. These are Captain Wood's men.

"If Moorosi has not received help from others," Griffith says, "it'll be only a matter of ousting him from his mountain stronghold, which I am confident we can achieve in a short time."

Leading his men across the hills toward Raisa's village, Lerothodi is confident that the Baphuthi will yield when they see his forces arriving. Just as Moorosi fled when he saw him arrive at the Telle River, he will retreat once again.

But Lerothodi's forces meet with strong resistance. Instead of fleeing as he thought they would, the Baphuthi fight back. Lerothodi realizes this battle might not be as easy as he thought. As Moorosi's men fire on him, he urges his men to go on the attack.

Moorosi's men, heavily outnumbered and outgunned, fight back vigorously, determined not to yield.

Soon what started out as a skirmish turns into a wider battle and the front line turns into a scene of chaos. Amid war cries, spears are flung through the air and rifle shots are fired from both sides. At times it becomes difficult to tell one group from the other.

Slowly the Baphuthi yield their ground.

Suddenly the battle turns and the Baphuthi retreat rapidly.

A runner brings Lerothodi the news that a bullet has struck his uncle Chief Lenkoane, a brother of the late chief Moshoeshoe. A horrified Lerothodi makes his way forward through the mass of dead and wounded men.

By the time he reaches Lenkoane, the advancing warriors, flush with success against the Baphuthi, have moved on. The shouting from the advance warriors already is becoming quieter with distance as Lerothodi reaches down and examines his uncle. The bullet has pierced his heart.

Lerothodi carries his uncle's body back toward the village, tears streaming down his face. As he stumbles across the rock-strewn earth, still slippery from the rain, he recalls the days he and his brothers spent as children, swapping stories with their uncle in the kraal before they set out to herd their family's cattle.

Before he reaches the village, he lays down the body. He is angry at the men who have robbed him of one who was like an older brother to him. He looks up and sees another body being brought back from the front lines, followed by another. Soon nine bodies lie in a row, a silent testimony to the horrible reality of this day.

The bodies convey a message as nothing else can: The lives of his family and friends are little more than a means to an end in the whites' strategic game. The adventure of war that would yield them bounty has turned into the horror of conflict. By his efforts on this day, the white government has won, and he has lost.

As he looks again at his uncle's body, Lerothodi finds his emotions driven in a direction he never envisaged.

As his men herd around him the 1,500 cattle they have captured in the fighting, their cheering and delight mock him.

Is this war against Moorosi really worthwhile?

Quthing — Saturday, March 22, 1879

The war has become as real for Moorosi as for Lerothodi.

Four of Moorosi's sons and two of his grandsons were among the 30 killed in the skirmish with Lerothodi. Even this hardened man, who has seen much warfare over his 80 years, is bowed down by the suffering, particularly as it came at the hands of a man whom he thought was a friend.

Now he knows without doubt that he and his people are alone in their fight against the white invaders. Lerothodi has turned on him.

But that realization serves to make him more resolute.

Either he will win, as the Zulus did, or he and his people will be destroyed. He can see no middle way. But he is confident they will win. The bones he threw just last night told him that with courage he will emerge the victor. But some of the bones lay at an angle, indicating it will be a tough and long fight. There might be setbacks. That prediction has already started to come true.

He has assembled another line of warriors in the hills between his mountain stronghold and Griffith's camp at Phaladi's Village. Should they fail to stop the invaders, he will muster them on his mountain, from where they will beat back the colonial forces and retake their land.

He will fight to the finish. And he and his people will win.

Transkei — The same day

The ravine called Rebel's Kloof proves as intimidating as Brabant had been told. It has sides as steep as a house. He instructs his men to put two spans of eight oxen on each wagon for double the power on the rough road at the ravine's base.

In addition, each wagon has 50 men with drag ropes to pull it along.

After much toil, the men make it through the ravine. They employ the system for another two ravines that prove almost equally as difficult. Eventually they reach the Kraai River, which they are to cross before moving north toward Basutoland, only to find it filled to the banks.

Seeing a mill, Brabant approaches the owner, a Mr. Douglas. "Have you any idea how we can make it across the river?" he asks. "We can fix double spans of oxen to our wagons and get them across. But my concern is with our supplies, which we need to keep dry. The wagons will become extremely wet when we drag them through the water."

"I have a boat I can let you use," Douglas replies. "My only stipulation is that you bring it back to this side when you are done."

The men unpack the wagons and take down the canvas covering, carry the supplies down to the river's edge and stock as many of the items as they can in the boat, leaving just enough room for two men to row. And they will certainly have to row. The swiftly flowing river threatens to drag them downstream should they stop rowing.

They succeed in moving the first set of supplies and return to the bank for another load. Soon the ferrying becomes routine. As night falls, the men continue, assisted by the light of their lanterns.

Quthing — The same day

Even though the guns sent by Brabant have failed to arrive and no word has been received from Brabant, Griffith remains determined to waste no time. The rain has let up, leaving the roads and paths soggy but passable. It is hot, but not intolerably so — and it is better weather for a war than the winter months of June, July and August.

"We need to move now," he tells Ayliff and Southey. "Our scouts report that Moorosi has fled to his mountain. We are likely to encounter skirmishes, such as the one yesterday, as we clear out the rebels trying to hold their positions between here and the mountain. But before long we will have to take the mountain."

Ayliff suggests that Griffith wait for a report from Brabant and for the guns to arrive. The stronger the force, the better the chances for immediate victory. "We do not want to conduct a prolonged battle," he tells Griffith. "The longer it takes, the more it will cost the government. Already your need for supplies and ammunition and the men's pay is making inroads into our treasury."

"I agree," Griffith replies. "That is precisely the reason we should move quickly. The longer we delay, the more we give Moorosi a chance to settle in and defend his position. And the more costly the war becomes. With our native contingent, we are strong enough to take on Moorosi and defeat him soundly even should Brabant and the guns never arrive."

Southey suggests they might want to wait to hear whether Brabant is moving from Barkly into Basutoland. "I've heard nothing from Brabant or from the government authorities, who should know where he is," Griffith responds. "I've not heard where the cannon are. But I'm sure they are on their way. If we leave today, we should reach Moorosi's Mountain in a day or two and will likely meet them there. If we leave only when we know Brabant is there and when the guns arrive, we will have lost that many days simply waiting here."

Ayliff nods. He is unsure which is the best course and is content to leave the planning to Griffith.

Griffith adds, "I do not want Brabant to arrive at the mountain before we do. I am in command here and I don't want him to take any action without me. As you know, colonel, Wood's column is moving southeast from Ongeluk's Nek to prevent Moorosi escaping to the north. They will help keep him on his mountain. It might be his fortress, but it also might prove to be his prison. We will trap him there and root him out.

"Again, I have to say, I believe we need to move now."

"Very well," Southey responds. Griffith is commander in chief and it is pointless to argue with him, even though Southey is convinced that they should wait for word of Brabant and the guns.

"But before we set out with the full force," Griffith says, "I will lead members of the yeomanry against the enemy position that scouts report to the north of us. We will set off at first light tomorrow."

The news reaches Maitin by way of a messenger sent from Masitise.

"The Reverend Ellenberger wants you to know that MaLebenya has recovered from her wound," he says. "He sees it as a miracle. Soon she will be able to walk around and, except for a scar on her side, be like any other person.

"Give her a few weeks to recover fully, he says. And then he will conduct a wedding ceremony for you when you can get there."

The cloud has lifted. Life has become worthwhile for Maitin once more.

Transkei — Sunday, March 23, 1879

The supplies — biscuits, coffee, salt, tinned salmon, clothing and ammunition to feed and equip an armed force for weeks — have been ferried in stages across the raging Kraai River through the night and into the day. Instead of rowing the boat across, soldiers pull it on a long rope while another sits in it and guides it.

To Brabant's delight, the men accomplish the task without losing any loads.

Quthing — The same day

At 5 a.m. Griffith sets off with 300 yeomanry and 100 Mfengu. They have not gone far when a scout reports that the stronghold is occupied by about 60 Baphuthi under Ratsuanyane, who, having fled from Lerothodi's forces, have gathered in caves in the hills along the Silver Spruit River, many with their families.

Griffith calls for volunteers to storm the caves with Lieutenant Badger and Captain Nesbitt. Ten step forward. At 8 a.m., Griffith, seated on his horse, takes up a position on a hill opposite the caves. The day is clear and he has a good view. He waves his sword in the air and orders an advance. The yeomen, all mounted and armed, descend to the valley in the strict formation that reflects their British-based training. They ride up the hill, toward the caves. On an order from Griffith, they raise their rifles and shoot toward the caves. Puffs of smoke fill the air.

The Baphuthi emerge from hiding, move down the hillside and respond with their own fire. Soon a battle is raging in the valley below the caves.

After two hours of firing, Griffith's forces capture 27 horses and kill three of the Baphuthi, but are unable to get close to the caves.

Griffith gives the order to retire. They are to rest for a few hours and return to the attack in the early afternoon, this time in a more determined manner.

"I want you to demonstrate that fighting spirit that I believe you have," Griffith tells the men. "You are to tolerate no resistance. Advance on the caves and root them out. We are stronger than they are and I want you to prove it."

Griffith moves among the men, encouraging them and explaining to some of the 10 volunteers where he believes they could have acted more aggressively.

More volunteer for the second round of fighting. Among them is Sergeant Thomas Muldoon, with Southey's yeomanry group, who declares his determination not only to fight, but to lead the way. "I will show those black savages who are the superior fighters," Muldoon says. "You will not find me wanting, sir."

Griffith thanks him. "Now that is the sort of spirit I want to hear and I want to see demonstrated this afternoon," he says.

At three o'clock, the yeomen gather in formation and prepare to attack once more. Griffith waves his sword. The men advance. The Baphuthi are ready.

As shots ring out on both sides, Muldoon moves faster than his fellow yeomen, leading the charge on horseback up the slopes to the caves. He waves his sword, yelling to his fellow troopers to follow. The Baphuthi warriors, who have moved out of their caves once more, fire on the approaching men.

Seeing a Baphuthi ready to throw his spear, an excited Muldoon jumps from his horse and runs toward him. The yeoman stops, raises his rifle and loads it. The warrior hurls his spear and Muldoon has no time to fire. The spear strikes him in the side, tearing a gash just under his heart. He falls.

As the skirmish continues, the Baphuthi slowly give way. Eventually they flee, leaving about 30 bodies lying on the hillside.

The yeomen capture 64 horses, sheep and goats. They climb up to the caves where they find some 50 unarmed women, whom they release.

By the time the Baphuthi have fled and his compatriots reach him, Muldoon is bleeding profusely. He has no strength to staunch the wound with his clothing.

He raises his head slightly, mumbles a few unintelligible words before allowing his head to fall to the ground. He is the first colonial casualty of the war.

The messenger arrives at the mountain to deliver the news to Moorosi.

"Two of your grandsons were killed, one of your sons was shot and 27 of our people were killed in a battle in the caves on the Silver Spruit River today," he tells him. "It was not a good thing to see. Seeing the bodies lying there made me feel so sad that I still am sick from it," he says.

Moorosi's eyes fill with tears. "Let my people come here, to the mountain," he says. "They will be safe here. The white soldiers will not be able to defeat us here."

Transkei — Monday March 24, 1879

Brabant leads his men alongside the Bell River, calling at farm houses along the way to find the best way to cross the mountain ahead, a major obstacle as he heads toward the Basutoland border on the path Griffith instructed him to follow.

He is hesitant to tell his men what he hears. Local residents say if he encounters a snow storm on the mountain he and his men will never be heard from again.

Near the foot of the mountain, Brabant encounters another obstacle. The Bell River is flowing swiftly. Although the horses will be able to swim across it, he does not have the use of a boat to ferry the supplies across, as before.

In addition, some of the horses are ailing. Brabant decides to leave the wagons, the sick horses and most of the men behind. He selects 100 of his best men to scout the mountain and map out a path. He tells each to take food for 10 days. Packing his tent and blankets on his pony, he loads six horses with ammunition.

"How far do we still have to go?" asks one of the selected men.

"I have no idea," says Brabant. "As far as I can tell, no one has been this way before. But I hope that once we scale this mountain, we should be able to move fairly quickly into Basutoland and, from there, meet up with Colonel Griffith."

Quthing — The same day

After spending an uneasy night camped on the battlefield that saw Muldoon fall, Griffith's yeomen awaken to a cloudy morning. Taking turns, they dig a shallow grave on the side of the mountain where they lay their colleague's body to rest.

"This shall henceforth be known as Muldoon's Place," Griffith says. "Now, let us move on to revenge his death and destroy these men who dare rebel against the Queen and everything for which she stands."

Spurred on by revenge and Griffith's encouragement to kill more of the enemy, the men wave their swords and march in formation across terrain that never has suffered the sounds, the smells and the savagery of modern warfare. Until now.

A mile away, the soldiers reach a village, now deserted but which, they learn from captured prisoners, had been under a chief named Motsapi. Using similar tactics to those employed against Sarhili, Griffith instructs his men to seize food supplies, capture sheep and goats and destroy the community. The soldiers cheer as the thatched roofs catch fire, sending bright orange plumes into the morning air.

By the time they move northward, the village, until a few days ago home to a contented family community, is little more than a circle of blackened stones.

Griffith tells Colonel Minto, commanding officer of the 3rd Yeomanry, and Captain Davies, leading the Basotho contingent to move eastward, across the mountains. The yeomanry under Southey will accompany him on the road and they will meet at the mountain.

Quthing — Tuesday March 25, 1879

Leaving Ratsuanyane's deserted village where they camped for the night, Griffith's 400 men, with their tents, food and ammunition, move north.

Here the road is little more than a rough track along the side of the hills. The sharp curves and the steep slopes render it treacherous for the heavy loads of the colonial troops. Should any wagon veer off the narrow path it stands the risk of rolling 500 feet downhill and crashing into the river.

Many of the supplies have come a long way. They were first delivered to the nearest railhead at Queenstown, 150 miles away in the Cape Colony. Now, in the last stretch to Moorosi's Mountain, the wagons slow to less than a walking pace.

After some hours of travel, they reach Thomas's shop. The two brick buildings — Thomas's house and his shop — will be converted to a hospital and quarters for some of the men.

They drop off supplies at Thomas's Shop and Griffith leads a contingent the 15 miles to Moorosi's Mountain, encountering no resistance on the way.

"I want you to set up camp here," Griffith tells the men. "Pitch the tents on this side of the mountain. When the others arrive, they will camp on the other side of the mountain so that we surround it and prevent all chance of the enemy's escape."

"Look how flat it is on top," Peter Brown says to his colleague Robert Scott, as he looks up at the 1,200-foot mountain. Both have just arrived with the Cape Mounted Riflemen from Palmietfontein, summoned by Griffith who reasoned that, having made good progress against the Baphuthi, it is no longer necessary to keep the additional troops there; he will need them at the mountain.

"You could put a whole village up there," responds Scott. "The flat part must extend for more than half a mile."

"Moorosi and his men are up there," Brown says. "You can't see them from here, But, wait a minute. Right at the top you can see a rectangular shape that looks like a stone hut. There, on the right, near the end of the flat top. It looks small from here, but it must be fairly big."

"Can't say that I can see it," says Scott. "You must have better eyes than me. The story is that the top of the mountain, which we can't see from here, is crowded with cattle, sheep and goats, stocked with grain, small arms and ammunition and is defended by at least 300 men," replies Scott.

The men's eyes follow the outline of the mountain from the top to the right to where it descends 600 feet from the crown in a series of ledges on which stone-and-earth walls have been built before leveling out into a hollow that the men dub "the lip."

From the lip, a plateau extends to the right for about 1,200 feet to a large rocky outcrop they call "the saddle" — because it looks like one. From the saddle, the mountain dips down again to the right to an area they call "the nek" (the Dutch-derived South African word for neck) because it lies between Moorosi's Mountain and another mountain on the right that rises 500 feet.

From the edge of the plateau above them, the mountain slopes 600 feet down to where they are standing.

"I know these natives are an uneducated bunch of ruffians, but they have built up their defenses on that mountain quite well," says Brown, casting his eyes back on the flat mountain top. "I have to admit that it is impressive."

"It certainly is," replies Scott. "The mountain side to the left of the plateau, which looks like a cliff — over there — is almost perpendicular and impossible to climb. I hear it is like that on the other side, too."

"Looks like the only way we can get to the top is from the right, along the plateau to the lip and up between the ledges," says Brown. "I assume there is a passage that goes up among the rocks on the slope to the top."

"There has to be," says Scott.

"But I am told that the chief has built stone walls blocking the path. Together, they look from here like a stony cliff. We are going to have to climb over those or get around them to get to the top."

"There must be a path through them," replies Scott. "Moorosi and his people must be climbing up and down there all the time.

"If they can do it, so can we."

London — Thursday, March 27, 1879

A debate is being held in the House of Commons today on the actions of the country's representative in the Cape Colony, Sir Bartle Frere.

"Throughout the last two years, Sir Bartle Frere appears to have attributed all native misbehavior in any part of South Africa to the machinations of Cetshwayo, but there is no evidence to support such a theory," says Edward Knatchbull-Hugessen, a former Under-Secretary of State for the Colonies, and a member of the opposition Liberal Party representing Sandwich.

"The only conclusion to be drawn from the facts is, as far as I can judge, that Cetshwayo is to Sir Bartle Frere what 'Old Bogey' is to naughty children. He appears to have Cetshwayo on the brain, and to have acted accordingly.

"In the course of the debate, the House has heard much of the Old Testament. I wish they would not forget the New, in which it is written that they who take the sword shall perish by the sword; and that there will be no further persistence in the attempt to force Christianity down the throats of the Zulus at the point of the bayonet.

"Sir Bartle Frere — whose eminent services to the country I desire to acknowledge — made an initial error in this matter, and the government has fallen into one of equal magnitude, which I fear will not be easily, if at all, explained away; I am confident that the course which the opposition has felt bound to take (in opposing these adventures) will meet with the ultimate approval of the English people."

Quthing — Saturday March 29, 1879

In an effort to clear the northern part of Quthing of Baphuthi, Captain Wood and his men have been on patrol, moving south from Ongeluk's Nek and capturing cattle, sheep, goats and horses.

Where they encountered resistance, they fired at the rebels. In almost all cases, they eliminated the resistance; in several cases they killed men whom they believed were among Moorosi's leading supporters. The only Baphuthi left are hiding in deep ravines.

In their sweep south they have captured 2,900 cattle, 6,000 sheep and goats and 490 horses reducing the Baphuthi wealth in northern Quthing, counted in cattle, to a fraction of what it was.

In the southwestern part of Moorosi's territory Lerothodi's forces have captured large amounts of livestock from the Baphuthi and the area appears deserted.

"It seems many have fled across the Orange River into Kornet Spruit and the main concentration of rebels is on this mountain," Griffith tells Maitin. "Our job now is to oust them from it. For that, however, we need the big guns."

He stops, places his hands on his hips and leans his body backward. His mustache ripples.

"Where are the field-guns? Did Brabant send them through Palmietfontein as I requested? And where is Brabant anyway? How long does it take for him to get here? Will he ever reach here? We need to complete this operation as quickly as we can. Every day is costing money yet we cannot launch an attack on the mountain without the guns."

Maitin suggests that the men might find it difficult to bring the field-guns along the steepest part of the track leading to Thomas's Shop.

"An excellent point, my dear Mr. Maitin," says Griffith, controlling himself after what he realizes might have been an unreasonable display of emotion. "Will you kindly send word to Sofonia Moshesh, who has 300 men of the Basutoland Native Contingent with him here, that I would like him to send his men to widen the road so that the guns can be brought along it."

Quthing — Tuesday, April 1, 1879

The 50 white triangular tents dot the slopes at the base of Moorosi's Mountain like sentries on guard. Men move among them drinking coffee, eating biscuits and talking of their anticipated attack. Now and then laughter and loud talk from one group attracts others. The joking helps reduce the tension as the men await the first attack any of them have made on a stronghold so well defended.

The men also have their complaints. Rain over the last few days has caused their tents to leak and some who have blankets have to resort to using them as tents.

The leaky tents nevertheless are temporary homes to two troops of Cape Mounted Riflemen under Captain James Murray Grant who served as staff officer to Griffith during the eastern Cape wars; two regiments of Cape Mounted Yeomanry, one under Colonel Southey and the other under Colonel Minto; and 100 Mfengu from Herschel under Captain Hook and Captain Davies. Nearby, 1,900 Basotho under Lerothodi camp in the open or in huts vacated by the Baphuthi.

All the fighting men fall under the command of Griffith. His first move has been to establish a sentry on the top of the saddle facing Moorosi's Mountain to guard against a surprise attack from the mountain. He also has positioned men on the mountain slopes opposite Moorosi's fortress.

Griffith outlines his thoughts to Ayliff, who is staying at Thomas's Shop and is visiting Griffith today. "I believe I have the troops to do the job," he tells the native affairs secretary. "But I have to devise a way to break through these stone-and-earth walls. As we approach the walls, Moorosi's men will fire on us and be able to see us before we see them."

"How will you stop them from doing that?" Ayliff asks.

"I will need to precede the storming of the mountain by using the two seven-pounder guns and rockets I ordered. They can break down the stone walls, causing them to topple, and also hit the Baphuthi hiding behind them. Without the big guns, we will be unable to break through the stone walls. With them, victory will be ensured."

"I leave the prosecution of this war in your capable hands, colonel," Ayliff says. "But I must urge on you the importance of bringing this war to a speedy end."

Griffith calls Hook, the colonial captain in charge of the Mfengu contingent, into his tent. "We cannot waste any more time. We must have those seven-pounders. Brabant is supposed to have sent them through Palmietfontein. I haven't seen them. I haven't seen Brabant either; he should have been here by now."

"Perhaps he has been delayed by the rains, colonel," says Hook.

"Yes, yes. I realize that the route that I instructed him to use from the southeast is narrower and less passable in bad weather than the one we used. Also, he needs to clear the area should he encounter rebels on his way here.

"But I see no reason he should not have cleared those obstacles by now. I cannot understand what is delaying him."

"I'm sure Brabant would not purposely delay his journey," Hook ventures.

"Yes, that is true. Yet we cannot afford to wait any longer," Griffith continues. "Our men are restless. Our supplies will not last forever. The longer we wait, the more time and money we waste.

"I particularly need those guns. We cannot launch an assault on the mountain without them. I want you to travel south and find the guns. Once you find them, bring them here by forced marches. I need the guns. And I need them now."

Natal colony — Wednesday, April 2, 1879

For a couple of months, General Chelmsford, determined that the defeat of the British army at Isandhlwana should be avenged and the Zulu leader Cetshwayo defeated, has been gathering supplies and reinforcements in Natal colony. Additional support troops have been pouring into the colony from England.

Today, Chelmsford takes the first move in his plan to reverse the Zulu victory. He leads 16,000 white troops and 7,000 black troops to relieve a small garrison of British troops who have been holed up for months at Eshowe. He is successful.

Some 200 Zulus die and the garrison is relieved.

The victory gives Chelmsford new determination to advance on the Zulu capital of Ulundi with one large column.

But it will be some time before he can make the advance; the roads are bad and there is little pasturage for the oxen and horses along the sides of the roads.

Quthing — The same day

Moorosi is angry when he learns so much of his people's stock has been captured, either by Lerothodi or by the colonial troops. The cattle represent considerable wealth to the Baphuthi people and a reserve food supply. But he is confident the losses can be reversed.

"Once we defeat the invaders, we will get our cattle back," Moorosi tells his people who are gathered outside his hut. "Our task now is to protect the cattle we have here on the top of the mountain, preserve our food, and see that the colonial soldiers do not climb this mountain and take us captive."

He stretches out his hand, symbolically embracing the mountain top.

"We can drink from the water in our two wells. We can survive for a long time on the corn we have stored here. We can drink milk from the cows we have driven up to the mountain top. We can slaughter some of them to eat. And we can climb down the mountain at night, when the white men are sleeping, and gather more food and cattle when we need it."

His listeners express their approval.

"I will sit now and then in my chair on the far side of the mountain where I can see the soldiers below."

His listeners smile. They have seen the natural indentations on the cliff top on the western edge of the mountain that provide two seats like legless chairs. Many have climbed down to sit in the "chairs," where they can look some 600 feet straight down to the river bank below. For some, sitting in the chair makes them giddy as they look down the steep slopes. They shudder to think what it would be like to slip and fall. This slope is the most sheer around the mountain.

"But, although we must be patient and wait," Moorosi says, "you also must know that soon we will be called upon to fight. You have seen the white tents down there. They will try to drive us this mountain.

"We are not sure when they will attack. So we are going to have to be ready and watch for them. You all have weapons. Other rifles and all the ammunition you will need is stored in that hut." He points to a rectangular stone structure, about 20 feet by 10 feet, which also has food supplies.

Moorosi turns and faces southeast, looking toward the summit of the mountain immediately behind his hut.

"Raisa will appoint men to take turns to stand at the top of the mountain, over there, where they can see all that the colonial troops are doing. They will warn us when an attack starts.

"When the colonists and the Basotho traitors attack, we will take up positions around the mountain top and behind the stone walls. I will assign the positions."

Moorosi appoints Mofana, a grandson, as head of a team that will guard the water spring at the eastern end of the mountain. Other teams will guard another spring and areas around the perimeter.

The best fighting men will guard the stone-and-earth walls.

"I will assign men to positions along the walls. Some will roll rocks onto our attackers. Others will shoot over the walls or through the holes in them at the invaders. Do not wait for them to get close. Shoot them as soon as you can reach them with your rifles.

"We will use our rifles because they can reach across the plateau to where the white men are; we will use our spears only if we cannot stop them with the rifles and they get close to us.

"The best shooting position will go to Maketa."

Moorosi points to a short man with a colorless face. An albino, he has the facial features of his people, but does not share their skin tones. His skin is devoid of all color, his hair an off-white color and his eyes gray.

Maketa has been accepted as special among his people. Although many albinos cannot see well, Maketa's sight is exceptional. Since he reached the age at which he could aim a gun he has been honored for being the best shot among all the Baphuthi people. So much so, that Moorosi presented him with a Winchester repeating rifle, the best of all the people's firearms.

Now Maketa is ready to use his skills to defend the only way of life he knows and the king he respects.

Transkei — Saturday, April 5, 1879

Brabant has reached the source of the Bell River high in the Drakensberg mountains where a broad plateau at the top of the mountain range provides a wide view of the mountains below that stretch toward the Orange River.

They camped last night at the northern end of the plateau, which Brabant estimates is 7,000 to 8,000 feet above sea level. The cold was intense and the men found it difficult to sleep. This morning their blankets are frozen as stiff as boards.

Captain Dell, riding up front, reconnoitres the path by which they will descend into the valley of the Buffalo Valley. He returns to report to Brabant.

"The descent is several hundred feet and is almost sheer," Dell says. "There is a faintly marked native footpath winding down the face of the mountain. A stream, which must be the head waters of the Buffalo River, falls over a precipice into the immense gorge down which we have to travel."

Brabant wonders whether progress is possible, but he knows there is no other way to reach the country below. He turns to the men gathered behind him.

"Follow me in single file. I suggest you allow plenty of space between you."

As Brabant leads his horse behind him, he has constantly to stop and crouch down to allow stones dislodged by the men above him to clatter down over his head. But he keeps moving so he does not detain those behind him. Dr. Comming, their 69-year-old surgeon, insists on riding down while the others dismount and lead their horses down. "I have seen service in many parts of the world," he says. "And I know I can do this."

The descent seems to take hours. The men, their legs aching, reach the valley safely. Even Comming makes it to the bottom on his horse.

Ahead of them is a narrow canyon. The men will have to constantly cross from one side of the river to the other to find space to ride.

Brabant has two concerns. One is that if heavy rains blow in, they will be trapped. His other worry is that his column has crossed into Quthing and could come across groups of rebels who could cut them off or shoot at them from above.

Quthing — Sunday April 6, 1879

Cheers surround them as Hook and Lieutenant Best arrive shortly before sunset with the two seven-pounder muzzle-loading guns sent by Brabant. Hook says he met Best on his way to the mountain and helped him move quickly.

Griffith calls his senior officers to his tent. "We have been camped here for nearly two weeks," he says. "Now that we have the seven pounders and the rocket launchers, there is no reason to wait for Brabant to reach here. Also, another troop of Cape Mounted Riflemen arrived a few days ago. We are ready to go forward.

"Here is how I plan to launch the attack."

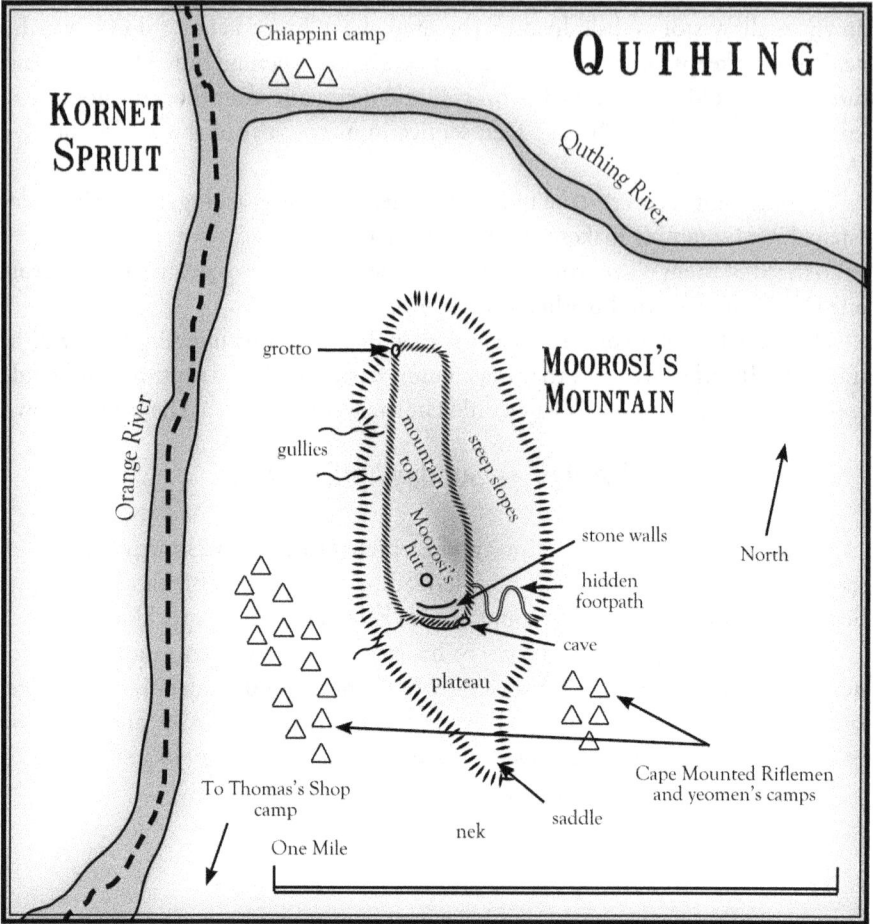

Chiappini camp

QUTHING

KORNET
SPRUIT

Quthing River

Orange River

grotto

MOOROSI'S
MOUNTAIN

gullies

mountain top

steep slopes

Moorosi's hut

stone walls

hidden footpath

North

cave

plateau

Cape Mounted Riflemen
and yeomen's camps

To Thomas's Shop
camp

One Mile

nek

saddle

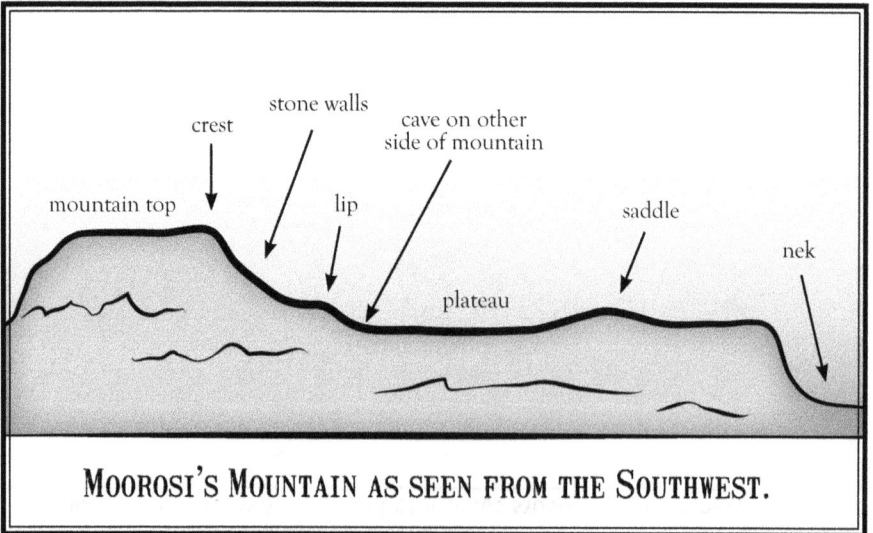

crest

stone walls

cave on other
side of mountain

mountain top

lip

saddle

nek

plateau

MOOROSI'S MOUNTAIN AS SEEN FROM THE SOUTHWEST.

XII

Quthing — Monday April 7, 1879

Shortly after dawn, Griffith calls his men together on the grassy parade ground at the foot of the mountain. He outlines their progress in the fight against Moorosi and his plan of action. Scott and Brown join their colleagues, wondering whether Granville, still stationed in Palmietfontein, is wishing he were with them at the scene of the action.

Also listening is Secretary for Native Affairs William Ayliff, who has ridden to the mountain from his quarters at Thomas's Shop.

"We estimate the rebel chief Moorosi to have 200 to 300 followers with him on the mountaintop," Griffith says, standing with his back to the mountain. "The mountain, as you can see, is inaccessible on three sides. We are calling the face behind me, the only accessible part, the 'attacking side.' It is steep and consists of a succession of three ledges, or tiers, one above the other. The Baphuthi have made excellent use of these natural ledges by building flanking walls on them.

"The walls are constructed of stone and earth and have been arranged with great skill. They are three to four feet high, but stand on ledges that vary from five to seven feet high. So we are faced with three tiers, one behind the other, each of which has a total height of nine to 12 feet. As you have no doubt observed, Moorosi's men are well armed and some are positioned behind the ledges.

"It would appear that these fortifications cannot be taken by assault without a great loss of life. As a result, I made up my mind when we arrived to invest the place and await the arrival of the two seven-pounders. They will be able to break down the walls and expose the enemy.

"In the meantime, while retaining the investment here, I have posted pickets day and night around three sides of the mountain, as many of you know who have been assigned those duties. I did not assign anyone to guard the far side as it consists of a perpendicular krantz that no one can climb.

"Let us remember, too, that the men on the mountain are not the only rebels. Others are scattered around the countryside, hiding in caves and in the steep mountain valleys all around us. So I have also sent out patrols of mounted Basotho in different directions to scour the country and harass the rebels wherever and whenever they could be found. These patrols succeeded in capturing 2,000 head of cattle, 2,000 sheep and goats and 400 horses."

The men cheer.

"On the west bank of the Orange River, the chief Lerothodi captured 2,000 head of cattle and 100 horses at a cost of two men wounded. He has also sent in six stands of arms, taken from rebels who surrendered. Six of the rebels were killed.

"I must also mention the good work of Captain J. G. Wood of the 1st Yeomanry. He and his men captured 700 head of cattle, 1,000 sheep and 50 horses with no casualties.

"Captain O'Connor has been working for 50 miles up and down the Orange River, clearing the country of rebels. In some cases they dislodged the rebels from strongholds capable of holding 500 men. They found large preparations for a siege.

"Essentially, therefore, the territory has been cleared of rebels. Now we are about to complete the task with an assault on the stronghold here.

"It has been a rather tedious and trying duty to besiege the mountain over the past 12 days, but, as I am sure everyone here knows, the two seven-pounders arrived yesterday, brought here by Lieutenant Best. Now we can execute our plan.

"We will launch the attack tomorrow."

Griffith points to a cleared position among the tents. "About noon today, the field-guns, mounted on the same carriages on which they were towed here, will be drawn into position on this cleared ground, just out of Baphuthi rifle range, but close enough for the shells to reach the stone walls.

"Tonight we will fire eight rockets on to the mountain fortress. That will soften the enemy and warn the Baphuthi of the kind of attack they can expect.

"Later tonight, under cover of dark, the assaulting party — number 4 and 5 troops of Cape Mounted Riflemen under Captain Grant, assisted by Captain Surmon, numbering about 60 men, and about 100 members of the 3rd regiment of yeomanry under Colonel Minto — will move into a cave at the base of the mountain. You cannot see it from here, but it is near the first line of defenses," he adds, turning and pointing behind him. "It is under cover from the enemy's fire and also of our guns."

Brown, who is with No. 5 Troop of the Cape Mounted Riflemen, turns to Scott. "Hear that? That means I'll be joining them in the cave," he says. "I'll be among the first to storm the mountain." He smiles with pride.

"Better you than me," replies Scott.

Griffith continues. "The storming party is to wait in the cave till the fortifications have been well shelled. Their advance will be sounded by a bugle call.

"The supports will be three other troops of the 3rd Yeomanry under Colonel Southey. They will take up position on this side of the plateau. They will shelter from Baphuthi fire under the rocky overhang before I give the word for them to join the Riflemen who by then will have emerged from the cave, marched on to the plateau and headed toward the stone walls.

"In addition, I am ordering the 2nd Yeomanry to furnish three troops as supports and three more as reserves to Captain Grant. They will take up their positions on the knoll, or saddle, on which we have set up the picket.

"The Basotho under Lerothodi will take up position on the western side of the plateau, not far from our tents.

"To summarize: At sunrise tomorrow, around 6 o'clock, we will start pounding the mountain with the guns. Once these formidable weapons have subdued the enemy and opened a way for us to attack, the men in the cave under Grant will rush forward up the path to the top, to be shortly followed by those troops who are on this side, on the knoll and west of the plateau. I suspect that most of the rebels will flee ahead of you. Your march to the top should be relatively easy.

"When you reach the top, you will take prisoner all who surrender and you will find and arrest Moorosi.

"I see no reason we should not be able to accomplish these tasks in one day. We could even be having breakfast with Moorosi tomorrow.

"As a result, we will end this siege before the Easter festival which starts on Friday. I cannot promise that you will be home for Easter; but I am confident that you will be on your way home by then."

The men arranged before Griffith are quiet. Scott shakes his head, but to most of the men, the plan seems a sound one. In any event, it is not their place to question their commander's strategy, but simply to carry it out.

"I suggest we assemble in small parties to discuss the arrangements for the attack in more detail. After that, we will retire to our quarters and rest for what will be a concerted and successful action," Griffith concludes.

"Oh, and I would strongly discourage you from drinking anything but coffee in the next day or two," he adds. "When we are victorious, there will be plenty of time to celebrate."

The men, grumbling in response, make their way back to their tents.

"We're going to trounce them," Brown tells Scott, increasingly excited at the opportunity to see action. "Those savages might be good at piling up stones, but after our big guns destroy their walls, they will be exposed like naked people. I will have great fun shooting them. Remember what they did to Van Hohenan and Evans? To me, they are little more than dogs, wild rabid dogs who serve no good purpose and deserve to be put down."

Scott is skeptical and unimpressed with Brown's bravado.

"The men who ripped Van Hohenan and Evans apart were the Gcaleka," he responds. "These are the Baphuthi."

"They are all the same," counters Brown.

Scott ignores the comment. "I'm not convinced it's going to be that easy. Have you looked at those walls through spy glasses? Do you realize how many there are? They look fairly thick. It must have taken them months, maybe years, to build them. You think we can destroy them in a few minutes?"

But Brown remains confident.

"We've seen nothing moving on that mountain, beyond a few goats and horses, for days now. When the shells fall on the walls, the only reaction is a cloud of dust.

"In any event, we don't have to destroy them all. We have only to pulverize them enough to make those poor miserable scoundrels run for their lives. They will be so scared. It will be great fun to pick them off with our rifles."

As they walk back to their tents, the men notice a trooper sitting alone on a rock near the camp.

"Who is that?" Brown asks.

"I am told his name is John Brome," Scott replies. "They say he is a volunteer farmer from Komgha who signed up recently. He never talks with anyone. He just sits around looking sullen and morose."

"He doesn't look excited about storming the mountain," adds Brown. "I'm so excited that I'm not sure I will able to sleep."

Quthing — Tuesday, April 8, 1879

Shortly after 3 a.m. Grant leads the main attacking group along the neck between the saddle on Moorosi's Mountain and the mountain opposite.

The troops trudge over the uneven ground and, after crossing the neck, turn left toward the mountain, headed for the cave. They move as quietly as possible. As far as they are aware, they have not been detected by Moorosi's men who, they assume, are still asleep.

About halfway to the cave, the moon rises over the surrounding mountains, casting a glow across the scene. Now it is easier for the men to find their way.

Now and then, a stone slips under a boot and clatters its way down the slope. The men pause, as if doing so will prevent the sound being heard. But that does not help. The sounds have alerted the Baphuthi to the soldiers' advance. Aided by the moonlight, the Baphuthi roll rocks down the mountain toward them.

"Run for the shelter of the cave!" Grant shouts.

Many stumble as they run through the grass and over the rough rocky ground. When they reach the overhang, they huddle together. Here they will wait, ready to storm the stone walls as soon as they hear the signal.

Grant counts those who are with him. Thirty-three, including Brown, Captain Surmon and Lieutenant Mitchell, are from the Riflemen and 13, including Captain Smith, from the 3rd Yeomanry. Colonel Minto is absent.

Brown has noticed that Brome, the sullen man, is among those who failed to join them. "Where are the rest?" he asks. "About 160 were supposed to have been here, now there are only 46. Why aren't they here?"

"They will join us later," Grant replies, unsure of the reason.

Cut to a third of their appointed number, the men feel a sudden sense of foreboding and loneliness; so few for such an important task.

As the first rays of sunlight creep across the mountain, four more men scramble across the ground to the cave, bringing the number to 50. "We must perform our assigned duty without the rest of our troops," Grant says. "It is our duty to take the mountain, whether they join us or not."

At dawn, as the artillery men move into position, Griffith stands on the saddle overlooking the plateau. In an attempt to identify with his troops, he is wearing a regular trooper's uniform rather than an officer's dress.

Griffith looks across at Colonel Southey, who is of the same rank, but today has to take his orders from him as the commander. Griffith has insisted on advancing on the mountain quickly, believing that the available troops are sufficient, dismissing Southey's suggestion that they wait for Brabant.

Griffith stands silently. In this pause, the opportunity to stop and think without interruption forces itself upon him. As the crescent of a rising sun appears across the mountains, in the silence, before the first shot is fired, Griffith ponders the mountain in front of him.

How did he get here? Why is he here? What does all this mean?

He answers the questions. He is implementing justice. Opposing the rule of law must have consequences.

He must perform his duty to his country, his fellow colonists and his Queen. And he will.

At 6 a.m. Griffith signals to Lieutenant Best to begin the firing. A soldier loads a shell into the muzzle of the first gun, another rams it down and a third pulls the lanyard that ignites the primer, which, in turn, ignites the powder in the shell and shoots it 500 yards across the plateau and at the mountain. The fourth man in the team stands back, ready to assist.

The explosion — deafening to those who are close by — is followed by a cloud of white smoke that temporarily hides the path of the shell from the men firing the cannon. As the smoke clears, Best raises his spy glass to examine the walls. The shell has fallen short.

The second cannon also fails to reach its target.

Best adjusts the guns' tilt. The men clean the barrels before firing them again.

After several adjustments and several volleys, the shells pound into the walls.

"Think of it as a cricket ball," Best tells his assistants. "You do not want to bowl a fast ball that has a flat trajectory, but a slow ball that rises into the air. You want to lob it high so that it falls both on the walls and on the men behind them."

The men, working with clockwork precision, continue firing each gun alternately, sending an average of three to four shots into the stone walls every minute.

The Baphuthi stay in their positions behind the stone walls, watching as the cannon balls fly toward them. Moorosi has stationed himself in the front schanzes. Several of his sons take up positions behind the walls on the western side.

The noise of the gunfire, the smell of gunpowder and the white smoke drifting toward the mountain alarm the warriors. It hurts their ears, offends their senses and represents a new form of warfare. It is loud and comes in waves. When the first seven-pound shells slam into the walls and nearby rocks, shaking the ground like an earthquake, they feel fear.

But, after a while, they note that the damage is limited. In the time between volleys the men crouch down and run to pick up shell fragments. They return to their posts and examine this new type of firepower that spies have heard the colonists refer to as the steel guns.

"Let them fire their large guns with the smoke and noise," Moorosi says. "They will not harm us. Our defenses are strong. If you see part of a wall that has been damaged, repair it, but make sure you are not hit by another shell." The chief adds that his men should hold their fire; those operating the guns are out of range.

The shelling continues for what seems like hours. Each time a hole is punched in one of the walls, the Baphuthi rush to repair it.

After firing about 100 rounds, Best orders the artillery to stop. Griffith, having noticed a number of Baphuthi scurrying up to the top of the mountain, is convinced the enemy have been driven from their positions behind the walls.

At 8 a.m., the commander in chief gives the order to sound the advance.

As the bugle sounds, Grant and Surmon instruct the men to line up outside the cave where they are still out of range of Moorosi's rifles. From there, they are to march toward the point from which they will advance on the stone walls.

The troops line up in rows. From a distance, they look like toy soldiers: black velvet corduroy trousers, blue jackets with white sashes and brown helmets with the golden royal insignia. Each carries a Martini-Henry rifle. At their head, a soldier holds high an embroidered flag that reads, "Onward to Victory."

"Let's show that old chief and his followers their time has come," Grant shouts.

"Go, Cape Mounted Riflemen! Go, Yeomanry! Storm the mountain!"

The men set off in double time, their ankle boots crunching the ground below, sending stones scattering. They advance in formation, but yell freely. Some shout "hurrah for the Queen" while others scream obscenities at the enemy. They have 250 yards of ground to cover to the first tier of stone walls. After 50 yards, they come within direct range of the Baphuthi rifles.

Moorosi cannot believe his eyes. These crazy white soldiers, dressed in outlandish costumes that make them ideal targets in the early sunlight, are advancing toward his warriors as though they want to die. They don't duck or weave, but keep in formation. "Look at me," they are saying, "Here I am. Shoot me please."

He is only too pleased to oblige.

"Keep firing," Moorosi shouts as he and his best marksmen maintain a barrage of fire. He calls the men in the tiers above to join in. There is no need for them to remain farther up the mountain as a reserve. Maketa, the albino, aims his Winchester and scores his first hit.

The Mounted Riflemen march on undeterred. But as they approach closer to the walls the bullets begin grazing some and piercing others through their clothing. One shot knocks Surmon's revolver away as it enters his side. He falls. As the 57-year-old captain, blood oozing from his side, struggles to claw his way back to the safety of the cave, the rest ignore him, retain their formation, and march relentlessly forward.

As they get closer not only bullets but also stones, rocks and even huge boulders bound toward them down the mountainside.

Grant sees 100 of Minto's yeomen appear on the plateau from the direction of the saddle and he beckons to them to join the assault. It now becomes clear to Grant what happened; rather than move on to the cave early this morning, Minto instructed his men to hold back until the order was given to storm the mountain.

Grant's men cheer at the sight of reinforcements, but soon Minto's men come under intense gunfire. Unlike Grant's men, who are approaching from the side, Minto's men are moving directly toward the walls and well within rifle range. "The bullets are whizzing about us like hail," one yells back to the soldiers at the saddle.

Leading Minto's yeomanry, Lieutenant H.A. Reed moves out ahead and looks back, urging the men to follow him. He has not moved more than a few yards when a bullet fired from a stone wall strikes his face, penetrating behind the right eye. He collapses, dead.

Seeing him fall, most of the men hold back, but about 15 continue to advance undaunted, leaving Reed lying where he fell. Moments later, Sergeant John Edwards and Private John Paschke are also hit. The two injured men scramble behind a lone rock, some 40 feet from the stone walls.

Unaware that the yeomanry under Minto are being gunned down, the soldiers under Grant arrive on the plateau in front of the walls. Grant instructs them to change to a wide shoulder-to-shoulder line, facing the enemy.

"On to victory," Grant shouts. "Advance to the walls and climb them! Go, Riflemen, go!"

The men, now facing the Baphuthi head-on, rush forward. The firing is intense. Many scream as they are hit in the arm, chest or leg. Some fall; others stumble in an attempt to find cover. Brown dodges from side to side, trying to make himself a difficult target.

Above them, the soldiers see an array of gun barrels poking through loopholes in the stone walls, filling the air with smoke and the acrid smell of gunpowder. Some consider firing into the walls above them, but they realize that stopping to load and aim their rifles will make them even better targets.

A side group led by Grant works its way up to the rocks at the north end of the stone walls where the walls are shorter and easier to reach. Climbing the rocks, they reach the base of the first tier and soon are staring directly into the loopholes. The Baphuthi stab at them with spears through the loopholes and throw rocks over the top of the walls. The colonial soldiers fire at them with their pistols.

Private George Rogers clings to the face of a rock, waiting for the opportunity to fire his pistol through one of the loopholes. As soon as the spear is removed, he determines, he will fire through the hole. Suddenly a shot comes from a point farther down the stone wall and Rogers falls, pierced by a bullet in his right eye.

Corporal Charles Martindale jumps down and picks him up in his arms. As he carries Rogers to safety, Martindale is shot in the leg and collapses, bleeding profusely. He drops Rogers, who is now close enough to drag himself to safety among the rocks. From there, Rogers watches in frustration as the man who helped him tries to drag himself to shelter, but is unable to do so.

On the plateau, the rest of Grant's men break formation and run forward to the closest cover — the ledge below a stone wall, where they can shelter.

From under the ledge, the men realize that the wall — built above the ledge — is a lot higher than it appeared from a distance. And the walls are intact. The cannon have had minimal impact.

The walls are bristling with men brandishing spears, some being thrown in front of them. Bullets, rocks and stones add to the onslaught, making it highly risky to move out from the ledge.

If they hunker down under the ledge, they are safe. But any attempts at venturing out are met with gunfire and more rocks.

"We can't climb this," Brown yells in frustration. "We're trapped. These men are crack shots. And they all fire one after the other, leaving no time between bullets. As one set of men load, the others are shooting."

A soldier, running from sheltering under one ledge to another alongside, is met with a hail of gunfire. The shower of bullets creates so much dust that the soldier is temporarily hidden. He makes it to safety, but no one follows him.

The men assess the situation. They count 12 wounded among them and a couple of men lying in the open — likely dead and at the moment not retrievable.

The men still able to fight are caught in a situation from which it seems impossible to escape without exposing themselves to extreme danger.

Aware that he probably has crossed the border into Quthing, Brabant is on the watch for rebels. So far, he and his group of 137 have seen no signs of them.

The valley has begun to widen more, making the going easier. The weather is clear. Brabant insists the men need to move as fast as possible to meet Griffith at the mountain. They are making good time when the men, hungry for meat after living on sparse rations, find a wide and deep cave filled with 200 sheep and goats. The men seize some of them. "These will supply us with meat," one says.

As they return, Brabant notes, "Because we are tired, let's spend the night here where we can defend ourselves. But we must press on early tomorrow."

When Lerothodi sees the colonial soldiers falling to the enemy fire, he tells his men to stay where they are and not to join the storming of the mountain. They can fire their rifles at a distance, he tells them.

He is still angry at the Baphuthi people for killing his uncle. But when he sees the Baphuthi keeping the white soldiers at bay, and when he sees the futility of scaling the stone walls, he realizes that joining in the assault would be folly.

Lerothodi also is having second thoughts about supporting the government. He still shares a degree of empathy with Moorosi and the king's attempts to preserve his people's way of life and to prevent the government taking over the running of his country. Although Griffith is a fine man and speaks well to him and his father, he watches with concern as Griffith leads his white colonial soldiers in this fight against an old patriarch whose main concern is for the freedom of his people.

"This is a different Griffith," he thinks to himself. "He was a man we all admired. Now he is waging a war against our brothers."

The reserve troops stationed below a ridge at the southern edge of the plateau are in disarray. As they watch the main advance become pinned down by surprisingly accurate enemy fire, they break ranks and scatter to avoid being told to join in the assault on the mountain. Soon no officer can say he has the troops under control.

The two wounded troopers sheltering behind a rock on the open plateau — Edwards and Paschke — lie in pain, grateful that they are still alive, but uncertain how they will be able to make it back to safety.

There is scarcely enough room for both men to fit behind the rock. Paschke's right leg, struck twice by Baphuthi bullets, is exposed. He pushes toward the center of the rock, pulling in his leg but causing Edwards to push out his leg on the other side, making it visible to the Baphuthi marksmen. "Pull in your leg," says Paschke. As Edwards does, a bullet strikes the ground in the spot where his leg had been.

They sit huddled together, fearful of moving without risking their lives.

After two hours, Edwards and Paschke become desperate. Both men have staunched their wounds, but they have been able only to lessen the flow of blood and not stop it completely. Dehydrated, drenched in blood and drained of strength, they continue to lose more and more blood.

Their wounds need treatment urgently.

They consider moving out and trying to make it to safety. "I'll go first," Edwards says, dragging himself out from behind the rock. He screams as a bullet strikes him in the arm. He seeks the shelter of the rock once more.

Now he is nursing two wounds. One in his leg suffered when he first was hit on the open plateau, and now another in the arm.

"I thought the firing had stopped," Edwards tells Paschke, talking slowly and carefully as the pain from his new wound starts to make itself felt. "But they are still there. What can we do?"

Edwards tries to pull himself up, catching a glimpse of the men hunched together behind the ledge, but collapses. A bullet whizzes over his head.

"The others are trapped under a ledge and we are trapped here."

The men realize they have nowhere to turn.

Edwards winces in pain as he looks down at his leg and sees flies settling on the caked blood. "The only reason Moorosi's men have stopped firing," he says slowly, gasping for breath, "is that no one is in their line of sight. As soon as we move, they will fire on us. And they are good shots."

Paschke, blood still oozing from the wounds to his side and his leg, lies quietly next to him. "I feel weak," he moans.

"We'll die here if we do not have a doctor and water," Edwards says slowly, the pain from the two wounds also sapping his strength. He has torn off his shirt and bound it around the deep bullet wound in his leg. The shirt is saturated in blood. He fears he is in danger of passing out from the loss of blood and dehydration.

"Do you have water?" he asks.

"No," Paschke replies, barely able to speak.

"Send a doctor!" Edwards screams toward the ledge,

"It's too dangerous," a yeoman yells back.

"Then bring us water," Edwards yells. "Water! We'll die without water."

Paschke is quiet. His face is drained of color and he is fading fast. Edwards must try to save him — and himself. Summoning all the strength he has left, he screams again for water.

The soldiers under the ledge hear Edwards's screams. They ignore them. They cannot afford to risk their lives because someone needs water.

As the minutes turn into hours, the men sheltering under the ledge turn to their task, which remains to scale the walls. Cowering here will accomplish little. They become restless, feeling guilty about failing to fulfill their duty, but afraid of being killed. As they discuss how to storm the wall, they note that the firing appears to have stopped. They need to resume their attack.

Corporal L.W. Bean volunteers to lead the way. He steps out from the safety of the ledge and turns to face the wall. Using indentations in the rock face, he clambers upward. As he reaches the bottom of the stone wall, he grabs the muzzle of a Baphuthi rifle protruding from a loophole. But the rifle is wrenched back, out of his grasp. A rock hurled over the wall hits Bean, causing him to fall backward, to the ground. He creeps under the protection of the ledge once more, telling his fellow soldiers what he did.

"That's not the way to do it," says Private William Braine. "We must get up there and get them where they are hiding behind the walls. If Bean can grab a rifle, it must be possible for us to make it over the wall."

Before anyone can stop him, Braine adds, "I am going up there." He runs a short distance away from the rock face on to the open plateau, turns and hurtles himself toward the wall. He scrambles up the rock face, clinging to hand-holds. With a supreme effort, he pulls himself up and over two intersecting walls, trying to push them down as he does so.

Braine is lost from sight to the men below. For a moment they believe he might have succeeded. An outburst of firing behind the wall convinces them, however, that he likely has not. When he does not return, they are sure of it.

Corp. Charles Crole — more senior than those around him — suggests doing it differently. "We need to move out where we can see the walls, and fire at the men above us," he says. "Private Braine has shown us that we can scale that wall if we are really determined. But we need to suppress the enemy fire first."

The men weigh up the suggestion. Having come under the fire of the enemy, they are unwilling to expose themselves to it again.

"They will not only fire on you, but will hurl down spears, rocks and stones on you," Trooper Peter Morley ventures. "I am ready to do what I can do to follow orders, but we will achieve nothing by being killed."

Others agree.

"If we all go together, we will not all be killed," Crole says. "I will show you how it can be done, just follow my example."

Trooper J. Broad tugs at Cole's arm and stops him. "You stay here," he says. "You already have suffered a bullet wound to your arm. Let me go." He cocks his rifle and walks forward, away from the safety of the ledge. Before he can turn around and aim toward the walls, a sharp crack of rifle fire emanates from above him and a bullet strikes him in the side. He collapses.

Morley and two other men run forward and drag Broad back to safety. The bullet has torn a hole in his chest. The men bind up the wound and make Broad as comfortable as they can under the ledge. But they doubt he will survive the loss of blood without medical help. And where will he receive such help now?

No one suggests venturing out into the open again.

It is approaching noon. Edwards's screaming from behind the rock starts up again and becomes more intense.

"Water. Water. We need water," he screams. "We'll die without water."

He repeats his plea, fueled by delirium.

"Water. Water. We need water. Water, water, water."

He shouts, over and over again.

"I can't stand this any longer," says Brown. "Those men need our help. Has anyone got water?"

A trooper hands him a half-filled canteen. "Here, you can have my water. But I wouldn't go there if I were you," he says.

Brown ignores the comment, drops his rifle and darts into the open. As he runs across the 40 feet of open space to the rock, the gunfire erupts once more and stones are pelted toward him. The men watch as he reaches the rock.

"Give Peter the water first," Edwards says. "He needs it more."

Brown bends down alongside Paschke. He shelters partly behind the rock, although his back can still be seen from the mountain.

Paschke drinks it all.

Brown takes a big breath and tears back to the shelter of the ledge. "Does anyone have more water?" he asks. "I need to help the other man."

"Here," says one of the troopers.

Once again, Brown runs across the open ground. This time he kneels alongside Edwards, exposing himself to the gunfire. As the bullets fly past him, he pours water into the trooper's mouth.

Edwards is still drinking when a bullet strikes Brown in the right arm, smashing the bone and knocking the canteen out of his hand. Brown picks up the canteen with his left hand before the precious liquid is lost and continues pouring water into Edward's mouth.

He has almost finished when another bullet punches a hole in the canteen, spilling the water on the ground. Almost immediately afterward, another shot hits Brown in the thigh, knocking him back. He pulls himself up once more and, narrowly avoiding being hit, limps back to the safety of a different ledge, closer to a path of escape.

When he sees Brown's plight, Sergeant Major Edmund Baron Hartley responds. At 32, he's an accomplished surgeon and runs the hospital at Thomas's Shop. After arriving from Britain five years ago and serving as a district surgeon in Basutoland from 1874 to 1877, he was appointed surgeon to the Cape Mounted Riflemen and recently served in the Ngqika and Gcaleka wars.

Hartley creeps under the ridge to the north of the plateau, ducks behind a sheltered rock and back under the overhang until he reaches Brown. He dresses Brown's wounds as best he can.

"Are there any more wounded?" Hartley asks.

"There are a number of wounded where I was under the ledge," replies Brown. "And there are two unfortunate souls sheltering behind that rock," he adds, pointing out their position. "I received my wounds when I carried water to them. I fear that they might not survive unless they are rescued soon. But you're our surgeon and I don't think you should risk your life trying to reach them."

Hartley nods. "We should get you to camp as soon as possible."

Together, the men scramble down the hill. Edwards' renewed groans and cries of "Water, water, water" slowly fade into the distance.

As Hartley binds up Brown's wounds, Scott strides up, relieved that his friend, although wounded, is safe and appears likely to recover. "Why are the others still there? Why didn't they follow you out?"

"It is hell out there, Robert," Brown replies, pausing to regain his breath. "I came out a different way. They would be risking their lives by trying to do the same.

Those savages are good shots, particularly the albino."

Brown tells Scott how he risked the firepower himself when he took water to the two injured men trapped behind a rock. "I nearly lost my life," he adds. "I suppose it was a foolish thing to do. But someone had to help them. "

Scott regrets that he, too, could not help the men trapped under the ledge.

It is afternoon when Southey, whose reserve troops have seen no action today, approaches Griffith on the rocky outcrop. "If you feel it is expedient for me to do so, I will lead my reserve troops in support of the men trapped under the wall," he says.

Griffith thanks him, but turns down his offer. "It's just too dangerous right now," he says. "But I might take you up on that offer a little later. I have an idea that I need to discuss with some of my men. I believe it just might help us to gain the upper hand and enable your troopers to resume the assault on the mountain."

So far, Moorosi's defense has worked flawlessly. The heavy stone walls have proven an effective barrier, both against bombarding from the seven-pounder cannon and from attempts by the soldiers to scale them. His men have fired well, killing a number of the enemy, pinning two behind an exposed rock, and trapping many more under the ledge.

This battle is proving to be easier and less painful than he had feared.

He walks down a path and along a trench where two walls intersect. In front of him lies the body of Braine, riddled with shots. The men leave the body where it has fallen, stepping around it to assume their firing positions.

"We will remove the body when the battle ends," Moorosi says. "I know that will be soon. The whites cannot do anything against us now. They're too afraid."

He addresses a number of the men behind the wall. "You are doing well," he says. "Maketa, your shooting has been good."

He turns to Lehana. "How many of our people have been hurt?" he asks.

"Only one or two," replies Lehana. "No one has been killed and the injuries are only slight. They are easily treated."

The casualties are nothing like those his people suffered in earlier clashes on open ground, when they numbered the dead in the twenties and thirties.

"We are winning," replies Moorosi. "Many among the enemy are dead. And the cost to our people has been small. I chose well when I chose this mountain to make my people's fortress."

Griffith outlines his plan to his special assistant Arthur Barkly, who normally serves as the magistrate at Mohale's Hoek. "I would like your assessment of my idea," he says. "First let me outline the background. Our problem this morning was that we were unable to lob the shells right into the enemy. We need to drop the shells behind those stone barricades where the enemy is."

"You might have to adjust the trajectory," says Barkly.

"Our men tried several times this morning to do that, but without any real success," Griffith responds. "Part of the problem is that we are too far away to aim the guns accurately enough. I suspect that by the time the shells reach the walls they also have lost some of their power."

"Are you proposing moving the cannon forward?" asks Barkly. "That would be dangerous. It would expose the artillery crews to the gunfire. "

"No, I am not suggesting that, Mr. Barkly. Here is my idea. We take the time-fuse shells and use them in the same way you would use hand grenades. The men could run up and lob them over the walls. The shells will explode behind the walls and the shrapnel will cause severe injuries."

Barkly's eyes light up.

"That would silence the gunfire, at least for a while, and give our men the chance to climb the walls," he says.

"Indeed."

"But surely the men lobbing the shells will be exposed to gunfire when they rush the walls?"

"That is the risk we have to take. Would you kindly ask Lieutenant Best whether this plan is feasible? He understands the guns and the shells better than I do. If he says it is, obtain some men who will serve as volunteers to carry it out."

Best confirms that the plan is a good one and says he will explain it to the men. He walks to the men who were to have been the second and third assault waves.

"Here's the plan," he tells them.

Scott, who has joined his fellow reserve troopers, listens carefully to Best's plan. He recognizes it as an opportunity to play a meaningful role in the battle just as his friend Peter Brown has done. The first to volunteer, he moves forward without hesitation.

"I will go," he says.

Three others follow his example. The men walk to the cannon where Best hands each two ready-fused seven-pound shells.

"Once you reach the walls, you will need to light the fuses," he explains. "The shells will explode nine seconds after you light them. Hold on to them for about five or six seconds and then throw. Those villains won't know what has hit them. Each of you should hurl your shells in different places. With six explosions along the line of fire, we should be able to make a big dent in the enemy ranks."

Barkly adds his advice. "Obviously you are going to come under heavy fire as you approach the walls," he tells the men. "I suggest you run as fast as you can and zig-zag as you go. The quicker you can cover that ground, the less likely you are to be hit. You will have the advantage of being a moving target. Run fast enough and by the time you have reached the walls they will be only loading their rifles.

"You should get as close as you can; even climb at least some way if that is possible so you can land those shells right in the enemy's midst. Get as close as you can as quickly as you can.

"Sergeant Scott, you are the leader. The rest of you should follow his instructions. When he tells you to run, run. When he tells you to throw, throw.

"Now go. Good luck to you all."

Scott is aware the mission has extreme risk. He will have to avoid Baphuthi gunfire until he reaches the safety of the ledge where he can light the fuse, then step out and throw the shell high enough to get over the wall and quickly enough to avoid any impact from the explosion.

"I want you to take cover to avoid injuries from any premature explosions," he tells the men who have been assigned him. "I will go first. Remember that even though we might be hit we can still lob those shells. We are risking our lives for our fellow soldiers. If we can succeed, they will be able to complete the mission."

Scott places the two shells in a bag slung across his chest. He sprints across the open plateau before reaching the wall. He has not gone far before the firing starts. The Baphuthi are able to load their rifles quicker than he thought. He wonders what kind of firearms they are using.

A bullet hits the ground alongside him; too close, he reckons. His fear gives him added speed. Even though the weight of the shells slows him, he reaches the wall in good time. And without being hit.

The soldiers sheltered against the rock wall to the right stare in amazement as Scott runs toward them.

"What is he trying to achieve?" asks one. "He doesn't even have his carbine with him."

"Maybe he is a negotiator and we are going to have a cease-fire," suggests another, enlisting a chuckle from the men.

"I'm amazed he hasn't been hit," adds a third. "He's a lot braver man than I am."

Panting from the run, Scott pauses under the ledge to regain his breath.

He turns to the soldiers.

"I'm going to lob shells over the schanzes," he says. "Others will follow me. We'll cause panic up there and the enemy will scramble up the mountain for their lives.

"Once that happens, you will be able to storm the walls. But, for now, I need you to move further down the ledge to avoid the effects of the explosion."

The men, filled with a mixture of admiration for Scott and apprehension for themselves, move lower down. They fear that, even should the shells remove the gunfire threat, it will not prove easy to scale the walls. But they remain committed to carrying out their assigned duties if it is possible to do so.

"Now for the tough part," Scott says to himself, aware his every move is being watched by the three other volunteers with shells and by the men who will assault the walls.

He removes the first shell from his bag and lights it.

Holding it in his right hand, he finds a protrusion on the rough wall. He counts slowly to seven as he pulls himself higher and places his feet in niches in the rock wall so that he is in a higher position to lob the shell over the schanzes above him.

"..five, six, seven," he says to himself.

He lobs the shell in the air, watching as it flies over the stone wall above him. When he hears loud shouting from the Baphuthi above him he knows the shell has landed in the intended spot.

The Baphuthi were mystified as to Scott's intentions when they saw the trooper running toward them. "He has no gun," observed Maketa. "Why is he running here?"

Only when Scott lobs the shell and it makes a fizzing sound as it flies over the wall, do the Baphuthi realize what Scott is doing.

"Out of the way," Maketa yells as the shell lands alongside him. He recognizes what it is and starts to run in the opposite direction. Before he has moved more than a couple of paces, he looks back because the shell has not exploded.

Maketa runs back, seizes the shell, and tosses it back over the wall.

Scott watches as the shell is thrown back. He runs forward and picks up the shell, determined to lob it back before it explodes.

"Watch out," he screams, running back toward the ledge with it.

The men, frozen with fright, brace themselves for the explosion.

Scott looks down at the shell and stops. As he reaches the safety of the ledge, he removes the fuse. He shows it to the men. "It failed to fire," he says. The soldiers breathe a sigh of relief.

Scott reaches into his bag for the second shell.

This time, he will count to seven, pause slightly, and then lob the shell. The closer he can get to having the shell explode exactly as it hits the ground the less chance the Baphuthi will have to throw it back.

This time, just in case he did something wrong last time, Scott makes sure he lights the fuse correctly.

He grabs on to the rock wall and starts hoisting himself up it. As he does, Scott looks at the shell in his right hand and realizes too late that the fuse is defective. Suddenly the shell explodes in his hand, instantly shattering it. The cap on the shell bursts off, puncturing his left leg. Other pieces of shrapnel cut into his body.

Pieces of the shell fly toward the soldiers under the ledge. Several hit Trooper Morley, who failed to move lower down as Scott requested. He screams in pain and falls. His fellow soldiers run across to assist him.

The explosion not only has severely injured Scott, it has caught his shirt on fire. He falls to the ground, slapping at the flames with his left hand in an attempt to put them out.

Horrified by the turn of events, the other three bomb carriers run forward to take his place.

"Stay there!" Scott shouts to them. The firing has stopped as the Baphuthi on the ledges above watch in amazement as the flames surround Scott. But Scott is aware that the firing could resume at any minute. Nevertheless, the three men continue to run forward, determined to help him.

Summoning every ounce of strength he has left, Scott barks at them: "I am ordering you to stay there!"

As the men — unwilling to disobey an order — hesitate, Scott remembers the drill he had been taught should his clothes ever catch on fire, something he had considered highly unlikely at the time.

He drops to the ground and rolls over and over, setting fire to a patch of grass. The flames go out, but in his manic effort, Scott continues rolling. He does not realize how close he is to the edge of the plateau.

He rolls over an incline and falls 25 feet to the valley below.

Griffith is dismayed.

His plans have gone awry. How many times in the past had he not made similar plans and seen them carried out? True, now and then there were hitches. Not every plan works right. But never before had they all gone wrong, as these have.

He looks across at the Basotho under Lerothodi who fired their rifles from a distance, but did not get within range of the enemy. It is clear that they were reluctant to get involved. That was another disappointment on this unfortunate day.

Yesterday, as he planned the attack, he was convinced the big guns he so desperately needed would blast their way to victory. They did not.

Yesterday he visualized his men assaulting the stone walls, overwhelming the Baphuthi fighters and climbing relentlessly to the top of the mountain. Now he has 50 soldiers pinned under a ledge, two seriously wounded men sheltering behind a rock, an unknown number killed, and a Basotho fighting force unwilling to fight.

Yesterday he was convinced his men's bravery and ingenuity would gain him victory. Now even a brave act by a sergeant has fallen flat.

Yesterday, his men were fit and eager to fight. Now even the men being held in reserve are in a state of panic.

Yesterday he told his men they would take the mountain and cause the Baphuthi to flee. Now his men are the ones on the run.

This is not the type of warfare he knows. He has fought the enemy on open ground and undulating hills. He has pursued them in thick bush. But assaulting a mountain fortress is entirely different. Griffith had no idea it would be this tough. True, his men fought bravely. They showed extreme courage. But the task was too great for them.

Enough recriminations, Griffith concludes. They can wait. Now he must rescue the situation. He must engineer a withdrawal before more lives are lost.

He is considering how to effect that withdrawal when Grant climbs the saddle to speak with him.

"I have to report that the attack we launched from the cave has failed," he says.

Griffith simply nods. He does not want to speak out of fear that his emotion will show in his voice. He has run out of ideas.

Grant stands silently alongside him, unsure whether to continue speaking. Griffith clearly is hurting. His disappointment, anger and humiliation are apparent despite his silence. Griffith gathers his composure. His task now is to save his men pinned under the ledge. He asks Grant to instruct Best to resume firing the cannon. "The men need to be withdrawn. We have to provide them with cover so that they can retreat."

Grant is doubtful. "With all respect, colonel, what kind of cover can we provide? The cannon had little impact when we used them this morning," he says. "They did not stop the enemy from firing effectively at us. I see no reason they will have an impact now. Why don't we wait until dark?"

Suppressing his immediate reaction to repeat his instruction and insist it be obeyed, Griffith forces himself to override his emotions and to think rationally, something he has tried to do his whole life but which he finds hard to do right now. He coughs, then continues. "Yes, yes. You are right. Let us not use them until dark. That is what I meant to say. If we wait until the sky starts to darken and we fire the cannon then, it will be more difficult for the enemy to see and fire at our men. Not only will their sight be limited, but as we fire the cannon in the failing light, they will also be disoriented."

He desperately hopes the maneuver will work.

Scott moans in pain as his fellow bomb carriers reach him. One bends down to examine him.

"He is alive," he says. "I don't know how he did it, but he is alive." The man looks up at the cliff and shakes his head in amazement at Scott's ability to survive not only having his hand blown off, his thigh torn apart, and his clothes catch on fire, but also plummeting down the mountainside.

The men lift him up gently and place him on a blanket. They lift the blanket and carry the injured soldier over the stone-covered ground toward one of the tents where the surgeon, Hartley, is waiting.

It is growing dark as the commander's final battle plan of his disastrous day takes shape.

Griffith has decided that not only should they shell the stone walls, but they should keep up a steady rifle fire as well. He places the reserves in position.

"It is not important whether you hit the enemy," he tells them. "I know that is almost impossible to do from this distance, particularly as they are hiding behind the walls. Your job is to keep firing, one after the other in quick succession, so that they are distracted. At the same time the cannon will be fired. That, combined with the failing light, should draw their attention away from the ground in front of them so we can get our men to safety and bring down the wounded."

Close to 7 o'clock, as the sun dips over the mountains, Griffith gives the order to start firing. The hills echo with loud explosions interspersed with the pop of rifle fire. White smoke drifts across the plateau as the men scramble down the mountainside in small groups. The Baphuthi taunt them to return.

"Come and get us."

"Here we are."

"Why are you running away?"

Grant, looking worried, strides up to Griffith.

"I must report, colonel, that Sergeant Edwards and Private Paschke, who are both badly wounded, are still lying under cover on the plateau," he says. "I think it is safe to bring them down now that it has become dark. Unless you disagree, I will give orders that it be done.

Griffith nods. "Go ahead."

"Also, I need to report, sir, that Captain Surmon is missing," Grant adds.

"He is one of our finest men," responds Griffith. "A great leader and popular among the men. When last did you see him?"

"He was among those who stormed the mountain; he was the senior officer who led the men. But we lost sight of him in the fighting. Perhaps he is among those sheltering against the wall, although no one has reported seeing him there."

A Basotho man runs up to the camp. "My master is lying badly wounded in a cave," he says, pointing toward the side of the plateau. "I'll show you where to go."

A group of volunteers follow the Basotho man, who has remained faithfully at Surmon's side for the entire day. The captain, badly wounded, can barely speak. The men carry him carefully to a tent that has been set up as a field hospital.

As darkness sets in, with the heavy firing still under way, Griffith orders the unhurt men to return to the ledge and to bring down the wounded. Many are suffering from gun wounds; those unable to walk are carried down the mountain slope while the others are assisted over the rough terrain.

By half past eight all dead have been brought down from the mountain, except Braine, whose body still lies on a path behind the stone walls. Also left behind on the plateau is a tattered flag, trampled under foot as the men scrambled to save their lives. The words, "Onward to Victory" are barely discernible in the dirt.

Griffith orders the shelling to stop. Best reports that 125 shells were fired during the day. "That is more than I fired during the whole Gcaleka campaign," Griffith says. He adds, to himself, "and that campaign I won."

As lanterns flicker in the tents, and the men huddle outside around fires to counter the cool temperature that has set in, the mood is somber as the men reflect on the lost battle. Tired and sore, those not injured sit around drinking coffee, relating to their fellow soldiers how tall the ledges and stone walls were, how it was impossible to climb them and wondering how they will ever take the mountain.

"We failed," says Thomas Reeves, a member of the Cape Mounted Riflemen who spent the day under the ledge. "They are calling it a check and a 'slight repulse', but I say we should look at it for what it was. It was a failure."

"Perhaps," replies James Gorman, who was one of the reserves. "But we were not disgraced. We didn't turn and run. We did what we were ordered to do. And we did it as best we could."

"But no amount of bravery can take away the fact that we failed," says Reeves. "Imagine what the people in the rest of South Africa are going to say about this. Think what the Basotho people are going to think of us. We failed. It was a grand failure that will have repercussions around the country. If not the world.

"Just look at what has happened. We and another 500 of us sat here for 12 days, doing nothing but waiting for those useless toy guns to arrive. In the meantime, the enemy on the mountain were adding to their stone walls. They saw us down here. They knew what we were going to do. When we attacked they were ready for us.

"And then what do we do? Do we shell the walls for a full day? No. We fire a few shots into those stone walls. They have no effect. And then we stop firing. Instead of us advancing under a cover of heavy fire, not a shot was fired after we came in range of their fire.

"The fact is that our officers were much more surprised than we were at the resistance offered. We underrated the enemy and the usual consequences followed. And we didn't do it on the cheap. I hear that £200,000 was spent on keeping us here before the cannon arrived."

"That is lot of money to spend on doing nothing, " Gorman says.

"Not just on doing nothing; in preparing for a failure."

A third trooper joins in. "I want to know why the Yeomanry didn't join us. We had to rush through that hail of gunfire while they sat back. Group of cowards."

"You can't blame them," says Reeves. "They saw what was happening to us. Apparently they were firing over our heads and I am sure that helped when we stormed the mountain. If it had not been for them, maybe none of us would have been alive to sit around this fire tonight. If they also had stormed the mountain, there would have been no fire from below to cover their charge. And if they had tried to reach the first stone wall none would have come out alive."

Not far away men of the Yeomanry also gather to discuss the day's events.

Comments one, "I know they're saying we're cowards. I am not a coward. I would have stormed that mountain if I had been ordered to do so. I thirsted for blood and I would have thought no more of shooting a native than I would a dog."

"Perhaps you would have," another replies. "But I don't mind admitting I was a coward. I tell you I'd rather be a frightened Peter than a dead Peter."

Senior officers, all on the front line in today's fighting, sit around their own fire, holding their own post-mortem inquiry into the day's events.

"I think Colonel Southey should have been in charge," says Captain Fincham. "He has the confidence of more officers and men. I've seen him in action and he is always cool, cautious and observant. He stands up solidly in the face of danger and he has undaunted courage."

"You're right," says Captain Leach. "He is quick to notice opportunities and to avail himself of them."

Fincham continues, "The problem with Griffith is that he has worked among the Basotho so long that he has inoculated himself with the Basotho nature. He has become like them, and I don't think he really wants to fight them.

"His old fire is quenched; instead of acting quickly, he has become deliberate. It is almost as though he is doing what he must do and not what he wants to do. He is cautious and slow. He lets opportunities slip past him."

"I agree," says Leach. "He's impassive. It's excessively annoying — and I might add discouraging — when you're dealing with him."

"He's excellent as a political chief," says Fincham, "but a worse selection could not have been made for the military chief. He never really allowed the guns to do their work of breaching the walls.

"He didn't acquaint himself with the task that he required the force to execute. If he had, surely he would have realized it was nothing short of stark madness to order men to charge up the face of a hill at those stone fences. It was worse than foolhardiness to send the men there only to discover that the enemy position was unassailable. It was a foolish sacrifice of valuable lives, to say nothing of those who were injured."

As the officers continue their discussion, Brome, who is thankful that he was not ordered to take part in the assault, leaves his fellow soldiers and wanders down to the temporary morgue. Among the bodies in it is that of Paschke, who died shortly after being brought down from his spot behind the rock.

Brome walks to a series of tents in which some 25 men lie with wounds. In one tent, four are from the ranks of the Cape Mounted Riflemen who stormed the mountain: Trooper J. Broad, Sergeant W. F. Cole, Corporal Charles Martindale and Captain James Surmon, who is suffering from a serious gunshot wound to the lung. Edwards, who sheltered behind the rock with Paschke, is also there.

They appear to be the most seriously hurt.

Brome feels their pain as if it were his own. He watches Hartley, the surgeon, tend to the men. When Hartley is done, and leaves the tent, Brome inquires of the men's condition.

"I don't like to say it, but the men in this tent are not expected to survive," Hartley says. "We will still fight to save their lives and I have instructed that, if possible, three of them be taken to the hospital we have set up at Thomas's Shop. But Surmon is too seriously injured to move. I have instructed that he not be disturbed.

"Most of the wounded in the other tents are expected to survive. They are suffering from gunshot wounds to the legs, arms and face. Three were struck in the head by rocks hurled from the mountain.

"I'll have to amputate the limbs of three of the men in the morning when it is light. One of those is Scott, whose right hand is too severely injured to save."

With Brome following close behind him, Hartley enters another tent and crouches at the side of Brown's stretcher. "Your body will heal, but I am sorry to have to tell you that you will not be able to use your right arm again," Hartley says. "Your fighting days are over. Your age of 45 counts against you, too. I suggest you retire on pension."

Brown, tired and suffering severe pain, has learned that war is less than the adventure he remembers from earlier years. Killing barbarians proved not to be that exciting or rewarding.

"I will accompany you and some of the other wounded men to Aliwal North where you will be cared for at the hospital," Hartley says.

Brome lingers at the entrance to the tent after Hartley leaves. Brown, looking for someone to blame for his suffering, calls to him, recognizing him as the loner who spoke with no one.

"Did you ever become involved in the assault?" he asks.

Brome is quiet for a moment. "No. I was not ordered to do so."

"You should have volunteered, to make up for those who were ordered to join us but did not do so," says Brown. "If we had more men we might have won. It's sad that so many of them were too cowardly to join us."

Brome does not respond. He has no answer. Perhaps he is a coward. If he could leave the camp and go home now, he would. When he signed up as a volunteer, he regarded it as his patriotic duty. He told his wife it would be an honor to serve in the military, to protect his fellow men and to defend their farms and settlements from native attacks. But what he once thought would be little more than a police patrol has become a death mission. Although he cannot bear to see his fellow soldiers suffering, he realizes he is pleased he did not volunteer.

"I am sorry. I hope you get better," he mumbles.

He pushes open the tent flap and leaves.

Brown calls out to him.

"Come back. I am sure you'll get another chance. We're not going to stop this war until we win. Get out there and kill those rebel good-for-nothings. Do your duty to God and country!"

Brome nods, turns and leaves once more.

"War stinks," he mutters as he walks away. "I am sorry I ever signed up for this. I don't want to be part of it."

Griffith walks in and out of the tents of the wounded men, commiserating with them and thanking all for their valiant efforts.

He walks across to the group of Cape Mounted Riflemen who less than an hour ago were discussing the failure of the mission. "I have never seen anything quite like the way you stormed that mountain," he says to them. "Observers from the colony tell me they would have traveled 200 miles to see that sight. You are a brave and honorable group of men and I am proud of you.

"But, as I am sure you have concluded, storming the mountain without heavy artillery does not work," he says. "The seven-pounders were ineffective, mere toys. The ascent is more difficult than one would have thought from looking through even good glasses from the bottom of the hill.

"So my plan now is to starve out these people. They will not be able to survive for long without food and I am not sure how much water they have up there."

The men wonder why they had to endure so much pain and death before Griffith came up with that plan.

Brabant's men reach a small hill, which offers a defensible position. They set up a camp below a few unoccupied stone huts, which offers clear evidence that they are in the settled part of Quthing and that some Baphuthi have fled their homes. After setting out a few sentries, Brabant lets the men enjoy a dinner of grilled mutton. Soon the men fall asleep in the huts, unsure how far away they are from their objective — Moorosi's mountain.

Quthing — Wednesday April 9, 1879

Scott lies in the tent. He must face a cruel reality, he says to himself. He has lost a hand. He will never be able to use that hand again. Never again. This wound, unlike others, will never heal.

In addition, his leg is throbbing and he wonders how that will heal or whether it, too, will have to be amputated, a routine procedure for severe leg wounds.

Yesterday he was proud to be strong and energetic; today he feels a quarter of a man. He cannot help thinking that he is suffering because he volunteered to undertake a duty that should never have been attempted. He thinks of the other sufferers in the assault, men who also were the victims of an ill-considered assault plan. They did not trust Griffith's battle tactics on the eastern frontier; they should have known better than to trust them here.

Running through his mind are the words of the poem *The Charge of the Light Brigade* by Alfred Tennyson, written to commemorate a similar crazy mission undertaken by the British in 1854. One verse in particular comes back to him.

Someone had blundered:
Theirs not to make reply,
Theirs not to reason why,
Theirs but to do and die.

When he had learned them by rote at school the words were little more than a cascading rhyme. Now Scott finds himself thinking for the first time of the meaning behind those words.

Someone had blundered.

Griffith, perhaps? He had rushed without thinking into the battle, refusing to wait for Brabant's forces. Would it really have been so bad to have waited a day or a week? Or did Griffith want to take all the glory?

None of the soldiers could question Griffith's orders.

Theirs not to make reply

No one could question whether Griffith had looked carefully into the battle plan, whether he was sure that the walls could easily be scaled, whether he had even taken time to consider what he was doing.

Theirs not to reason why

They had rushed into battle, like madmen, into a storm of gunfire.

Theirs but to do and die.

At least he is not dead.

Scott hears voices in the tent alongside.

"Who is here?" he asks.

"Barkly is doing the rounds," responds a voice.

Barkly — the magistrate from Mohale's Hoek who is now Griffith's staff officer — is making it a point this morning to talk with the wounded men in the tents. It is unpleasant for him to see their injuries. But he knows the men appreciate the company and he believes it is a boost to morale.

Barkly is carrying a box of biscuits sent to him from his wife who is in Mohale's Hoek. The men appreciate the biscuits. Camp food has consisted only of corn and meat for days and the monotony has made some men reluctant to eat.

As he squats down beside Scott, Barkly notices that the bandage on the sergeant's arm has fallen off. Scott's hand and some of his lower arm have gone; all that is left is a stump, with the bone exposed. The bleeding has stopped and is congealed on the stump, and the bandage is covered in blood. "Let me help you with that," Barkly says, carefully putting the bandage back in place and tying it on.

Scott avoids looking down at the stump. "At least I have another hand," he says, trying to be cheerful. "I will have to learn to write with my left hand now."

Barkly ventures a smile. "You see, it's not as bad as it could have been," the magistrate says, not sure whether that is the right thing to say.

Scott looks into Barkly's face. This is the man who passed on to him Griffith's idea of lobbing the shell over the wall. Scott holds no animosity toward him, but he would like to know why Griffith and Barkly — and the others in the upper ranks — acted when they did. Today he is even wondering why they are fighting at all. He tries to shake off those thoughts.

Theirs not to reason why

Barkly is talking again, saying something about being sorry and about the brave way in which Scott hurled the shell behind the enemy fortifications. But, although he feigns interest, Scott pays no heed to what he hears.

"Tell me again why are we fighting this war," he says. "Why do we want to kill these people? Why are they so bad?"

Barkly is taken aback at Scott's cynical tone. Soldiers do not ask those sort of questions. If they did, wars could never be fought. If each soldier followed his own conscience or his own thoughts on how to fight the war, the result would be chaos. A soldier must follow orders and adopt the same attitude toward the enemy as his officers. If he starts to tolerate the enemy, problems can arise. He must believe the enemy to be evil and worthless, otherwise he will be an ineffective fighter. Few sane humans want to kill fellow humans — for any reason. The only way they will kill is if they see the others as expendable inferior beings.

"We are defending ourselves and our government from a rebellious chief who has declared war on *us*," he replies. "He disobeyed the law by helping his son escape from jail. He refused to surrender his son and then he attacked our troops across the Telle River and sacked the magistrate's offices.

"We cannot let acts like that go unpunished. He is a rebel, a thief and a trouble-maker. He must be brought to book. We are fighting for justice."

Scott sighs. "I suppose I knew that," he says. "But I keep wondering whether we could not have tried talking with him and tried to persuade him to give up his son. After all, this is his country. These are his mountains. These are his people."

"That might be so, sergeant, but we are bringing civilized rule to this uncivilized, barbarian part of the world," Barkly replies. How, he ponders, could this fine soldier, this gentleman, speak as though he almost supports the enemy? The pain and resulting delirium can be the only explanation.

"We are helping these savages live better lives. We are bringing light into their world of darkness," he continues. "Besides, the old chief would not listen to reason," Barkly adds. "And he was the one who started this war, not us. He attacked us first. Even the Basotho do not like Moorosi and are cooperating with us in our fight against him."

"I did not see many Basotho fighting on the mountain yesterday," Scott replies, his voice becoming weaker.

"You may not have seen them, but they are on our side. Anyway, you need to get rest and should not be getting yourself excited. You performed a valiant deed for your country yesterday and you should be proud of yourself. It is people like you who make this world a better place. You are a true hero."

Scott closes his eyes. Perhaps when the pain subsides and he learns to write with his left hand he will be able to feel the pride.

His not to reason why

He drifts into sleep and Barkly creeps quietly out of the tent.

As he continues to assess the results of yesterday's assault, Griffith notes the death toll has reached four — so far — and the wounded 17, four of whom might not survive. The casualties, killed and wounded, amount to almost one-fourth of the hundred or so men who stormed the walls.

"We will have to arrange a burial for the dead," he tells Barkly. "I am sure you can find a chaplain to conduct the service. Choose a site for a cemetery."

Griffith prepares a report for Prime Minister Sprigg in Cape Town, including a request for the government to send as many men as it can spare.

He adds, "I have seen nothing of Colonel Brabant, who left Kraai River camp about eight days ago, and was supposed to be working his way down the Buffalo River to join me at this place."

Griffith also asks that a full hospital be established at Thomas's Shop Camp. Two more ambulance wagons are urgently required, he adds.

"I also require several hundreds rounds of ammunition, sent up without delay. Supplies for at least a month for eight or nine hundred men will be required."

Moorosi also is conducting an assessment of the battle. He is proud of his men, of the way they fought and of the victory they achieved. He walks around the huts and the caves on the top of the mountain and ascertains the damages his men suffered. After listening to their reports, he summarizes the results.

"Motsapi, you were injured in the arm by a bullet when you were occupying the front position behind the wall; Mofullufullu, you were also hit in the arm by a bullet; Hlukana, you received a wound in your leg from a piece of a cannon shell that landed close to you in the trench behind the wall; Moshibidi, your hand was hurt by a cannon shell."

"These injuries are minor and they will heal. You all fought well and you killed and injured a number of white soldiers. I am proud of all of you. Maketa, I am proud of you, too. You shot well and accurately."

The albino man smiles.

"We won that battle, but the white men are still there. Their tents are still there. You can all see them. The lion is still ready to pounce, and he is going to pounce on us again. But we are nimble antelope who will defend ourselves.

"Others of our people are hiding in caves along the rivers where they have defended themselves and are ready to fight in the way we have fought.

"When the whites eventually realize they cannot defeat us and give up and leave our land, we will join our brothers and sisters who are hiding in the caves and together we will take back our country and live in freedom once more.

"Now we must build up the walls where they have been damaged. We must make them higher and stronger so that when the next attack comes we will be able to repulse it as well as we did today.

"Soon the lion will become tired of pouncing on us and hurting himself without hurting us. His wounds will be too great. He will limp away and look for other antelope. But before that happens he will try again. We must be ready for him."

Quthing — Friday, April 11, 1879

Having reached the headwaters of the Buffalo River, known to the local people as the Sebaphala, Brabant has picked up the pace. At noon, his men stop for a meal.

One explores ahead and runs back to Brabant.

"We are only about five miles from the mountain," he reports. "I can see the tents around it." The men need no encouragement to pick up the pace and cover the five miles as quickly as possible.

Late in the afternoon Brabant arrives at the mountain. Griffith comes out to meet him.

"I am pleased to see you," he says.

"Have the guns arrived?" Brabant asks. "I sent them through Palmietfontein."

"They have," replies Griffith. "They arrived on Sunday, we set them up on Monday. On Tuesday we fired them and stormed the mountain."

"You stormed the mountain? You didn't wait for me to arrive?"

"I believed we could scale those walls with comparative ease," Griffith responds. "I did not think your presence and any additional troops would have changed anything. My senior advisers agreed with me.

"It was only when our troops reached the spot just below the walls that we realized what we were up against."

"You found that the guns were ineffective, did you not?" Brabant asks.

"Yes."

"If you had waited I would have told you that Captain Giles is bringing a 12-pounder," Brabant responds. "That likely will be more effective against the stone walls and will make the job of the storming troops a lot easier.

"In addition, I have brought 140 men with me. Had you had them as well, you might have succeeded."

"I am not sure whether any number of troops would have helped. We might only have suffered more casualties. When the storming party reached the first line of schanzes, they found it was impossible to scale them or pull them down."

When Griffith relates how Scott tried to throw the shells behind the walls but blew off his hand, Brabant asks, "I'll ask our surgeon, Dr. Comming, to take a look at him. He saw many gunshot wounds when he served in the British Legion in Spain."

Comming emerges from Scott's tent. "I've stopped the bleeding," he says. "He will eventually recuperate. But I must tell you that he was in great danger of bleeding to death. I'm glad we arrived when we did. Had we arrived any later, I don't think we would have saved him."

Quthing — Thursday, April 17, 1879

Ellenberger is taken by surprise at the hostilities at the mountain. When he saw the guns being transported past Masitise, he thought the battle would be some weeks off. Perhaps, he thought then, it could still be prevented. He knew more soldiers were on their way from Palmietfontein and he had heard that troops under Brabant were still to arrive.

When word reached him that a battle had already taken place, with loss of life and injuries on the government side, he was disappointed at being unable to negotiate a settlement. He realizes that more warfare probably lies ahead — unless he can step in and prevent it. He believes there is still hope for a peaceful settlement of the conflict, particularly in the wake of the failure of the attack on the mountain. Earlier, the government spoke confidently of defeating the Baphuthi, making them unlikely to seek any sort of settlement. Now they might be thinking otherwise.

So today he has come to the mountain to talk to Griffith to try to advance such a settlement.

"I am told that a number of Baphuthi people in caves and other hiding places want to surrender themselves and give up their arms," he tells Griffith. "Among them are a group who belong to Lehana's Ward and live up the river not far from my mission station at Masitise. They do not believe they have done anything wrong and do not want to fight against you."

As far as he can ascertain, Ellenberger adds, the stock under that group's control had originally consisted of 6,000 head of cattle, 6,000 sheep and goats and 700 horses. Of those, 2,000 head of cattle and 100 horses were captured by Lerothodi.

Griffith welcomes the news.

"Thank you for the information," he tells Ellenberger. "Thank you, too, for taking the time and effort to travel here to tell me. As you see, we have the mountain surrounded and we have a couple of guns in position.

"My plan now is to starve them out. They will become so hungry that they will be forced to surrender. This, I believe, is a more effective way of solving this problem and will involve less loss of life on both sides. But to do that I need more men and more firepower here and I am ordering that from the government."

Ellenberger nods. "Your approach might be the right one from a military perspective, but I believe that if you and the Baphuthi talked to one another and tried to understand each other we might avoid further conflict.

"As I said, several people in Lehana's district are ready to surrender. If you are prepared to reach a compromise with them, it is possible we could persuade more to stop their rebellion against the government. Offer them more autonomy, perhaps. You might have to give up something to achieve peace, but it'll be worth it.

"I am sad to see the lives that were lost among your troops in your attempt to scale the mountain. I believe a more peaceful way out of this confrontation can be found. Consider why this battle started and whether those issues can be resolved.

"I wish I could once again have you and King Moorosi together on the Wodehouse bench where you could talk. Perhaps you can achieve a compromise. I am sure that the Baphuthi will also be willing to compromise if you sit together with them and talk.

"The more you talk, the longer you keep the killing at bay and the closer you get to preventing more killing. Remember, we must be peacemakers, not war makers."

Griffith appreciates what Ellenberger is saying, but he remains a dedicated government official with the responsibility of carrying out his duty, which is to punish Moorosi, his family and his followers for rebelling against the government. But perhaps, as Ellenberger suggests, he could start with those hiding in the caves. They might be more amenable to compromise than Moorosi.

Before he leaves the mountain, Ellenberger visits the wounded men, including Captain Surmon. He prays for them.

After the visits, he seeks out Maitin.

"If you would like to accompany me back to Masitise — and if Colonel Griffith will allow you to take off a few days — I am sure we can arrange a nuptial celebration for you and your bride," he says. "Our church is available and I believe she has recovered enough to stand at the altar."

Maitin is delighted.

Griffith suggests in a letter to Ayliff, who is still at Thomas's Shop, that Austen, who remains the magistrate of the Quthing district, be told of Ellenberger's statement that there are Baphuthi in the mountains who want to talk peace.

"Of course," he tells Ayliff, "all those who have taken a leading part in the rebellion will have to be tried for sedition. But many others have apparently only fled to the mountains from fear of their chiefs, and to get away from our forces.

"I think all the people who have not taken a leading part in the rebellion should be allowed to come in and give up their arms."

Quthing — Friday, April 18, 1879

Ayliff, responding to Griffith's suggestion, provides written instructions concerning those Baphuthi who wish to surrender that:

They hand over themselves and their arms to the government;

In surrendering, they are not exempted from trial should evidence be found justifying trial for any crime or aid in the rebellion;

If they agree to these terms, they should be placed in safekeeping and prevented from communicating with Baphuthi still in opposition to the government.

Hardly a compromise. But better than nothing.

Quthing — Wednesday, April 23, 1879

As part of his plan to seek the surrender of those not on the mountain whom Ellenberger mentioned could be willing to compromise, Griffith has turned his attention to a cave along the banks of the Silver Spruit River in which Lehana is said to be hiding. Even if he would not compromise or surrender, Lehana must be captured, not only because of his role in starting the war, but because he is undoubtedly helping to supply Moorosi on the mountain.

So it is that Griffith has sent 75 men under Captain Clough to seek out Lehana and his followers, charging them to use force only if Lehana refuses to surrender.

Today, after a march lasting most of the night, Clough, directed by the Baphuthi informer, is leading a party of men into a deep ravine called Quanatu. It is daybreak as Clough and his small band of troopers approach the spot. The informer points down the ravine. "That is where they are hiding," he says.

There, under a sheer rock face, 40 or 50 men led by Lehana have built a stone wall across the cave entrance. About a foot thick, it is loopholed in the same way as the stone walls on the mountain and has a narrow space at the top. Above this is another cave, a sort of second story, into which the men climb using a long pole set alongside the lower cave.

As Clough's party winds its way into the ravine, they see men watching them from the upper slopes opposite the cave. The watchers make no attempt to attack, even as the colonial soldiers commandeer a dozen horses and 16 sheep in the ravine.

As Clough approaches the cave, he divides his men into three groups. Two are to take up positions upstream and downstream, blocking the escape routes. He will lead the main party of 30 men toward the cave.

About 30 yards away from the entrance, Clough positions his sharpest shooters and waits, as arranged, for the arrival of Austen. "Mr. Austen understands the people and the terrain," Clough tells Captain Kemper. "I am waiting for his best judgment on whether I should launch an assault. I don't want to make the same mistake that was made in storming Moorosi's Mountain."

No one mentions calling on the Baphuthi to surrender.

The colonial soldiers wait with intense anxiety. They are talking nervously when a bullet is fired from the cave, striking the ground near one of the men. The soldiers dive for cover, from where they fire back, hitting two men who have stuck their heads out from behind the stone wall to fire more effectively. The injured Baphuthi duck behind the wall. Their heads have been grazed, but the injuries are not serious.

The Baphuthi continue to fire through the loopholes. After several exchanges, the soldiers are retreating as Austen arrives. He assesses the situation.

"I don't believe you should attempt to launch an assault on this cave," he tells Clough. "It is too well fortified. Should your men storm the lower tier of schanzes, they would be completely cut up by the men in the upper cave. They could destroy you." He, too, is afraid to see the disastrous attack on Moorosi's Mountain repeated.

"In addition, we have no medical men and no stretchers to carry the wounded," Austen continues. "This is one of the best-fortified caves that I have seen and I don't think we can take it. I suggest you withdraw."

Clough reluctantly agrees. As the troops withdraw, they fire a last time toward the cave, and hit one of the men. They also fire toward the Baphuthi scouts on the top of the mountain, hitting one of them, too.

"We chased away the government soldiers," Lehana says. "All we had to do was to fire a few shots at them and they became afraid and ran away. We are safe here where we can stay until the war is over. We must tell my father. He will be pleased."

Quthing, Thursday, April 24, 1879

Hearing that their father has been seriously wounded, Captain Surmon's daughters, Elizabeth, 24, and Evelina, 23, have arrived in camp. They are distraught. Their mother, Maria, died two years ago at the age of 41 when their family was living at Palmietfontein police station and they do not want to lose their father, too.

They ask directions to his tent where they promise they will watch over him and help nurse him to health in spite of the serious nature of his wounds. "He must not die," says Elizabeth. "He turns 58 on June 18th and we want to celebrate his birthday with him."

Cape Colony — Saturday, April 26, 1879

Debate on the failed attempt to storm Moorosi's Mountain has begun throughout the Cape Colony. Scapegoats are being sought. A loss cannot simply be accepted as a loss. Someone has to be held responsible.

To the white settlers, politicians and editorial writers, the explanation cannot be that the colonial forces were beaten by a better prepared force with a better strategy operating from a better position. It cannot be that the troops were out-shot and outwitted. It cannot be that Moorosi is a more wily fighter than anyone had thought. Surely, it cannot be that a native fighting force proved itself to be better than the Cape men trained in guerrilla warfare.

Yet the attack failed. There must be an explanation.

One of those looking for an explanation for the embarrassing loss is Under Secretary for Native Affairs Richard Bright, who is acting for Ayliff in Cape Town during the secretary's absence at the scene of the war in Basutoland.

Bright peruses the telegrams and early reports from the war front, looking for the reason. He sees references to "strongly built fortifications" in a number of the telegrams and suddenly an explanation presents itself.

The explanation lies not in what occurred on the day of the battle. It lies in what happened before the battle, in the building of the mountain fortress. How was it possible for Moorosi to build these defenses without the authorities in Basutoland stopping him?

Such a system of strong stone fortifications must have taken considerable time to build. Yet Austen failed to inform the government of it. Inexcusable.

Bright checks with Sprigg, who agrees he should write to Griffith.

After outlining his theory about the cause of the failure, Bright concludes: "I am directed by Government to inquire: (1) How is it that the building of such fortifications was allowed; (2) What steps, if any, were taken to prevent their being constructed; (3) What reports were made to Government from which they could have gathered that such a formidable series of defenses existed at Moorosi's Mountain; and (4) Whether any explanation of his intentions was demanded of that chief."

That should place the blame squarely where it lies.

Aliwal North's *The Northern Post* also suggests the blame lies with Austen — not because he failed to warn about the stone walls, but because he shot two Baphuthi men.

"We do not wish to anticipate the results of an inquiry, which no doubt Parliament will institute, but we must say that Mr. Austen will have to show strong grounds for firing the two fatal and unnecessary shots, and for deserting his post so precipitately and without first warning the traders or giving the loyal and faithful people in the district an opportunity of declaring for the government.

"The question is: Could the rising of Moorosi, which has occasioned the loss of so many valuable lives, have been avoided by tact, prudence and courage; or did it break out in spite of the exercise of those qualities by the magistrate?

"For Mr. Austen's own sake, we trust there will be a searching investigation."

To the *Burghersdorp Gazette*, it is all Griffith's fault.

"The brave and gallant Southey was the proper officer to have had the command-in-chief. He possesses the confidence of officers and men, and his conduct in action has shown him to be cool, cautious, observant; intrepid in danger and of undaunted courage; he is quick to notice opportunities and prompt to avail himself of them.

"New associations have metamorphosed Mr. Griffith and have inoculated him with the nature of the people he has been placed among…He is excellent as a political chief; but all parties agree that a worse selection could not have been made for a military chief."

To the missionary community, the blame lies with the disarmament measure pushed through Parliament by Sir Bartle Frere, a measure they vigorously opposed.

The missionaries are convinced the war with Moorosi was unnecessary and was caused by the disarmament act: "We would respectfully ask, even if it is not our duty to express our doubts in this momentous question, that the government should reconsider this serious question, as far as it concerns the Basotho."

From his vantage close to the action, Ayliff has had time to ponder the effectiveness of Griffith's leadership in the assault on the mountain. He has concluded that Griffith conducted himself well. At no stage did he quarrel with Griffith's tactics. Some say Griffith should have waited for Brabant to arrive or that he should have ordered more powerful cannon or that he should have demanded that the soldiers climb the walls. Their suggestions, however, were all made after the fact. No one can conclusively demonstrate what would have worked.

Ayliff is upset at the casualties suffered in the attack. The latest death toll is seven, a figure that is too high. When added to the injuries suffered by nearly 20, some of whom have lost limbs, the battle was costly, both in men and money. Ayliff remains concerned at the mounting financial expense of the war effort. More men, more food supplies and more ammunition all cost money — and the colonial budget is far from overflowing.

But is the solution to take the command away from Griffith? Would someone else fare any better?

Ayliff has read the comments in the newspapers that arrived here over the past couple of weeks. The variety of reasons given for the failure indicate that others believe that all the blame cannot be laid at Griffith's door. Ayliff is not ready to suggest to Sprigg that Griffith be replaced with another commander. Starving the rebels out seems to be a reasonable approach. He will give the man another chance to prove himself. He conveys his views to Under-Secretary Bright who will represent him to Prime Minister Sprigg.

Sprigg also has been gathering the reports of the attack on Moorosi's Mountain. Some are from Griffith, Grant and Maitin outlining the course of the battle and how it was lost. Others are reports in newspapers throughout the colony, such as the Cape Town dailies *The Cape Argus*, and *The Cape Times*, as well as the *Queen's Town Free Press*, the *Burghersdorp Gazette* and Aliwal North's *Northern Post*. They have been trickling in over the past two weeks, providing more details.

As Sprigg reads through them, he gains a picture of an undertaking gone seriously awry. Before the attack, his officials had assured him there was little chance the attack would fail. The reports detail a disaster.

A report in the *Queen's Town Free Press* is written by a trooper who took part in the battle. "On the 8th one of the most grievous mistakes ever made in warfare in this colony was made by Commandant Griffith in ordering the attack on old Moorosi's Mountain. We had to own we had suffered a severe and humiliating defeat, without killing a single combatant on the enemy's side."

In the words of *The Cape Argus*, "There seems no room for escape from the observation that the military measures directed against the recalcitrant Moorosi have resulted in fiasco, while the attack upon his stronghold can only be described, in its own small way, as a disaster of serious moment.

"The result will doubtless shake the faith of those who have long held it as gospel that the colonial man, left to himself, will make short work of any African native who may dare to defy his arms."

Sprigg grunts. "Coming on the heels of the Zulu defeat, this is extremely embarrassing," he tells Bright. "I can understand it — although not appreciate it — if a battle is lost against a bloodthirsty warrior with thousands at his disposal. But to lose to an old chief with a ragtag group of barbarians who live in the mountains...

"Now some, like *The Cape Argus*, are saying that we should withdraw; that we should let Moorosi go unpunished, that we should not complete what we started, that we should wave the white flag of surrender. I cannot accept that argument. One way or another, we have to remove Moorosi from that mountain."

Bright nods. "I cannot agree more," he says. "Imagine the impact a withdrawal would have on the Basotho people, and perhaps all the natives in South Africa."

The next step, Sprigg concludes, is to determine what went wrong, who is to blame for the disaster and how those mistakes can be corrected and Moorosi defeated.

Sprigg has read the *Northern Post* report criticizing Austen and has seen the letter from the missionaries blaming the disarmament act. He has listened to Bright's argument that more should have been done to prevent Moorosi building the stone walls. But he is inclined to blame Griffith. He was the commanding officer. He devised the strategy. The blame must lie with him.

Argues *The Cape Argus*: "Whatever Mr. Griffith is, he is not a professional soldier. There could, therefore, have been no suppression in giving the chief command, when it came to military measures, either to Colonel Brabant or Colonel Southey, whichever may be senior, both being soldiers by training, and both enjoying more confidence than Mr. Griffith has lately been able to command."

When Sprigg suggests the fault lies with Griffith, Bright, as instructed by Ayliff, defends the colonel. "He is a fine man, a good leader and an excellent soldier," Bright replies. "Do you not recall the actions he took in subduing Sarhili? He beat Sarhili handily, sending him into hiding and freeing up the territory for white settlement. Not only that, but he understands the Basotho people, having worked among them for many years."

"So what are we to do?" asks Sprigg. "Should we replace him with Colonel Brabant or Colonel Southey?"

He pauses, thinks for a while, then adds, "In the meantime, however, I am inclined to follow your suggestion and leave Griffith where he is and to accept his plan of starving out the rebels. I will accede to his request for more troops, ammunition and guns to prevent the rebels restocking their mountain. I believe one must give a man the right tools to complete the job. Will you see his request is acceded to?"

Bright nods. "It will be my first order of business today," he says.

Quthing — Saturday, April 26, 1879

In the past few days, several Baphuthi have approached Austen in his temporary office near the Masitise mission station and offered to surrender. If they fall within the guidelines drawn up by Ayliff, Austen accepts the men's offer.

The magistrate keeps a careful tally of those who have surrendered. So far the tally is 104 men, 119 women and 234 children. In addition, 52 women and 125 children who were living with the rebels in caves in the area have surrendered in nearby villages, leaving their men to continue fighting. Austen realizes that these numbers are only a fraction of the 5,000-strong Baphuthi people.

Quthing — Sunday, April 27, 1879

With an apparent stalemate reached in the war, Ellenberger goes ahead with the formal opening of his church. He had hoped that Moorosi would have been able to attend, but the king clearly cannot do so.

Among the special guests is Georges Steinheil, now 21, who recently joined the missionaries at Morija. He made this journey specially to see the new church inaugurated and visit with Fred and Emma Ellenberger, even though he had been warned that war was being waged in the area. "It was worth making the visit, in spite of the dangers," he says.

"As I am sure you can see, things here in the south of the country are quiet," Ellenberger says. "Several Baphuthi here have surrendered.

"But I have had to close my mission station at Sibaphala, which is closer to the scene of the fighting — temporarily, I trust."

The men discuss the war, with Ellenberger explaining the causes behind it and how he tried to avert it, but could not persuade Moorosi to give up his son Lehana, nor could he persuade the authorities to allow Lehana to surrender by offering him a lesser sentence.

"So am I to believe that this war is being fought because one man was sentenced to jail for advising people not to pay taxes, escaped from prison and now will not give himself up?" Steinheil asks.

"Yes, that is the immediate cause," replies Ellenberger. "But the real reason for the war is to determine who holds the power in Quthing. Neither side wants to cede ground and at this stage it is difficult to see how we can bring back the peace we had here for so long. But I will keep trying to do what I can to avoid more deaths on both sides."

"If anyone can do it, you can," says Steinheil. "They don't call you the fire extinguisher for nothing."

"But sometimes," Ellenberger responds, "the fire is too great for even the best extinguishers."

Transvaal — Monday, April 28, 1879

The resolution is just what Frere likes to hear. Passed at public meetings in Rustenberg and Potchefstroom in the Transvaal colony, they refer to the Zulu war, but echo the sentiments of many whites toward South Africa's indigenous peoples, including the Baphuthi. The resolution, addressed to Frere, reads in part:

"We take the liberty of expressing our unqualified approval of the measures adopted and defined by your Excellency in regard to the Zulus, which we, and, indeed, all who have the least knowledge of the character of the colored races in South Africa, must admit to be the proper course, for they never will be civilized, much less Christianized, if governed by their native chiefs and it will, therefore, prove a blessing to the savages to be under the rule of a strong Christian Government, whereby the peace of the country can and will be maintained."

Quthing — The same day

The days on the mountain are often cloudy as autumn approaches, but they are still pleasantly warm. They are punctuated by the pop-pop sound of guns fired by pickets whenever they see people moving around behind the walls. At times, too, when the soldiers move too close, the Baphuthi shoot back. For the most part, however, the firing back and forth, which has resulted in no injuries, is simply an indication that both forces are on guard.

The higher altitude on the mountain top means the nights are a little colder than in the valley below. Frost settles on the ground before the sun rises to thaw it.

In spite of the cooler temperatures, the Baphuthi work on the walls largely during the hours of darkness to avoid attracting fire from the colonial pickets. Using crowbars, they dig stones out from the ground on the mountain and build the walls even higher. Where the walls are weak, they strengthen them.

The Baphuthi have heard through informants that more ammunition is being sent for the cannon and they want to strengthen the walls so that it will be harder to break them down once the soldiers decide to use the big guns again.

They also want to make sure that should the soldiers ever get close to the walls they will be unable to climb them.

Griffith has ordered the men to remain vigilant. He knows the Baphuthi are masters at slipping down the mountain and returning with supplies so he wants to prevent them doing so. But Brabant, settled in at the mountain and advising Griffith, is not convinced that starving out the Baphuthi is the best way. It will take too long, he suggests, and will cost the government too much. Brabant believes it is possible to storm the mountain again with the troops that they now have and remove Moorosi by force.

Griffith disagrees. In any event, until the arrival of the additional men and ammunition that he ordered, he is unwilling to discuss further action. "With all respect, you were not here when we made that first attempt," Griffith tells Brabant. "We cannot storm the mountain unless we can breach the schanzes."

"We could use ladders," replies Brabant. "We could place them against the walls and scale them in that way."

"Placing the ladders against the walls would be impossible. The enemy would fire on the men and roll stones on them," Griffith responds. "They would be killed or wounded before they could set the ladders in place. Even if the ladders were in place, the men climbing them would themselves become targets.

"There is no other way but to break down the schanzes. But the seven-pounder guns could not do it and I believe even the 12-pounder guns will be unable to do it. This mountain is such an extraordinary natural fortress it is almost impregnable. It would be hard to take even if we had many guns and unlimited ammunition."

But Brabant is adamant. "I believe that if we can get four big guns, or even three, into position on the heights facing the mountain, the fire will become too hot for anyone to live up there. Once the 12-pounders and the ammunition get here, we could start pounding them day after day. If we do that, we will ensure that nothing can live on the mountain. I feel certain of that."

"My strategy right now is to starve Moorosi out," Griffith says, believing that is not only the most practical way to fight this war but also the most humane — for both sides. Recalling Ellenberger's encouragement to be a peacemaker, he adds, "Later today I am going to send a messenger to Moorosi to send down his women and children, who will be protected should we use force against him again."

Moorosi sees a messenger below the walls with a white flag. "Mr. Griffith wants you to send down your women and children," the Basotho man explains.

So that's it. He wants to take away some of his bargaining power. Two of paramount chief Letsie's daughters are married to one of his sons. By sending the women down the mountain into the arms of the government he will no longer have them to use as a lever against Letsie; no longer will they be exposed to government fire.

"Tell Mr. Griffith that I will not let any of my people leave their home here on the mountain," he says, ordering his men to make the walls even higher.

Quthing — Wednesday, April 30, 1879

Ordered to the front by Prime Minister Gordon Sprigg at Griffith's request, the men are trickling in from all parts of the eastern frontier. They report first at Thomas's Shop before continuing to the mountain where they pitch their tents alongside those already there.

Many of the newcomers are members of three special units set up by the legislation passed last year at Frere's urging: A Yeomanry Force; Volunteers organized to defend the colony; and the reorganized Cape Mounted Riflemen.

Among the newly arrived Riflemen is Granville. Separated from Scott and Brown for some time, he is anxious to hear of them. He soon learns that they were among those wounded in the storming of the mountain three weeks before, that Brown's injuries have forced him to retire on pension, and that Scott is still at the hospital at Thomas's Shop, recuperating from the amputation of his hand.

Granville visits Scott who tells him his story and the story of how Brown helped carry water to two men who subsequently died.

"Why do you think the attack failed?" Granville asks.

"I think partly it was because many of the men failed to obey the command to storm the mountain," Scott responds. "The yeomanry individually are good men, but they are not disciplined. Remember when we complained about the lack of discipline in the old Mounted Police in its worst days?"

"I certainly do. Talk about a rag-tag army."

"Well, here it was the same," Scott continues. "Not only were they lacking in discipline themselves, but, with few exceptions, they were badly led."

"I gather that our old friend Griffith is the commander."

"Yes, and I am afraid he is not much better than he was before. I think the lack of discipline can be traced back to him. He just does not know how to ensure that his orders are strictly carried out. It seems as though he has made as great a mess of this as he did of our movements in the Gcaleka war. And he was ably assisted in his mess-making by the greater part of the yeomanry and burghers."

"The result was our most ignominious defeat so far."

Scott grimaces. "I am afraid the pain in my arm is coming on again. I am sure we will talk again soon," he says as he curls up on his bed.

Quthing — Thursday, May 1, 1879

The only vulnerability Moorosi feels is his ability to survive on the mountain. A concern is that the grain supplies have been running low. Some replenishment has been possible from men who have slipped through the enemy lines and collected grain stored in villages and caves, but the amount that one man can carry is limited and even several men cannot carry the amount of food needed for what looks like being a long siege through the approaching winter.

As the corn and other food supplies dwindled during the summer, cattle became the group's main supply of food. But, in addition to those that have already been slaughtered for food, a number of cattle have been dying. Some that wandered too close to the edge of the mountaintop were struck by stray cannon shot during the bombardment and a few have been hit by bullets, but other cattle that should have been healthy have also died. He is unsure why.

Moorosi needs, therefore, to gather more cattle as well as corn. He does not want his people to starve when they have so successfully defended themselves against an attack.

Answers are at hand. It's harvest time and corn should be in plentiful supply; the challenge is to get it up on the mountain in sufficiently large amounts to see them through the winter and into the next summer.

He knows, too, that cattle are available in the surrounding areas, even if they have to commandeer them. But the problem is obvious: The constant patrolling and pickets, who regularly open fire when they see any movement on the approaches to the mountain, make it challenging to bring corn and, more especially, cattle up the mountain path.

Indeed, a few men have been shot and some have died from injuries received in their attempts to herd cattle through the enemy lines.

Moorosi calls his senior advisers to him. "We need to find a way to gather more food supplies and particularly more cattle," he says. "You are all aware of our problem. We cannot get more than a few people off the mountain at a time and they cannot get the cattle past the soldiers. Does anyone have a suggestion?"

Lehana, who has joined his father on the mountain and who is coordinating the gathering of supplies, speaks. "We were able to get up here in the darkness. We mingled with Lerothodi's men, who sheltered us and then, when it was dark, we climbed up the side paths. We heard gunfire from the enemy, but we were not shot."

Moorosi agrees. "Yes, but herding cattle up here is a lot more difficult than moving people up here. Cattle don't understand that they have to move quickly. They don't know how to hide behind rocks and duck when the bullets start flying. They take their time and they are big targets.

"Another thing. Go yourself to the rock at the highest part of the mountain behind us here and look down. You will see there are more men guarding the mountain than before. It is becoming dangerous for our men to leave and return to the mountain. They can do so only in small numbers. They can't bring enough grain and cattle to keep us going through the winter."

As the men continue to discuss the situation, a strategy begins to emerge. "I have a plan," Moorosi says. "I need 10 men to help me accomplish it."

Quthing — Sunday May 4, 1879

Picket duty on the saddle facing Moorosi's Mountain, particularly at night, is becoming a chore.

"This is one of the most boring things I've ever done," Granville says to Sergeant James Corfield before setting off to start his shift. "Picket duty during the day, as you have been doing, is all very well. But at night it is quite different. You stand up there, on that saddle, and you look at the mountain and its stone walls. You cannot see very well in the darkness, particularly when there is no moon, so you rely both on sound as well as sight to try to detect movement.

"Should you happen to detect someone moving around, you fire generally in their direction. Soon they disappear and all is quiet again.

"It is like waiting for a mouse to come out of its hole.

"It is deathly still up there. The nights are cold and you pull your coat around you. Below, hundreds of men are asleep in their tents. You cannot talk to the next picket as he is too far off.

"I must confess I have dozed at times. It is dull, boring and meaningless work."

Corfield can offer no antidote. He wishes him good luck anyway.

Granville climbs the saddle where he and two others are on picket duty for the night. Tonight's full moon provides them with a better-than-usual view of the stone walls. They are to stare at the ghostly grey barricades for the entire night — if they can stay awake.

He guesses it must be around 11 p.m. and he is already starting to feel sleepy when Granville hears a noise behind him. He looks around. He can hardly believe what he sees. Lit by the moon, a Baphuthi man armed with a spear is moving toward him. Somehow the man succeeded in climbing undetected off the mountain and up the knoll behind the pickets and is now almost upon him.

Granville raises and cocks his rifle. He sees other Baphuthi climbing the knoll. "Enemy upon us!" he shouts.

He fires into the warriors below, hitting one. He swings around and realizes more men are climbing up the hill from the front. He and his fellow pickets are being surrounded. They fire repeatedly, shattering the night stillness with the popping sound of gunfire, but the Baphuthi warriors keep coming.

A Baphuthi flings his spear toward Roger Warren, the soldier alongside Granville. The spear finds its target and Warren slips and falls over the edge of the knoll. Baphuthi men, holding their spears above their heads, run toward the spot where he has fallen where they plunge more spears into his body to ensure he is dead.

The rapid gunfire arouses the men in the tents. They tumble out of their beds, grab their revolvers and rifles, and head out of their tents toward the gunfire.

Best and his men run to the cannon, which are positioned behind the knoll. In the moonlight, they can see men moving around on the plateau and can hear gunfire, but they are unsure how many men are attacking and exactly where they are coming from.

Best instructs his men to fire the cannon over the saddle on to the plateau, hoping to deter those who are there from moving forward.

Taken by surprise and without clear direction, the colonial troops are not sure what best to do in the chaos.

The sound of gunfire puts Moorosi's plan into its second phase.

The first phase started three days ago when about 10 men began moving down the mountainside on their way to find grain and cattle in the nearby villages. They went individually, slipping out under cover of darkness.

For the past three days they have collected baskets of grain recently harvested and left in villages by people who surrendered or fled, or that were given them by villagers hiding in caves. They also have rounded up 50 head of cattle, which they are ready to herd up the mountain.

During the day, the men hid in places where they could see the tents, but could not be seen. Now whistling and whooping as they herd the cattle ahead of them, the men push forward to a path up the mountain. With the government soldiers focused on defending the pickets, Moorosi's other men urge the cattle — many of them oxen laden with grain — to climb quickly up the mountainside. It does not matter if they make a noise. The whole area is alive with noise. Nor are the men concerned the cattle might be seen. They are concerned only with moving quickly.

Griffith's staff officer Arthur Barkly takes charge in the absence of anyone senior to him. He calls for the men to join him in climbing up to the scene of action. At the base of the saddle, they come across a soldier covered in spear wounds.

"It's Charles," says one. "The poor man is in a bad state."

"Do you know him?" asks Barkly.

"Yes, it's private Charles Peterson. We shared a tent. Look at his injuries."

He counts 10 puncture wounds.

Although unconscious, Peterson is still alive and Barkly instructs some of the men to carry him down the mountainside to the field hospital.

The base of the saddle is swarming with soldiers firing at the Baphuthi, who are fleeing toward the stone walls. Barkly instructs them to give chase. "Line up here in skirmishing order," he says. "When I say 'advance,' move toward the walls."

The men line up, carrying their weapons at their sides, and march quickly forward, leaving an equal distance from each other. Approaching the plateau below the stone walls, the men, now visible in the moonlight, brace themselves for enemy fire and prepare to fire back. But the Baphuthi seem to disappear. Suddenly, the soldiers find they have no enemy to confront.

"They have fled," Barkly says. "We have trounced them and sent them scurrying away. Well done, men."

He instructs his men to return to their camp. It is nearly midnight and quiet is returning to the mountain.

"That just shows you that once we have them in the open they become frightened and run away," Barkly says as the men walk back to the camp. "I am only sorry that Warren was killed and poor Peterson was so severely wounded. But I suppose that every victory comes with a cost."

As the Baphuthi men herding the cattle reach the top of the mountain, they are greeted with rejoicing. King Moorosi's ruse worked. The whites were thoroughly deceived. The cattle will provide them with meat for many weeks and the grain is sufficient to keep them going for two or three months.

About 4:30 a.m. the moon sets and darkness descends on the mountainside. The men who launched the attack on the pickets and have been hiding in the rocks at the base of the mountain return up the trail.

They report that not one warrior was hurt and they killed one white soldier and possibly two.

The warriors join their fellow Baphuthi in packing the grain into a rectangular thatched-roofed stone hut where it will be protected from the rain and wind. The rest plan a celebratory feast tomorrow when they will slaughter a stolen ox.

Moorosi smiles with satisfaction. The whites will never oust him from his fortress.

XIII

Cape Town — Tuesday, May 6, 1879

When white settlers gather in homes, stores and town meetings in the eastern Cape, events in the Quthing War have become a central topic of discussion. As soldiers return with first-hand stories of the battle and observers arrive home to tell what they saw, they provide fodder for newspaper reports and add a new dimension to the debate.

Why has this quarrel over the payment of hut tax turned into a major dispute? Why is the disarmament law not being enforced to prevent rebelliousness like this? Why has Moorosi not been brought to book? Why is it beyond the powers of the colony's best soldiers to oust this old chief from his mountain fortress?

The settlers fear that if the battle against Moorosi is lost, the result will be outbreaks among the rest of the Basotho people, leading to a wider war and greater casualties than the Gcaleka and Ngqika battles.

The discussions center not on whether the government's policies are right or wrong, but on what is wrong in implementing the policies, accepted as right.

Thus: The disarmament act is not wrong; it is the way it is being imposed that is wrong. "It was quite possible to have carried out the disarmament measure without forcing the natives into hostilities," writes the *Burghersdorp Gazette*.

Similarly, the war is not wrong. It is how it is being fought that is wrong.

Increasingly, Griffith, seen as ineffective and indecisive, is taking the brunt of the blame. Instead of procrastinating, he should have acted when Moorosi's people crossed the Telle River and confronted them in Palmietfontein, the editorial writer for the *Gazette* argues. As a departmental officer too much cannot be said in praise of Mr. Griffith, but as for his military reputation, even his friends will not dispute that the least said about it will be better for his credit, the writer says.

"Now that the assault of the position has failed, the force is to return to the waiting system. Mr. Griffith expects that the Yeomanry will wait before the mountain until the enemy are starved to surrender. We are surprised that he does not propose that they shall wait there until the moldering hand of time shall remove enemy and barricades and all. It would be equally sensible.

"With all due deference for Mr. Griffith's presence on the field of action, we do not think that it is in his power, with the men at his command, so to invest the mountain that the enemy will be shut out from supplies reaching them.

"Besides, it is a dangerous game he is playing; the proofs he is giving of the colonial forces being unable to dislodge a handful of Moorosi's men cannot have the effect of strengthening the loyalty of other Basotho tribes. We are sure he might render the colony a far greater service by resigning the command and returning to his office of Political Agent."

The Northern Post of Aliwal North, which previously blamed Austen for the war, is now equally scathing of Griffith's command.

"The sad roll of five killed and 27 wounded speaks sufficiently to the losses sustained by our men, whilst, on the other hand, not one of the enemy is known to have been killed.

"The story, however, of Mr. Griffith's bungling does not end with the fiasco of the assault. In every other particular he was unprepared. No provision was made for the wounded, not a stretcher nor an ambulance was on the spot, not even a bed to lie the poor fellows on, nor a single 'medical comfort.' We have at our disposal all modern appliances of warfare, and yet we are absolutely reduced to confess our inability to take the mountain by force, and resort to starving the 'garrison' out...

"A few gallant men do not make a glorious campaign but one incompetent officer may ruin the prospects of the bravest army that ever took the field."

Quthing — Wednesday, May 7, 1879

One of those gallant men breathes for the last time at 10 a.m. today. At Captain James Surmon's side are his daughters, Elizabeth and Evelina, who watch in desperation as the wound that pierced his lung and caused him a month of intense suffering eventually takes his life. He will not live to see his 58th birthday.

Granville hands the women a letter written to them by one of the Cape Mounted Riflemen: "Pardon me if I intrude on this your privacy on the occasion of your sad bereavement. I have long known you both and I could not conscientiously allow this opportunity to pass without expressing my heart-felt sympathy.

"Although I speak individually allow me to say that I convey the sentiments of the troop and many would fain express their wishes as I have done were they privileged to do so. Your father has endeared himself to many in this troop and most particularly in the gallant and soldier-like act on the occasion on which he met his death wound. May God in his providence overlook all for good in the humble prayer of your sincere friend."

Quthing — Monday May 12, 1879

The colonial camp at the mountain has settled into a tedious daily routine of manning pickets. An occasional patrol into the countryside relieves the boredom.

The lull gives Griffith the opportunity to catch up on his paperwork. In his civilian role, he has received Austen's response to the request from Under Secretary for Native Affairs, Richard Bright, to explain how Moorosi was allowed to build fortifications on his mountain. Griffith must forward Austen's response to Bright and include a cover letter.

In his report, Austen explains that in May 1877 he introduced Hope to Moorosi and they found the mountain in a fortified condition. At the time, he strongly advised Moorosi to move down from his mountain.

Austen says he had warned the government repeatedly about Moorosi and his fortified mountain. "I have faithfully kept Moorosi before the Government for more than 20 years, and pointed out the danger he was to the colony," he writes.

"This is the first example in our colonial warfare in which we have had to encounter such determined opposition and good engineering generalship. We were all, more or less, taken by surprise."

The Surmon daughters, having watched their father buried at the mountain, arrive at Masitise where they will spend a few days with the Ellenbergers.

Expressing his sympathy for their loss, the missionary vows to do what he can to bring the war to a peaceful end so as to prevent more tragedy — on both sides.

Quthing — Wednesday, May 14, 1879

Reports say that rebels led by Lehana have returned to their caves along the Silver Spruit River after fleeing to the mountain fortress following the aborted attack by Captain Clough three weeks ago. To ascertain the truth of the reports, Griffith dispatches a mounted patrol of eight volunteers under Lieutenant J.J. Dunn.

The men ride up the deep valley before off-saddling and tethering their horses. Dunn walks about 300 yards to scout the area. He stops.

"Take a look at this," he says, indicating a footprint in the soft sand. "This tells me that a barefooted Baphuthi was here recently," he says. "He was almost certainly a rebel." Dunn instructs a soldier to return to camp and ask Sergeant Frost to join them with more men "as it seems to me this is a nasty place."

The man rides off. The others return to their horses to wait.

"I'm tired of waiting. I'm going further up the kloof to look for the savages," says trooper Frederick Von Brombsen of the Herschel Mounted Volunteers.

"You are to wait here until our reinforcements arrive," says Dunn.

"No, I am going on my own," replies Von Brombsen, walking off toward where the rebel stronghold is believed to be.

"I order you to return," Dunn shouts after him. "Come back this instant!"

Von Brombsen swings around and shouts back, "No native has ever molded a bullet to kill me."

"I suggest you heed the words of Lieutenant Dunn," shouts Corporal Webster, another member of the group.

Ignoring both men, Von Brombsen strides boldly up the valley. Dunn, afraid he will be blamed for any fate that might await Von Brombsen, follows him.

"You must obey my order," he shouts. "You cannot do as you like. You are a soldier under my command and you must obey my order."

Von Brombsen continues to walk up the valley, forcing Dunn to watch at a distance as the volunteer soldier looks in a cave under a rock and finds it empty.

Dunn, catching up with him, tries again. "I order you to return to where we off-saddled. You must return now. I order you to go no further." Ignoring him, Von Brombsen walks toward another cave across the valley.

Surprised by the man's disobedience and intrigued to find out where he is going, the five other men in the patrol follow at a distance. As Von Brombsen enters the cave, he is hit in the chest by a bullet. He collapses, yelling, "I'm shot. I'm shot."

The men fire at the cave. Their fire elicits no response and they retreat. Shortly after they reach the place where the horses are tethered, Sergeant Frost arrives with reinforcements. After consultation, Dunn and Frost conclude it is imperative that they retrieve Von Brombsen's body.

"Cover us," Dunn tells the men. They fire round after round toward the cave as Dunn and Frost reach the body and carry it down the hill.

"I think our wisest plan now is to return to camp," Dunn says. "We have used up most of our ammunition. I am afraid the foolish actions of one of our volunteers who thought he knew better than me has led to the failure of this mission."

The death of another government soldier with no corresponding progress in the war reinforces Griffith's frustration. Not only does the mountain remain unconquered, but the Baphuthi appear to be reinforcing their cave hideouts in the countryside and even building new ones in areas he believed to have been emptied.

He needs to turn the war around. He needs a victory, even a small one.

Griffith identifies three major centers of resistance. Obviously one is the mountain. Another are the rebel holdouts up the Silver Spruit where Lehana apparently is once again hiding in a cave that appears almost as impregnable. A third is a labyrinth of caves some 15 miles east along the Quthing River, in which patrols report an unknown number of rebels, led by Letuka and Raisa, are hiding.

Griffith's plan now must be to destroy the two other main centers of resistance while investing the mountain. He will begin with the caves up the Quthing River, which appear more vulnerable than those occupied by Lehana.

He will send Brabant to subdue the rebels in the caves, giving him 85 of the best Cape Yeomanry, including Captain Andrew Jones, and 100 Basotho under the command of Captain Henry Lee Davies and Inspector George Moshesh of the Basutoland police. To provide every assistance, he will even let Brabant take one of the seven-pounders to blast at stone walls. He assigns Lieutenant Best and seven men from the Cape Mounted Riflemen to ensure the gun is correctly used. If successful, the foray will not only provide him with the victory he needs, but also serve as a warm-up exercise for an attack on Lehana's hideout — and possibly the mountain itself.

Quthing — Thursday, May 15, 1879

Raisa walks out of a natural passageway at the entrance to the cave into the crisp air outside. He looks down the gorge where his fellow Baphuthi have built themselves strong fortifications at the entrances to a series of caves alongside the Quthing River in which they are living.

He thinks back two years when it also was harvest time and Hope wanted to punish him for destroying MaLebenya's corn field.

After Moorosi settled the matter, Raisa reflects, the territory became quiet and they were able to live in peace. Then the trouble started again when the government tried to force Lehana to see that his people paid hut taxes. After that was settled by Bowker, the government jailed Lehana, saying he had helped steal cattle. When Lehana escaped and rumors of war were rife, Raisa feared he would be targeted by the government as a known opponent. So he and his family fled first to the mountain fortress and then retreated to these caves for safety.

Letuka, Moorosi's son, who moved from supporting to opposing the government, is living with his family in a cave on the slopes of the valley above them.

The people hoped the white government would not find them here, but they protected the caves just in case.

The rebel position, Brabant realizes after reaching the valley in mid-afternoon after several hours ride along the banks of the Quthing River, is much stronger than he had expected. Situated in a deep gorge, it is protected by natural rock surroundings, steep slopes and bush cover, as well as by fortifications.

As his troops pitch their tents for the night on a spot high above the river, Brabant sets out to reconnoiter the area, descending a narrow trail that winds down the slope of the gorge toward the river below.

The gorge, about 200 yards deep and 600 yards long, becomes narrower at the other end and its sides progressively steeper until the cliffs are almost sheer. Although the side of the gorge down which he is descending is wider and easier to follow, it is covered at the bottom by a large mass of boulders interspersed with bushes. On the opposite side of the river are several cellar-like caves behind stone walls that the Baphuthi have built.

On the slopes of the gorge opposite him, Brabant spots a cave on a semicircular rise halfway up the slope of the gorge that appears to be the rebels' main holdout. Giving the appearance of a miniature version of Moorosi's Mountain, the entrances to the cave are fortified with loopholed stone walls.

The cave can be reached on only one path, which leads up the slope to a narrow rock platform, surrounded by several more small caves, also defended by stone walls and boulders. The way to storm the cave complex, Brabant decides, would be to rush up the slope and destroy the stone wall that closes off the entrance.

Brabant is struck by the quietness of the valley. Apart from the sounds of his men settling into their camp on the high ground behind him, he hears no voices or sounds of movement coming from the caves.

Best, who brought the seven-pounders by horse team from the camp at Moorosi's Mountain, descends the path. Brabant points to the defense complex.

"We are going to have to pummel these stone walls with the gun until they are damaged enough to afford us access," he says. "Then we will drive the rebels to the back of the caves or force them to flee and possibly surrender."

"I'll set up the gun in the morning," says Best.

"No, I think we should start shelling them now, before it gets too dark to see," Brabant replies. "You can be sure that they already know we're here. We need to hit them before they better their position or try to escape."

Best returns to the camp where, assisted by seven gun operators, wheels the gun into position on a level spot opposite the main cave on the side of the hill. Soon they are lobbing shells into the stone walls around the cave.

Letuka's thoughts are shattered by the sound of the large gun. The blast echoes through the valley, breaking the afternoon stillness.

In the cave the children are crying, the women are looking worried and the men are reaching for the guns that they have stored there. He tells his people that they should not be afraid, and should not run outside. The shells from the big gun will not hurt them, the walls are strong and the government soldiers will not be able to get into their caves.

They failed to destroy the walls at the mountain and they will not destroy the walls here. He will see to it.

"They are not responding," Brabant says. "They are apparently not there. I assume they have all gone to the caves along the river." He calls to Lieutenant James Gray. "I want you to take a group of yeomen down this slope, to the river. Once there, skirmish through the boulders and bush and flush out the enemy. Move quickly and we can get this done before dark."

Gray's men clamber down the slope. Brabant follows at a distance. Soon after the yeomen cross the river at the bottom, a volley of gunfire issues from the caves. As the yeomen scramble to gain cover among the bushes and boulders, a bullet strikes Corporal James Mack in the leg. The wound is shallow and he succeeds in limping back to safety across the river. The rest of the men continue to advance toward the caves, their rifles at the ready, under shelter of bushes and boulders.

Gray, moving into the open ahead of the other men and away from shelter, is shot through the arm. He falls. The field surgeon crosses the river and, carrying his medical instruments, runs to his assistance. It is the first time the young surgeon has been called upon to render aid and he is eager to perform his duty. He kneels down alongside Gray and starts to dress his wound.

"Shouldn't you move him under shelter first?" shouts Brabant, observing from across the river. Moments later, a bullet strikes a rock less than a yard from the surgeon. He drops his bandages and instruments, and runs in fright to the river. In his haste to cross, he slips on a rock and plunges into the cold water. Laughing at the surgeon's panic and bumbling antics, a couple of troopers help him out of the water.

Brabant, also amused, orders the attack on the caves to cease and two men to assist Gray back to the camp. It is late in the day and becoming dark as they ascend the hill to their bivouac.

"Tomorrow we will pluck rebels out of their caves rather than fish surgeons out of the river," Brabant pledges to amusement from the men — except the surgeon.

Shortly before the men retire to their tents, Brabant hears a shot, followed by shouting. Brabant runs to the area of the shooting, only to find that one of the men had accidentally shot Private Rousch in the foot.

"Let's concentrate tomorrow on shooting the enemy and not ourselves," Brabant responds.

So far, with the surgeon's slip and now the wounded foot, this patrol is turning into more of a comedy show than a military action, Brabant fears. He is determined, however, that tomorrow will be different.

Quthing — Friday, May 16, 1879

In the morning, Best directs his cannon fire at the caves on both sides of the gorge, pounding the stone walls. Brabant is hoping that the shells will break down the walls, but, as was the case yesterday with the cave halfway up the hill, there is no sign the shelling has any effect.

After an hour, Brabant orders Best to cease firing and orders the 100 Basotho under Davies to advance up the river toward the caves. Their mission is to plunder the Baphuthi supplies. Brabant does not order the Basotho to attack the Baphuthi as he suspects they are sympathetic to them, but he is confident they will seize food supplies as they will be able to keep part of them.

The Basotho seize large supplies of recently harvested grain stored by the Baphuthi under the cliffs on both sides of the river. They meet with no resistance.

On their return, Brabant compliments the men on their action and gives them half of the grain to divide among themselves as remuneration for their work and tells them they can take the rest of the day off.

The next step is the removal of the men, women and children from the caves.

Brabant then turns his attention once more to the cave halfway up the hill which he has become convinced is home to a large number of Baphuthi even though they have not revealed their presence. "I would like you to storm the cave by climbing as quickly as you can up the path," he tells the men. "Once there, you should punch a hole through the stone walls that guard the entrance. The men will be trapped inside and you will be able to force them to surrender and capture them, or, if they will not yield, kill them."

Carrying their carbines, the men clamber up the steep slope until they reach the narrow rock platform outside the cave, where they pause, ready to rush at the stone walls. They are surprised when they suddenly come under fire, not from people inside the cave, but from farther up the gorge, 250 yards away.

The men rush at the stone walls, pushing on them in an attempt to topple them and also to get inside to escape the gunfire. But the walls cannot be pushed over. The only effective way to break them down would be stone by stone, starting at the top. But that would take time; and the men are being shot at.

Brabant, standing near the top of the path up the hill to the cave, takes in the scene. The rebels doing the firing are concealed behind rocks and bushes, providing them with cover, whereas his men are crowded together on a rock ledge fully exposed. Mindful of the loss of men to Baphuthi fire on Moorosi's mountain nearly six weeks ago, he orders his men to retreat.

As the soldiers move off the rock platform and down the hillside, one volunteers to return and try again. "We are willing to go ahead and storm the cave," he says. "If you order us to do so, we will obey your orders. I am sure we can succeed."

"You are a brave man," Brabant responds. "But I am ordering you to withdraw. The fire is too heavy and well directed and I am afraid we cannot storm the cave without loss of life."

Brabant orders the men to return down the narrow path. He lets them go ahead of him and waits until the last man, Captain Howard Sprigg, brother of the Cape Premier, is ready to move. Sprigg gestures to Brabant to go first.

"No, you go first," Brabant responds.

Sprigg declines. "No, you are more senior in rank than I am. You go first."

With that, a bullet tears open the sleeve of Sprigg's coat. "Here we are in range of the enemy's gunfire and we are both standing on ceremony," he says. "Let's put off the discussion till a more favorable opportunity." Sprigg puts his hand on Brabant's back and pushes him, causing him to half-slide and half-run down the slope.

A moment later, Brabant finds himself lying on his back and caught up in a tangle of bushes and sand. He is unable to move either up or down. "Help," he shouts. "I am afraid I am stuck. I have never been an active climber and now I'm getting paid back for my neglect."

Sprigg calls to the men to climb back up and help Brabant. After several attempts at freeing him, they settle on dragging him downhill by his ankles as the best method to get him moving again.

It works, although Brabant is sharply scratched on the arms and legs and is embarrassed by the indignity.

Back at their camp, a trooper cannot resist commenting, "Let's concentrate tomorrow on putting our feet into the enemy's caves instead of into the hillside."

The comedy show, Brabant reckons, is still on. This time, he is the subject.

Brabant asks Captain Howard Sprigg to take a small group of men and scout around the caves along the river for more information.

Sprigg returns in the late afternoon with a captive: an old woman whom he dubs "princess." Pressed for information, the woman, whose real name is MaTsekelo, tells Brabant that a number of Baphuthi are living at the upper end of the gorge, an area that he has not yet reconnoitered.

Frustrated that he has achieved little since arriving here yesterday, and realizing that the attack on the caves will be challenging, Brabant decides to give the rebels one more chance.

"Princess, you see the firepower we have. You see that big gun over there. It can fire shells that can knock down the walls in front of your caves. We are ready to go along the river banks tomorrow and kill all who will not surrender.

"So, I want you to return to your chief or headman and ask him whether he is prepared to surrender. Tell him I am giving him one more chance to come out and cooperate with us before we attack the caves and destroy him and his people. He has until an hour after dawn tomorrow to let me know he is surrendering. If I do not hear from him by then I will order my troops to attack the caves."

"I will go with your message," MaTsekelo says. She leaves as the sky darkens.

Quthing — Saturday, May 17, 1879

Letuka, ensconced in the cave halfway up the hill, laughs when he hears MaTsekelo's message, which she delivers shortly after dawn.

"Why are you bringing us this message from the white men, old woman?" he asks. "Have you become a spy for them?"

The woman explains that she was captured by one of the white men and that she had no choice but to go to their camp. They told her to deliver the message.

"He wants us to surrender?" Letuka says. "We fire at them and chase them away from our caves, they run away and slide down the mountain in their fear, and now they want us to surrender? Why would we do that?"

Letuka laughs again, even more loudly.

"I know these white men. I thought they were good men and I even worked with them until I learned that their real motive is not to help us, but to take away our land from us, to destroy us as a people and to force us to work for them. Now they even have some of the Basotho helping them. These Basotho have stolen our grain, but we have more stored away. These white men think it is easy to defeat us. They think they can show off with their big guns and their rifles and march around in their fancy clothes and we will obey them because we are afraid of them.

"But did it work when they marched on my father's mountain fortress? It will not work here either. Tell them we will not surrender."

"Very well," Brabant says when MaTsekelo conveys Letuka's response. "If that is the way he wants it."

He thanks the woman and tells her she must stay with the Basotho contingent for safety until the battle is over, which, he assures her, it soon will be.

Soon the seven-pounders are firing toward the caves once more. Shells arc into the air. Some hit the walls, but to little effect. More shells fired farther up the gorge have little impact. For most of the morning the heavy gunfire echoes around the narrow ravine. Shell after shell pounds the caves. Now and then Best adjusts the trajectory to make sure they have the strongest impact possible.

But, apart from breaking holes in some walls, the gunfire achieves little.

After several hours the shelling stops and the gorge is quiet.

At midday Brabant consults with his senior men. "What is our next move, gentlemen? How do we force these people to surrender? We have pounded their fortifications once again this morning, but I am afraid we have not created enough damage. And, in any event, we have run out of ammunition for the gun so we can make no further use of it. We found in the last two days that a direct assault is unlikely to be successful without a heavy loss of life.

"I need ideas."

"I have an idea," says Jones. "I have served in the Royal Engineers and we used dynamite. What I suggest is that we throw dynamite into the caves. We could start by throwing charges from above down the cleft of the rock into the cave on the side of the hill. That should effectively blast a hole in the wall."

Brabant turns to Best. "Did we bring dynamite with us?"

"A small quantity. We can obtain more from the main camp."

"Let's try it out before we send for more," Brabant says. "Captain Jones, seeing you have experience in this type of warfare, why don't you climb to a point above the cave and do as you suggest?"

Carrying heavy charges bound in rags, Jones climbs to the top of the hill. There, he balances on a ledge and lights the first stick and drops it toward the entrance to the cave. The dynamite fails to ignite. He lights the second stick, dropping it, too, down the cleft.

After the first stick of dynamite lands on the ground outside the wall, but fails to explode, the men in the cave move toward the entrance to examine it. They have just started to look at it when the second charge falls just within the wall.

Letuka sees that the stick is burning. Seizing it, he runs to a nearby bucket of water. As he places the dynamite in the water, the charge explodes, turning the bucket into shrapnel, hurling the men against the walls and to the floor of the cave.

The cave falls silent.

Letuka looks down at his right hand, which has been shattered. He cannot hear anything, nor can he feel any pain, but the wound is bleeding and his hand has turned into a mass of blood and bone. The men brace themselves for another blast. When it does not come, and the smoke clears, they try to ascertain the extent of the damage.

A man lies motionless on the cave floor. Letuka looks across at him. He is dead. Another six men have been wounded.

Letuka, still feeling no pain, stares at his hand. "This is a new kind of weapon," he says. "We have no answer for these kind of weapons."

Minutes later, as his hand starts to throb with searing pain, Letuka passes out, collapsing on the floor next to the body of his friend.

Jones reports to Brabant that the second charge blasted away part of the stone wall, but he has no way of knowing whether it caused any damage inside the cave.

"I am glad it worked," says Brabant, who has been giving Jones's idea some thought. "But before I proceed, I need permission from the government to use dynamite. I am concerned that we might not just break down the walls, but will kill the people behind them and that this kind of warfare might be frowned upon.

"Jones, take a message to the camp at Moorosi's Mountain. You are to go to Colonel Griffith and Mr. Ayliff, the secretary for native affairs, and ask them whether they will authorize the use of dynamite to blast our way into the caves," he says. "Explain to them that the caves here are protected by stone walls in the same way that the mountain is."

Jones mounts his horse and sets off.

While he waits the several hours that it will take before Jones returns, Brabant clambers down the hill. At the bottom he discovers a cave on the left of the entrance to the gorge that he had not noticed before. It, too, is well fortified. He sends yeomen to ascertain how many people are hiding in it.

As the yeomen approach the cave, the men inside, led by Raisa, fire on them. A small battle ensues, with neither side making any gains.

As he watches the action, Brabant calls to Captain Sprigg.

"I think it is clear that the way this cave and its fortifications are configured, it is all but impossible to gain entry with rifle fire," he says.

"We have to try another method. While we await word about the dynamite, I want you to assemble a group of men. They are to light a fire outside the cave. Dampen the branches if necessary so that they produce an abundance of smoke. Build it so that the wind will blow the smoke into the cave. Let's smoke them out."

Soon smoke is billowing into the cave. The men hear sounds of coughing and talking from inside.

As the smoke wafts down a narrow passageway that leads into the main part of the cave, it sets the men, women and children inside coughing and spluttering.

For a while, they are content to wait it out. But soon dense smoke fills the front portion of the cave, forcing those inside to close their eyes and making it harder to breathe. They know that to move outside will invite the soldiers to shoot at them and is likely to result in their being seriously wounded or killed. Yet the only way out is through the entryway.

The Baphuthi move to the back of the cave, where it is easier to breathe. But they know they are trapped.

Raisa calls four men and a boy to him. "Listen to what I tell you to do," he says.

Jones returns from the mountain carrying several sticks of dynamite. "Both Mr. Ayliff and Colonel Griffith agree that we can use the dynamite," he tells Brabant.

"Excellent work, Captain. We will tackle that task later. Right now, we are concentrating on this cave. We might have some success with this idea of mine to smoke the enemy out of his lair. Why don't you store that dynamite somewhere safe and then join us here? You are a man of considerable experience and we need you to help us here first before we use the dynamite again."

Four men and a boy emerge from the cave, shouting at the men not to shoot.

"We surrender," they say. "All our people want to surrender."

The soldiers drop their rifles to their sides, ascertain that the men and boy are unarmed, and arrest them. The men, now prisoners, tell them that the people inside are having trouble breathing, some are dying and they need help. The men move to the entrance of the cave and peer in through the smoke.

"Help us, please help us, we cannot breathe," Raisa cries down the passageway, between coughs.

"We want to surrender, but you need to come in here and help us to come out as we are dying from the smoke. Please you must come and help us."

The colonial soldiers douse the fire with water. When the smoke has cleared enough to enter the cave, they do so.

Among the first in the cave is Jones, accompanied by one of the Baphuthi men, now a prisoner. He has volunteered to show Jones where the people are and who among them needs the most help. The other soldiers follow Jones in single file down the narrow passageway.

"Those of you who can must come out and surrender," Jones shouts into the darkness as he enters the large interior of the cave. "You will be safe outside and you can —" A large stone hits him on the head. He puts his hand to his head and falls to his knees. A bullet fired from the dark recesses at the back of the cave passes above him, hitting the man behind Jones in the eye.

Jones staggers to his feet, his head pounding, and fires back.

"They are not surrendering; they are shooting at us," he shouts. "It is a ruse. Get out of here! Now!"

As they lurch backward, tripping over one another, the men fire repeatedly to cover their retreat. Raisa and his followers fire back. For a few minutes, the bullets fly in all directions, ricocheting off the stone walls.

Outside, the soldiers curse themselves for falling for the trick. They angrily relight the fire, which takes a while to get going because so much of the wood was doused with water.

As darkness falls, and no more people emerge to surrender, the soldiers return to their camp, leaving the fire to smolder. They will build it up again tomorrow.

Quthing — Sunday, May 18, 1879

The morning begins for Brabant when Davies enters his tent.

"I went to the caves early today — unarmed," Davies, who speaks the local dialect, says. "I said I came in peace and spent some time talking with the Baphuthi people. One of the headmen, Raisa, has offered to surrender with all of his people."

"His people did that yesterday, too," Brabant replies. "But it was a ruse. He wanted our men to enter his cave so he could fire on them. Ignore him."

"I don't think it's a ruse," Davies replies. "He and his people are coming out from the caves along the sides of the gorge, carrying their belongings."

"Why are they doing that?" Brabant asks. "We failed to oust them yesterday with the smoke and now they've suddenly changed their minds? I smell a rat."

"They told me that nine of Raisa's men were killed in the firing in the cave," Davies says. "Apparently one of them shot and killed one of his own men in the confusion. That and the fear of suffocation that many of the people felt, apparently gave Raisa second thoughts. When I spoke with him and suggested it would be a good move to surrender, he decided to give up before more people die."

Brabant's demeanor changes. Without his having done anything this morning, other than wake up, victory is at hand.

"Well done, my good man."

Davies continues. "The Baphuthi people say that another of the headmen, named Letuka, also wants to surrender."

During the day, hundreds of Baphuthi stream out of the caves to an area the yeomen mark out. They are told they are prisoners and will be taken back to the camp at Moorosi's Mountain and, from there, to the camp at Phaladi's village.

Quthing — Monday, May 19, 1879

The camp surgeon, eager to prove his worth after his slip in the river, carefully binds Letuka's wounds as the headman's followers join the rest of the prisoners.

Before leaving the area, Brabant, determined that the cave fortifications will never be used by the rebels again, orders his men to destroy the stone walls with dynamite and dismantle what is left by hand. He also orders them to gather all the Baphuthi grain.

A count reveals 15 Baphuthi were killed during the skirmishing, in Raisa's cave, and by the dynamite thrown into Letuka's cave. In addition, 82 fighting men, of whom 10 are wounded, 18 youth and 310 women and children are taken prisoner. Among the prisoners are two families of Khoisan people, the original inhabitants of the rugged country, who live among the Baphuthi and have sided with them. In addition, 13 horses, 207 sheep and goats, 49 stand of arms and 40 spears are seized. A large quantity of tobacco and about 50 bags of thrashed-out grain are destroyed.

Looking at the prisoners and the booty, Brabant realizes the cave fortifications were far more extensive than he had thought. If the Baphuthi had not surrendered, he could have faced a long siege.

The 400 prisoners are escorted by the yeomen back to Moorosi's Mountain.

"I am sure this capture will materially affect the war," a triumphant Brabant says to his men. "I strongly expect that Moorosi will offer his surrender when he learns what has happened here." What he does not notice is that, as the group nears Moorosi's Mountain amid great excitement from the men at the camp, Letuka and Raisa — accompanied by a few others — slip quietly away, heading for a path up the mountain.

Quthing — Saturday, May 24, 1879

The cool autumn nights are starting to make themselves felt at the mountain and William Ayliff, the secretary for native affairs, says he will leave for Cape Town on Monday to attend to matters that have been accumulating in his absence.

He tells Griffith he had hoped to see an end to the war, but that looks unlikely any time soon. Although he is satisfied with Griffith's decisions, he adds that it is imperative that victory be achieved as soon as possible.

"The war is proving costly," he says. "The 600 men camped here have to be supplied and fed. The ammunition costs are growing.

"Colonel Brabant thought his victory up the river would lead to surrender at the mountain, but that has not happened and is unlikely to do so. I know you believe your plan to starve out the rebels will work in the long run, but it will bring with it a heavy toll in monetary costs and the government is reluctant to bear that burden. We are growing impatient.

"So I have to urge you to consider the value of time. Your forces have been increased and once they are at their full strength I must ask you to move as quickly as possible to destroy the rebel strongholds, both here at the mountain and any remaining in the surrounding countryside."

Griffith weighs his options.

It is unlikely that another assault similar to the last one would be successful.

It is clear now that starving the rebels out will take too long; they keep mysteriously adding to their supplies and do not appear to be likely to run out of grain and cattle any time soon.

An answer would be to secure the Baphuthi's surrender in the way that Brabant did in the Quthing River valley. That would answer the government's demand and, though the government might not care, it would help to answer Ellenberger's challenge to him to become a peacemaker rather than a war-maker — a challenge he takes seriously as he has deep respect for Ellenberger.

But how to get the Baphuthi to surrender? Brabant's capture of 400 rebels raised morale among the colonial soldiers, but has had no effect on Moorosi, who remains defiant. And methods Brabant used in the river valley cannot be used here.

Before he solves this problem, Griffith must put together a force to clear out the other remaining major center of resistance: the fortress that Lehana has constructed on the banks of the Silver Spruit River.

Quthing — Sunday, May 25, 1879

The weather this morning is bitterly cold, with frost covering the ground. Hundreds of colonial soldiers gather on the parade ground among the tents for a Sunday service at 11 a.m. to be conducted by the Rev. Joseph Start, a Wesleyan minister from the Eastern Cape. Start arrived in the camp just as it was getting dark last night after leaving Bensonvale on Friday morning, staying overnight with the Ellenbergers at Masitise and visiting the injured men, including Scott, at Thomas's Shop yesterday afternoon.

The men sing several hymns, including "Rock of ages, cleft for me," "Oh, for a thousand tongues to sing," and "Jesu, lover of my soul." Every now and then the singing is drowned out by the sound of cannon fire, but the firing is stopped for the minister to deliver his sermon.

As his text, Start has chosen Acts 26:18, "To open their eyes, and to turn them from darkness to light, and from the power of Satan unto God, that they may receive forgiveness of sins, and inheritance among them which are sanctified by faith that is in me."

Presenting the war as a battle between Christianity and heathenism, he prays that the Baphuthi might turn from their sinful ways. He prays, too, for strength for the colonial soldiers, never questioning that what the men are fighting for is right and true and that what the Baphuthi are defending is heathen and wrong.

The sounds of singing through the brisk morning air attract the attention of the Baphuthi.

"It's a church service," Moorosi says. "They are singing to God."

"Is God on their side?" asks Letuka.

"I have heard the missionary say that God is a loving God," Moorosi replies. "They say He is not the God of the white people only. He is the God of all people and so He is the God of the Baphuthi people, too. We might look different on the outside, the missionary told us, but we are the same on the inside. He loves us as much as He loves them and He does not want us to be hurt."

"Do the white people think God will help them and not us?"

"They think God is on their side and not on ours," Moorosi replies. "But I think God will help us. The missionary Ellenberger says that God loves us."

He walks back to his hut and digs among the amulets he has gathered over the years — a baboon's foot, an ox tail, a bone from an antelope — to find a leather-bound Bible given to him by Ellenberger. He pages through the Bible before placing it on the ground once more, alongside the lucky charms. Together, they will strengthen him and his people.

London — Monday, May 26, 1879

Concerned at the cost of the Zulu War and the lack of progress, and with the prospect of confederation becoming ever more remote, the British government appoints Sir Garnet Wolseley as its supreme military and civil commander in South Africa. He is regarded as the most outstanding soldier-administrator that Britain possesses and the man who can swiftly bring the war to an end and avenge the defeat at Isandlwana.

Frere and Chelmsford will both be subordinate to him on the battlefield.

The appointment, relayed by telegraph, angers Chelmsford, who feels he is on the point of achieving victory over Cetshwayo.

He determines to push onward toward the Zulu capital at Ulundi before Wolseley arrives in South Africa by ship from London. Chelmsford reckons he has more than a month.

Quthing — The same day

Now that the area on the Quthing River is cleared of rebels, Griffith sets his sights on Lehana's holdout along the valley of the Silver Spruit River.

He has selected 80 men from the 2nd regiment of Cape Mounted Yeomanry, a mountain gun under Best and about 100 Basotho and Mfengu fighters to attack Lehana's caves.

"If Brabant can do it, so can you," he tells Southey." The force I am sending with you is similar in size."

As Southey and his retinue leave, Griffith moves to the camp at Thomas's Shop where, away from the daily distractions at the mountain, he plans to catch up on his paperwork. His main task is to report to Prime Minister Sprigg on the success of Brabant's patrol — and to gain some credit for ordering it.

"To me it is a perfect wonder that there were so few casualties on Colonel Brabant's side," he writes.

"The success of the patrol is no doubt due to the determination of Colonel Brabant, who would not be beaten by any difficulties and thus persevered until he had accomplished his object. The results of this patrol will no doubt tend to dishearten the rebels who are still holding out in Moorosi's Mountain and will also, I think, induce many others to surrender."

He does not really believe this. So far, Brabant's success seems to have had little effect on Moorosi. And the tactics used by Brabant cannot be adapted to the mountain, where the people cannot be smoked out and dynamite would appear to be an ineffective solution.

But at least Griffith will gain time by telling the government in Cape Town that a significant victory has been achieved. He hopes that, when Southey's patrol returns, he will be able to add another victory to the tally.

Quthing — Tuesday May 27, 1879

After spending most of yesterday reconnoitering along the Silver Spruit River, Southey has determined that hundreds of Baphuthi, presumably led by Lehana, are hiding at the end of a deep ravine in six caves, linked with one another by a passageway behind a series of stone walls. The caves lie below a 50-foot rock face and are covered by thick bushes. Access can be gained only by climbing large rocks.

The attack, Southey determines, will start today and will be similar to that used by Brabant. He instructs Best to fire cannon shells at the walls to unnerve those hiding inside and to deter them from firing back.

With the gunfire backing them, the colonial soldiers, lined up shoulder to shoulder in a wide arc, advance on the fortress, firing as soon as they are within range. Southey directs the men to attack the smaller of the caves first. When the men advance on the holdout, he orders Best to cease the cannon fire, afraid that the shells might hit his own men.

The men climb the rocks, maneuver through the entrance in the stone wall, and enter the cave. Holding their long-barreled rifles on their shoulders, they wait to allow their eyes to become accustomed to the dim light before advancing more deeply into the cave. Soon they realize it is empty.

As they move from cave to cave along the passageway between them, they find each new cave is empty. Eventually only one cave — the largest — is left. As they approach it, the men are blasted with a volley from behind the stone wall guarding it. They climb back down to the valley below.

"They are all in that one cave," Southey tells his men. He orders Best to bring the gun closer and to use it to break down the walls while the yeomen keep up their firing to prevent the Baphuthi rebuilding the wall.

This time, perhaps because of the short range, the big gun is more successful. In places the shells knock down the tops of the stone wall. The Baphuthi try to repair the damage, but heavy firing from the yeomen prevents them from achieving much success. Nevertheless, the Baphuthi continue to fire from behind the walls, turning every advance by the yeomen into a retreat as they are forced to find safety. The result is a stalemate.

By nightfall, the yeomen are tired and hungry after fighting furiously during the day, yet gaining little ground. Hundreds of Baphuthi are still in the cave.

Southey orders his men to withdraw, but stations two sentries outside the cave.

Following Brabant's lead, Southey orders that a fire be burned at the entrance.

The topography makes it unlikely that much smoke will enter the cave, but Southey is concerned that the inhabitants might leave during the night and reasons that blocking the entrance with fire will keep them from doing so.

Under cover of darkness, the yeomen gather logs, building a huge fire in front of a gap in the stone wall that is the only way out of the cave.

"Keep the fire going all night," Southey instructs the pickets. "They will not be able to get out without being severely burned. Tomorrow we will enter the cave."

The heat from the fire permeates the first few feet of the cave and the blaze lights up the interior. Lehana assesses the results of the day's fighting. Five men are dead, three struck by colonial fire over the top of the damaged wall, and two struck by stones loosened by the cannon fire. Another two men lie badly wounded.

In the recesses of the cave 300 men, women and children huddle together. Some have lived here for weeks; others came from adjoining caves when the firing began. The cave is stocked with grain and pumpkins that will keep them fed for months. The 10 horses in the cave appear to be in good shape, being kept at the back of the cave, away from the gunfire.

"The enemy forces have left two men to guard the cave," Lehana says to his warriors. "They have built a big fire that makes it impossible for us to go out and come back in. I want you to continue firing at those two men during the night. I know there is only a small moon and it is difficult to see them in the dark. But you must keep firing, even if you use up a lot of our ammunition.

"I need another set of volunteers. Come here and I will show you what to do."

King William's Town — Wednesday, May 28, 1879

Several men should be rewarded for their bravery in the April attack on Moorosi's Mountain, says Defense Department head Colonel Jarvis. He recommends Scott be promoted to officer and that Brown be given £10.

The members of the artillery troop who carried away their wounded comrades under fire, and those who remained with Captain Surmon when he lay wounded under fire and finally brought him away "would, in the army, be very likely to be decorated with the Victoria Cross. But as this assault resulted in the repulse of our forces, I could not advise that any public demonstration should be made in favor of those engaged," he writes to the colonial secretary in Cape Town.

"A money grant to those who especially distinguished themselves will, I hope be considered sufficient reward and encouragement to others."

Quthing — The same day

The heavy firing from the cave echoes around the steep-sided ravine throughout the night, amplifying its sound and keeping Southey's men awake until the early hours of the morning when they fall asleep through sheer exhaustion. The two sentries fire back occasionally, but feel little fear from the Baphuthi bullets, which fall some distance in front of them.

Shortly before dawn, the firing stops. An eerie silence descends on the ravine.

As the sky starts to lighten, and shortly before he is to be relieved by the rest of the yeomen, one of the sentries calls to his partner.

"Look there, on that path leading out of the ravine," he calls. "Aren't those people running through the bushes?"

"Yes, you're right."

The first sentry fires on the fleeing people, who quickly move out of sight.

As the early dawn glow turns into the light of day, the soldiers douse the fire and Southey walks carefully to the cave entrance, pausing now and then to check whether it is safe to proceed. Several men accompany him, rifles at the ready. They encounter no gunfire, however, and enter the cave.

Inside, Southey finds three bodies and two badly wounded men sitting close to them. Five men emerge from the back of the cave, holding their hands high in a sign of surrender. Soon they are followed by scores of women and children.

The yeomen accompanying Southey take them into custody and escort them to the camp.

Questioned by Southey, the men say the rest of the men in the cave fled in the early hours of the morning. Eighteen were wounded, but were able to walk and accompanied the fleeing men. They point to a break at the far end of the wall, away from the fire and out of the sentries' sight, explaining that the men, led by Lehana, were able to take down the stones without being heard because of the sound of the gunfire. It took some time to demolish a section of the wall, but they were able to leave before daylight.

"Where did they go?" asks Southey.

The men point up the ravine and over the mountains. Spotting a group near the top of a mountain, Southey dispatches several yeomen to pursue them.

The yeomen return to the camp in the afternoon. They report that they chased the rebels for seven miles, trying to cut them off. They shot and killed two, but the rest scattered in all directions. They turned back because the horses were exhausted and the terrain too mountainous.

"We need to abandon our attempt to hunt the enemy," Southey tells the men. "Not only has our meat supply run out, but I also have received a note from Commander Griffith telling me to return to camp as soon as possible."

Quthing — Thursday, May 29, 1879

Shortly after midnight, in the dim light of the half moon, 150 Baphuthi silently creep down the southeastern path on their mountain fortress. They have no need for more light than the half moon provides; they know the area well and are able to find their way over rocky outcrops, among the bushes and through the long grass with comparative ease.

Leading them is Letuka, Moorosi's son, who, having escaped from Brabant, is now living on the mountain. The gnarled stump at the bottom of his arm, left when his hand was blown off 11 days ago by a stick of dynamite, has begun to heal but is still painful. Indeed, the pain spurs him on; it was a major reason he agreed to lead this group, whose mission is to attack the colonial soldiers camped at the junction of the Orange and Quthing rivers. His injured hand means he will not be able to shoot or throw a spear, but he will lead his fellow Baphuthi, who are dressed for war and carry spears, shields and guns.

Moorosi has told them that attacking the isolated camp would be revenge for the attack on Letuka and Raisa in the caves and would serve as a warning to the colonists not to venture on such sorties any more.

Watching from the rock "chair" on the northern edge of his mountain top, where he can look down a vertical incline to the area where the Quthing and the Orange rivers meet, the king saw the soldiers set up their camp four days ago.

The soldiers make a good target. Not only are they relatively few in number, but their distance from the main camps means help would take an hour to arrive.

The warriors cross a low point on the Quthing River, turn south and walk toward the Orange River. Ahead of them white pyramid-shaped tents, lit by the moon, stand starkly against the dark background of the night sky. They move closer under cover of the bushes, which are thicker and taller near the river bed.

Four sentries are standing in a trench behind a short stone wall 15 yards from the camp and 60 yards from the Orange River.

The Baphuthi stop. As planned, a group breaks off and climbs the slope behind the camp. Looking down, the scouts obtain a good picture of the camp layout. Now and then they hear the sentries in the trench behind the stone wall talking. One laughs, another lights a cigarette, a third sips from a mug of coffee. Their guns lie alongside them. They appear relaxed.

The scouts return to the main body of fighters. Together they move away from the camp until they are out of hearing of the soldiers. After hearing the scouts report on what they have seen, Letuka instructs the fighters to continue on the path that runs along the Quthing River and to attack the sleeping soldiers.

"Tear down the tents and attack the men sleeping in them," he says. "We must move before the white soldiers have time to organize. We will attack from this side, away from the sentries. We will do our work without getting into lines."

The men laugh. Whites are always getting into lines, writing things down, following orders unrelated to reality. The Baphuthi have no need for such things. The warriors creep forward, their bare feet silent on the rocky path leading to the camp.

Trooper C. F. Meyer, one of 12 sentries, reckons it must be around 2:30 a.m. Four more hours to go before the bugle announces the end of his duty. He cannot see the other sentries, but he assumes they are as bored as he is, wishing they could be asleep in their tents as are the other men in the 48-strong regiment posted here just four days ago as part of the forces around the mountain, charged with isolating the Baphuthi on the mountain and ensuring that help does not reach them from Kornet Spruit, just across the river.

Thirty minutes ago, his commander, Captain A. L. Chiappini, had checked in with him, saying he was about to go to bed and wanted to ascertain that all was quiet. Meyer assured him it was.

Meyer reaches into his pocket for a cigarette. He puts it in his mouth and prepares to light a match when he hears the sound of a breaking bough. He looks behind him, near the river bank. It is probably an animal, a jackal perhaps. Another noise follows, this time the swishing of branches. In the pale moonlight, he makes out a movement in the bushes. It must be a fairly large animal.

Then he sees it's no animal. A hundred to 200 men, most carrying spears and some bearing guns, are running from the bushes along the river toward the tents.

At first, he cannot comprehend it. The moonlight creates a ghostly picture and at first he thinks he must have fallen asleep and is dreaming. But, as the scores of Baphuthi continue to rush forward, his mind stirs itself into action.

Meyer fires in their direction. Realizing he cannot achieve much with one rifle against a horde, he runs the 100 yards down to the camp to waken Captain Chiappini. He reaches Chiappini's tent, which is closer to the stone wall than the others, at the same time as the Baphuthi arrive at the first row of tents.

"We are being attacked by natives," he says. "There are hundreds of them!"

Chiappini rolls out of bed. He has just fallen asleep and has to shake himself awake. Perhaps, he thinks for a moment, Meyer is wrong. Perhaps these are the friendly natives, the Mfengu, moving through the campsite on their way elsewhere.

But as he leaves his tent, his doubts end. He is glad he ordered the men to sleep with their arms loaded.

"Out of your tents!" Chiappini screams toward the tents not yet attacked. "Go to the schanz!" referring to the stone wall.

The men awaken, instinctively grab their rifles, and scramble out of their tents, some dressed more fully than others. Chiappini orders them to run. "Get to safety, go to the schanz," he repeats, running for cover himself toward the stone wall.

For more than 20 of the men in the tents attacked first, the order comes too late. The Baphuthi surround their tents, cut the guy ropes and spear the men trapped in the collapsed tents.

From the stone wall breastwork, 16 men raise their rifles and fire toward the attackers. The Baphuthi, wearing few clothes in spite of the night cold, are not only difficult to see, but are also moving constantly. The soldiers fire again and again toward the warriors, being careful not to direct their fire into the tents themselves. Now and then a scream confirms they have hit a Baphuthi.

The warriors continue to plunge their spears into the side of the tents, which are now stained red with blood. Even as they fire, the yeomen of the 3rd regiment watch in horror as their comrades are slaughtered.

After intense, seemingly endless, stabbing into the canvas, the Baphuthi — satisfied that no one can be alive in the tents any longer — turn toward the stone wall, flinging their spears, many now covered in blood, and firing toward the soldiers. The spears reach the trench, striking and wounding some of the soldiers.

The persistent fire from the yeomen forces the Baphuthi back. After a while, they regroup and rush forward again, but are repulsed and driven back once more.

The chaotic noise arouses the Burghersdorp Troop, a group of volunteers from the Cape Colony camped on the opposite side of the Orange River. They run to the banks of the river; a soldier with a bugle sounds an advance.

"Listen, the bugle is blowing and help is coming," Letuka says. "We have done enough. Let us return to the mountain."

The warriors abandon their attack and follow the path along which they came. Some are carrying wounded fellows. One carries the body of a warrior killed by a soldier's bullet. They move as fast as they can toward the mountain.

Joined by the Burghersdorp volunteers, who have crossed the Orange River, the men under Chiappini hunker behind the stone wall. They remain for several hours, afraid that the Baphuthi will return, perhaps in greater numbers. They make no attempt to go to the destroyed tents; they are convinced none of their colleagues could have lived through the slaughter they have just witnessed.

The birds are the first to greet the approaching dawn, doing so with a cheeriness that mocks the scene of destruction around them. Soon they are followed by the chirping of insects and the buzzing of flies.

As the first rays of the sun light up the scene, the men of the 3rd Yeomanry Regiment are greeted with a horrific sight.

Tents attacked by the Baphuthi are in shreds, covered in pools of blood. Bodies, some half covered in canvas, lie at angles, some crouched in a fetal position to which they turned as they tried to avoid the spear thrusts. Broken spears, guns, blankets, clothes, pots and water bottles are strewn in a circle of chaos.

As the yeomen peel away the canvas, they hear groans. "Some of these men are still alive," says one.

Chiappini springs into action. "Get these wounded men some help," he says. "On the double! Also, we need to know how many men we lost and how many have been injured."

As Chiappini picks his way through the debris, he sees teeth scattered about and wonders whether they came from his men or the Baphuthi attackers. At the edge of the scene of carnage he spies drops of blood on the ground. A bit farther on he notes more. He calls to a couple of his men. "Follow the blood trail," he says.

A man reports back. "We have six men dead and fifteen wounded, seven of them seriously," he says. "Three of the wounded are in dangerous condition. James Kannemeyer has a bullet wound in his left eye, Thomas Louwens has four bullet and eleven spear wounds, and Andrew Johnston a bullet wound.

"We also found the bodies of three Baphuthi."

"Get our wounded men to the hospital tent as soon as possible," Chiappini replies. "Leave the bodies of the Baphuthi here. They are likely to come and retrieve them once we have moved out. We will take the bodies of our men back to the main camp for a decent burial. Once you have seen to all of that, break up camp and clean up as much of this mess as you can. I am leaving to report to the officers."

Quthing — the same day

In some ways, the order — sent by telegram to Palmietfontein and brought to Thomas's Shop by express post overnight — comes as a relief to Griffith. It informs him that he is to hand over his command to Colonel Brabant tomorrow.

No reasons are given, but Griffith knows what they are. He has been roundly condemned for the failure of the attack on the mountain. He has made only limited success in ousting the rebels from their cave hideouts. His plan to starve out the rebels is showing no signs of progress; the men keep supplementing their supplies. As a result, the government has lost faith in his ability to end the war speedily.

The only real success in this war has been Brabant's taking of the cave stronghold up the Quthing river. So why not give overall command to him?

Griffith accepts the verdict, but he has two thoughts. One is whether any other officer could have done better. No one had come up with a better plan when he launched his attack. True, he could have waited for Brabant to arrive, but would Brabant's help really have made any difference?

The other thought is that Ayliff could have been more forthright while he was here. Obviously Ayliff had considered removing him even as he was expressing his confidence in him. So be it. Ayliff obviously had to consult with the government in Cape Town before dismissing him.

His day is about to become worse. A trooper brings him the news of the attack on the Chiappini camp.

Griffith is devastated. Not only is the news of the deaths and wounding of the yeomen in the early hours of this morning itself horrifying, but he suspects that, although he was not there and had placed Brabant in charge, he will bear responsibility for the attack. After all, he was the commander in charge and had instructed the camp to be set up there. This attack will be seen as another reason to consider Griffith's work at the mountain a failure.

Griffith returns to the mountain. After hearing more details of the vicious attack, he orders a court of inquiry to look into it.

The court, he stipulates, should begin its proceedings tomorrow morning, minutes after he hands over command to Brabant. He appoints Captain J. T. O'Connor of the Cape Mounted Riflemen, now stationed at the mountain, as the president of the court, and recently arrived Captain George E. Giles and Captain Howard Sprigg as members.

He is confident that the proceedings will clear him of blame.

Quthing — Friday, May 30, 1879

Members of the court of inquiry gather in a somber mood. As they do, they learn that Andrew Johnston, wounded in the attack, died last night, bringing the death toll to eight.

First to give evidence is Chiappini, who says he received orders from Captain Minto on Sunday, the 25th of May, to form a camp at the junction of the Quthing and Orange Rivers to assist in the investment of Moorosi's Mountain.

"I pointed out to Colonel Minto at the time that it was a dangerous position on account of its isolation, and also because there was no favorable site for a camp," Chiappini says. "Colonel Minto told me that it was the commandant's order that a camp should be formed there."

Chiappini outlines the attack. He is followed by Meyer and two yeomen.

In his evidence, Minto, commander of the 3rd yeomanry, says Griffith instructed him to send a detachment of his regiment to set up a permanent camp at the junction of the Orange and Quthing rivers to guard entry to and from the mountain. He therefore dispatched the group under Chiappini.

"Owing to the rugged country, the enemy were enabled to come quite near the pickets before they were discovered, and rushed on to the camp at once, stabbing into the tents with their spears," he says. He praises the stand taken by the men as "most heroic." From all accounts, Captain Chiappini behaved splendidly, and kept his men well together. "Had this not been done, the whole detachment would in all probability have perished," Minto adds.

Griffith asks to be heard. "If the men had not been sleeping in tents they would not have been as vulnerable to attack," he says. "I do not know why the men were sleeping in tents. I gave no orders that tents should be used."

Minto responds: "Commandant Griffith told me that tents were to be erected on the site. It was, after all, a permanent site."

"But I gave no order that tents should be erected," replies Griffith.

"Yes, sir, you did."

O'Connor, as president of the court of inquiry, intervenes. "Colonel Minto, do you recall Colonel Griffith using the word tents?"

After thinking deeply for a moment, Minto slowly replies, "I recall him giving instructions that a permanent camp was to be established on the site," he replies.

"But did he use the word tents?"

Minto ponders the question for a little longer. "The order from the Colonel-Commandant of the Field Forces to me about forming a camp was a verbal one.

In the course of the conversation on the subject I was told the camp was to be a permanent one. And the men were to be made as comfortable as possible."

"I must ask again," says O'Connor. "Did Colonel Griffith use the word tents?"

"Although I cannot be certain that tents were actually mentioned, the impression on my mind was that tents were to be taken, and I accordingly gave the order that they were to be taken."

Griffith is satisfied. As far as he is concerned, Minto has conceded that he took it upon himself to use tents.

O'Connor asks Minto to put his account of Griffith's order in writing by Sunday, when the inquiry will issue its report.

Quthing — Saturday, May 31, 1879

George Whitehead steps down the path to the Orange River, pulling his coat around him. A member of the Cape Mounted Riflemen, he was ordered to join the troops at the mountain two weeks ago as part of a new supplementary force of 300, consisting of Riflemen as well as members of the Cape Mounted Yeomanry.

Since his arrival Whitehead has found the days becoming cooler and the nights intensely cold. The tents offer little protection from the freezing temperatures, although they afford shelter from strong winds that whip through the valley.

The thick layer of frost that formed overnight crunches under his boots as Whitehead approaches the river, which is flowing slowly now that the summer rains have stopped.

A soldier at the river introduces himself as William King. A farmer in the Cape Colony who volunteered for duty in Basutoland as a member of the Yeomanry, he also arrived two weeks ago. He and Whitehead talk as they stoop down to the water, washing their faces between words.

"We were supposed to relieve other members of the yeomanry who wanted to return home," King explains. "But when we arrived here, Griffith didn't release them and when Brabant took command yesterday he told them they must stay on.

"I hope that means we'll see action soon. Ever since we arrived here we've had nothing to do. If we continue sitting around like this, the enemy will come off the mountain and attack us in our tents the way they did those men up the river."

"That attack shows you how this war is being fought," replies Whitehead. "We do nothing except serve on guard duty and wait for the enemy to attack us."

King nods. "Already, I miss my family and my farm," he says. "I wonder if my wife and children are well. Although the harvest is over, there is always something on the farm to keep you busy. Here, there is nothing to do."

At the main camp, Maitin concludes that his work is done at the mountain. He held an important position as Griffith's aide; now he will go back to being a clerk and translator. He will return with Griffith to Maseru. With him will be his bride of a month. Now they will be able to live together and even have a family.

In the campaign, Maitin felt it was his duty to stand by Griffith, just as he had stood by Hope, in spite of everything, and later by Austen.

As the situation changed from confrontation to colonial obsession with winning the war, Maitin saw Griffith change. The senior magistrate, once so proud, so efficient, so calm, and so dedicated to impartial justice, stumbled as a commander. Losing the assault on the mountain unnerved him. He lost his way. He lashed out at others, determined to be shown to be right, even when he knew he was to blame.

He watched as Griffith moved from being an administrator and a peacemaker, a task at which he excelled, to being an army commander and a war maker, at which he failed. Griffith had left his area of competency for a position for which he was not suited. That was why, Maitin assumes, he had heard unfavorable reports of Griffith's leadership on the eastern frontier. There, too, he had been called upon to be a destroyer, not a diplomat.

But Maitin continued to stand by Griffith, dutifully preparing reports to the government, ensuring that the commander kept appointments, and acting as a buffer when demands on his time grew too great.

Had it not been for Griffith, for whom he will continue to work in Maseru, Maitin might have quit Quthing months ago when he became disillusioned with the war, even though he would not have had a job. But, not one to voice his opinions against those in authority, he said nothing then and will say nothing now.

Yet his unexpressed views on the conflict run deep. Born and raised in Basutoland and the son of French missionaries, Maitin knows the Baphuthi people. He understands that Moorosi's resistance runs deeper than his desire to remain king. It is driven by the powerful force of culture and the duty of leadership his culture has bestowed on him. Rooted in land, language and custom, the Baphuthi culture, like all cultures, cannot be changed by decree, by force, or by self-will. It is the very essence of who the king and his people are.

He sees that force in MaLebenya, too.

Although she has moved beyond tribal custom to try to adopt the British way of life, her culture still is part of her. She might have disagreed with what Raisa had done and what Moorosi is doing, but in her heart she remains a Baphuthi and feels a strong affinity with her people.

Maitin, too, has deep cultural roots. He remains a European and will always be a European.

By marrying MaLebenya, he will become partly Baphuthi, just as she has become partly European. But neither he nor she can lose their cultural base. That base, that essence of who they are, can be modified, but it cannot be eliminated. Their customs and ways of thinking and their languages will continue to direct their lives no matter what they do or where they go. And they will respect each others' way of life. Their lives together will mix two cultures, drawing on the best that each has to offer. They will not destroy or try to supplant either of them; to try to do so would invite disaster.

Those cultural differences, Maitin believes, are at the root of the war against Moorosi.

The colonial government's real aim is to take over the Baphuthi people's land and use the people as a ready form of cheap labor. But, to put a moral face on it, the government says it wants to bring a civilized way of life to people who lack it. The Baphuthi people, the government says, would be uplifted materially and morally by having to follow European standards and later, having learned the European ways, would adopt those standards as their own. Light would be brought into the Baphuthi darkness. The Baphuthi would become Europeans in black skins.

But Maitin knows, even were such a motive genuine, cultural change is impossible to achieve through the force of an alien government. Cultures might change over time through interaction with other groups, but such change can take generations and even then would not be complete.

The ideal outcome would be to establish a joining of cultures as equals, each understanding and respecting the other, sharing what they have in common and recognizing and honoring what is different between them and what neither can change. They will compromise, seek a middle way and combine the best of their two cultures. They will not seek to destroy or to dominate. It will not always be easy, but it will be fulfilling and, above all, peaceful.

But that will not happen here in Quthing. Not between these two peoples. This is a cultural clash, not a drive for cultural collusion. One side will win the battle for the land and the control of the people living on it.

Should the Baphuthi win and the colonial government leave, the conflict will be gone and the status quo restored. One language, one land, one way of life.

Should the colonial government be the victor, however, and attempt to impose its cultural norms on the Baphuthi people, they will have to dominate them by force as the Baphuthi's culture can never be expunged by the orders of white magistrates or the spoils of war. Unless the Baphuthi people are annihilated — an outcome too horrible for Maitin to contemplate — the cultural clash will remain.

Any outcome that involves a cultural compromise and a union of equals seems so remote that Maitin can never envisage it happening. He hates what is happening in Quthing and will be pleased not to be directly involved in it any longer.

The attack on Chiappini's camp has made Brabant, on his second day in command, even more determined that the war should be ended — soon. That is the reason he was chosen to take over from Griffith and he will make sure that he does not disappoint the government.

Brabant, 40, is a man of action.

Three years ago he founded the Buffalo Corps of Rifle Volunteers in East London, and led it during the Ninth Frontier War. A couple of months ago he led his men through almost impassable rivers and deep ravines to reach Moorosi's Mountain. And, while Griffith sat at the mountain, Brabant completed a successful mission against hundreds of Baphuthi hiding in caves along the Quthing River.

His record shows he knows what needs to be done, he is not afraid to do it and he knows how to achieve it.

He must act now. He does not have the options Griffith had. The cost of doing nothing has risen — and not only the political and economic costs. The mountain must be taken, Brabant affirms, not only to remove Moorosi and his followers, but also to prevent them from attacking the Cape forces and potentially reasserting control over the land.

In addition, the winter cold has set in and it may snow in coming weeks.

Brabant's troops are at full strength and he does not see any reason to sit around and wait for the Baphuthi to become hungry and surrender.

"I plan to storm the mountain again as soon as additional ammunition arrives," he tells his officers. "This time we will employ a 12-pounder M .L. R. Armstrong, which is on its way here, as well as the 7-pounder M .L. R. mountain guns. And I intend to use them as they are supposed to be used, with strong and sustained bombing. They will blast the stone walls so effectively that the way will be cleared for our men to reach the top and declare victory. Southey showed in his attack on Lehana's fortress that the big guns can be successful in breaking down the walls."

"Do you know when the additional ammunition and the 12-pounder will get here?" Captain Davies asks.

"I am expecting them any day. In the meantime, we need to be ready. I could make the decision to move as soon as the big gun arrives. Before I do, however, I need a group of men to patrol as close to the stone walls as they can and report back to me on the most practical way to attack the walls.

"Do I have any volunteers for this mission?"

Davies walks toward the river where he sees Whitehead and King.

"I have a task for which you might like to volunteer," he says.

Quthing — Sunday June 1, 1879

Griffith spends the morning preparing his report on the court of inquiry. Although he addresses it to Brabant, it will form a part of the official record of events and will be sent to the government in Cape Town and eventually to London.

"It appears that the picket in question was taken by surprise, in consequence of the sentry or sentries not having given the alarm in sufficient time to allow the men to turn out of their tents," he writes. "It is also my duty to bring to your notice the unheard-of proceeding upon the part of the officer commanding the 3rd regiment of yeomanry in allowing the pickets to take tents with them.

"The very object of the picket was frustrated in his allowing them to do so; this picket was posted for the purpose of watching the rebels and preventing either egress or ingress to the mountain, and this could only be done by the picket taking up certain positions after nightfall — the mere fact of pitching tents, of course, exposed the position of the picket and gave the rebels the opportunity either of invading or attacking it, and it appears they were not slow in taking the latter course.

"I was absent from the camp, which I had left in charge of Colonel Brabant, from the morning of the 26th May to the morning of the 29th, having gone on duty to the camp at Thomas's Shop, and was therefore not aware that the picket in question had taken their tents with them, which, had I been aware of, I should most certainly have not allowed."

That should do it. He has distorted the facts enough to clear his name — at least as far as the attack on the Chiappini camp is concerned — and is ready to return to Maseru to resume his former post.

He has had enough of this war. He sees it as having transformed him from a just, caring and honest gentleman to an unjust, uncaring and dishonest rascal.

Quthing — Monday, June 2, 1879

Shortly after the sun sets, but before it becomes too dark, Whitehead and King, accompanied by three other members of the Cape Mounted Riflemen, set out on their assigned task. With Whitehead in the lead, the five men creep slowly up the hill toward the stone walls. They approach from the southwest, hoping to be out of sight of the Baphuthi — and out of range of their gunfire should the warriors see them in the light of the dusk and the quarter moon.

Their plan is to shelter under the ledge and follow it eastward, stepping back now and then to view the walls above.

Drawing closer to the walls, the men instinctively walk more quietly. Coming within range of the Baphuthi rifles, they are bracing for the first shot.

They reach the ledge without incident and begin to step out into the open to look up to examine the stone walls. They see the occasional Baphuthi above them, peering at them from above the walls. But no one shoots.

Gaining more confidence, the men edge farther into the open. They estimate the height of the walls, the loopholes and the occasional breaks between them, envisioning how and where the walls can be destroyed or overcome.

The Baphuthi watching them remain unmoved.

"They know we are here, but I think they understand we are only looking," Whitehead whispers to the four men behind him. "They assume we will launch an attack only in the daylight. Do not raise your rifles. Keep them at your side so that it is clear we have no intention of attacking them."

"This is a little eerie — and not just because of the darkness," King says. "I feel any minute now they could start shooting at us."

"If that happens, get behind the ledge," Whitehead responds. "We can escape their fire within seconds. But the main thing is to show that we have no ill intentions. Remember, we are only looking."

The men's inspection reveals embankments of solid earth with heavy stones placed in front of them. Most have a double row of loopholes, near the base and near the top. The men conclude that should the outer facing of the walls be knocked away, the Baphuthi would still have earth behind which to shelter.

Satisfied they have made a careful inspection, King suggests moving off.

"Before we go, let's make sure we have seen all we need to see," Whitehead, emboldened by the lack of Baphuthi response, tells the soldiers gathered around him. "Do you see how we could climb up the rocks, scramble over the walls, which will then be in a state of disrepair after being hammered with the 12-pounder, push our way through the earth embankments and get into the trenches behind the walls?"

"It will be difficult, but not impossible," responds King. "We could — "

He stops in mid sentence as a spear swoops past him and embeds itself in the heart of Peter Ferreira, a member of the Cape Mounted Riflemen standing next to him. The air is filled with yells and whooping as a group of Baphuthi rush out of the semi-darkness on their right, heading directly toward them on the plateau, firing and throwing spears.

The men realize that while they were looking at the wall structures, the Baphuthi had come down from the mountain almost alongside them. Now it is clear — too late — why the warriors behind the walls made no attempt to fire.

Once again, the "ignorant barbarians" have outwitted the colonial forces.

The white soldiers turn and run, leaving Ferreira lying on the ground. They have no doubt he is dead.

"Run to that ridge ahead of us," Whitehead yells. "Get behind it, raise your rifles and give these natives what they have coming to them."

The soldiers have a 20-yard lead over the Baphuthi, but the fleet-footed warriors are shortening the distance and flinging spears toward the men.

As he runs, King turns to watch his pursuers. In doing so, he fails to see a rock ahead of him. He strikes it with his boot, loses his balance and falls forward. The others continue running toward the ridge, unaware King has tripped and fallen.

King pulls himself up. A sharp pain in his knee tells him he is injured, but he is determined to make it to safety behind the ridge. His four-and-a-half foot long Snider still in his hand, he slowly pulls himself up on to his legs, in spite of the pain. He staggers only a few feet forward, however, before three Baphuthi surround him. They seize him, grab his rifle, and hold his wrists behind him.

"You will come with us," they say. "You are our prisoner."

Quthing — Tuesday, June 3, 1879

The wagons carrying the ammunition roll into camp and the men cheer. They know the ammunition is key to their next moves against Moorosi — and they are ready to seek vengeance on the Baphuthi. Their vindictiveness has been spurred by the attack on Chiappini's camp, and strongly advanced by King's seizure.

"We will move at first light on Thursday," Brabant tells his officers. "We will pummel the stone walls with intense bombing for 48 hours until we have evidence that the cannon are having an effect. We will accompany the bombing with sustained volleys of rifle fire.

"In fact, I suspect that the rebels will scamper to higher ground as soon as the walls start to crumble and they find they cannot rebuild them under the withering fire both from the cannon and from our rifles. Then we will rush the fortress.

"Sergeant Whitehead led a group of valiant men to a position just below the stone walls yesterday. He was able to confirm that it is possible to storm the enemy's position once we have destroyed the walls with cannon fire. The foray was not without incident. As I am sure you know by now, the men returned with valuable information, but a soldier was killed and another taken prisoner by the enemy."

The men are interrupted by shouts from the mountain. They look up to see a pole sticking up from behind the walls. On the end is King's severed head. As they watch, King's headless body is thrown over the wall to the ground below.

It is one thing to watch a friend die in battle. In a sense, it is part of the high-risk game that a soldier knowingly plays, the rules of which are etched out in a mutually agreed code. We shoot at you; you shoot at us. You try to capture us; we try to capture you. You stand to die if we win; we stand to die if you win. But severing a man's head breaks the rules.

"We will remember this when we finally get to attack them," Whitehead vows, tears welling in his eyes when he recalls the friend he had known for only a couple of days but with whom he felt he had shared a year's worth of adventure.

The Baphuthi no longer are simply an enemy. They are now a hated enemy.

Moorosi is proud of what his people have achieved in the last week.

First, there was the victory his son Letuka won in the attack on the camp at the junction of the Quthing and Orange rivers. As he looks down from the northern end of his mountain home, Moorosi notes that the tents are gone.

"You avenged the deaths of our people in the Quthing River caves," he tells Letuka. "The white men showed in that attack how cruel they can be to our people. They tried to smoke our people out of their caves and they threw an explosive at you and caused you to lose your right hand and other people to be killed. Even now it is healing only slowly, and will never be right. It will forever be a reminder to you of the cruelty that the white people show toward us."

"My hand is now a stump," Letuka says. "The white doctor bound it up and our doctors have put a potion on it, but the hand cannot grow back.

"I am angry at the white people for what they have done, not just to me but to our people. At least I survived. Others did not. They died slow painful deaths from the explosive. But I am pleased that I was able to lead my people to one of their camps and to show them how it feels when you are attacked, how your people die and how you grieve for them."

Moorosi agrees. The attack on the camp was not their only recent victory.

"After we captured one of their men last night, we showed them today what it means to fall into the hands of the enemy," Moorosi continues. "We showed them what we think of the people sent here to kill us."

Moorosi calls his people to him.

"We have killed some of the men sent here to kill us," he says. "We have killed them as they lay sleeping in their tents. We have cut off the head of one of them and killed another with a spear. But we cannot rest. I see that the government people have brought a bigger gun to their camp. I see the men marching around.

"They are about to attack us again. They will aim that bigger gun at our defenses. We are to build up the walls if they are damaged. And if they are foolish enough to try to storm our walls again, we are to shoot at them as we did before.

"I want those who are guarding the walls to be on watch all the time. No one is to return here to the top of the mountain at meal time. The women will bring the food to you. You are to stay on watch continuously. When it is time for you to be relieved so you can sleep then someone else will take your place.

"And when the white men attack, we must all be there, all of us who can fight, must fight." He turns to look at Letuka, his eyes falling on the stump that once was his son's hand. "Some of us cannot fight well, so the rest of us must fight even harder. Now, those who are not watching on the walls must get some sleep tonight because our spies tell us the government people will attack us tomorrow."

As the men move toward their huts, the mountain shakes from the pounding of the 12-pounder gun. "They are attacking sooner than I thought," Moorosi shouts to his men. "Forget what I said about sleep. Everyone, to the walls!"

Brabant plans to pound the mountain for a couple of days using the stronger more effective 12-pounder Armstrong gun, set up in the camp 1,500 yards from the walls, backed by the two 7-pounders, until the schanzes have been destroyed.

One of the 7-pounders, manned by Best, has been placed across the Orange River to the southwest of the mountain, from where the top of the mountain can be seen 1,800 yards away.

The other 7-pounder, manned by a team under Corporal Collingwood, has been placed on the northeast side of the mountain. Although it is in a shaky condition and is inaccurate, it will cover an attack planned for that side of the mountain.

After pounding the walls for several hours, the 12-pounder proves it is more effective than its smaller cousins. It shatters parts of the first tier, which consists of two parallel stone walls with earth between them and loopholed at intervals, causing the stones to tumble on both sides, some rolling down the mountainside. By 1 p.m. a large portion of the stone walls flanking the path up the mountain is in ruins.

The bombing encourages Brabant, who orders the firing to continue until dark and to resume tomorrow. But, after 87 rounds have been expended, the firing from the 12-pounder stops. Captain George E. Giles, who brought the gun with him and is now in charge of the artillery in the field, walks up to the men handling the gun. "Why have you stopped?" he asks.

"The copper lining of the vent has become bulged up and that is impeding the firing," the men report. Giles examines the vent, which must be clear if the firing is to be at full force. "Keep firing and make every effort to keep the vent clear," he says.

The men fire several rounds, but each successive discharge closes the vent even more. "Stop firing," Giles says. "It seems only to be making matters worse. Let's do all we can to clear this vent."

The men work on the vent all afternoon. By the evening it has been partially cleared — enough for the firing to be effective — but the lining is severely bulged and cracked. "I'm afraid that damage might be done to the gun if we continue to fire it before it is re-vented," Giles tells Brabant.

"Well, re-vent it then and let us get on with the firing at dawn," Brabant replies.

"We cannot do that without the proper tools," Giles replies. "They might have them at Thomas's Shop Camp, but that will mean a delay of a day or two. Otherwise, we might have to wait for them to come from Aliwal North."

"We cannot wait that long," Brabant replies. "We have made considerable progress in tearing down the walls and, if we stop even for a day, the enemy will rebuild them. No, Giles, we must keep pounding those walls. Even if it damages the gun, we need to continue firing at first light tomorrow."

Giles says he will bring the seven-pounder manned by Collingwood from its position on the northeast side of the mountain back into the main camp on the southwest and use it to supplement the firing. Brabant doubles the picket on the saddle and orders constant carbine fire should they see the enemy attempting to repair the walls. The full moon will help them see until it sets during the early hours of the morning.

He is confident that he is on the verge of success.

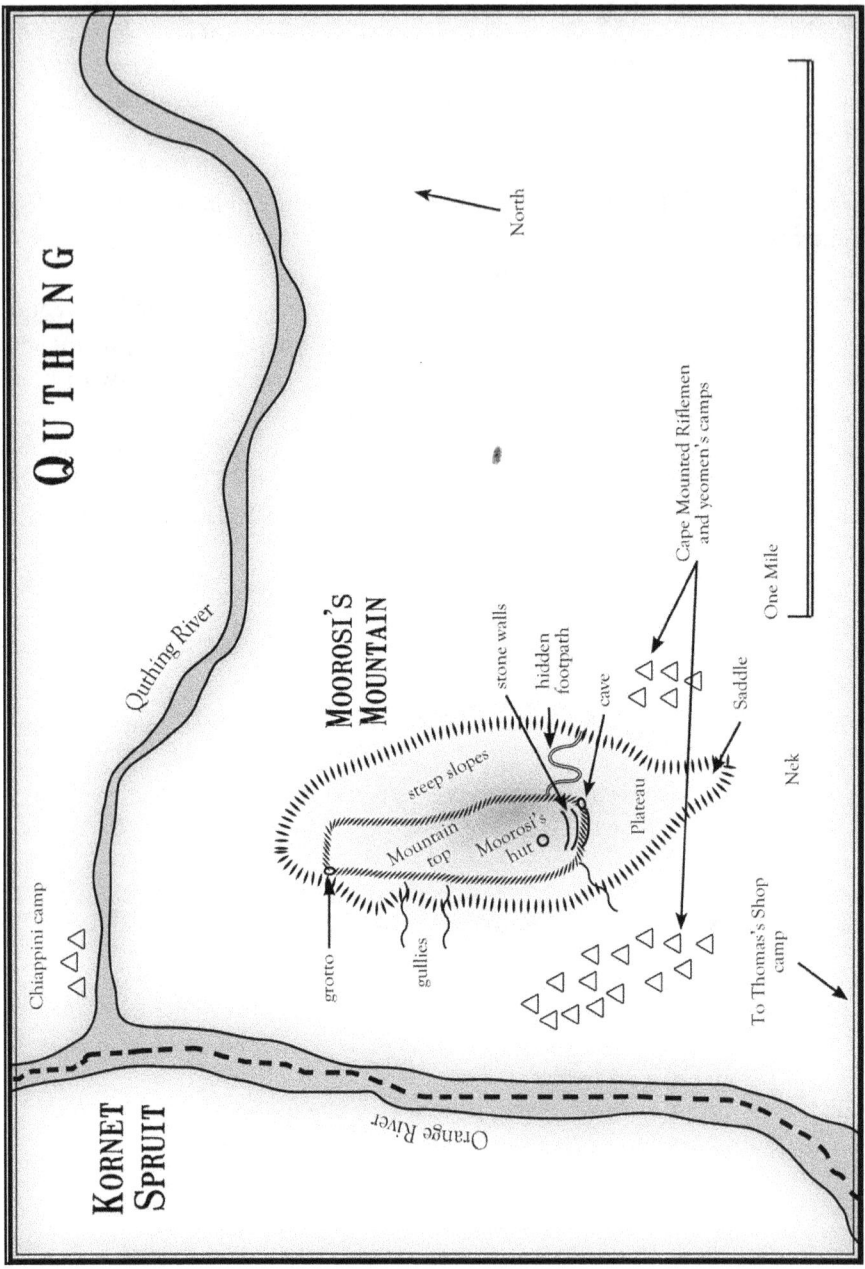

QUTHING

North

Quthing River

MOOROSI'S MOUNTAIN

stone walls

hidden footpath

cave

steep slopes

Mountain top

Moorosi's hut

Plateau

grotto

gullies

Saddle

Nek

Cape Mounted Riflemen and yeomen's camps

One Mile

Chiappini camp

KORNET SPRUIT

Orange River

To Thomas's Shop camp

XIV

Quthing — Wednesday, June 4, 1879

At dawn, Brabant discovers that the Baphuthi have been busy in the night rebuilding the walls, most of which have been restored to their former strength, rendering his task more formidable. He needs more time, but winter is coming and he believes it is imperative to attack soon.

Working during the night, Giles' men have removed the copper lining of the vent in the 12-pounder, making the gun useful for the time being although the problem with the vent is still causing a long delay between firings. Brabant orders him to pound the mountain during the whole day and into the night, this time using the 7-pounder under Best in addition to the 12-pounder.

"Tonight, we will again direct a heavy volume of small-arms fire at the schanzes," Brabant adds. "After the moon sets, you will use the 7-pounder to lob star shells to light up the walls and enable the men on picket duty to see their targets and prevent the enemy from rebuilding them.

"I will order the attack at dawn tomorrow."

After a few rounds, the copper lining in the 12-pounder is blown away, meaning that there are no longer delays in firing the gun. But each successive discharge slightly scores the surface of the vent hole, causing a larger escape of gas and reducing the gun's accuracy.

At 8:30 a.m., the 7-pounder is brought into position alongside the 12-pounder.

Although less accurate, the 12-pounder is able to fire 170 rounds of segment shell during the day, breaching the walls in several additional places and adding to the damage that the Baphuthi were unable to repair during the night. Some of the flanking walls are almost destroyed.

The success of the guns gives Brabant confidence. As he gathers his officers in the late afternoon, he explains that he will use a different strategy from that used by Griffith. He will send groups to act as feints on either side of the mountain, diverting the enemy's attention. As the enemy moves to the sides, the main group will storm the center.

Brabant assembles the men into three groups of 150 each.

The first group, consisting of Cape Mounted Riflemen, the 2nd Cape Mounted Yeomanry and 25 Fort Beaufort burghers, as well as a small group of Mfengu, is to move up a gully on the south-western, or left, side of the mountain.

"Your attack will be a feint," he says. "You are there to divert the enemy's attention. Only should the opportunity offer, should you convert it into a real attack."

The other feint will take place on the slopes on the south-eastern face, or the right side, from where Baphuthi have been seen emerging, Brabant says. He is convinced there's a hidden route to the top unguarded by stone walls; he wants the men to find it and advance as far as they can.

For this attack he orders troopers from the Cape Yeomanry to take the lead and Captain Henry Davies to follow with 500 Basotho. "You will be covered by one of the seven-pounders," he tells the men. "We will aim the fire above and ahead of you.

"I want you to advance as far as you can, but your goal is not to take the mountain. That is the purpose of the men who will storm the main walls. Your role is to make the enemy think your advance up the path is our main attack.

"If you encounter severe resistance, which is entirely possible, you will respond. But let me repeat that you are essentially a diversionary tactic, not a main advance force.

"Once we can confirm that the two diversionary groups have successfully attracted the enemy's attention, we will send the main body across the plateau to scale the walls and take the mountain in that way. It will be more effective than from the sides."

Brabant selects 150 men to storm the mountain. Of them, 50 are from the Cape Mounted Riflemen, 75 are from the 1st Cape Mounted Yeomanry and 25 are volunteers from the Cape Colony. Many, like Brabant, were not involved in the first attack.

The men are eager to set off. They want this war to end and they want Moorosi and the cruel men he leads to be killed. If they can, some swear, they will cut off the savages' heads themselves.

"You are my main body of troops," Brabant tells the men. "I have chosen you to attack the stone walls.

"You will not attack them alone or without help. The stone walls will have been weakened by the cannon shells we will fire today and they will be lightly manned by the enemy because of our diversionary tactics."

An additional group of burghers from Colesberg and Burghersdorp are stationed at the Chiappini campsite, Brabant adds, where they will cut off Baphuthi who might try to flee in that direction. A group of sharp-shooting burghers from Bedford will line up along a ridge at the side of the plateau to provide added firepower.

Brabant turns to address all the men. "All of you in all the groups will parade at 6 a.m., just before daybreak. We set off at dawn."

Whitehead, selected for the main attacking force, is nervous. He has heard from Scott and Brown what good shots the Baphuthi are. He has also experienced a stealth attack from the Baphuthi himself two days ago in which he narrowly escaped with his life.

He shares his fears with Captain Andrew Jones, who threw dynamite in Brabant's attack on the caves, and also has been chosen for the main storming party.

"Don't you worry," Jones replies. "Remember how you were taken by surprise the other night when you surveyed the stone walls?"

"How can I forget? I am afraid we will be facing the same thing here."

"Well, it will be the same thing, only the opposite," Jones says. "Just as you did not expect those men to attack you from the side, so the Baphuthi will not think we are attacking from the front."

"I hope you are right."

"I know I am. Also, we will have the larger gun pounding the walls. They will not be able to simply stand there and fire at us as they did last time. As for me, I will be protected; I have my lucky rabbit's foot charm with me and it has never let me down." He pats the outside of a pocket and smiles.

Brome, lingering in the background when selections are made or volunteers are called for, is pleased that he is not chosen for any of the groups. He knows he might be called upon as part of a back-up group when the fighting becomes fierce, but for now he is happy to be on the sidelines.

Quthing — Thursday, June 5, 1879

As dawn breaks, the cannon resume their blasts on the lower tier of stone walls, large parts of which remain breached as the Baphuthi were unable to rebuild them effectively during the night.

Amid the screams of shells and mortars, concussion of explosions and whistle of rockets, the men in the diversionary force on the right led by Davies, reach the base of the mountain and attempt to find a path to the top. They soon find the going steeper than they had thought. Taking big strides, they climb up jagged rocks that form a series of irregular steps. Soon they are winding up the mountainside in a zig-zag pattern, heading north, then south and north again as they climb upward.

Above them, the cannon shells crash against the rocks, sending stone splinters cascading around them and overriding the sounds made by the men as they climb in single file. Unopposed, the men make good progress. They can no longer see the crest of the mountain as it is hidden from their sight by the ridge above them.

After about 30 minutes of climbing, the men hear gunfire and see puffs of white smoke above them as bullets fly over their heads. They press on, acting as targets to divert the Baphuthi attention. Now and then they stop to fire above them, another means of drawing attention away from the stone walls in the front.

The men charged with advancing up the gully on the left of the mountain are unable to progress far. The ravine is steep and when the Baphuthi hurl boulders down the gully, the Basotho led by Davies return to their starting point.

But they fire repeatedly, trying to divert the attention of the Baphuthi away from the center and toward them.

Forty minutes after they began their climb, the leading men on the right face reach a level 40 yards from the first tier of a series of three sets of stone walls above them. But their path, which now leads north, is only two feet wide, with an almost perpendicular rock face on their left and a precipice on their right.

The Baphuthi roll boulders down the path toward them and fire in their direction. Two of the 3rd Yeomanry troopers, who are leading the Basotho, are struck by bullets. William Hannan is hit in the stomach and Henry Leonard in the right thigh. Seized with pain, they lie in the path, unable to move. Some of the yeomen move forward to try to help the wounded, but there is little they can do.

The other members of the yeomanry fall back, urging the Basotho to go ahead of them. As the firing intensifies, Mphelekane, one of the 500 Basotho who had formed the main part of this attack on the right side of the mountain, is struck by a bullet; he dies within minutes. Musi suffers a gunshot wound in the right arm, Mekwane a gunshot wound in the knee and Penoki a gunshot wound in his chest.

The sight of the men being hit is too much for the remaining Basotho, who turn and flee down the mountainside. Halfway down, they stop and fire every round of ammunition they have above the heads of the yeomen on the path above them. Their hearts were not in this mission — and now their lives are in danger. The promises of being able to keep the cattle taken in the war and their arms in spite of the disarmament act appear hollow. This war is real. They could die. It is not a game.

With the Basotho gone, the yeomen move slowly forward on the path, firing repeatedly ahead of them. The Baphuthi fire back, retreat up the path and disappear around a curve. The yeomen follow them. Ten yards past the curve they face a group of Baphuthi behind a stone wall blocking the path, their rifles cocked and pointing in their direction.

Brabant sees smoke from gunfire emerging above the gully to his left and to the right. The sound of continued firing to the right suggest his plan is succeeding.

He directs his senior officers to ready the main assault troops. They gather 70 of the 150 for the first wave. The other half will follow once the walls are taken and will help in the final push to the top.

Brabant notes some Baphuthi remain at their posts behind the stone walls, but he assumes that most are occupied in diverting the forces on the right and left.

The 70 troopers, under Captain J. T. O'Connor, are assembled behind the saddle. Among them are Whitehead and Jones.

"You are the advance force," O'Connor tells them. "Once I give the signal, Captain Pope will lead you to the plateau. You will rush 500 yards to a ridge of rock running parallel to, and 25 yards from, the first stone wall. There you will wait a few minutes before gathering your breath, sizing up the scene, and making the final rush for the schanzes.

"Those at the forefront of the advance will be able to make use of a scaling ladder that will be carried there by two of the troopers. They will be able to climb up it, confront the enemy, and clear the way for the rest to follow.

"Judging from the appearance of the walls, we hope to be able to take the schanzes without much opposition.

"Once you have taken the lower schanz, the next force, consisting of 80 men, will follow you with more ladders and climb the walls up to the next level. From there you will advance higher and eventually take Moorosi himself."

The men form up, rifles at their sides, and edge forward still behind the saddle. Their view directly ahead of them is blocked by the saddle, but they can see the smoke and hear the shooting from the right side of the mountain where their comrades are fighting on the cliff trail.

At 8:30 Brabant orders the first wave of the main storming party to advance. "Onward to victory!" he shouts. The men hesitate. O'Connor is about to repeat the order when the cannon fall silent.

Brabant calls to an officer. "Tell them I need them to keep up the firing," he says. "We have to cover our advance."

The officer returns in a few minutes.

"The guns have broken down," he says.

"What? Both of them?"

"Yes, sir. The carriage of the 7-pounder is totally disabled and ammunition for the 12-pounder is running low. Captain Giles wants to reserve the ammunition for any further advances that might be made later in the day."

Moorosi moves from group to group in the trenches behind the stone walls, encouraging his warriors to keep up the firing and not to be distracted.

"They are trying to attack us from the sides," he says. "We can hold them off. Stand in the places that I gave you and don't go anywhere else."

"Why do you think they've stopped the cannon fire?" Jones asks Whitehead.

"They likely have broken down the walls enough for us to make it through," Whitehead replies. "They don't want to fire into the walls when we're scaling them."

O'Connor again gives the command to advance. The men emerge from behind the saddle and line up in a broad wave that stretches across the plateau, with their leader, Captain Pope, on the right flank. They stride forward, rifles at the ready.

They have advanced only a short distance when they run into a hail of bullets. They press on, but have covered only 100 yards of the 500-yard-long plateau when Pope is shot through the forearm. With flesh ripped off his arm and the bone exposed, he turns back toward the saddle. A number of volunteers also turn.

Jones and Whitehead, on the far left flank, are unaware of what has happened to Pope. They hear rifle fire, move at a slight jog across the bare rock with the rest of their group, making good progress. They hear rifle fire but are unsure at first whether it is coming from the pickets on the saddle behind them or the walls ahead of them. Soon they know it is from the walls as bullets kick up the dust.

Some of the soldiers stop, load their rifles and fire back. But they soon realize they present better targets when they stop, so they press forward. As they proceed into the teeth of the heavy and accurate rifle fire, a number are hit.

Unwilling to continue against the withering fire, many of the men turn and head back toward the saddle. No amount of persuasion or degree of command will convince them to return to the plateau.

Others, including Jones and Whitehead, continue forward, heading, as instructed, toward the shelter of the ridge 25 yards from the walls. As they get closer, fire directed at them from all the lower schanzes, including those that appeared to be demolished, gains in intensity. This was not supposed to happen. The Baphuthi were supposed to be thinned out. Yet, the troopers are finding, the warriors' firepower is severe, scathing and spot-on.

As more men are hit, any pretense of a marching order is gone. The men scatter, some running back to the saddle and others darting for the ridge ahead.

Not all reach the ridge. A few yards away, Sergeant J. Robinson, of the 2nd regiment of Cape Yeomen, falls, shot dead through the heart.

Behind him, Whitehead and Jones evade the bullets, and keep moving forward. "No good turning back now," Jones says. "We can make it to the ridge. Imagine the natives' surprise when we show up right in their midst. They will —"

Jones falls to the ground, struck by a bullet to the head. As Whitehead leans down to tend to him, a bullet whistles past his ear. With bullets flying around him, Whitehead calls to those already behind the ridge for help.

The soldiers on the cliff trail on the mountain's right side stop in their tracks as they see the Baphuthi behind the wall ahead of them ready to fire. "Enemy ahead!" the yeoman leader yells to the men behind him. "Fall back!"

The men scramble back, still in single file. They hear the crack of rifle sounds and, seconds later, see puffs of smoke drifting into the air ahead of them. Turning and heading downhill, they recall Brabant's words, "You are essentially a diversionary tactic, not a main advance force."

Clambering back down, the men reach the next set of rock steps. They kneel and fire toward the warriors who have climbed over their wall and are now sheltering behind the rock steps at the end of the path.

The two groups of fighters, each behind rocks, size one another up. Neither group wishes to move forward or backward. Occasionally a shot is fired.

They can hear the sounds of a blistering fire fight coming from the plateau.

Whitehead remains fully exposed to enemy fire as he kneels to help Jones. He tears off the bottom of his shirt and uses it to try to staunch the blood from the wound on Jones' head. His efforts meet with little success.

"You can make it," he pleads with Jones. "Don't leave me now. We have been together too long for you to leave now."

"Get to safety," Jones replies, breathing deeply. "Take care of yourself."

"I will stay with you," Whitehead says. "I will see to it that you get help."

A shot scrapes Whitehead's trousers and strikes Jones in the arm.

"Go on," Jones pleads, intense pain coursing through his body. "Don't lose your life because of me."

Whitehead looks back toward the ridge; no one is responding to his calls for help. He shouts, "Is there a doctor there?"

Surgeon-Major Edmund Baron Hartley, who made it to the ridge with the initial wave of men, looks up from tending to the wound of a man resting against the ridge. "Yes. I am a doctor," he shouts.

"A man is lying out here, badly wounded," Whitehead responds.

Hartley quickly secures the bandage to a wounded man under the ridge and runs zig-zag 20 yards across the plateau toward Jones.

Whitehead, realizing he can do little more to help Jones, runs toward the ridge, shouting back, "You are in good hands, my friend. I will see you again soon."

With bullets flying on either side of him, Hartley staunches the blood, stretches into his side pack, retrieves a bandage, and winds it around Jones's head. Jones, who is losing a lot of blood, needs to receive more medical help soon.

Hartley picks up Jones and staggers back toward the saddle, across the exposed ground over which the men were so recently marching. A bullet strikes Jones as he lies in Hartley's arms. This time it hits his leg.

After carrying Jones for 200 yards, Hartley moves out of range of the enemy fire and behind the shelter of the saddle rock where stretcher bearers take Jones back to the camp.

Aware that his services are needed behind the ridge where several men are lying wounded, Hartley turns around and runs back across the plateau, successfully avoiding the bullets directed toward him, returning to the ridge. There, he dresses the wounds of eight men hit by enemy fire on their march to the ridge.

Most seriously wounded is Trooper C. Lewis of the 1st Cape Mounted Yeomanry who, Hartley realizes, is in imminent danger of bleeding to death from a wound in the arm. He makes Lewis as comfortable as he can, hoping he will survive.

Hartley cannot risk carrying another man across the plateau as he did Jones. Not only would he risk being hit himself, but his experience with Jones has taught him that the man he is carrying could himself be hit.

"You are doing good work," Moorosi tells his men. "We are keeping them from reaching the walls. Makuta, your shooting has again been accurate. How many have you shot?"

"I am not sure, my king, but I have hit a lot of them. These people are not very clever. What are they thinking when they run at us? Do they think we will not shoot them? Do they have herbs that they think will stop the bullets from entering their bodies?"

Moorosi laughs.

"The white people believe they can do anything," he replies.

As he moves among the men crouched in the trenches behind the stone walls, Moorosi checks on how many have been injured. Some have been struck by exploding shells and a few have been grazed by bullets, but the injuries are not serious and no one has been killed.

"Keep watching," he says. "We do not want to drop our guard at any time. Even if they are not moving now, they might decide at any time to rush at the walls again. We must be ready for them."

"We were instructed to move from here and storm the walls," Whitehead says to the men crouching behind the ridge. "But to do so, we will have to cross the 25 yards ahead of us. We will be completely exposed to enemy fire. It is inviting death. They fire with great accuracy and they seem to be familiar with every inch of ground between the saddle and the schanzes. Almost every man that tried to make it to this ridge was fired at. Now that we are closer to the walls, it will be worse."

"We have had to run the gauntlet," says Private Andrew Hemple. "I don't want to do that again."

"Look at what happened to Robinson," responds another. "Shot dead just as he was about to reach here."

In spite of the blistering attack from the walls, Captain O'Connor orders the second wave of 80 men at the saddle to advance. But most refuse to move, willing to suffer the consequences of disobeying orders rather than face death.

Believing that he should lead by example, O'Connor moves out on the plateau.

"Follow me," he says, waving at them with his hand. But only a handful do. O'Connor leads them across the plateau, evading the Baphuthi gunfire. Incredibly, they make it to the ridge, where they join those already there.

O'Connor completes a quick head count. Of the 150 men in the two waves, only 78 — the bulk of them from the first wave — have reached the ridge. But a number of those are injured and unable to fight.

As the highest ranking officer with the men behind the ridge, O'Connor takes command. He asks for volunteers for the attack on the walls that lie just 25 yards ahead of them.

"I would be prepared to go," says Captain Douglas. "But only if I had a strong force of men with me."

O'Connor ponders issuing an order to storm the walls, but fears that most of the men would refuse to do so. As he is pondering his next steps, three troopers from the Cape Mounted Riflemen take up the challenge and volunteer to creep closer to the wall.

"We may be able to gain some information," says Sergeant Graham. "Or we may be able to get a shot at them."

"I am not ordering you to go at this stage," says O'Connor. "But if you are prepared to do so, I will not stop you."

Accompanied by Private Jones, a brother of Andrew, the captain shot earlier in the head, and Private J. R. Handyside, Graham moves ahead. Near the wall, a shot blasts Handyside in the foot. He reaches down, grabbing at his foot with his hands. "Help," he cries. "Please help me."

Captain Dalgety, using the ladder carried to the ridge, climbs to the top of the ridge, and helps Handyside down, narrowly escaping being hit by bullets.

As the men return to safety, O'Connor decides he has had enough for now. "Under these circumstances, I deem it best to abandon further attempts at assaulting the mountain at this stage," he tells the men.

"Any further attempts will only result in great additional loss of life, without achieving any real advantage.

"We will wait here until one or both of the assaults on the left and right prove successful. Then we can make a rush at the stone walls, which by then should be empty."

As the rifle fire near the front of the mountain dies down, the members of the distraction force on the right assume the main assault has been a success and therefore that their job as a distraction force has ended.

Slowly, the soldiers move back down the path, all the while holding their arms at the ready. The Baphuthi do not follow them.

The men pinned behind the ridge, tired, dejected and disillusioned, also note the silence and wonder what has happened in the distraction attacks on the flanks of the mountain.

Shortly after noon a Basotho messenger, who has succeeded in braving the gunfire, hands a note to O'Connor from Brabant. In it, he asks how many casualties his group has suffered and asks about the feasibility of storming the mountain stronghold after dark.

O'Connor retrieves pen and paper from his pack.

"In addition to the wounded who have already left with Dr. Hartley, there are three yeomen and two Cape Mounted Riflemen lying wounded behind the ridge, and Sergeant Robinson is dead," he writes. "I consider the attack at this point to have failed as so many of the stormers are still behind."

The Basotho messenger returns. He is soon back with a reply from Brabant: "I order you to retire as quietly as possible after it becomes dark. Send the dead and wounded down first. I regret our casualties and I would not feel justified in risking further loss."

As darkness descends, Giles orders the 12-pounder to resume firing to cover the retreat from the ledge. The ammunition is dwindling, but it is more important now that it be used to enable the men to return to the camp.

With the 12-pounder firing, O'Connor signifies that the men can retreat, warning the men to be as quiet as possible. But their movements soon attract the attention of the Baphuthi who, assisted by the light of the moon, open up an insistent fire. When he realizes what is happening, O'Connor orders the men still behind the ridge to fire on the stone walls to cover their comrades' retreat.

One of the men still under the ridge, William Sluyter, who left his farm at Beaufort on the eastern frontier a few weeks ago to join the yeomanry, looks across at Robinson's body lying just yards away. He seethes with anger when he sees what the natives have done to his fellow farmer. With darkness descending and only the light of the moon to aid the Baphuthi shooters, he feels now is the time to help in some way, Sluyter moves from the shelter of the ridge, runs to Robinson's body and picks it up, determined to carry it back to the camp.

Struggling to hold the dead weight in his arms, his knees buckling under the strain, Sluyter carries Robinson's body down the slope. He has not gone far when he is struck in the back by a bullet. He staggers forward, dropping Robinson's body, and falling to the ground. The one casualty has become two.

The remainder of the men make their way as quickly as they can down the mountainside, back to their camp. As they do, Baphuthi jump down from the walls and run toward the ridge, stopping now and then to fire in the direction of the departing men.

When the colonial soldiers are about halfway down the mountainside, they hear shouts behind them. They turn around to see the Baphuthi warriors, standing in front of the stone walls, laughing and chanting victory songs.

Quthing — Sunday, June 8, 1879

They bury their comrades at a graveyard by the Orange River with a view of the mountain on which they died. They chisel crosses and names on stone slabs and set them up as gravestones.

The lines chiseled below the cross on one of the gravestones sum it up: "Capt. A. P. Jones, No. 1 Troop C. M. R., Wounded June 5, Died June 7, 1879."

After digging the grave, placing Jones' body — and his unlucky rabbit's foot alongside it — in a crude coffin, and covering it with earth, others help Whitehead raise the heavy gravestone. They repeat the procedure for three others and ask a soldier to say a prayer to serve as a funeral service.

They have done all they can for the men who served alongside them, who took the bullets that so easily could have hit them. Perhaps these men even died in their place. "Had I been on the right side of him and not on the left, I — not Jones — would have been hit in the head," Whitehead says ruefully as he stares at the slab.

"I will not forget him; he was a fighter brave enough to admit he was afraid and courageous enough to overcome his fear."

But being brave did not rescue these men from death. And their deaths did nothing to gain victory. Did these men, therefore, die in vain? It is difficult for the survivors to come to any other conclusion. They walk silently and slowly back to the camp. There, in a tent, the leading officers, conducting a post-mortem on the attack, have to admit the storming of the mountain two days ago, like the first, was an unmitigated failure. They achieved nothing; they got nowhere; they set back their cause.

At last count, 10 died. Not counting the wounded, the assault was more bloody than the first, in which seven died. The campaign against Moorosi is becoming worse, not better.

Slowly, the colonial troops are being forced to admit that they have seriously underestimated their enemy. The Baphuthi are smarter than the whites imagined. They have better rifles and are superior shots. They understand the terrain better. Their fighting tactics work better in the mountains of Basutoland than the colonial troops' British-style military methods.

Moorosi is proving to be a wily fighter, hunkered down on a virtually impregnable mountain fortress.

What can be done?

Discussing the events with the senior officers in Brabant's tent, O'Connor, leader of the storming party, is dejected. "We all hoped this would be a success," he says. "Indeed, it plainly appeared to promise success."

He pauses. The words are difficult to say. "I sincerely regret that it failed."

"Why do you think we failed?" asks Brabant. "Was it the quality of our men, many of whom were found wanting when it came to acting bravely under fire? Or was our strategy at fault?"

"The men lacked training," volunteers Southey. "I think that is one of the major causes of the disastrous failure. They failed to obey orders, they were undisciplined and untrained."

"I agree," responds O'Connor. "Almost half of the men under my command simply refused to march across the plateau and take the mountain. Had they all obeyed orders we might have succeeded. I think that nothing short of a regiment of steady, well-trained soldiers will succeed in capturing this mountain stronghold.

"The ascent is difficult, steeper and more challenging than we had thought. The fortifications that the mountain offers in its natural state are in themselves formidable. Even without the stone walls, the enemy has the advantage of being able to fire down on the troops below and they can hide behind the rock formations that provide shelter. The vast towering height of the mountain effectively becomes visible only from the ridge behind which we sheltered. There you gain a different perspective on just how massive it is, how strong the fortifications are, and how difficult it is to ascend.

"When you add to this the years spent by the Baphuthi laboring on building the walls and studying the best form of defense, the natural fortifications become even more formidable. Any attempt to take the place by storm must result in a more or less serious loss of life. That is all there is to it. We cannot succeed without our troops being prepared to risk their lives in large numbers. A lot will die, but those who don't will break through the enemy defenses."

Brabant sighs. "I thank you for your perspective, with which I agree. Here's my view, which is similar to yours. I believe that the mountain is so strongly defended that nothing but a considerable body of regular troops — not yeomen, not volunteers, but regular troops — provided with heavy guns, in good condition, of course, and proper siege material would have any chance of taking it.

"We have found in this attack that irregular troops, such a volunteers, might be admirably suited for service in the open field, but they can seldom be relied upon for the attack of a strongly fortified position like this mountain. The very qualities that make them so valuable in the one case militate against their efficiency in the other.

"The looseness of formation and individual initiative that make men so formidable in open country, however rough it may be, are quite out of place where solidarity and strict discipline are the essentials of success. Under such conditions of strict discipline it is difficult for a man to turn round or seek shelter when an order is given to him to advance."

For now, Brabant decides, he has to revert to Griffith's tactics of keeping Moorosi and his followers besieged atop their mountain. He must ensure they do not sneak in any food, that they have no access to the springs at the base of the mountain and that they do not launch any further attacks. He will maintain a ring around the mountain that watches Moorosi continuously and may help to drive him into eventual surrender. The old man cannot last there forever. Can he?

Brabant believes he must also continue Griffith's strategy of ousting other rebels from their mountain holdouts.

"Every one of those cave strongholds is a supply depot for the mountain," he adds. "We must visit them and persuade the people to surrender and seize their grain and other food supplies or we must blast them out."

In a telegram relayed from Palmietfontein, Ayliff is adamant that the second failure to take the mountain should not deter the government. It remains determined to win the war at all costs.

He writes to Brabant to tell him that the government's idea is "that you keep possession of the country and that you do not withdraw one inch from the position taken up, the government not describing the manner in which this shall be done...In case of communication with the rebels being opened up, and terms asked for by the rebel chief, his sons, or subordinate chiefs, those only admissible by the government will be an unconditional surrender."

To help implement Ayliff's instruction to hold his ground, Brabant requests an additional 300 Cape Mounted Riflemen from the frontier districts of the Cape Colony to supplement and enlarge the troops at his disposal. Using the additional men, Brabant will be able to rotate the troops regularly, preventing them from becoming bored, and have about 450 men in the field at any one time.

Another action Brabant will take is to consult the colony's top military planners in Cape Town and ask them for a strategy to oust Moorosi from his fortress.

Those steps are the best he can take right now, particularly with winter rapidly approaching. Already, the first snowfall has covered the higher peaks of the mountains and there is a chance it will soon reach Moorosi's Mountain, making further attacks even more forbidding.

London — Tuesday, June 17, 1879

The mounting cost of Moorosi's War is straining the Cape Colony's deficit and the British will to fund it. In isolation, it would not have raised as much concern, but it comes on the heels of the eastern frontier wars of the past two years and the Zulu war this year.

These adventures bring little direct benefit to Britain. Not only are they costly, but they have bogged down the move to confederation, aimed at moving the region to self-sufficiency so it will no longer rely as much on Britain for financial help.

Sir Michael Hicks-Beach, the Conservative politician who took over from Lord Carnarvon as the colonial affairs secretary, writes to Frere, asking him to abandon a conference with the other colonies, but to meet with only his ministers and submit proposals to the Cape Parliament for a South African union or confederation.

Hicks-Beach insists that the matter is urgent. A major reason is money.

"This country, which has already in various ways borne a large part of the cost of the proceedings which have resulted in the acquisition and pacification of these territories, without receiving any direct benefit in return, cannot be expected to undertake the responsibility of their future government and defense," he writes.

Whatever the Cape Colony might decide to do, Hicks-Beach says, the British forces will be removed from the areas of the native insurrection and stationed only as a garrison at or near Cape Town, "for the defense of a naval station of great importance to the interest of the whole empire."

The message is clear: Members of the British parliament no longer want to fund wars in South Africa. The Cape Colony must pay for its own defense force ultimately as part of a confederal government. Britain will retain and fully fund only a naval defense station at Simon's Town, near Cape Town, which, guarding the sea route from Britain to India, is of vital interest to it.

But financial cost is not the only issue on the minds of the British parliament.

This afternoon Hicks-Beach has just taken his seat in the House of Commons when the member for Dungarvan in Ireland's County Waterford, Frank Hugh O'Donnell, an Irish nationalist active in denouncing abuses of British power in South Africa, rises to ask him a question. O'Donnell refers to reports in *The Graphic*, a London publication, of plunder and destruction of native villages in South Africa and similar reports in London newspapers *The Standard* and *The Daily News*. He quotes, too, from a report in which Sir Arthur Cunynghame, former commander of the British and colonial forces on the eastern frontier, says, "I desire to point out that the condition of the Ngqika women and children has become most deplorable."

Great indignation also has been caused, O'Donnell says, by reports that the Basutoland insurgents are "being driven out of their caves by smoke and dynamite." He wants to know whether Hicks-Beach "has sent any specific instructions to the British authorities in South Africa on the subject of burning and plundering native villages, smoking out refugee insurgents, and similar alleged practices?"

Hicks-Beach replies, "I do not think an illustration in a newspaper is of sufficient importance to base an opinion upon as to what is occurring in South Africa.

"I do not know that it is true that several hundreds of native villages have been plundered and destroyed since the rising of the Ngqika to the present time, nor do I believe there is any practice of the kind going on now.

"No doubt, in the war many of these villages may have been destroyed as a necessary part of military operations; but I do not believe that in any case they have been destroyed where it has not been necessary for that reason to do so."

He says the condition of these women and children "is due to other causes besides the destruction of villages; they were humanely treated afterwards."

As to the mode in which the Basutoland insurgents were dealt with, Hicks-Beach says, "I know nothing; but however painful it might be to drive them out by smoke, yet I will venture to say that is a more humane process than driving them out by starvation.

"Even if these reports be true, at any rate, it would appear that the surrender of these insurgents was secured with very little loss of life, whatever operations may have taken place."

Cape Town — The same day

The Cape Colony Prime Minister Gordon Sprigg proposes to his cabinet that they respond to Hicks-Beach's letter to Frere in only about two weeks. That will give them time to consider what their response should be.

The colony's own financial situation is a more important issue to the colonial government at present than that of Britain, Sprigg tells his cabinet ministers. The preliminary figures of expenditure for the colony over the last financial year, which will be released publicly in the next few weeks, reflect a loan of £650,000 for an item marked as "native rebellion."

"This figure is a third — yes, a third — of our total debt of £2 million," Sprigg adds. "And almost all of it is being spent on the war against Moorosi.

"This loan is a big jump — something like 32 percent — from the £490,000 we borrowed for native rebellions in the last fiscal year," the prime minister continues. "And may I remind you that last year we were fighting wars on the eastern frontier.

"Let me point out, too, that nearly all the rest of our debt was incurred on public works," Sprigg says. "Most of these — such as our largest single expense,the £1.28 million we spent on expanding our railways — will become income-producing investments. In addition to railways, we invested in harbors, bridges, buildings, telegraphs, and so on. These loans will pay for themselves in future income.

"But the war is neither income-producing, nor a financial asset. We must conclude this war before it swamps us in debt that will never yield us any returns.

"For now, we can at least make up for it to a small degree by making the people of Basutoland pay toward the war. After all, it is their people who rebelled and forced us to wage it." On Sprigg's orders, the government sends a telegram to Arthur Hubbard, the accountant in the magistrate's office in Maseru, instructing him to transfer £12,500 from the Basutoland Treasury to the colonial government.

King William's Town — Wednesday June 18, 1879

Colonel S. P. Jarvis, overseeing the colonial forces as commandant-general from his quarters in King William's Town, has read Griffith's report on the massacre at the Chiappini camp. He concludes that the commander must bear at least some of the blame.

He notes in an official response that Griffith refers to the camp as a "picket," whereas Colonel Minto states that his orders were to form a "camp." As the orders were conveyed orally, he cannot verify what exactly Griffith did order.

But Jarvis concludes that the men were a detachment or outpost from the headquarters camp and not an outlying picket. Had a picket, or sentry post, been set up, it would have not involved the erection of tents, and it would have been of short duration. Also, the distance from the post to the headquarters meant that it was not a picket that would be relieved daily.

"As an outpost two or three miles removed from the main body and not relieved daily, I think Colonel Minto was justified in allowing tents to be taken.

"The mistake seems to have been in pitching the tents too near cover, and exposed to surprise by the enemy, before sufficient defense was prepared to protect them.

"I hold that if it was meant to be a picket it was improperly posted — exposed to surprise — kept out far beyond the usual tour of picket duty and out of reach of support from the main body.

"As an outpost it should have thrown out its own advanced picket in support of the sentries, and to cover its own camp. All orders for such duties should be recorded in writing."

Griffith — the proud master of precise procedure and detailed directive — has been found wanting.

Cape Town — Saturday June 21, 1879

Sir Bartle Frere, opening the first session of the sixth parliament of the Cape Colony, is blunt: "I deeply regret to be unable to announce to you that peace reigns upon our borders and in the neighboring colonies," he says.

"The Colony of Natal is still passing through a period of great anxiety. A war of considerable magnitude is being waged against a barbaric power, which has for years silently but steadily grown in strength, until that strength has become seriously and actively dangerous to the peace and prosperity of South Africa. I trust that the speedy and complete success of the British arms will have the effect of crushing a military organization, hostile not only to the advance of civilization, but also to the material interests of South Africa, and that such a firm, enduring, and honorable peace will alone be established as may give to South Africa that assurance of permanent security which is indispensably necessary for the attainment of progress.

"I regret to have to state that military operations are still rendered necessary by the attitude of certain chiefs upon the northern border of the colony, and by the rebellion of the long discontented Baphuthi Chief Moorosi, in Basutoland. In both cases the operations are being carried on solely by colonial forces, of whose gallantry the colony may be justly proud.

"Many casualties have unhappily occurred, chiefly amongst the Cape Mountain Riflemen and Cape Mounted Yeomanry, both of which forces have borne themselves throughout with distinguished gallantry. The colony has to deplore the loss upon the northern border and in Basutoland of some of her bravest sons. A speedy termination of hostilities is expected; but it will be necessary to make permanent provision for the defense of that part of the colony to ensure the maintenance of peace in the future.

"The defensive forces of the colony are in a satisfactory condition, taking into account the recent organization of a large portion of the forces. Any feeling of dissatisfaction which prevailed amongst a small section has disappeared, and the force which has been organized as the Cape Mounted Riflemen is fast approaching a condition of the highest efficiency. "

London — Friday, June 27, 1879

Newspaper reports about the use of dynamite in Moorosi's war continue to be published in London, leading to concern among members of Parliament.

The reports are raised again today during question time in the House of Commons. John Whitwell, member of Parliament for Kendal, rises to ask Colonial Affairs Secretary Sir Michael Hicks-Beach whether he has inquired about reports that Colonel Brabant, with a detachment of Cape Mounted Yeomanry, "threw explosive dynamite and fired cannon into a cave occupied by Basotho and their women and children."

Hicks-Beach replies that the operations in Basutoland are being undertaken solely by the Cape Government and are not funded by money controlled by the House of Commons.

"I have received some despatches from Sir Bartle Frere, the governor of the Cape Colony, detailing some of the occurrences of this war; but nothing relating to the employment of dynamite under the circumstances mentioned," he says.

"If I thought for a moment there was any necessity to do so, I should forward a remonstrance to the Cape Government; and if there was any case calling for inquiry, I should direct such inquiry to be made. But I have neither the right nor the wish to interfere with individual officers in the services of the Cape Government."

Quthing — Monday, June 30, 1879

Winter is making itself felt down into the valleys of Quthing. Freezing nights and cold wind-blown days combine to cause less than desirable conditions for pursuing any sort of military action. As testimony to the onset of winter, today it snows at Moorosi's Mountain.

Following the second assault on the mountain, Brabant has resorted to Griffith's starve-them-out strategy, a plan in which the winter weather may be counted as an asset. But to make it work he sends out regular patrols to sniff out and destroy rebel strongholds in Quthing and also in Kornet Spruit, from where he believes many of Moorosi's supplies come.

Quthing — Wednesday, July 2, 1879

For weeks Brabant has led patrols into the surrounding areas to search out rebels and to destroy food supplies that can be sent to the mountain, but tonight, with winter weather reducing the patrols, Brabant is sitting around a fire at camp headquarters, swapping war stories with his senior officers.

He recalls a patrol a week ago up the Quthing River to caves near its source at Qacha's Nek in the Drakensberg mountains.

"We gained the ridge of the Drakensberg in the evening and we were forced to bivouac there in a snow drift," he tells about 20 officers gathered around the fire. "The cold was severe. We were glad when the dawn came and we could move on.

"After scrambling down the valley, we came across the tracks of a large herd of cattle, but the men leading the cattle were too quick for us. We followed them at a distance and saw them drive the cattle into a cave.

"We reached the cave only to find bodies of the cattle, which had been stabbed by the natives to prevent their falling alive into our hands. The men had all disappeared into the caves, which were honeycombed by passages underground and between an immense mass of boulders at the foot of the valley.

"The whole place was so large and the only passages we could find were so small that it would evidently be madness to send men to certain death in them."

Brabant pauses, looking around the circle of listeners. He is pleased to see they are clearly impressed with his story. Now for the really good part.

"In the middle of the day my servant brought me some lunch and while I was preparing to eat it, and had seated myself on a convenient rock, Captain MacLean came up and remarked that he would advise me to select another seat as the one I had was in a direct line with one of the narrow slits in the boulders a fairly short distance from us that were used as loopholes by the enemy.

"I took his advice, luckily, and moved off a few yards. Presently, some of the totties (Hottentots) came up and one of them in passing sat down for a moment on the rock I had previously occupied. A shot was fired from the loophole pointed out to me by MacLean, and the man fell, shot through the head.

"Several shots were fired in our direction, but there were no more casualties.

"We had to carry the dead tottie slung across a pony across the Quthing River, which ran at the foot of the valley, and finally buried the poor fellow on a grassy flat where we made our camp."

The men urge him to tell more of his stories. Brabant is pleased to oblige.

"On another expedition, we were using pack oxen to carry the mountain guns for the first time. I sent into the Herschel District specially for eight or 10 of these oxen, including two for myself. We found them most useful for carrying the guns.

"One of the bullocks actually fell off the narrow path on which we were traveling and rolled down the steep hillside, taking the gun with him."

The listening officers gasp.

"We naturally thought we should never see the bullock alive and should be lucky if we recovered the gun, but to our amazement bullock and gun turned up half an hour afterward having been brought up by the friendly natives who had been sent to look for him."

His listeners laugh and applaud the story.

"Here's another story," Brabant continues. "I am sure you will enjoy this one.

"When we reached Masapuli's village, in search of rebels, we camped on the roof of a cave in which the rebels were hiding. The stratum of hard rock between us and the enemy was not more than 10 or 12 inches in thickness, so we determined to attempt to blow it up close to its edge, so as practically to make a breach behind the known entrance, which was as usual walled up with large stones.

"We had brought jumpers and hammers with us and we proceeded to drill holes for blasting. So near were we that we could distinctly hear the enemy singing and carrying on a war dance below us.

"We exploded two or three charges of dynamite and powder before night, sufficient to show the enemy that our getting on to them was only a matter of time. We placed a Mfengu guard on, and were having our supper very comfortably when the enemy made a sudden rush from the cave, dashed through the line of Mfengu and got clear away, leaving one or two badly wounded men behind.

"As soon as they were a fair distance away the women and children came out of the cave and gave themselves up, well aware that they were sure of good treatment."

The men laugh, but beneath the humor is the realization that, even in the outlying areas the war is reaping as many setbacks as victories.

Brabant is not the only government officer dispatching patrols into the countryside to flush out the rebels. Police sent by Austen from the new magistrate's office have had several successes in ousting Baphuthi from caves. The Basotho policemen, who have remained loyal to the government in spite of the war, also have seized cattle, goats and sheep.

The forays have led to several arrests. Interviews have convinced Austen that Moorosi is still being supplied with cattle seized in the area by headmen loyal to him and smuggled up the mountain.

Lehana has become the leader of an underground ring that maintains constant communication with Moorosi and supplies the king with food on the mountain. He travels regularly between the mountain, villages and cave holdouts.

Everywhere he goes, he hides his presence as best he can, aware that there are those who will disclose his whereabouts to the government. He remains elusive, determined not to let his guard fall.

Lehana is part of Moorosi's overall plan to hold out until the government gives up its siege, which he is confident must happen before too long. As the government troops withdraw, Moorosi will follow them and chase them off his land. He will then link up with those living in the caves. In that way, the Baphuthi king will be able to take over his land once more.

The standoff between the opposing forces has developed into a determination on both sides that they will stay in position until they prevail. Each is waiting for the other to yield. Yet each is determined not to be the one to yield.

Zululand — Friday July 4, 1879

Although Sir Garnet Wolseley has been in Natal for a week and is said to be on his way to take over command in Zululand, Lord Chelmsford decides he will attack Ulundi today. He will not allow Wolseley to arrive from England, take over, and claim victory.

Chelmsford and his force of thousands have been advancing steadily on Ulundi over the past few weeks and are only a day's march from the Zulu capital when they are attacked by 20,000 Zulus armed with spears.

As the Zulu impis descend on them, the soldiers hold them at bay with their rifles. The British soldiers fire into the waves of advancing warriors, preventing the

Zulus from reaching close enough for spear-to-bayonet combat. The Zulus run over the bodies of their fallen comrades in an attempt to get close to the soldiers, but are repulsed. Eventually, they retreat and the British, cheering wildly, move on to Ulundi, where they find the great kraal deserted. Although parts of Zululand remain unconquered, the taking of the capital means the British have won the war.

It means, too, that Chelmsford, and not Wolseley, has achieved the victory.

News of the Zulu defeat will renew the confidence of the whites in the Cape Colony that the back of the black resistance can be broken.

Quthing — Saturday, July 5, 1879

For some time Brabant has been trying to devise a way to keep the men on sentry duty warm at night. The cold is intense and a sentry cannot stand by a fire. It would make him a target and it would dull his night vision, which needs to be firmly fixed on the mountain. But the sentries are complaining bitterly about the cold.

Brabant issues them extra rations of rum, confident that the alcohol will help warm their bodies. But the complaints continue.

One of the men offers the commander a suggestion, one that he had heard some years ago while serving in winter conditions on the eastern frontier. "I have heard that onions are useful in warding off the cold," he says.

"Really?" Brabant responds. "It so happens that we have just received a large supply of onions from the colony. I suppose there is no harm in trying it out."

Brabant issues a large onion with the regular supply of biscuits to every man on picket duty.

It works. The onions, he finds, supply the warmth that the rum failed to do.

Quthing — Sunday July 6, 1879

After conducting the regular Sunday service at his new church, Ellenberger sits down with the Baphuthi Christians who help him run his mission station.

"This war and the deaths that have resulted have me extremely worried," he says. "I have temporarily closed our outstation along the Silver Spruit river and invited the Christians living there to move here. I am afraid that they will get caught up in the war, even though I know that Moorosi has no quarrel with them. Here they will be safe."

One of the Baphuthi Christians, Philemon Seboka, says he cannot understand why the whites, who are a Christian people, are fighting a war against them.

"As our wise king Moshoeshoe said many years ago: Before the white people came, we fought because we had no other examples than the wild animals. When we first heard the Gospel we put away our weapons because we thought war would not be possible by people who call themselves Christian.

"But now we see those who profess to be the children of Him who said, 'Love your enemies,' taking pleasure in fighting.

"They work this evil without anger, mixing wisdom with it. I can make no sense of it except that war must be a rod that God does not choose to break because he will make use of it still for the chastisement of men. The great chief wished peace. He said he knew war could produce no good. That is what Moshoeshoe said and I myself see it happening now in our land. I can see what he said is true."

"The wise Moshoeshoe was right," Ellenberger says. "And you are right, Philemon. Jesus told us that we must be peacemakers, that we must love our enemies. That is one of the most important commands he gave to us. It is sad to watch the people who profess to be Christians failing to follow what Jesus said. But you must not stop believing what Jesus said because you see a bad example.

"It is as important to be peacemakers when we are dealing with our family and our friends as it is between us and other people who are different from us or who disagree with us. Even if they hate us and want to kill us, we must still love them."

Seboka shakes his head in disbelief.

"But they are not following what you say. This shedding of blood is no good." His eyes pleading, he asks, "Can you not stop it?"

Ellenberger explains that he talked with the government people in an effort to prevent the war. He says he was critical of the colonial authorities for their action, which he regarded as hasty and precipitous. He had even tried to get the government people to sit down with Moorosi and try to find a compromise that could achieve peace. He had offered to serve as a negotiator.

"But I was unsuccessful," he says. "Now there have been two attacks on the mountain and many attacks on the people hiding out in caves. Many lives have been lost on both sides and still no peace is in sight. Perhaps it is a good time for both sides to see reason.

"If I can get the king and the leaders of the colonial army to sit down on the Wodehouse bench and even if we have to talk for days I am sure we can get them to agree on many things and to stop fighting. Each side will have to give up something, to make sacrifices, but that is the only way we can have peace."

His listeners nod in agreement. They have come to respect Ellenberger's ability to bring about peace between feuding people, having seen it work in their lives and in the lives of those around them.

"It would be good if you could stop the war," Seboka adds.

"Now I know that, much as I would like to do so, I am unlikely to get them to come here to Masitise and actually sit on the Wodehouse bench," Ellenberger continues. "But I will talk once more with the people on both sides and encourage them to come to some sort of compromise.

"Before I speak with the government, I would like to talk to King Moorosi about what compromises he is prepared to make and what he can do to try to achieve peace. Can anyone help me to speak with King Moorosi? The mountain is ringed by the colonial army, but I know it is possible to get up the mountain to see the chief. Does anyone know how I can do that?"

"I do not think you must go on to the mountain," Seboka says. "It will be too difficult and you will put yourself in harm's way. But I can get a message to King Moorosi through one of my people. What should I tell him?"

After outlining his proposal to Seboka, Ellenberger sets off for the mountain, where he hopes to be able to talk with the colonial military leaders about the same time that the message is being conveyed to Moorosi.

London — Monday July 7, 1879

It is question time in the House of Commons in the British Parliament. Sir Wilfrid Lawson, Liberal member of parliament for Carlisle, rises to ask a question of the Secretary of State for War, Colonel Frederick Arthur Stanley, a member of the cabinet of Conservative Prime Minister Benjamin Disraeli.

Lawson fashions his question in parliamentary format, addressing the secretary in the third person.

Sir Wilfrid: Does the secretary have reason to believe the statement of a Cape newspaper, the *Watchman*, that in the Moorosi campaign our forces had smoked to death nine men and boys in a cave; and if so whether Her Majesty's Government have given any sanction to this war being carried on in this manner?

Colonel Stanley: I will communicate with the Secretary of State for the Colonies; but my impression is that these officers belong to the colonial forces.

Sir Michael Hicks-Beach: With the permission of the House I will reply to the hon. Baronet. I have seen the paragraph which he has quoted. The forces engaged in the war against Moorosi, to which it relates, are not in any way responsible to my right honorable and gallant friend, nor, indeed, to Her Majesty's Government. They are in the pay and employment of the colonial government of the Cape; and, with regard to their actions, I could only remonstrate with the Cape Government, if I saw any necessity for doing so.

"It appears, however, that what occurred was this. Certain persons, Basothos, occupied a cave, and it was found necessary to dislodge them.

"They stated they were ready to surrender, and some of the colonial forces entered the cave with the view of helping them out when they were fired upon. Then it was that the fire was re-lit at the entrance to the cave, and these deaths occurred."

Quthing — Tuesday, July 8, 1879

Brabant is preparing for an early-morning troop inspection when a sergeant-major looks into his tent. "The missionary from Masitise is here," he says.

"Send him in."

"Thank you for agreeing to talk with me," Ellenberger, carrying a large leather-bound Bible, says. "I would like to talk to you about a compromise to end the war."

"Compromise?" Brabant responds. "You missionaries always take the side of the natives against the government. I suspect you want us to surrender, not settle."

"That is not what I am suggesting," Ellenberger responds. "I know it is difficult to talk about settlement in the middle of a war. The issues are forgotten; people want only to fight to win and nothing else. They do not remember why the war started in the first place, nor do they try to understand the enemy's motivation. Or even their own motivation for that matter. They want only to win.

"Neither side wants to back down and be seen as losing. Honor and pride are at stake. I understand that. But now you have lost two assaults on the mountain and lives have been lost. The war has caused much suffering.

"I am sure the government wants the war to end. I am sure King Moorosi wants the war to end. We all want the war to end. And I think the way to end it is through a negotiated settlement. I think you might find that Moorosi might meet you somewhere in the middle. You might have to give up something, and Moorosi might have to give up something, but you will both gain an end to the war, which is what we all want.

"Reverend Ellenberger, I am not the government," Brabant says. "I only work for the government. My duty is to obey orders, to carry out what the government decides. The government minister, Mr. Ayliff, has told me that we will accept nothing but unconditional surrender from Moorosi. The government wants us to defeat Moorosi. And, I assure you, we *will* defeat Moorosi."

"But there is another way," Ellenberger counters. "I am convinced that if you talk with King Moorosi you might be able to work out a compromise, or settlement, of some sort. Mr. Bowker, who served for a time as the resident magistrate in Maseru, was able to work out such a compromise in a previous confrontation between the government and Moorosi. He did so with wisdom and tact and prevented the outbreak of hostilities."

A look of urging in his eyes, he pleads with Brabant. "Does it not make sense to talk to Moorosi again and to reach some sort of agreement that can prevent more people being killed on both sides? Can I ask you, instead of continuing this war, to seek a negotiated agreement as Mr. Bowker did?"

"What did Bowker achieve in the long run?" Brabant asks, a hint of anger in his voice. "He was an appeaser and didn't solve the underlying problem. Once Lehana was released, he was up to his old tricks again, spurring on people to rebel against the government. Bowker should have punished Lehana and Moorosi properly. Then the rebellion would have been squashed and we would not have had to go to war.

"In any event, as I said, you are speaking to the wrong person, reverend. I am doing what I was instructed to do. I am a soldier first, and an honorable one at that. I and the men I command are fighting for our country, our Queen and our God."

The statement touches a nerve in Ellenberger. "Queen and country perhaps. But God?"

"Yes, these people are unchristian and heathen, reverend. Surely you, of all people, understand that? They are a mass of savagedom. They are lazy. They are thieves and, like the other black people in this country, are incapable of acquiring civilization. We all know that."

"I would not describe the Baphuthi as heathen, nor are they savages," Ellenberger responds. "Most are not Christians, but they do have a strong moral code based on family and community of property, similar to that of the children of Israel. They seldom commit serious crimes, and murder is rare among them. Their family bonds are strong.

"And even were the Baphuthi all heathens and savages, I do not believe that is a reason to try to destroy them. Jesus never gave us instructions to wage war against those who are not Christian, even though they might be our enemies. On the contrary, he instructed us to love our enemies — not to tolerate or ignore them, but to love them.

"He made clear what our attitude should be in all he said and did.

"He gave us the Golden Rule: Do unto others as you would have them do unto you.

"He said if you live by the sword you will die by the sword.

"He said if you are attacked you should turn the other cheek.

"He said the meek will inherit the earth.

"He told the story of the Good Samaritan, showing that love for your neighbor means that Christian love crosses cultural boundaries.

"He refused to resist the Roman authorities, even when they arrested him.

"I could go on. Everything Jesus did and said spoke of loving others, not hating others — and certainly not waging war on them."

Brabant responds: "God helped the children of Israel win their wars against the heathens surrounding them. And let me tell you that the bishops of the church support us in this war. They have been here to encourage us. They believe God is on our side. They understand that these people are infidels, that they have rebelled against the government and they must be brought to justice. They tell me that this is a just war, a war of good against evil."

Ellenberger opens his mouth to disagree but lets the colonel continue.

"The noblest thing you can do is to fight — and die if necessary — for your country," Brabant adds. "That is what we are doing. What we are doing *is* noble. Our church leaders say there are times when war is justified. This is one of them.

"You say we should negotiate with these barbarians. But if we let them continue their rebellion through some sort of compromise or settlement, as you suggest, they will rebel another time, again and again. They will continue to refuse to obey us. These people are rebels, they are traitors. They want to wage war against us and we have to defend ourselves. They will kill us if we give them half a chance.

"Even you might be pleading to us for protection should that happen."

"I do not think they are a warlike people," Ellenberger says. "They, in turn, want to protect themselves against you, whom they see as the invaders. Perhaps they believe God is on *their* side. Surely God loves them as much as He loves you.

"War is the most uncivilized of human pursuits and the most unchristian way of trying to solve problems. Anyone who says he is a Christian and goes to war is not following the clear instruction from Jesus. It's as simple as that. By fighting against your enemy you are disobeying Jesus.

"In any event, that action has already been taken," Ellenberger continues. "The war has begun. Now we must turn to the next solution. I must believe even you — and your church leaders — would prefer to see this conflict resolved before more people die. Surely a peaceful settlement is the best outcome.

"You still can solve this problem in a civilized and Christian way through compromise. If you do, you will be a hero, colonel. You will have achieved something of which you can be truly proud."

"Let me repeat, reverend, Mr. Ayliff has told me that the government will accept nothing short of unconditional surrender from Moorosi. Those are my orders."

"Nevertheless, if you present a good case to Mr. Ayliff for compromise, he might agree to a settlement or a conditional surrender of some sort," Ellenberger says. "Let me appeal to you: If the chief comes with a proposal aimed at a conditional surrender — a compromise — would you please consider it, not just for his sake, but for your sake, for the sake of peace, for the sake of your Queen and, yes, for the sake of God?"

Brabant sighs. It seems the only way he can get rid of Ellenberger is to placate him. "Very well. Should that occur, I will consider it, as far as I am able to do within the confines of my jurisdiction, but I don't believe Moorosi will concede anything."

Ellenberger persists. "All I ask is that you listen and that you weigh carefully the alternatives — continuing what looks like a war that will drag on for a long time without resolution, costing more and more in lives and money, or achieving a negotiated settlement through compromise.

"You could then pass that plan on to Mr. Ayliff, who may well agree to it, and you will have helped to end the war."

Ellenberger hopes he has planted a seed of compromise toward settlement on the colonial side. He is confident, too, that another seed of settlement has been planted on the top of the mountain. And he desperately hopes the two will find their way to meet somewhere in the middle.

Moorosi's first wife, Masakale, is perturbed. She might be older than all the women on the mountain, but she can set them all an example when it comes to prodding their husbands to fight for their nation. If she detests anything, it is to see a man who is vacillating, weak and subservient.

"Why have you set up a white flag behind the stone walls?" she asks as she walks up to a group of advisers sitting around Moorosi.

"Have we not fought off the enemy? Have we not killed many of them? Have we not shown them to be weak fighters?

"And now you want to surrender?

"Could we have done more? Could we have fought harder? Could we have killed more of the enemy? What kind of man are you that you want to give up?"

Moorosi looks around at his advisers and realizes they are probably asking similar questions. He turns back to Masakale. "We are not surrendering. Our men have performed well. We have scored many victories for our people. I am very happy with what they have done."

"Well, why then, have you put out the white flag?"

"Listen what I say to my people and you will learn."

He pauses, making clear that it is important that Masakale, his other wives and his advisers all understand what he is about to say to them.

"As you know, the coming of winter has reduced the amount of food available to our people," Moorosi continues. "Our supplies of grain are being reduced and it is becoming harder to replenish them."

During harvest, Moorosi says, the Baphuthi men were able to sneak down from the mountain on to unguarded grain fields and supplement their supplies.

"But now, as you know, there is no grain left to be harvested. The only supplies we can obtain are those stored in villages, but those supplies have been reduced by the flight of people. Our Baphuthi people hiding in caves along the river valleys also need grain to keep alive. They cannot give it all to us. As you have seen, too, the colonial forces have stepped up their patrols and have increased the number of men on picket duty. It is harder now for us to leave and return with food supplies.

"We also have eaten many cattle and goats. Others have died from the cold at the top of the mountain. We have fewer left.

"As you know, Letsie failed to support me as he said he would."

Already, Moorosi continues, he has asked about 200 of the Baphuthi men and about the same number of women and children to leave the mountain under cover of night and to shelter in caves where they can find food more easily and from where they will emerge to take back the country once the colonial forces accept defeat. He has been sorry to hear that some have been killed or captured by the whites and the policemen and the soldiers who work for them, but most of them remain in hiding.

"My son Lehana is with them," he continues.

"You 300 men who remain on the mountain are, like you Maketa, among our best shots and our strongest warriors. There are enough of us here to defend the mountain stronghold. I know we can defend ourselves. That does not worry me. But those of us who remain have to be careful how we use our food supply to make the best of what we have."

His wife Masakale nods. "We have been working to enable the supplies to last as long as possible. The women have developed clever ways of providing food." One of the ways is to take a few of the hides set aside to provide clothing and convert them into fragments that are ground, like corn, between two stones and boiled to form a nourishing soup. "It is good. I drink it every day. Look at me. Am I not strong? Am I not healthy?"

"Yes, I am proud of what you women have done," says Moorosi. "But last night, when it was dark, a messenger from the missionary Ellenberger came to talk with me. He says we must talk peace with the white fighters. We must be willing to make some changes so there can be peace. He says if we are suffering so are the white people. And I know that to be so. We have had reports from Mfengu who have heard the white soldiers saying they are unhappy. They want to go home; they do not like the cold weather.

"We would like to see an end to the war. So would they.

"So, reverend Ellenberger says, we must talk to them about peace. We must look for a way to meet them halfway and they will also want to look for a way to meet us halfway. We meet in the middle and there you have peace."

Moorosi says the colonial forces have been thwarted twice in their attempts to take the mountain. They must be frustrated. Surely, he reasons, they will not be foolish enough to attack a third time. They will not be satisfied with guarding his mountain month after month. They are looking for a way out.

Moorosi recalls the missionary Ellenberger talking to him about how much he desired people to live in peace and how Jesus had spoken of loving your enemy and peacemakers being good people.

Perhaps he will have to give up something and seek a compromise, which was so favored by Moshoeshoe. Perhaps peace will work.

"I will talk with them," he tells Masakela, "and perhaps we can get an end to this war and bring about peace."

"But you have put up a white flag," Masakela replies. "To the white people that means we want to surrender. We cannot give up now. We are winning. We are not losing. Only losers surrender."

Moorosi is about to respond when a messenger runs up. "The white chiefs are calling for you," he says.

Moorosi walks down the path toward the pole with the piece of white material fluttering at the top. He recalls how he had found the white cloth among the supplies taken months ago from Thomas's Shop. How long ago that now seems.

Across the plateau he sees three men — all dressed in the finery that marks them as senior officers — standing and looking toward him.

"Are you ready to surrender?" an officer shouts.

"I want to talk about peace," Moorosi replies.

Brabant, accompanied by Colonel Southey and Captain Tainton, who will act as interpreter, move forward slowly across the plateau.

"I am confident that Moorosi would not raise a white flag under false pretenses," he says, "but I have to be careful that it is not a clever decoy and so I have given instructions for a group of troopers to stand guard. You never know how sly these savages can be, do you? To them, lying and deception come naturally."

The three men walk slowly forward until they are below the stone walls.

"I want to talk peace," Moorosi repeats.

After a brief parlay, Tainton turns up to face Moorosi. "Are you then willing to give up your arms, come off the mountain and surrender?" he asks.

"I want you to promise that, if I come down off my mountain and do not fight against you, you will not punish me for anything you say I've done," Moorosi says.

Tainton speaks briefly once more with Brabant and Southey before replying. "We cannot promise you that. You have broken the law and you must be punished for that. You have rebelled against the Cape colonial rule and we cannot allow you to go unpunished."

Moorosi is insistent.

"No, I want peace. I am giving in. I will not fight you any longer. I will not send my people out to attack you. But I do not want you to punish me. I want to live in any village that you choose for me. I want us to live in peace."

The three officers hold a short discussion after which Taiton shouts back, "Come down off the mountain and we can sit down and talk about the terms of your surrender."

Now it is Moorosi's turn to suspect trickery and deceit.

"I and my mountain are one," he says. "Why do you want me to come off my mountain? I have given in. I have told you that I have given in if you agree not to attack me. Now it is time for you to say what you will do.

"I want peace. You say that I am a child of the government. The government is my father. So now I have given in to my father. I swear before the great God that I have given in. Why must I come down? I want peace. What more do you want from me?"

The colonial officers hold another discussion at the base of the wall.

"He says he has given in and we must not attack him, but he wants to go unpunished and presumably continue to be the chief here. It doesn't make sense."

Brabant agrees. "This is typical of the way these people think. He raises a white flag. He tells us we have won. He tells us he has surrendered. That seems clear to me. But he does not want to come off the mountain. What, then, does a surrender mean? How can we have won if he does not want to leave the mountain?"

Tainton offers his explanation. "I think he is trying to say that he will not fight against us any longer if we do not fight against him any longer."

"But that is not a surrender," counters Brabant.

"It is not a surrender," replies Tainton. "He did not use the word surrender."

"He is telling us that we have won, but I think he also believes that, in a sense, he has won. In other words, it is a stalemate.

"As he keeps repeating, he wants peace. He is asking us to be benevolent to him, as a father is to his child. He says he has already been punished. Now he wants peace and he does not want us to punish him any longer. He wants to be free to live in any village we choose for him."

"I have no authority to debate the issue," Brabant says. "The only authority I have is to accept an unconditional surrender."

The words of Ellenberger that Moorosi would likely offer a compromise return to him. But he deems such a suggestion impractical. How can he be certain that

Moorosi will honor such a peace and not continue fighting?

Tainton moves away from the officers, takes a step toward the wall, and looks up at Moorosi, patiently waiting alongside the white flag.

"We will accept nothing but the unconditional surrender of you and all the men on the mountain," he says. "Colonel Brabant says he has no power to decide on anything else, but he will report to the government."

Masakela's words ring in Moorosi's ears. "Only losers surrender."

He realizes these men do not want compromise as Ellenberger said they might. They want to defeat him. What they want is for him to give up, to hand himself and his people over to the government so they can be punished.

They have already said they want to take his arms away from him so he will never be able to defend himself and his people again. Should they resist the order to give up their weapons, he and his family members and the other chiefs and headmen of the Baphuthi people will be sent to the Cape to work on the breakwater.

The Baphuthi people will be forced to work on the white farms that will be established on their land.

If that is what he has to do to achieve compromise, he does not want it.

Honor is more important than that form of so-called settlement.

Freedom is worth enduring a cold winter and a depleting food supply.

The Baphuthi way of life tastes better than all the food in the world.

Even death would be better than to surrender and be punished by the government. But Ellenberger said he should talk to the government about achieving peace through compromise. So he will present his part of the bargain one more time.

"I want to stop the fighting," Moorosi says. "I want peace."

But Brabant has no intention of talking any further.

"I will give you half an hour to get back to the top of the mountain. At that time, the white flag must be taken down," Brabant says.

The white officers walk back to their camp.

"I think we are close to winning this battle," Brabant says. "Clearly the man is suffering. His people are hurting, their food supplies are dwindling. He wants all this to end.

"When he says he wants peace he really is saying, I want to surrender. But surrender on his terms. He is only halfway there. He cannot take that full step of surrender. But, as he suffers even more, he will realize that surrender is the only way to prevent further suffering. It is all a matter of time.

"Ellenberger must have relayed a message to Moorosi about compromise, as he did with me. But we cannot make the concessions Moorosi demands of us. He must be the one to give up more before we can talk about any sort of compromise."

As Moorosi makes his way back up the path to the mountain top, Maketa runs up to ask him what has happened. When he hears, he is pleased. "I am glad you did not surrender," he says. "We will win. I will go and take down the flag."

"No, leave it there," Moorosi replies. "I want to show them that I am ready to talk peace, that they are the ones who want to continue the war.

"I heard that the missionary was here a few days ago and that he spoke to the commander Brabant. Perhaps they will listen to the missionary in the way the magistrate Bowker listened to him and brought about a peaceful settlement when they wanted to send my son Lehana to the breakwater.

"We conceded at that time that they could sentence Lehana. Bowker conceded that they would not punish him by sending him to prison in the Cape Colony.

"We both gave up something to achieve something better. We had a time of peace after that. Then last year they sentenced Lehana to prison in the Cape Colony and to work on the Cape Town breakwater. They tried to wipe out the peaceful settlement that Bowker had achieved.

"Now they do not want to concede anything. They want to punish not just Lehana, but me and all my people, too.

"Perhaps if they see that flag is still there they will think again.

"But the longer it stays there the more it makes me realize that they do not want to talk peace. They want only to talk war and only to defeat me and my people.

"We must not let them do that."

XV

Cape Town — Thursday, July 10, 1879

Sprigg is hoping that ways to bring the war to a speedy end will emerge from a seven-member committee of Parliament, called the Committee on Basutoland Hostilities. Chaired by John Merriman, which is holding hearings into the "origin and conduct of the hostilities in Basutoland." From Tuesday, the day on which it first sat, it has taken evidence on the background to the war at Moorosi's Mountain.

Today Secretary for Native Affairs William Ayliff tells the committee that he reached Moorosi's country on March 18. He took no part in military movements, deferring to Griffith as the commanding colonel who was responsible to the Commandant-General in King William's Town.

S. Cron Wright (a committee member) asks: "We'd like to know the real reasons that led to the forces being taken to Palmietfontein."

Replies Ayliff: "What led to the Yeomanry being taken there was the report of Mr. Austen of Moorosi's movements."

"Did the government ask Mr. Griffith whether he could settle this differently without the presence of an armed force?"

"Yes, and Mr. Griffith tried to do so. The papers will show all that. Letsie sent his son, Lerothodi, over to Moorosi's, but no good came of it."

It is late afternoon when Ayliff concludes his testimony. The hearing adjourns.

Quthing — Tuesday, July 29, 1879

The white flag, tattered and torn from the harsh winter and the winds that blow restlessly across the mountain, continues to fly in its spot behind the stone wall. The three days grace for which Moorosi asked to discuss the terms of surrender have now stretched into three weeks and all that Brabant has heard from the chief is a message from Lemena that indicates Moorosi has hardened his attitude.

According to Lemena, Moorosi says, "You talk of peace. Yes, peace for the whites, but not for my people; you would not even let me die in peace in my country, where I wish to end my days.

"I prefer to die on my mountain than surrender on your terms."

Brabant remains convinced, in spite of Ellenberger's impassioned argument, that the only way to achieve resolution of the war is not "peace discussions" but to continue to invest the mountain until the chief is starved into submission — the same conclusion that Griffith reached.

Yet Brabant's task is becoming more challenging each day. Six months since colonial troops first arrived to oust Moorosi from his mountain fortress, and two failed attacks later, the siege of the mountain is stalled, leading to growing dissension among the volunteers who are tired of enduring the monotonous, cold and dreary duty at the mountain, which seems to be achieving nothing.

Some of the men have been at the mountain for six months. Their boots have become battered by the constant walking on the rocks, but they are unable to buy boots at the camp and have not been issued new footwear. Blankets had been discarded on the way up to the mountain in the summer so that the horses would not be too heavily weighed down. Now the men need them on the cold winter's nights and don't have them.

Food is scarce, although the soldiers are able to sustain themselves with meal and meat bought by government agents in the Orange Free State and sent to them. Coffee and tea also have run out and sugar is a luxury.

"I cannot stand this any longer," Douglas Sampson, a volunteer, tells Alex Granville. "The boredom is punishment enough, but in addition we have to survive this winter without the benefit of a house warmed against the cold by a roaring fire. To endure such conditions for a day is not much to ask, for a week it becomes arduous. But for weeks on end, it is simply not worth it."

"That is only part of the problem," Granville replies. "I think another problem is that you volunteers are good men, but you are not well organized. I have noticed many volunteers showing bad discipline. And not even that is their fault. You are simply badly led and I cannot blame you for feeling bored. You need the discipline to feel you are performing a useful role in this war."

The man's view is shared by most of his fellow volunteers. They view the war as expensive and mismanaged. The two attacks on the mountains failed, the men believe, because of a lack of firepower, needlessly sacrificing the soldiers' lives. So slovenly is the siege being conducted, the men complain, that even wagons carrying supplies to the camp have been attacked by rebels. A week ago a party of five wagons was ransacked near Thomas's Shop and 60 oxen were stolen.

The men also have no guarantees they will be compensated for wounds or disabling injuries. In case of death, they do not know whether provision will be made for their widows and children.

As a result, some volunteers are quietly drifting off and returning to their homes in the Cape Colony.

Dissension is particularly rife among the contingency from the district of Stockenstroom, who insist that they will leave en masse at the end of the month.

The dissension has spread to the Cape Mounted Riflemen, some of whom are applying for discharge, asserting their time of service has expired. But Brabant, who can exercise more control over the Riflemen than over the volunteers, has refused them permission to leave.

Brome decides the time has come to join the others wishing to leave, but, wary of the consequences and of being called a coward, he does not want to sneak off. He approaches Brabant and requests a discharge.

"I cannot allow you to leave," Brabant says. "You are to serve out your term as a proud member of the Cape Mounted Riflemen as the other 500 members of the CMR are doing. When you joined up you must have known what it would involve."

"Yes, sir, but we were told we would be policemen, not soldiers. And since I have been here I have realized that we are not protecting anything of ours. The Baphuthi have no intention of invading my farm and our colonial land. They are bent only on preserving what they have.

"I have changed my attitude toward them. I see them now as good, brave people, fighting for what is their own just as I thought I would be fighting for what is my own when I signed up.

"Now I realize they have no evil intentions against us; we have evil intentions against them."

Brabant scowls. He grabs Brome by the collar and shakes him.

"We are not evil people, soldier," he says sternly. "I will not have you say that. The rebels on that mountain over there are the evil people.

"We are noble people advancing a noble cause. We are fighting for our country, for our fellow countrymen and ultimately for the Queen we love and respect. She is not evil and we are not evil. Anyone who thinks we are evil deserves to be thrown into an insane asylum.

"You should be whipped for speaking like this."

As Brabant grabs the other side of his collar with his other hand and shakes him even more vigorously, Brome realizes he has gone too far.

"I am merely giving my reasons as to why I would like to be released from my duties, sir. I should not have used the word evil, sir. If you say I cannot leave and that I must stay, I will perform the duties to which I am assigned, sir."

Brabant releases his grip on Brome's collar.

"Very well. But be warned if I find you to be questioning our motives and to be rebellious, you will be severely punished. I will not tolerate this sort of dissent within my ranks.

"I refuse your request for discharge. You get back there and fight in the way you are instructed to fight. I will not tolerate any insubordination. Do you hear me?"

"Yes, sir."

London — Friday, August 1, 1879

Opposition to events in South Africa is increasing in the Liberal Party, which is growing increasingly confident it can replace the Conservative government of Benjamin Disraeli in the general election to be held next year. The Liberals under William Gladstone oppose what they view as the expansive, aggressive and immoral actions of the colonial government and the spending of large sums of British money in pursuing those actions. As a result, South Africa is once more the subject of a debate today in the House of Commons.

Joseph Chamberlain, an influential Liberal who represents Birmingham, suggests a royal commission be appointed to look into the wars in South Africa "which have resulted in large annexations of territory and increase of responsibility in spite of repeated protests from successive British governments."

Chamberlain says he is disappointed that the people of the Cape Colony seem intent only on extending their territory into the native areas, to act cruelly toward the native people, and to spend British money. "The history of South Africa seems to be a history of periodic native wars," he adds, quoting Sir William Molesworth as saying that the colonists are 'possessed with an insane desire for worthless empire.'

"From 1871 to 1879 this country has paid £3,316,000 for wars in the Cape, Natal and the Transvaal and has received back only £163,000. The ordinary revenue of the Cape Colony is only about £750,000 a year and that of Natal, where the Zulu war was fought, about £250,000, and I do not see how the three million pounds now overdue and the five or six million for the Zulu War is to be repaid out of that."

The legislation to take away weapons from all natives, Chamberlain says, "led to the rebellion of Moorosi, whose submission the colonists have tried to compel by the use of dynamite to drive him from the caves in which, with his women and children, he had taken refuge. This proceeding is unknown in civilized warfare and it has brought lasting disgrace on the perpetrators.

"Some of the actions almost make a man ashamed to be an Englishman.

"I am glad, however, to believe that none of these excesses have been committed by British troops. They were due entirely to colonial troops and to a class of adventurers almost peculiar to unsettled colonies who always come to the front in connection with lawless deeds.

"It is one of the most distressing consequences of these wars with inferior races that they have a tendency to brutalize all who are concerned in them and practices unheard of in civilized warfare were openly avowed and defended in the course of these miserable contests."

A white man had been sentenced to three years for shooting a native without cause yet a native man had been sentenced to 20 years for the "simple act of rebellion," Chamberlain says. "These things, although perhaps not done by men of our blood, were done by people under our authority, and we are morally responsible for them, so long as English soldiers are employed and English money expended in protecting the colonists from the results of their injustice and wrongdoing."

Chamberlain adds that a confederation would lead to a policy in which Dutch influence would be predominant "and we have learned what that means from Sir Bartle Frere's earlier despatches, which stated that the Dutch Boers derived their notions of the rights of the natives from accounts in the Old Testament of the dealings of the Hebrews with the tribes whom they encountered."

W. H. James, who represents Gateshead in the House, suggests the remedy is plain: No assistance of a military kind should in future be given to the colonists.

"I disapprove of the policy of Sir Bartle Frere, who has encouraged the sending of troops to the colony," he says. He is convinced the wars will continue unless the British government refuses to pay her soldiers in South Africa.

Justin M'Carthy, the member for Longford, Ireland, agrees, adding, "The wars of South Africa always began in the eagerness of the colonists to obtain the land of the natives. Now it is time to put a stop to that, or if they will not put a stop to it, then to accept that as their national policy and once and for all drop their hypocrisy on the score of Russia and other powers who believe in their manifest destiny to fulfill a certain civilizing mission."

E. Jenkins, the member for Dundee, says the British troops should stay to protect the blacks. If the British withdrew an inevitable result "would allow a war of extermination to go on between the whites and native races. Every humanitarian sentiment in the country would revolt from such a course. We are responsible as a nation for the position of our fellow-countrymen there and we cannot allow them to commit any acts which will be discreditable to the nation."

Sir Michael Hicks-Beach, the colonial secretary, responds that the underlying cause of the outbreaks of violence in the Cape Colony is not the colonists' greed for the natives' land, "but the movement of the whites to the north and the movement of the blacks to the south." He does not believe, Hicks-Beach adds, that the policy of disarmament has anything to do with Sarhili's outbreak or that of Moorosi. The disarmament policy, he says, has been carried out "with the utmost care and caution by the Cape government."

There is a general rising among the native people, Hicks-Beach continues, who clearly bases his approach on what he has heard from Frere. The small number of whites in the Cape Colony are scattered among the native majority and would be "comparatively powerless in the event of an outbreak."

W. E. Forster, the member for Bradford, says he believes the House of Commons and the country are united on the question "which is that our relations with the Cape Colony must be put on a different footing; that we will not join in unjust wars and that we should not be responsible for the ill-treatment of the natives."

Adds Arthur Mills, member for Exeter: "The colonists should be told that they must fight their own battles and pay their own bills."

The debate ends without action being taken on Chamberlain's motion that a royal commission be appointed to investigate the wars in South Africa.

Maseru — Wednesday, August 6, 1879

With Britain making clear it no longer wants to fund Moorosi's war and with the war's costs straining the Cape Treasury's coffers, Ayliff has told Griffith he needs to consider increasing the Basutoland hut tax from 10 shillings for each hut to £1.

Griffith wants to consult the magistrates and the people first, believing that the unsettled nature of the country because of the war against Moorosi and the disarmament act makes this time a bad one to double the tax burden.

In spite of being removed from his post as commanding officer and being rebuked for his actions in the attack on the Chiappini camp, Griffith remains a dedicated public servant. As such, he believes he cannot remove himself from bearing some responsibility for the war and still resolutely seeks ways that he can use his position to bring about an end to the conflict.

Convinced that cutting off Moorosi's supply sources remains the best, most humane, and most effective way to end the war, he has instructed Arthur Barkly — who returned to his position as magistrate in Kornet Spruit when Griffith left the mountain — to move the Baphuthi refugees in his district several miles away from the Orange River to prevent them from secretly supplying Moorosi across the river. Barkly is also to seize their weapons.

Lehana continues to occupy the holdout along the Silver Spruit River, where he has linked up with a Thembu leader named Madusela. They are replenishing their supplies and sending some north to the mountain. They add to their stock by regularly crossing the Telle River into the Cape Colony to seize cattle.

"The more the government tries to shut down our supplies, the more we will come up with ways to outwit them," Lehana says.

Cape Town — Thursday, August 7, 1879

Today Colonel Bowker is giving evidence to the committee on Basutoland hostilities and is telling the chairman John Merriman that he believes that disarmament "would unite every black face in South Africa against us."

Do you not think under any circumstances there would always be a division in case of any rebellion, the same as in India and North America in the past among the native tribes? — I think if there is anything calculated to unite the natives, it is this disarmament act; it is moral castration.

Cape Town — Tuesday, August 26, 1879

Anxious to extricate the government from the morass into which the war against Moorosi has thrust it and hearing little of meaningful progress from the mountain, Prime Minister Gordon Sprigg is taking a more active role in trying to end the war. He has asked Major F. W. Nixon, a British military officer and an engineer, and Colonel Jarvis, the commandant-general of colonial troops, to travel to the mountain.

Between them, and the anticipated report from the committee on Basutoland hostilities, Sprigg hopes they will devise some way to end Moorosi's rebellion.

The committee inquiring into the hostilities in Basutoland is meeting for its 14th day. On most days members have discussed the war among themselves and heard no evidence. But today Emile Rolland, acting resident magistrate in Maseru for 13 months and now inspector of schools in Basutoland, is testifying.

Merriman: "Do you think Moorosi's disaffection will spread?"

"As long as the question of disarmament is present in the minds of the Basotho, there is every chance of the disaffection eventually spreading."

Committee member John Irvine asks, "Can you suggest anything that would be likely to lead to a conclusion of our difficulties there with Moorosi? You are aware he has already made some overtures for peace?"

"I do not think it would be consistent with our prestige to accept anything but an unconditional surrender. His proposal is conditional surrender, that he is to be allowed to locate himself in any village that may be selected and that he should receive no punishment. If that were done, however, it would injure our prestige. The only thing that can be done is to invest the mountain, if it can be invested. I believe it never has been properly invested. The rebels have always been able to run in supplies at night, and they are doing so still and will continue to do so until we build a wall around the mountain."

"You think there is nothing for it but to fight it out to the end until Moorosi surrenders?"

"Yes, I do not see anything else."

Transkei, Thursday, September 4, 1879

"Look at what is happening in Basutoland," Hamilton Hope tells Mhlonthlo, the paramount chief of the Mpondomise, in whose territory he serves as magistrate. "Chief Moorosi has opposed colonial rule and now he is finding himself at war with the government. He has had some victories, but this is a war he cannot win. The government will eventually conquer him and destroy Moorosi and his people.

"This is what happens when native people will not listen to the government, when they are not obedient and they try to say they, and not the magistrate, are in control of the people.

"The chief wouldn't listen to me. I warned him many times he would pay a high price for not accepting government rule over his people. Now he's paying that price.

"I hope you take this as a lesson for you and your people. Listen to me, accept that the government comes first and you come second and you will enjoy peace."

Mhlonthlo is unimpressed with Hope's thinking, but will cooperate. For now.

Cape Town — Friday, September 5, 1879

The committee inquiring into the hostilities in Basutoland is calling it quits. After meeting 16 times, poring over masses of paperwork, obtaining evidence from a few people and failing to hear evidence from Griffith or Austen, it has been unable to reach any conclusions on the causes of the war or what can be done to solve it. The legislative session is drawing to a close, they have other work to do, and they are anxious to return to their constituencies.

So today members present their final statement to the government.

"Owing to the late period of the session and the press of legislative work, as well as the large mass of correspondence bearing on the subject, which is, until printed, in a very inconvenient form for reference, the committee do not feel themselves in a position to submit a report of a nature suitable to the importance of the subject."

They add that a searching inquiry should be instituted and presented to Parliament at its session next year.

After spending almost 100 hours deliberating and listening to evidence, the members dissolve their committee. They have nothing to add to the debate.

Quthing — Monday, September 8, 1879

Major F. W. Nixon, armed with a budget of £200 and accompanied by two royal engineers and eight mining experts, arrives at the mountain today to meet with Brabant, who returned last night from a patrol into the surrounding hills.

"I have been sent here by the prime minister," Nixon tells Brabant, "to devise a military strategy in which Moorosi's Mountain fortress can be taken, probably using mining methods."

Brabant is skeptical. He is aware that Nixon served in the Ngqika-Gcaleka war as an officer in the most professionally trained corps in the British Army, but he is not in the mood for far-fetched suggestions.

"I have heard some unusual ideas about how this war should be waged," Brabant tells Nixon. "Apparently some planner offered to blow up the mountain so that its mighty mass should fall into the gorge at the junction of the Quthing and Orange rivers.

"The planner claims that this colossal scheme has the great recommendation of utility, for the waters of the rivers thus dammed up would form a mighty reservoir from which the neighboring country could be well irrigated."

"I have heard of that plan," Nixon says. "I agree that it is somewhat outrageous, but I will look at a less spectacular way in which we can blow up at least part of the mountain."

Accompanied by Brabant, Nixon examines the fortress from all angles, occasionally using an opera glass. He takes notes. He talks with men in the camp, learning of slack discipline, inadequate training and low morale among the volunteers. He hears how Moorosi has successfully supplemented his grain and cattle on the mountain with regular forays that take the colonial troops by surprise.

He is told, too, that the attacks on the stone walls were ineffective because the men were not prepared to risk their lives in running in a group across the open space between the ridge and the walls.

An attack by a strong force of determined men, he is told, would result in loss of life, but the Baphuthi firepower would be inadequate to restrain all of them. The question, his informers add, is whether the government is prepared to order such an attack or wants to try some other method.

Nixon learns, too, of the abortive attempt by Scott to hurl cannon balls behind the stone walls and of the dynamite attacks by Brabant on some of the occupied caves he encountered on his patrols.

He instructs the mining experts to look at the feasibility of using dynamite to dig a tunnel under the mountain and gain access to the walls in that way.

By evening, the engineers have reached several conclusions. They meet with Nixon. "We could hew a gallery from the cave at the northwestern base of the mountain in such a direction as to place a mine under the first scance," one of the mining engineers says. "The resulting blast would blow a huge hole in the wall."

"I agree," responds Nixon. "That blast would certainly succeed in driving off the defenders and our men could scramble up the side of the mountain unchallenged and make their way over the collapsed wall. The moral effect of firing such a mine successfully would be great.

"But would it materially assist the attack?

"I would imagine that the blast would make the slope even steeper and therefore make it even harder to climb. And the difficulty of the attack would only have begun because the lines of the second and third schanzes are above. Could those be blasted away?"

"We could not get near enough to them," the miner says.

Further discussion reveals the engineers have no other suggestions.

"So what you are saying is that mining operations would not help much," Nixon says.

The men agree.

Nixon walks to Brabant's tent and summarizes his conclusions.

"Mining operations will be of no avail," he says.

"What do you think we should do then?" Brabant asks.

"My view is that the first action you should take is that the first scance should be breached by a couple of guns of moderate caliber, say 9 or 12 pounders."

"That is what we did in the last attack," Brabant responds. "The problem is that no sooner do we blast away the structure than they rebuild it."

"I understand you had some success last time when you consistently blasted away at the walls for many hours," Nixon counters.

"Yes, that is true, but —"

"The pounding by the guns should be followed by a force of 500 men," Nixon continues. "They could be positioned under the ridge and near the cave before advancing on the wall in a determined attack.

"This might lead to the certain sacrifice of perhaps a tenth of their number.

"For such an attack well disciplined men, accustomed to act together and ready to follow where they are led are absolutely necessary, for the advance from each scance in succession would have to be made under fire up a steep ascent."

"That is your conclusion?" Brabant asks. "Essentially we throw 500 men at the walls, assume that 50 will be killed and thereby take the mountain?"

"It is. But I must add that your officers agree that the colonial forces, as at present organized and disciplined, are not to be depended on for such an attack."

Quthing — Thursday, September 11, 1879

Commandant-General Jarvis arrives on horseback after a 10-day ride from King William's Town. Prompted by Sprigg and his desire to win the war as soon as possible, he is here to discuss strategy with Brabant.

He is scouting around the area when Sergeant Corfield approaches him, believing that he is speaking with Jarvis's servant.

"The men are miserable," he tells Jarvis. "They want an end to this ridiculous war and they want to go home. Soon."

Aware the soldier does not realize he is talking with the commander of the colony's armed forces, Jarvis listens as Corfield outlines his complaints, the lack of discipline in the camp, and the general malaise.

It is a sobering introduction for Jarvis and, with morale this low, makes him reconsider whether Brabant is indeed the best person to be managing the war.

Quthing — Friday, September 12, 1879

For the first time, Whitehead has been assigned night picket duty. It is a pleasant change; not only will it relieve the boredom, but it will give him an insight into life on the saddle at night.

He reports for duty and is told the officer in charge has not yet arrived. "I'm not really sure when he arrives," a soldier says, "as I am often asleep by that time."

"Asleep? Aren't you supposed to be keeping watch?"

"We take turns to keep watch. Nothing much ever happens during the night, especially when it's this dark."

Whitehead soon determines that none of the men has his rifle loaded.

"What would happen if the Baphuthi were to suddenly surprise you?" he asks. The men grunt in reply, but Whitehead cannot make out what it is they are saying.

Soon most lie down behind the sandbags that form the first line of defense and fall asleep, leaving two men to keep a lookout.

Whitehead decides he will remain on guard behind the breastworks, keep his rifle loaded and not succumb to the malaise of the others. Ahead he can see, reflected against the lower stone walls, the flickering light of a Baphuthi fire.

Lemena is hungry. He has been sitting around the fire, his gun at his side, for many hours, but has not received the meal that he was promised.

"I am going to get the food myself," he says. As he climbs the path to the summit, he pulls his blanket around him to ward off the evening chill. At the mountain summit, he enters his hut and searches for food.

The noise awakens Moorosi.

"Why have you left your post?" he asks.

"I am hungry. No one brought me my meal."

"Do not worry about food. You can eat later. Get back to your post. What if the government men attack us? Is your stomach more important than our lives?"

Lemena turns and heads down the path to the stone walls.

"I will shoot you if you do this again," Moorosi shouts after him.

"I have enemies everywhere," Lemena grumbles, throwing up his hands in the air. "The whites want to shoot me. The Mfengu fighting with the government want to shoot me. And now my own king wants to shoot me."

About an hour after Whitehead takes up his picket position, a man arrives who identifies himself as the officer in charge, a corporal named Ben Masoopie. Whitehead soon warms to the man's friendly spirit and sense of humor.

"Are you trying to see men over there?" Masoopie asks.

"Yes, but all I can see are the reflection of the fires."

The two peer across the shadowy plateau, their eyes concentrating on the walls and the fires behind them.

"I think I see something moving there," Masoopie says, pointing to the bottom of the first stone wall.

"Yes, yes. I see three Baphuthi men moving toward us!"

He grabs his rifle, takes aim and fires. Whitehead fires as well. Although he cannot see any movement, he assumes that Masoopie's vision is better than his.

Bright sparks indicate returning gunfire emanating from the stone walls.

A still hungry Lemena arrives back at his post in time to hear a rapid succession of fire emanate from the saddle. He hunkers down behind the stone wall.

"What are they firing at?" he asks.

"We're not sure," a man responds. "But we are firing back."

"They're firing at nothing," laughs Lemena. "The darkness makes the white men's eyes work backwards. When we send men down to fight them, they don't see them. But when we are not sending men to fight them, then they see them."

As the Baphuthi bullets whistle toward them, the men on picket duty suddenly spring awake. "Stand to your arms," Masoopie shouts, standing straight up, with his bayonet in one hand and folding his arms. His wide hat, blue serge jacket, leggings and pose remind Whitehead of Napoleon.

The men, woken from their sleep, raise their rifles and fire toward the stone walls.

The Baphuthi hold their fire, preferring to save their ammunition.

After a while the pickets stop firing and the mountain quiet returns. Soon, most of the men wrap themselves in their blankets and fall asleep.

"At least that gave them something to do," says Masoopie.

In the early hours of the morning, before dawn, the men on picket duty awaken and, before they leave, fire off a volley of shots toward the mountain — largely, Whitehead gathers, to prove that they have done something during the night.

"Stop your firing, you are keeping us awake," Moorosi shouts across in English at the men on picket duty.

"Won't you let a man sleep? Do you hate me because I am old and ugly? If you don't stop firing, I'll come down and spear you."

"You'll go back quicker than you left, you old scoundrel," one of the men shouts, not appreciating the humor in the king's remarks.

The men on picket duty fire off another round.

Lemena joins in the conversation. "Now you have woken me up, I am going to have something to eat," he says, his laughter wafting across the plateau.

The Baphuthi retain their vigilance, fearful that the colonial soldiers could launch another attack at any time.

But, his attempt at a settlement having failed, Moorosi feels the need to do more than wait for another assault on his fortress. He must break the stalemate and go on the attack.

He sits down with his leading advisers. "We must do something," he says. "We cannot sit here and wait for them to attack us again. And all the time they are building up their forces. It is time for us to go on the attack ourselves."

Assisted by his advisers, the king devises a radical plan of action aimed at swinging the war in his favor.

Masitise, Sunday September 14, 1879

The number of refugees gathered around the Masitise mission station grows as the war drags on. Some have come because they are unwilling to fight whereas others have been brought here after being wounded. All find a place to stay.

The mission station is a neutral site that neither side would dare attack. So Ellenberger does not question whether the wounded and asylum seekers are anti-government, pro-government or innocent Baphuthi caught up in the battle. Here he protects them, provides for them, and prays for them.

Among those who have gathered today in the crowded church is a young Baphuthi man whose right lung was pierced by a bullet. For seven weeks, Ellenberger tended to the wound and saved the man's life.

Sitting alongside him is a 5-year-old grandson of Moorosi whose left humerus was shattered by a bullet. The missionary extracted six pieces of bone from the wound, dressed it regularly and bandaged the arm in such a way that the boy recovered its use. Ellenberger closed the wound, now quite clean, by grafting skin on it.

The result has been higher attendance at church services and a growing interest in Ellenberger's message.

"I am delighted to tell you that a revival has broken out here at Masitise," he tells the congregation in today's service. "You have come here to seek peace from war and you have found the Prince of Peace. In the past few weeks we have added 90 new converts. I am pleased that, in this painful chapter in our history, we have found the One who would have us never fight any more wars, the One who would have the whole world be at peace with one another, as we are in Masitise today."

Quthing — Tuesday, September 16, 1879

The men have been asleep for less than an hour when they are awakened by fire from the direction of the saddle.

"It is just the pickets proving they're there before they sleep," laughs Granville, who is sharing a tent with Corfield. "It sounds more serious than that," Corfield replies, jumping out of his bed and leaving the tent.

Granville stays to tie his laces and, by the time he leaves the tent, cannot see in the inky darkness where Corfield has gone, but realizes that the exchange of fire between the saddle and the mountain is more intense than usual. He kneels behind the earthworks that guard the camp, his rifle at the ready. He can see a mass of men around the saddle but holds off firing as he is unsure in the darkness whose side they are on. The scene is one of utter confusion.

The plan devised by Moorosi and his advisers appeared to be a sound one. Relayed by a messenger to loyal Baphuthi in the surrounding countryside, it was for 180 warriors, accompanied by 20 pack horses, to leave the caves in which they were living, to travel to the base of the mountain and, from there, launch an attack on the colonial forces in the dark, taking them by surprise in the early hours of the morning. The government men could be expected to be ready for an attack from the mountain, but not from the surrounding countryside.

Once the attack began and the government soldiers were diverted, Moorosi would send his men down the mountain. Together the two forces could kill large numbers of soldiers sleeping in their tents, just as they had done in the attack on the Chiappini camp.

Late yesterday, the outlying warriors left their caves. They timed their move so that they would arrive at the mountain at night when they would camp in the dark at the bottom of the cliffs on the northern face, unseen by the colonial forces. From there, in the early hours of the morning, the plan was that they were to launch an attack on the colonial encampment.

But as they arrive in the darkness early today, creeping quietly along under a cliff, they walk into a group of Mfengu dressed in distinctive white blankets given them by the colonial forces. The Baphuthi are nonplussed. No one was supposed to be camped here; the messenger from Moorosi was clear about that.

True, no one was — until 300 Mfengu relief forces from the Cape Colony arrived yesterday and moved here under orders from Brabant.

When the Mfengu, sleeping in the open, see the Baphuthi, they open fire.

"What's going on?" yells Corfield, arriving amidst an eruption of gunfire.

"A group of Baphuthi are trying to get up the mountain," a soldier shouts. "The Mfengu have caught them . They're firing on them and so are we."

Corfield stares into the darkness, making out the forms of men on the far side of the plateau. As he readies to fire, he asks, "How do you know who is who?"

"The Mfengu are the ones in the white blankets," the soldier says. "Don't fire at them. Fire at anyone else who is black."

The shooting on all sides is less than accurate, given the darkness and that both groups are moving. Nevertheless, some of the Mfengu bullets find their target and a few of the 20,000 rounds fired randomly by the colonial troops find their quarry. Soon several Baphuthi lie dead on the mountain slopes.

But the gains are not all on the Mfengu and colonial sides.

A Baphuthi charges a Mfengu and stabs him in his arm with his spear. The Mfengu falls. The Baphuthi grabs his blanket and pulls it around him. Others follow his lead, stabbing the Mfengu, who drop their blankets in the confusion as bullets whizz around them.

The chaotic firing and stabbing continues until a bank of mist rises from the Orange River and wafts across the plateau, reducing visibility to zero. The fighting stops. The Baphuthi escape up a path to the top of the mountain.

Moorosi walks down the path to greet the arriving warriors.

They tell him seven men are dead and several wounded, but most of the men and the horses they brought with them have made it through enemy lines.

"Why are you wearing white blankets?" Moorosi asks. "Our people do not wear white blankets."

"Let me tell you," says one. "These blankets, they are bullet proof."

Quthing, Thursday September 18, 1879

After a week's stay in camp, Colonel Jarvis sets off on his return journey to King William's Town. The week has been a revealing one for the man who heads the colony's defense operations. A sergeant's unintended complaints were reinforced later when several members of the Cape Mounted Riflemen, who had been at the mountain for months and believed their terms of duty had expired, applied to him to be discharged. He had let them go.

He held talks with Brabant about the progress of the war and was briefed on Nixon's visit. He was woken early one morning as the Mfengu beat off the Baphuthi.

Pondering the findings of his trip, Jarvis has to admit that little progress to end the war is being made and morale at the camp is extremely low. He has few solutions to suggest to the prime minister beyond looking for a new commander at the mountain with a bolder plan of action.

Quthing — Friday, September 26, 1879

Spring has arrived at the mountain. The last of the snow has disappeared from the peaks and the frost has gone from the valleys. The weeks are filled with sunshine, reflected in the ripples on the river, alongside which the willow reeds are turning green with new foliage. Spring flowers add to an almost idyllic scene.

For the newly arrived volunteers from Queenstown, Cradock and Berlin life at the mountain is pleasant and at times seems like a picnic. They enjoy fishing in the river, which yields barbel and yellowfish, which gain their name from their gilded scales of pale gold, and weigh from one to 20 pounds.

But the tranquil scene is a false front. Discontent among the volunteers is growing. The contingent from the town of Stockenstroom, already soured six weeks ago, are on the brink of deserting. Saying they agreed to serve only until September 25, and that the new volunteers are able to relieve them, they want to return to their farms to plant corn. Almost 100 sign a petition urging Brabant to let them go.

Brabant, who wants to secure as tight a ring as he can around the mountain to cut off Moorosi's supply lines, asks them to stay until November 15, saying it is essential they be there to complete the war. Some reluctantly agree, but others leave.

Maseru — Wednesday, October 1, 1879

Monitoring Moorosi's war from his post in Maseru, Griffith is developing a new concern.

He is worried that the war will spread to the rest of Basutoland as a result of growing anger over disarmament.

When the policy was first mooted, the Basotho were led to believe that if they fought on the side of the government they would be allowed to keep their arms. Now it is clear from the way the measure is being implemented that the Cape authorities are determined to disarm all black people under their jurisdiction, whether they assist the government or not. Many Basotho now fear they will soon be in the same position as Moorosi.

Griffith believes that the disarmament policy is a recipe for disaster in

Basutoland and is afraid that if Moorosi's war is not concluded soon all of Basutoland will follow his example and be at war with the colony.

He will write to Sprigg to warn him how serious matters have become.

Cape Town — Monday, October 6, 1879

Griffith's warning letter and increasing pressure from Parliament convince Sprigg he needs to do even more to end the war against Moorosi. Thus far his long-distance attempts at a solution have fallen short. Brabant had no proposals beyond investing the mountain, the Committee on Basutoland Hostilities produced nothing of value, and Jarvis was unable to devise any plans for victory after his visit to the mountain.

"It is imperative that we devise a solution to end the war in Basutoland," Sprigg tells Ayliff. "You know, as I do, that we cannot allow events to continue as they are driving our colony more into debt and drifting into a wider conflict in that territory. We need to end this costly escapade."

Ayliff nods in agreement.

"As I see it, we have two issues to deal with," Sprigg continues. "The one is the ongoing war against Moorosi. The other is the resistance to disarmament among the Basotho people.

"Right now the war is our top priority. We must bring it to a conclusion. Once we have done that we can start implementing the policy of disarmament in the territory to make such rebellious acts as this by Moorosi impossible in the future. But we must deal with the war first.

"Some three months ago we were told that Moorosi was hurting and had offered to talk with us about ending the war. But he is still on his mountain, defying our best forces to come and get him.

"We have tried artillery bombardments. They have been ineffective. We have tried storming the mountain. That has failed twice. We have tried blockading the enemy's supplies and that, too, has not worked; in spite of our blockade the chief rushed more cattle on to the mountain in September.

"We need to try another method.

"You will recall that about six weeks ago we commissioned a report by the royal engineers. I have just received a copy of the report, prepared by Major F. W. Nixon. He says mining operations are of no avail and that storming the mountain with a large force is the only way to achieve victory."

"Storming the mountain did not work the first two times," says Ayliff.

"You are right," Sprigg replies. "But he is not only suggesting storming the mountain. To succeed, he says, we need men who will follow orders so much that they will be willing to give their lives if necessary.

"I have received reports, too, that the volunteers are unruly and their morale is low. Jarvis spoke of it and Colonel Brabant writes that they are questioning their agreements to serve and that many want to return home.

"So I am giving orders that the volunteers be recalled. I want to get rid of all of them. I want only the enlisted troops to do the fighting.

"In addition, we should replace Colonel Brabant — who, as you say, like Colonel Griffith, has failed to oust Moorosi from his mountain — with a new commander who will be under orders to turn the Cape Mounted Riflemen into a force that can take the mountain. I welcome suggestions as to who that new commander should be.

"I believe, too, that now also is the time for me to enter the fray, not just in giving orders, but in person. I plan to travel to the mountain in the next few weeks, observe the situation at first hand and, I hope, talk to Moorosi personally.

"I believe that a lot of the chief's inspiration to rebel came from the Zulus. If the Zulus could defeat the white men, he must have reasoned, he could do so, too.

"But now that the Zulus have been defeated, he must be having second thoughts. I'll tell him it is useless trying to defy the strength of the government.

"Should my talks for some reason fail, I will hand over charge of our troops to a new commander and instruct him to implement the Nixon plan.

"But before I visit the battlefield I will stop over in Maseru and talk to the chiefs and the people there. Bearing in mind Griffith's concerns about the people opposing disarmament, I will explain the law to them in terms they can understand and tell them disarmament is in their own best interests. I am sure that they will hand in their arms voluntarily after I talk with them."

Quthing — Wednesday, October 8, 1879

Although his plan to attack the colonial troops failed, Moorosi remains convinced he needs to take the offensive in the war. He must not be content simply to watch the white troops camped around his mountain. He must drive them off, sending them back to the Telle River and into the Cape Colony.

So it is that, since the end of September, he has called in all remaining fighting men from the cave hideouts along the rivers. Lehana is back on the mountain, ready to lead attacks when called upon by his father to do so.

"Now that the good weather has arrived, it is time for us to move," Moorosi tells Lehana and Letuka. "We must not just sit back and wait for the government to attack us again. We must go out and attack them. We must frighten them and drive them away from the mountain. Then perhaps they will be prepared to talk to us about peace.

"They have sent one of their big guns away; our men have learned through spies among the Mfengu that it has been sent away to be repaired. Soon it will return. Before that happens, we must attack them.

"Our people here on the mountain are still strong. We have cattle and grain supplies. Our ammunition supplies are plentiful.

"We must start with a big attack. We must launch it while the government soldiers are asleep."

Letuka reminds his father of the great victory they achieved in the attack on the camp at the junction of the rivers where the whites were killed in their tents.

"Let us do that again," Moorosi says. "They have set up another camp there. Although it is better guarded, we can attack it again.

"Let's go and attack it tonight, my son. You can lead the attack again, the way you did before. We must creep up to them in their tents and attack them in the way we attacked them before. That will frighten them and when we threaten more attacks they will run away from the mountain."

Letuka is eager to obey. "We will go tonight."

Quthing — Thursday, October 9, 1879

Letuka returns with his band of fighters to the mountain in the early hours of the morning. "We fired on the men at the camp where the rivers meet," he reports to Moorosi. "We could see the white tents even though it was dark.

"They fired back, but it was too dark for them to see us.

"Then suddenly, from behind us, the Mfengu came and fired on us. They were right behind us before we knew it and took us by surprise. We were forced to run away and return to the mountain."

"Very well," Moorosi says. "We must do better next time. We cannot allow the Mfengu fighters to stop us again. This is the second time they have ruined our plan.

"But perhaps we can achieve our aims without killing any soldiers. We will do so by approaching the other camps around the mountain in a strong force at night when the government's rifles are of no help to them as they cannot see us well enough to shoot at us. We will creep up on them without them even knowing we are there and show them that we are able to attack them and kill them if we want to do so. We don't have to kill any of them, just frighten them.

"When we have them afraid we will tell them they must talk to us about a settlement or else next time we will not just creep up to their tents, but also kill them before they know what is happening."

Quthing — Friday, October 10, 1879

Quietly, their bare feet making no noise on the rocky ground, 50 Baphuthi slip off the mountain at 1 a.m. . They elude the colonial pickets, who have no idea they are there, and move around the sleeping soldiers' tents. Unseen, they steal sticks of dynamite from the ammunition dump.

Quietly, they creep quietly back up the mountain, leaving only their footprints — and less dynamite — as evidence of their silent demonstration of power.

"We found their tracks this morning," Brabant tells his senior soldiers. "I am amazed they did not try to shoot at us. We can only assume that this was a practice for a larger attack, which could come any day now.

"The lesson is that these men are capable of creeping up on our tents at night without us even being aware of their presence until they are right on top of us, that they are likely to do so again, and we must be ready for them.

"So I want you all to sleep dressed in your uniforms, ready for any emergency.

"On the positive front, I am pleased to say that I am expecting the 12-pounder gun, which has been repaired in Aliwal North, to arrive here tomorrow and two mortars and plentiful supplies of food will follow in a few days."

As the Cape Mounted Riflemen wander off to their tents after Brabant's talk, they air their complaints. It is all very well, they say, for Brabant to talk about being ready and to sleep in their uniforms, but, after almost eight months at the mountain, their uniforms are a bit the worse for wear.

"No new clothes for three months now," Corfield says to Granville. "Look at us. Look at our uniforms."

He tugs at his breeches, which are torn in numerous places and into which he has sewn part of a blanket, and at his black velvet corduroy shirt, which has buttons missing and which he has sewn up where it was torn at the elbows.

"Our boots are damaged from continually walking over the stones and rough ground. I have started wearing my socks over my boots to protect my feet."

He pushes his foot forward to display his socks covering his boots. The others laugh. "Me, too," says one, pushing his foot forward.

"Have any of you had bad dreams?" asks Corfield. "I had one in which I dreamed I came face-to-face with Moorosi and I was fighting with him."

"Who won?" asks Granville.

"It was a tie. I screamed at him and woke myself up."

"I also had a dream about confronting the chief," offers John Brown of No. 4 Troop. "I dreamed I saw Moorosi, and he objected to be captured, so I laid forcible hands on him. Then I was awoken by Booty, who shares my tent, who was returning my blows with vigor."

The men laugh. "Did Booty say anything to you about it?" asks one.

"Yes. He objected to my having a loaded carbine alongside me at night."

Maseru — Thursday, October 16, 1879

The Basotho start arriving early in the morning, assembling on a gently sloping hill above the colonial government headquarters in Maseru, where they have been told the leader of the Cape Colony will address them at the annual pitso. By 10 a.m. some 8,000 have assembled. Many carry brightly-colored umbrellas to shield them from the summer sun. Others sit or stand alongside their horses.

"This body of cavalry is almost as numerous as that which Marlborough had at Blenheim," Sprigg tells Griffith as he walks to the spot at which he is to speak.

After a missionary, the Rev. A. Mabille, says a prayer, Griffith introduces Sprigg, telling them he has traveled all the way from Cape Town to tell them of his plans for the future of the Basotho people.

Mojela reads a translation of a message from Letsie, who, clearly believing this meeting is important enough for him to attend, is seated in front of his people. The message diplomatically praises the government and, harking back to the reason the British took over the running of Basutoland in the first place, talks of the "peaceful protection of Her Majesty."

Sprigg steps forward. A ripple of laughter passes through the audience. Noticeably shorter than Griffith, Sprigg wears a tweed suit and a straw hat. Draped around the hat is a light scarf that falls behind his head as a cover from the sun. To the Basotho he looks awkward and out of place. Is this truly the leader of the Cape Colony? How quaint he is.

But soon Sprigg's words turn the Basotho from amusement to anger.

After saying the government is pleased that the Basotho "have taken no part with the rebel Chief Moorosi," Sprigg tells them that the hut tax will be doubled next year. Instead of paying 10 shillings, they will now pay one pound.

Not a way to win over your audience. Nor does it help when Sprigg suggests that "the proposals that the government is making are not for its own advantage, but simply for the advantage of the people here, and that every penny that is raised by taxation amongst you will be spent for your own good and your own advantage." Already, the Basotho people are convinced that a greater proportion of the hut tax leaves Basutoland for use by the government elsewhere — including its use in the war against Moorosi. They simply do not believe what Sprigg is saying.

But the remarks that Sprigg makes next really get his audience fired up.

The government has decided that the Basotho people need to surrender their arms, he tells them.

"This is not a harsh, or unjust, or unkind measure on the part of the government; it is done simply for the good of the people themselves.

"I would ask you, the Basothos, what use you have for guns in this country? Can you in ordinary times do any good with them? I feel sure that you will admit that you cannot do any good in ordinary times; but then I would ask you, can you do any harm with the guns, not only to the white man but to yourselves?

"I need only point you to what is going on in Moorosi's district and at his mountain; and I would ask you now whether you do not think it would have been a good thing if all Moorosi's people had been disarmed a year ago?

"It is the belief of the government that if Moorosi and his people had not possessed guns they would never have gone into rebellion; but this is perfectly certain that, having gone into rebellion, if they had possessed no guns they could not have held the mountain against our forces for half an hour.

"The government feels sure that you are thoroughly as loyal and faithful to it and that it is your intention to be faithful in the future, as you have been in the past. But the government knows that there have been tribes thoroughly as loyal and faithful to the government as you are this day, who have yet gone into rebellion, when they had at one time no intention of fighting against the government.

"The government feels that, like the rest of the natives in South Africa, you possess very much the character of children, and the government knows that children cannot at all times trust even themselves; that they are led away by excitement, and that when the war fever is abroad in the land, the natives often become infected by it, and without the slightest intention of going into rebellion they are drawn into it, and then they use these guns, which they had no intention of using, for the purpose of fighting against the government and their fellow creatures."

The looks on the faces of his audience should warn Sprigg that his words are not being well received. Their silence is a warning that indignation is building. But he continues, speaking of establishing a small Basotho militia force that would be armed and would put down any disturbances.

"The government wants you to become like the white man, and not to regard it as a proof of manhood that you possess guns. If you go into the larger towns of the colony, or across the sea to England, you will find that few white men have guns, but a small portion of the population only is armed for the defense of the country and that is what is in the mind of the government as being suitable for Basutoland, that such a force should be raised here under European officers and under the direction of the government and the government would be able to protect the Basothos against any attacks from within or without, and then there would be no occasion for the people generally to carry arms."

Sprigg tells the Basotho that the government believes they will be loyal to the queen and are too wise to fight as the Gcaleka, Ngqika and Cetshwayo did.

"War is the greatest curse and horror that can inflict a people," he says, "and I think that it would reflect great discredit upon you, the Basotho nation, and upon the government if by any steps which should be taken upon one side or the other a war should result in this beautiful country.

"I ask you to believe that the government knows better than yourselves what is good for you, and when the order is given by the government that the guns shall be surrendered, I ask you to render cheerful obedience to that order, believing that it will work for your ultimate good and tend to your prosperity as a people."

After warning the men about the dangers of brandy and declaring that the government will do all it can to prevent its introduction in Basutoland, Sprigg ends with an invitation to the people to speak out and not be quiet.

Sprigg sits.

Letsie and the senior chiefs are silent. For them, it is expedient not to speak — by a custom all Basotho understand, they will leave the sentiments to be expressed by the junior chiefs and they will speak later.

Mabusetsa: "With regard to the hut tax all I have got to say is that it is a difficult order to obey. Most of the people will be too poor to pay it; you might order us to pay two or three pounds instead of one pound, but we still would not have the money to pay it."

Tsita Mofoka: "We have never hesitated to follow the government. We were quite prepared to fight against Moorosi in case he should point his guns at the queen. We are dogs and we do whatever we are ordered to do. Now we hear our guns are to be taken away. I am only sorry that I am black today; I think that being black is a very great misfortune. The reason I say it is a misfortune is that although you may be following the government ever so faithfully, it turns round upon you and says, you do not belong to me, just because you have a black skin."

Tsekelo Moshoeshoe, a brother of Letsie: "We are to be disarmed, not because we have done any evil, but just because our color is black.

"To take away our arms would be to tear our hearts from inside our bosoms. Perhaps it is true as Mr. Upington said in Parliament we are the natural enemies of the white man because we are black."

With the junior chiefs having had their say, the responsibility moves up the line to Letsie's son Lerothodi: "This matter of the hut tax is a very serious one to some of us poor Basotho. I am a poor man, and I have now ten wives; that will make ten pounds that I have to pay.

"The ten-shilling hut tax has already hurt Moorosi, who is a son of Moshoeshoe. What is the one-pound hut tax going to do to us? Are we going to rebel like Moorosi?

"We have guns now and we never have done any harm with them. We have used them for good. When the government called on us to use our weapons to keep order in our country, we have always obeyed.

"When Mr. Griffith asked me to assemble my people to wage war for the government, we agreed to do so. In just the past few months, I led two thousand of my men in the war against King Moorosi. We drove him and the Baphuthi people back to their mountain stronghold. We helped in the siege against his mountain.

"You were pleased to use us then. Now you want to take away our weapons so we can never use them again in the service of the government. How do you expect us to keep law and order in this country if we are turned into women by being deprived of our arms?"

Sprigg waits for the interpreter to complete the translation, then replies, "I want to thank you, chief, for your help against Moorosi. He is acting like a naughty child and needs to be taught a lesson. We will defeat him and we will take away his weapons when we have defeated him so he cannot defy us again.

"But we think it is better for you that you do not have weapons in the future. Although you might have used them for the government, you might also use them in the wrong way and we cannot trust you not to use them badly. We think it is for your own good that you give them up. In that way you will live better lives and we will all live in peace."

Lerothodi is not satisfied with the answer.

"No, you who call yourself the Leader of the Whites, you want to make us powerless by taking away our guns. Then when you have done that you want to make slaves of us, our wives and our children. We have always obeyed the government up to now. But if you tell us to surrender our arms we will not obey that law."

Letsie, the paramount chief, finally speaks. Unwilling to be as explicit as the junior chiefs or to address Sprigg directly, he uses an idiom to condemn the disarmament law. "The government wants to cut off our claws. The women cut off the nails of a little baby when they grow too long and it scratches at its face, and I want you, Colonel Griffith, to ask whether we scratch out our own eyes, or whether we scratch out the eyes of the government with these nails of ours?"

Griffith announces that the principal chiefs will meet with Sprigg tomorrow in a smaller meeting in the Maseru schoolroom to continue the discussion.

Maseru — Wednesday, October 17, 1879

Sprigg addresses the group of chiefs, not all of whom are here. Letsie has sent a message that he is too ill to attend, as have his brothers Molapo and Masupha.

"No speaker yesterday appeared to understand the reasons that influenced the government in shaping the policy it proposes to carry out," the prime minister says.

"Tsekelo said the Basotho people were treated in this way, which he seems to regard as harsh, because they are black. It is not because you are black, but because you are children. You call the government your father and it is as your father that I speak to you today. Some of you think it makes a man of you to have a gun. The government, your father, does not think so. The past history of the native races has shown that it makes wild beasts of them."

Sofonia rises to "express clearly our misgivings about the disarmament act," adding that "the real fault the government has found with us is our color. A black man is not accorded equal rights with a white man. We have been told all the money collected in Basutoland would be for Basotho, but it is taken away and men from the colony are paid with it without our being consulted. I say it is because of our color."

Adds George Moshoeshoe, "I suddenly forgot my color, which God gave me, and I thought, how is it possible that we can get into parliament, being black? And I quickly answered my own heart and said, 'Is it thought that we are foolish and stupid, and would not be able to choose men fit to represent us?' If we are British subjects, does the queen possess us as men or cattle?

"We are like a black pot and I wish to see the queen's government take the black pot and wash it white. I am not speaking for myself, but for these poor people crying for their guns who believe it is good for them to keep them."

Tsekelo rises and says, "If the government thinks that by taking away a few rotten guns it will prevent war, I don't agree with it. The real remedy is to take away all the causes of dissatisfaction that are likely to produce war and to satisfy all grievances. Quarrels, not the possession of guns, are the real causes of war."

Others offer similar sentiments to that of Seeta, who says, "We love our guns and we beseech to be allowed to keep them. I repeat, I beseech you, I beseech you."

Sprigg replies to Tsekelo that the possession of guns, not quarrels, caused the Zulu and the Gcaleka to rise up against the government.

He shows no signs of being influenced by the comments. He concludes, "So there may be no mistake on the subject, let me say that the policy of disarmament is still the policy of the government. You may rest assured that the government will stand firmly by that policy. We think that the European race is endowed by the Almighty with superior intelligence; we know at least that we have had the blessings and advantages of a superior education, and we feel that that casts upon us a greater responsibility to use the advantages which we possess in raising those people who have been placed by nature in humbler circumstances."

Anger over Sprigg's remarks spreads quickly among the Basotho. And the rebellion by Moorosi is being seen in a new light.

Quthing — Friday, October 19, 1879

The test set by Moorosi early today is for a band of Baphuthi to see whether they can evade the Queenstown and Mfengu pickets on the Quthing River side of the mountain. They climb down the hidden path on the southeastern side of the mountain, unnoticed by the pickets, and begin to walk around the mountain.

But minutes later, shots are fired their way. They return and report to Moorosi that it seems that the pickets are becoming more vigilant, but an attack on the men sleeping in the tents is still feasible.

"I have shown them we can attack them and cause many to die if we want to do so," Moorosi tells his advisers. "Now I must talk to them again about a settlement of this war. Perhaps they will listen to me this time."

Quthing — Monday, October 20, 1879

Brabant takes comfort in knowing that, although the Baphuthi have made sorties into their ranks, they have not yet launched their anticipated all-out attack on the headquarters camp. He is determined to be patient and put on as strong a face as he can, particularly as Sprigg is due to arrive soon.

"I need hardly remind you that the last thing we need is a successful attack by Moorosi on our forces while he is here," he says. "They are increasing their incursions into our camps, but we are becoming better prepared for them.

"Last night several of the enemy tried to pass our lines and were fired at. I would like to remind you — "

Brabant is interrupted by shouts from sentries closer to the mountain.

"Moorosi has put up a white flag on the lower scance," a man yells.

"We have seen the flag before," says Brabant. "But we will send an interpreter up there immediately to find out what it is he wants."

XVI

Quthing — Tuesday, October 21, 1879

Brabant prepares to send a translator to find out why Moorosi has put out another white flag. But he is preempted by the Baphuthi themselves, who send two men with the flag across the plateau to the headquarters camp. In the front, carrying the flag, is a short man dressed in a red nightcap and a white blanket, likely taken from the Mfengu in the recent clash. Behind him strides a tall man who identifies himself as the youngest son of Moorosi.

Through an interpreter, they say they have shown great restraint in not attacking the colonial forces, even though they have demonstrated their ability to infiltrate their ranks. But, they say, Moorosi would like Brabant to talk with him personally about peace.

After much parleying, Brabant goes up to the first stone wall.

"I would like to talk to you again about reaching a peace accord with you," Moorosi tells Brabant, with Tainton once again interpreting. "But I am afraid of you killing me and my people if we do so. I want an assurance that we will be able to live in peace on our land if we do agree to a peace treaty."

"I have already made it clear to you that we require nothing but your unconditional surrender," Brabant replies. "But the prime minister, the man who runs the government in Cape Town, will be here soon. He might agree to talk with you."

Moorosi agrees to wait until Sprigg arrives.

Quthing — Friday, October 24, 1879

The troops in the camps around Moorosi's Mountain have never been as organized and as obedient as today. Their sudden devotion to duty springs from one source. The prime minister is here, having arrived yesterday in an eight-horse omnibus after a journey from Maseru, accompanied by Griffith, Austen and Barkly.

With Sprigg, too, is 38-year-old Colonel Zachary Stanley Bayly, appointed earlier this year as commander of a unit of the Cape Mounted Riflemen. He is a rising star in the new defence department set up at Frere's prodding last year. Although a newcomer to the military and better known as the owner of the Pig and Whistle tavern in Kimberley, Bayly was in charge of a unit of men who repulsed a Gcaleka attack at Holland's Shop during the Ninth Frontier War two years ago. He also commanded a victorious battle at Umzintzani in Natal Colony.

Sprigg's avowed purpose in visiting the battlefield is to see the scene of operations for himself, hold talks with Brabant, other senior officers, and, if it can be arranged, Moorosi. While he is here he will appoint Bayly as the new commander of the colonial troops, in place of Brabant.

The troops believe their future at the mountain will be determined by these talks, which could lead to either a peace treaty or a resumption of hostilities.

Sprigg asks Brabant about the feasibility of another assault.

"I do not think it's advisable," Brabant replies. "My men are disheartened and very weak in numbers. The volunteer burghers are useless for an assault."

"You have no special plan to oust Moorosi?"

"Not right now. The only suggestion anyone has come up with is to storm the mountain with hundreds of men who are willing to die if necessary. That is essentially Nixon's plan. But even if I am given the additional men willing to undertake the task, I do not think I would be justified in risking a certain loss of life and possible failure for my own glorification."

"How would you feel if I replaced you with Colonel Bayly, whom I have asked to join me here?"

"I think that, if he can get his regiment together and bring it here with him, he will have a much better chance of success," Brabant replies.

"Very well, that is settled then. Colonel Bayly will take over the command of the troops. But before he does, I would like you to arrange a meeting for me with Moorosi, similar to the one you told me you held with him earlier. He is expecting me to talk with him, is he not?"

"Indeed, he is, Mr. Prime Minister."

"I am confident he will listen to reason, as the Basotho people did when I addressed them recently in Maseru, and that he will surrender. Then we can settle this war without having to call on Colonel Bayly."

Brabant dispatches a messenger to take a white flag to the mountain and tell Moorosi that the prime minister would like to talk with him.

About 30 minutes later, the two men who earlier brought Moorosi's white flag from the mountain arrive. The king, they say, wants Sprigg to meet with him on the mountain.

"No. It is better if the chief comes down from the mountain and meets with the prime minister here," Brabant says.

The men return to the mountain, confer with Moorosi, and march back across the plateau once more.

"King Moorosi says that he is a dog and the prime minister is a lion and the dog objects to talking with the lion in the lion's territory," the man who identifies himself as Moorosi's son reports.

Sprigg and Brabant assure the men that Moorosi will be safe if he comes down from the mountain to talk to them. The messengers return to the mountain, but return with the same message: The prime minister must come to the mountain, this time adding that old age is also a factor in Moorosi's plea.

"Very well," Sprigg says. "I will go to the mountain."

A look of concern flashes across Brabant's face. "With all respect, sir, you are putting yourself in the path of danger," he says. "You must understand that these men are ruthless. They are masters of deceit and trickery. You would be risking your life by going on to the mountain. I can give you some protection, but the mountain is filled with armed men ready to shoot at a moment's notice.

"Once up there you will be absolutely in his power. He can murder your whole party without any fear of immediate retaliation."

"But did you not go up to the mountain to talk with him?" asks Sprigg.

"Yes, sir, but I am paid to take such risks. It is part of my duty to run such risks. It cannot reasonably be said to be part of your duty."

"Thank you for your concern, colonel," Sprigg replies. "But I will go to the mountain. Please arrange for me to meet with Moorosi tomorrow morning."

Quthing — Saturday, October 25, 1879

In all his years of leading men in battle, Brabant never has been this anxious. As he walks alongside Sprigg across the plateau to the mountain, he half expects a shot to ring out and to hit one of them. Accompanied by Colonel Bayly, Captain O'Connor, two senior officers and a translator, they comprise a small group and make easy targets; as part of the agreement, Moorosi has stipulated that if any other government men should go beyond the saddle "they will be shot like dogs."

Brabant does not breathe any more easily as they walk along a path that leads behind the first stone wall to the point where the white flag was first raised. This is the appointed place at which Sprigg is to talk with Moorosi. And here, Brabant shudders to think, they could be attacked and brutally murdered and no one could help them.

The meeting place is set between a rock, the point where the first and second stone-wall tiers meet at an angle and the mountainside. Here, Moorosi, dressed in his cloak and hat and accompanied by 15 of his senior advisers, takes a seat on a box. Sprigg, Brabant and Bayly sit on chairs that have been carried for them by the senior officers. Moorosi's son Letuka, an adviser to Moorosi named Qhamane, and two other men sit on rocks opposite them.

None of the men on either side is armed. Moorosi has learned how sensitive the white men can be to the carrying of arms and he wants to make it clear that he is sincere about discussing peace. He is pleased to see that Sprigg, for his part, instructed none of his group to bear weapons.

After an exchange of pleasantries, Sprigg, through an interpreter, tells Moorosi that he might not be aware yet, but the Zulus have been conquered.

"They have been completely suppressed," he says. "Cetshwayo has been captured and he is in jail in Cape Town. I saw him there before I came here."

Moorosi shows no reaction. He already knows.

"Also, your own Basotho people are against you. They have been assisting the colonial forces and there are even some Basotho left in the colonial camp where they are ready to fight against you."

Again, Moorosi is little moved. He knows how much support he has received from the Basotho people and how few are against him. Only a few weeks ago his people were able to supplement their supplies, including more ammunition, with the help of Basotho. Moorosi also knows the few Basotho left in the colonial camp are not eager to fight him.

"You cannot hold out much longer, chief," Sprigg continues. "You are isolated, alone and cannot summon help from anywhere. We will continue to surround this mountain and make it impossible for you to obtain food, water or wood."

Moorosi knows he is isolated, but not as isolated as Sprigg thinks he is. He also is confident that his people are better armed — and better marksmen — than the Zulus. He has a mountain fortress that the Zulus did not have. He has held out for six months and can hold out much longer. In addition, he has the means to win this war. Already, he has shown the government how easy it would be to attack the soldiers at night.

"So now I am giving you the opportunity to surrender to my government and to that of Letsie, your king," Sprigg adds.

"I am interested in hearing how we are to surrender," Moorosi replies. "But I must ask you why you refer to me surrendering to Chief Letsie. I am surprised you say that he is my king because I am the king of the Baphuthi, whereas Letsie, he is the king of the Basotho."

Sprigg ignores Moorosi's assertion.

"We want to offer you the opportunity to surrender. You must not take false hope in the attack you made on May 29th when your people ruthlessly killed 21 of our government's soldiers. That attack is not going to help you win this war."

Moorosi is angered at Sprigg's attitude.

"I did not ask for this war," he says. "It is you who have sent men here to kill me and my people. We attacked the men in the tents at the meeting of the rivers because you attacked us in our caves. We could have attacked many more of your soldiers in their tents, but we didn't do so.

"If you will take your soldiers away everything will be peaceful again. You said we were going to discuss peace, so please tell me why you are sitting here and telling me these things about me killing your people. You sent men here to kill my people; I am only defending my people."

"I am saying that if you and your people continue to kill our soldiers by hiding on the mountain, we shall send in additional soldiers and punish you. There is no way that you can avoid dying a painful death."

"I kill your soldiers only because they are attacking me," Moorosi reiterates. "Now I am asking you to give me your opinion on how I should surrender. I am asking you how we can go back to having peace in my country. But you are not talking to me as a leader. You must remember that I am a king, too, just as you are. The way you are talking is not the way to talk to a person who might conquer you. You are talking to me like a child not as a leader equal to you."

"You are not a leader equal to me," Sprigg responds, sitting straight up as his anger rises. "I am the Prime Minister of the Cape Colony and no chief is equal to me.

"You ask how you should surrender. I will tell you. You should surrender to me and the government will do whatever it wants to do to you. That is what surrender means. Give in now and you will no longer be subject to bombardment from our guns, you will no longer have to suffer here on the mountain, trying to obtain enough food to keep you alive.

"Surrender comes with a price. You cannot surrender and expect the government to allow you to go free and continue your rebellious ways. You have done wrong and must hand yourself over completely to the government or else face the consequences. That is what surrender means. It means you give up and we declare victory."

"I will never surrender to you on those terms," Moorosi says. "I will fight you and I will defeat you."

The two men debate for three hours. But they make no headway.

The talks stall.

Finally, Sprigg says, "I will give you one more chance, Moorosi. Will you offer your complete surrender?"

Moorosi is adamant. "Not if it is on your terms. It is no good us talking any longer. You do not want to discuss a way in which we can live peacefully together. You want me to hand myself over to you like a slave."

Moorosi stands. "I am leaving now. We will continue to defend ourselves against the people you sent here to kill us. We will do so until you realize you cannot defeat us. The people you sent to kill us will themselves be killed. Those who do not die will be so afraid that they will run away, like a dog with his tail between his legs."

Sprigg also stands. "I am warning you, Moorosi. You are choosing death. What you choose is what you will get. And it will not be long before you get it. I am appointing Captain Bayly here to be in charge of our soldiers. The day he starts to attack you it will be the end of you, your arrogance and your tiny nation. Your necks will be broken on this mountain. Even though you think you are invincible, we will conquer you."

"I will face the consequences," Moorosi replies as he starts to walk away. "I will rather die on this mountain than surrender to you on your terms."

Moorosi turns and makes his way back up the mountain.

"I will give you one more chance," Sprigg says as the Baphuthi leader walks off.

Moorosi stops and turns to face him.

"I will give you and your people until nightfall to surrender unconditionally. Every man who comes down from the mountain before the sun sets tonight will be regarded as one who has surrendered."

Sprigg leads his contingent down the mountain path to the camps below. Moorosi leads his group to the mountain top.

Each leader returns to his people to tell them the result.

The sun sets with no Baphuthi coming down from the mountain. The talks are over. The war goes on.

Quthing — Sunday, October 26, 1879

At 11 a.m., as Bayly formally takes over command of the troops from Brabant, the soldiers turn out to see a display of colonial bravado aimed at sending a message to Moorosi. A shell fired from the 12-pounder incredibly falls right into the spot where the parley was held yesterday. Three other shots are fired. They are less accurate, but succeed in hitting the stone walls near the meeting spot.

Quthing — Tuesday, October 28, 1879

Sprigg hands Bayly a copy of Nixon's report and points out the main suggestion — that a body of well disciplined and well trained men make the assault on the mountain.

Bayly agrees. "With your permission, I would like the three yeomanry regiments to leave when Brabant leaves. Also, let the burghers go home. I have seen enough of them in the short time I have been here. We have no need for those untrained complaining volunteers who scare at the sight of a sheep.

"And most of the Basotho who are still left here can leave, too. Their hearts are not in this war and, from what I've gathered in the few days I've been here, as many of them side with Moorosi as are against him.

"But I do need more Cape Mounted Riflemen. I need a larger force to do an effective job. I will also need an improved supply of food and supplies for my men and for their horses. We do not want them to go hungry or have inadequate clothing and boots.

"Finally, I need a few weeks to train these men properly and to ensure that this time we do not have any laggards or cowards among them. They will risk their lives, but they will do so in the service of their country.

"With the weather improving every day, we should be in a good position to mount a solid attack that will bring the chief and his followers to their knees."

Sprigg is impressed with Bayly's professional approach and determination.

"Your requests are approved," he says. "You can start moving out the men you do not want immediately and training those you do want. I will leave tomorrow for Cape Town, knowing this command is in good hands. I expect to be able to report to the next session of Parliament that we defeated the Baphuthi and are in control of their land."

"I am confident you will be able to do so, Prime Minister."

Brabant enters the tent. "I am leaving now, Prime Minister," he says. Trying to avoid any intimation of the bitterness he feels, he turns to Bayly. "When you have been a month here, colonel, and know the mountain as I know it, and if you find you are unable to achieve anything, I will come up again and relieve you."

"Farewell, colonel," Bayly responds. "I will bear your words in mind."

Sprigg's party leaves camp for Thomas's Shop, where he will stay before returning to Cape Town. The troopers relax in their tents surrounding the mountain. The tension has noticeably lessened.

Following Bayly's orders, the volunteers still in the camp prepare to leave for home. The full-time soldiers have been told they will undergo strict training in the next month before launching another assault on the mountain.

For now, they are happy to enjoy themselves.

They open their rations of whisky and soon the sounds of their revelling echo across the mountains.

As the party continues into the night, the pickets are eager to join. Some take off early. After all, who will know? All the senior officers are with Sprigg at Thomas's Shop, now named Fort Hartley in honour of the doctor who established the hospital there. A few of the pickets remain on duty, with the promise that they will be relieved a little later so they can join in the revelry, too.

Moorosi has abandoned his plan for an all-out attack on the colonial soldiers. The response to his latest attempt to infiltrate the camp has persuaded him that the soldiers are guarding themselves better, meaning that an assault on them could lead to large losses among the Baphuthi. He does not want to risk such a setback. Instead, he will launch smaller surprise raids on the soldiers even as he guards the mountain and replenishes his supplies.

So it is that, as midnight approaches, a number of Baphuthi climb down the mountain and steal through the bush at its base in a wide semi-circle to approach the pickets from behind the saddle.

The full moon helps them find their way easily and the noise of the soldiers' shouting and singing covers any sounds they make.

They creep behind the sentries, load their rifles and fire on the men on the rocky promontory above them.

The few pickets still on duty fire back and a couple run to the noisy camp ground to summon help.

By the time help arrives the fighting is in full swing as white soldiers, their backs toward the mountain, fire on their black attackers who are behind the saddle. In a short lull, a picket turns and sees movement on the moonlit mountain.

"They are doing it again," he shouts. "They are moving cattle up the mountain. Scores of them."

The pickets turn their fire toward the mountain, but are forced to watch their backs, too, as the Baphuthi behind them continue to fire.

Soon spears are being flung toward them from behind the saddle.

As more men arrive from the camps, the Baphuthi retreat.

But the attack has served its purpose. The cattle disappear behind the rocks at the top of the mountain.

Moorosi is delighted at his new wealth.

"Forty-seven," he shouts. "Let that white chief tell us we cannot survive for much longer. We will show him he is wrong."

Quthing — Tuesday, November 4, 1879

The wagons that rumble into camp are loaded with a five-and-a-half-inch mortar, 16-pound shells and other supplies. Granville, who by now has developed expertise with mortars, assists Captain William Bourne to off-load the mortar. Bourne — among those who arrived with Bayly — was a leader during the Ninth Frontier War two years ago.

Granville remarks that morale in the camp has improved since Bayly took command a little more than a week ago. New life seems infused into the men by cricket matches, athletic sports and shooting contests.

"You should have been here earlier," he tells Bourne. "Morale was all but absent. The men thought the war could not be won without the loss of many lives and even then they were not sure it could be won at all. The volunteers' heart was not in it. Now, with the volunteers leaving, the mood has changed. You don't hear as much about it being impossible to take the mountain."

The men are instructed to check out the mortar and place it in position with the other guns on the south-western side of the mountain, 1,000 yards from the stone walls.

"Look how old it is," Granville says to Bourne. He points to the inscription on the gun: G.R. 1806 for George Rex, or King George III. "It's 71 years old."

Bourne nods. "One of the men told me it has performed service at Cape Town for many years. It stood outside the museum."

Granville laughs. "So we attack the enemy with a museum piece do we? Let's check the fuses that came with it."

When the men find the fuses that came with the gun do not work, they spend several hours transforming 7-pounder fuses. They work. Problem solved.

Next they place iron bands around the carriage so that it will stand up to steady use over many days. "Don't want the old girl falling apart on us," Granville says.

Granville and Bourne return to assist with the off-loading of the wagons. It is starting to rain and the rest of the supplies have to be put under shelter.

In the wagon load are 25 scaling ladders, each 10 feet in length, 24 inches wide and with sides one and half inches deep. Built in Aliwal North, they are equipped with iron sockets two inches long at each end to link the sections. Ropes to tie them together are included.

Granville wonders how the officers can even think the ladders and ropes can help them scale the walls in the face of Baphuthi firing. "Fat lot of use these will be," he says to Bourne as they carry the ladders to a new stone building in which they will be stored along with the ammunition. "If you ask me, these are suicide devices. Want to die? Place one of these against the walls and climb. You'll get your wish.

"Also, they're badly made. Well designed, but not put together very well. To make them stronger, we're going to have to tie two of them together."

"Well, let's try them out anyway," Bourne replies. The men link two of the ladders together and place them against a nearby ledge. They collapse before anyone can stand on them. Other ladders 15 feet long that they find in the wagon are stronger.

As they are working out how the ladders can be put together, Lieutenant Springer walks up, offering to be of assistance. "We might be able to get these to work," he says. Assisted by Bourne and Granville, he cuts the wider ladders to half their width, removing the iron joints, and tying them up with raw ox hide.

"Why didn't they build them like that in the first place?" Granville asks.

Bourne is silent. He is in deep thought. He looks at the ladders.

"Don't you agree?" Granville asks; clearly Bourne's thoughts are elsewhere.

Granville continues, trying to attract Bourne's interest once more. "I still don't know how useful those ladders will be, even though they are stronger now. They will serve only to expose us more to the enemy. Must we prove again that storming the mountain doesn't work?"

Bourne remains silent.

"Don't you agree?"

Bourne recovers from his thoughts. "Yes, yes. I understand what you are saying," he says. "But I have an idea that I must pass on to the colonel."

"What is it?"

Bourne walks off without replying.

Quthing — Sunday, November 9, 1879

Normally Sunday is like any other day at the mountain. But not today. On cleared ground near the camp stands a man in the light rain, dressed in a black shiny robe down to his feet with baggy "lawn" sleeves tied with a black ribbon at the wrist, from which a white ruffle projects. He wears a crimson doctor's hood.

Dr. Webb, bishop of Bloemfontein, leads the men in a hymn and prayer and delivers a short sermon. Webb prays for the men's safety and success at war and leaves them with a number of hymn books. The men, ordered by Bayly to attend, appear moved by the service.

In the evening, the sound of hymn singing wafts from several tents. But while the other men sing or simply talk together, Brome sits alone in his tent.

The service has had a strong impact on him, but perhaps not in the way Webb intended.

Months ago, when he signed up to join the Cape Mounted Riflemen, he believed it was his patriotic duty to defend his family and his property against those who would take it away from him. Fighting against heathen people was the right Christian thing to do.

But the harsh reality of the battlefield has focused his thoughts in ways he did not expect. Brome wonders how Webb can pray for the white soldiers' safety when they are setting out to kill other people also made in the image of God. In praying for the whites, he was, in effect, praying for blacks to be killed, wasn't he?

Is that what Christians are supposed to do?

Quthing — Thursday, November 13, 1879

The Rev. Ellenberger has cancelled all his plans for today. Emma is giving birth to their tenth child and the fifth to be born in the Masitise cave house. With Ellenberger's expert medical assistance, the birth is uncomplicated. As Emma holds the newborn in her arms, Frederic sits alongside her.

"We will call him Victor," Emma says. "And we will always remember that he has been born not far from the sound of gunfire."

"Indeed," Ellenberger replies. "Let us pray he will grow into a peaceful world where men will realize that to do good to one another rather than harm helps us all be better people."

Quthing — Sunday, November 16, 1879

The yeomanry and the other volunteers have almost all gone. Convinced the mountain is impregnable and having no desire to add their lives to the 90 who have died trying to achieve the impossible, they were pleased to agree with Bayly's order to leave. Now only 50 of these minimally trained militia men remain.

Bayly is pleased to see them go. Taking Moorosi's mountain is a job for professional soldiers. The new commander has assembled a force of 275 members of the Cape Mounted Riflemen, 40 Border Guard volunteers — the best he could find among the hundreds who had been at the mountain — and 460 black soldiers, whom he will use as a back-up. The black soldiers include 260 Thembu and 150 Mfengu from the Cape Colony. Only 50 of the 2,000 Basotho under Lerothodi remain. The others have either been dismissed or have drifted away.

Bayly announces the mountain will be stormed in four days — on Thursday, November 20. To prepare the way, he orders a constant bombardment.

"Starting tomorrow morning, I want the mortar to be kept in action day and night for the next four days," he tells Bourne and Granville. "We will use it in conjunction with the other cannon, which will also be kept in constant action. During the day we will punch into those stone walls with the 7-pounders and lob shells into the trenches behind them with the five-and-a-half pounder. At night, the 7-pounders will fire star shells that will light up the mountain. I want to give those damned barbarians no rest. By the time we are ready to attack they will be tired and disoriented and will lack the spirit to fight back."

Quthing — Wednesday, November 19, 1879

It is not only the screaming of the shells and mortars every three or four minutes throughout the day. It is not only the explosions and the shaking of the ground. It is not only the star shells that repeatedly light up the night. It is not only the damage being done to the walls, which constantly have to be repaired. It is not only the clouds of smoke from the gunfire that blanket the mountain and the pungent smell of gunpowder that accompanies it. It is not only the danger to the Baphuthi themselves, several of whom have been injured and a number killed.

It is the combination of all these factors that is unnerving Moorosi's warriors.

For three days now, it has been difficult to relax during the day and is hard to sleep at night. They lie awake, anticipating the next blast, hoping each will be the last so they can sleep. Eventually they succeed in sleeping for a few hours. But with each passing day they are becoming more sleep deprived and disoriented.

The extent of this gunfire also is greater. Because the government forces have moved the mortar closer to the mountain, they are able to reach farther than the crest of the mountain. Some of the shells are landing in the living area on the flat mountaintop. The men have moved the cattle to parts of the mountaintop that are safe behind rocky outcrops and have learned how to avoid the worst of the shelling.

Moorosi, however, is finding it increasingly difficult to persuade his men of the necessity to hold on. The bombing, he tells them, eventually will stop. The whites will run out of ammunition and will become tired of firing the guns all the time. But Moorosi's men continue to leave the mountain in a steady trickle. More than half the 500 who were guarding the mountain when the war started have left, finding refuge in caves or villages deep in Baphuthi territory or in Kornet Spruit.

Those who are left are his best fighters and his finest marksmen and Moorosi remains convinced they can defeat the white forces. He does not need a large army, as the whites seem to do. All he needs is a courageous force, one that can fire with pinpoint accuracy, anticipate the movements of the whites and outwit them. He still has such a force.

"The whites' big guns can reach a little distance beyond the crest of the mountain," Moorosi points out in a evening talk with his men. "The rest of the area is safe. If you move away, you will find that the guns are only noise and cannot hurt you.

"When you go down to the walls to defend us, keep using the ox hides that I have given you. Hold them over your heads and they will protect you from the pieces of shell that explode against the rock behind you and in the air. It is working well and saving lives.

"We need to keep defending the mountain. The whites will become tired of firing the guns at us. If they try to storm our walls again, we will defeat them.

"They will be the ones to surrender. Not us."

Moorosi stands, prompting his listeners also to stand.

"Come, Lemena, show us we are not afraid."

Lemena raises his spear, brandishing it in the air.

"You, Moorosi, great and mighty king!" he chants. "You, who have an army."

He turns to face the rest of the men who also raise their spears.

"Griffith sent his forces," he shouts.

Beating time with their feet and waving their spears, the men chant a responsive chorus: "We destroyed them!"

"The soldiers came."

"We destroyed them."

"The burghers came."

"We destroyed them."

Soon the men are dancing from side to side across the mountain top. Their singing grows louder.

"The big guns came."

"We destroyed them."

"Brabant sent his forces."

"We destroyed them."

"The mounted police came."

"We destroyed them."

Lemena turns to face Moorosi once more. "You, the great and mighty king! You, who have an army! When will they dare to repeat their attack?"

"We will destroy them! We will destroy them! We will destroy them!"

As the sound of their final shouts echo across the valley, and the men sit down, the artillery fire stops. The men wait, bracing themselves for the next firing. It takes a while. After 15 minutes, another blast rocks the mountain. They wait again; this time even longer. After a while it stops altogether. Says Lemena with a broad smile, "They must have heard our war song and have given up."

Granville shakes the mortar from side to side on its carriage as though that will fix it. But the firing mechanism appears to have failed. He has no idea how to repair it.

He has kept a careful count of the firings since they put the museum piece to use three days ago. The gun has fired 367 times, an average of once every 10 minutes during the daylight hours. Although old, it has been the most effective of the large guns. But now the mortar's work appears to be over.

"I think this old lady has finally succumbed," Granville says to Bourne.

"But it has been effective," Bourne replies.

"Yes, we have achieved what Bayly wanted," replies Granville.

A bugle sounds: The men are to assemble at the parade grounds for an important address by Colonel Bayly.

Bayly stands on a slight rise, looking down on the 500 men assembled below.

"For some weeks now, we have been developing our plan to take the mountain," Bayly tells them. "We have reconnoitred every part of it. We have examined every gully, every rock and every bush. We received a plan of action suggested by Major Nixon who also spent some time examining the mountain. I also was assisted by Captain Bourne, who had an idea for an attack that I have incorporated in our plans. You'll hear about that later."

Bourne looks across at Granville and smiles.

"Those of you who wish to have them will be issued with long Sniders and bayonets in place of the carbines you have been carrying up to now. I think you will find those more effective against the enemy, who appear to have newer and more efficient weapons than we have had.

"Now the time has come to implement our plans. Moorosi's Mountain will be taken tomorrow by the Cape Mounted Riflemen!"

The men dutifully cheer. At least Bayly seems confident.

"Five parties will storm the mountain," Bayly continues. "One will assault the mountain from the front, crossing the saddle and attacking the stone walls. That party will consist of 25 members of the Wodehouse Border Guard, who are among the few remaining volunteers. Eighty Mfengu under the command of Lieutenant Muhlenbeck will storm the mountain from the ridge on the east of the plateau.

"You will take up your positions about 350 yards from the first row of stone walls in the darkness and will launch your attack at dawn tomorrow. The firing of a rocket over the mountain will be your signal for attack. You will proceed under the element of surprise as most of the Baphuthi are likely still to be asleep, recovering from the massive fire power we directed their way.

"You will storm the walls, ascend them and overpower the enemy."

The men are quiet. Members of the guard cast ominous glances at one another, aware of the casualties that took place on the two previous assaults — and with a force that numbered considerably more. They wonder why they have been singled out for this attack. Bayly has made it clear that the Cape Mounted Riflemen are his elite troops, yet they — the few volunteers left in the camp and the Mfengu fighters — are being chosen to storm the mountain.

Sensing the men's unease, Bayly continues.

"You have the option of obeying these orders or leaving camp at once," he says. "I will not tolerate anyone taking part in the storming party who is not wholly committed to the task at hand. We have no room for the craven and chicken-hearted."

The men maintain, at least outwardly, a calm determination that helps one to bolster the other. They have come so far, endured so much, that now they are willing to risk almost anything to end this war.

Bayly repeats his offer, allowing the men time to move if they wish to do so.

Silence. No one moves.

"Thank you. I know you will do your duty.

"But, although it will be the main one, these men will not be our only storming party," he continues. "And the same options apply to all of you. Either you are with me or you are against me. If you are not prepared to take part in this mission, leave now. I want only the men committed to doing their duty to God and country."

Brome stays frozen in place. He rephrases Bayly's words in his mind, "We want only those men committed to doing their duty to God *or* country."

Now is his chance to opt out. Now is his chance to choose God above country.

But he cannot do it. His legs will not move. He is unwilling to fight, but more afraid to stand alone and say so. The pressure from Bayly, the officers as well as his colleagues form a powerful force that overrides the conviction that following these orders is morally wrong. He will go with the crowd. He will choose country.

Whitehead and Granville, for their part, realize this is a desperate engagement. They are being called upon to put their lives on the line.

The men are all silent. No one wants to be seen as a coward. They look at one another. They stay where they are.

"Very well. Four other parties will ascend the mountain from the sides, on the east and west, in a large circle from right to left around the mountain. These parties will move off when the moon sets at midnight tonight, which is in a few hours. The darkness will give them the opportunity to take up their positions unseen by the enemy. Once in their positions, they will wait for daybreak before attacking. When the rocket is fired to signal the advance, they, too, will swing into action.

"Two parties will attack on the eastern side of the mountain. Each will consist of two troops of Cape Mounted Riflemen. You know who you are.

"One party will be under the command of Captain Montague. It will consist of 181 officers and men. They will ascend the mountain from the cave in which men under Captain Grant hid before ascending the mountain in a previous assault. It is now known as the commandant's cave or Grant's Cave.

"The other party, 100 yards farther down the mountain, will climb up a fissure on the eastern side of the mountain called Bourne's Crack, a low piece of rock in a krantz, 100 yards to the right of the cave. It will be led by Captain Bourne, who will be assisted by Lieutenant Springer, Lieutenant Sutherland and Lieutenant Hatton. It will consist of 174 officers and men.

"Each man will carry 70 rounds of ammunition slung around his neck. Your rifles will be equipped with bayonets. You will be given fuller instructions later tonight.

"Another party will be headed by Lieutenant Allen MacLean and will consist of those Mfengu who are not in the first party. They are to scale the mountain up a path at the back, or north-east of the mountain, at the area known as 'the spring,' a fountain at the back of the mountain. We believe this footpath is used by the Baphuthi to move to and from the mountain and was used in the attack on the Chiappini camp. It is steep, but we hope to use the element of surprise strongly here and when you attack, as I have mentioned, we expect most of the Baphuthi to be asleep.

"As in the case of the first party, I expect absolute devotion to duty. You too, have the option of following orders or leaving at once."

No one moves.

"The final party, consisting of Mfengu, Thembu and Basotho, will attack up the gully on the southwest front of the mountain and will be led by Captain Hook."

"Now return to your camps. You are free to talk among one another and make a noise this evening if you wish. The enemy will think we have forgotten about them. But once it is midnight, and the moon has set, I want you to move about as silently as possible by placing your socks over your boots. Let the enemy think you are asleep.

"As your arrival on the top awakens the Baphuthi, they will come running down the paths that lead to the stone walls, thinking that will still be our main point of attack. But you'll be attacking from behind. Use your new Sniders to the best of your ability. Dress as you wish, but every man must carry a rifle, a revolver and ammunition.

"I am expecting every one of you to show no quarter to the men on the mountain. Should you come across any women or children, you are not to molest them in any way. But you are to do your utmost to oust Moorosi and his band of rebels from their mountain stronghold. Do not hold back in any way. If you must shoot, then shoot. We will not win this battle by talking; we have tried that. We will not win it by taking prisoners; we have taken a number already.

"We will win this war only by using our fire power. I am relying on each of you to give it his all.

"With that in mind, I am offering tonight a reward of 200 pounds for the capture of Moorosi. Dead or alive. The same for Lehana. Two hundred pounds. Dead or alive. A reward of 25 pounds, with promotion, goes to the first man on the top of the mountain. There will be other rewards for meritorious acts. Now go and enjoy yourselves for a couple of hours. It will not be long before the Cape Mounted Riflemen take Moorosi's Mountain."

The men dutifully cheer and move off.

Moorosi is tempted to let his guard drop. The bombing has stopped and nothing has happened. His men's morale has been sapped, they are tired from lack of sleep and they are demoralized because many have left the mountain.

As Moorosi walks slowly around the mountaintop, he peers down on the camps where he can see the men moving around like ants finding a new food source. They appear agitated and excited. For the last few weeks they have trained more vigorously.

The whites attacked before after one or two days of sustained bombing. Now they will do so again. There are fewer of them, but they seem better prepared. He recalls Sprigg's words, "I am warning you, Moorosi. You are choosing death...Your necks will be broken on this mountain. Even though you think you are invincible, we will conquer you."

Such is the white men's bravado. They think they are more clever than anyone else. They are convinced their soldiers, marching up and down to nowhere, are the best. They consider their military strategy to be superior.

Moorosi has proven over and over that the white soldiers can be beaten. His warriors have defeated government raids on their caves. They have repulsed two attacks on the mountain. His people have smuggled men, food, oxen and water on to the mountain by outwitting the white commanders. His men have used guile to outwit the whites' grandiosity. They have shown that the whites can act without thinking and are easily distracted.

Yet he cannot shake the sense that this attack will be different. For one thing, the bombing was more intense. Also Bayly seems more determined and the soldiers appear to be more organized and more active. He assigns more sentries than usual to guard the stone walls.

"Be aware that they probably will attack in the early morning," he says. "That is what they did before. They will not attack after the moon has set tonight, because they will be unable to see what they are doing, but they might attack once the sun begins to rise tomorrow."

He tells most of his men to sleep tonight in the trenches behind the stone walls. He wants them to be ready, he says, whenever the attack might come.

The men assigned to the guard agree, even though it is a tough task to peer into a quiet dark motionless world for hours and stay awake.

Bayly has forbidden the sale of liquor at the colonial camp for several days, but a few of the men have brandy and whisky that they stored away earlier, which they share with their colleagues.

A gallows humour helps the men prepare for the morning's challenge, particularly those who have been assigned to the frontal assault.

"What are you going to drink?" asks one. "It had better be a stiff one, if you can find one, while you have the chance. One of Moorosi's men may stop you from enjoying another for some time to come."

A number of the men, unable to sleep, are writing letters to be taken in the next post, many fearing it is their last word home. The married men write messages that, should they die, will be sent to their wives. In the quiet of the night, the men are all too aware that tomorrow could be the last day of their lives.

XVII

Quthing — Thursday, November 20 1879

The moon sets just after midnight and the stars are all that remain to bathe the bush around them in a soft, eerie light. The sergeant-majors move from tent to tent, waking the men who have fallen asleep and alerting the others.

"Now then, fall in quickly and make as little noise as you can," Bourne says as Granville tumbles out of his bed.

"Seems like I had no sleep at all," Granville says.

Dark forms glide about the camp as the men assemble, as instructed, at the parade ground, where a roll call is taken, one of the quietest Granville has ever heard.

"Left turn, slow march ahead," a sergeant major instructs them under his breath. In single file, they creep along the side of the mountain. Hardly a sound breaks the stillness of the night except for the stealthy tread of the men or the clatter of a pebble, dislodged accidentally, as it bounds over the rocks. All are concerned not to tip off the Baphuthi, whom, they hope, are all asleep.

Bourne instructs Granville to follow right behind him. At his side are Lieutenants Springer, Sutherland and Hatton as well as Whitehead.

"We will make our way along the eastern side of the mountain," Bourne explains. "Fifty Basotho will carry ladders for us as we make our way to the bottom of the two ways to the top. Two Basotho will carry each ladder, one at each end. Twelve ladders will be assigned to our group, who will climb up the one fissure, and 12 to Montague's group, who will climb up the other path, the one from the cave. We have one ladder to use as a spare.

"Once we reach the bottom of our path, we will place our ladders against the mountainside and use them to climb a series of six natural giant rock steps that ascend the mountain. I have identified these steps as a way of scaling the mountain.

"But we can't get up them without the use of the ladders as each giant rock step is six to eight or possibly even 10 feet high; we can't tell for sure until we get there."

Granville glances at Bourne. So this was his plan. Why could he not have told him of it?

"By using two ladders roped together," Bourne continues, "we will be able to climb up to the top of the first step. More ladders will be handed up to the men who have made it on to the step. They will rope those ladders together and place them on the next step. Once the ladders are in place, they will climb to the top of the second step.

"And so we will go until we reach the top of the sixth step.

"Once there, we will have put in place a series of ladders that will take us to the top.

"Montague's group, on the left of us, will use their ladders to try to scale their

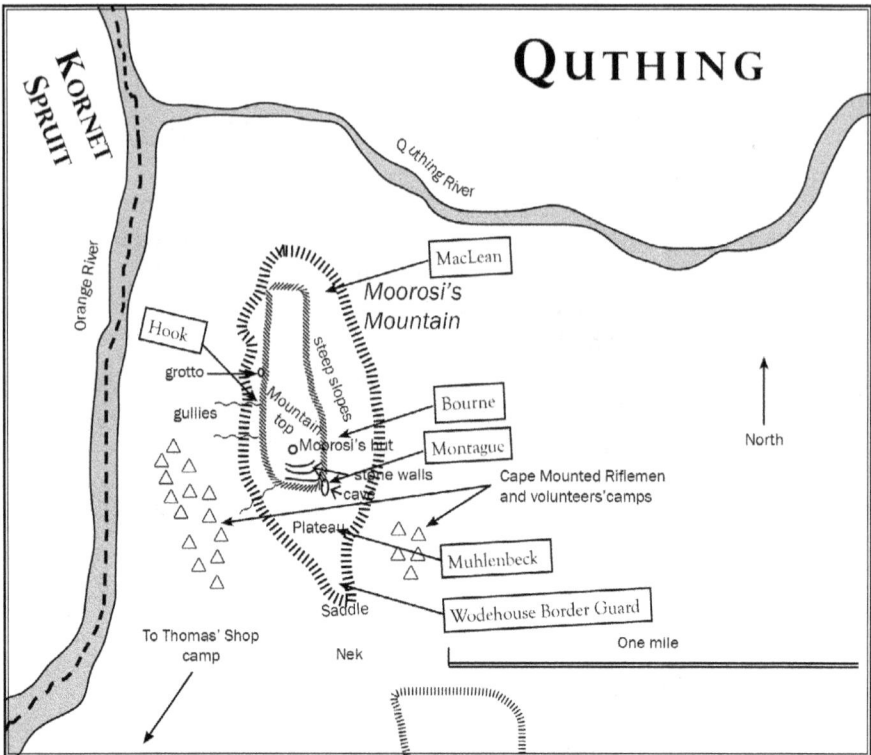

path. They do not have the benefit of natural steps as we do, so they likely will have a harder task.

"When the ladders are in place and we are poised unseen on them one behind the other, we will wait until dawn when a rocket is fired. That will be the signal for the three other parties to storm the mountain from the front and sides. The enemy will rush to the walls to fire at the attackers in the way they did in the previous two assaults.

"At that point, we will be climbing on to the mountaintop from our positions on the ladders. Once on the top, we will assemble and move across the mountaintop to attack the enemy from behind.

"If the other group — the troop on our left — is successful in reaching the top, both of our groups will reach the top at the same time, establishing a large force up there.

"Right, men, let's go."

The men set off, making their way across the mountain slope toward the attack points, steadily climbing higher up the mountainside. In the darkness, they trip over rocks and stumble into holes. Every now and then one tries to stifle his scream of pain as he slips on a rock and twists his ankle.

The outline of the mountain, which the men can just make out, looms alongside.

Granville cannot resist breaking the silence. He moves forward along the line of soldiers to walk alongside Bourne.

"Why," he asks him in a whisper, "didn't you tell me of your plan to attack up the giant steps?"

"Colonel Bayly asked me not to tell anyone," Bourne replies. "He has heard that plans like these have a way of getting out and reaching Moorosi. We have to realize, he said, that there are spies among the black people and that we are not always careful when we speak in front of them. We tend to act as though they're not there.

"Also, he said, if the Wodehouse Border Guard and the Mfengu know that their storming of the walls from the front is only a diversionary tactic, they will not do it well. It has to seem like the real thing.

"That is why Bayly acted as though the ladders would be used by the main storming party to climb the stone walls. Truth is they are all being used by us and the main storming party will have none."

"But you could have told me," Granville protests, his voice rising. "I would not have told anyone."

"Shhh," Bourne replies, realizing he is speaking too much and placing his finger on his lips. "Strict silence," he whispers. "Our voices carry in the quiet mountain air."

Granville nods.

After traversing the mountainside for about 30 minutes, they reach an overhanging ledge. Here, they stop for a few minutes' rest.

"Where are the natives carrying the ladders?" asks Bourne. He instructs Whitehead and Springer to find out.

As they double back, the men hear a clattering noise and shouts from the Basotho who have dumped the ladders, ropes and ammunition on the ground and are shouting to the Baphuthi on the mountain.

"Stop the shouting," Whitehead says as they reach the Basotho. "If you do not want to help us, don't. But stop warning the Baphuthi."

As the Basotho continue shouting, Whitehead and Springer raise their Sniders. Whitehead fires a warning shot.

The men are quiet as they stare into the barrels of the guns.

"That's better," says Whitehead.

"Now do as you were told. Pick up the ladders."

The Basotho run off down the mountain into the dark of the night. Whitehead fires another shot in their direction.

"Don't waste your ammunition," Springer says.

"What do we do now?" asks Whitehead.

"Let's take one of the ladders up to the ledge and tell Bourne what happened."

Bourne is unmoved. "We continue as before. We are well rid of those turncoats. We will still climb the mountain. Even though the Baphuthi have been warned that we are on this side of the mountain, they might not be aware of what we plan to do.

"And, even if they are aware," Bourne continues, "there are no defences on this side of the mountain. No stone walls to overcome. When we climb to the top we will step on to level ground. We might have lost some of the element of surprise, but we can still succeed in making it to the top of the mountain, which proved impossible on the front face."

Bourne turns to face the men. "Our mission continues as planned with only one difference. I want volunteers to pick up the ladders, rope and ammunition and carry them to the bottom of the paths. The rest of us will continue on."

Hook's group is making its way up the first stretch of a steep gully on the western side of the front face of the mountain at 1 a.m. when the commander hears whispering among the Thembu and Mfengu fighters assigned to his command. Their attitude to his orders and some of the words he overhears lead him to believe that a number will refuse to fight and might even turn their Sniders on the Cape Mounted Riflemen.

He selects 50 Mfengu whom he is confident are loyal and orders the rest to move away from the mountain. It is better to lose their potential help than to risk their treachery, particularly as his assignment is largely a diversionary tactic.

Alerted by the Basotho who had been carrying the ladders, Raisa is taking command of the Baphuthi on the mountaintop. He reports to Moorosi.

"It's another attempt to distract us," Moorosi says. "Just as they did before, when they tried to attack us on the other side, they want us to move away from the front walls and concentrate our attention here. They won't be able to climb up these sides of the mountain. "If you see them approaching the top, those who are here can throw down rocks on them and shoot at them if necessary to stop them, but we must concentrate our attention on the front walls."

Fifty members of the Cape Mounted Riflemen scramble down the western side of the mountain, pick up the ladders abandoned by the Basotho and carry them to the point at which they are to start scaling the mountain.

It has taken them 90 minutes from the camp to reach this point, far longer than planned. They are tired from lack of sleep and carrying the ladders. Soon, the rocket will be fired to signal the start of the attack and they have not yet set the ladders in place, let alone climbed on to them. But it is still dark and they have time if they work as fast as they can.

The men under Bourne are able to assemble the ladders and place them on the first slopes. But as they climb up, they find that the ladders collapse easily. With four men on them, they bend and break apart. In addition, some ladders are shorter than others, making it more difficult to join them. The only solution, they find, is to tie them together, overlapping one ladder with another so they are not as long but are stronger.

Lashing the ladders slows them down, but within 45 minutes the men are making good progress. So far, the men whisper to one another, the Baphuthi are quiet.

"They don't know what we're doing," Whitehead says to Bourne. "They probably didn't hear the Basotho warning them."

The soldiers above the commandant's cave, led by Montague, make faster progress than Bourne's men.

But progress has its downside. By the time they have set the third set of ladders in place and are readying the fourth set, they come close enough to be seen by Baphuthi, peering over the edge above them.

The Baphuthi hurl down stones and boulders, as well as stone-filled hides, forcing the soldiers to duck for cover.

As a Baphuthi peers over the edge above them, one of the Cape Mounted Riflemen raises his Snider and shoots. His aim is true. The warrior falls forward and his body falls down the mountainside, hitting against the rock cliff.

The soldiers, stunned by the incident, watch for more heads to appear above them. None do, but the reality of their task is starting to hit home. This is indeed a matter of life and death, of shoot or be shot, as Bayly had said it would be.

Brome, assigned to the group under Montague, assists his fellow soldiers in placing the ladders, secretly hoping the plan will not succeed and he will be able to turn around and go back to his tent.

As the men continue to place the ladders, the stone and rock attack from above gains in intensity. A large rock crashes down, striking a boulder just above a group of men before bounding over their heads and splintering on the rocks below. A fragment hits a Mfengu man, sending him, doubled up as a ball, down the hillside.

Hit by another rock, a ladder spirals down the mountain slope, clattering to the ground below. As a replacement ladder is handed up to them, the soldiers realize they are now one ladder short and might not make it all the way. Suddenly the mission is looking a lot more difficult.

When the Baphuthi push a dead cow over the edge, narrowly missing one of the men, but striking another ladder and sending it, too, tumbling down the mountainside, the troopers call on their leader, Montague, to abandon the climb. He agrees. The venture has become too risky.

"They are going back down," Raisa says. "We have stopped them. The white soldiers' tactic to divert our attention didn't work. We must go and help to guard the front walls because they will soon attack us there."

The frontal assault of the stone walls appears to the men assigned the task to be an invitation to almost certain death. At least they are to storm the mountain while it is still fairly dark, giving them some hope they can avoid the Baphuthi bullets.

Shortly after 2 a.m., the 25 members of the volunteer Wodehouse Border Guard file up to the saddle. Here they join the 80 Mfengu fighters who are to attack up the "spring" path on the right of the mountain under Capt. MacLean.

As the group under MacLean move off, Captain Muhlenbeck addresses the men under his command who are to attack from the front.

"You are to wait here until ordered to move," he says. "As soon as I give the order you are to storm the mountain and make as much noise as you can. Shout, scream, yell. In that way, we will encourage one another.

"Obviously the enemy will concentrate their attention on us. But the darkness will prevent the enemy from seeing you effectively.

"You are to run to the walls, climb them and attack the Baphuthi as they stand behind the schanzes. Does everyone understand our task?"

The men respond in chorus, "Yes, captain," with little enthusiasm.

With no light more than the starry skies above, and ordered not to talk but to wait until ordered to move, the men become drowsy. By 3 a.m. many are asleep.

With the men under Montague abandoning their assault, the task of reaching the summit falls on those under Bourne.

Bourne whispers, "I believe they might be thinking that our only attack is the one Montague is leading," he says. "I don't think they have seen us here. Keep working as quickly and as quietly as you can. Pass the word along, but don't raise your voices."

He scrambles down to the other group. "You must continue. I do not want you to stop," he tells Montague.

"But," Montague protests, pointing up the gully. "It has become extremely dangerous up there. We don't have the benefit of the giant steps that you do and they can see us more easily than they can see you."

"No matter. You need to make it appear that you are still climbing," Bourne says. "The Baphuthi seem to think that you're the only ones placing ladders on this side of the mountain. Let's keep it that way. If my group can avoid being seen, we can creep up and surprise them."

Montague instructs his men to continue.

Their cessation of the climb, however, has given the Baphuthi the impression that the soldiers have abandoned their plans to try to ascend the mountain at that point. Most turn away and return to the front stone walls.

Bourne returns to his group, who have almost completed placing the ladders on the giant steps that form "Bourne's Crack."

After tying them together and putting them in place, they climb the ladders and gather in groups on the ledges at the top of each step, waiting for the signal from Bourne to get on to the ladders and climb to the top.

When the last ladder is readied for its placement on the final step, Springer volunteers to go first.

"I will go up and place the final ladder. It will fall a little short," Springer tells the men. "But I am taller than all of you and I will be able to clamber up the remaining distance more quickly."

"As soon as Springer starts climbing up the last ladder, you should follow him," Bourne tells the men. "When we're on top, the plan is to fix bayonets and march in formation to the south-east and take the enemy from behind.

"You should take the lead from Springer. Follow what he tells you to do.

"Remember, there is a big reward for the man who captures or shoots Moorosi."

Able now to see his way more clearly in the morning light creeping across the mountain, Springer clambers his way up the ladder over the final stretch of rock.

Behind him, the men, aware that Springer is likely to receive the reward for being the first on the top of the mountain, are eager to be right behind him and among the first on the top of the mountain, perhaps even beating Springer to it.

They bunch on the ladders, threatening to break them. But, although they bend under the weight, the lashed-together ladders hold.

The rocket signalling the start of the attack on all fronts is fired at 4 a.m. Springer finds hand holes in the 15 feet of rock above the top ladder and pulls himself up. At the top of the last rock step, he reaches up to a narrow ledge to his left about four feet from the top of the mountain. He pulls himself up.

But Springer has come within view of the Baphuthi, who cannot see down this fissure from the edge of the mountain, but can see the ledge.

Springer looks up and sees two Baphuthi men, both with raised rifles in their hands, above him.

One cocks his rifle and points it at Springer's head.

"Don't come up here or I will shoot you," the man says.

"Well, fancy seeing you here," replies Springer, reaching down for his revolver. "I would not shoot if I were you, because I might shoot you first."

Before Springer can lift his gun, however, the Baphuthi fires.

When the rocket is fired to signal the advance, Muhlenbeck orders the men under him to move away from behind the saddle and to storm the walls from the ridge on the right of the plateau.

Still groggy from their sleep, the volunteers find the fear of death suddenly overtaking the fear of disobeying a command. None moves forward.

"You go first," one says, rising to his feet.

"I would prefer it if you went first."

"I said advance!" Muhlenbeck shouts, frustrated by the men's failure to move. He was told he was getting the best trained and most courageous men available, even though they might be volunteers.

Now they simply stand there.

"Advance!" he screams. "I am instructing you to advance! Now, damn you, Now!" The men stay where they are.

The soldiers gathered just below Springer watch in horror as the Baphuthi warrior takes aim at their lead man and pulls the trigger.

The crack of the rifle is followed by a puff of white smoke that drifts into the air above them. The bullet penetrates Springer's shirt. But it only grazes his shoulder. Stunned, Springer hesitates.

The second Baphuthi fires. This time the shot is off its mark and hits a nearby rock. Springer raises his revolver and, before either of the two Baphuthi can fire again, shoots one, hitting him in the heart. The other Baphuthi, unaware of the presence of the men on the ladders below, runs off.

The body of the struck Baphuthi falls to the ledge alongside Springer, bounces off and rolls down the mountainside. It hits and breaks two ladders tied together lower down the mountain and knocks the men off them. The soldiers tumble down the mountain alongside the body of the Baphuthi warrior.

They pick themselves up and find they have suffered only minor injuries. "It's as well we were near the bottom and did not have far to fall," comments one.

Ignoring the body lying in the bushes, the men gather two more ladders, rope them together and put them in place.

By the time they are done, the men ahead of them are following Springer, climbing to the top of the mountain.

Angered and frustrated at his men's refusal to follow his orders to storm the mountain from the front, Muhlenbeck wonders how he can get them to do so. The sky is becoming steadily lighter, making it easier for the Baphuthi to aim.

"Very well. I will show you the way," Muhlenbeck shouts, believing that, given the lead, the men will follow.

Muhlenbeck sets off on the 350-yard stretch of open plateau.

James Corfield, carrying a carbine, with his water bottle and bag at his side and extra cartridges slung around his neck, follows him. He and Muhlenbeck are alone.

As shots ring out from the stone walls, Corfield trips over a rock, landing behind a small ledge. But it provides little shelter and he stands up and sprints ahead once more.

The sound of the 12-pounder fired from behind him frightens him. He seeks shelter behind a nearby rock about 120 yards from the base of the stone walls.

The men following Springer pull themselves up to the ledge and on to the mountaintop, encountering little resistance from the Baphuthi.

Within five minutes, scores of Cape Mounted Riflemen are on the top of the mountain. The rest scramble up the ladders, but in their eagerness, too many men climb on them and the ladders break. Nevertheless, using the broken ladder steps, and pulling themselves up the mountainside, the men make it up.

The men in Montague's group abandon their attempts to reach the top by their path and climb up the broken ladders behind Bourne's group. In spite of his reluctance, Brome joins his fellow soldiers in clambering to the top of the mountain, joining 200 already there.

Bayly's plan is working. Only about 30 of the Baphuthi are on the mountaintop. The rest are behind the stone walls defending against an attack from the front.

The Baphuthi on the mountaintop find shelter behind a stone wall originally built near the crest of the mountain to counter an attack from the front. They squat behind it to fire from the other side on an enemy attacking them from the rear.

When they realize what is happening, scores of Baphuthi leave the trenches behind the front walls and climb to the crest of the mountain where they join their compatriots behind the stone wall.

Bourne, taking command of all the colonial soldiers on the mountaintop, shouts, "Remember your orders! Get into formation!"

The soldiers form a line, their bayonets at the ready.

"Forward march!"

They are all here now. Granville, Whitehead, Bourne, Springer, Brome and the rest of the Cape Mounted Riflemen.

They are joined by MacLean's group who climbed the path at the spring. With them, too, are the men under Hook who climbed the gully on the western side.

The colonial soldiers, numbering almost 400, form a long line around the edge of the mountaintop. As they move forward, the soldiers set fire to the thatch covering the huts. Soon huge flames light up the mountaintop with an orange glow.

The Cape Mounted Riflemen cheer as they march toward the Baphuthi hiding behind the stone wall, holding their bayonet-tipped rifles before them.

Brome, caught up in the fervor, marches with them. Farther down the line, Whitehead and Bourne stride purposefully forward.

When the soldiers on the mountaintop are 50 yards from the wall, Raisa moves forward, raising his hands in a gesture of surrender. The soldiers pause. The firing stops and an eerie silence settles over the scene as the Baphuthi and the soldiers alike are unsure how to react.

"Take two paces forward," Bourne says in his best military voice. Raisa does not respond. He shrugs his shoulders, indicating he does not understand.

"I said take two paces forward."

Raisa responds by raising his hands in the air as high as he can. His palms reflect the glow of the fires destroying the huts.

The soldiers, unwilling to let any Baphuthi escape punishment, yell, "Give no quarter! Bayly said to give no quarter!" For weeks, they have recalled the time when the severed head of King was displayed behind the front stone wall, how the men in the Chiappini camp were slaughtered, how the Baphuthi killed the pickets guarding the saddle, and ways in which they were repeatedly embarrassed by men who have outwitted and outfought them.

"Give no quarter," they were told. And no quarter will be given.

Without warning, a soldier fires. Raisa, shot in the chest, collapses.

The Cape Mounted Riflemen rush forward with even more determination.

Caught up in the frenzy, they lose any constraints they might have had to play by the rules of organized warfare, firing furiously and with abandon in their eagerness to extract vengeance and pour hatred on these "savages."

The organized march turns into a chaotic contest to determine who can extract the most carnage in their rush forward.

No quarter will be given.

Lemena emerges from behind the stone wall on the mountain crest, runs forward and flings his spear toward Brome. As the spear tears a superficial wound in his leg, Brome feels a rush of anger fired by intense fear surge through his body. He must kill or be killed.

Before the Baphuthi man can fully recover his balance, Brome runs at him with his bayonet. Lemena turns in an attempt to avoid the blow. Brome feels the resistance as the sharp steel point enters Lemena's side, just below his heart. He watches as Lemena's face reflects the pain. With blood oozing from the wound, Lemena buckles over and falls.

As Brome withdraws his bayonet from Lemena's body, he gasps at the blood covering it, and then looks down to see the man he has bayoneted bleeding profusely. He recognizes Lemena. The awful realization of what he has just done strikes him.

He has killed a man.

Not just any man. The intelligent man with the cheeky sense of humour that they all liked, even though he was the enemy, even though he was regarded as a savage. The man of justice. The man of pride in his people.

For a moment, as Brome stands affixed, looking at Lemena's lifeless body, he no longer hears the noise of the battlefield.

In his senses, the players in the deadly drama around him pause in mid-action. Life stands still.

He has killed a man.

A man who did him no personal wrong. A man who deserved to live.

As the fighting continues to rage, no one notices Brome standing transfixed, staring in disbelief at his blood-covered bayonet and the man who lies unmoving on the ground below him.

He has killed a man.

Bourne is of a different mind.

Thrilled with the knowledge that his "six-steps" plan of attack worked, he fires at the Baphuthi, now fleeing from behind the wall. He has no doubt now that the Cape Mounted Riflemen have won this war, and he is the one responsible.

He savors the sweet smell of victory in this do-or-die game.

Whitehead, too, is indulging in the high-risk high-adventure thrill of battle. He narrowly avoids a bullet, then smiles with satisfaction as he watches the Baphuthi scatter. Never before has the adrenalin pumped through his body as it is right now.

Screaming in fear, Baphuthi run down the mountain toward the stone walls that form the front tiers, hoping the edifices will provide some protection.

Some, panic stricken, jump over the side of the mountain, falling to their deaths on the rocks below.

Two dozen Baphuthi succeed in escaping the fighting and jump down the edges of rocks, hiding in small groups under the edges where they plan to stay until they can slide down a gully when the soldiers have left.

Others incredibly make it down the mountain, slipping and sliding down the gullies on the western side.

The rest continue to fire from behind the walls at the crest of the mountain, determined to resist to the end, even as the soldiers surround them.

Soon Baphuthi bodies lie everywhere as the Cape Mounted Riflemen continue their mass killing spree

The few women and children left on the mountain, spared by the rampaging soldiers, stand in a huddle, begging for mercy and wailing uncontrollably as they watch their fathers, husbands, brothers and sons bayoneted and gunned down.

Bourne and Whitehead find themselves caught up in the contagious spirit to destroy. They are true soldiers now. Any last vestige of compassion has left them. Their conscience that would insist that killing another person is wrong is silenced.

The commanders have lost control and are unable to devise any sort of Baphuthi surrender, even if they wanted to do so. The mountain has been commandeered by an out-of-control group of white desperadoes who have been sent to kill and destroy and now are determined to do so with gusto.

No quarter will be given.

A hut in which the Baphuthi had stored ammunition explodes in a huge ball of flame, sending fragments of wood, stone and bullets into the air.

The colonial soldiers, who duck as the fragments fly around them, succeed in avoiding most of the shrapnel. For a while the explosion disorients everyone on the mountain, but soon the killing resumes, the bodies pile up and the chaos continues.

Down on the plateau, all is quiet. Corfield huddles behind the rock, wondering how long he will be stuck here. He hunkers down as the firing on the top of the mountain intensifies. He waits for the bullets to fly around him.

There are none.

As the firing continues, he raises his rifle and gingerly looks out. He looks toward the mountain. There, just below the crown, Lieutenant McMullen is waving the Cape Mounted Riflemen's flag and a surge of relief flows through his body. Somehow they have taken the mountain.

A minute or two later he has joined Muhlenbeck near the base of the stone walls. "The firing is not coming from the Baphuthi, but from our men firing into the schanzes from the top," Corfield says in amazement. "How did they get there?"

"They used scaling ladders to climb up the steep sides of the mountain," Muhlenbeck explains. Our task in storming the walls was to act as a feint, to divert the Baphuthi attention away from the gullies. I couldn't tell you that earlier because we wanted our attack to look genuine."

"Feint, my eye," says Corfield. "The volunteers fainted, is what happened. Fat lot of good they were. As it was they did absolutely nothing."

Muhlenbeck is silent. He hopes the men's failure to follow his command and his lead will be overlooked in light of the tremendous victory.

The Baphuthi still alive behind the walls on the mountaintop, surrounded on all sides, fight back furiously. Confused by the sudden onslaught that seems to have come from nowhere, they try desperately to hold their ground, flinging their spears and firing toward the colonial troops as they attack them.

They are hopelessly outnumbered. Soon the trenches behind the stone walls are awash in blood. Bodies lie everywhere.

Less than an hour after the attack began the firing on the mountaintop dies down.

Smoke continues to pour from the smouldering huts, covering the mountain in a thick black cloud.

Strewn across the mountain top, scores of Baphuthi bodies lie at angles and pointing in haphazard directions, some piled on top of one another, some in groups, others alone, gunned down or bayoneted as they tried to run to safety.

Some bear begging looks on their faces, their hands raised in a desperate last-minute plea for mercy.

The bodies of a few women and children, killed by flying shrapnel, lie among those of the men.

Dead and dying cattle are strewn across the mountain top.

Two bodies lie inside a torched hut, burned beyond recognition.

Whitehead glimpses a white object in the ruins of the ammunition hut. As the smoke starts to clear, he sees it is a skull built into the side, placed there, he assumes, to act as a talisman to protect them against the white soldiers. He shivers as he realizes it is probably the skull of his friend William King.

The top of the mountain, now fully lit by the morning sun, has mostly fallen silent, but the talking and laughter of the colonial soldiers, delighting in their victory, can be heard as they tour the remains of Moorosi's village.

They pick up pieces of earthenware pots blown apart in the fighting.

They shiver at the site of the body of a vicious dog, snarling its teeth in a post-mortem threat.

They wonder at the way the Baphuthi survived for so long on the mountain.

In a shallow cave on the mountain top, they etch the date and their names into the rock with the tips of their bayonets as a lasting testimony to their prowess.

The men are joined by Bayly, dressed in a deer-stalking hat, cardigan jacket and yellow riding cords tucked into his socks, standing next to the Union Jack erected alongside the mountain's crown.

Bayly beams with delight, proud that his plan worked and that the colonial troops have suffered so few casualties.

Before long, Bayly and most of the soldiers clamber down the mountain, ready to celebrate.

But first Bayly must tell the world of his success. In his tent, he pens a message for onward transmission to Cape Town:

"I assaulted the mountain on the 20th inst. from five different positions, all parties leaving camp for their respective positions at the dip of the moon.

"The mountain was ours at a quarter past four o'clock a.m....Moorosi at present not turned up."

In a rocky outcrop on the north-western side of the mountaintop, three Baphuthi men, who escaped the battle scene as the fighting erupted and have been watching the carnage from a distance, head toward the mountain's northern edge.

One, a lot older, is slower than the others. A son walks in front and the other son behind him. They vied for the right to be heir to the kingdom. Now, with their lives and the existence of their people in the balance, that dispute is forgotten as the three seek a hideout where they will not be found by the soldiers.

Their people have been decimated. Most of what they fought for has been lost. But they are still alive, and while they are still alive their nation is still alive.

Lieutenant McMullen seizes a Baphuthi, one of few taken prisoner in the capture of the mountaintop. "Where is your chief?" he asks him angrily. "Where is Moorosi?"

The man fails to answer. He wants to say he does not know where his king is, but he is afraid he might make the soldier even more angry if he does.

McMullen places his carbine under the man's chin.

"Tell me, where is Moorosi? You must know where he is. Tell me!"

No response.

"I will shoot you if you don't tell me!"

The man remains silent, frozen with fear.

McMullen fires his carbine, blowing the prisoner's head to pieces.

No quarter will be given.

Concerned that Baphuthi who fled at the outbreak of the fighting might still be hiding on the mountaintop, Whitehead decides not to join the other soldiers leaving the mountain. He will search the rocky outcrop on the north-western side of the mountain for stragglers.

As Whitehead draws closer to the outcrop, he spots a couple of Baphuthi sticking their heads out from behind a rock. He is right. Not all the enemy are dead. Not all have fled. Is the war then really over?

"What has happened to Moorosi?" he wonders. "Has someone claimed the £200 reward for his capture? As he is pondering these questions, he hears gunfire from the rocks where he saw the Baphuthi. Running across the uneven ground toward the noise, he follows a path through the outcrop, where he finds Private Thomas Swash lying on his side behind a rock. "Three natives fired at me," he says. "One of the shots hit me." He points to a growing patch of blood on his thigh. "They went down that path."

The war is not yet over.

Two soldiers, also attracted by the sound of gunfire, arrive at the scene.

"You go down the path," one says to Whitehead. "We'll carry Private Swash to a place where he will be safer. But be careful. We heard that the natives dropped a charge of dynamite over the ledge. They might try to set it off at any time."

Along the narrow path, Whitehead sees the three Baphuthi heading for a protruding rock. He raises his carbine and fires. The man at the back falls — "like a slain ox," Whitehead thinks to himself.

Moving past the body, Whitehead follows the path, which twists around large rocks, narrowing as it winds its way along the western side of the mountain. Around a corner, on the north-western corner of the mountaintop, Whitehead comes to a shallow grotto, about 10 feet high, near the edge of the cliff that plunges a sheer 1,500 feet to the valley at the confluence of the Orange and Quthing rivers.

He stops. A man he suspects is Lehana kneels at the grotto, his rifle at the ready. He is looking away, down to the valley below, and has not seen him.

Whitehead creeps quietly forward and sees a grey-haired man sitting in the grotto. He raises his rifle. Aiming at the man's chest, he pulls the trigger. The old man reels backward. Whitehead reloads his rifle.

At the sound of the shot, Lehana wheels around. Seeing Whitehead, he loads his rifle. But, before Lehana can fire, Whitehead fires again, this time sending the bullet into the old man's neck. The man rolls forward, slumping to the ground.

Lehana fires moments after Whitehead's second shot. Whitehead ducks. The shot, which would have struck him in the face had he not moved, pierces the badge on Whitehead's cap, splitting it in two as it knocks his cap off his head.

When Whitehead raises his rifle to return Lehana's fire, the warrior jumps up and takes off on the path, back toward the mountaintop. Whitehead follows. In a short time, he draws close to him and the two exchange shots. Lehana runs off once more and Whitehead tries to follow him further, but loses the trail.

He is returning along the path through the rocks, on the edge of the mountain, when the dynamite that the soldiers warned him had been dropped over the edge explodes on his right, a few yards ahead of him.

The blast causes Whitehead to lose his footing and sends him reeling backward. He falls and finds himself rolling down a slope. He makes a desperate attempt to grab hold of bushes and grass to stop his slide, but is unable to cling to them for any length of time; some slip through his hands, others pull out from the soil by the roots as he grabs on to them.

He continues to slip 30 yards downhill without being able to appreciably stop, sliding toward the edge of a sheer cliff edge. He stares down in fear. He is about to careen over the edge and plunge to his death on the rocks 1,500 feet below.

As the colonial soldiers reach the lower slopes of the mountain and look back on where they have been, they break out into cheering and laughing,

"When I look at the way we came up, I cannot believe we actually did it," says Robert Kennan.

"I was confident we could make it up the crack — and we did," says Bourne.

Brome walks quietly alone. He is not proud of what he did.

It is true no one can call him a coward. No one can accuse him of failing to perform his duty. He has been a gallant soldier, serving his country. But a profound sense of guilt is tearing at his soul. He served his country, but he fears he did not serve God.

He killed a man.

He plunged his bayonet into him, robbing him of his life. A man who did him no wrong. Nothing now can bring that man back to life. He cannot go back in time to reverse his action. This deed — this wrong deed, this evil deed, this murderous deed — will haunt him forever.

He killed a man.

Walking slightly behind Brome, Granville is looking forward with eager anticipation to returning home now that the war is over. He is ready to return to dull boring England once more.

Suddenly it strikes him. No one has spoken of the Baphuthi king. Where is Moorosi? Was he captured during the fighting? Did he die? Granville is not alone in his thoughts. Around him, men are picking through the bodies, searching for anyone who looks as old as the king. Now and then one picks up a body and carries it down the mountain to Bayly, hoping they will earn the reward.

Whitehead stops his slide by digging his boots into the ground and against a rock just before reaching the cliff edge. He lies there clutching the mountain, panting. He can feel his heart pumping. Stunned, but only slightly hurt, he regains his footing and climbs carefully up the slope to the trail.

Although most of the white soldiers have left the mountain, Whitehead is not convinced that the battle is over. Lehana —assuming it were him — is still at large. A number of Baphuthi are likely also still on the mountain and could be hiding until the colonial forces leave, enabling them to retake the mountain.

Whitehead continues to scout the mountaintop.

Eventually the troopers leave and Whitehead suspects he is alone — except for the few remaining Baphuthi.

It is party time at the camp ground and the liquor, banned by Bayly for the last few days, is now flowing freely. They are alive. They won. The threat has gone. They will soon be going home. Could the situation possibly be any better?

But not all the men are accounted for. Bourne still has not found his friend. He hopes Whitehead survived the battle in good shape.

Whitehead has been keeping guard on the mountaintop for some hours, but has caught only occasional glimpses of Baphuthi. When he fires at them, they disappear and he is unable to find them.

It is 4 p.m. when a sentry arrives. "You have been reported missing," the sentry says. "All the rest of the men have been accounted for. Our forces have only two seriously injured. I'm told Private Swash was wounded and is not expected to survive. Private Corfield was hit in the shoulder joint. One Mfengu is dead. We wondered whether you had been injured, or even killed, but I am pleased I found you here unhurt. You can go back down to the camp; I'll take over the guard duty here."

Whitehead, tired and relieved to escape the pungent odor of the carcasses of cattle, horses and heaps of human bodies, walks down the mountain path.

The scene on the way down is as sickening as that on the top. Baphuthi bodies lie strewn behind the stone walls.

In the trench behind the lowest wall a Baphuthi with white hair and a colorless face is among a dozen bodies. He lies at a grotesque angle, making his body look even more strange and out of place. Whitehead realizes this is the albino who many said was such a good shot. He will shoot no more now.

Whitehead feels a twinge of emotion. This man did his best for his people, as he saw it. He defended them with his ability to shoot. One who would have been an outcast in many societies, he served people who cared for him. Now all he did has come to nothing. In the end, all that mattered was he was on the side that lost.

At the camp, Whitehead walks to Bayly's tent and asks to see the colonel.

"What do you want with me?" asks Bayly.

"Beg your pardon, colonel. I am wondering if anyone has found Moorosi," Whitehead says.

"No, a number of people have brought me bodies, but none of them was Moorosi. We assume he died on the mountain, but no one has claimed the reward."

Whitehead tells Bayly how he stayed at the top of the mountain, keeping the remaining Baphuthi at bay. "I did not realize it at the time, but I suspect now that a man I shot up there might have been Moorosi, lying in a shallow cave. I did not get a chance to look properly at him because I was shot at by a man guarding him."

Out of the corner of his eye, Whitehead sees that James Neville, of the Wodehouse Guards, is standing outside listening. Neville leaves, calling a few Mfengu soldiers to accompany him.

Whitehead continues his report to Bayly, but he is interrupted by a spate of gunfire from the mountaintop. The men leave the tent and look toward the mountain gullies. They see a group of Baphuthi jump down the edge of the mountain, clambering down what remains of the ladders, and run off toward the river.

"Those were the men I saw on the mountain," Whitehead says. "The sentry let them get away."

"I am sure one of those men was Lehana," says the Quthing magistrate Austen who has been at the mountain since the attack began. "The one who started it all appears to have escaped. But I'm told that almost all of Moorosi's other sons have been killed as well as most of his followers."

He adds that he climbed the mountain earlier and, knowing the men involved, identified the bodies of Letuka, who was lying on a path toward a rocky ledge, Motsapi, a son of Moorosi who was reputed to be a splendid shot, Masepuli, a nephew of the chief, and Thladi, a grandson of Moorosi and one of the prisoners who was forcibly released from the prison at the residency.

"I also know that Muntsu, who hid for a long time in a cave before joining the rest on the mountain, was killed, as was Lemena. Indeed, Moorosi's whole family appears to have been wiped out, except for Lehana.

"But I have no idea where Moorosi himself is. I did not see him or his body."

A Mfengu man carries a body of an old Baphuthi man. He lays it down before Bayly. "This is Moorosi," he says.

"No, I am afraid it is not," Bayly replies. "He is an old Thembu chief."

Angry at not qualifying for the reward, the Mfengu man dashes the lifeless head to pieces with a thick fighting stick that he carries.

Later that afternoon, Neville — the man who had been listening at Bayly's tent when Whitehead was reporting — arrives with the body of an old man, which

Mfengu have helped him carry down from the mountain. Whitehead follows them to the tent.

"How did you get this body?" Bayly asks.

"After the fighting had died down, I realized there were Baphuthi left on the mountain," Neville says. "So I went back up to the mountain. As I arrived at the top, I saw a native drop over a ledge of rock and run round a narrow footpath, about a foot or two wide. I fired at him. He ran toward a shallow cave.

"I was joined by a Mfengu policeman and we ran toward the cave, but the cave was protected by three or four armed people. They fired at us and the Mfengu was wounded in the hip. Another Mfengu arrived and told the Baphuthi to come out in their language, but they did not respond.

"We moved away from the cave.

"Later Sergeant Paterson of Yeomanry joined me. He had dynamite with him, which we threw toward the cave entrance. The Baphuthi moved off and we entered the cave where we found this body with wounds on the neck and the ribs. He had crawled in there to die. We thought it looked as though it could be Moorosi's body."

"Yes, that indeed is the chief," Bayly says. "Well done, Private Neville, you will receive the 200-pound reward."

Whitehead, convinced Neville's story was a fabrication, is quick to protest.

"I am sure I shot that man while I was guarding the mountain after everyone left," he says. "He looked like this man, old, short and wrinkled, but with fine, almost European features. He bore himself with dignity, even when he was shot.

"Now Private Neville, who heard me talking, has gone up to the top of the mountain, found the body and claims the reward."

"I cannot give you the reward based simply on a story like that," Bayly tells Whitehead. "The reward must go to the man who brought me the body."

"But that is the man I shot," counters Whitehead.

"I shot Moorosi."

Neville protests. "*I* shot Moorosi. I brought down his body," he insists.

Bayly is more convinced by Whitehead's explanation than that of Neville. He realizes, too, that Neville made no mention of shooting the Baphuthi leader until Whitehead claimed he had done so. But he has made his ruling. The man who brought him the body will get the reward.

Nevertheless, he hands Whitehead 25 pounds. "Here is compensation for you. The important thing is we defeated the wily old chief. He won't be around any longer to defy the law. You can be proud of that."

Bayly instructs the men to move away and to take Moorosi's body with them.

"I do not want it lying here," he says.

At the top of the mountain, the thatch roof of the hut that Moorosi occupied is charred and the top layers of rock that form the hut itself is blackened. It is deserted now and likely will be forever.

On the ground, unaffected by the fire, alongside a group of charred amulets, lies the Bible given to the chief by Ellenberger. A large rectangular hut is found to contain six to seven tons of gunpowder.

Other huts contain a plentiful supply of corn and other food. Clearly, the soldiers conclude, the Baphuthi could have held out for a long time.

Moorosi's body is carried out of Bayly's tent by a group of soldiers. They laugh as they parade the king's body around the camp. As they return from their parade, a soldier shouts, "Cut off his head the way they cut off King's head."

Bayly sends an updated report to Cape Town:

"Moorosi turned up; was shot through the neck at the first assault, and managed to creep into a cave where he was found about three hours after, dead. The whole affair is over; it only requires a few natives, assisted by a small party of the Europeans, to patrol the country."

Speaking to his senior officers, Bayly outlines his victory.

"By our count, 70 of the chief's warriors died in the fighting. A considerable number, possibly 120, fled down all sides of the hill in the deficient light when they saw the war was over, but every man of importance, except for Lehana, is now believed to be dead.

"Moorosi lost 16 sons and nine grandsons. In addition, 12 men and seven or eight women have been taken prisoner.

"These people will not be giving us any trouble any more.

"Like Moorosi, the Baphuthi tribe has been decapitated. It will disappear into the sands of history.

"I have given instructions that tomorrow the stone walls should all be dynamited so that the stones and earth cover the bodies of the dead Baphuthi in the trenches.

"Bodies lying on the top of the mountain should be dynamited. I want no trace to remain of the defences or of the bodies.

"The Cape Mounted Riflemen have done us and themselves proud in helping us to bring down an uncivilized rebellious barbaric leader who dared defy the colonial government.

"Springer was named a captain the moment he stepped on the top of the mountain. Captain Bourne, who was in charge of the storming party, will be gazetted for a brevet majorship.

"I hope this will be a lesson to those who are insane enough to rebel against a constituted authority of the British government.

"Our colonial forces will always prove a safeguard of peace in the exact proportion of their ability to strike terror and destruction to any misguided tribe. God save the Queen."

Queenstown — Monday November 24, 1879

Early today, four days after the end of the battle, the body of Private John Brome, Cape Mounted Riflemen, is found in a bed at Queenstown Hospital where he had been taken after complaining he was ill on his return from Moorosi's Mountain. He committed suicide by shooting himself.

Quthing — Saturday, November 28, 1879

For a week, colonial soldiers, working in 24-hour shifts, dismantle the stone walls and clear the mountain. It is unpleasant work. Cattle, dead and dying, immense quantities of bones and human bodies have to be removed. A powder magazine containing six or seven tons of gunpowder is blown up.

The men successfully complete the task.

"It looks quite decent and respectable," Granville says as the colonial soldiers are discharged.

But the soldiers themselves look far from respectable as today they start straggling back to the colony through the mountains.

As nearly all their horses died during the campaign, they are forced to ride on bullocks, wagons or even walk. Their clothing is tattered and their boots are falling apart. Some have part of their blankets sewn into their breeches.

"A fine crew we look," Whitehead says.

"Our clothing is only one aspect of the bad way we were treated," says Granville.

"I think it would have been a gracious act, which I would have valued, if they had offered me something to acknowledge the service I rendered. Bayly called on us to give the attack everything we had and that our country would be proud of us. Well, we did give it our all. Now we are left with no thanks. But I'm sure Bayly will get his praise."

"At least I received 25 pounds for my trouble," says Whitehead, "although I spent it all on drinks for everyone in camp on Thursday night."

XVIII

By February 1880, hundreds of Baphuthi who surrendered or were captured during the nine-month war, and who are able to handle pickaxes and spades, are employed at the magistracy and on the public roads. Among them is Mafetudi, Moorosi's chief messenger, who surrendered before the end of the war.

Those Baphuthi who found sanctuary with the Ellenbergers remain at Masitise. The rest, defeated and disillusioned and their numbers decimated, abandon their ancestral homeland, finding new homes in the isolated mountains of Basutoland where they teeter on the edge of survival as a nation.

Lehana, putative heir to the kingdom, is the only one of the Baphuthi leaders known to have escaped uninjured at the end of the final assault and, following a brief return to the mountain, is reported to have left Quthing for Matatiele.

After an outcry by missionaries, Moorosi's head, which was sent to King William's Town, is returned to the Baphuthi for burial with his body.

The highest medal of honor that a British or colonial soldier can earn — is awarded to three colonial soldiers.

- Peter Brown for his actions in carrying water to two wounded men sheltering behind a rock in the first attack on Moorosi's mountain.
- Robert George Scott for his action in volunteering for the dangerous assignment of throwing shells behind the enemy lines.
- Dr. Edmund Baron Hartley for bravery and devotion to duty in attending to the wounded under fire and carrying Captain A. P. Jones to safety.

They are presented with little fanfare, partly because the medals were won in the first two failed attempts to oust Moorosi from his fortress and partly because of growing public disillusionment with the war itself.

A number of settlers conclude the destructive war against Moorosi and the Baphuthi people achieved nothing of value or honor for the colony. Moorosi was not only a valiant warrior but an outstanding military strategist and an engineer of great merit, they add.

Indeed, rather than averting further conflict, it is not long before the Cape Colony's victory creates new, more widespread, strife. The wider conflict is sparked when the colonial government draws up plans to sell much of the conquered land in Quthing to white colonists. The government argues that selling the land will recover a portion of the costs of the war and will show other black nations that rebellion will not go unpunished. The Basotho are furious; Letsie sends a petition to the Cape Parliament on May 14, 1880 strongly opposing the plan for white settlement.

Ellenberger supports Letsie, pointing out to the colonial government that the confiscation of Quthing land is contrary to Moshoeshoe's original arrangement with the British. Other missionaries join the opposition to the plan.

But the protests fall on deaf ears. The missionaries' appeals merely serve to anger Governor Sir Bartle Frere and the Cape Colony government who press on with their plans.

Anger over the white-settlement plan is intensified by opposition to the disarmament act, which the colony moves to enforce in Basutoland.

In September 1880 the new Liberal British government — led by William Gladstone, which ousted the Conservatives under Benjamin Disraeli in April, 1880 — recalls Sir Bartle Frere to England, citing strong differences with his policies. But even the removal of the architect of the disarmament act and the white settlement plan fails to deter the colony.

When in December 1880 the Cape government appoints a commission to inspect Quthing with a view to dividing it up for white settlement, the Gladstone government in Britain steps in and instructs the colony to abandon the plan. The colonial government reluctantly complies.

But the damage has been done. Fueled by the white-settlement plans, attempted implementation of the disarmament act, and growing fear that the colony will turn on them as it did on Moorosi, rebellion grows among the Basotho.

The growing unrest in Basutoland reaches into the Transkei — to Hamilton Hope, the first magistrate in Quthing and now the magistrate at Qumbu.

On October 23, 1880, at Sulenkama, near Qumbu, Hope prepares for a meeting with leaders of the Mpondomise people at which he will insist that the people help him to fight Basotho rebels in the north, even though Mhlonthlo, their king, has said he cannot do so now as his wife, a daughter of Sarhili, has just died.

Charles Brownlee, chief magistrate of Griqualand East, warns Hope his move is risky. Mhlonthlo, he says, has a "treacherous and unreliable disposition" and could side with the rebels rather than cooperate with Hope.

In response, Hope says he will be true to the chivalrous traditions of his family and name and will proceed. "I believe I can perform an important service to my country and I am prepared to incur any risk in accomplishing this end," he says. "My opinion is that as in a game of cards, having led my king of trumps, if anybody in the game holds the ace, I lose the trick, and, if not, my king wins."

The meeting is attended by four white officials — Hope, his clerk A. Davis, and two young officials Charles Henman and Robert Warren — and 900 Mpondomise.

Their king, Mhlonthlo, invites Hope and the officials to sit in a circle. Even though he will not lead his people, he is prepared, he says, to hand them over for Hope's final orders on sending an armed force against the rebels.

"I am now putting you in Mr. Hope's hands," Mhlonthlo tells his people. "He will tell you what to do and you must obey him."

Mhlonthlo takes Davis by the hand and leads him away, saying he wishes to speak with him.

At this prearranged signal, a warrior named Mahlangeni plays the ace of trumps. He seizes Hope's long beard from behind and, pulling up his head, stabs him in the breast. He also stabs Henman and Warren.

The three die in minutes.

Hope's clerk, Davis, is spared as his father and brother serve as missionaries to the Mpondomise and Mhlonthlo's fight is only with the government and, in particular, its magistrate, Hamilton Hope.

Hope's death certificate is signed by Emile Rolland "brother of widow Emma Cecile Hope."

Hope's successor also does not escape the growing turbulence in Basutoland.

In January 1881, John Austen, still serving as the colonial magistrate in Quthing, is called upon to deal with an anti-government group who have crossed into the territory. The group includes a small number of Baphuthi living in the mountains, bent on revenge against the colony for the Moorosi war.

Austen mismanages the ensuing battle and is killed in a clash on a plateau just south of Moorosi's mountain. A Baphuthi decapitates Austen in retribution for the mutilation of Moorosi's body. He sends the severed head to Letsie.

In spite of the conflict, Fred Ellenberger, the man of peace, continues his work at Masitise, living in the cave house and conducting services at his 400-seat church. He expands his outstations from three to 12 and many Basotho who move into Quthing become Christians under his and Emma's ministry.

Growing unrest in Basutoland turns into the "Gun War" against the Cape Colony. On August 25, 1881, Griffith, unable to implement a new colonial policy on disarmament, is given a year's leave prior to retirement. Maitin, working for the colony in Maseru, is obliged to resign in January 1882 to escape an unacceptable transfer that he believes is victimization for his political views.

Faced with an uprising across Basutoland it cannot put down, the Cape Colony, on March 18, 1884, formally withdraws from Basutoland, which reverts to its earlier status as a British protectorate. The Basotho achieve the only successful revolt against the Cape Colony, and the colony loses everything for which it fought against Moorosi — and more. Basutoland never becomes part of the Cape Colony, nor of South Africa. Today it is the independent kingdom of Lesotho.

To view pictures, documents and photographs, visit: www.moorosi.com